CONSTITUTIONAL ORIGINS, STRUCTURE, AND CHANGE IN FEDERAL COUNTRIES

A Global Dialogue on Federalism
Volume I

CONSTITUTIONAL ORIGINS, STRUCTURE, AND CHANGE IN FEDERAL COUNTRIES

EDITED BY JOHN KINCAID AND G. ALAN TARR

SENIOR EDITOR JOHN KINCAID

Published for

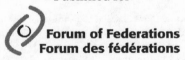

Forum of Federations
Forum des fédérations

and

iacfs

INTERNATIONAL ASSOCIATION OF
CENTERS FOR FEDERAL STUDIES

by

McGill-Queen's University Press
Montreal & Kingston · London · Ithaca

© McGill-Queen's University Press 2005
ISBN 0-7735-2849-0 (cloth)
ISBN 0-7735-2916-0 (paper)

Legal deposit first quarter 2005
Bibliothèque nationale du Québec

Printed in Canada on acid-free paper that is 100% ancient forest free
(100% post-consumer recycled), processed chlorine free.

McGill-Queen's University Press acknowledges the support of the Canada
Council for the Arts for our publishing program. We also acknowledge
the financial support of the Government of Canada through the Book
Publishing Industry Development Program (BPIDP) for our publishing
activities.

Library and Archives Canada Cataloguing in Publication

Constitutional origins, structure, and change in federal
    democracies/edited by John Kincaid and G. Alan Tarr; senior
    editor John Kincaid.

    (A global dialogue on federalism; v. 1)
    Includes index.
    ISBN 0-7735-2849-0 (cloth)
    ISBN 0-7735-2916-0 (paper)

    1. Federal government. 2. Democracy. 3. Constitutional history.
    I. Kincaid, John, 1946- II. Tarr, G. Alan (George Alan) III. Forum of
    Federations IV. International Association of Centers for Federal Studies
    V. Series: Global dialogue on federalism; v. 1.

JC355.C663 2005   321.02   C2004-907149-1

This book was typeset by Interscript Inc. in 10/12 Baskerville.

Contents

Preface

This volume on constitutionalism in federal countries is the inaugural contribution to a series of practical books on federalism being published as a part of the program "A Global Dialogue on Federalism." The goal of this Global Dialogue is to engage participants from around the world in comparative conversations and debates about core themes and issues of federalism, with the aim of building an international network that enables practitioners, students, scholars, and others to learn from one another, share best practices, and enhance their understanding of the prospects as well as the problems of federalism as a mode of governance in today's world, especially in relation to democracy, freedom, prosperity, and peace.

The Global Dialogue is a joint program of the Forum of Federations and the International Association of Centers for Federal Studies (IACFS). The Forum is an international network on federalism that seeks to strengthen democratic governance by promoting dialogue on and understanding of the values, practices, principles, and possibilities of federalism. The IACFS is an association of centres and institutes throughout the world that maintain a research and teaching focus on political systems that have federal features. The direction and content of the Global Dialogue program are overseen by an editorial board, which consists of representatives of the Forum of Federations and the IACFS as well as other experts. The theoretical underpinnings and practical application of the Global Dialogue are outlined subsequent to this preface in a chapter explaining the program's conceptual framework.

The work of the Forum of Federations and the IACFS is part of a broader endeavour to build and strengthen democracy through federalism when and where appropriate. As a mode of governance that seeks to combine self-rule for regional and minority interests with shared rule for general and common purposes, federalism is necessarily of interest to advocates of democracy. This is particularly true in a world in which the vast majority of political states are multinational, multilingual, multireligious, and/or multicultural. Indeed, there has been a tremendous upsurge of interest in federalism since the emergence of a new wave of democratization in the late 1980s. This worldwide interest in federalism is directly linked to movements promoting greater democracy and decentralization and to the simultaneous trends toward globalization and regionalization evident throughout today's world.

Given the dominance of statist ideologies during the past two centuries, however, federalism has often been viewed as a stepchild less worthy of attention and cultivation than the seemingly natural children of modern nationalism. Consequently, while there is a long history of federal-democratic experience in a few countries, such as Australia, Canada, Switzerland, and the United States, there is little practical experience with democratic federalism in most countries, and there are problematic experiences in a number of fledgling federal democracies. In turn, there is a paucity of accessible literature and information on comparative federalism and a dearth of intellectual capital available for investment in research and teaching about the many varieties of federalism worldwide.

The series of books, being published as one important product of the Global Dialogue program, seeks to create informational capital and to fill gaps in our comparative knowledge by providing as balanced a view as possible of theories and practices of federalism in various countries around the world. It does so by exploring comparative and contrasting theoretical and practical perspectives, with each volume focussing on a particular aspect of federalism through the examples of selected countries that reflect federalism's diversity, including its strengths and weaknesses.

Our aim is to produce books that are accessible to interested citizens, political leaders, government practitioners, and students and faculty in institutions of higher education. Each chapter, therefore, seeks to provide an overview of its country's federal constitutional system in a way that covers all relevant, important information without overwhelming detail while also providing some analysis of the rationales and workings of the system and also indicating how well or poorly the system functions in relation to its constitution and its society.

This first volume of the series begins at the beginning, so to speak, with the constitutional systems of twelve federal countries. Future volumes will be devoted to the allocation of powers and competences in federal polities, legislative and executive governance in federal systems, fiscal federalism, foreign affairs in federal countries, and other important themes, with a somewhat different mix of countries being represented in each volume.

Given the extent of the Global Dialogue program, we have many people to thank. We are grateful to Ralph Lysyshyn, former president at the Forum of Federations, for his commitment to the program in its embryonic state and infancy. We offer thanks to the co-editor of this book, G. Alan Tarr, for his invaluable help in launching this inaugural volume. We wish to acknowledge the contributors to this volume and their institutes for their dedication in hosting events, writing the chapters, and helping us to lay the foundation of the program. Thanks are due also to participants in the twelve country roundtables and in the international roundtable, whose input helped to shape the content of the chapters.

We wish to thank, as well, colleagues who read and critiqued drafts of the chapters contained in this book: Joachim Amm, Technical University Dresden, Germany; Dirk Brand, Provincial Administration, Western Cape, South Africa; Maureen A. Covell, Simon Fraser University, Canada; Frank Delmartino, Katholieke Universiteit Leuven, Belgium; John Dinan, Wake Forest University, United States; Lawrence S. Graham, University of Texas at Austin, United States; Bede Harris, University of Canberra, Australia; Hans Hirter, University of Bern, Switzerland; G. Gopa Kumar, University of Kerala, India; Samuel LaSelva, University of British Columbia, Canada; Wolf Linder, University of Bern, Switzerland; David Samuels, University of Minnesota, United States; Robert Sharlet, Union College, United States; G. Campbell Sharman, University of Western Australia; Jurg Steiner, University of North Carolina, United States; and Ian Stewart, Acadia University, Canada. The assistance of these individuals is much appreciated, but they are, of course, not responsible for any deficiencies remaining in the chapters.

We would also like to thank our colleagues and associates at the Forum of Federations and at the International Association of Centers for Federal Studies. Without their assistance and expertise, the program and the present book could not exist. We wish to acknowledge the work of Forum staff Barbara Brook and Abigail Ostien, as well as Rebeca Batres-Doré, Rupak Chattopadhyay, Paul Morton, Karl Nerenberg, Nicole Pederson, and Carl Stieren. Thanks are due also to Brandon Benjamin, Benoit Charron, Terry A. Cooper, and Jared Gardner for their work on behalf of this volume at the Robert B. and Helen S. Meyner Center for the Study of State and Local Government at Lafayette College, Easton, Pennsylvania. We also want to acknowledge the Map and Geospatial Information Collection at Dalhousie University, Canada, for permission to use the maps in this book. Finally, we thank the staff at McGill-Queen's University Press for all of their assistance in producing the volume and working with us to ensure the success of this first book in the series.

On behalf of the Global Dialogue Editorial Board
John Kincaid, senior editor

CONSTITUTIONAL ORIGINS, STRUCTURE,
AND CHANGE IN FEDERAL COUNTRIES

A Global Dialogue on Federalism: Conceptual Framework

RAOUL BLINDENBACHER
AND CHERYL SAUNDERS

I find it personally quite a paradox that federal states have been in existence for at least two hundred years, but that as far as I know, it is only in the last few years that these states have decided to meet each other as federal states and to exchange knowledge and experience.

Guy Verhofstadt, Prime Minister of Belgium[1]

The impetus to begin such an exchange between federal countries came in 1999 at the first International Conference on Federalism in Mont Tremblant, Canada, at which more than 500 elected officials, civil servants, academics, and private-sector representatives from 25 countries participated. Only three years later, more than 600 representatives from 60 countries participated at the second International Conference on Federalism in St. Gallen, Switzerland, in 2002. This work will continue through the International Conference on Federalism in Brussels, Belgium, in March 2005 and through such conferences in the future.

While sharing experiences may seem to be an obvious way to improve government systems and mechanisms, surprisingly, it has not been common practice among federal or constituent-unit governments. The large international conferences on federalism have opened the doors for officials and other experts to engage in such exchanges and to build an international network on federalism.

In an effort to maintain and deepen this initiative, the Forum of Federations and the International Association of Centers for Federal Studies launched the program "A Global Dialogue on Federalism." This program provides opportunities for the large international conferences to thoroughly and comparatively explore core themes on federalism. The resulting publications, such as this book, aim to fill the gap in the corresponding literature.

In a world that today is undergoing political, cultural, economic, and social change at an unprecedented rate, federal systems are experiencing continuous transformation. They are therefore faced with the need to develop an ability to learn and adapt in order to cope with the challenges they face. Although the circumstances in each federation are different, many of the problems they face are common to all. The experiences of other federations allow us to foresee more clearly the likely consequences of various arrangements. Learning comes not only from the successes but also from the difficulties of other federations.

However, no single federal model is applicable everywhere. One cannot simply transfer an institutional model from one country to another without taking into account the varied conditions. Therefore, a different approach is required. A more effective means of improving federal governance is through "learning from each other."[2] One important distinguishing factor of this approach is its emphasis that all participants be regarded as equal partners in the exchange of experiences. This self-evident but, in practice, often neglected consideration is a fundamental condition if participants are to share and listen openly and, in turn, become inspired to create new applications of the federal idea. A further distinguishing factor of this learning approach, which is of particular importance for federations, is the ability to create suitable forums where the participants learn not only for themselves but also for their institutions and their countries.

The conceptual framework of the program "A Global Dialogue on Federalism" is designed to embrace this idea of learning from each other. The program entails a comparative exploration of a dozen core themes in federal governance. Through a series of themed roundtables, participants representing diverse viewpoints in a representative and diverse sample of federal countries search for new insights and solutions. The new information emanating from the roundtables is used to produce comparative materials for worldwide distribution.

The program adapts a process in which participants expand their individual as well as their institutional knowledge through a "knowledge spiral."[3] In this learning process, new practical and theoretical knowledge is integrated with the aim of fostering a collective vision in order to develop new solutions for specific problems. These are then transformed into measures producing practical action. In the Global Dialogue program, this is accomplished in four interconnected stages by which knowledge is disseminated, internalized, externalized, and finally transformed.

DISSEMINATION STAGE

During the first stage of the process, referred to as the "dissemination stage," participants in the program are introduced to the latest thinking on the chosen core theme. The goal of this stage is to ensure that all participants have the opportunity to engage in the learning forum as equal partners with the same level of knowledge.

In the Global Dialogue program, the mechanism for the dissemination of knowledge is the "theme template." It is comprised of an introduction, which summarizes the essence of the latest research, a set of crosscutting analytical questions, and an internationally comprehensive set of questions covering institutional provisions and how they work in practice. This document is produced by a leading expert on the theme, referred to as the "theme coordinator." He or she also identifies the federal countries whose contributions would ensure the theme's adequate exploration from many perspectives. The theme template is distributed to participants in all of the featured countries.

INTERNALIZATION STAGE

The purpose of the second stage, the "internalization stage," is to enable the participants to reflect on their own experience in light of the contemporary research provided in the dissemination stage. For the Global Dialogue program, this takes place at a country-focused roundtable held in each featured country. The selected participants gather to share their expertise relating to the theme-template questions, providing diverse viewpoints within the contexts of their countries. In order to create the optimum conditions for the participants to learn successfully from each other, two prerequisites should be fulfilled.

First, how participants are selected has a direct impact on the success of the learning process. Rather than placing the priority on hierarchical position, participants are selected to ensure that, as far as possible, all points of view and all experiences related to a given topic are represented. This is known as "triangulation."[4] By looking at a topic from all angles, representatives are able to develop the most accurate picture of the subject. In addition, it is important to select highly committed and knowledgeable people.

A second and equally important prerequisite for the successful implementation of this learning process is the application of an appropriate type of communication. According to the theory of group dynamics,[5] "dialogue" is the most appropriate type of formalized communication for this learning approach. In this context, dialogue means "a free flowing of ideas through a group, allowing the group to discover the insights not attainable individually."[6] In contrast, individuals involved in "discussion" put forward and defend their point of view, which they consider to be the best solution. When individuals in a group open themselves to learning from others, they can explore and bring to the surface the full wealth of their thoughts and experience in an unfettered way, going far beyond their individual opinions.

EXTERNALIZATION STAGE

During the "externalization stage," participants share their reflections and identify patterns and new insights from the prior stage of introspection. The goal of this stage is to have individuals become more receptive to new ideas and points of view so that they can see and interpret their own social and political realities in new ways. In the Global Dialogue program, this stage is facilitated by an international roundtable that features key questions of international importance from each country roundtable. The participants are selected based on their ability to effectively represent their country's question. In this way, the participants share knowledge gained from their reflections at the country roundtables and go through a process of finding patterns and differences and seeking new insights. The diversity of the countries and viewpoints offers participants a broad understanding of the theme, allowing for a truly comparative dialogue.

TRANSFORMATION STAGE

To ensure that the knowledge gained at these events does not end with only those who participated in them, the knowledge spiral proceeds to the "transformation stage." This stage integrates the reflections from the country roundtables and new insights from the international event into a comparative whole, thus building on the progress already made and creating opportunities to use the material for the next twist of the spiral. The diverse Global Dialogue program publications and website fulfil this function.

The present volume is one key example. It provides a thorough review and in-depth analysis of the role of federal constitutions through country examples, ending with comparative observations. Each country chapter is intended to capture the key issues, areas of consensus, and major disagreements related to the featured theme, using the theme template as a guide to ensure comparability across countries.

The Global Dialogue program also produces a booklet series that provides an entry point to each corresponding book by highlighting the insights, key issues, and items of international interest that arose at the country and international roundtables. This format allows publication in multiple languages and reproduction as changes in the featured countries warrant. Program materials are also available on-line.[7] A further significant function of the website is its discussion forum, which enables additional people around the world to become involved in the Global Dialogue.

As noted above, using the knowledge spiral as a conceptual framework for the program, "A Global Dialogue on Federalism" is an attempt to enhance individual as well as institutional learning. It is a significant addition to the work of the international conferences on federalism, enabling federal states and constituent units to learn from each other. Similarly, the program's publications will fill a gap in the contemporary literature in federal studies and will provide a rich foundation of knowledge for future conferences. Readers of this book are therefore challenged to use the knowledge gained in order to inspire new solutions, thereby strengthening democratic governance, and to join the many participants of roundtable events around the world in order to expand and strengthen the international network on federalism.

NOTES

1 Guy Verhofstadt, "Inaugural Speech," paper presented at the Second International Conference on Federalism, St. Gallen, Switzerland, 27-30 August 2002.

2 Raoul Blindenbacher and Ronald L. Watts, "Federalism in a Changing World: A Conceptual Framework for the Conference," *Federalism in a Changing World: Learning from Each Other*, ed. Raoul Blindenbacher and Arnold Koller (Montreal and Kingston: McGill-Queen's University Press, 2003), pp. 19–20.

3 Margit Osterloh and Sigrid Wübker, *Wettbewerbsfähiger durch Prozess- und Wissensmanagement: Mit Chancengleichheit auf Erfolgskurs* (Wiesbaden: Gabler, 1999).

4 Donald T. Campbell and Donald Fiske, "Convergent and Discriminant Validation by the Multitrait-Multimethod Matrix," *Psychological Bulletin* (Washington, DC: American Psychological Association, 1959), pp. 81–105.

5 William N. Isaacs, *Dialogue and the Art of Thinking Together: A Pioneering Approach to Communicating in Business and in Life* (New York: Doubleday, 1999); Edgar H. Schein, *Process Consultation Revisited: Building the Helping Relationship* (New Jersey: Prentice-Hall, 1998).

6 Peter M. Senge, *The Fifth Discipline: The Art and Practice of the Learning Organization* (Sydney: Random House Australia, 1998), p. 10.

7 The Global Dialogue website can be reached via www.forumfed.org.

Constitutional Origins, Structure, and Change

G. ALAN TARR

A constitution ordinarily embodies a society's fundamental choices about government. The constitution designates offices, specifies how these offices are to be filled, allocates powers and responsibilities between the various offices, indicates the aims for which political power is to be exercised, and – in most instances – elaborates the individual rights and, sometimes, group rights that are to be protected against violation by government. In some instances, a constitution eloquently articulates a country's aspirations and becomes a source of pride and a symbol of national unity for its citizens.

When a country adopts a federal system, it necessarily embraces complexity in government, and the tasks of the federal constitution are correspondingly multiplied over those of a unitary system. The constitution in a federal system designates the component units of the federal system; it also may specify procedures for the inclusion of additional units or, perhaps, for the merger or secession of existing component units. The federal constitution also determines the range of discretion available to the component units of the federal system in creating their own polities: namely, the extent to which they are free to make their own decisions about their respective forms of government, the purposes for which political power will be exercised, and the rights to be protected. More generally, the federal constitution allocates power between the federal (or confederal or national) government and the component units, determining which powers are the exclusive prerogative of each government and which powers are shared. When powers are shared, the federal constitution usually defines how conflicts among the governments with regard to these powers are to be resolved. More broadly, the federal constitution regulates the relations among the component units and between the federal government and these units.

Needless to say, the constitutional arrangements within federal systems differ across federations because countries can choose among a variety of alternatives in deciding how to structure their governments, allocate powers, diffuse responsibilities, and safeguard rights. Federal democracies may be presidential or parliamentary. They can be two-party systems or multi-party systems. They can be integrative or devolutionary, bringing together preexisting governmental units or transforming a previously unitary state into a federal one, or they may even combine integrative and devolutionary features. They may allow component units to create constitutions and design their own governments, or they may mandate the form of these governments in the federal constitution. They may give constitutional status and independent powers to local governments, or they may make them subject to the constituent units. They may create purely territorial constituent units, or they may form units designed to accommodate territorially concentrated minorities.

Typically, the constitutional choices made by a country reflect its distinctive history, its political culture, and the character of its populace. Of particular importance is the country's prior constitutional history. If the current constitution is not the country's first, then experiences under earlier constitutions will influence the design of the current one. The constitutional choices that a country makes also may reflect the political thought of the founders, especially their understanding of the particular challenges confronting the country and of the aims the country should be seeking to achieve. Constitutional diversity may be found not only among federal democracies but even within them because constitutional arrangements may change over time and because subnational constitutions may embody different values and establish different institutional patterns. Finally, federal constitutions may evolve in response to changes in circumstances or changes in the reigning political forces in the country, and they may change dramatically when the populace replaces one constitution with another.

Because constitution making represents the most fundamental exercise of political choice, constitution makers are well advised to seek the broadest possible perspective on their drafting task. They will, therefore, find it useful to survey the constitutional choices that other countries have made, to assess how well these choices have worked, and thereby to learn from and benefit from the experiences of these countries. This comparative perspective is valuable also for those engaged in implementing, rather than designing, constitutional regimes. This volume seeks to contribute to informed deliberation on constitutional matters by presenting overviews of the constitutional arrangements in twelve federal democracies, thereby enabling public officials, scholars, and students to learn from the constitutional experiences of other federal democracies.

The present volume focuses on Australia, Belgium, Brazil, Canada, Germany, India, Mexico, Nigeria, Russia, South Africa, Switzerland, and the United States of America. Each chapter was written for this volume by an expert from the respective country after consultation with practitioners

and academic and nonacademic experts on his or her country's constitution. Each chapter thus provides an up-to-date description and analysis of
the constitutional origins, structure, and development within a particular
federal democracy. A concluding chapter highlights constitutional com-
monalities and differences, the range of choices available to constitution
makers in federal systems, and the consequences of various constitutional
choices, thereby facilitating comparative analysis and mutual learning.

Informing the analyses of constitutionalism within the twelve countries is
a series of questions that are important to understanding constitutional arrangements in any federal system:

- Why was the country's federal constitution constructed the way it was,
  and what were the principal philosophical, historical, or political reasons
  for doing so?
- What, if anything, is unique or different about the country's federal constitution compared to other federal constitutions around the world?
- What, essentially, is the role or function of the constitution in the country's federal system?
- How successful is the constitution in terms of (1) longevity and durability, (2) adherence of governments and politicians to its provisions,
  (3) political and social stability, (4) support for the constitution by the
  people, (5) democracy, (6) individual and/or communal rights, (7) economic performance, and (8) potential for positive future development?
- What are the major reasons for the success, partial success, or failure of
  the federal constitution or constitutionalism in the country?
- Is the federal constitution generally compatible or incompatible with the
  country's society and political culture, and is the federal constitution supported by an underlying federal society or political culture in the country?
- How has the constitution evolved over time, and why?
- Where is the country's constitutional debate going, and what are the
  likely future trends for the country's federal constitution?

Examination of the twelve federal democracies highlighted in this volume reveals a wide range of constitutional experiences. Some mature federal democracies – for example, Australia, India, and the United States –
have created durable constitutions that have not required fundamental reform. In contrast, other mature federal democracies have chosen to recast
or modernize their constitutional foundations, as Switzerland did in adopting a new constitution in 1999. Still other mature federal democracies
have had to confront new challenges to their constitutional orders – Germany in the wake of reunification and Canada in response to the rise of
separatist sentiments in Quebec – that have encouraged consideration of
fundamental constitutional reforms.

Other federal democracies are involved in the difficult task of creating a durable constitutional order after a period of dictatorship. In some instances – for example, Russia in 1993 and South Africa in 1996 – the new constitutions represent the country's attempt to fashion a viable constitutional democracy. In other instances – for example, Brazil since 1988 and Nigeria since 1999 – the challenge is to restore constitutional democracy after previous constitutional arrangements failed or were overthrown, leading to military takeover and dictatorship.

Finally, some long-standing federal democracies, such as Belgium and Mexico, are in the midst of significant constitutional change that is designed to strengthen the authority of the component units of these federations. In these countries, the final federal balance and the constitutional arrangements underlying it remain a matter of contention.

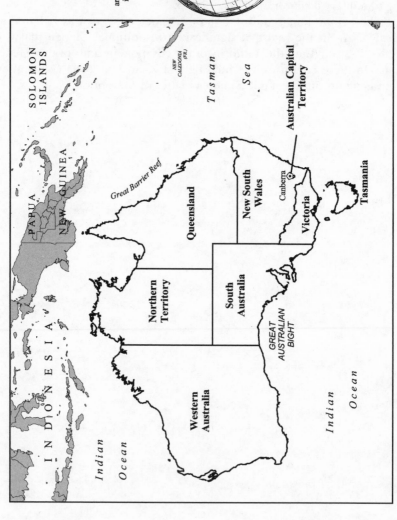

Australia

Capital: Canberra
Population: 20 Million
(2004 est.)

Boundaries and place names
are representative only and do not
imply any official endorsement.

N

500   0   500

Kilometres

Sources: CIA World Factbook; ESRI Ltd;
Times Atlas of the World

SOLOMON
ISLANDS

PAPUA

NEW GUINEA

INDONESIA

NEW
CALEDONIA
(FR.)

Tasman

Sea

Australian Capital
Territory

Great Barrier Reef

Queensland

New South
Wales

Canberra

Victoria

Tasmania

Northern
Territory

South
Australia

GREAT
AUSTRALIAN
BIGHT

Western
Australia

Indian

Ocean

Indian

Ocean

Commonwealth of Australia

CHERYL SAUNDERS

Australia's Constitution was negotiated during the last decade of the nineteenth century and came into force on 1 January 1901. Its federal features were substantially influenced by United States federalism, as then understood. Nevertheless, the Australian Constitution was distinctive from the outset in ways that were recognized during the drafting and that have become more prominent over time.

Australia's Constitution combines United States-style federalism with British institutions of parliamentary responsible government, creating a different dynamic for decision making within and between the spheres of government. The framers of the Constitution initially feared that these two sets of principles would be antagonistic, and indeed, accommodation has not always been easy. More significantly, however, with federalism and responsible government came different approaches to constitutionalism. One involved the limitation of power in an entrenched, written constitution. The other was highly pragmatic, favouring flexibility and efficiency over written constitutional rules. The tension between the two is still reflected in Australian constitutionalism. Those parts of the Constitution that create the legislature and the executive leave considerable discretion to the institutions of government. Attempts to apply constitutional restraints to them, even in the name of protecting democratic principles, have met considerable resistance.[1] Few rights are secured through the Constitution; the framers, in the British tradition, assumed that rights could be protected by the Parliament and the common law. Few limits are placed on decision making by the states beyond those necessitated by federalism itself.

By contrast, those parts of the Australian Constitution – namely, allocating power for federal purposes, providing for social and economic union, and establishing the judicature, originally considered an incident of federalism[2] – are taken very seriously. Federal limits on the power of the

Australian Parliament are given effect through judicial review. A separation of federal judicial power has emerged as a considerable constraint on the legislature in ways that now go well beyond the protection of the independence of a judicature that monitors the boundaries of the federal division of power.[3]

There is one other distinctive characteristic of Australian constitutionalism. Australia's constitutional system, as the High Court has occasionally observed, is the product of evolution, not revolution.[4] There has been no break in the legal order since European settlement, which itself was built on a foundation of English law, deemed to have been absorbed by the Australian colonies. The Constitution originally derived its binding force from an act of the British Parliament. It was democratically advanced, by the standards of the time, as befitted a new, relatively egalitarian nation. Otherwise, there was neither need nor incentive for the framers of the Constitution to be particularly constitutionally creative. The Australian federation was largely a response to considerations of economic advantage and shared interests in defence and immigration, although recent historical work has drawn attention to the rise of national sentiment as well.[5]

Even after federation, the same evolutionary process enabled Australia to achieve independence without constitutional change or any break in legal continuity. In consequence, the Constitution retains some outward signs of earlier colonial status, including the continuing link with the British monarchy. Even more significant to Australian federalism was the impact on Australia's internal constitutional arrangements of the Commonwealth's assumption of authority to exercise Australia's external sovereignty as the imperial power withdrew.

THE FEDERAL CONSTITUTION
IN HISTORICAL-CULTURAL CONTEXT

Australia has been a federation for more than 100 years.[6] The polity comprises six states, two self-governing mainland territories, and some external territories. The national population of 20 million is spread over 7,682,300 square kilometers. Most of the population lives in eight large cities around the perimeter of the land mass and on the island of Tasmania. These cities are the capitals of the respective states and territories. The dominant ethnicity is Anglo-Celtic, and the dominant language is English. The society is multicultural, however, especially in the Southeast, where post-Second World War migration from southern and eastern Europe, Asia, and Africa has produced considerable diversity. In addition, there is an indigenous population of Aboriginal and Torres Strait Islander peoples, now representing about 2 percent of the total population. The predominant religion is Christianity, with a mixture of Protestants and Roman Catholics, although all denominations are in relative decline. Australia is an affluent society whose gross domestic product was US$23,100 per capita in 2002.[7]

Federation

Federation took place on 1 January 1901 after a decade of intermittent negotiation. At this time, the territorial distribution of the population was much the same as it is today but on a smaller scale. British settlement had begun in 1788 with the establishment of a penal colony at Sydney Cove. By 1890 Australia comprised six self-governing British colonies, which subsequently became the original Australian states. Formally, therefore, federation brought together six distinct polities, each of which needed to be persuaded to surrender a measure of its autonomy. The Constitution still shows signs of this negotiation process. In particular, it includes concessions to Western Australia, which, as the most remote colony, was a reluctant participant.[8]

Nevertheless, there was a considerable degree of preexisting unity between the colonies, which provided an impetus for federation and helped to form its character. The vast majority of the population were settlers from the British Isles. The four eastern colonies began as part of the settlement of New South Wales, which was gradually subdivided during the first part of the nineteenth century. All six colonies constituted parts of the same empire, which tended to administer them collectively. Even before federation, there was a degree of intercolonial collaboration through meetings of premiers and other government officials. Discussion of federation had been underway in a desultory fashion since the middle of the nineteenth century.

The eventual impetus for union came in response to a range of factors, the most dominant being (1) the need for defence at a time of concern about French, German, and Russian activity in the Pacific; (2) the attractions of a common market; (3) the desire to control immigration; and (4) less tangible feelings of incipient national unity. The distance between Britain and Australia brought other subtle pressures to bear as well, including the advantages of a single final Australian court of appeal as an alternative to the Privy Council based in London.[9]

An early attempt at a weak form of confederation was made in 1885 with the establishment of the Federal Council of Australasia, involving most of the Australian colonies and Fiji but not, importantly, New South Wales.[10] The council was still operating when the movement for a more effective form of federation began. The first step was a conference in 1890, involving representatives from all Australian colonies and New Zealand, to determine how best to proceed. Thereafter, the nature of the federal settlement and the terms of the federal Constitution were effectively determined by two constitutional conventions. The National Australasian Convention in 1891 was comprised of delegations of members of Parliament from each of the six Australian colonies and New Zealand. This convention agreed on a draft constitution, on which the final Constitution was ultimately based, although the 1891 draft never came into effect. No agreement had been reached on the process for its adoption and, once the convention adjourned, more pressing economic and political priorities monopolized the attention of governments and parliaments. Following a revival of the federation movement by forces both within and outside the colonial parliaments, a second convention, the Australasian Federal Convention, took place in 1897–98. The somewhat more popular character of the issue at this stage was reflected in the composition of the new convention. Four of the five participating colonies sent an elected delegation, although the fifth, Western Australia, once more sent members of Parliament. Moreover, the enabling legislation of the four colonies that had elected their delegates called for a referendum on the draft constitution before it could be sent to the imperial Parliament for enactment.

Although the process was more complicated than originally envisaged, it was ultimately effective. The convention agreed on a draft constitution, which, despite minor but important subsequent changes by both an Australian Premiers' Conference and the British Parliament, was essentially the instrument that came into effect on 1 January 1901. By this time, the sixth colony, Queensland, had reentered the federation movement and had passed an act to authorize approval of the Constitution by referendum. Western Australia eventually passed an enabling act as well, although New Zealand never did so.[11] In due course, therefore, the Constitution was approved by referendums in all six Australian colonies. By the standards of the time, this was a relatively popular process although, to modern eyes, the franchise was restricted, and the voting turn-out was low.

Upon federation, the six Australian colonies became the original states of the Commonwealth of Australia. At this time, the whole of the Australian land mass was divided between these states. After the first decade of federation, however, South Australia ceded its Northern Territory to the Commonwealth. In 1978 this territory became self-governing. A second self-governing territory, the Australian Capital Territory, was carved out of New South Wales for the seat of government in a compromise between Victoria and New South Wales that is enshrined in the Constitution itself.[12] The Constitution recognizes that a territory (although probably not the seat of government itself) may be established as a new state and that new states may be created from existing ones.[13] Although there have been occasional pressures to create new states, this has never happened largely because the Constitution requires the consent of the Parliament of any state whose territory would be diminished by the change.

In the 1990s, however, there was a serious debate on statehood for the Northern Territory, in time for the centenary of the Constitution. This was driven by several factors. By definition, a territory has less autonomy than a state. Moreover, as the Australian Constitution has been interpreted, some constitutional safeguards do not apply to territories.[14] On this occasion, the movement to have the Northern Territory granted state status failed largely because of the inadequacy of the constitution proposed for the new state and the process by which it was developed. It seems likely that, at some stage in the future, the Northern Territory will seek statehood again. If this occurs, one issue to be resolved will be the number of senators to be elected from the new state.

There is no provision for secession. The Preamble to the Constitution Act refers to an "indissoluble federal Commonwealth." A secession movement nevertheless took place in the 1930s, when Western Australia voted to leave the Commonwealth.[15] Western Australia had been a reluctant participant in federation partly because of its geographical isolation from the rest of the country. It also considered itself economically and politically disadvantaged by federation. The secession movement failed in the face of British reluctance to alter the Australian Constitution in order to recognize secession of a state at a time when Australia was on the cusp of independence. Support for secession was defused by establishing the Commonwealth Grants Commission in order to make equalization grants to claimant states more systematic.[16] There has not been a serious secession movement since then.

The Constitution

The Commonwealth Constitution is relatively short, comprising 127 sections and 11,908 words. Its two principal goals, both satisfactorily achieved, were to establish a federation on a basis to which all colonies were prepared to agree and to provide for the institutions of national government. The temper of the Constitution was broadly democratic, again judged by the standards of the time. Both chambers of the Commonwealth Parliament were to be directly elected. The qualifications for both voters and members were to be the same in the Senate as in the House of Representatives. The Constitution offered some mild encouragement for extension of the franchise to women, which had already taken place in two colonies.[17] In the end, however, consistent with the philosophy underpinning this part of the Constitution, the decision was left to the discretion of the Commonwealth Parliament. On the other hand, "aboriginal natives" were not to be counted for constitutional purposes, including the calculation of the size of state representation in the House of Representatives.[18] This discriminatory provision was not removed until 1967.

At least two distinctive characteristics of the Constitution can be attributed to the circumstances of its framing.

The first characteristic concerns its substance. Australia's Constitution draws on the common-law constitutional traditions of Britain and the United States. The Australian colonies were established along British lines with institutions of parliamentary responsible government. It was natural to provide similar institutions for the new national government. The federal part of the Australian Constitution, however, drew extensively on the Constitution of the United States, popularized in Australia through the work of James Bryce.[19] The United States' influence extended not merely to the manner of the division of federal powers, conferring specific powers on the centre and leaving the residue to the states, but also to the idea of an upper house, or Senate, in which the states are equally represented; to a written constitution representing fundamental law, which can be changed only by a process involving both national and state consent;[20] to the concepts of federal jurisdiction and a distinct federal judicature; and even to the terms and structure of the Constitution. One consequence, probably unintended, has been judicial interpretation of the Australian Constitution as embodying a three-way, albeit asymmetrical, separation of powers, including a strict separation of judicial power from the federal government's executive and legislative branches.

The combination of federalism and responsible government has generally been regarded as a success. It involves tensions of at least two kinds, however. Most obviously, there is potential for conflict between the principles of parliamentary responsible government, in which the government relies for office on the support of the lower House of Parliament, and a powerful Senate with authority to reject all legislation, including financial legislation, thus putting the government itself at risk. Even at the time of the framing, this difficulty was foreshadowed. It was captured in a prediction that "either responsible government would kill federation, or federation would kill responsible government."[21] The particular problem of disagreement over financial legislation was the subject of a key compromise during the conventions of the 1890s, which restricted the power of the Senate to amend key categories of money bills but left its power to reject them in place, thus failing to overcome the difficulty altogether.[22] Following a constitutional crisis in 1975 involving the Senate's power to reject financial legislation,[23] a range of proposals for change was publicly debated; none, however, has been put in place.[24]

Tension between the British and American constitutional traditions, as embodied in Australia's Constitution, is reflected in Australian attitudes toward the role of a constitution and of courts in interpreting it. An uneasy compromise has been reached by restricting the content of the Constitution to the essential requirements for operating a federation and establishing national institutions of government. Australians tend to disagree over the important question of whether the purpose of constitutional rules is to empower governments or to restrain them in the exercise of power. The Constitution provides no express protection for individual rights, although a handful of limits on Commonwealth or state power have a similar effect. There is satisfaction in many quarters with the considerable degree of flexibility left to elected institutions under current arrangements. At the same time, however, Australians expect the courts to enforce the boundaries of federal power with regard to both the national and state spheres of government. Judicial decisions that derive further limits on power from the separation of judicial power[25] or from the institutional logic of representative government[26] also attract some, although far from universal, approval.

The second circumstance of the framing of the Constitution that has had a profound and continuing effect on its character is the manner of its making. Australians used a relatively popular process whereby the people, organized in their colonies, voted to approve the draft. This process is now complemented by the procedure for change, which requires approval by the people voting both nationally and in the states,[27] following the example of the Constitution of Switzerland. From this perspective, Australia's constitutional experience raises a question that is familiar in many federal systems: whether authority for the Constitution lies with the people organized nationally or with the people organized in states. In Australia this question has had no practical significance. From one perspective, in any event, the answer is neither. The Constitution originally gained its effect as fundamental law as a statute of the then sovereign British Parliament. Although the British Parliament is no longer sovereign, in outward form the Constitution remains a section of a British statute. After the formal renunciation of British sovereignty, in the Australia Acts 1986, the High Court began to attribute authority for the Constitution to the Australian people.[28] This was done both as a convenience and as a justification for implied limits on power, in the style of *Marbury v. Madison*.[29] For this purpose, the "people" invariably are conceived as organized nationally. This may be significant for the nature of Australian federalism, but it is also clear that observations of this kind have been made without any implications for federalism in mind.

The rather casual process by which authority for Australia's Constitution moved from the British Parliament to the "people" points to another characteristic of the Constitution and of Australian constitutional culture. As the High Court has occasionally observed in considering comparative case law, unlike its counterpart in the United States, the Australian Constitution is the product of evolution, not of revolution. Australia became a federation without achieving full independence, and it achieved full independence without a break in legal continuity. This history, in turn, has had some important consequences. First, the Constitution builds upon, and in many respects assumes, a preexisting common law.[30] There is and always has been a single Australian common law, declared by the High Court in its capacity as the court of final appeal. Second, many important constitutional rules lie outside the Constitution. These include, for example, the rules establishing effective Australian independence, most recently set forth in the Australia Acts 1986. Third, the attitude toward constitutionalism that underlies the preference for evolution affects Australia's approach to constitutional change. Major changes tend to be made without alteration of the constitutional text or with as little alteration as possible. The result is a constitution that is quite misleading about how key aspects of the system of government work. On the face of the Constitution, for example, the queen is a dominant figure, whose responsibilities within Australia are performed by a governor general. The prime minister and the Cabinet, the effective executive decision makers, are not mentioned at all. Political parties are referred to only in passing, in the context of a relatively minor change to the procedure for filling casual Senate vacancies, implemented in 1977. None of the institutions of intergovernmental relations, including the Council of Australian Governments, is mentioned in the Constitution.

CONSTITUTIONAL PRINCIPLES OF THE FEDERATION

Federalism

On the face of the Constitution, Australia is a dual federation in that it is understood as involving two spheres of government, each with a complete set of governing institutions and corresponding allocations of power. Thus both the Commonwealth and each state has its own legislature, executive institutions, and courts. Legislative, executive, and judicial powers are divided between the Commonwealth and the states for federal purposes. The constitutional arrangements for the judiciary depart from this model (1) to the extent that the Constitution enables the Commonwealth to confer jurisdiction on state courts, if it so chooses,[31] and (2) by creating the High Court as the final court of appeal for all Australian courts in all matters. The dualist features of the federation have recently been held by the High Court to present some difficulties for the constitutional validity of certain types of intergovernmental cooperation.[32]

Australia is not a dual federation, however, if dualism is understood as two spheres of government exercising powers in isolation from each other and inhibited from legislating for each other. It is possible to characterize the federation in other ways as well if attention is focused solely on the Constitution. Thus some provisions of the Constitution mandate or facilitate cooperation: The Commonwealth has power to make laws on additional matters referred to it by state parliaments,[33] the Constitution authorizes intergovernmental agreements in relation to borrowing,[34] and the Commonwealth has a right, born of convenience at the time of federation, to make use of state courts and state prisons for federal purposes.[35] The division of federal and state powers, which leaves substantial legislative and taxation powers to the states, creates real potential for competition between jurisdictions in relation to taxation and public policy more generally. The fiscal imbalance, to which the Constitution itself makes a direct contribution by denying the states power to impose customs and excise duties, offers the opportunity for regulatory federalism.

With hindsight, it is apparent that the Constitution created a federal framework that was capable of development in a variety of ways. The actual operation of Australia's federal system over the course of more than 100 years has been the result of political developments and judicial decisions occurring within a relatively flexible framework. The concept of dual, in the sense of coordinate, federalism has long been discredited by judicial decisions.[36] In practice, a vast range of cooperative arrangements has substantially modified the formal constitutional allocation of powers.[37] Commonwealth dominance of tax resources and the reliance of the states on revenue transfers have prompted occasional speculation that Australia is moving toward a system of regulatory federalism in which the principal state role is to administer Commonwealth programs. This is an overstatement; the states still retain sufficient constitutional and political power to compete with the Commonwealth for electoral advantage and policy choice.

For like reasons, it is difficult to characterize the Australian federation as either centralized or decentralized, inclined toward either unity or diversity. At the time of its establishment, the federation was relatively noncentralized, with considerable potential for policy diversity, which was not necessarily realized because of the relative homogeneity of the states. Over the century that followed, Australia became significantly more centralized in practice, tending to value uniformity at the expense of diversity. The Commonwealth has progressively assumed more responsibility in areas originally considered the domain of the states, ranging from human rights and the environment to education, health, housing, and transport. The causes are various: the fiscal dominance of the Commonwealth, an expansive interpretation of Commonwealth powers by the High Court, the Court's own role as the final authority on the form of the single Australian common law, and the Commonwealth's assumption of responsibility for foreign affairs as Australia achieved independence. This last development ultimately led to an interpretation of the Commonwealth's external-affairs power in a manner enabling the Commonwealth to make laws to incorporate any international treaty obligations of Australia, which contributed further, and controversially, to the centralization of the federation.

Centralization is not always the result of unilateral Commonwealth action. In some areas, of which corporations law was for a long time the prime example,[38] uniformity of policy making, legislation, and administration is effectively achieved through intergovernmental cooperation, facilitated by the dynamics of parliamentary government, giving rise to the phenomenon of executive federalism.

Status of the Constituent Political Communities

The principal constituent polities of the Australian federation are the six original states. The constitutional provisions relating to them establish the Australian federation as remarkably symmetrical. Despite substantial differences in population size, from 6.6 million in New South Wales today to only 470,000 in Tasmania, all original states are equally represented in the Senate and guaranteed minimum representation in the House of Representatives.[39] These provisions may not be changed without a referendum in which majorities are secured in the state affected. In addition, the constitutional powers of the present states are the same. The Commonwealth is constitutionally precluded from discriminating between states in taxation and from giving preference to particular states in laws of trade, commerce, or revenue.[40] These are important features of the Australian federation. It is unlikely that the colonies would have agreed to unite on any other basis.

The Constitution provides some protection for the states, their constitutions, and their territorial limits. Both "state" and "original state" are defined in the Commonwealth of Australia Constitution Act 1900, which established the Constitution. The Commonwealth Constitution expressly preserves state constitutions, albeit subject to its other provisions.[41] State boundaries cannot be altered without the consent of the Parliament and a majority of electors in the state concerned.[42] Any alteration of the constitutional provisions dealing with state boundaries requires a referendum in which a majority in the affected state or states approves the proposal. Judicial doctrine prevents the Commonwealth from using federal power to threaten the continued existence of the states or their capacity to function.[43]

The institutions of state government are created by the respective state constitutions. They are largely autonomous from Commonwealth institutions; even state governors are appointed by the queen on the advice of state governments rather than through the governor general. While state constitutions are subject to the Commonwealth Constitution, the latter includes relatively few restrictions on the structure and organization of state government. With a few exceptions, there is no obvious framework of national principles with which state institutions must comply.

The principal exception derives from the structure of the judicature. The potential for state courts to exercise federal jurisdiction has been held by the High Court to prohibit the states from structuring or empowering their courts in a way that would be incompatible with their position as component parts of the Australian judicature.[44] The High Court of Australia, established by the Constitution at the apex of the judicature, also has profound significance for state government. Most obviously, it may declare state laws and state constitutions to be contrary to the Commonwealth Constitution. However, it also declares the common law of Australia and develops it in a manner consistent with the Commonwealth Constitution.[45] In addition, as the final court of appeal in state as well as in Commonwealth matters, the High Court is the final interpreter of state legislation and of state constitutions.

The Constitution allows some variation in the position of new states vis-à-vis the original states, the extent of which has not yet been tested because no new states have been created. New states have no guarantee of equal representation in the Senate or of minimum representation in the House of Representatives. On the contrary, the Constitution provides for the admission of new states on "such terms and conditions, including the extent of representation in either House of the Parliament," as the Commonwealth Parliament sees fit. Through this mechanism, the Commonwealth could exercise some control over the content of the constitution for a new state. The Commonwealth might also be able to vary the federal division of powers in relation to a new state,[46] although there is some uncertainty over the extent of Commonwealth power in this regard. This differential treatment of categories of states reflects a pragmatic judgment on the part of the framers of the Constitution that the original states would only join on conditions of equality but that there was no reason to extend these concessions automatically to later additions to the federation.

Territories, Localities, and Indigenous Peoples

The constitutional position of the territories is different. The two mainland territories, the Northern Territory and the Australian Capital Territory, govern themselves through their own elected institutions. For purposes of the day-to-day operation of the federal system, they are treated as virtually equivalent to the states. Nevertheless, there are institutional and constitutional differences. The governor general appoints the head of state, or the administrator, of the Northern Territory. The system of government in the Australian Capital Territory is designed to avoid altogether the need for an office of this kind; in extreme circumstances, however, the governor general would perform any necessary function. The Self-Government Acts of the territories are ordinary statutes of the Australian Parliament and may be changed by this Parliament. The Australian Parliament may override territory legislation even within areas of territory responsibility, as occurred in 1997, for example, after the Northern Territory passed legislation to legalize euthanasia. These differences between the constitutional status of the states and territories carry through to other parts of the Constitution. In particular, the provisions of the Constitution dealing with the composition of the Australian Parliament do not extend to voters in the territories, the strict separation of judicial power does not apply fully in the territories, and the relatively few other limits that the Constitution places on the powers of the Commonwealth and the states do not apply to the Commonwealth acting in the territories or to the territory governments themselves.

There are about 800 local government authorities in Australia. However, local government is not mentioned in the Commonwealth Constitution. Rather, it is established and regulated by each state, generally in legislation, although each state constitution now recognizes the state system of local government and provides some minimal protection for it. The question of whether local government should be recognized in the Constitution has been a political issue since the 1970s. Change has been resisted partly because it might adversely affect state power and partly because, in Australia, local government is relatively weak. A referendum to recognize local government in the Commonwealth Constitution was rejected in 1988 by large majorities.

The Constitution now makes no mention of the indigenous peoples of Australia. At the time of federation, Aboriginal Australians were specifically excluded from Commonwealth power under the Constitution and from any population count taken for constitutional purposes. The former reflected a view that indigenous peoples were a state responsibility; the latter was simply racist. Following a 1967 referendum, passed with an overwhelming majority both nationally and in all states, these references were repealed, giving the Commonwealth power to make laws for "the people of any race for whom it is deemed necessary to make special laws."[47] The "race power" is a concurrent power, and both Commonwealth and state laws now affect Aboriginal Australians.

Indigenous law was not recognized by the common law of Australia until relatively recently. This changed in 1992 to the extent that *Mabo v. Queensland (No. 2)*[48] held that the common law would, in some circumstances, recognize indigenous title to land. *Mabo* was followed by Commonwealth legislation providing a regulatory framework for indigenous land claims. Other significant changes in Aboriginal governance also took place in the late decades of the twentieth century. These included the creation of an elected national institution, the Aboriginal and Torres Strait Islander Commission, with responsibilities for both representing and delivering services to indigenous peoples; the conferral of some opportunities for self-governance on particular Aboriginal communities either on their own lands or through local government structures; and the execution of land-use agreements of various kinds between Aboriginal groups, governments, and the private sector. None of these arrangements have a base in the constitutions of either the Commonwealth or the states.

The Allocation of Powers

The Commonwealth Constitution enumerates the powers of the federal legislature and the federal judiciary. Federal executive powers have been defined by judicial interpretation in a manner analogous to federal legislative powers.[49] Subject to the Commonwealth Constitution, the states have plenary powers under their respective state constitutions. The notion that the states have residual power is the consequence of this arrangement. The 40 powers allocated to the Commonwealth can be broadly categorized as concerned with trade and commerce, foreign affairs and defence, and selected social powers, including powers in relation to marriage and divorce.[50] Key powers on which the Commonwealth draws for much of its legislation deal with trading and financial corporations, external affairs, and interstate and overseas trade and commerce. Police powers generally lie with the states, although federal criminal law is significant and growing in response to international developments. There is a federal police force in addition to the more general police forces of the states.

The model for the division of legislative powers draws on that of the United States. Most Commonwealth powers are concurrent in the sense that they may be exercised by the states as well. The principal exception is the exclusive Commonwealth power to impose customs and excise duties.[51] In the event of inconsistency between Commonwealth and state law in an area of concurrent power, the Commonwealth law prevails.[52] Inconsistency is defined broadly for this purpose to include not only laws that are directly in conflict with each other but also circumstances in which a Commonwealth act purports to cover an entire legislative "field," leaving no room for state legislation.[53]

Although the Constitution places relatively few absolute limits on the powers of the Commonwealth or the states, these limits have proved significant. Some are designed to secure economic union. These provide some protection for the internal common market and some guarantee of interstate mobility.[54] Other express limits on power require the Commonwealth (but not the states) to provide for the payment of "just terms," or compensation, in connection with the acquisition of property and to provide some protection for religious freedom.[55] In addition, the sections of the Constitution that create the institutions of government and Parliament imply limits on both Commonwealth and state power to impair freedom of political communication.[56]

The only other governmental institution contemplated by the Constitution is an Interstate Commission.[57] This was originally conceived as a watchdog to monitor the provisions of the Constitution dealing with the common market. It was a Commonwealth rather than an intergovernmental institution in that it was to be established by the Commonwealth and that its members were to be appointed by the Commonwealth. Although the Interstate Commission has played an intermittent role in Australian federalism, it has been relatively unimportant. No Interstate Commission presently exists, and this is unlikely to change.

Jurisdictional Conflicts

Jurisdictional conflicts between the Commonwealth and the states are fairly common. When they occur, they tend to be significant, although major conflict cannot be described as either frequent or severe. Questions of jurisdiction may be raised in any court, whether Commonwealth or state, by governments or by private parties with an interest sufficient to meet the Australian requirements of standing. This is implicit in the common-law constitutional model and recognized, somewhat obliquely, by Covering Clause 5 of the Commonwealth of Australia Constitution Act. If a constitutional issue is raised, Commonwealth legislation requires that notice be given to the attorneys general of all Australian jurisdictions to enable them to decide whether to intervene and whether to seek removal of the case to the High Court. A case in which a significant constitutional question is raised is likely either to begin in the High Court as mandated by its original jurisdiction or to be removed to the High Court. In any event, it is likely that the High Court will finally deal with such matters on appeal. The courts play a significant role in enforcing the limits of the Commonwealth Constitution with respect to both spheres of government, and there are relatively recent cases invalidating both Commonwealth and state legislation on constitutional grounds. In 1995, for example, the High Court held that Commonwealth legislation regulating the employment contract between two parties, one of whom was also in a contractual relationship with a "trading corporation," could not be supported as a law with respect to trading corporations and was thus invalid.[58] In 1997 the High Court held that state business-franchise license fees are excise duties, which may not be imposed by the states in accordance with the Constitution.[59]

There are no particular mechanisms, other than the normal political and administrative processes, to forestall jurisdictional conflicts. The cost and disruption of constitutional litigation no doubt offer some incentive to avoid conflict or at least to keep it out of the courts.

FEDERALISM AND THE STRUCTURE AND OPERATION OF GOVERNMENT

Institutions of Commonwealth Government: General

Both the Commonwealth and the states have parliamentary systems: Members of the government must be members of Parliament; governments must have the "confidence" of the lower House of Parliament; and a governor general or governor representing the queen acts as a largely nonexecutive head of state, formally exercising power on government advice.

Despite the historical imperative favouring a parliamentary system, one consideration gave the framers of the Constitution pause before they would mandate responsible government for the Commonwealth. This was concern about whether federalism and responsible government were compatible. Their concern centred on potential for conflict between a House of Representatives with the composition and powers of the Senate, on the one hand, and the requirement that a government have the support of the House, on the other hand. The draft of the Constitution that emerged from the convention of 1891 left the question of responsible government open. One of the most significant changes made by the convention of 1897–98 was to reintroduce a requirement that ministers be members of Parliament.

The Constitution is characterized also by a separation of federal powers. This has become an important principle but remains subordinate to the central requirements of parliamentary government. The conclusion that the Constitution requires a separation of federal powers has been drawn by courts from the structure of the Constitution and, in particular, from the division of the first three chapters between the judicial, legislative, and executive branches of the federal government.[60] The separation of powers, however, is "asymmetrical." Parliamentary government assumes that the legislative and executive branches interlock and that legislation overrides executive power. The judicial branch, on the other hand, enjoys a strict separation of judicial power, which distinguishes courts from other institutions of government, precludes bodies other than courts from exercising federal judicial power, and restricts the federal courts to the exercise of federal judicial power.

A system of checks and balances emerges from this institutional structure, although it was not necessarily a design feature of the Constitution. Courts may declare actions of the executive illegal and may invalidate acts of Parliament. Governments appoint judges; courts require funding, pursuant to appropriations approved by parliaments; and judges can be removed through a combination of legislative and executive action on the grounds of "proved misbehavior or incapacity."[61] With regard to relations between the executive and the legislature, the legislature may withdraw confidence from the executive, while the executive may dissolve the lower House of the legislature by advising the governor general to do so. New laws must be passed by Parliament, which is also expected to play the usual role of scrutinizing executive action. In practice, the Senate has made the Commonwealth Parliament more effective in this regard because, for reasons explained below, the Senate is generally constituted differently from the House of Representatives.

The governor general also operates as a check to the extent that he or she has "reserve" powers exercisable without or against government advice. In reality, this check is limited: The prime minister effectively selects the governor general, although the formal appointment is made by the queen; the reserve powers are few; and their exercise is always controversial. Nevertheless, there have been times in Australian history when the governor general has influenced the outcome of events, most notably in 1975, when Prime Minister Whitlam, who had a majority in the House of Representatives, was dismissed from office after the Senate blocked the passage of key financial bills.

The Parliament[62]

The Commonwealth Parliament has the powers traditionally allocated to the legislature in a common-law parliamentary system subject to the division of powers for federal purposes. In other words, the Parliament must make or approve all laws, including tax laws, and must appropriate monies for expenditure by the executive government.

The Parliament is bicameral, and considerations of federalism affect the composition of both houses.[63] The Senate consists of a minimum of six senators for each of the original states; the number may be increased and is presently twelve, but the equal representation of these states must be maintained. The total size of the House of Representatives is required to be approximately twice the size of the Senate, and the Constitution requires the total number of seats to be allocated between states, in proportion to population, before divisions into constituencies are determined.[64] Constituencies need not be equal in population, but current legislation limits population variation to 10 percent above or below the average. A federal constituency may not cross the borders of a state, and each original state is entitled to a minimum of five members of the House of Representatives, irrespective of population.

The self-governing status of the two mainland territories has made some small difference to the scheme. These territories are represented in both houses of the Parliament but pursuant to Commonwealth legislation rather than by constitutional right. Territory representatives are not subject to many of the constitutional requirements that apply to representatives from the states, including the rules that senators have fixed six-year terms, that in general half the Senate faces election every three years, and that the total number of members of the House is linked to the size of the Senate.

The Senate has almost coequal powers with the House. The exceptions are that it may not initiate bills imposing taxation or appropriating monies and may not amend taxation or key appropriation bills. In addition, the Constitution provides a procedure for breaking deadlocks between the Senate and the House in relation to both ordinary legislation and constitution-alteration bills, which, after an extended process – including, in the case of ordinary bills, a double dissolution of both houses – ultimately gives the edge to the House of Representatives.[65] Nevertheless, the Senate is a relatively powerful chamber even though, unlike the United States Senate, it has no special, additional constitutional powers of its own.

Since federation, senators have generally voted in accordance with their party allegiances rather than on state lines or with a view to state issues. However, this does not mean that the Senate is irrelevant to Australian federalism. At the very least, its composition ensures that there are more members from the smaller states in the Commonwealth Parliament than there would be otherwise. Thus the smaller states have a larger voice than they would have had in the respective party caucuses, and there is a larger pool of members from the smaller states on which to draw in selecting the ministry and constituting parliamentary committees.

In other respects, too, the Senate has had a profound effect on the operation of the Commonwealth government. Whereas the House is composed of members elected for maximum three-year terms from single-member constituencies through a system of preferential voting, the Senate consists of an equal number of members from each state, half of whom are elected for fixed six-year terms every three years through a system of proportional representation that regards each state as a single electorate. Typically, representation of parties in the Senate is very different from that in the House, and it is unusual for either the government or the opposition parties to have a majority of seats. Hence governments cannot assume that their legislation will be enacted, and government action tends to be subjected to more severe scrutiny in the Senate than in the House. The Senate thus constitutes a real, if not always consistent, check on the will of the government that draws its authority from the House of Representatives. Australian opinion is typically divided over whether this should be so. In 2003 the incumbent Australian government established an inquiry into how the deadlock procedures might be modified to ensure that the will of the House of Representatives is more likely to prevail. While the results were still unknown at the beginning of 2004, the evident lack of public interest in or enthusiasm for such a change make it unlikely that the proposal will be taken further.

The Executive

The executive government of the Commonwealth comprises the prime minister and the ministers, all of whom must be members of the House or the Senate and who depend for office on the confidence of the House. As Australia has a constitutional monarchy, the executive also comprises a governor general, representing the queen and appointed on the advice of the prime minister. Formal executive power is vested in the queen and exercisable by the governor general.[66] In practice, pursuant to unwritten constitutional convention, the powers of the governor general are exercised on the advice of the executive government unless, exceptionally, a discretionary or "reserve" power of the governor general comes into play. Also pursuant to convention, the executive government is responsible to the Parliament for the conduct of the business of government according to the principles and practices generally associated with responsible government in the British parliamentary tradition. The powers of the executive are those normally exercisable by executive government in a common-law parliamentary system, again subject to the division of jurisdictions for federal purposes. Thus the Commonwealth executive derives powers directly from the Constitution (e.g., to dissolve the House of Representatives), from statutes, and from the inherent powers of the executive recognized by the common law. Although some matters fall within state rather than federal executive power, the Commonwealth executive has the powers normally exercisable by a national government, including the powers to enter into international treaties, to declare war, and to make peace.

There is no constitutional requirement that the states be represented in the Commonwealth executive. In practice, however, the ministry usually includes at least one member from each of the six states. The position of head of state in the Australian federation is complicated by constitutional monarchy. The queen is the single head of state for the whole of Australia. To this extent, she plays a role in relation to the states as well as to the Commonwealth. In practice, however, she has seven separate representatives in Australia, each of whom has an effectively discrete role in relation to his or her jurisdiction. Thus the queen appoints the governor general, on the advice of the prime minister, without consultation with the states. The queen also appoints each state governor, on the advice of the state government, without consultation with other jurisdictions. A state governor plays the role of governor general if there is no incumbent or if for some reason the governor general is not available. This may be explained by the fact that, formally, both the governor general and the governors represent the same monarch. If Australia becomes a republic, this link will be removed and there will be a question about how, if at all, the federal structure of Australia should be reflected in the new arrangements for a head of state.

The Courts

The Constitution divides judicial power between the Commonwealth and the states and contemplates two distinct court hierarchies, united at the apex by the High Court. Federal judicial power includes matters arising under the Commonwealth Constitution and under federal laws, matters involving parties or governments in different jurisdictions, and matters in which the Commonwealth is a party.[67] This jurisdiction may be conferred on either federal or state courts. During the first half-century of federation, the Commonwealth made extensive use of state courts. Since the 1970s, however, the federal court system has been progressively developed to the point where there is now a clear federal court hierarchy, comprising a Federal Magistrates Court, a specialist Family Court, and the Federal Court of Australia, below the High Court itself. The governor general appoints members of the federal judicature on the advice of the Federal Executive Council, which is always accepted.

The highest court is the High Court. It has both appellate and original jurisdiction. Constitutional matters may be taken to the High Court as mandated by its original jurisdiction, although they may also commence elsewhere. The High Court has appellate jurisdiction from both federal and state courts, now subject to a requirement that the High Court itself give special leave to appeal the decision. Courts, including the High Court, may declare acts of either the Commonwealth or state parliaments to be void on constitutional grounds, but they have no advisory jurisdiction. Within at least the federal government, such jurisdiction would be contrary to the separation of judicial power.

The role of the High Court as final court of appeal gives it significant authority in state matters: The High Court is the final arbiter on issues arising under state constitutions; it finally interprets state legislation; and it declares and develops the common law. The states thus have a significant stake in the predilections of High Court justices. However, there is no constitutional role for the states in appointments to the Court. Since 1978 Commonwealth legislation has required Commonwealth attorneys general to consult with their state counterparts before making an appointment. The effect of this change is difficult to gauge. It is symbolically significant and may be presumed to have made some difference in practice, weak though a mere requirement to "consult" may be. No concept of state representation in the High Court has developed in Australia. There are two states from which a High Court justice has never been drawn, and the present seven-member court has five justices from one state, New South Wales (all of whom are men). The composition of the court is emerging as a controversial issue. Ironically, other federal courts have a more substantial presence in the states. They have registries and resident judges in most states, drawn from the legal communities of the states concerned. The High Court itself is based in the national capital, although it has regular hearings in the state capitals.

State Institutions

State institutions are broadly similar to those of the Commonwealth: Most states (except Queensland) have a bicameral legislature; state ministers are members of the state Parliament and depend on the lower House of Parliament for their continuation in office; each state has a governor representing the queen who acts on the advice of the state executive; and each state has a court system able to declare actions of the state executive to be unlawful and acts of the state Parliament unconstitutional.

There are some institutional differences between the Commonwealth and state constitutional systems. One is that state constitutions are generally easier to change and, in some cases, have no higher status than ordinary law. A second is that the states do not have a constitutionally entrenched separation of powers. Thus, while there is a general expectation that state courts exercise judicial power, there is no constitutional rule to inhibit its exercise by, say, a tribunal or to restrict state courts exclusively to the exercise of judicial power. A third difference concerns the upper houses of the state parliaments. The rationale for the Australian Senate, which still informs its composition, does not exist in the state sphere. State legislative councils originated in the design for colonial governance, whereby a relatively conservative upper house in a bicameral legislature was permitted to represent propertied interests and to operate as a check on the lower house. Although these times have passed and the franchise for upper houses is the same as for lower houses, most states still struggle to identify a useful role for the upper house that does not merely replicate the views of the lower house nor inappropriately stymie the upper house's decisions. To this end, a different electoral system is now used for many state upper houses (typically, proportional representation) to enable representation of a wider variety of interests. Most state upper houses also have lost their legal or effective power to reject money bills and, thus, to threaten the continued existence of the government.

Typically, each state has a complete court hierarchy, beginning with lower magistrates or district courts and culminating in a supreme court. State courts exercise federal as well as state jurisdiction. Judges are appointed by the state governor on the advice of the relevant government. There is no Commonwealth influence over state judicial appointments. Moreover, even though state courts can exercise federal jurisdiction, the Commonwealth has limited capacity to influence the composition of state courts for this purpose. The Commonwealth is expected to "take state courts as it finds them" subject to any implications that can be drawn from the Commonwealth Constitution.[68]

Consistent with common-law method, the decisions of the higher courts of each state hierarchy are binding on courts below. The decisions of other state court systems are not binding but are likely to be persuasive, particularly in the interpretation of intergovernmental legislative schemes. This apparently decentralized judicial system is substantially modified by decisions of the High Court, which are binding in all state systems, resulting in a homogenizing effect that tends to increase the likelihood of a state's judicial decisions proving persuasive in the other states.

Relations between States

The Constitution provides a minimum framework for comity between states in the interest of ensuring national unity on key matters. Provision is made for giving full faith and credit to all state laws and judicial proceedings throughout Australia.[69] Other constitutional provisions inhibit protectionism in interstate trade and provide some mobility rights.[70] States are territorially restricted in their capacity to legislate for other states.[71] The Commonwealth has the power to make laws for the service and execution of judicial process throughout Australia and has done so.[72] Suits between residents of different states arise in federal jurisdiction, although they are generally dealt with in state courts.

There is a vast network of intergovernmental ministerial councils, which proliferated in the last half of the twentieth century. With one partial exception, none is specifically authorized by the Constitution. The exception is the Australian Loan Council, through which government borrowing is coordinated in Australia and which is established by an intergovernmental agreement authorized by Section 105A of the Constitution. There is no constitutional prohibition on compacts between states. While Commonwealth-state cooperation is the norm, agreements are sometimes made between the states alone without giving rise to particular problems.[73]

FISCAL AND MONETARY POWERS

Taxation

With two important exceptions, the Constitution allocates general taxation authority to both the Commonwealth and the states. In this sense, it is a competitive system. The exceptions are customs and excise duties, which are allocated exclusively to the Commonwealth. These taxes have been interpreted by the High Court as denying the states power to impose any taxes on goods. This development also inhibits the states from imposing taxes on natural resources within their territories or in the offshore areas adjacent to a state to the extent to which such taxes can be characterized as imposed on the production of the resource.[74] However, state ownership of these resources within the states' own borders and within the three-mile territorial sea[75] entitles them to collect royalties on the use of these resources.

The taxation powers of both the Commonwealth and the states are constitutionally restricted in various ways. Commonwealth taxes may neither discriminate between nor give preference to states or parts of states.[76] The states are limited in their authority to tax with extraterritorial effect unless a connection can be established between the state and the subject matter of the tax.[77] Neither order of government may tax each other's property. States, and thus local government, may not tax the Commonwealth at all, although the Commonwealth may and does tax the states.

In practice, taxation has become centralized through political action that has largely been upheld by the courts. Most significantly, the Commonwealth unilaterally assumed a monopoly on income taxation during the Second World War through an interlocking series of acts, challenges to the validity of which were largely dismissed, twice, by the High Court. The Commonwealth has retained this monopoly ever since then although, as a matter of law, the states now may, if they so wish, reenter the income-tax field.[78] In the late 1990s, the states agreed to forego additional state taxes in return for Commonwealth agreement to allocate to them the proceeds of the goods-and-services tax. The states still impose some taxes, however, including property taxes, gambling taxes, payroll taxes, and some stamp duties. In the financial year 2001–02, state and local government taxation comprised 18.4 percent of total taxation revenue; Commonwealth taxation comprised 81.6 percent.[79]

Borrowing

The original constitutional design left both the Commonwealth and the states with independent borrowing authority. Even at the time of federation, however, there was concern about the level of debts incurred during the colonial period for the provision of costly infrastructure, such as railways. There was a question of whether the Commonwealth should take over state debt and whether, as a quid pro quo, state borrowing should be subject to some form of national control. Agreement to this effect was reached in 1927, when the Constitution was amended to authorize agreements between the Commonwealth and the states with respect to the debts of the states.

The first agreement established an intergovernmental ministerial council, the Loan Council, to coordinate the borrowing of all governments. It provided that, during the currency of the agreement, the Commonwealth would borrow monies for the states in accordance with Loan Council decisions. With some modifications, this scheme lasted for more than 60 years, although it became increasingly less effective as states developed new methods of financing capital works and as semigovernmental authorities that fell outside the definition of states for the purposes of the agreement raised capital for themselves. A major revision of the Financial Agreement in 1995 restored the capacity of each government to borrow on its own behalf but requires that borrowing programs be fully disclosed and subject to Loan Council surveillance. This mechanism, coupled with the political discipline now imposed by the ratings agencies at a time when fiscal restraint on the part of government is fashionable, so far has proved effective in controlling borrowing levels.

Allocation of Revenues

From the outset of federation, it was expected that the Commonwealth would have more revenues than it needed and that the states would have less as a result of exclusive Commonwealth power over the imposition of custom and excise duties. The framers of the Constitution were unable to agree on a lasting system of revenue redistribution. The Constitution, therefore, makes detailed provision for revenue redistribution only for the first ten years after federation. The only obligation beyond this period was for the Commonwealth to distribute its "surplus revenue" to the states each month on such a basis as the Commonwealth Parliament deemed "fair." This section of the Constitution has proved entirely ineffective because the Commonwealth has been able to organize its revenues to avoid leaving a "surplus."[80]

Revenue redistribution, nevertheless, takes place pursuant to Section 96 of the Constitution, which authorizes the Parliament to grant "financial assistance" to any state "on such terms and conditions as the Parliament thinks fit." The Commonwealth relies on this authority to make both general and specific-purpose payments to the states. This is the mechanism used, for example, to pay the states proceeds from the goods-and-services tax. Typically, general-revenue payments are affected by an equalization formula. The concept of fiscal equalization is long-standing. From the outset, the Constitution allowed Western Australia, as a special concession, to continue to impose customs duties, at diminishing rates, for the first ten years of federation. Payments by the Commonwealth to less affluent states began shortly after the operation of this section of the Constitution came to an end.

The present system of equalization can be traced to the 1930s, when the Commonwealth established an independent Grants Commission to advise on levels of payment to claimant states. The objective of fiscal equalization is to enable each state to provide services at standards comparable to those of other states without imposing taxes and charges at levels appreciably higher than those of other states. To this end, the Grants Commission recommends a "factor" for each state, which takes into account both its revenue capacity and its expenditure needs. The total general-revenue funds made available by the Commonwealth to the states is distributed between them in proportion to state population numbers, adjusted by the equalization factor. In 2003 three states were donors and three were recipients of fiscal equalization funds. Typically, donor states are critical of the system of fiscal equalization; however, successive attempts to impose limits on the extent of equalization through alteration of the methodology have failed.

Spending of Revenues

The Constitution requires money spent by the Commonwealth executive to be appropriated by law "for the purposes of the Commonwealth."[81] This stipulation does not limit the matters for which monies may be appropriated.[82] Expenditure is another matter, however, because it engages the executive power. The High Court has held that the Commonwealth's executive power is limited by reference to the enumerated heads of legislative powers plus additional matters peculiarly appropriate to a national government. Expenditure on scientific research is an example of such "national" power.[83]

Limits on the Commonwealth's power to spend do not affect the range of purposes for which grants can be made to the states or the conditions that may be attached to them. It is clear from the judicial interpretation of Section 96 that although the states may not be forced to accept grants, grants may be made for any purpose and subject to any conditions as long as the conditions at least do not contravene one of the few absolute limits on Commonwealth or state power.[84] It is not clear whether the conditions attached to grants are legally enforceable against a state once a grant has been accepted. In practice, the question does not arise because the threat of withholding other grants from an offending state is an effective sanction.

The High Court has held that the Commonwealth's power to spend is not affected by the prohibition against giving preference to a state in a "revenue" law.[85] The Constitution provides, however, that any Commonwealth "bounty" on the production or manufacture of goods must be imposed uniformly throughout the Commonwealth.[86]

Monetary Policy

Monetary policy is effectively assigned exclusively to the Commonwealth. "Currency, coinage and legal tender" are included in the list of Common-

wealth concurrent powers. An absolute prohibition in Section 115 precludes the states from coining money. The central bank, the Reserve Bank
of Australia, is not established by the Constitution but under Commonwealth legislation. There is no practice whereby the states are represented
in the governing organs of the bank.

FOREIGN AFFAIRS AND DEFENCE POWERS[87]

Responsibility for foreign affairs and defence lies almost exclusively with the
Commonwealth. This is the result both of constitutional design and of the
manner in which Australia acquired independence. The states were effectively fully independent. The authority of the imperial power in relation to
foreign affairs and defence gradually passed to the Commonwealth, and the
understanding of the meaning of the Constitution was adjusted accordingly.

The governor general is the commander in chief of the armed forces[88]
and acts, in this capacity, on Commonwealth government advice. The
Commonwealth Parliament has power to make laws for defence,[89] and the
states are precluded from maintaining any naval or military force without
the Parliament's consent.[90] The Commonwealth alone possesses the international legal status to speak for Australia.[91] Commonwealth executive
power extends to making and ratifying treaties, declaring war, and making
peace. Effectively, there are no limits on this power. However, treaties of a
legislative character require implementation by a parliament, whether
Commonwealth or state, before they can be given effect in Australian law.
The legislative power of the Commonwealth Parliament over external affairs enables it to implement international commitments subject to relevant restrictions on power elsewhere in the Constitution.[92] The expansion
of the subjects of international treaties, coupled with judicial recognition
of the scope of this power, has had a profound effect on the federal division of powers.[93]

Formally, the Australian states have little or no authority in these matters. To the extent that state governments have executive power that might
impinge on external affairs, it is subject to the exercise of Commonwealth
power to the contrary. State parliaments may legislate to implement treaties, but such legislation is subject to any inconsistent Commonwealth law.
In practice, nevertheless, the Australian states engage in a wide variety of
arrangements with other countries or parts of countries. Such arrangements have less than formal treaty status. States also maintain offices in
some overseas countries, notably the United Kingdom and the United
States. The Australian states are parties to recent agreements between Australia and New Zealand, providing for the mutual recognition of standards
for goods and occupations and the execution of child-protection orders.
The Commonwealth also has a constitutional obligation to protect states

against invasion and, "on the application of the executive government of
the state, against domestic violence."[94]

The increase in the range of matters of international concern that characterized the last decades of the twentieth century led to demands for
greater cooperation and consultation between the Commonwealth and the
states on external affairs. In a parallel development, there has been pressure for greater involvement of the Commonwealth Parliament in decisions
about treaties that traditionally were left to the executive. Following some
significant procedural changes in the 1990s, pending and existing international commitments are made more transparent. International agreements
are now tabled in the Parliament before Australia finally accedes to them
and are scrutinized by a parliamentary committee. An intergovernmental
Treaties Council has been established to consider international agreements
of particular interest to the states. The states may participate in international delegations negotiating treaties on behalf of Australia by agreement
with the Commonwealth. There is an understanding that state parliaments
may implement treaties when the matter is predominantly of state concern.

CITIZENSHIP, VOTING, ELECTIONS, AND PARTIES

At the time the Constitution was written, there was no formal legal category of Australian citizen.[95] Rather, Australians were subjects of the monarch of the United Kingdom. To the extent that the Constitution refers to
status at all, therefore, it refers to "subjects of the Queen."[96]

The Constitution confers power on the Commonwealth Parliament to
make laws for "naturalisation and aliens."[97] After the Second World War, as
component parts of the former British Empire moved to create separate
national citizenships, the Commonwealth Parliament enacted a citizenship
law, presumably relying on the naturalization power. Citizenship in this
sense is purely a Commonwealth affair. The predominant means of acquir-
ing citizenship is by birth in Australia to at least one parent who is either an
Australian citizen or a permanent resident of Australia. New applications
for citizenship are made to the Commonwealth and granted by the Commonwealth without consultation with the states.

There is no clear concept of dual citizenship in the sense of distinct state
and Commonwealth citizenships. However, an argument for dual citizenship could be made. The people voting in states agreed to the original
Constitution. Approval of the people voting in a majority of states remains
necessary for constitutional change. Petitioners to the House of Representatives identify themselves as "citizens" of the states in which they reside.
There is a concept of state residence that attracts both the right and the
obligation to vote in state and local elections.

The Constitution establishes the institutions of Commonwealth government but makes little lasting provision for the rights to vote and to stand for election. In one view, this is because the Constitution is "facultative"; in other words, its principal purpose is to create the institutions of the state and to empower them to act. An alternative interpretation is that failure to provide for such matters reflects disagreement about what the voting requirements should be at a time when two of the six states had already extended the franchise to women although the others were reluctant to do so.

The only constitutional provision that deals with voter qualifications in a way that has substantive effect is Section 41, which prohibits the Commonwealth from preventing a person with the right to vote in a state election from voting in an election for the Commonwealth. This section was intended to protect the voting rights of women in elections of the Commonwealth Parliament immediately after federation and has been held to be transitory in effect.[98]

Section 41 aside, the scheme of the Constitution is intended to confer power on the Commonwealth Parliament to prescribe the qualifications for voters for the House and the Senate after an initial period during which, for convenience, the laws of the relevant states were used. The Parliament exercised this power in 1902, and Commonwealth law has governed these matters ever since. The power is probably not completely at large, as it seems likely that implications drawn from the Constitution now protect at least universal adult suffrage.[99] This is prescribed in the Commonwealth Electoral Act in any event, with the minimum voting age being eighteen. British subjects who are not Australian citizens but who acquired the right to vote in Australian elections before the cut-off date of 1984 still possess the right to vote in Australian elections. Voting is compulsory. Ironically, in these circumstances, citizenship education has been much neglected, although some steps to remedy this acknowledged problem were taken in 2001 in connection with the constitutional centenary.

The constitutional scheme is similar in relation to candidacy for election to the Commonwealth Parliament. State laws were initially used, but the Parliament has power to prescribe the qualifications of candidates and has done so. This power is subject to the disqualifications stipulated in Section 44. These preclude, for example, Australians who are also citizens of another country, including the United Kingdom, from standing for election to the Commonwealth Parliament.

In its original form, the Constitution made no reference to political parties. There is now one such reference, which is the result of a successful referendum in 1977. Section 15 requires that a casual vacancy in the Senate be filled by the relevant state parliament with someone from the same political party as the senator who had held the seat. This change reflects the significance of party numbers in the Senate, particularly since the introduction of proportional representation. The provision is a complicated one, having been drafted to deal with the possibility that the retiring senator had changed party allegiance in mid-term or that the appointee was not, in fact, the relevant party's preferred candidate. This section of the Constitution makes it clear that party allegiance is to be determined at the date of election and that another choice must be made if an appointee is dismissed by the party before taking up the seat.

PROTECTION OF INDIVIDUAL AND COMMUNAL RIGHTS[100]

Neither the Commonwealth nor the state constitutions include a bill or charter of rights. At the time the constitutions were written, countries under the British constitutional system were satisfied that rights could be protected adequately by other means. Unlike other comparable countries, now including the United Kingdom itself, Australia has continued to adhere to this view. Successive attempts to introduce a national bill of rights have failed, although a bill to provide statutory protection for rights was before the Legislative Assembly of the Australian Capital Territory at the beginning of 2004, with a view to implementation by July 2004.[101] Consistent with this somewhat complacent view of the ordinary legal system's capacity to protect rights adequately, there has been no general incorporation into Australian law of international human-rights instruments to which Australia is a party. Australian law is assumed to be in compliance with them. Corrective action is possible, although not always forthcoming, if, as sometimes happens, this assumption is shown to be misplaced. In the case of some instruments, specific incorporating legislation has been passed. The Commonwealth's Racial Discrimination Act 1975 is an example. This legislation applies to both the Commonwealth and the states, although in its application to the Commonwealth, it has the force only of ordinary law.

The Australian Constitution imposes a few specific limits on the powers of the Commonwealth or of the states that have an effect akin to the protection of individual rights. In particular, Commonwealth legislation authorizing the acquisition of private property must provide for the payment of "just terms"; any trial on indictment for an offense against the laws of the Commonwealth must be by jury; Commonwealth power is restricted in the interests of freedom of religion; and neither the states nor, probably, the Commonwealth may discriminate against subjects of the queen on the basis of state residence in a way that would detract from the requirements of Section 117.[102] The High Court has tended to characterize these provisions as systematic limits on power rather than as free-standing individual rights. It is a minor distinction but a distinction nevertheless. Using this analysis, for example, the Court has held that the requirement for trial by jury is significant for the justice system as a whole and, therefore, may not be waived by an accused if it is otherwise applicable.[103]

Other limits on the powers of parliaments and governments have been drawn from the parts of the Constitution establishing the institutions of government. Thus the collective effect of sections of the Constitution establishing the institutions of representative and responsible government has been held to limit the power of either Commonwealth or state parliaments to burden "political communication."[104] For the same reason, the Constitution probably provides some protection for universal adult suffrage and for the fairness of electoral boundaries, at least for Commonwealth elections. The separation of federal judicial power under the Constitution also provides some limited protection for aspects of the judicial process. It has been held, for example, that the separation of judicial power would preclude Commonwealth legislation that had the effect of a bill of attainder.[105] Despite the similarity of the effects of these doctrines to what in other countries and systems might be described as civil and political rights, in these cases, too, the High Court has maintained the distinction between limits on power and rights.

Many of these restrictions on power are linked in some way to political participation in the institutions of government and thus apply principally to citizens. Some others apply also to noncitizens, however, depending on context. In particular, the requirement of "just terms" for the acquisition of property and the protections drawn from the separation of federal judicial power are available to all individuals affected by a relevant Commonwealth law.

CONSTITUTIONAL CHANGE

The Constitution prescribes a two-step process for change involving both the Parliament and Australian voters. Only the Australian Parliament can initiate a bill to change the Constitution. Normally, both houses of Parliament must pass such a bill. It is possible, however, in accordance with the process prescribed by Section 128, for the governor general to put to referendum a bill that has been passed by one house twice. In practice, this deadlock mechanism operates only if the government is prepared to advise the governor general to act, which is unlikely to be the case if the house has rejected the bill. In any event, rejection of such a bill by one house of the Parliament does not augur well for the fate of the proposal in a referendum.

A bill to alter the Constitution that has been passed by the Parliament must be approved in a referendum before it becomes law. Normally, approval in a referendum requires the support of a majority of voters nationally and of a majority of voters in a majority of the states. Australians who live in the territories are counted for the first of these purposes but not for the second. Alterations that would change the representation of an original state in either house or the provisions of the Constitution relating to state boundaries must also be approved by majorities in the states concerned.

It has proved difficult to amend the Constitution through this procedure. Forty-four proposals for change have been put to the voters since federation, but only eight have passed. Of the eight successful proposals, several were very minor, and all were confined to quite specific purposes. The referendum record appears to have discouraged governments from seeking to amend the Constitution. Equally, the record of success in referendums has declined in recent decades. The last referendum to approve proposed changes was in 1977, when three out of four proposals were passed. Four others were rejected in 1988, however, with historically large majorities. Two further proposals, to add a preamble to the Constitution and to establish a republic, were rejected in 1999. Among the possible explanations for this record of constitutional change are the highly adversarial character of the process, lack of understanding of proposals for change, and the conservatism of Australian voters on constitutional issues.

Effective change in the operation of the Constitution has been achieved largely by two means. One is political action. This is facilitated by the extent to which the Constitution leaves key matters for resolution to the Australian Parliament after making initial provision for them. Political change has also been effected by cooperation between governments – for example, through use of the Commonwealth's power to make laws on matters referred to it by a state parliament. A recent reference of power by the states to the Commonwealth, for example, enabled the latter to enact a national-corporations law. The second means by which effective constitutional change has taken place is judicial interpretation. Although the courts are relatively conservative in their interpretation of the Constitution, judicial interpretation has contributed to a significant expansion of Commonwealth power over the course of 104 years. The interpretation of the external-affairs power, for example, to enable the Australian Parliament to implement treaty commitments has given the Commonwealth broad power in relation to the environment, labour standards, and human rights.

CONCLUSION

Like most federal constitutions, the inspiration for Australia's Constitution came from a range of sources. Some of the Constitution's original features, however, were intended to suit peculiarly Australian conditions. Over the course of 103 years, moreover, it has developed in a way that has made it distinctively Australian.

In some respects, the Constitution has been remarkably successful. It brought and has peacefully kept together all parts of a geographically very large country, resisting at least one serious attempt at secession. It has functioned as the principal constituent instrument during more than a century of stable democratic government. It has been flexible enough to adapt to dramatically changing circumstances, including transition to Australian independence. It has provided a framework for government within the limits of which Commonwealth, state, and territory communities have developed and flourished.

However, partly because of its longevity, the Constitution has become increasingly irrelevant to the structure and operation of Australian government, at least for those who regard the purpose of constitutions as being to structure power and control its abuse. In contrast with, for example, the attitude of Americans to the Constitution of the United States, the Australian Constitution attracts relatively little reverence, or even respect, from Australians. Typically, Australians claim to know very little about it. Public education is difficult because the text of the Constitution seems to have relatively little to do with the practice of government.

Australians also have a love-hate relationship with federalism. Anecdotal evidence suggests that there is a widespread view that Australia does not need a federal form of government and that a system of national, state, and local governments represents "overgovernment" in a country of 20 million people. Nevertheless, this view rarely translates into a willingness to support a referendum to increase Commonwealth power. It seems improbable, moreover, that voters in the smaller, more distant states would ever favour a change that would finally entrust all decisions of government to a single national government dominated by the most populous states on the East Coast.

In the final decade of the twentieth century, the main subject of constitutional debate in Australia was whether, when, and how to establish a republic in the sense of breaking Australia's links with the Crown. Apparently, the referendum failed largely because of the perceived deficiencies of the alternative arrangements that would have been put in place. Whether to establish a republic will likely continue to be a dominant constitutional issue in the early part of the current century not because it causes particular practical difficulty but for symbolic reasons. The debate has a federal dimension, not fully recognized in the proposal unsuccessfully put to referendum in 1999. In a future referendum, there could be questions, for example, of whether it is important for the constituent units of a federation, as well as its centre, to be involved in selection of the head of state. An alternative, possible subject of constitutional debate in the future is the constitutional protection of rights. This seems an obvious issue in a country that, alone in the common-law world, now has no systematic rights protection. Federalism complicates this debate, too. A legislative bill of rights, enacted by the Commonwealth, is likely to be more acceptable in the Australian constitutional culture but would override inconsistent state law and attract state opposition for that reason. In the face of this difficulty, for the foreseeable future, rights protection in Australia is likely to be left to the traditional mechanisms of the Parliament and the courts, developing the single Australian common law.

NOTES

1 *Lange v. Australian Broadcasting Corporation* (1997) 145 ALR 96.
2 *Attorney-General of the Commonwealth of Australia v. The Queen* [1957] AC 288 (PC).
3 Brian Opeskin and Fiona Wheeler, eds, *The Australian Federal Judicial System* (Melbourne: Melbourne University Press, 2000).
4 *McGinty v. Western Australia* (1996) 186 CLR 140.
5 John Hirst, *The Sentimental Nation: The Making of the Australian Commonwealth* (Melbourne: Oxford University Press, 2000); Helen Irving, *To Constitute a Nation: A Cultural History of Australia's Constitution* (Cambridge: Cambridge University Press, 1997).
6 For a review of Australia's operation to mark the occasion of the constitutional centenary, see Robert French, Geoffrey Lindell, and Cheryl Saunders, eds, *Reflections on the Australian Constitution* (Sydney: The Federation Press, 2003).
7 This calculation of gross domestic product is based on current purchasing power parity; see the Organization for Economic Cooperation and Development (OECD), http://www.oecd.org/dataoecd/48/5/2371372.pdf, accessed 20 April 2004.
8 Section 95 enabled Western Australia to continue to impose customs duties after federation, on a diminishing scale, for 10 years.
9 Appeals to the Privy Council nevertheless remained an option until they were progressively restricted, to the point of effective extinction, in 1968, 1975, and 1986.
10 Federal Council of Australasia Act 1885 (Imp). South Australia was a member for only two years.
11 Under Section 121, New Zealand, or any other country, may still be admitted to the Australian federation as a new state. There is an express reference to New Zealand in Section 6 of the Commonwealth of Australia Constitution Act 1900 (Imp), which now has no legal significance.
12 Section 125.
13 Sections 121 and 124.
14 Alvin W. Hopper, "Territories and Commonwealth Places: The Constitutional Position," *Australian Law Journal* 73 (March 1999): 181–218.
15 Gregory Craven, *Secession: The Ultimate States Right* (Melbourne: Melbourne University Press, 1986).

16 Commonwealth Grants Commission Act 1973; Commonwealth Grants Commission, *Equality in Diversity: History of the Commonwealth Grants Commission* (Canberra: Australian Government Publishing Service, 1995).

17 Section 41. The two colonies were South Australia and Western Australia.

18 Section 127.

19 James Bryce, *The American Commonwealth,* 1st ed. (Indianapolis: Liberty Fund, 1888); John S.F. Wright, "Anglicizing the United States Constitution: James Bryce's Contribution to Australian Federalism," *Publius: The Journal of Federalism* 31 (Fall 2001): 107–29.

20 In Australia, unlike in the United States, however, both national and state consent were signified through a referendum, with the people directly voting both nationally and in state communities.

21 John Quick and Robert Randolph Garran, *The Annotated Constitution of the Australian Commonwealth* (1901; reprint, Sydney: Legal Books, 1976), p. 127.

22 Section 53.

23 Geoffrey Sawer, *Federation Under Strain* (Melbourne: Melbourne University Press, 1977).

24 House of Representatives Standing Committee on Legal and Constitutional Affairs, *Constitutional Change: Select Sources on Constitutional Change in Australia, 1901–1997* (Canberra: AGPS, 1997).

25 *Lim v. Minister for Immigration, Local Government and Ethnic Affairs* (1992) 176 CLR 1.

26 *Lange v. Australian Broadcasting Corporation* (1997) 145 ALR 96.

27 Section 128.

28 *Australian Capital Television Pty Ltd v. Commonwealth* (1992) 177 CLR 106.

29 *Marbury v. Madison,* 5 US 137 (1803).

30 *Lange v. Australian Broadcasting Corporation* (1997) 145 ALR 96.

31 Section 77(iii).

32 *Re Wakim; Ex parte McNally* (1999) 198 CLR 511 and *R. v. Hughes* (2000) 202 CLR 535.

33 Section 51(xxxix).

34 Section 105A.

35 Section 120.

36 *Amalgamated Society of Engineers v. Adelaide Steamship Co.* (1920) 28 CLR 129.

37 Martin Painter, *Collaborative Federalism: Economic Reform in Australia in the 1990s* (Cambridge: Cambridge University Press, 1998).

38 Under Section 51(xxxvii) of the Constitution, corporations law is now Commonwealth law, following a reference of power by the states to the Australian Parliament.

39 Sections 7 and 124 respectively.

40 Sections 51(ii) and 99 respectively.

41 Section 106.

42 Section 123.

43 *Austin v. Commonwealth of Australia* (2003) 77 ALJR 491.

44 *Kable v. Director of Public Prosecutions (NSW)* (1996) 189 CLR 51.

45 *Lange v. Australian Broadcasting Corporation* (1997) 145 ALR 96.

46 This view is expressed by Chris Tappere, "New States in Australia: The Nature and Extent of Commonwealth Power under Section 121 of the Constitution," *Federal Law Review* 17 (1987): 223 at 248–49.

47 Section 51(xxvi).

48 *Mabo v. Queensland (No. 2)* (1992) 175 CLR 1.

49 *Victoria v. Commonwealth and Hayden* (1975) 134 CLR 338.

50 Marriage and divorce were included in the list of Commonwealth powers due to the desirability of uniform laws of marriage and divorce between states; see Quick and Garran, *The Annotated Constitution*, p. 608.

51 Section 90.

52 Section 109.

53 *Viskauskas v. Niland* (1983) 153 CLR 280.

54 Sections 92 and 117 respectively.

55 Sections 51(xxxi) and 116 respectively.

56 *Lange v. Australian Broadcasting Corporation* (1997) 145 ALR 96.

57 Section 101.

58 *Re Dingjan; Ex parte Wagner* (1995) 183 CLR 323.

59 *Ha v. New South Wales* (1997) 189 CLR 465.

60 *R. v. Kirby; Ex parte Boilermakers' Society of Australia* (1956) 94 CLR 254 (HC); *sub-nom Attorney-General of the Commonwealth of Australia v. The Queen* [1957] AC 288 (PC).

61 Section 72.

62 For a review of the operations of the Parliament prepared for the constitutional centenary, see G. Lindell and R. Bennett, eds, *Parliament: The Vision in Hindsight* (Sydney: The Federation Press, 2001).

63 See generally, Brian Galligan, *A Federal Republic: Australia's Constitutional System of Government* (Cambridge: Cambridge University Press, 1995).

64 Section 24.

65 Section 57.

66 Section 61.

67 Sections 75 and 76.

68 *Federated Sawmill, Timberyard and General Woodworkers' Employees' Association (Adelaide Branch) v. Alexander* (1912) 15 CLR 308; *Leeth v. Commonwealth* (1991) 174 CLR 455; *Kable v. Director of Public Prosecutions* (1996) 189 CLR 51 per Gaudron J. at 103, per McHugh J. at 110-11.

69 Section 118.

70 Sections 92 and 117.

71 *Union Steamship Co. of Australia Pty Ltd v. King* (1988) 166 CLR 1.

72 Section 51(xxiv).

73 Martin Painter, *Collaborative Federalism* (Melbourne: Cambridge University Press, 1998).

74 *Hematite Petroleum Pty Ltd v. Victoria* (1982) 151 CLR 599.

75 Title to resources within the three-mile territorial sea is vested in states by the Commonwealth Coastal Waters (State Title) Act 1980.

76 Sections 51(ii) and 99.

77 *Broken Hill South Ltd v. Commissioner of Taxation (NSW)* (1937) 56 CLR 337.

78 Cheryl Saunders, "The Uniform Income Tax Cases," *Australian Constitutional Landmarks,* ed. H.P. Lee and George Winterton (Melbourne: Cambridge University Press, 2003), 62–84 at 62.

79 Australian Bureau of Statistics, *2001–02 Taxation Revenue,* document 5506.0, 23 May 2003, p. 4.

80 *New South Wales v. Commonwealth* (1908) 7 CLR 179.

81 Section 81.

82 *Victoria v. Commonwealth and Hayden* (1975) 134 CLR 338.

83 Ibid., 397 (Mason J.).

84 *Victoria v. Commonwealth* (1957) 99 CLR 575, per Dixon C.J. at 605-11.

85 *Deputy Federal Commissioner of Taxation (NSW) v. W.R. Moran Pty Ltd* (1939) 61 CLR 735 (HC).

86 Section 51(iii).

87 See generally, Brian R. Opeskin and Donald R. Rothwell, eds, *International Law and Australian Federalism* (Melbourne, Melbourne University Press, 1997).

88 Section 68.

89 Section 51(vi).

90 Section 114.

91 *New South Wales v. Commonwealth* (1975) 135 CLR 337.

92 Section 51(xxix).

93 *Commonwealth v. Tasmania* (1983) 158 CLR 1.

94 Section 119.

95 See generally, Kim Rubenstein, *Australian Citizenship Law in Context* (Sydney: Law Book Co., 2002).

96 Section 117.

97 Section 51(xix).

98 *R. v. Pearson; Ex parte Sipka* (1983) 152 CLR 254.

99 *McGinty v. Western Australia* (1996) 186 CLR 140.

100 See generally, George Williams, *Human Rights under the Australian Constitution* (Melbourne: Oxford University Press, 1999).

101 Human Rights Bill 2003.

102 The somewhat unwieldy Section 117 provides that a "subject of the Queen, resident in any State, shall not be subject in any other State to any disability or discrimination which would not be equally applicable to him if he were a subject of the Queen resident in such other State."

103 *Brown v. The Queen* (1986) 160 CLR 171.

104 *Lange v. Australian Broadcasting Corporation* (1997) 145 ALR 96.

105 *Polyukhovich v. Commonwealth* (1991) 172 CLR 501.

Belgium

Capital: Bruxelles (Brussels)
Population: 10.3 million (2003 est.)

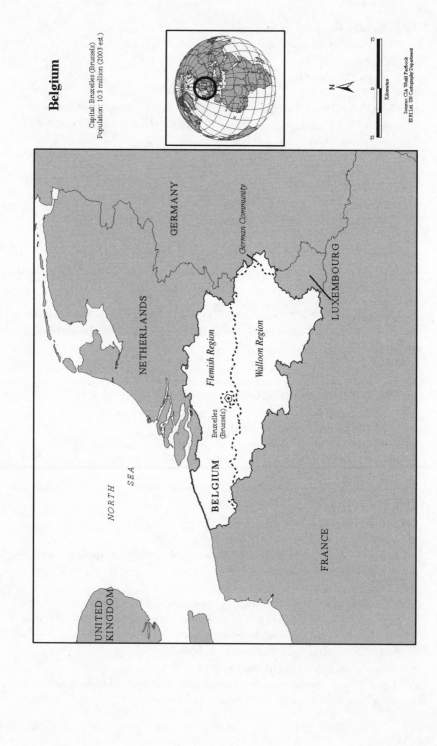

Sources: CIA World Factbook
ESRI Ltd. UN Cartography Department

Kingdom of Belgium

KRIS DESCHOUWER

Belgium is a small – 32,500 square kilometers – but densely populated country with 10 million inhabitants. The country was born in 1830, when the southern part of the 15-year-old United Kingdom of the Low Countries seceded from the north. There were two major reasons for the south to break away: religion and language. The southern part of the Low Countries – which became the Belgian state in 1830 – was homogeneously Roman Catholic, whereas the northern part was predominantly Protestant. Furthermore, the elites of the south spoke French, whereas Dutch was the dominant language of the United Kingdom of the Low Countries.

Although the Belgian elites of 1830 spoke French, this was not the language spoken by all Belgians. The division line between the southern Latin and the northern Germanic parts of Europe runs right across the Belgian territory, dividing the country into a French-speaking southern part and a Dutch-speaking northern part. The two main language groups are not of equal size; roughly 60 percent of the Belgians speak Dutch, 40 percent speak French, and 0.6 percent speak German.

The country created in 1830 was a totally new construction. Parts of the territory had been together as parts of larger entities (i.e., France, Austria, and the Holy Roman Empire), but Belgium as such has no history going further back than 1830. In the beginning, the country was not federal but a classical unitary nation-state. Federal Belgium is much younger and the result of a long, gradual process of territorialization of the relations between the two language groups.[1] The movement toward federalism started in the north. The reason for this is obvious: The Belgium of 1830 adopted French as its single official language. Requests for the right to use Dutch in public affairs and especially in education were accepted very slowly. During the First World War, linguistic tensions reached a high point. Dutch-speaking soldiers had to serve in an army in which the leading officers were Francophones. As well, Dutch-speaking elites collaborated with the German occupying forces to obtain the right to offer some courses in Dutch at the University of Ghent. The Flemish Movement[2] began to make clear demands for "cultural autonomy." By 1918 it had become pretty clear that the unitary nation-state of 1830 would not survive. This is illustrated by the oft-cited letter of 1912 to King Albert from the Francophone Jules Destrée: "Sire, there are no Belgians anymore, only Flemings and Walloons."

The years after the First World War were marked both by the granting of universal (male) suffrage, which led to the Dutch-speaking demographic majority becoming the majority in the Parliament, and by the beginning of an administrative reorganization of Belgium on the basis of language. Three language areas were defined: Dutch-speaking, French-speaking, and the bilingual area of Brussels. The latter is important. Brussels is located north of the linguistic borderline and was historically a predominantly Dutch-speaking city. After it was chosen as the capital city of Belgium, it rapidly became predominantly Francophone.

The limits of the linguistic areas were defined on the basis of a language census, to be conducted every ten years. Given the higher status of the French language and its dominance in the Brussels area, the censuses moved the linguistic borderline toward the north. The bilingual area of Brussels also expanded into territory that had been Dutch-speaking. Thus, rather than continuing to rely on the census, Dutch speakers demanded that the linguistic borderline become fixed. This was done in 1963, and it has not changed since then. The borderline between the language areas was used subsequently to define the limits of the constituent parts of the Belgian federation.[3]

The constitutionalization of the new organization of Belgium, and especially the move toward a federal structure, began in the 1970s. In hindsight, there seems to have been a logical progression toward federalism, but the process of change has been erratic rather than deliberately aimed at a federal outcome. It is not easy, and perhaps not even possible, to find the "point of no return," the change that made a federal outcome for Belgium unavoidable. Among the important stages were the first demands for cultural autonomy in 1918, the language laws of the 1920s, the internal division of the Catholic Party in the 1930s, the division of public radio and television along language lines in 1960, the fixing of the linguistic borderline in 1963, the linguistic division of the Department of Education in 1965, and radical changes in the Belgian political parties in the 1960s and 1970s.

The first major reform of the Constitution came in 1970. The basic principles of the future federal country were laid down, but this was done more as an attempt to avoid further devolution than as an attempt to find a federal-type solution for the tensions between the north and south. The constitutional reform of 1980 can be considered the fundamental step toward a federal Belgium, as it gave Belgium's constituent parts real and important powers: namely, a parliament (though not yet directly elected) and a government. Subsequent reforms were built on these foundations, and in 1993 a new Article 1 of the Belgian Constitution was introduced, stating explicitly that Belgium is a federal country. Since 1995 (1989 in Brussels), the regional parliaments have been directly elected.

Federalism in Belgium is thus the result not of a deliberate choice but of incremental conflict management. In fact, the movements that defended devolution of the unitary Belgian state were the first to use the notion of federalism. Federalism, which for these groups meant decentralization and autonomy, was originally favoured by those rejecting the existing state. The use of the term "federalism" as the official term for the Belgian system is a remarkable change.

Belgium's federal system came into being following piecemeal reforms meant to pacify ethno-linguistic tensions. This means that the framers of the Belgian Constitution did not find their inspiration in existing models of federalist countries. The Belgian federation did not result from the implementation of a blueprint. No one invented or imagined the new Belgium. It is the product of subtle compromises between two divergent visions of how the old unitary state had to be reformed. The Belgian Constitution, therefore, is totally silent about the meaning or the goals of federalism. Federalism just happens to be the system of government that emerged, to some extent as the unwanted consequence of the search for a way to keep two increasingly divergent parts of the country together.[4]

The following description is a snapshot of federalism in Belgium in 2003, at a time when – like at any time since the 1960s – several proposals for reform were on the table.

A DOUBLE AND ASYMMETRICAL FEDERATION

Probably the most striking feature of the Belgian federation is its double nature.[5] Belgium is a federation of language *communities* and also of territorial *regions*. This double federation is the result of the different views of Dutch speakers and French speakers on the ideal configuration of the country. The first demands for devolution came from the Dutch speakers and were based on defence of their language. The Dutch speakers wanted autonomy granted to two language communities. In this scenario, Brussels – situated north of the linguistic borderline – would have been incorporated into, or at least intimately linked to, the Dutch-speaking, or Flemish, community. The Francophones defended granting autonomy to regions, which meant that Brussels (with a population that was 85 percent Francophone) would have become a region in the Belgian federation rather than being part of the Flemish community.

Whereas the Francophones of Brussels opted for division by regions as a way of defending their language, the Francophones of Wallonia – the region south of the linguistic borderline – wanted an autonomous Walloon region for economic reasons. In the nineteenth century, the southern part of Belgium was one of the first industrial areas of Europe, but since the 1950s it has faced the consequences of industrial decline. As the Flemish elites gradually came to occupy more positions of power in the Belgian state (as a result of both their demographic weight and their increasing economic weight), the Walloon elites began to fear that the Belgian state would not take into account the specific needs of the Walloon region.[6] For this reason, they wanted a regional autonomy that would give them more control over economic matters.

These were the opposing views on Belgium's reorganization when tensions between the language groups increased in the 1960s. A complex set of tensions exists between the north and south (and Brussels) resulting from divergent views on the use of language, the different social and economic composition of the regions, and different political landscapes in the north and south. The north is dominated by a Christian-democratic party and the south by a socialist party, whereas in Brussels in the early 1970s a Francophone party concerned with defending the French language was the strongest political faction. There was consensus on the need to reform the unitary state, but fundamental disagreements remained about how this should be done. The north defended autonomy for the two main language communities and wanted to incorporate Brussels into the Flemish community. The south wanted autonomy for three regions, both to secure economic self-rule for Wallonia and to defend the French language in Brussels.

A double federation provided a way out of this deadlock. Belgium created both language communities and territorial regions. The three regions are Wallonia, Brussels, and Flanders (without Brussels). The Flemish community may exercise its powers in the Flemish region and in Brussels, and the French community may exercise its powers in the Walloon region and in Brussels. The German-speaking community also received autonomous status and may exercise its powers in the German-speaking area that is part of the region of Wallonia. Because the regions and communities overlap to a large extent, the basis for the Belgian federation is indeed territorial. But exceptions to this rule were needed to solve the problem of the status of Brussels, which is now a full-fledged region. Because of the dual nature of Belgium's federation, the Flemish community has been able to retain its presence in Brussels and the Francophones have been prevented from using their majority in the city to dominate the Dutch speakers.

There is no hierarchical relation between regions and communities in Belgium. Both are on an equal footing as constituent units of the Belgian federation. Yet how they function is asymmetrical in several respects. In the first place, the Brussels region is defined as having a different status. Its official name is the Brussels Capital Region, reflecting (at least for the Dutch speakers) that it is not the same kind of region as Flanders and Wallonia. The rules produced by the Brussels regional Parliament are called "ordinances," whereas the other regions (and communities) issue "decrees." The federal government may in principle nullify an ordinance, but this would be politically unthinkable because of the need to respect a linguistic balance in the federal government (as discussed below). Courts may rule on the constitutionality of ordinances but not of federal laws or decrees. Unlike the other two regions, Brussels has no constitutive autonomy, which means that it may not determine how its government institutions function. The reason for this is to protect the Dutch-speaking language group in Brussels. In the Brussels regional Parliament, 17 out of 89 seats, and two out of five ministerial positions, are reserved for Dutch speakers. The authority to change this requirement resides only with the federal government. By contrast, Flanders and Wallonia are free to determine the number of seats in their regional parliaments, the number of ministers, the electoral system, and so on. Yet, in all substantial matters, the Brussels region has the same powers as Flanders and Wallonia.

Another and very important example of asymmetry is evident in the relationship between the Flemish region and the Flemish community. Because Flanders wanted to be a community and also to maintain its link with the Dutch speakers of Brussels, the government institutions of the Flemish region and the Flemish community have been merged. Both remain constitutionally defined entities but with a single parliament and a single government. The Flemish regional Parliament (118 seats) is directly elected by the inhabitants of the region. The Flemish community Parliament is composed of these 118 regional MPs and an additional six Dutch-speaking MPs elected in Brussels from a list of Dutch-speaking candidates during the election of the Brussels regional Parliament. The Flemish regional and community parliaments meet (as the "Flemish Parliament") to deal with both regional and community matters. The members elected in Brussels vote only on community matters. There is also a single Flemish government, which deals with both regional and community matters, but a Dutch-speaking minister living in Brussels may be given responsibility only for community matters. The Flemish government needs at least one such minister living in Brussels, as this minister symbolizes the link between Flanders and Brussels through the language community.

Among Francophones, there has occasionally been some debate about the possibility of organizing the relations between the French region and the French community along the same lines, but the government institutions of the French have remained separate. There is a linguistic link between the Walloons and the Francophones of Brussels, but the linguistic identity of the French is not as strong as that shared by the Flemish. Thus the Belgian federation has five constituent units: Flanders (community and region), Wallonia (region), Brussels (region), the French community, and the German-speaking community. The Walloon regional Parliament has 75 directly elected members. The Parliament of the French community is composed of these 75 Walloon MPs and 19 Francophone MPs from the Brussels regional Parliament. The German-speaking community has a directly elected community parliament with 25 members.

THE DISTRIBUTION OF POWERS

The powers allocated to the regions and communities are not detailed in the Constitution but listed in so-called special laws. This technique was invented in 1970, when the principle of devolution toward regions and communities was first written into the Constitution. At that time, no agreement on powers for the regions was possible, especially given the ongoing debate on the status of Brussels. Therefore, the Constitution introduced the paraconstitutional device of special laws. The Constitution lays down the basic principles for the powers of the regions and communities, specifying that the details may be established by special laws. These special laws must be adopted by both houses of the Parliament with a two-thirds majority that also comprises the majority of the members of each language group. This procedure is easier and faster than changing the Constitution itself, although the threshold of support required for adopting special laws is higher. The use of special laws has become very common since 1970. Not only the details of the statutes and powers of the regions and communities have been laid down in special laws, but also their fiscal arrangements.

As noted above, the Belgian federation was not deliberately formed. Rather, it represents the (provisional) end point of a set of institutional reforms intended to pacify tensions between the north and south by devolving powers to regions and communities, thereby avoiding deadlock or ongoing conflicts in the national arena. Each reform was meant to solve an immediate problem. Thus the Constitution contains no clear view on the basic philosophy or general goals of the Belgian federation. The federation continues to evolve, but neither the next step nor the final stage is known (or agreed upon). This fact is nicely illustrated by the very confusing way in which the (remaining) residual powers of the federal state are defined. Article 35 of the Constitution says that the federal state has only those powers granted by the Constitution, but thus far the Constitution has not specified minimal federal powers because they have not been agreed upon. Article 35 also says that regions and communities have residual powers under conditions specified in a special law. However, this special law has not yet been formulated because, according to the Constitution, this special law must *follow* the inclusion of a list of minimal federal powers in the Constitution. In practice, then, the regions and communities have only those powers explicitly granted by the Constitution and by special laws, and the residual powers reside with the federal state even though the Constitution says that they do not.

The piecemeal construction of the federal polity and of its Constitution has led to some awkward ambiguities. Several times the Constitution says that a matter needs to be settled "by a law." Strictly speaking, a law is a rule adopted by the federal Parliament because the regions and communities issue decrees or ordinances. Yet the intention of this constitutional rule is to clarify that an executive body may not settle the matter alone. Therefore, legal theory has accepted that whenever the Constitution requires a "law," the term may also be read as "decree" or "ordinance" if the matter pertains to the powers of regions or communities and if the article requiring a law was introduced after 1980.

In general, the powers allocated to the regions and communities are fairly broad, although the federal state has retained a number of mechanisms of control, especially in fiscal matters. The existence of both regions and communities requires a clear division between the different types of powers that may be given to each of them. In principle, the distinction is easy to make: The regions receive powers that can be organized on a territorial basis, whereas the communities receive powers related to individuals (see Table 1). In matters of social and employment policy, however, there is room for interpretation. If powers related to social security were to be devolved, they might as well be given to both regions and communities.

It is interesting to note that both regions and communities have been granted far-reaching powers in international relations. Indeed, both have the right to engage in international relations and to conclude treaties and agreements of cooperation on all matters that fall within their regional or community powers, including international trade.

Although both exercise powers related to persons rather than to territory, the powers of the communities are territorially bounded. Thus the Flemish and French communities of Belgium are not composed of all the speakers of each language irrespective of where they live. The Flemish community may not, for instance, open schools outside the Flemish and Brussels regions, and the French community may not operate in Flanders. These restrictions are a result of Belgium's division – since the 1920s – into language areas. These areas have consequences for the use of language by public authorities but not by individuals. The Constitution clearly ensures the free use of language. However, the Constitution and the language laws oblige government institutions to use the language (or languages) of a region in their communications with its citizens. Individuals may be required

Table 1
The powers of Belgium's regions and communities

Regions (Flanders, Brussels, Wallonia)	Communities (Flemish, French, German)
Area-development planning (e.g., town planning, monuments and sites, and land policy)	Cultural matters (e.g., defence and promotion of language, arts, libraries, radio and television broadcasting, youth policy, and leisure and tourism)
Environment (protection and waste policy)	
Rural development and nature conservation (e.g., parks, forests, hunting, and fishing)	Education
	So-called "personalized" matters in which the use of language is important (e.g., health policy and assistance to individuals)
Housing	
Water policy (production and supply, purification, and sewerage)	Use of language (except for those localities with special status – i.e., with language "facilities")
Energy policy (except for national infrastructure and nuclear energy)	
	International cooperation within the limits of their powers
Subordinate authority (administrative control and finance of public works)	
Employment policy	
Public works and transport (e.g., roads, ports, and public transport)	
International cooperation within the limits of their powers	

to use a specific language only if they hold a public position; for example, civil servants in local government must be bilingual if they have contact with the public in Brussels. There is no regulation, for instance, governing how shop owners may erect public signs.

The overlapping of the two language communities in Brussels is a very peculiar example of nonterritorial federalism. Individuals do not officially belong to one of the two language communities. There is no subnationality based on language-community identity. In Brussels both language communities offer services (e.g., schools, cultural events, and social programs), and the citizens have the right to choose among them. They may make mixed choices, and they may always change their choices. For the election of the Brussels regional Parliament, voters must choose from lists of either Flemish or Francophone candidates, but they are always free to choose which list to vote from.

There remains considerable disagreement about the imposition of a territorial (and thus strongly regional) organization on Belgium's linguistic communities. The Dutch speakers defend this strict division into linguistic areas because they have experienced the dominant power of the French language and the "frenchification" of Brussels and its surrounding areas. The Francophones would prefer a more "personal" interpretation because there are Francophones living in Flanders (especially in the Brussels periphery) who cannot be served by the French community. That Francophones in Flanders define themselves as a meaningful minority reinforces the fear among the Flemish that they will lose control of the use of language in Flanders. By comparison, Flemings living in Wallonia do not regard themselves as a linguistic minority, reflecting a tradition of the Dutch adapting themselves to the French. The division of the Belgian state into both regions and communities is thus clearly a compromise but not one that has served to fully reconcile the divergent views of the country's linguistic communities.

CONFLICTS AND COOPERATION

The Belgian federation is the result of numerous (and often failed) attempts to avoid ongoing conflict. The decentralization of powers came about in response to the demand of the constituent parts that they be permitted to develop their own policies without having to take into account the will of the other lingusitic communities. Yet, even though the federal structure has reduced tensions between the language groups, the potential for conflict remains high. In addition to linguistic tensions, Belgium also faces conflicts typically occurring in federal states: conflicts of power and conflicts of interest.

Conflicts over the distribution of powers are settled in a judicial way. This may take two forms. First, such conflicts may be prevented by the legislative section of the Council of State (Raad van State/Conseil d'État), which renders an initial opinion on all proposed legislation, whether it emanates from the federal or the federated entities. Although the Council of State is a federal court (as justice is still a federal matter), it has separate linguistic chambers.[7] It verifies that all proposed laws, decrees, and ordinances comply with higher legal rules, including, of course, those laid down in the Constitution. The advice of the Council of State is not binding, but it is an important warning and does have a political impact. Second, if a conflict over distribution of powers arises after a law, decree, or ordinance has been issued, it is settled by the Court of Arbitration (Arbitragehof/Cour d'Arbitrage). This court is composed of 12 judges (6 Dutch-speaking and 6 French-speaking), all of whom are appointed by the federal government on the Senate's recommendation. Half of the judges are former politicians, and half belong to the judicial profession.

Conflicts of interest (i.e., conflicts involving lack of agreement on the substance of laws, decrees, or ordinances) are more problematic because they require that a political solution be reached in an institutional setting that is complex, subject to the maintenance of subtle equilibriums, and

replete with divergent interpretations. These conflicts are most likely to occur between the Dutch and French poles of Belgium's bipolar federation
and, in practice, have to be solved by means of an agreement between
them.[8] The typical cause of such conflicts is a proposed law or regulation
by one entity or by the federal government that another entity fears will affect it negatively. In order to deal "officially" with conflicts of interest, the
Concertation Committee was created. This committee, which must be per-
fectly balanced linguistically, is composed of the federal prime minister,
five ministers of the federal government, and six members of the regional
and community governments. Either the federal government or the government of one of the federated entities may bring a potential conflict to
the committee, a move that suspends the debated decision for 60 days. If
the committee is unable to reach a solution by consensus during this time,
the suspension is lifted and the conflict remains unsolved.

Although appealing to the Concertation Committee is the only official
way to deal with conflicts of interest, this method is rarely used. In practice,
the presidents of the governing parties, who meet regularly with the prime
minister, deal with the prevention of such conflicts. Indeed, the absence of
federal parties in Belgium obliges the governing parties to be active in two
arenas (the regional and the federal) and to resolve the potential conflicts
between the arenas among themselves.

The bipolar character of the Belgian federation often blurs the difference between conflicts of power and conflicts of interest. If the language
communities disagree on how the Constitution, a law, a decree, or an ordinance should be interpreted, a ruling by a court may not settle the disagreement. As a divergence of views, and hence a conflict of interest, the
disagreement is a political problem. If the interpretation of a regulation remains contested, it needs to be reformulated and thus renegotiated. It
needs a political solution.

The division of powers has produced fairly homogeneous sets of powers
for the communities and regions because the aim of state reform was not
to foster cooperation but to avoid the obligation of having to find a common solution for both sides of the country. Thus there are very few concurrent powers and no hierarchy of regulations. Federal laws and regional and
community decrees have the same status. Belgium is clearly a dual federalist system. Yet the implementation of this system is different from that of
other dual systems. Given that important powers have been decentralized
to fairly small territories within a small country, the need for coordination
is high. The existence of two types of constituent units – linguistic communities and territorial regions – also reinforces the need for cooperation.
That some powers are clearly concurrent also makes cooperation unavoidable. Health policy, for instance, is a community responsibility, whereas social security (including health care insurance) is a federal responsibility.

Social security also includes unemployment insurance, but employment policy is regional. Transportation is regional, but the railway system is federal. Public transport is regional, but many people commute – by public transport – from Flanders and Wallonia to Brussels.

Given that maintaining federal control of all powers was not an option, other techniques and strategies for cooperation have been established.[9] The most common form of cooperation is the conclusion of a cooperation agreement between one or more entities. The Special Law of 1988 allows the regions, the communities, and the federal state to draft such agreements of cooperation "notably in view of the creation and common management of common services and institutions, the joint exercise of powers or the development of joint ventures."[10] Agreements may be horizontal or vertical, and they may be optional or compulsory. The latter might seem strange, but the technique has often been used to ensure that the transfer of powers to regions or communities does not lead to major discontinuities. Once agreed upon, a transfer becomes effective only when the regions and/or communities have concluded an agreement of cooperation to deal with the details of the transfer and how the task will be performed in the future. This was done, for instance, when responsibility for public transport was transferred from the state to the regions.

One cooperative agreement deserves extra attention. This agreement organizes how Belgium and its regions and communities are represented in the European Union (EU). Within the European Union, Belgium is a member state and may be represented only in the Council of Ministers. Yet numerous matters regulated by the EU are the responsibility of the regions and communities. An agreement of cooperation, however, allows Belgium to be represented in EU decision making by a regional or community minister rather than by a federal minister. Once the regions and communities have agreed on the view that will be defended, one of the regional or community ministers (they alternate) may sit in the Belgian chair in Europe. When Belgium chairs the Council of Ministers, a regional or community minister may also be the chairperson. If the federated entities cannot reach consensus on an issue, Belgium abstains from voting.

This mechanism of cooperation functions very well. Regions and communities tend to readily agree on the views to be defended in Europe. Indeed, the EU plays a very important role in obliging the Belgian regions and communities to work together in a constructive way. Although the EU did not play an active role in settling Belgium's conflicts and in creating a federal state, its mere presence now fosters cooperation between regions and communities that wanted, and still want, to conduct their own policies freely.

Although the regions and communities possess a high degree of constitutional autonomy, paradoxically their political autonomy remains limited. One reason for this situation is explained above: the continuous need, and

sometimes the obligation, to cooperate. Another reason is the absence of
federal political parties. All the Belgian parties are community-based and
thus seek votes only in their own language communities. Belgium has two
party systems, and the balance of power in these two systems is different.
However, the absence of federal parties obliges the regions and communities to form governmental coalitions that are *congruent* with the federal coalition. It is very unlikely that a major political party will govern in one arena
yet be the opposition party in another arena because in both arenas it is
dealing with exactly the same community parties rather than with the community or regional sections of those parties. Indeed, governmental coalitions have always been (with some minor exceptions) congruent in all
arenas. As well, the federal government has always been *symmetrical*, in the
sense that parties of the north and south belonging to the same ideological
family have always been together either in government or in opposition.
For these reasons, the political autonomy of the regions and communities
is limited. They may not go in wholly different directions because their governing parties also have to govern in the federal arena and thus to maintain the federal consensus.[11]

Since 1993 the Constitution has included the principle of "federal loyalty." This principle is not detailed in the Constitution, and there are no
formal obligations to comply with it. In fact, the notion enters Belgian debates only when one of the constituent entities feels that the other is exceeding the limits of its powers (i.e., when a conflict of interest arises). This
is typically the case when Flanders pushes for more autonomy, testing the
limits of its designated powers, or when the Francophones try to circum-
vent their obligation to limit the actions of the French community to Wallonia and Brussels or try to avoid the requirement for bilinguism. The
federal government never refers to federal loyalty, although federal loyalty,
or at least federal cohesion, is secured at that level (yet always by politicians
elected only by the voters of their own communities).

Born of conflict, the Belgian system of government comprises a very complex and symmetrical set of federated entities with a wide range of powers.
Making the system work requires a high degree of mutual cooperation.
Both communities have numerous veto powers and may veto proposed
changes whenever they want. Built on mutual goodwill, the system provides
greater incentives to work together than to act unilaterally. The latter does
occur regularly, however, as a consequence of the divided-party system, in
which all politicians represent only their own communities and thus only
one of the two sides of public opinion. Yet, in the absence of federal parties,
the combination of regional governments, community governments, and
the federal government necessitates a willingness to continue working together. However, because of the communities' veto powers, there is the risk
that if one player refuses to cooperate, the system will rapidly move toward

conflict. Nevertheless, if one level of government is locked in conflict, the whole system ceases to function, and the price must be paid by all the partners. This explains why Belgium, despite sometimes experiencing deep crises, always finds (indeed, has to find) a negotiated solution.

STRUCTURE OF THE FEDERAL GOVERNMENT

Since 1830 Belgium has been a bicameral parliamentary monarchy. The parliamentary system was changed in 1993 to adapt the composition and role of the Senate to the new federal features of the country. The House of Representatives now has 150 members, elected in 11 constituencies. The number of seats per constituency depends on the number of inhabitants and is adjusted every ten years. The maximum term of the House is four years, but it may be dissolved earlier by the king (i.e., by the federal government).

The Senate has a fairly complex composition. Forty senators are elected directly: 25 Dutch speakers and 15 French speakers. Inhabitants of Flanders and Wallonia have to vote for candidates from Flemish or French lists respectively, while the inhabitants of Brussels and its peripheral areas may choose which of the two lists they will use.[12] An additional twenty-one senators are members of the community parliaments: ten from the Flemish community Parliament, ten from the French community Parliament, and one from the German community Parliament. The numbers per party depend on the distribution of votes for the directly elected senators. The third category of senators are the coopted senators: six Dutch speakers and four French speakers. They are selected by the directly elected senators and the community senators (still based on the electoral results per party). Finally, the heir to the throne may be a member of the Senate. In its composition (excepting the membership of the royal princes), the Senate reflects the division of the country into language communities. The regions are not directly represented in the Senate.

Belgium's federal structure, however, is reflected in the House of Representatives. Each member of the House (and the Senate) clearly belongs to one of the language groups. This group is defined by the location of the constituency in which a member has been elected (again the territorial principle). Each member elected in the Brussels constituency indicates a chosen language group by taking his or her oath in that language. There is no possibility of remaining neutral. The division into language groups is necessary to ensure the double majorities required for the acceptance of special laws. It also serves as a protective device: If three-quarters of the members of a language group demand it, consideration of a proposed bill may be suspended. The federal government then has 30 days to propose an alternative text. Called the "alarm bell procedure," this measure was introduced in 1970 but has never been used.

Belgium's bicameralism is not symmetrical: The powers of the Senate are specified and therefore limited. Only on matters related to fundamental state structures, international treaties, and the monarchy does the Senate have the same powers as the House of Representatives. The Senate's powers in the first of these three areas are especially important, as the Senate is required to approve any reform of the Constitution, any special laws altering the status or the powers of regions or communities, and any laws dealing with the organization of the judicial system. The Constitution clearly indicates that only the House is responsible for granting Belgian nationality, for laws regulating the responsibility of ministers, for the budget, for fixing the number of personnel in the military, and, importantly, for granting or rescinding confidence in the federal government. In all other matters, the House has final responsibility. Although the Senate may ask (with the support of at least 15 members) to have a second look at any bill that the House has accepted, the House retains the last word.

The Belgian federal government exercises both executive power and, with the Parliament, legislative power. The government's composition, which reflects the desire to balance the relationship between the two main language groups, is described in some detail in the Constitution. The maximum number of ministers in the federal government is fifteen. Seven of these have to be Dutch speakers and seven French speakers. This arrangement allows for perfect parity, as the prime minister is considered to be linguistically neutral. In practice, however – although the prime minister plays the role of go-between and needs the full acceptance of both language groups – he (or she) comes from Flanders. This reflects the larger size of the Flemish population and the fact that (so far) the largest political party of the country has been Flemish. To the 15 ministers, a number of secretaries of state (junior ministers) may be added. The rule of linguistic parity does not apply to them. Usually there are two or three secretaries of state and generally a higher number of Dutch speakers than French speakers.

The (quasi) parity of the federal government is an important device, although not the only device, obliging the two language groups to cooperate in government. Even more important is the unwritten rule that government decisions be made by consensus, never by voting. As long as the parties of the two language groups that together hold a majority of the seats in the House are able to work together, the government can function. If one of the parties (language groups) explicitly refuses to accept a proposal, the government can no longer function. The only option is to negotiate until there is agreement again.

According to the Constitution, the king appoints the members of the federal government. When the Constitution deals with the role of the government, it refers to "the King." Yet the king has a constitutionally limited role, as no act of the king has any value unless it is cosigned by a member of the government. The role of the king has gradually declined to make way for the domination of the political game by the political parties and their elected members. The political composition of the government is not the choice of the king but the result of negotiations between the political parties. In practice, the party leaders choose their own ministers, and they make sure in the first place that these are acceptable to the other parties. There have been a few instances of proposed ministers being refused by the king, but if views are truly divergent, the political party seeking to place one of its members in government will be able to do so.

Although the ministers of the regions and communities are not appointed by the king, but formally elected by the respective parliaments, the prime ministers of these governments take an oath before the king. The political procedure for the formation of regional and community governments is similar to the procedure used by the federal state. In the case of the federal government, the king first appoints an *informateur* to determine what can be done to form a government with the elected parties and to suggest the name of a prime minister. The proposed prime minister is agreed upon by a number of parties who hold a majority in the Parliament and want to form a coalition. Subsequently, the king will appoint this potential prime minister as *formateur* and ask him or her to form a new government.[13] The role of the king in this government-formation process is largely ceremonial. In the case of regional and community governments, the parties agree among themselves, without this ceremonial appointment of an *informateur* or *formateur* by the king.

In 1990 the refusal of King Beaudoin I to sign a bill on the liberalization of abortion – accepted by a majority of the federal Parliament – further reduced the king's political influence. Because the bill was an initiative of the Parliament, rather than of the government, the proposal had not been cosigned by King Beaudoin I. When the law was passed, he told the prime minster that his conscience would not allow him to sign the bill and that a solution had to be found. Use was then made of an article in the Constitution that allows the Parliament to state that the king is unable to govern. (To guarantee continuity, the federal government takes over the powers of the head of state in such cases.) Thus all federal ministers signed the bill, including the Christian-Democrats who had opposed the bill in the Parliament, thereby allowing the law to be enacted. One day later, the Parliament stated that King Beaudoin I was able to govern again. The problem was solved, but at the same time, it was proven that the king no longer has substantial political power. In his private communications with members of the government, he might be able to make suggestions or voice discontent, but final decisions are made by the government and thus determined by agreements between the coalition partners. Yet, because the relations between the ministers and the king are private, it is very difficult to assess, and to verify, the king's real role.

In a divided country like Belgium, one might expect the king to play a unifying role. Yet keeping the country together by building a complex federal state based on subtle compromises and built-in obligations to cooperate was the work of the political elites of the second half of the twentieth century, not of the king. In fact, for a very long time the king was extremely reluctant to support devolution, fearing that it could eventually mean the termination of the Belgian state. But the political elites convinced him that devolving powers to communities and regions was the best way to keep the country united.

The king's role as a symbol of the monarchy, one of the only remaining truly Belgian institutions, is also difficult to sustain. The monarchy is widely accepted by the people, but the Francophone background of the royal family has led to increased criticism from the Flemish, who were more supportive of the monarchy in the past. Demands that the (already-very-limited) role of the king be reduced are perceived by the Francophones as one more attempt to further erode Belgian unity, and there is an extreme reluctance to open this debate. Given that no agreement can be reached on the issue of formally changing the king's role, the status quo seems to be the best solution for all.

Clearly, the cornerstone of Belgian unity, and that which guarantees the relatively smooth functioning of the federal system, is the federal government and, more specifically, the leadership of the parties in the federal coalition. These parties are also (with minor exceptions) the parties ruling in the regional and community arenas. Since the introduction of substantial reforms in 1988 that gave real powers to the federated entities, the level of tension between the language communities has clearly declined, and the stability of the federal government has been remarkable. However, because of the communities' numerous veto powers and the obligation for all parties to work together, the potential for deep and intractable conflict remains high.

Both the stability and the daily functioning of the Belgian system are thus determined by the elite. The role of the population is limited. Indeed, the Constitution makes no provision for holding referendums. The Constitution states that all powers emanate from the nation and that the nation is represented in the Parliament. Only the Parliament, therefore, is the voice of the sovereign people. Thus a referendum could never be binding. Besides the constitutional limits on a referendum, there is a major political impediment. A referendum is a device favouring majority rule, whereas the decision-making processes in Belgium rely on negotiations, common agreements, and mutual vetoes. The use of a majority-based device would be disruptive, bypassing all the built-in protections for Francophones at the federal level. A system in which decisions required the approval not only of a majority of the people, but also of a majority of the federated entities, would be extremely complex given the existence of both regions and communities and would still be at odds with the basic principle of elitist consensus seeking. There has, however, been one (nonbinding) referendum: In 1950 the population was asked whether King Leopold III could return to the throne. The majority of respondents voted "yes," except in Wallonia and in Brussels. The king finally had to resign. This experience with a referendum that did not offer a solution but rather a clear illustration of the disruptiveness of a majority-based approach in a bipolar nation explains the reluctance to organize referendums, even if they are nonbinding.[14]

Despite the devolution of major powers to the regions and communities, the role of the federal government and its political parties remains crucial. This is one of the ironies of the Belgian system. The federal government has retained its authority because a number of important powers still reside with the federal state. The judicial system has remained completely federal, which means that federal courts enforce all the laws, including the decrees and ordinances of the regions and communities. The federal government has maintained responsibility for important economic tools, such as labour-market policy and price regulation. The social-security system is also entirely federal. Flanders has voiced demands for further devolution of federal authority, but the Francophones do not wish to move in that direction, especially when it comes to social and fiscal powers.

FISCAL POWERS

How fiscal powers are exercised in the Belgian federation clearly reflects its organization as a double federation of regions and communities and its reliance on an open-ended and constantly adjusted process of piecemeal changes in light of the tense relations between the north and south. Because the devolution of fiscal powers did not occur at the same pace as the devolution of policy-making powers, until 2002 centrally collected taxes were redistributed to the regions and communities. In 2002 a reform of the special law regulating financial measures introduced a higher level of fiscal autonomy for the regions. Inspired by the stronger fiscal capacity of Flanders and its better economic situation, the Flemish demanded even further autonomy. But Francophones are very reluctant to see an additional increase in subnational fiscal autonomy because they fear that the resulting fiscal competition would put Flanders – the only region able to reduce taxes – in an even stronger position.

The double federation and its asymmetrical organization have a number of direct consequences for Belgium's fiscal organization.[15] Both the French and the Flemish communities are present in the Brussels region, but the inhabitants of Brussels are not required to choose a community identity. The communities, therefore, do not know who their own citizens are. The total population of the Brussels region is known but not the number of members of each of the communities. Thus, in Brussels, taxes are regarded as coming from each community in proportion to its approximate weight: 20 percent from Dutch speakers and 80 percent from French speakers. Powers of taxation are transferred to territorial regions rather than to linguistic communities precisely to avoid the problems occasioned by the dual linguistic make-up of Brussels. If one community decides to introduce a tax, it may do so only in cooperation with the other community, which means that the communities do not really have autonomous taxation powers.

The communities, therefore, are predominantly financed by federal funds composed of three elements: financial transfers, a compensation for the formerly shared radio-and-television tax, and a fund related to the number of foreign students in each community's education system. This mixed and very ad hoc arrangement nicely illustrates how Belgium's financial organization is the result of political compromises rather than of well-defined principles.

The financial transfers comprise value-added-tax (VAT) transfers and a personal-income-tax transfer. Each year an amount to be transferred to the communities is determined based on the level of the transfer in 1989 and adapted to the consumer price index. In 2002 it was agreed that beginning in 2012, the amount of the transfer would also be adapted to growth in gross national income. Until 2012 an annually increasing transfer payment will compsensate the communities for the difference between the amounts transferred under the old system and under the (more generous) new system. The amount transferred to each community is also adapted to changes in the size of their student populations, as the communities' major expense is the organization of their school systems. There is no need for a mechanism to ensure consensus in the distribution of these funds because they are based on the needs (number of students) of each community. Nor did the 2002 reform introduce such a mechanism. Rather, the amount transferred to each community was substantially increased and linked not only to the communities' needs but also to their taxation capacities. The first measure was clearly a response to a demand from the French community, and the latter to a demand from the Flemish community.

The amount of personal-income-tax revenue transferred to the communities was fixed by the Special Law of 1989 and is adapted yearly to growth in national revenue. The proportion given to each community is based on its personal-income-tax contributions, with the distribution of taxes collected in the Brussels region fixed at 80 percent for the Francophone community and 20 percent for the Flemish community. The VAT and personal-income-tax transfers constitute the bulk (approximately 90 percent) of the communities' financial means. Of less significance are payments to compensate for the radio-and-television tax that used to be transferred to the communities and funds provided in proportion to the number of foreign students in each community (higher numbers in the French community).

The regions also receive transfer payments from the federal state, but since 2002 they have had greater fiscal autonomy than the communities. The federal income taxes transferred to the regions are handled similarly to the personal income taxes given to the communities. The amount of the transfer was fixed in 1989 and is adapted yearly to the consumer price index and to growth in gross national income. The distribution of federal income taxes among the regions is based on each region's fiscal capacity. Regions with a personal-income-tax revenue below the national per capita average receive an equalization transfer. The amount, fixed in 1989 and indexed accordingly, is multiplied by the number of inhabitants in a region and by the percentage of difference between the per capita personal-income-tax revenue of the region and that of the country as a whole.

The regional autonomy introduced in 2002 permits the regions to introduce lump-sum reductions or increases in the amount of personal income taxes collected. Regions also have the right to reduce taxes in matters related to regional powers. This means, for instance, that they may introduce their own fiscal measures to implement environmental policy. The fiscal autonomy of the regions, however, is bound by measures that seek to prevent too much fiscal competition between the regions. The tax reductions or increases introduced by the regions are set at 6.75 percent of the personal income tax collected in each region. The Special Law of 2002 also states that regions must refrain from unfair tax competition but fails to define exactly what this means. Obviously, any interpretation will be a matter of ad hoc political negotiations.

Regions also control a number of their own taxes: on gambling and betting, the opening of drinking establishments, automatic betting devices, gifts, registration of real property, automobile registration, and possession of radio and television sets. Because these taxes used to be federally administered, the federal state deducts the lost tax revenues from the personal income taxes transferred to the regions. The regions are also free to set the base amount for real estate taxes (also collected by the federal state and by municipalities). These measures allow the regions to conduct a fiscal policy of their own but only within the strict limits set by the Special Law of 2002.

All the regulations governing the Belgian federation's fiscal organization are recorded in special laws rather than in the Constitution. The Constitution does not even include a general principle or guideline for enacting fiscal policy. Nor do the special laws implement any such principle. Rather, they reflect temporary agreements between economically distinct regions and communities that have voiced different fiscal demands. The north pushes for more autonomy, and the south for more solidarity. The only possible outcome in a dual federation whose constituents have mutual veto powers is a detailed agreement reflecting a middle ground.

PROTECTION OF MINORITY RIGHTS

It goes without saying that the position and protection of minorities is a crucial issue in Belgium. It is also a very sensitive issue. Although creation of the federal system was based on mutual agreement following numerous negotiations, each of the two major language groups has a different view on the legitimacy of the current situation and on its position and future in the system.

The gradual transformation of the unitary state into a federal-type state was an answer – or rather a set of answers – to the tensions resulting from the new Belgian state's choice of French as its single official language in 1830. Because of this measure, the Dutch speakers can be considered Belgium's first minority. They were not a demographic but a political, sociological, and psychological minority.[16] In turn, the Dutch speakers requested protection against their political marginalization under the new language policy. The protection was instated gradually, first by recognizing Dutch as the second official language and, beginning in the 1920s, by delimiting the geographical areas in which Dutch or French would be the only official language. An obvious territorial organization was thus used to give the secondary language a secure area. The fixing of the linguistic borderline in 1963 reinforced protection of the Dutch against a sociologically dominant language, and this arrangement was subsequently preserved by the formation of a federal state comprised of both regions (avoiding further expansion of the Brussels region into Flanders) and communities (allowing the Flemish a formal link with the Dutch speakers of Brussels).

The second minority is formed by the French speakers. They are a demographic minority, who gradually became – as a result of extending the suffrage and implementing measures to protect the Dutch speakers – also a political minority. In 1971 when the Belgian Constitution created three regions and three language communities, protective measures for the French minority were written into the Constitution. These measures stipulate that half of the Belgian federal government (except the prime minister) must be composed of Francophone ministers. They also give the Francophone group in the federal Parliament the power to veto (the "alarm bell procedure") any bill considered harmful to them. "Parity," or a 50-50 distribution of administrative positions between the two main language groups, has also been used as a protective device in selecting judges for the Court of Arbitration and in appointing the members of the Concertation Committee. Reforming the special laws that are the basis of the Belgian federation requires a double majority: two-thirds of the votes in both houses of the Parliament and a simple majority in each language group in the Parliament. Again this prevents political domination by the Dutch-speaking demographic majority. The obligation of both language groups to cooperate and their possession of mutual veto powers are the key protections for the French-speaking minority.

The establishment of two main language communities and three regions in 1971 created a third minority group as well: the Dutch speakers of Brussels. As a region, Brussels is predominantly Francophone, and deciding on an equitable organization of its government institutions took a long time. Only in 1988 was an agreement reached on Brussels.[17] The agreement accepts the status of Brussels as a full-fledged region, with only symbolic exceptions to that principle, as discussed above. It accepts the limitation of Brussels to the boundaries set in 1963, which means that areas outside of Brussels remain in the Flemish region and thus in the area where Dutch is the official language of the authorities. It allows for direct election of the Brussels regional Parliament but with guarantees for fair representation of the Dutch-speaking parties (since 2002, this has meant reserving 17 seats out of 89 for the Dutch). It also guarantees the Dutch-speakers an equal number of ministers (except for the prime minister) in the Brussels regional government.

Each language group perceives and interprets these institutional devices differently. The Dutch speakers insist that the arrangements regulating Brussels must be seen as mirroring the devices for protecting the French speakers in Belgium. Indeed, the basic protective principles are the same: parity and veto power. The Francophones generally insist that Brussels cannot be seen as mirroring Belgium because the balance of power between the two language groups in Brussels is much more unequal (15 percent Dutch and 85 percent French) than the balance in Belgium as a whole (40 percent French and 60 percent Dutch). They prefer to speak of protection of the Dutch-speaking *minority*, whereas the Dutch speakers prefer to speak of fair compensation for having constitutionally relinquished their majority status within the Belgian state. Francophones also often complain that obligating large numbers of civil servants in Brussels (e.g., judges and police officers) to be bilingual amounts to unfair and excessive discrimination in favour of the Dutch speakers.

Until 1963 movment of the linguistic borderline according to the language censuses reflected the higher status of the French language. When the linguistic border was fixed in 1963, a number of Francophones just outside the Brussels area remained once and for all in the Dutch-speaking part of the country. Under the old system, six municipalities would have been added to the bilingual area of Brussels. To compensate for the new arrangement, "language facilities" were introduced for the inhabitants of these six municipalities and for the inhabitants of ten more municipalities with significant linguistic minorities along the language border. These minorities would remain once and for all on one side of the border and thus, beginning in 1971, clearly belong to one of the three regions. Some of these municipalities are located on the Francophone side of the border and offer facilities for the Dutch speakers. The request for facilities, however, first came from Francophones in Flanders, particularly those living in the Brussels periphery. The facilities ensure individual inhabitants the right to communicate in their own language with a public authority, even if this is not the authority's official language. If a minimum number of parents request it, the local municipality must offer primary education in the other language. These are clearly exceptions to the rule of territoriality in determining the official use of language and can be seen as special devices protecting linguistic minorities.

Here again there is controversy over the definition, interpretation, and extent of these rights. Among the Flemish, the language facilities are seen as a temporary exception to the principle of territoriality, a means of accommodating the linguistic minorities until they learn the language of a region sufficiently to be able to communicate with the public authorities. Because the use of language is constitutionally free, the language laws regulate only the languages used by the public authorities. There is no limit on the use of any language in any other sphere of life. Although the facilities have been entrenched in the Constitution, Flanders regularly demands their removal because they are an exception to the general rule. The Flemish argue that the relation between the language groups has been settled by the federal organization of the Belgian state. Indeed, within the existing system, the Francophone minority is protected at the federal level, and Dutch-speaking minorities are protected within French-dominated areas.

Among the Francophones, opinion on the language facilities is fundamentally different. They regard the French speakers in Flanders as a minority in need of the same formal protection that the very small Dutch-speaking minority in Brussels has received. They absolutely reject the idea that the facilities should be seen as a transitional measure. On the contrary, they see the facilities as protecting fundamental rights that should not be limited to the minority groups that received them prior to 1963 on the basis of the last linguistic census. Today the six municipalities in the Brussels periphery have a Francophone majority but are officially governed in Dutch. Furthermore, there are other municipalities with significant Francophone minorities that receive no protection at all. There are also (still) Francophones living in the major Flemish cities of Antwerp and Ghent. Belgium's Francophones refer to international law – particularly the Council of Europe's Framework Convention for the Protection of National Minorities – in demanding better protection in general for the Francophones in Flanders. They define the French speakers of Flanders as a minority that deserves proper cultural protection, whereas the Dutch speakers argue that linguistic rights should be based on a clear link between territory and the use of language. The Dutch speakers, therefore, do not agree that explicit linguistic or cultural rights should be given to minority groups living in the Dutch-speaking part of the country. The Francophone position on granting such rights would also mean better protection for Dutch speakers in the Walloon region, but this group does not present or organize itself as a minority and does not claim this protection.

In 2002 the Council of Europe adopted a motion urging Belgium to accept the idea of language minorities in the regions but added that this should be done in a manner consistent with the existing principles and constitutional spirit of minority protection in Belgium. However, because there is no commonly accepted definition of "national minority" in Belgium, the issue remains unsettled. This is why Belgium has not yet ratified the Framework Convention for the Protection of National Minorities.

Meanwhile, tensions persist between the Francophones and the Flemish over the interpretation of the language facilities. In the only municipality where Flemish parents have requested primary education in Dutch, the French community has refused, meaning that the Flemish community must finance the school. In the Brussels periphery, the Flemish community finances Francophone primary schools but insists on retaining control of the pedagogical inspection of these schools. The Flemish government, which has administrative control of the municipalities with facilities for Francophones, prefers to grant linguistic rights in a very restricted way, which leads to continual conflicts between the Flemish regional government and the Francophone executives of these municipalities. The French community government offers subsidies to Francophone publications distributed in the Brussels periphery, although the Court of Arbitration has ruled that this goes beyond the powers (actually beyond the territory) of the French community. The Flemish government has launched ambitious plans to promote the Flemish character of the periphery and has officially declared that there is no linguistic minority in Flanders. These never-ending conflicts will not be resolved as long as both language groups have a fundamentally different interpretation of the standing of language groups and language minorities in Belgium.

One additional minority must be mentioned: the German speakers of Belgium. Comprising a fairly small community (0.6 percent of the Belgian population), the German speakers are concentrated in a few municipalities in the Walloon region. They have received constitutional status as a community within the Belgian federation and possess the same powers as the two larger communities. The German community has a directly elected parliament and its own government, and one of the community's MPs sits in the Belgian Senate. This community is very small, but its rights are not contested. The community leaders themselves, however, regularly voice their ambition to be granted more autonomy and also to receive the regional powers that now reside with the Walloon region.

CONSTITUTIONAL CHANGE AND FUTURE PROSPECTS

Since the early 1960s, the Belgian Constitution has been the object of proposals for change, and it has indeed been changed often since then. There were major leaps in institutional reforms in 1970, 1980, 1988, 1993, and 2002, plus many minor changes in between. Yet it is not easy to change the Constitution. To do so, one first needs a list of articles that may be changed. When the houses of both the Parliament and the federal government accept the same list of articles for revision, the Parliament is automatically dissolved. The newly elected Parliament may then change the Constitution, but changes are restricted to only the articles that were listed for revision before the election. A constitutional change requires a two-thirds majority in both the House of Representatives and the Senate. The search for a two-thirds majority, either when forming a new government or when trying to introduce constitutional changes, has become a constant theme in Belgian politics.

This procedure for changing the Constitution was established in 1830. It is clearly not a federal procedure because approval from the constituent entities is not formally needed for a constitutional change. Only the federal houses of Parliament need to approve. Yet in practice, federal principles have been built into the procedure of constitutional change by the wide use of special laws, which are introduced and changed according to a different procedure than that used for constitutional changes. In one respect, the threshold for changes to special laws is lower than for constitutional changes because dissolution and reelection of the federal Parliament is not required. Special laws may be changed, sometimes eventually several times, by a single legislature. However, in another respect, the threshold is higher because changing a special law requires not only a two-thirds majority in both the House of Representatives and the Senate but also a majority in each language group. In practice, this means that the governments of the regions and communities must accept the proposal. Consensus on changing a special law is sought in the federal government among the political parties governing in all arenas. The reforms of 2002 – involving changes both to the Constiution and to special laws – marked the first time that the governments of the regions and communities, together with the party presidents, had played an active role in the negotiations.

The reforms of 2002 were definitely not the last. In the future, one can expect more alterations both in the distribution of powers and in fiscal arrangements. There are plans to reform the Senate again, but the bulk of these reforms will be achieved by changing the special laws rather than the Constitution. It is hardly possible, however, to predict the future direction of changes because of the fairly long list of issues on which there is strong divergence with respect to the future evolution, and even perception, of the present situation. Flanders is economically the strongest region and has a longer tradition of claiming (a larger degree of) autonomy. At present, Flanders is demanding more fiscal autonomy, decentralization of parts of the (still completely federal) social-security system, decentralization of all powers related to traffic (e.g., speed regulations and railways), more powers related to employment policy, greater constitutional autonomy for the regions and communities, and abolishment of the linguistic facilities for the Francophone minority in the Flemish municipalities of the Brussels periphery. The two largest Flemish political parties officially defend the idea that Brussels should not be a full-fledged region but governed by the Flemish and French communities of Belgium. Far-reaching autonomy for Flanders as a region in Europe seems to be the ideal outcome, and further devolution and reduction of the federal state's powers are steps toward this end.

Among Francophones, the ideal future looks very different. Further devolution of powers is not seen as important. The Francophone political elite defend maintaining the status quo in the distribution of powers and in fiscal regulations (especially those governing the federal social-security system). Attempts by Flanders to become more economically autonomous are seen as efforts to undermine the basic solidarity between the north and south. Yet, when it comes to defending the rights of linguistic minorities, the Francophones would like to see protection of the Dutch speakers in Brussels reduced and protection of the French speakers in Flanders increased. The Francophones would also like Brussels to remain a full-fledged region and its territory eventually to be expanded to its peripheral areas, which presently belong to the Flemish region.

In the future, the Belgian federation will continue to be a complex compromise, the result of divergent, and even incompatible, views of the future and divergent interpretations of the current situation. There is no such thing as "the Belgian federation." There are two ideas of Belgium's present and of its future. Today it survives by combining these ideas in a complex compromise. Whatever the future brings, one can be almost certain that any changes will involve a Belgian constitutional compromise.

NOTES

1 Alexander Murphy, "Linguistic Regionalism and the Social Construction of Space in Belgium," *The International Journal of the Sociology of Language*, no. 104

(1993): 49–64; Alexander Murphy, "Belgium's Regional Divergence: Along the Road to Federation," *Federalism: The Multi-ethnic Challenge*, ed. Graham Smith (London: Longman, 1995), pp. 73–100.

2 The label "Flemish" refers to the language and the area north of Belgium's linguistic division line. Historically, the term "Flanders" referred to the western part of the region, but it was gradually used to refer also to the provinces of Antwerp and Brabant (originally the County of Brabant) and to the province of Limburg (the Dutch-speaking part of the former Princebishopry of Liège).

3 More details on the history of Belgium and on the evolution of its linguistic tensions and solutions can be found in Els Witte, Jan Craeybeckx, and Alain Meynen, *Politieke Geschiedenis van België van 1830 tot heden* (Brussels: VUB Press, 1997); Xavier Mabille, *Histoire politique de la Belgique: facteurs et acteurs de changement* (Brussels: Crisp, 1986); Kenneth McRae, *Conflict and Compromise in Multilingual Societies: Belgium* (Ontario: Wilfrid Laurier University Press, 1986).

4 Maureen Covell, "Political Conflict and Constitutional Engineering in Belgium," *International Journal of the Sociology of Language*, no. 104 (1993): 65–86; Kris Deschouwer, "Falling apart Together: The Changing Nature of Belgian Consociationalism, 1961–2000," *Acta Politica* 37, special issue on "Consociationalism and Corporatism in Western Europe: Still the Politics of Accommodation?" (Summer 2002): 68–85.

5 For a more detailed overview of the Belgian political institutions, see André Alen and Rusen Ergec, *La Belgique fédérale après la quatrième réforme de l'Etat de 1993* (Brussels: Department of Foreign Affairs, Trade and International Development, 1998); Guido Craenen, ed., *The Institutions of Federal Belgium: An Introduction to Belgian Public Law* (Leuven: Acco, 1996); Marc Uyttendaele, *Regards sur un système institutionnel paradoxal: Précis de droit constitutionnel belge* (Brussels: Bruylant, 2001).

6 Michel Quévit, *Les causes du déclin wallon* (Brussels: Vie Ouvrière, 1978).

7 Jérôme Sohier, "Chambres flamandes et chambres francophones: Divergences et dissonances," *Le Conseil d'Etat de Belgique: Cinquante ans après sa création*, ed. Bernard Blero (Brussels: Bruylant, 1999), pp. 699–731.

8 André Alen et al., *Les conflits d'intérêt: Quelle solution pour la Belgique de demain?* (Namur: Faculté de Droit, 1990).

9 Johanne Poirier, "Formal Mechanisms of Intergovernmental Relations in Belgium," *Regional and Federal Studies* 12 (Autumn 2002): 24–54; Maarten Theo Jans and Herbert Tombeur, "Living apart Together: The Belgian Intergovernmental Cooperation in the Domains of Environment and Economy," *Public Policy and Federalism*, ed. Diermar Braun (Aldershot: Ashgate, 2000), pp. 142–76.

10 Translated in Poirier, "Formal Mechanisms," 36.

11 Kris Deschouwer, "Waiting for 'the Big One': The Uncertain Survival of the Belgian Parties and Party Systems," *Res Publica*, no. 2 (1996): 295–306.

12 This in an exception to the rule that the French community cannot be present in Flanders. The constituency of Brussels does indeed contain a part of Flanders

outside Brussels, and the Francophone voters can vote for a Francophone representative in the Senate. Dutch speakers living in Wallonia cannot do so.

13 The general rule is indeed that the *formateur* becomes the prime minister, although there have been two *formateurs* (in 1980 and 1987) who finally let someone else become the prime minister.

14 Mark Van den Wijngaert, "De volksraadpleging van 12 maart 1950," *De Re Ferenda: Een meta-juridsiche conflictanalyse van het referendum,* ed. F. Fleerackers (Gent: Larcier, 2001), pp. 131–44.

15 Magali Verdonck and Kris Deschouwer, "Patterns and Principles of Fiscal and Financial Federalism in Belgium," *Regional and Federal Studies* 13, no. 4 (2003): 91–110.

16 Val Lorwin, "Belgium: Conflict and Compromise," *Consociational Democracy: Political Accommodation in Segmented Societies,* ed. Kenneth McRae (Toronto: McLellan and Stewart, 1974), pp. 175–94; Aristide Zolberg, "The Making of Flemings and Walloons, Belgium, 1830–1914," *The Journal of Interdisciplinary History* 5, no. 2 (1974): 180–235.

17 Els Witte, André Alen, Hugues Dumont, and Rusen Ergec, *Het statuut van Brussel: Bruxelles et son statut* (Ghent: Larcier, 1999).

Brazil

Capital: Brasilia
Population: 178 Million
(2004 est.)

Brasilia, the Capital, is situated within the Distrito Federal.

Boundaries and place names are representative only and do not imply official endorsement.

N

500   0   500
Kilometers

Sources: ESRI Ltd.; CIA World Factbook;
Times Atlas of the World

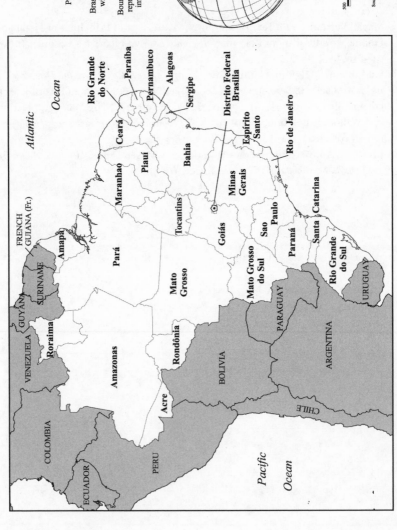

Atlantic
Ocean

FRENCH
GUIANA (Fr.)

SURINAME

GUYANA

VENEZUELA

COLOMBIA

ECUADOR

PERU

Pacific
Ocean

CHILE

BOLIVIA

PARAGUAY

ARGENTINA

URUGUAY

Rio Grande
do Norte

Paraíba

Pernambuco

Alagoas

Sergipe

Distrito Federal
Brasilia

Espírito
Santo

Rio de Janeiro

Ceará

Piauí

Bahia

Minas
Gerais

São
Paulo

Santa Catarina

Rio Grande
do Sul

Paraná

Maranhao

Tocantins

Goiás

Mato Grosso
do Sul

Mato
Grosso

Pará

Amapá

Roraima

Amazonas

Rondônia

Acre

Federal Republic of Brazil

CELINA SOUZA

Brazil has been a federal country for more than a century. With a land area of 8,514,215 square kilometers, Brazil has a population of about 178 million and an annual population growth of 1.4 percent. The urbanization rate is 81.2 percent. In 2002 Brazil's gross domestic product (GDP) amounted to approximately US$451 billion, and its GDP per capita was $2,582. According to the 2001 Census, most Brazilians (54 percent) declare themselves white, followed by mulatto (39.9 percent), black (5.4 percent), Oriental (0.5 percent), and indigenous people (0.2 percent). The great majority said they belong to the Roman Catholic Church (73.6 percent), followed by those who said they belong to no religious group (7.4 percent). Because the country was colonized by Portugal, Brazil's official and predominant language is Portuguese.

Brazil is under the aegis of its seventh constitution, drafted between 1987 and 1988 as a result of the country's return to democracy after almost 20 years under a military regime. Brazil has had a variety of federal arrangements and has experienced periods of authoritarianism and democracy. The country's main social conundrums (regional and social inequality and poverty), while of concern to constitution makers since the 1930s, have not been vigorously addressed by any political system.

This chapter discusses why Brazil has had difficulties maintaining a stable federal democracy that is capable of preventing periods of authoritarian rule, reducing social and regional inequality and poverty, and reconciling social democracy with the constraints of the world economy. I argue that the main problems Brazil faces today are due more to governmental difficulties in changing policy priorities and dealing with economic constraints not foreseen by constitution makers than to deficiencies in the Constitution itself. There is a gap between the areas constitutional governance explicitly covers and politico-economic circumstances, and the latter still continue to take precedence over constitutional mandates.

CREATION OF THE FEDERATION
AND RECENT DEVELOPMENTS

Federalism was introduced in 1889 and laid out in the 1891 Constitution. Unlike in many federal polities, federalism in Brazil was never a response to deep social fissures along ethnic, linguistic, and religious lines, and the country has never had a civil war. During colonial times, Brazil's unity was threatened by Spanish, Dutch, and French invaders, but they were all defeated. Separatist movements were relatively common only during Portugal's domination, but at the beginning of the nineteenth century the unity of the country was not an issue. For these reasons, there is no constitutional provision for secession, and the 1988 Constitution states only that no constitutional amendment may abolish the "federal structure of the state." Because the unity of the country is not threatened, the Constitution states that "all power emanates from the people" (Art. 1), not from the nation as a community with a common history, from the state as organized under one government, or from the constituent units as member states of the federation, signalling that Brazil's federal system is built on the principle of individualism rather than communalism.

The federation was created with 20 provinces previously established by a unitary state. Brazil is now comprised of 26 states plus the Federal District (Brasília) and 5,561 municipalities. Since the promulgation of the 1988 Constitution, pressure for territorial subdivision has come from municipalities, not from states. The country is officially divided into five regions: North, Northeast, Centre-West, Southeast, and South.

There is a consensus that regional inequality is Brazil's major constraint against federalism and that regional economic concentration worsened during the 1990s. Data show the existence of three "Brazils" composed of: (1) an area covering seven states in the South region that, together with the Federal District, share a high level of human development; (2) an area starting in Minas Gerais and extending northwest that has a medium level of human development; and (3) an area composed of the states of the Northeast region plus the states of Pará and Acre that is characterized by low levels of human development.[1]

Regional economic disparity decreased slightly under the military regime that governed from 1964 to 1985. However, this decrease can be attributed neither to centralization of public resources nor to authoritarianism but rather to good economic performance during decades of accelerated economic growth. Economic growth rates of almost 10 percent a year for more than a decade allowed decision makers to adopt policies aimed at decreasing regional inequality.

FEDERALISM AND CONSTITUTIONALISM
IN PREVIOUS CONSTITUTIONS

The characteristics of Brazil's federation and constitutionalism can be better understood by examining the country's previous constitutions. This is because the constitutions mirror major political and territorial pacts made throughout the country's history and because each new constitution, while expressing changes in the political regime, retained or strengthened the constitutional mandates of previous constitutions, with few exceptions.

Debates on the territorial division of power began before the end of colonial rule. The main goal of the republican movement was federalism, not freedom. Nevertheless, together with decentralization, federalism and freedom were presented as synonymous. The option of federalism, despite mirroring the US model, was not simply a copy of its predecessor because its adoption was preceded by debate and because the provincial elites were in favour of decentralization, which was seen as better achieved by a federal than a unitary system. Although US institutions such as the presidential system, federalism, and judicial review were adopted and remain the bases of Brazilian political institutions, and although the Weimar Constitution influenced the trend in Brazil toward constitutionalizing social rights and benefits, Brazil has built its own constitutional history. The 1988 Constitution expresses a constitutional tradition developed throughout the writing of seven constitutions.

Brazil first promulgated a written constitution in 1824 following its achievement of independence from the Portuguese Empire. This Constitution devolved administrative powers to the existing 16 provinces although they had no formal or informal political autonomy. This decentralization was seen as paving the way for federalism.

The 1891 Constitution, promulgated after the republic had been set up, accomplished the decentralization promised by the republican slogan "centralization, secession; decentralization, unity." Economic resources were channelled to a few states, which shows that the federation was born under a concentration of resources in a few states.

Brazil's experience of isolated, or dual, federalism ended in 1930 with a coup led by a civilian, Getulio Vargas, as a result of regional disputes over the presidency. One of Vargas's first measures was to write off the states' debts to the federal government, including São Paulo's enormous debt incurred from subsidizing coffee growers. In 1932 Vargas sponsored an electoral reform that, among other things, increased the political representation of smaller states in the Chamber of Deputies. Initially conceived to counteract the power of a few states, this principle of representation remains one of the bases of Brazilian federalism.

The 1934 Constitution, promulgated as a result of the 1930 coup, introduced the constitutionalization of socio-economic measures to clarify that Brazilians had several social and economic rights. It also expanded intergovernmental relations by introducing several measures allowing the federal government to grant resources and technical assistance to subnational units. The municipalities were permitted to collect their own tax revenues and received half of their revenues from one of the state taxes. Nevertheless, the 1934 Constitution was unable to survive conflicts between measures increasing economic intervention and social spending, on the one hand, and the strengthening of regional elites and Congress, on the other.

The Constitution of 1937 was conceded by Vargas after he took power in a military coup. This coup was deemed necessary to combat communism and the oligarchies, the latter nourished by the impossibility of decreasing the importance of regional interests in Congress, and to build political and administrative unity in order to advance socio-economic modernization. Vargas closed down Congress and the state legislatures and replaced all elected governors with intervenors. Subnational governments lost revenue to the federal government, which was granted the right to regulate Brazilian exports and interstate exchange. By denying the regional oligarchies the right to prescribe their trade rules, Vargas paved the way for industrialization. Nevertheless, horizontal imbalances remained: By 1945 three states possessed more than 70 percent of all state revenues.[2]

In 1945 Vargas was overthrown by his war minister after pressures from the military and after calls for a liberal democracy arose as a result of the worldwide wave of democratization that followed the end of the Second World War. The 1945 election was won by General Dutra. Vargas won the following presidential election in 1950 and governed Brazil under democratic rule until 1954, when he committed suicide as he was about to be overthrown by the military.

The drafting of the 1946 Constitution was influenced by liberal ideals. However, they did not last long given the urgent need for rapid economic growth under the aegis of the federal government. As democracy and decentralization have always gone hand in hand in Brazil, the revenues of municipal governments increased. The Constitution introduced a scheme requiring higher territorial units of government to share revenues with lower units in an attempt to address the issue of vertical imbalance. Horizontal imbalance was partially addressed by designating federal revenues to be spent on Brazil's poorer regions. These measures, however, were of limited effect due to the disproportionate growth in federal activities, an increase in the number of new municipalities, inflation, and the nonpayment of federal quotas to states and municipalities.

The 1946 Constitution is still Brazil's longest-lasting constitution. Its measures and the democratic regime that it regulated survived several crises: Vargas's suicide, the resignation of President Quadros in 1961, and the accession of Quadros's vice president, Goulart, to the presidency despite the hostility of the military and the entrepreneurs. However, democracy did not survive the major economic and political crisis of the mid-1960s, and a military coup followed, finding Brazil's government among the wave of dictatorships that ruled Latin American regimes during this time.

The military did not immediately issue a new constitution. Only in 1967 was a new constitution promulgated, and in 1969 it was again changed through a constitutional amendment. The 1967-69 Constitution, together with a 1966 fiscal-reform law, boosted the centralization of political power and public finance. Competitive elections were forbidden for federal and state executive positions and for the mayors of state capitals and municipalities considered "national security areas" or "mineral sites."

By the end of the 1970s, the fragility of the military regime became apparent and the country's economy began to slow. The military allowed direct elections for the state governors in 1982 and tried to pacify local elites by gradually increasing federal transfers to municipal governments. Financially weak, the military started to lose support.

CREATION OF THE 1988 FEDERAL CONSTITUTION

Redemocratization started in 1985, and a new constitution was designed to end authoritarian rule. The Constitution's key political and policy objectives were to create a just and solidary society, to guarantee national development, to eradicate poverty and marginalization, to reduce social and regional inequalities, and to promote the wellbeing of all people without prejudice and discrimination. In response to pressure from social movements, in particular from minority communities, the Constitution's preamble and several articles address the issue of prejudice and discrimination. Surprisingly for a country in the process of freeing itself from a military regime, restoring or maintaining democracy is not among the Constitution's stated objectives, although Article 1 does declare Brazil to be a democratic state and several mechanisms were created to guarantee the maintenance of democracy.

Creation of the 1988 Constitution was coupled with enthusiasm and optimism about the country's future. For 20 months, Congress and Brasília were the centre of Brazilian life, engaging in a visible exercise in democracy and political participation. The rules determining how the Constituent National Assembly (CNA) would function were the first signal that drawing up the constitution was going to be a bottom-up process: Instead of only one committee to design a draft, there were 24 subcommittees, which later merged into eight committees and finally into a systematization committee of 97 members, as well as plenary sessions with two rounds of voting. One innovation in the rules was to allow the proposal of amendments to come from outside Congress if up to 30,000 voters signed a petition. This was widely used by social movements and corporatist organizations for lobbying. In another attempt to encourage popular participation, citizens were invited to send their suggestions for the Constitution by post. The bottom-up intentions of the constitution makers proved successful: 122 popular amendments were signed by more than 12 million voters, and 72,719 suggestions from individuals were sent to Congress.[3] Popular participation was a key element of the transition to democracy and became an important instrument for the legitimization of redemocratization.

The 1988 Constitution is more detailed than its predecessors. When approved, it had 245 articles plus 70 articles in the title on Transitional Constitutional Measures. It is divided into nine titles: Fundamental Principles, Fundamental Rights and Guarantees, Organization of the State, Organization of the Powers, Defence of the State and of Democratic Institutions, Taxing and Budgeting, Economic and Financial Order, Social Order, General Constitutional Dispositions, and Transitional Constitutional Measures. This range of legislative matters reflects the tradition of constitutionalizing whatever is considered important but also constitutes a reaction against the military's contempt for constitutional mandates and constraints. With the approval of constitutional amendments, the Constitution was expanded to 250 articles plus 94 articles in the title on Transitional Constitutional Measures, which is similar to the number of articles found in the Indian and the South African constitutions.

The Constitution stipulates not only principles, rules, and rights, but also a wide range of public policies. The title on Economic and Financial Order, for instance, regulates the liberal principles of the state and also provides guidelines both for urban and agrarian policies and for private financial institutions. The title on General Constitutional Dispositions similarly details the limits imposed on the federal government to finance the creation of new states and provides for other matters then considered important that had been ignored by the military regime. The Transitional Constitutional Measures created a new state, upgraded two territories to the status of states, and regulated specific issues regarding civil and military service, the judiciary, and public administration, although each of these is also detailed in the Constitution's main body. The title on Defence of the State and of Democratic Institutions allows the president to take exceptional measures if democracy is threatened.

The 1988 Constitution is unique vis-à-vis other Brazilian constitutions. First, it was not based on a draft drawn up by experts, as happened in 1891 and 1934, nor did it mirror previous constitutions, as in 1946. Second, previous constitutions were a result of conclusive political processes and the inauguration of a new order, whereas the 1988 Constitution came into being as part of the political process of transition to democracy. Third, and directly related to federalism, the CNA was free to decide whether to abolish the federal system, an option previously prohibited.

The 1988 Constitution was not influenced by any particular ideology or any foreign power. Although there was no constitutional debate, such as occurred among the US founding fathers, one can say that the 1988 Constitution was the result of political momentum, marked by a need to legitimize democracy. This meant reconciling conflicting interests among old and new actors given that the transition to democracy was still in progress. This is also why the Constitution has several mandates requiring further regulation either by ordinary or by complementary law, as happens in Switzerland, despite being very detailed. Consensus was the way forward given the lack of a clear political or ideological majority.

For these reasons, the constitution makers had several incentives to design a federation in which power is decentralized and in which several unequal but competing power centres have the strength to play a part in the decision-making process. All of these factors promoted unprecedented constraints against a previously centralized federation.

In many senses, the 1988 Constitution contrasted with previous constitutions, particularly (1) in providing more resources to subnational units, (2) in expanding societal and institutional control over the three orders of government by increasing the power of the legislature and of the judiciary and by recognizing the role of social movements and of nongovernmental institutions in controlling the government, and (3) in universalizing social services, especially access to health care, which until then had been restricted to those who had formal jobs. However, the 1988 Constitution maintained certain characteristics from previous constitutions, such as (1) the trend toward constitutionalizing a wide range of issues, which has also been maintained in the constitutional amendments approved so far; (2) the strengthening of municipal governments vis-à-vis their state governments, as also happens in South Africa; (3) the trend toward uniformity in subnational orders of government, particularly state governments, which has tied their hand on the introduction of policies closer to their priorities; and (4) the failure to overcome regional and social inequalities despite the existence of policy mechanisms in the Constitution designed to offset these inequalities.

CONSTITUTIONAL PRINCIPLES OF THE FEDERATION

Federalism

Unlike many federations, Brazil is a three-tiered federation, as is Belgium. This is because the municipalities were never a creation of the states and because the 1988 Constitution incorporated municipalities, together with the states, as part of the federation, reflecting a tradition of municipal autonomy and little state control in municipal matters.

The federal, state, and municipal governments have their own legislative and executive institutions, and the federal and state governments have their own courts. The states are represented in the Senate but are not formally represented in the federal government, which is referred to in the Constitution as "the Union." However, informally there has always been a tradition of having the states' interests represented in the federal executive through political appointments that often reflect a combination of party memberships and the state interests of those who support the president's governing coalition.

Even though the 1988 Constitution decreased the number of cases in which the federal government may intervene in state affairs and in which the states may intervene in municipal affairs, the Constitution still permits federal and state intervention, subject to approval by the legislature. Federal intervention was widely used only in the early years of the republic and by Vargas to reduce the powers of subnational political elites. Federal intervention may occur if there are threats to national unity, public order, the republic, or the democratic order and if state and municipal finances require reorganization. When an intervention has been declared, no constitutional amendment may be approved.

Since the 1988 Constitution, it has been difficult to describe the Brazilian federation as either centralized or decentralized, as is also true of Australia's federation. The Brazilian federation has been marked by federally centralized policies and by constraints on the subnational freedom to introduce legislation, a freedom also restricted by juridical interpretation. Moreover, few constitutional powers are allocated to the states and municipalities, as also happens in Mexico and South Africa. At the same time, state and municipal governments now enjoy considerable administrative autonomy, responsibility for policy implementation, and a share of public resources they had never enjoyed previously.

Status of Constituent Units

Constitutionally, each constituent unit has the same powers as those granted to constituent units in the United States and Mexico (i.e., Brazil has adopted symmetrical federalism in a socio-economically asymmetrical polity). Two main factors have stimulated this symmetrical federalism. First, the rules governing subnational jurisdiction, revenue, and many public policies comprise detailed sections of the Constitution, unlike in the United States and Australia, for instance. Second, the Federal Supreme Court systematically requires the state constitutions and laws to reflect the federal Constitution, thereby imposing a hierarchical interpretation of constitutional norms even though the Constitution does not state this explicitly.

Unlike in Australia, India, Mexico, Switzerland, and the United States, where amendments to federal constitutions have to be ratified by state legislatures or by the electorate, there is no such requirement in Brazil. Rather, it is assumed that the states' representation in the Senate guards their interests.

The states have their own constitutions, which were promulgated in 1989. The drafting of these constitutions followed the same rules applied to the federal Constitution, as did their approval and further amendments. Although state constitutions are not bound by federal constraints, except that they must adhere to the principles in the federal Constitution, most of them replicate federal mandates, as in South Africa. Attempts by those drafting state constitutions to create rules not explicitly considered by the federal Constitution have generally been overturned by the Federal Supreme Court. This is because both the 1988 Constitution and its further amendments are highly detailed and because of the Federal Supreme Court's view that the state constitutions and laws should reflect the federal Constitution.

Elections for the president, for governors, and for Congress and state representatives take place simultaneously every four years. Two years later, mayors and municipal councillors are elected simultaneously to four-year terms. Reelection of those occupying executive positions was introduced in 1997, with only one reelection permitted. For federal and state executives and in municipalities with more than 200,000 voters, a second round must be held if no candidate receives a majority of the popular vote. All legislatures are elected through a system of open-list proportional representation, except for the Senate, which relies on a variant of the first-past-the-post rule.

The Allocation of Powers

Brazil's constitutions have always defined the jurisdictions of the three orders of government, and the 1988 Constitution furthered this trend. The Union holds the largest number of exclusive powers, including those that are most important, as is the case in Russia. Although residual powers reside with the states, as in the United States, Australia, and Mexico, the high degree of detail in the Constitution leaves little room for the states to make use of their residual powers. Concurrent powers are listed in Article 23 of the Constitution. Although these powers cover a wide range of issues (see Table 1), gaps remain between what the article says and how its provisions are put into practice. If a state government introduces legislation regarding an issue on the list of concurrent powers and if federal legislation on the same issue is later approved, the federal legislation prevails. Unlike in many federations, with the notable exception of India, Brazil's federal executive retains most of the legislative authority regarding concurrent

Table 1
Exclusive and concurrent powers in Brazil

Level of government	Spending category
Union only	Defence
	Foreign affairs
	International trade
	Currency, banking
	Use of water resources
	National highways
	Planning: national and regional
	Guidelines: urban development, housing, sanitation, urban transport
	Postal service
	Police: federal and frontier areas
	Regulation of: labour, energy, interstate commerce, telecommunications, insurance, interstate transport, mining, employment, immigration, citizenship, and native rights
	Social security
	National statistical system
	Guidelines and basis for national education
Union-state-local (shared)	Health and social welfare
	Services for disabled persons
	Historic, artistic, and cultural preservation
	Protection of the environment and natural resources
	Culture, education, and science
	Forest, fauna, and flora protection
	Agriculture and food distribution
	Housing and sanitation
	Combating poverty and social marginalization
	Exploitation of minerals and hydroelectricity
	Traffic safety
	Small-business improvement policies
	Tourism and leisure
State only	Residual powers: any matter not assigned to federal or local orders by the Constitution
Mainly local	Preschool and primary education
	Preventive health care
	Historic and cultural preservation
Local only	Public transport (inner-city)
	Land use

powers. The long list of powers shared by the three orders of government, most of which cover public policies, might suggest that the drafters of the Constitution intended to broaden the scope of cooperative federalism in Brazil. However, this has not happened because the capabilities of subnational governments to carry out public policies are highly uneven.

Police powers are also regulated by the Constitution. The federal government is responsible for the federal police and for the railroad and highway police forces. The states are responsible for military and civil police forces and for a fire brigade linked to the state police force. The Union finances these two police forces and the fire brigade in the Federal District. Local governments may, if they wish, have a municipal guard to protect their assets and services. Municipal guards may not carry weapons, but there is pressure to arm them because of increasing urban violence.

The rights and duties of the military forces and of the federal and state police forces are detailed in the Constitution, as are those of civil servants. Coupled with rules and procedures governing public administration, these regulations reflect the trend in Brazil toward constitutionalizing whatever is considered important as well as the strength of certain lobbies in the CNA.

The logic governing the distribution of powers in the Constitution is paradoxical: On the one hand, a decision has been made to decrease the federal government's revenues to amounts lower than those received by the other orders of government; on the other hand, the federal government's legislative role and jurisdiction have been increased. It seems that the constitution makers, given Brazil's two long periods of authoritarianism, were still influenced by the notion of an all-powerful federal government.

Although the Union enjoys considerable legislative and assigned powers, scholars differ on how powers have been informally divided among the three orders of government since redemocratization. There are those who argue that the Brazilian political system is blocked by state interests given the informal power that the governors have over their state delegations in Congress.[4] Others have pointed out the federal executive's success in dealing with Congress.[5] Another view is held by those who regard the current features of Brazilian federalism as strengthening democracy through the creation of several, albeit unequal, power centres that compete both among themselves and with the federal executive.[6] From this perspective, because the federal and subnational governments share powers, increasing the powers of subnational political elites, in particular the state governors, does not diminish the role of the Union.

Constitutional lawyers argue that the balance of power favours the Union because of its central role in many public policies, the lack of financial resources of poor states, and federal legislation ensuring excessive uniformity among state governments.[7]

Certain analysts argue that the balance of power within the federation favours local governments given the historical and current strength of Brazilian municipalities, although their financial strength and their role in implementing social policies can be considered a matter not of federalism but rather of decentralization.

Neither mechanisms nor institutions to regulate intergovernmental relations are provided for in the Constitution. A paragraph in Article 23 states
that a complementary law should be issued regulating cooperation among
the three orders of government, but this has not been on the agenda and
has yet to be done. This is not to say that intergovernmental relations are
nonexistent. Subnational governments share federal taxes, the municipalities share state taxes, and there are some social policies, particularly
regarding health care and primary education, for which the federal government provides guidelines and resources according to rules determined
by federal legislation. With the exception of these policy areas, intergovernmental relations are highly competitive, both vertically and horizontally, and marked by conflict. Cooperative mechanisms only come into
being with federal support. Although there are several constitutional
mechanisms for stimulating cooperative federalism, such as concurrent
policy areas, Brazilian federalism tends to be Union-dominated and frequently competitive.

Power conflicts between the three orders of government and their legislatures are resolved by the Federal Supreme Court through judicial reviews
provided for in the Constitution. Governors may initiate judicial reviews, as
may the president, the Senate board, the Chamber of Deputies board, state
assembly boards, the general public prosecutor, the bar association, political parties with representation in Congress, and union and business con-
federations. Governors have been the most active initiators of judicial
reviews. Paradoxically and until very recently, judicial reviews proposed by
state governors have not normally been an attempt to defend the states'
autonomy vis-à-vis federal legislation but rather have called for federal juridical intervention against measures taken by the state assemblies.

The 1988 Constitution and subsequent decisions by the Federal Supreme Court have given uniformity to state laws that comply with federal
objectives; thus state and municipal interests are consistent with a federal
rationale, and there is constitutional and legal homogeneity despite varying state and municipal interests.

THE STRUCTURE AND OPERATION OF GOVERNMENT

General Institutions

Brazil has always had a presidential system, except for during 14 months
between 1961 and 1963. Nevertheless, some attempts have been made to
introduce a parliamentary system, including during drafting of the 1988
Constitution and in the early 1990s, when a plebiscite was called to change
the system.

Except during authoritarian periods, the separation of executive, legislative, and judicial powers has been a prominent principle in the Constitution, which provides detailed rules concerning the jurisdiction and functioning of these powers. However, as in many other presidential countries, the executive branch has become the main proposer of legislation.

A system of checks and balances prevails. The Federal Supreme Court may declare laws issued by the executive to be unconstitutional and may overturn Congress's decisions. The judiciary's revenue comes from the federal budget approved by Congress. Regarding relations between the executive and the legislature, Congress has to approve: (1) international treaties; (2) peace agreements and declarations of war; (3) exceptional presidential decisions to preserve democratic order, provided for in the section of the Constitution on Defence of the State and of Democratic Institutions; (4) the Union's accounts; (5) referendums and plebiscites; and (6) the use of water and mining resources in indigenous areas. The Chamber of Deputies may initiate procedures to impeach the president, with the Senate holding responsibility for passing judgment in such cases. The Senate has a broader role in implementing checks and balances among the three powers (as detailed in Article 52 of the Constitution). It is responsible for ruling on the removal of members of the Federal Supreme Court, ratifying certain appointments of officials by the president, and deciding on issues regarding any internal and foreign loans to the three orders of government.

Federal Legislature

The federal legislature is bicameral. Congress is made up of the Chamber of Deputies and the Senate. There are 513 federal deputies and 81 senators. Each state and the Federal District elects three senators to serve eight-year terms. In the Chamber, the number of seats per state is determined by population, with a minimum of 8 and a maximum of 70 seats, and in practice each state acts as an electoral district. Given the enormous population differences among states, this rule results in highly disproportionate representation, with São Paulo's 24 million voters electing 70 representatives (one deputy per 350,000 voters), while in Roraima, Brazil's smallest state in terms of population, 186,000 voters elect 8 eight representatives (one deputy per 23,000 voters). The overrepresentation of smaller units was introduced in 1932 to counterbalance the power of the states of São Paulo and Minas Gerais in the federation. It has been maintained ever since.

Like most legislatures, Congress must approve laws proposed by the executive. It also has to vote on the budget tabled by the executive. The Senate not only shares most of the Chamber's powers, as in Australia, but also has constitutional powers of its own.

Since redemocratization, no president has achieved a majority in Congress; consequently, presidents have had to build coalitions of several parties represented in Congress in order to pass legislation. This is crucial for constitutional amendments, when a qualified majority is required.

As mentioned above, the Union holds a considerable amount of constitutional power, including power to propose legislation and to introduce and change public policies. This does not mean, however, that Congress is a minor player, particularly given the constitutionalization of a wide range of issues. Congress has also played an active role in scrutinizing public issues, having set up several commissions of inquiry in recent years.

Federal Executive

The federal executive comprises the president and ministers. The 1988 Constitution increased the executive's powers, which now encompass 25 items of Article 21. The areas covered by these powers range from those normally overseen by executive governments in a presidential system (e.g., foreign affairs, national defence, and monetary policy) to several specific policies on which the executive provides guidelines. There is no constitutional measure requiring cooperation or consultation between the Union and the states on matters concerning the Union's jurisdiction.

Although the Constitution increased the number of individuals entitled to propose legislation – Congress members, the president, members of the Federal Supreme Court, the attorney general, and citizens, the latter if a petition is signed by at least 1 percent of the national electorate distributed among at least five states – the Union has exclusive jurisdiction to initiate legislation on 29 subjects detailed in Article 22. These include civil, commercial, penal, electoral, agrarian, maritime, aviation, space, and labour laws, citizenship, macroeconomic measures, public utilities, the postal service, foreign and interstate commerce, indigenous populations, social security, and general rules for bidding. The Union's jurisdiction to print money is exercised through a nonautonomous central bank without representation from the states. Article 22 stipulates that only the Union may pass legislation on the following areas in which municipal, state, and Union powers are concurrent: hydroelectricity, traffic and transport, mining, and education. This apparent contradiction reflects the Brazilian trend toward uniformity among the three orders of government and a quest for national standards.

Article 23 states that the three orders of government are concurrently responsible for preserving the Constitution and democratic institutions and also lists several policy areas in which the three orders share jurisdiction. Article 24 lists 16 matters that may be concurrently legislated by the Union and the states (but not by the municipalities). These include taxation, finance, control of the economy, budgeting, urban laws, use and protection of natural resources and the environment, and imprisonment.

Federal Judiciary

There has always been a division of powers between the federal and state courts; thus the constituent polities are not represented in the federal judiciary. Brazilian constitutionalism has never been influenced by traditional or religious law, and no demands have ever been made for the recognition of traditional, communal, or religious courts. The constitutions have always reflected a civil-law tradition, like those of Mexico and Quebec.

The federal judiciary comprises several court networks: the Federal Supreme Court, the Superior Court of Justice, regional federal courts, labour courts, the Electoral Court, and the Military Court.

The Federal Supreme Court is the federation's highest court. Since 1988 it has enjoyed the juridical-political attribution typical of a constitutional court, but it also judges certain cases of appeal. Its jurisdiction includes: (1) judicial reviews of federal and state laws and rules; (2) deciding conflicts between the federal government and the states, between two or more states, and between state governments and their state assemblies; and (3) judicial reviews of municipal legislation considered unconstitutional. This means that the Supreme Court may declare federal, state, and municipal laws unconstitutional and therefore null and void. It has no advisory jurisdiction. The Superior Court of Justice has the jurisdiction to rule on administrative conflicts between two or more of the constituent units.

The Supreme Court has 11 members appointed by the president subject to Senate approval. Members of all other federal and state judiciary branches enter the service through a selection procedure open to all law graduates. Federal and state judges may be removed only by their peers, except for those sitting on the Supreme Court, who may be removed only by the Senate.

STATE INSTITUTIONS

As in South Africa, Brazil's state political institutions are similar to those of the Union, except that they are not bicameral. The number of state deputies and their pay ceilings are determined by the federal Constitution. Although the states enjoy relatively little constitutional power, they (1) levy the highest tax, determining its rate in absolute terms (this is a value-added tax that, unlike in many federations, is under the states' jurisdiction);[8] (2) administer more public resources than they did before redemocratization; and (3) enjoy greater administrative freedom. Nevertheless, given the economic disparity among states, their financial and decision-making capabilities are highly uneven.

As with the separation of powers at the federal level, the separation of state powers is constitutionally guaranteed. Each state has a court hierarchy, with a judge generally based in each large municipality, and a state tribunal. Members of the state tribunal are appointed by the governor subject to the approval of the state assembly. State courts exercise only state jurisdiction because there is a regional federal court in each state. Labour courts in the states also belong to the federal court network. Decisions by state courts may be reviewed by superior federal courts.

There is no constitutional provision regulating relations between the states. Unlike in many federations, such as Australia, Belgium, Germany, Mexico, and South Africa, the Brazilian federal government has no formal or informal intergovernmental council, and relations between the states have been marked by great competition, particularly in attracting investment. There is only one interstate council, which is made up of the states' secretaries of finance, but this council is not mentioned in the Constitution.

Article 43 states that for administrative purposes, the Union may create special regional agencies, run by the federal government, with the aim of decreasing regional economic and social disparities. Based on Article 43, the governors of less developed regions have a seat on a federal council that decides on federal fiscal incentives for investors to locate in these regions. This mandate has not yet led to coordinated federal actions nor has it contributed to alleviating regional inequality.

More recently, as a result of pressure from the media concerning urban violence, the federal government has sponsored a joint program with the federal and state police forces, public prosecutors, and judges designed to ensure that they work together. As with other programs, this program was initiated by the Union, which is providing federal resources to stimulate state cooperation and adherence to the program. Nevertheless, there are few examples of cooperation between the Union and the states and among the states.

Municipal Institutions

The rules that apply to municipal governments, including those concerning financial resources, are written in the federal Constitution. The autonomy of municipal governments has always been preserved by Brazilian constitutions under democratic regimes. However, Brazil's deep-rooted inequality affects local autonomy and resources as well as the capacity of municipalities to implement policies.

The rules for municipal elections are stipulated federally. The number of councillors varies from a minimum of 9 to a maximum of 55 according to population size, as determined by the Constitution. Councillors' pay ceilings are also determined federally. Moreover, the 1988 Constitution states that the municipalities have to issue their own constitutional rules, known as Organic Law.

Since the mid-1990s, municipal governments have become the main providers of health care and primary education, following rules and using earmarked resources determined by constitutional amendments. The reason for this federally supported municipalization of public services was to guarantee local citizens access to health care and education based on national programs and minimum standards. In terms of their adherence, this transfer of responsibilities to municipal governments has been a success. This success can be credited to a policy favouring a complex system of intergovernmental relations and transfers that combines incentives and sanctions. The health care program injects additional resources into the municipal purse, and the education program penalizes municipalities that fail to improve school attendance rates at the primary level. This transfer of policy implementation has reduced conflict among municipal governments for federal resources. And intergovernmental relations are now more common between the Union and the municipalities than they are both between the Union and the states and between the states and their municipalities.

Intermunicipal relations have developed rapidly in recent years. The municipalities have created hundreds of consortia through which they share the costs, equipment, and personnel required to deal with issues such as health care, environmental protection, and economic development.

Municipalization is not limited to the transfer of responsibility for policy implementation to local governments. It also gives local communities a share of decision-making responsibility regarding the provision of local public services. The 1988 Constitution contains several mechanisms enabling grassroots movements to participate in certain decisions and to oversee public matters, particularly at the muncipal level. Participatory forums stimulated by the 1988 Constitution, federal legislation, federal programs, multilateral organizations, and municipal governments themselves are now widespread in Brazil's local communities in an attempt to increase local democracy.

FISCAL POWERS

Taxation

The Constitution grants taxation authority to the three orders of government. Some taxes are exclusive to one order, others are collected by the Union and shared with states and municipalities, and others are collected by the states and shared with their municipalities. The Constitution does not grant any order of government the autonomy to introduce a new tax without an amendment to the federal Constitution, although there are a few exceptions, such as the imminence of a war or the need to finance the social-security system, the latter requiring the enactment of a law. The rates and rules for certain taxes, including state and municipal taxes, are determined by federal legislation. Royalties paid by companies for the natural resources they use are collected federally and redistributed to states and municipalities that produce minerals, oil, natural gas, and hydroelectric power.

Two constitutional tax principles are worth mentioning. First, Article 150:IV prohibits any order of government from taxing another order's property, income, or services, thus guaranteeing intergovernmental immunity from these taxes. Second, Article 145, Paragraph 1, bases taxation primarily on the ability-to-pay principle rather than on the benefit principle, stipulating that taxes "whenever possible, shall be graded according to the economic capacity of the taxpayer," which signals that the tax system should be predominantly redistributive. This principle, however, may be applied only to direct taxation, whereas the bulk of taxes levied are indirect.

The Constituent National Assembly's promotion of fiscal decentralization was an exercise in political and constitutional engineering for which there were several reasons. First, there was consensus among participants in the CNA on weakening the federal government financially. The challenge was deciding how to divide resources among the country's unequal and diverse regions. Second, there was consensus on rejecting whatever had been done by the military regarding the centralization of resources, which entailed confronting the federal executive. Paradoxically, the federal executive did nothing at this time to prevent its financial losses. Third, economic issues such as the public deficit, inflation control, and globalization – issues that would later confront the new democracy – were on neither the drafters' nor the country's agenda given the enthusiasm at the prospect of restoring democracy. The importance of the 1988 Constitution rests on the fact that the decision to increase the financial role of subnational governments was made not by the government but by the constitution makers.

The drafters' responses to demands for decentralization were very positive. Today subnational governments collect 32 percent of all taxes collected in the country. With transfers from federal taxes, they are now responsible for 43 percent of tax revenue. In terms of spending, subnational governments are responsible for 62 percent of payroll expenditures and for 78 percent of public investment.[9]

Borrowing

To be able to borrow, federal, state, and local governments must (1) obtain the approval of their legislatures; (2) submit their requests to the Central

Bank, which sends a report to the Senate recommending approval or rejection of a request; and (3) receive Senate approval. However, in 1996 a major scandal was disclosed involving certain states and municipalities that were making improper use of a mandate in the 1988 Constitution that allowed subnational governments to issue bonds in order to pay for debts contracted before 1988. The bonds could be issued only when the courts recognized the debt as pertinent. Because of the high rates of inflation before 1994, politicians had overestimated the amount of these debts still owed to creditors and had apparently used the excess financial resources for other purposes. As a result of this scandal, the Senate set up a Parliamentary Inquiry Commission. Although the commission failed to start procedures to punish officials responsible for the misuse of financial resources, there were important consequences. Several new rules and laws were passed restricting subnational debts, and the Senate issued a self-binding resolution that delegated some of its powers to the Central Bank and opened the way for the promulgation of the Fiscal Responsibility Law in 2000. This law imposes limits on public-sector debt and on payroll expenditures and prohibits the federal government from covering new debts contracted by subnational governments.

State and municipal governments may borrow from the market and from from federal financial institutions, although the rules and restrictions on borrowing are now tougher.

Public debt has always been a serious constraint, and subnational debt was of major importance until the 1990s. The states were the largest debtors, with 42 percent of the public-sector debt in 1997, when the federal government launched a program to renegotiate the states' debts. Although a part of their debts was transferred to the federal government and another part was renegotiated with the federal government, the states' capacity to fulfil their obligations to the Union has been a matter of concern.

ALLOCATION AND EXPENDITURE OF REVENUE

Despite the constitution makers' efforts, concentration of revenue in the Union has continued, particularly since the constitutional amendments approved in the 1990s, as has the concentration of economic activities in a few regions. However, this does not mean that a system of regional equalization was not pursued by the drafters of the 1988 Constitution.

The 1988 Constitution introduced complex mechanisms for intergovernmental tax transfers. Federal revenues from income tax and from the tax on industrial products are shared through participation funds established for this purpose. The states receive 21.5 percent of these tax revenues, 85 percent going to the North, Northeast, and Centre-West regions and the remaining 15 percent to the South and Southeast regions. The formula for determining state shares is based on population size and an inverse of per capita income. The municipalities receive 22.5 percent,[10] 10 percent going to the state capitals and the remaining 90 percent being calculated using a formula based on population size and per capita income. All these rates and formulas are stipulated in the Constitution. These formulas, however, do not compare to the extensive systems of equalization payments provided for by the Canadian and the German constitutions.

There are also schemes for federal transfers to subnational governments. Approved by constitutional amendments in 1996 and 2002, these transfers enable subnational governments to carry out national policies such as health care and primary education. Grants are also sent by the federal government to specific subnational governments. These grants, known as negotiated grants, were of great importance before the policy of tight fiscal control was implemented, and they were highly conditioned by the need to keep the federal governing coalition together.

Apart from the revenue-sharing scheme mentioned above, the 1988 Constitution also stipulates that 3 percent of the federal tax transfers should be used to finance programs in the North, Northeast, and Center-West regions. Furthermore, Article 165, coupled with Article 35 of the title on Transitional Constitutional Measures, attempts to provide for a more equitable and more transparent distribution of federal budget resources. The former states that national public revenue should be regionalized to ensure a more equitable distribution of federal spending on regions and on states. The latter stipulates that ten years after the Constitution's promulgation, the allocation of federal resources among regions and states should be proportionate to their populations. However, these initiatives have not decreased horizontal imbalance, either in absolute or in proportional terms.

FOREIGN AFFAIRS AND DEFENCE POWERS

Responsibility for foreign affairs and defence lies exclusively with the president and the Union. The president has supreme authority over the armed forces. According to the Constitution, military service is mandatory for everyone except women and clerics. The Constitution provides alternative service for those who argue against military service on religious, political, or philosophical grounds.

Congress has to approve presidential decisions concerning declarations of war, peace agreements, and granting foreign powers authorization to cross the national territory. Congress is also responsible for ruling on international treaties involving financial resources. The states have no authority in these matters. Trade, investment, and tourism promotion are carried out by federal ministries and agencies, although more recently certain states and large municipalities have established agencies to promote their interests abroad.

Regarding supranational institutions, Article 4 states that Brazil should pursue the "formation of a Latin-American community of nations." To date, there has been only one regional commercial agreement, the Mercosur, signed by Brazil, Argentina, Paraguay, and Uruguay. Joining the Free Trade Area of the Americas is now under debate. The states have no formal representation in these agreements, and they do not organize specific lobbies for or against supranational agreements.

PROTECTION OF INDIVIDUAL AND COMMUNAL RIGHTS

The Union is the only order of government authorized to legislate on citizenship, nationality, naturalization, migration, and extradition of foreigners. Dual citizenship does not exist; Brazilians are citizens of the Union alone, not of the states.

The title of the 1988 Constitution on Fundamental Rights and Guarantees is dedicated to individual and communal rights, with 11 articles and several chapters and sections. It assures all Brazilians and foreign residents the right to life, freedom, equality, security, private property, and religious freedom. Men and women are equal before the law. Bail is not granted in criminal cases involving racism, torture, drug trafficking, and terrorism or for crimes committed by armed groups acting against either the constitutional order or the democratic federation. There are also several articles protecting the rights of the accused and the imprisoned.

Social rights are also found in this title, including those related to education, health, work, housing, leisure, public safety, social security, protection of mothers and children, and help for vulnerable members of society. However, given the financial and economic difficulties Brazil faces, these rights are poorly protected. The protection of workers' rights is the main focus of this title's Chapter II on Social Rights, reflecting the strength of the unions during the democratic transition and the effectiveness of their lobbying in the CNA.

This title's Chapter IV on Political Rights regulates both voters' and candidates' rights and obligations. Women have had the right to vote since 1932. Chapter V of this title covers the creation and functioning of political parties, which must receive at least 0.5 percent of the valid votes in the Chamber of Deputies' last election. There is no public funding of election campaigns, although this is now under debate. Political parties are entitled to a party fund, financed in part by the Union, and to free access to television and radio broadcasting according to federal rules.

In the title on Social Order, Articles 231 and 232 of Chapter VIII regulate the rights of indigenous populations. They have the right to their own social organization, language, religion, and traditions and the right to live on the land they have traditionally occupied, as delimited by the Union.

The title on Defence of the State and of Democratic Institutions allows the president, with the authorization and participation of Congress, to suspend certain individual and collective rights if there are threats to democracy, such as the right to meet with others, the right to privacy in personal correspondence, and the right to freely come and go.

All state constitutions have a list of individual and communal rights, incorporating rights provided for in the federal Constitution as well as a few other rights. Like the Union government, the states do a poor job of protecting social rights due to financial constraints.

CONSTITUTIONAL CHANGE

Since the promulgation of the 1988 Constitution, its reform has been on the agenda of the federal and state governments and of multilateral and business organizations. These bodies have called for a broad constitutional review, particularly regarding privatization, the taxation and social-security systems, and workers' rights. They argue that the Constitution should be reformed to guarantee the country's "governability" and to make Brazil a global player with the ability to adapt to changes in the international environment. More recently, other arguments for constitutional reform have been used, such as the need to decrease government spending in order to free the country from its dependence on foreign resources and also to redirect resources in the fight against poverty. Many changes have been made, but they are more likely to tighten fiscal control than to free taxpayers, particularly businesses, from what they claim is a heavy tax burden preventing them from competing abroad.

The number of votes required for a constitutional amendment is low in comparison to the number required in other countries: three-fifths of the members of Congress. However, amendments have to be approved by two rounds of roll-call voting in both houses. Proposed constitutional amendments must be supported either by one-third of Congress members, by the president, or by more than 50 percent of the members in at least half of the 26 state legislatures. Provisions immune from amendment are the federal system; direct, secret, and periodic voting; the separation of executive, legislative, and judicial powers; and individual rights and guarantees.

The 1988 Constitution was promulgated on the condition that it be reviewed within five years, as stated in Article 3 of the title on Constitutional Transitional Dispositions. However, because those who advocated a total revision at the end of this review period were still poorly organized, only six amendments were approved. These amendments required an absolute rather than a qualified majority and are referred to as revision amendments.

Thus far the 1988 Constitution has been Brazil's most amended constitution. As of mid-December 2003, 42 amendments had been approved as well as six revision amendments. Despite being a constitution drafted with high levels of public participation, its main aim was to legitimize democracy; thus little attention was dedicated to economic issues. The great majority of the amendments, most of which have been approved, have come from the federal executive.

Constitutional amendments, however, have revised certain of the drafters' important decisions regarding subnational resources. These changes were mainly designed to (1) impose limits on the subnational freedom to spend resources, this being a requirement of the federal policy of fiscal control; (2) earmark specific resources to be spent on health care and primary education; and (3) decrease the amount of resources to be freely transferred from the federal to the subnational governments. Constitutional amendments have also either created new federal taxes or raised the rates of certain taxes not shared with the subnational governments.

Amendments passed in the mid-1990s were intended to address new issues such as globalization and the demand for fiscal constraint and poverty alleviation and to take the country in a new direction. However, old issues that had received special attention from the 1988 drafters (e.g., the country's regional inequality) have remained unresolved. This is not because of constitutional blockades but rather because this issue has never been on the government's agenda and thus lacks public policies to address it.

PROSPECTS AND TRENDS

Brazil's experience of seven constitutions in a century demonstrates the country's difficulty sustaining constitutional governance. Constitutional governance comes under threat when economic and political environments are restructured or are on the verge of major crises. Although the constitutionalization of a wide range of issues limits politicians' and governments' room to manoeuvre, the constitutions have often failed to sustain democracy and address Brazil's social and regional inequalities. In light of this, what are the prospects of the 1988 Constitution overcoming the political and economic constraints that still seem to prevent the political system from addressing Brazil's main problems?

The 1988 Constitution has strengthened the federation and provided for a broader role for government in key problem areas. Nevertheless, the constitutional design is now exposed to two types of tensions. First, new macroeconomic demands due to changes in the international environment have arisen, requiring tight fiscal control and budget surpluses. This has left little room to increase government spending on regional and social policies, thus heightening tensions between the pressures for fiscal control and the need to address regional imbalance and poverty. Second, the constitutionalization of several aspects of the country's life has resulted in tensions between the need for rapid responses to macroeconomic demands and the lengthy process of meeting these demands through consitutional change. Although changing the status quo requires long negotiations with Congress, the outcomes are usually positive for the federal government. However, the increasing degree of constitutionalization gives rise to many conflicts and judicial reviews requiring a decision from the Federal Supreme Court, including decisions about the constitutionality of legislation and sometimes even about the constitutionality of ordinary laws.[11] Congress is also under pressure from the federal executive to approve changes to constitutional mandates in order to adjust the country to a new economic reality and to fight poverty. These two types of tensions raise issues that may have an impact on the country's future.

The main problems currently facing Brazil's federalism and constitutional governance concern three issues. First and most important, Brazil is a federation that has always been characterized by regional and social inequality. Although the 1988 Constitution and those preceding it have provided several political and fiscal mechanisms for offsetting regional inequality and tackling poverty, these mechanisms have not been able to overcome the historical differences among regions and social classes.

Second, there has been a trend toward uniformity in subnational orders of government. Although the 1988 Constitution provides more freedom to subnational governments, other political, economic, and juridical forces restrict this freedom. Furthermore, a crucial issue in the states' decision-making freedom is how to reconcile the need for fiscal adjustment with the need for more autonomy for the constituent units and more federal and state investment in social and regional programs. The states' investment capacity is also bound by their debt payments. Another factor adversely affecting states is the opening up of Brazil's economy. This tends to make intergovernmental relations more complex, as it increases the differences between developed and less developed states. This also contributes to the current trend toward reversing previous, although timid, initiatives favouring economic deconcentration.

Third, there are few mechanisms ensuring vertical and horizontal coordination between the three orders of government. Coordination and cooperation have occurred only when the federal government has stepped in, although there have been some exceptional examples of cooperation between municipal governments. Coordination has become more important because municipal governments have had their financial standing upgraded within the federation vis-à-vis the states and have also been given responsibility for important social policies.

What are Brazil's prospects of solving its regional and social problems? First, although no separatist or antidemocratic threats are foreseen, it is uncertain that the country can continue to support substantial inequality among its regions and social classes. The implementation of constitutional normative principles aimed at a better regional and social balance might become part of the government's agenda if high levels of economic growth are achieved, as has happened in the past. Although the prospect of transforming constitutional principles into policies for regional and social development is not yet foreseeable even if fiscal policies become less important on the agenda, transformation is not impossible given that overcoming regional and social inequality has always been a priority of Brazil's constitution makers. Second, it is not impossible to foresee greater clarification of the role of the states in the federation. This is because the states' debts and problems, including their failure to fight violence and drug trafficking, are now on the agenda. Third, there is now a consensus that an in-depth review of fiscal and taxation mechanisms and of the role of each order of government in the federation is necessary. Enough short-term measures have been taken to alert decision makers that significant changes are needed. These changes, however, are likely to be preceded by broad debate involving governmental and private interests. How the resolution of significant conflicts of interest are likely to be negotiated is not yet foreseeable. Furthermore, changes in sensitive areas of interest are likely to create uncertainty among the electorate and investors.

Resolving Brazil's main problems depends less on federalism and on the Constitution itself than on addressing broader political conflicts, redefining policy priorities, and improving economic performance. Nevertheless, public policies to overcome a long history of inequality require governmental intervention and resources in a time when governments are seen more as a hindrance than as a solution and when the role of governments, particularly in the developing world, is being restricted to achieving budget surpluses to the detriment of increased public spending.

NOTES

1 See Instituto de Pesquisa Econômica Aplicada (IPEA) and Programa das Nações Unidas para o Desenvolvimento (PNUD), *Relatório sobre o Desenvolvimento Humano no Brasil* [Report on human development in Brazil] (Rio de Janeiro, RJ: IPEA and PNUD, 1996), pp. 15–20.

2 See Dennis Mahar, "Federalismo Fiscal no Brasil: A Experiência Histórica," *Política Fiscal e Programação dos Gastos do Governo*, ed. Fernando Rezende et al. (Rio de Janeiro, RJ: IPEA, 1976), pp. 241–80.

3 See Stéphane Monclaire, ed., *A Constituição Desejada* (Brasília: Senado Federal, 1991), pp. 39–40.

4 This view is shared, for instance, by David Samuels and Fernando L. Abrucio, "Federalism and Democratic Transitions: The 'New' Politics of the Governors

in Brazil," *Publius: The Journal of Federalism* 30 (Spring 2000): 43–61; Barry Ames, *The Deadlock of Democracy in Brazil* (Ann Arbor, MI: University of Michigan Press, 2000); Scott Mainwaring, *Rethinking Party Systems in the Third Wave of Democratization: The Case of Brazil* (Stanford: Stanford University Press, 1999); Alfred Stepan, "Brazil's Decentralized Federalism: Bringing Government Closer to the Citizens?" *Daedalus* 129 (Spring 2000): 145–69; and David Samuels, "Concurrent Elections, Discordant Results: Presidentialism, Federalism, and Governance in Brazil," *Comparative Politics* 33 (October 2000): 1–20.

5 See Argelina Figueiredo and Fernando Limongi, "Presidential Power, Legislative Organization, and Party Behavior in Brazil," *Comparative Politics* 32, no. 2 (January 2000): 151–70.

6 See Celina Souza, *Constitutional Engineering in Brazil: The Politics of Federalism and Decentralization* (Houndmills and London: Macmillan; New York: St Martin's Press, 1997); Celina Souza, "Brazil: The Prospects of a Center-Constraining Federation in a Fragmented Polity," *Publius: The Journal of Federalism* 32 (Spring 2002): 23–48; and Wayne Selcher, "The Politics of Decentralized Federalism, National Diversification, and Regionalism in Brazil," *Journal of International Studies and World Affairs* 40, no. 4 (Winter 1998): 25–50.

7 For an overview of constitutional lawyers' analyses of Brazilian federalism in English, see, for instance, Fabio K. Comparato, "Economic Order in the Brazilian Constitution of 1988," *American Journal of Comparative Law* 38 (Fall 1990): 753–72; Keith S. Rossen, "Brazil's New Constitution: An Exercise in Transient Constitutionalism for a Transitional Society," *American Journal of Comparative Law* 38 (Fall 1990): 773–802; Jacob Dolinger and Keith S. Rosenn, eds, *Panorama of Brazilian Law* (Miami, FL: University of Miami North-South Center, 1992); and Marcelo Neves and Julian T. Hottinger, eds, *Federalism, Rule of Law and Multiculturalism in Brazil* (Basil, Fribourg: Institut du Fédéralisme and Helbing and Lichtenhahn, 2001).

8 Constitutional Amendment No. 42, issued in December 2003, provides more resources for subnational governments but also limits the states' prerogative to determine the rate of this value-added tax.

9 José Serra and José Roberto Afonso, "Federalismo Fiscal à Brasileira: Algumas Reflexões," *Revista do BNDES* 6 (1999): 5–24 at 15.

10 Constitutional Amendment No. 42 increased this percentage from 22.5 to 23.5 but did not increase the percentage for state transfers.

11 Between 1988 and 1998, 1,935 judicial reviews were proposed. See Luiz Werneck Vianna et al., *A Judicialização da Política e das Relações Sociais no Brasil* (Rio de Janeiro, RJ: Revan, 1999), p. 63.

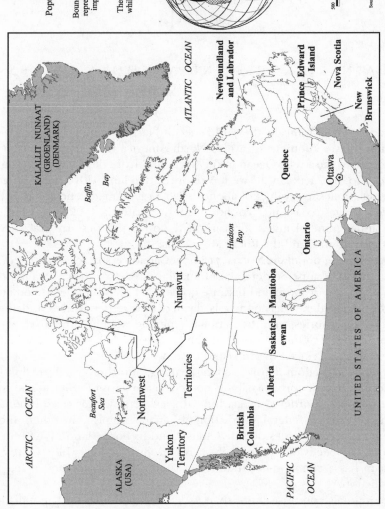

Canada

Capital: Ottawa
Population: 31.5 Million

Boundaries and place names are
representative only and do not
imply official endorsement.

The three northern territories,
while adminstrative divisions,
are not provinces.

N

Kilometers

500   0   500

Sources: ESRI Ltd.; National Atlas of Canada;
Times Atlas of the World

ARCTIC OCEAN

Beaufort
Sea

ALASKA
(USA)

Yukon
Territory

British
Columbia

Northwest
Territories

PACIFIC
OCEAN

Alberta

Saskatch-
ewan

Manitoba

Nunavut

Hudson
Bay

Baffin
Bay

KALALLIT NUNAAT
(GROENLAND)
(DENMARK)

ATLANTIC OCEAN

Newfoundland
and Labrador

Ontario

Quebec

Ottawa

Prince Edward
Island

Nova Scotia

New
Brunswick

UNITED STATES OF AMERICA

Canada

RAINER KNOPFF AND ANTHONY SAYERS

Canada is geographically the world's second largest country.[1] Its nearly 10 million square kilometers traverse North America from the US border in the south to the Arctic Ocean in the north and from the Atlantic Ocean in the east to the Pacific in the west. A resource-rich land with a 2002 per capita gross domestic product of about US$27,112,[2] Canada encompasses the world's longest coastline,[3] countless interior waterways, extensive forests, substantial mineral and hydrocarbon deposits, the western prairie, the northern tundra, and the Rocky Mountains.

With a 2003 population of 31,714,637, Canada is sparsely populated, all the more so because 80 percent of Canadians live in centres with a population of 10,000 or more and because 90 percent live within 320 kilometers of the US border. The country is divided into ten provinces and three northern territories, with the national capital located in Ottawa. The largest provinces are Ontario (12.3 million people) and Quebec (7.5 million); the smallest is Prince Edward Island (138,000).[4]

Quebec is predominantly French-speaking, and there are francophone minorities in every province, most notably in the parts of Ontario and New Brunswick that border Quebec. Indeed, New Brunswick is constitutionally bilingual, as is the federal jurisdiction of Canada. English, the other official language, predominates outside Quebec and its borderlands. Based on its history, Quebec is constitutionally a civil-law jurisdiction, while the rest of Canada has a common-law tradition. Criminal law is a matter of federal jurisdiction.

Aboriginals comprise more than 3 percent of the national population but are demographically more prominent in the West and the North. The Constitution groups indigenous peoples into three categories: "Indian," "Inuit," and "Métis." The Inuit live north of the tree line in the Northwest Territories, Nunavut, Northern Quebec, and Labrador. The Métis are of mixed Indian (Ojibway, Cree) and European (Scottish, French) ancestry.

In Canada's early history, the aboriginal "First Nations" encountered Christian settlers (Catholic and Protestant) from France and Britain. Subsequent immigration contributed to a much wider range of backgrounds, so much so that the concept of "multiculturalism" acquired constitutional status in 1982. Through the first half of the twentieth century, immigration was mainly from Europe. Now the majority of immigrants come from Asia, especially China and India. In 2001 Canada's most prevalent cultural groups were British (47 percent), French (16 percent), German (9.3 percent), Italian (4.3 percent), Chinese (4 percent), and Ukrainian (4 percent).[5]

Immigration has also affected Canada's religious composition.[6] The mainline Christian religions declined between 1991 and 2002 – Catholics from 45 percent to 43 percent and Protestants from 35 percent to 29 percent – partly because of postmaterial value shifts[7] but also because of the growth of religions favoured by non-European immigrants, especially Islam, Hinduism, Sikhism, and Buddhism. Canada has no official religion, although the preamble to its Charter of Rights acknowledges "the supremacy of God," and the Constitution protects certain publicly funded denominational schools that existed at the time of federal union.[8] However, the Charter guarantees "freedom of conscience and religion."

The Constitution of this sprawling and diverse country is dominated by two documents: the Constitution Act 1867 and the Constitution Act 1982. Formerly known as the British North America (BNA) Act, the 1867 statute transformed three colonies into a union of four provinces. The preunion colony of Canada, which gave the new entity its name, was divided into the current provinces of Ontario and Quebec. Nova Scotia and New Brunswick were the other two provinces at the time of "Confederation," as the 1867 regime came to be known. The Preamble to the BNA Act states the desire of the participating colonies to be "federally united into One Dominion under the Crown ... with a Constitution similar in Principle to that of the United Kingdom." Federalism, of course, bore no resemblance to the constitutional structure of the United Kingdom; it was an innovation borrowed from Canada's southern neighbour, the United States. Britain's principal contribution was its regime of constitutional monarchy and parliamentary democracy, in which executive power is formally vested in the Crown's representative – the governor general for Canada and the lieutenant governors for the provinces – but is actually exercised by a prime minister and cabinet "responsible" to the majority in the House of Commons and provincial assemblies respectively. This combination of federalism and parliamentary "responsible government" has shaped Canadian public life in decisive ways. Although this 1867 Constitution has withstood many quarrels, including the threatened secession of Quebec, it has proved to be remarkably resilient. Canada may be a young country by world historical standards, but it has one of the older modern constitutions. Among current federal regimes, only the United States (1789) and Switzerland (1848) have more durable constitutional orders.

Through a series of orders in council and subsequent BNA acts, Britain admitted more colonies and territories to the new union after 1867. British Columbia and Prince Edward Island (PEI) joined in 1871 and 1873 respectively. In 1870 Britain added the vast Northwest Territories (NWT). In the same year, the Canadian Parliament passed the Manitoba Act, creating the province of Manitoba out of part of the NWT.[9] In 1905 Ottawa similarly carved the provinces of Alberta and Saskatchewan out of the NWT. Earlier, in 1898, Ottawa had created a new territory, the Yukon, out of the NWT, something it would repeat with the creation of Nunavut in 1999. The last colony the British Parliament admitted as a Canadian province was Newfoundland (now called Newfoundland and Labrador) in 1949.

Although Canada's Constitution was determined largely by British legal instruments, by the early 1930s Canada had become a fully sovereign country in all but two respects. First, Britain's Judicial Committee of the Privy Council (JCPC) remained Canada's final court of appeal, responsible for, among other things, policing the federal-provincial division of powers. Second, Canada could formally amend important parts of its Constitution only by asking the imperial Parliament to make the changes. Appeals to the JCPC were abolished in criminal cases in 1934 and in civil cases in 1949. The "patriation" (or "bringing home") of the Constitution occurred in 1982, although one final enactment of the British Parliament, the Canada Act 1982, provides that no further acts of the British Parliament "shall extend to Canada as part of its law."[10] The Canada Act incorporates the Constitution Act 1982, which gives practical effect to patriation by establishing fully domestic Canadian amending procedures. In addition, the Constitution Act 1982 renames many of the previous constitutional documents, thereby underlining their domesticated status. Thus the various BNA acts became the Constitution Act 1867, the Constitution Act 1871, and so on. At least 26 documents are said by Section 52 of the Constitution to be part of "the supreme law of Canada."[11] Finally, the Constitution Act 1982 adds the Charter of Rights and Freedoms to the Constitution.

CREATION OF THE CONSTITUTION

The Constitution Act 1867

Confederation was stimulated by commercial aspirations, military concerns, and the desire to maintain local and cultural identities. Many proponents of the new regime considered the creation of a large, integrated British North American market to be key to achieving prosperity, although skeptics expressed the view, repeated ever since, that the centre (i.e., Ontario and Quebec) would be enriched at the expense of the periphery.[12]

Militarily, British North Americans had feared American expansion under the guise of "Manifest Destiny," a fear that was heightened by the outcome of the US Civil War (1861–65). As one father of Canadian Confederation put it, the American South had been "the best safeguard for British North America"[13] because of its reluctance to support expansion into slave-free territories. When the Civil War erased this "safeguard," many of Washington's postwar policies – the end of trade reciprocity,[14] the arming of the Great Lakes, and the construction of a canal around Niagara Falls for the movement of warships – were received in British North America as signalling annexationist intentions. Some kind of union of the British colonies, within the context of the British Empire, became an attractive solution. When the colonies were "all united," said George Etienne Cartier, a leading founder, "the enemy would know that if he attacked any part of those provinces ... he would have to encounter the combined strength of the empire."[15] The desire to carve out a political existence separate from the United States is a motivation that has animated Canadian public life ever since.

Of course, the founders could have achieved a common market and a more defensible regime by establishing a unitary state. To explain why British North Americans chose federalism, we must turn to another founding theme that remains at the heart of Canadian politics, namely the English-French tension that dominated pre-Confederation Canada. The 1867 Constitution was actually the fifth constitutional order devised to deal with cultural division in Canada. The other four, dating back to the Royal Proclamation of 1763, vacillated between attempts to assimilate the French population within a single unitary state and attempts to grant it a degree of autonomy under British rule. Nothing had worked, and the 1840 Act of Union – the penultimate of these constitutions – had proven so problematic that by the 1860s Canadians were prepared to consider a federal compromise between complete separation and complete unification of the two sections. Believing that federalism would work better if there were more than two provinces, the Canadians invited themselves to a conference that the maritime colonies were holding in Charlottetown, Prince Edward Island, in September 1864 to discuss the possibility of a maritime union. Having agreed on the merits of a wider British North American enterprise, the participants at Charlottetown met again a month later in Quebec City, where they produced a draft federal constitution. The maritime colonies increased the pressures for federalism not for the cultural reasons so prominent in Canada but simply because proud colonies did not want their identities and interests completely submerged in a new unitary state. Like the other causes of Confederation, provincialism and regionalism have remained enduring themes of Canada's public life.

The colonial delegations in these founding conferences were composed partly in anticipation of securing legislative consent for their handiwork. Political parties were then much less disciplined, and first ministers could not control their legislatures as easily as their modern counterparts often can. Thus such highly partisan figures as Charles Tupper, Nova Scotia's chief father of Confederation, knowing that it would be difficult to ram an agreement through his legislature, refused to attend the Charlottetown conference unless accompanied by the opposition leaders whose support he would ultimately need.[16] The draft that emerged from Quebec was debated in the legislatures of Nova Scotia, New Brunswick, Canada, Prince Edward Island, and Newfoundland. After it was approved, either in full or in principle, by Canada, Nova Scotia, and New Brunswick, a conference in London, England, made final modifications, and the British Parliament passed the BNA Act 1867. PEI continued its deliberations until 1873. Local debates also preceded the creation of Manitoba in 1870 and the admission of British Columbia in 1871. Newfoundland joined in 1949 following local referendums on the issue. British statutes or orders in council provided the formal framework in all these cases, but the reality was arguably a domestic constitution in imperial garb.

If local input and consent created the Constitution, presumably the same was required to change it. Yet the BNA Act contained no general amending procedure. It became a constitutional custom that Britain would make only those changes requested by Canadians – but which Canadians? The answer depended on how one understood the Confederation settlement. If the 1867 Constitution had created a new people, represented as such by the national government and in relation to which the provinces were subordinate administrative subdivisions, then Britain should make only those changes requested by Ottawa, paying no attention to the provinces. John A. Macdonald, a leading founder and Canada's first post-Confederation prime minister, held this view.[17] If, by contrast, Confederation was primarily a compact of two nations, English and French, then Quebec should have a veto over constitutional amendments. If, in yet another view, Confederation was a compact of equal provinces, then substantial amendments could not be made without equal (i.e., unanimous) provincial consent. These conflicting visions of the country later did vigorous battle from the 1960s on, as amendment politics came to consume Canadians.

Conflicting views similarly exist regarding the founding balance between centralization and decentralization. The American Civil War loomed large for the founders not only because its outcome increased the danger of American expansion, but also because it suggested to some of them the dangers of an overly decentralized federal system. Indeed, some prominent founders, such as Macdonald, would have preferred a unitary state.[18]

Knowing this was impossible, Macdonald sought as centralized a federation as he could achieve and looked forward to a decline in the significance and stature of the provinces over time. They would, he thought, be little more than "glorified municipalities."[19] Needless to say, not all of those who agreed to Confederation were of this centralist persuasion. A genuine federalist strain was present among the founders and would be prominent in post-Confederation politics.[20] Each side in this dispute would emphasize some parts of the Constitution and downplay others.

There was certainly plenty of constitutional ground on which centralists could stake their claim. For example, the residual power – the "Peace, Order, and good Government" (POGG) clause – is vested not in the provinces but in the federal Parliament, something Macdonald thought would prevent Canada from splitting "on the same rock which [the Americans] had done."[21]

Even more strikingly centralist – indeed, antifederal – are the powers of reservation and disallowance. Reservation allows the lieutenant governor of a province (a federal appointee) to reserve provincial legislation for Ottawa's approval or rejection.[22] Disallowance permits Ottawa on its own initiative simply to disallow provincial legislation.[23] Britain enjoyed similar powers of control with respect to the federal government but, by convention, never used them.[24] Eventually, similar conventions arose to prevent the reservation and disallowance of provincial legislation,[25] but these powers were certainly used against the provinces for some time.[26]

Other centralizing features of the Constitution include Ottawa's authority to (1) bring "local works" under federal jurisdiction by declaring them to be for the "general advantage of Canada or for the advantage of two or more of the provinces";[27] (2) enact "remedial legislation" if, in its judgment, a province has used its jurisdiction over education to infringe the rights and freedoms of denominational religious schools existing at the time of Confederation;[28] and (3) appoint judges to the higher-level provincially constituted courts.[29] Of particular importance is Ottawa's power to tax much more broadly than the provinces and to spend in areas of provincial jurisdiction. This "spending power" has at various times been a major lever of centralization. Such powers led K.C. Wheare to describe the Canadian constitution as "quasi-federal" at best.[30]

Those of a more federalist or decentralist persuasion could point to the fact that a significant list of powers was designated as "exclusively" provincial. These powers may not have impressed Macdonald, but for others they were an important reflection of the founding agreement that matters of primarily local concern must be left to the provinces. In this view, the major economic powers (e.g., trade and commerce, banking, and transportation), which were then seen as culturally neutral, could be left to Ottawa.

However, this was not the case for the culturally relevant matters that had agitated politics in Canada under the Act of Union from 1840 to 1867. Thus the culturally sensitive matter of education was assigned to the provinces; so were "property and civil rights," partly to protect Quebec's civil code from interference. Without some protected jurisdiction over these and like matters, neither Quebec nor the maritime colonies would have agreed to Confederation.

From this provincial autonomist perspective, the ability of Ottawa to interfere through such powers as reservation and disallowance was as contrary to the true spirit of the Constitution as it seemed to Macdonald to embody this spirit. In the decades following Confederation, the autonomists waged political battles against the use of such powers, ultimately rendering them dead letters.[31] They also successfully persuaded the JCPC to interpret provincial powers generously and federal powers narrowly. At one point, Macdonald's precious POGG clause had been transformed from a broad, residual grant of power into little more than a power to enact temporary emergency legislation.[32] Correspondingly, the JCPC gave the provincial power over property and civil rights such a broad interpretation that it could plausibly be called the true residual clause of the Canadian Constitution.[33] The interpretive pendulum has since swung back from this decentralist extreme but has never come close to the highly centralist end of the arc envisioned by Macdonald.

A constitutional division of powers, of course, interacts with evolving circumstances to produce the actual – and usually shifting – balance of power between the national government and the component units of a federal system. Thus, despite generously interpreted provincial powers, the federal government was dominant during and immediately after the two world wars. The "emergency power" branch of the POGG clause enabled Ottawa to legislate temporarily in areas otherwise under provincial jurisdiction, and it used its greater taxation and spending powers to influence the priorities of provincial governments through conditional grants.[34] Beginning in the 1960s, however, the provinces more fully exploited their constitutional space and, indeed, attempted to occupy or capture ground from the federal government. Conditional grants gradually gave way to unconditional transfers,[35] and the provinces emerged as major players in one of the world's more decentralized federations. As Ottawa tried to control its ballooning debt during the latter part of the twentieth century, it had its own reasons to limit spending in areas of provincial jurisdiction. At the dawn of the twenty-first century, the pendulum has begun to swing back in a somewhat more centralist direction, including more conditionality in fiscal transfers, although not as much as in virtually all other federations.[36] Constitutionally, and also in practice, Canadian provinces today are very far from Macdonald's glorified municipalities.

The Constitution Act 1982

The Constitution Act 1982 sought to counteract the decentralizing challenges of the late twentieth century. Not surprisingly, Quebec was a major
engine of decentralization, especially after its "Quiet Revolution" in the
1960s. The Quiet Revolution overthrew Quebec's traditional portrayal of
itself as the Catholic agrarian foil to English Canada's Protestant commer-
cialism. Henceforth, Quebec would be an aggressive secular competitor in
the commercial arena. This meant wresting economic powers from the
grasp of a federal government controlled by the English majority. In short,
the survival of French in Quebec came to be associated with a significant
decentralization of powers from Ottawa to Quebec. For some Quebecers, it
required outright secession, and in 1976 the separatist Parti Québécois
(PQ) was elected as the provincial government on the promise to hold a secession referendum, a referendum that the PQ held, and lost (by a margin
of 60 percent to 40 percent), in 1980.

At the same time, other forces of regional and provincial alienation gathered strength. Westerners, for example, had long nurtured grievances
against the majority in Ontario and Quebec, whose common interests often trumped those of the West.[37] By the 1970s, Canadian provinces generally were at a "high tide of 'province building'" that involved them in
competitive confrontations with Ottawa.[38] These forces led to a series of
conflicting proposals for constitutional reform that culminated in – although they were not all satisfied by – the Constitution Act 1982.

Pierre Elliot Trudeau, Canada's prime minister during much of this tu-
multuous period, was the driving force behind the Constitution Act 1982.
Trudeau's reforms implemented his long-standing strategy of employing
constitutional "counterweights" to offset the centrifugal forces in Canadian federalism.[39] Central to his strategy was the constitutional entrenchment of a Charter of Rights and Freedoms. Whereas the federal parts of
the constitutional structure emphasized what divided Canadians on territorial lines, Trudeau intended the Charter to underline what they had in
common. Moreover, Charter issues on which Canadians were divided
tended to be regionally cross-cutting and would thus ultimately be contested in a single national institution: the Supreme Court of Canada.[40] In
addition to enacting the Charter, the Constitution Act 1982 patriated the
Constitution by domesticating the amendment process.

Trudeau's reforms required one last amendment by Britain, which by convention would act only as Canada directed. Trudeau maintained that Britain
would act on the federal Parliament's recommendation alone, without any
provincial consent.[41] His depreciation of provincial involvement was consistent with the amending formula he proposed for the patriation package.
This formula embodied a regionalist logic, requiring that amendments pass

only with the consent of regional groupings of provinces, expressed either
through their legislatures or, significantly, through referendums initiated by
the federal Parliament. Trudeau was animated by a vision of the country as
composed primarily of individual citizens rather than provincial communities. This national community of individuals would be represented first and
foremost by the federal government and by the Supreme Court's implementation of newly entrenched individual rights.

Eight provinces vigorously opposed the entire package.[42] They saw the
Charter as transferring policy-making power from Parliament and provincial legislatures to a central court. They rejected Trudeau's proposal to
minimize their role in future constitutional amendments. Consistent with
their understanding of their current role in amendments, they also insisted that Britain could not pass the package without unanimous provincial consent, a formulation that satisfied both the two-nations veto desired
by Quebecers and the equal-provinces sensibilities of the others.[43] Indeed,
as intergovernmental negotiations broke down, the provinces launched legal challenges to Trudeau's proposed amendment in several provincial
courts of appeal. These were ultimately consolidated at the Supreme Court ·
in the *Patriation Reference*.[44]

Canadians in general did not share the opposition of their provincial
governments. Both patriation and the Charter were popular ideas, and
groups representing such constituencies as women, aboriginals, ethnic
groups, the disabled, and the aged had worked hard to get their favoured
rights included in the package. As provincial opposition mounted, the
Trudeau government solicited the support of these nongovernmental constituencies, often accepting their suggestions to strengthen and broaden
certain rights. Calling the Charter the "People's Package," Trudeau hoped
public support would justify passage of his constitutional amendments
without provincial consent.[45]

Partly owing to the Supreme Court's opinion in the *Patriation Reference*, a
compromise was reached.[46] Trudeau got his Charter but only with the addition of a "notwithstanding clause" enabling both federal and provincial
legislatures to override many of the guaranteed rights for renewable five-
year periods.[47] As for the main amending formula – there were five in all –
it required the consent of two-thirds (i.e., seven) of the provinces, provided
they collectively had at least 50 percent of the population of the provinces.
This 7-50 formula did not require the unanimous consent implied by the
equal-provinces vision of the country, but it treated provinces more equally
than Trudeau's regionalist formula, and consent would be expressed by
provincial legislatures, not by federally initiated referendums.[48]

All but one province agreed to this compromise package. Quebec dis-
sented, not least because the 7-50 amending formula conflicted with its

cherished (though contested) two-nations vision of the country (under which Quebec should have a veto over amendments)[49] and because the Charter's language rights threatened the province's legal protections of French.[50] Quebec's failure to endorse patriation and the Charter was a stain of illegitimacy on the Constitution, and when new governments were elected in both Ottawa and Quebec City, proposals were soon developed to bring the province "back into the constitutional family," especially by giving Quebec explicit constitutional recognition as a "distinct society" within Canada and by decentralizing some governmental powers. Once the Pandora's box of constitutional amendment had been reopened, however, it proved impossible to keep other constitutional demands at bay. The "special status" suggested by "distinct society" grated against the equal-provinces view widespread outside Quebec, and certainly other provinces also wanted any new powers that would go to Quebec. The West wanted to change the appointed, regionally based federal Senate into an elected institution with equal provincial representation – the Triple E (Equal, Elected, and Effective) Senate – something that offended Quebec's two-nations sensibilities.[51] Several constituencies worried that the constitutional victories they had won in 1982 would be watered down, while those who thought they had gained too little in 1982 wanted more attention this time. For example, aboriginals and women challenged the traditional categories of debate – two founding nations and equal provinces – preferring to speak of three founding nations and two founding genders.[52] Two major reform packages – the Meech Lake and Charlottetown Accords – were at the heart of this constitutional debate. Both failed, the Meech Lake Accord in 1990, when it did not gain unanimous provincial legislative support,[53] and the Charlottetown Accord in 1992, when it was rejected in a national referendum.[54]

THE PROVINCES AND OTHER ORDERS OF GOVERNMENT

One manifestation of Quebec's unhappiness was its desire for a more asymmetrical federal arrangement than that provided by the Constitution. Not that the provinces are constitutionally equal in all respects. The French and English languages have constitutional status for certain purposes in Manitoba, Quebec, and New Brunswick but not in other provinces. Provinces are allocated unequal numbers of seats in the regionally based Senate. Until 1930 the western provinces did not have control of public lands or resources, whereas other provinces did.[55] Section 94 of the Constitution, which has never been used, gives Ottawa a role in establishing uniform laws respecting property and civil rights in Ontario, Nova Scotia, and New Brunswick but not in the civil-law jurisdiction of Quebec. The federal power of remedial legislation to protect denominational schools has never applied in Newfoundland. In the most significant respects, however, the Constitution treats the provinces equally, assigning them the same powers. While Quebec wants its distinctiveness recognized, some provinces insist on equality. This contributes to a decentralizing dynamic in which any devolution in favour of Quebec must be extended to the other provinces as well, leaving Quebec's desire for special status unsatisfied and triggering further demands for decentralization.

For some Quebecers, the desire for asymmetry extends to outright separation. As noted above, in the 1980 referendum on this question, about 60 percent of Quebecers voted against separation. A second secession referendum in 1995, stimulated by the Quebec government's failure to achieve its goals in the Meech Lake and Charlottetown Accords, came within a whisker of being passed, with 50.6 percent voting "No" and 49.4 percent voting "Yes."

Not surprisingly, a widespread question was whether secession could be achieved constitutionally. Although the 1982 amending procedures provide for the creation of new provinces, they do not explicitly indicate how one could leave. However, in 1998, at the request of the federal government, the Supreme Court outlined elements of a secession procedure. Quebec could not legally separate through a unilateral declaration of independence, said the Court; a constitutional amendment would be required (although precisely which of the amending formulae would apply was left to another day). On the other hand, if Quebecers gave a clearly affirmative answer to a clear question on secession, the rest of the country would have a duty to negotiate in good faith.[56]

Short of secession, altering the number of provinces or provincial borders is now expressly governed by the 1982 amending procedures. Changes in provincial borders are covered by a formula for amendments that apply "to one or more, but not all, provinces."[57] Such amendments require the consent of the houses of the federal Parliament and of the Legislative Assembly of each province to which the amendment applies. The "extension of new provinces into the territories" and "the establishment of new provinces" are deemed to be of more widespread concern and are thus governed by the general 7-50 formula.

The Constitution Act 1867 gave the provinces the power to amend their own constitutions, and this provision reemerged, essentially unchanged, as one of the five 1982 amending formulae. The nature and content of provincial constitutions are left undefined, however, and are thus matters of some ambiguity and confusion.[58] Parts of these constitutions are found in the Constitution Act 1867 and in various constituent instruments that admitted or established later provinces, all of which are parts of the Constitution of Canada. Other parts – electoral laws, judicature acts, bills of rights, and the like – are found in ordinary provincial statutes. Still others are found in constitutional convention.

Obviously, the purely statutory parts of provincial constitutional law can be amended by ordinary legislation. What about those aspects of provincial constitutions that are found in the national Constitution? The provincial amending formula sets out one explicit limitation: The provinces' power to amend their constitutions does not extend to the lieutenant governor. Originally, this was a feature of Ottawa's predominance inasmuch as this federal appointee had the power to reserve legislation for federal-government approval. However, Canada's constitutional evolution has left behind such powers as those of reservation and disallowance. Moreover, while the federal Cabinet appoints the lieutenant governors of the provinces, it normally does so only after consultation with provincial governments.[59] The exemption of the lieutenant governor from the provincial amending power remains relevant, however, inasmuch as it has been judicially interpreted to secure the rudiments of representative parliamentary government. For example, because the Crown's representative is part of the legislative process, a province (or the federal government, for that matter) cannot transform itself into a direct democracy that legislates through initiatives and referendums. Legislation must be assented to by the Crown's representative, who can do so only upon the culmination of a representative assembly's deliberations.[60]

Another limitation on the power of some provinces to amend their constitutions arises out of Section 133 of the Constitution Act 1867 and Section 23 of the Manitoba Act 1870, both of which are parts of the Constitution of Canada. These sections, which mandate the use of both French and English in the legislative and judicial records of Quebec and Manitoba, have been held by the Supreme Court not to be among those parts of Quebec's and Manitoba's provincial constitutions that either province may amend unilaterally.[61]

However, each province may use its amending power to determine whether its legislature is composed of one or two chambers. Thus the five provinces that once had bicameral legislatures have abolished them.[62] Similarly, although prior to the 1982 Charter of Rights the Canadian Constitution specified a four-year limit for provincial legislatures, provinces extended this to five years through ordinary legislation.

As for interpretive authority over the Constitution, all laws, constitutional or otherwise, are subject to an integrated judicial hierarchy culminating in the Supreme Court of Canada. Thus, unlike in the United States, the Supreme Court is the final court of appeal for both federal and provincial law, including provincial constitutional law.[63]

Municipalities

If the provinces are Canada's second order of government, there are two contenders for the status of its third constitutional order: municipalities and First Nations. Most provinces have smaller populations than Canada's largest cities, and many cities are larger than at least some provinces. Canada is an urbanized country, and its cities play increasingly prominent economic, social, and political roles. Thus there are periodic calls to recognize municipalities constitutionally as a third order of government in the federal system and even to establish certain city-states.[64] All such proposals have failed. Municipalities remain the legislative creations of provincial governments. Most of their functions and responsibilities may be altered by provincial governments, as may municipal boundaries. Many provinces, notably Quebec and Ontario, have in recent years significantly restructured local government.[65]

The powers and manner of operation of municipalities are governed by provincial legislation. Cities generally have limited taxation powers – usually with respect to property taxes – but the provinces (and the federal government via provinces) make direct contributions to municipal budgets, most often in the form of grants tied to specific purposes (such as major infrastructure projects).

Municipalities usually select and organize their personnel and have control over their financial and legal existence within the bounds of provincial and federal legislation. They administer a range of services that include local road maintenance, waterworks, garbage collection, parks and recreation facilities, and libraries.

First Nations

Canada's indigenous First Nations have also called for recognition as a third order of government. Section 91(24) of the Constitution Act 1867 gives the federal Parliament jurisdiction over "Indians, and Lands reserved for Indians." In 1876 the Parliament passed the Indian Act, which set out the rules under which bands may engage in a variety of activities, such as governance, land use, and membership selection. The Constitution Act 1982 added two provisions on indigenous peoples. Section 25 provides that "[t]he guarantee in this Charter of certain rights and freedoms shall not be construed so as to abrogate or derogate from any aboriginal, treaty, or other rights or freedoms that pertain to the aboriginal peoples of Canada." More important, Section 35 states that the "existing aboriginal and treaty rights of the aboriginal peoples of Canada are hereby recognized and affirmed." Moreover, a 1983 amendment to Section 35 provides that "treaty rights" include "rights that now exist by way of land claims agreements or may be so acquired." These provisions signalled that aboriginal people deserve unique constitutional recognition and protection. Yet for many aboriginal groups, they did not go far enough in protecting and encouraging aboriginal title, rights, and self-government. Thus in 1992 an attempt was made through the unsuccessful Charlottetown Accord to constitutionally entrench aboriginal self-government and Senate representation as well as a veto for aboriginal peoples on any future constitutional amendments involving them.

With the failure of the Charlottetown Accord, attention turned to treaty negotiations and to giving First Nations self-government and greater control over their lands.[66] A treaty in British Columbia gave the Nisga'a Nation extensive self-governing powers, including taxation, land use, and bylaw powers.[67] Statutes such as the Sechelt Indian Band Self-Government Act, the First Nations Land Management Act, the Governance Act, and the proposed First Nations Fiscal and Statistical Management Act[68] gave First Nations greater control over governance, land management, and economic development. For the Inuit, the federal response was to create Canada's third territory, Nunavut, in which the majority of the population is of Inuit descent.

THE ALLOCATION OF POWERS

Sections 91 to 95 of the Constitution Act 1867 allocate powers to the federal and provincial jurisdictions. Section 91 begins with Ottawa's residual power "to make laws for the Peace, Order and good Government of Canada in relation to all Matters not ... assigned exclusively" to the provinces. To avoid the prospect of these provincial powers being interpreted too broadly, thus leaving too little authority to the federal government, the section then lists, "for greater certainty, but not so as to restrict the generality of the foregoing," 29 areas of exclusive federal jurisdiction. These cover most of the powers considered economically important in 1867, including jurisdiction over the public debt (Sec. 91(1A)), trade and commerce (Sec. 91(2)), the raising of money by any mode or system of taxation (Sec. 91(3)), the borrowing of money on the public credit (Sec. 91(4)), navigation and shipping (Sec. 91(10)), currency (Sec. 91(14)), banking (Sec. 91(15)), weights and measures (Sec. 91(17)), bills of exchange and promissory notes (Sec. 91(18)), interest (Sec. 91(19)), legal tender (Sec. 91(20)), bankruptcy and insolvency (Sec. 91(21)), patents of invention and discovery (Sec. 91(22)), and copyrights (Sec. 91(23)). Criminal law, which in the United States is predominantly a state jurisdiction, is a federal matter in Canada (Sec. 91(27)). Indians and their lands is another federal jurisdiction (Sec. 91(24)).

Section 92 then sets out 16 exclusively provincial powers, including direct taxation for provincial purposes (Sec. 92(2)), hospitals (Sec. 92(7)), the administration of justice (Sec. 92(14)), property and civil rights (Sec. 92(13)), and "generally all Matters of a merely local or private Nature in the Province" (Sec. 92(16)). Section 93 gives the provinces "exclusive" jurisdiction over education subject to the federal power of remedial legislation to protect the rights of denominational schools. The provincial list of powers has gained significance with the advent of the modern welfare state. While the federal government may have many of the most obvious economic powers, the provinces have jurisdiction over much social policy, including health care, welfare, and labour relations in provincially regulated sectors.

Jurisdiction over the administration of justice gives the provinces the "police powers" of prosecution and enforcement. Although Ottawa can appoint federal prosecutors for its own laws, it has done so only in limited areas, such as prosecutions under the Narcotics Control Act.[69] On the whole, provincial officials prosecute violations of both federal and provincial law. Similarly, under its jurisdiction over criminal law, Ottawa established its own police force, the Royal Canadian Mounted Police (RCMP). Some provinces have contracted the RCMP to act as their provincial police forces as well,[70] while others have established their own provincial forces. Municipalities usually have their own local police.

The judiciary serves as the ultimate arbiter of jurisdictional conflicts that cannot be resolved by intergovernmental negotiation and agreement or that are challenged by nongovernmental actors even when the governments agree.[71] When the JCPC was Canada's final court of appeal, it favoured a jurisprudence with separate "watertight compartments" for the two orders of government.[72] Given the JCPC's tendency to interpret provincial powers generously, this usually meant giving federal powers a restrictive interpretation. For example, the JCPC interpreted the broadly worded federal "trade and commerce" power to cover only international and interprovincial transactions, leaving the provinces to regulate intraprovincial commerce.[73] Indeed, at one point, the JCPC allowed the trade-and-commerce power to be used only as additional support for federal legislation whose primary constitutional support lay elsewhere.[74] Thus a power that on its face is broader than the American commerce power became very much narrower.[75]

The JCPC pursued its "watertight compartments" agenda in order to minimize the implicitly concurrent jurisdiction that arises when powers overlap (e.g., the inevitable overlap between trade and commerce and property and civil rights), thus protecting the provinces against indiscriminate applications of the federal paramountcy doctrine, which holds that valid federal legislation trumps valid but conflicting provincial legislation in areas of concurrent jurisdiction. At the same time, it ensured that the provincial compartments were not dwarfed by federal powers. Many of the federal pow-

ers have recovered from their low point during the JCPC era, and one consequence is greater overlap and thus more concurrency subject to federal
paramountcy.[76] The JCPC's "watertight compartments" are decidedly leaky.

In a limited number of cases, the Constitution explicitly provides for
concurrent jurisdiction. Section 95, for example, establishes concurrent jurisdiction over agriculture and immigration subject to the usual rule of federal paramountcy. By contrast, Section 94A, which establishes concurrent
jurisdiction over "old-age pensions and supplementary benefits," gives priority to provincial laws.

In addition to determining which government has the power to do something, the courts have, since the 1982 enactment of the Charter of Rights
and Freedoms, decided whether a power can be denied to both federal and
provincial governments. Before 1982, for example, if the issue was freedom
of religion or of expression, the principal question was which order of government could violate such a freedom.[77] Since 1982 neither has been permitted to do so. When the Charter came into force, provincial governments
and some observers worried that it would often entail the judicial resolution
of what were in fact matters of reasonable policy disagreement. When this
happened in areas of provincial jurisdiction, it was argued, the result would
be the substitution of uniform policy standards where provincial governments had previously been free to differ. Some centralizing influence of this
kind seems inevitable, although scholars disagree about the extent to which
it has materialized. Certainly, the Supreme Court has shown sensitivity to
the tension between the Charter and federalism and has worked to preserve
room for provincial policy-making discretion.[78]

Another limitation on the provinces long predates the Charter. Section
121 of the Constitution Act 1867 sought to establish free trade within Canada: "All articles of the growth, produce, or manufacture of any one of the
provinces shall, from and after the union, be admitted free into each of the
other provinces." This limitation, it is generally agreed, has been honoured
mostly in the breach.[79] In the past, this had something do with Ottawa's inability to use a weak trade-and-commerce power to enforce this principle
legislatively. Nowadays, when the trade-and-commerce power might be
more effectively exploited, its exercise is more a matter of political will. In
any case, provincial barriers to intranational trade are significant.[80]

THE STRUCTURE AND OPERATION OF GOVERNMENT

Parliamentary Government

The proverbial alien visiting earth would learn little about the workings of Canadian government by reading the Constitution. There he would find
lengthy discussions of the generally invisible governor general and provincial

lieutenant governors but no mention of the first ministers (prime minister federally; premiers provincially) who dominate the daily news. To learn the truth about Canada's governance, our alien would have to turn from the text of the Constitution to its conventions. Chief among these is the parliamentary convention of "responsible government," which requires the representative of the Crown to exercise the formal executive powers almost exclusively on the advice of the first minister and the Cabinet, who are members of the legislature and remain in power only with the "confidence" of a majority of their colleagues (in the "lower house" in bicameral legislatures). Through this convention, executive power passes from the monarch to the leaders of the democratically elected legislatures.

In adopting this system, the British North Americans rejected the starker separation of federal powers they saw in the United States. Certainly, the judiciary would be independent of the political branches, but the executive and legislature, although conceptually distinct, were much more closely integrated in a single institution.

The Canadian founders nevertheless embraced goals of liberal democracy that the American founders would have recognized. They wanted a regime of constitutional liberty that would promote self-government through elected legislatures and that would protect rights, including property rights. The American system, they thought, had become overly democratic in the populist sense and thus more dangerous to liberty. In their view, the British system of responsible government provided better liberty-protecting checks and balances.[81]

Many Canadians today would consider this view naive, pointing out that responsible government has generated highly disciplined governing parties that are controlled by the executive rather than the reverse. The Canadian House of Commons and the provincial legislative assemblies have become so executive-dominated that modern commentators sometimes apply the label of dictatorship,[82] echoing James Madison's dictum about the accumulation of all powers in the same hands being "the very definition of tyranny."[83] This exaggerates the Canadian reality. Among other things, power remains dispersed through the federal system itself and between the political and judicial branches. Moreover, even the so-called "trained seals" on the backbenches of government parties can be pushed only so far. Checks and balances are not absent in Canada, although there is no denying the very considerable and concentrated power of Canada's first ministers.

Bicameralism, which is traditionally conceived as a check on the power of lower houses, is also, in Canada, a potential check on executive power. Yet only the federal Parliament includes a second chamber. Ontario and Quebec each have 24 senators in the Senate, as do the four western provinces (six each) and the three Maritime provinces (Nova Scotia and New

Brunswick with ten each and PEI with four). When Newfoundland entered Confederation, it was given six senators. The Yukon, NWT, and Nunavut have one senator each.

The Senate has virtually identical powers to those of the House of Commons. Money bills may not be introduced there,[84] but the Senate may defeat them. The Commons may not override the Senate's veto except in the case of constitutional amendments, where it exercises only a suspensive veto.[85] As an appointed house in a democratic age, however, the Senate lacks the legitimacy to exercise these very considerable powers effectively.

On the assumption that the Senate would take care of regional representation in the federal Parliament, the House of Commons was supposed to be based on representation by population. Given the Senate's inefficacy, however, a degree of regionalism has crept into Commons representation. Constitutional amendments have ensured that no province has fewer members in the Commons than it has in the Senate and that a province's seats will not be reduced below 1985 levels.[86] The "senatorial floor" gives tiny PEI four seats, double what it would be entitled to otherwise. The 1985 "grandfathering" provision leads to overrepresentation in several other provinces, mainly at the expense of Ontario, British Columbia, and Alberta. This regionalization of the Commons, however, does not meet the need for effective regional representation in the federal government because most power lies in the Cabinet, not generally in the House.

Therefore, the Cabinet has borne much of the integrative burden within the federal government. From the outset, Canadian prime ministers, who choose their cabinets from among their partisan legislative colleagues, have made regional representation a central principle of "cabinet making," and strong regional ministers have been key to the success of many federal governments. In the past, religious representation also figured prominently in Cabinet selection, although nowadays characteristics such as race, ethnicity, and gender are more important. However, the Cabinet has not adequately filled the perceived need for effective provincial and regional representation, especially as more power has been gathered into the hands of the prime minister.[87] This has led many to call for reform of federal parliamentary institutions, including electoral reform, the creation of a Triple E Senate, or changes that would weaken party discipline (and hence executive authority) in the Commons.

What is true for the national Parliament is perhaps truer for the unicameral provincial legislatures, which do not experience even the sporadic limitations on executive power applied by the Senate. Moreover, the limited formal mechanisms for representing regional and provincial interests in the national Parliament have cleared the way for premiers to portray themselves as the best representatives of provincial interests in national politics.

In effect, the combination of federalism with increasingly executive-dominated parliamentary systems has produced the characteristic pattern of intergovernmental relations known as "executive federalism" (to be discussed in more detail below).

The Judiciary

Canada's judiciary is an integrated hierarchy composed of provincial courts, "superior courts," and federal courts. With some exceptions, all of these courts settle disputes arising under both federal and provincial law.

The purely provincial courts are constituted and staffed by the provinces under their Section 92(14) authority over the administration of justice. These lower trial courts deal with matters arising under provincial private law, but they also try more than 90 percent of cases arising under the federal Criminal Code.[88]

Moving up the hierarchy, we find the only courts mandated by the Constitution Act 1867 (Sec. 96). Composed of a trial division and a court of appeal in each province, these "superior courts" are also constituted by the provinces (Sec. 92(14)), but their judges are appointed (Sec. 96) and paid (Sec. 100) by the federal government. The trial division of these "Section 96 courts" hears the more important civil and criminal cases and may hold jury trials; the courts of appeal give authoritative interpretation to both federal and provincial law subject only to the ultimate authority of the Supreme Court of Canada.

Section 101 of the Constitution Act 1867 authorized, but did not require, the federal Parliament to establish a supreme court. Constituted in 1875, eight years after Confederation, the Supreme Court did not actually become "supreme" until appeals to the JCPC were ended in 1949.[89]

Section 101 also permits the Parliament to establish additional courts to hear cases arising under federal law, thus allowing the federal government to remove areas of federal law from the jurisdiction of the Section 96 courts and give them to federal courts. Ottawa has established two such courts: the Federal Court of Canada, which is responsible for federal administrative law, and the Tax Court.[90] With these exceptions, courts throughout the system can decide matters of both federal and provincial law, including issues of constitutional law that emerge in the course of ordinary litigation. All levels of the judiciary can invalidate – and sometimes even rewrite[91] – both federal and provincial laws on constitutional grounds subject to review by the Supreme Court.

The Supreme Court exercises its ultimate authority over constitutional law partly because it sits atop the appellate hierarchy. But the federal government can also pose "reference questions" to the Court. The provinces can similarly refer issues to the provincial courts of appeal, whose decisions can then be appealed to the Supreme Court. Many of Canada's most important constitutional decisions, including the 1981 *Patriation* and 1998 *Secession* rulings, were reference cases.[92] Formally considered "advisory opinions," these decisions are in practice given the same precedential weight as judicial opinions in appellate cases.

As one would expect for such a powerful body, Supreme Court appointments are subject to representational concerns. By law, three of the nine judges must come from Quebec; by convention, the other regions must be fairly represented. Appointment of judges is constitutionally a discretionary executive prerogative, falling in practice to the minister of justice and the prime minister, who receive behind-the-scenes advice from a variety of sources, including provincial bar associations. In the case of the Supreme Court, there have been many proposals to make the process more open and consultative and to include some provincial input. None have thus far succeeded.[93]

INTERGOVERNMENTAL RELATIONS

Intergovernmental relations are inevitable given interjurisdictional overlap, Ottawa's power to spend in areas of provincial jurisdiction, and the provincial premiers' claim to champion provincial interests in areas of federal jurisdiction.

Because parliamentary government concentrates power in the executive, intergovernmental interaction is dominated by an extensive system of "executive federalism" in which cognate ministers and/or their deputies meet to work out matters of common concern.[94] First ministers' meetings, which deal with the matters of highest importance, are particularly prominent and often conflictual, although their use depends on the preferences of federal prime ministers. In a real sense, the institutions of executive federalism are Canada's true "third order" of government. Although executive federalism is for the most part a constitutionally unofficial practice, Section 35.1 of the Constitution Act 1982 commits first ministers to calling a conference, to which aboriginal representatives have been invited, before amendments are made to any of the constitutional provisions concerned directly with aboriginal matters. Similarly, Section 49 mandated a first ministers' conference to review the new amending procedures within 15 years after they came into effect (i.e., by 1997). From a democratic perspective, executive federalism poses difficulties. Policy agreements transcending jurisdictional boundaries are reached by ministers in an entirely unofficial forum and then given a stamp of approval by their executive-dominated legislatures. Critics wonder what happens to democratic accountability.[95]

Constitutional influences on interjurisdictional relations at the level of society and the economy, rather than of governments, include the "mobility rights" guaranteed to Canadian citizens and permanent residents by Section 6 of the Charter. These rights, which apply only to natural persons, not corporations, include the right to move to and take up residence in any province and to pursue a livelihood in any province. Section 6 mobility rights are subject to valid provincial laws of general application and to reasonable residency requirements for the receipt of publicly provided social services. Provincial restraints on the professional activities of out-of-province residents have been held to be unconstitutional by the Supreme Court.[96]

The free movement of goods is not protected by the Charter, but Section 121 of the Constitution Act 1867 requires that "all articles of the growth, produce or manufacture of any one of the provinces shall ... be admitted free into each of the other provinces." This section "precludes customs duties between the provinces" but "has never been used to strike down non-fiscal impediments to interprovincial trade" and prohibits "only the crudest and most direct provincial restrictions on the mobility of capital."[97] As a result, interprovincial economic barriers are substantial.

FISCAL AND MONETARY POWERS

The federal government was given most of the obvious economic powers, including banking and monetary policy. In addition, Ottawa can flex its muscle within areas of provincial jurisdiction because of the "vertical imbalance" between its taxation and spending powers and those of the provinces. Ottawa may raise money by "any mode or system of taxation,"[98] but a province may impose only "direct taxation" and license fees.[99] Legally, direct taxes are imposed on those intended to pay them, while the direct payer of indirect taxes passes them on to others.[100] Given that the most important direct tax, the income tax, did not exist at the time of Confederation, the limitation of provinces to direct taxes reflected the founding perception that their responsibilities would be much less costly. This changed dramatically as provincial powers gained significance with the rise of the welfare state. Provincial social-policy responsibilities such as health care and education are hugely expensive.

Since Confederation, of course, provincial revenues have grown significantly. The income tax has become well established in both orders of government, and the JCPC gave provinces access to what might seem the quintessential indirect tax, the sales tax, by defining retailers as government collectors of a tax imposed directly on consumers.[101] Significantly, the provinces may also collect royalties from natural resources within their boundaries.[102] In addition, both orders of government may borrow money on their own authority without restriction,[103] and there is no constitutional stricture on deficit financing by any order of government.[104] Nevertheless, the revenues of provinces regularly fail to meet their constitutional expenses, whereas Ottawa takes in more tax revenues than it spends in its own areas of jurisdiction. Ottawa addresses this imbalance by spending in areas of provincial jurisdiction. This federal "spending power" is constitutionally implied rather than explicitly stated.

Ottawa's fiscal transfers address not only the vertical imbalance between itself and the provinces, but also the "horizontal imbalance" between richer and poorer provinces. These "equalization payments" are intended to ensure that citizens enjoy similar levels of government services in all the provinces. In effect, Ottawa uses its taxation and spending powers to transfer resources from so-called "have" provinces to the "have nots."

The principle of federal transfers to the provinces was established in Section 118 of the Constitution Act 1867, which early on provided for federal subsidies to provincial governments. This provision has since been repealed, but Section 36 of the Constitution Act 1982 states that the federal government is "committed to the principle of making equalization payments to ensure that provincial governments have sufficient revenues to provide reasonably comparable levels of public services at reasonably comparable levels of taxation." What qualifies as "reasonable levels" is, of course, open to interpretation.

FOREIGN AFFAIRS AND DEFENCE POWERS

Under the Constitution Act 1867, Ottawa has exclusive authority over "militia, military and naval service, and defence" (Sec. 91(7)). Moreover, it can enact temporary domestic-emergency legislation during and after wars under the emergency component of its POGG power.

Foreign policy is not as straightforward. Making treaties is a prerogative of the federal executive and requires no legislative approval. However, in the 1937 *Labour Conventions Case*,[105] the JCPC ruled that the power to enact any legislation necessary to implement a treaty followed the normal federal division of powers; thus only provinces may enact implementing legislation in their areas of jurisdiction. "While the ship of state now sails on larger ventures and into foreign waters," wrote the JCPC, "she still retains the water-tight compartments which are an essential part of her original structure." *Labour Conventions* remains the black-letter law. Today, however, where it remains unclear which government has the relevant legislative authority, the Supreme Court will sometimes be influenced by treaty obligations to find in favour of Ottawa.[106] As a consequence of the division of legislative authority to implement treaties, Canada often seeks the inclusion of a "federal state clause." Such a clause informs all signatories that the fulfillment of Canada's obligations may depend in part on the cooperation of provincial governments.

The federal government will also negotiate with the provinces prior to signing a treaty involving their jurisdiction in the attempt to bring them onside. Because the provinces have an interest in successful international trade negotiations, they increasingly cooperate in this area. This was true, for example, in negotiations under the General Agreement on Tariffs and Trade in the mid-1980s, the 1989 Free Trade Agreement with the United States, and the 1994 North American Free Trade Agreement.

Although provinces may not make full-fledged treaties, they have entered into international agreements in areas of provincial jurisdiction. Consequently, provinces, and most notably Quebec, have established a number of foreign offices to represent their interests. In the main, these offices are directed at encouraging investment and trade. Cooperation with the federal government, and even among provinces, is also the rule. However, Quebec's offices have had a more cultural and quasi-diplomatic role, particularly under separatist governments and especially with respect to relations with the francophone world.

CITIZENSHIP

The federal Parliament has exclusive jurisdiction over citizenship. The Constitution Act 1867 is silent about citizenship because Canadians were then simply British subjects. In 1947, as part of rising nationalist sentiment following the Second World War, the federal government introduced legislation establishing a statutory category of Canadian citizenship. The federal government's authority to define the requirements of citizenship is accepted by most scholars, but it is unclear whether the power is part of its jurisdiction over naturalization and immigration (Sec. 91(25) of the Constitution Act 1867) or an exercise of its general power to legislate for the "Peace, Order and good Government" of Canada.[107] Citizenship is granted on both the "law of soil" (*jus soli*) and the "law of blood" (*jus sanguinis*). Anyone born on Canadian soil is automatically a Canadian citizen. Children born abroad to a Canadian parent also have a right to Canadian citizenship (second-generation nonresidents lose their right to citizenship at the age of 28). Permanent residents may apply for Canadian citizenship if they have resided in Canada for three of the four years prior to application. Such residents also need to demonstrate adequate knowledge of Canada and of one of the official languages in order to complete the citizenship process. Since 1977 Canadians have been allowed to take foreign citizenship while keeping Canadian citizenship, thus permitting dual or multiple citizenship. All regulations and procedures related to citizenship are defined and administered by the federal government.

Despite its statutory status, citizenship developed a constitutional aspect with the enactment of the Charter of Rights and Freedoms. While most

Charter rights are extended to everyone in Canada, three rights are exclusive to Canadian citizens: democratic voting (Sec. 3), mobility (Sec. 6), and minority-language education (Sec. 23). In 1989 the Supreme Court ruled that discrimination on the basis of citizenship is unconstitutional,[108] but the Court subsequently upheld civil-service hiring and promotion preferences for citizens.[109] Discrimination on the basis of citizenship remains an unsettled area of Canadian legal and constitutional doctrine and is therefore certain to attract future judicial determinations.

VOTING, ELECTIONS, AND POLITICAL PARTIES

Although the Constitution is silent about the organization and behaviour of political parties, it does have provisions governing elections and electoral districts. The Constitution Act 1867 established the House of Commons and the provincial assemblies as elected institutions, provided for an initial distribution of seats (subject to readjustment after each decennial Census), and set the maximum period between elections (five years for the Commons and four years for provincial assemblies). As noted earlier, provinces amended their constitutions to increase the maximum term for provincial assemblies to five years. The 1982 Charter of Rights and Freedoms confirmed the five-year maximum duration of the Commons and provincial assemblies, except in times of emergency, and mandated that they sit at least once a year.

The Charter also guarantees "every citizen" the right to vote in elections for these assemblies and to stand for election.[110] The courts have held that the right to vote is infringed by too great a variation in constituency size but that the equally sized constituencies suggested by the "one person, one vote" principle are not required.[111] Deviation limits of plus or minus 25 percent have been upheld.[112] As far as the franchise is concerned, a reasonable age threshold for voting is constitutionally permissible, but the disenfranchisement of prisoners is not.[113]

Within these limits, each legislative body is free to administer and organize its own electoral operations, including the exact form of the franchise. All Canadian citizens 18 years of age or older are qualified to vote in federal elections, with the exception of officials responsible for running elections, which includes the chief electoral officer, the assistant chief electoral officer, and the returning officers in each electoral district (except when required to vote to break a tie on a recount). The same is true of provincial elections. Provincial governments monitor municipal elections, and the federal government, under the Indian Act (Secs 74–79), administers elections for band councils on Indian reserves.

Until 1996 voters were registered, or enumerated, in the lead up to each election. Since then a permanent database, the National Register of Electors, has been used to produce the preliminary voters' lists for federal elections, by-elections, and referendums as well as for provincial, territorial, municipal, and school-board elections when the relevant authority has a formal agreement with Elections Canada.

INDIVIDUAL AND COMMUNAL RIGHTS

Under the pre-1982 Constitution, there were few substantive, as opposed to jurisdictional, limits on Canadian governments. The federal government and the provinces of Manitoba and Quebec were constrained by the requirement to make provision for the use of either English or French in their legislatures and courts and by the requirement to produce the records, journals, and laws of these institutions in both languages. Similarly, some of the jurisdiction of the "superior" courts established by Section 96 of the Constitution Act 1867 is fully entrenched and beyond the authority of either order of government to alter or repeal.[114] In addition, beginning in the 1930s, certain judges of the Supreme Court, but never a majority, opined that an "implied bill of rights," protecting such principles as freedom of political expression, was inherent in the parliamentary system of government established by the Constitution.[115]

Parliament and three provinces (Alberta, Saskatchewan, and Quebec) also enacted statutory bills of rights applicable only within their own areas of jurisdiction. Although these statutory bills are still in force (and occasionally applied), the Charter of Rights and Freedoms has largely superseded them.[116] Unlike the statutory bills, the Charter applies within both federal and provincial jurisdictions. Its rights and freedoms are protected against abridgment by government, not by private actors, although the distinction is not altogether clear. Although the Charter does not explicitly incorporate international human-rights instruments, the Supreme Court sometimes uses international (and comparative) law and jurisprudence as interpretive aids.

The Charter's rights and freedoms are not absolute. Section 1 guarantees the Charter's rights and freedoms "subject only to such reasonable limits prescribed by law as can be demonstrably justified in a free and democratic society."[117] Section 4(2) allows a legislature to continue beyond the normal five-year limit because of "real or apprehended war, invasion or insurrection" if it receives the support of at least two-thirds of its members. Most dramatically, as a result of the 1981 compromise between Prime Minister Trudeau and the dissenting provinces during the patriation process, even unjustified laws can be immunized against the Charter for renewable five-year periods by including in them a declaration that the law shall operate "notwithstanding" certain Charter rights (Sec. 33). This notwithstanding clause was initially used extensively by Quebec, including in its omnibus immunization of all the province's legislation immediately after the Charter came into force. Elsewhere, the override clause is more apt to be seen as illegitimate. Nevertheless, it has been used in 16 pieces of legislation by provinces other than Quebec.[118] The clause has never been invoked by the federal government.

The notwithstanding provision protects laws only against the Charter's "Fundamental Freedoms" (Sec. 2), "Legal Rights" (Secs 7–14), and "Equality Rights" (Sec. 15). These sections include many familiar liberal-democratic rights. The fundamental freedoms, for example, are the classic freedoms of religion, expression, assembly, and association. The legal rights include the right to "life, liberty and security of the person," the right to counsel, the right to be presumed innocent until proven guilty, the right to protection against self-incrimination, and the right to protection against double jeopardy. The equality-rights section guarantees equality "before and under the law and ... the right to the equal protection and equal benefit of the law without discrimination and, in particular, without discrimination based on race, national or ethnic origin, colour, religion, sex, age or mental or physical disability." This provision contains unnamed grounds of discrimination analogous to the enumerated ones. The courts have found foreign citizenship[119] and sexual orientation[120] to be among these "analogous grounds."

One classically liberal limitation on government that was deliberately left out of the Charter is the protection of property rights. This has led some advocates of these rights to call for a constitutional amendment to include them and others to explore the interpretive possibility of bringing property rights within the guarantee of "security of the person."[121]

Not subject to the notwithstanding clause are the Charter's "Democratic Rights" (Secs 3–5), "Mobility Rights" (Sec. 6), and "Language Rights" (Secs 16–23). These more strongly protected provisions include additional rights common to liberal democracy, such as the rights to vote and to move about freely. Many of these "strong" rights, however, are more peculiar to the Canadian situation. The democratic rights, for example, speak mostly to the parliamentary system, limiting elected assemblies to five-year maximum terms and ensuring a sitting of the federal and provincial legislatures "at least once every 12 months" (Sec. 5). The mobility-rights section permits a government to engage in otherwise unjustified discrimination in favour of its own citizens if its unemployment rates are above the national average. The Charter's language rights clearly respond to Canada's ethno-linguistic history. Indeed, some of them were designed to invalidate language laws passed by the separatist Government of Quebec.[122]

Much of the Charter emphasizes individual rights. Its provisions generally guarantee rights and freedoms to "every citizen," or (indicating the protection of noncitizens as well) to "everyone," "every individual," or "every person." This individualistic orientation is true of the rights to use either official language or to have one's children educated in the minority language (i.e, French), which is why these rights jeopardized Quebec's policy of limiting individual rights of language choice in the name of collective survival. In certain respects, however, the Charter tends toward a group-rights vision. Thus the Section 15 guarantee of equality rights "without discrimination" immediately goes on to say that this "does not preclude any law, program or activity that has as its object the amelioration of conditions of disadvantaged individuals or groups." This provision permits group-based affirmative action, although it does not require it.

Similarly, the right to have one's children educated in the minority official language of one's jurisdiction is available only to two specified groups: (1) Canadian citizens for whom the minority language is their first language or (2) citizens who received their own primary-school education in this language in Canada. Moreover, the right to have such education publicly paid for applies only when "numbers warrant" – that is, when there is a sufficiently sizeable group. Additionally, the rights of denominational schools protected by the Constitution Act 1867 are, in an important sense, rights of religious communities.

The right to publicly funded denominational and minority-language schools are positive rights that require government action rather than simply inaction, as is the right to have the legislation of Quebec, Manitoba, New Brunswick, and Canada enacted and published in both official languages.[123] Positive rights to such social-policy goods as housing and health care are not explicitly mentioned in the Charter, and, as in the case of property rights, their advocates argue about whether to pursue them through constitutional amendment or judicial interpretation. The courts have certainly made interpretive forays into positive social rights. They have ruled, for example, that if governments choose to enact legislation prohibiting discrimination in employment, housing, and the like, they must extend the protections of this legislation to all groups covered by the Charter's equality-rights provision, including such unnamed analogous groups as gays and lesbians.[124] In the realm of health care, they have required governments to pay for interpreters for deaf patients.[125]

CONSTITUTIONAL CHANGE

The Constitution Act 1982 sets out five amending procedures, most of which were discussed above. The general amending formula (Sec. 38), governing all matters not explicitly covered by the other four, is the "residual" formula, which requires the consent of the Senate, the House of Commons, and the legislative assemblies of two-thirds (i.e., seven) of the provinces having 50 percent of the population. Section 42 provides a list of matters that are expressly covered by this 7-50 formula. These include the principle of proportionate representation of the provinces in the House of Commons, the powers and composition of the Senate and the appointment of its members, and the establishment of new provinces. Changes to provincial powers are also covered by the 7-50 formula, although dissenting provinces may opt out, in some cases with compensation, of any diminution of their powers (with the option to opt in later). In 1996, in response to the 1995 referendum on Quebec secession, the federal Parliament passed what Peter Hogg calls the "regional veto statute,"[126] which "loans" Ottawa's veto under Section 42 to each of five "regions": Quebec, Ontario, British Columbia, Atlantic Canada, and Prairie West. In each of the latter two regions, consent would be signified by the approval of two provinces with 50 percent of their region's population. This legislatively transformed the constitutional formula, giving a practical veto to each of four provinces: Quebec, Ontario, and British Columbia (because they coincide with three of the regions) plus Alberta (because it has more than 50 percent of the population of the three prairie provinces).

The second amendment formula (Sec. 41) specifies some matters – the office of the governor general and lieutenant governors, the right of a province not to have fewer members in the Commons than in the Senate, the use of English or French, the composition of the Supreme Court, and the procedures for amendments themselves – that require the unanimous consent of the federal and provincial legislative houses.

The third formula (Sec. 43) provides that a constitutional amendment applying only "to one or more, but not all, provinces" requires the consent only of the federal houses and the legislative assemblies of the provinces to which the amendment applies.[127] This includes altering provincial boundaries and amending the use of English or French within a province. The latter is an express qualification of the language clause in the unanimity formula, allowing, for example, other provinces to follow New Brunswick in making themselves officially bilingual without requiring the consent of all the other provinces. The fourth formula (Sec. 44) allows the federal Parliament, in matters not covered by other amending formulae, to amend "the Constitution of Canada in relation to the executive government of Canada or the Senate and House of Commons." Finally, the fifth formula (Sec. 45) enables provinces to amend their own constitutions. In addition, some observers argue that the 1992 referendum on the Charlottetown Accord established a convention that the formal amending rules be supplemented by referendums in the case of major amendments.[128] There have been several amendments under the provisions established in 1982,[129] but most constitutional adjustment occurs by way of judicial interpretation.

EMERGING ISSUES

Many of the perennial issues of Canadian public life – relations between Quebec and the rest of Canada, provincialism, regionalism, First Nations issues, and the like – dominated a public agenda of "megaconstitutional" change from the 1960s to the 1990s. With the failure of the Meech Lake and Charlottetown Accords, however, came widespread constitutional fatigue, and the 2003 election of a federalist government in Quebec dampened calls for formal constitutional change from this quarter. Indeed, the "C" word became one that many public actors assiduously avoid. Nevertheless, the yearning for substantial institutional change survived the declining appetite to achieve it through formal constitutional amendment. In effect, attention shifted from "large C" to "small c" constitutional change, or from constitutional amendment to legislative, bureaucratic, and interpretive reform.

The mid-to-late-1990s were notable for the degree to which important institutional change was achieved via ordinary legislation, a trend that seems set to continue. We have already noted, for example, Ottawa's 1996 legislative promise to use its veto over constitutional amendments to block any that do not have the consent of specified regional groupings of provinces, thus significantly altering the amending procedures. True, this change is itself not constitutionally entrenched, but given the conventional nature of Canadian constitutionalism, it may be politically difficult to undo. Four years later, in the spring of 2000, the federal government enacted the Clarity Act, which essentially underlined the Supreme Court's decision in the 1998 *Secession Reference*.[130] This Act requires that a clear question be passed by a clear majority of voters in any future referendum and stipulates some of the items that must be agreed to in a secession amendment.[131] We have similarly noted how the growing assertiveness of First Nations, in combination with the difficulty of dealing with their claims at a constitutional level, has led governments to offer legislative solutions such as that found in the Nisga'a Agreement.

More recently, a Royal Commission initiated by the Government of Newfoundland and Labrador suggested that the province has both benefited and lost as a result of joining Confederation in 1949. In particular, limitations on access to taxation revenue from offshore oil and gas production are seen as unfair by Newfoundland and other Atlantic provinces. It is quite likely that we will see legislative action to alleviate some of this discontent.

Legislative proposals also exist to address the interest among voters and governments in improving the accountability of Canada's political institutions. For example, the federal government has introduced a range of measures, including party-financing legislation and ethics guidelines, aimed at improving both the operation of political institutions and public perception of their operation. Prime Minister Paul Martin has indicated a desire to pursue other changes, including attempts to reduce party discipline in the Commons that will alter the nature of central institutions.

In the provinces, British Columbia has legislatively implemented fixed-term elections, and other provinces are considering doing the same. Equally dramatic, governments in British Columbia, New Brunswick, Quebec, and Prince Edward Island have initiated formal procedures aimed at assessing the democratic adequacy of their traditional "first-past-the-post" electoral systems, with other provinces soon to follow. Reform of provincial legislatures is also on the agenda. For example, a recent electoral redistribution report in Alberta raised the issue of a second chamber for the province. One can easily imagine a domino effect if electoral and legislative change occurs in a number of provinces. The implications for federalism are potentially complex. For instance, more proportionally elected provincial legislatures – particularly if they produce coalition governments – might, on the one hand, undercut the logic of executive federalism, which rests on executive dominance, and, on the other, provide premiers greater legitimacy in their negotiations with other federal actors.

As for intergovernmental relations, the current preeminence of social policy (e.g., health care) in provincial-federal interaction is reminiscent of the period before constitutional issues came to dominate executive federalism. The appeal of fiscal prudence, combined with federal surpluses, cements Ottawa's domination of these negotiations and may produce new types of intergovernmental agreements. External pressures, such as negotiations under the World Trade Organization, the Free Trade Zone of the Americas, and relations with the United States, may spawn new ways of reaching agreements on security as well as on international trade and encourage the federal government to assert its authority in this area. However, policies such as health care, which have serious implications for budgets and government direction, are so contested that a return to the bureaucratic cooperation of earlier times seems improbable. One area in which we might expect to see both greater activity and more conflict is with respect to municipal government. The new federal government has promised to provide financial aid to municipalities, many of which – notably large cities – face severe difficulties financing infrastructure. Settling on a mechanism for such assistance may prove controversial because federal intervention in an area of provincial jurisdiction will not sit well with many provinces and because the needs of municipalities are diverse.

Finally, much constitutional reform comes by way of judicial interpretation. The balance of power between the federal and provincial governments is constantly being adjusted by the courts. This is an old story, but now the growth in Charter litigation and the broadening of the Charter's application due to Supreme Court interpretation shape public policy in

new and often more publicly visible ways. Given that most public policy in
Canada has a federal (and constitutional) component, the growth of Charter politics will continue to affect the nature of Canadian constitutionalism
and federalism.

NOTES

AUTHORS' NOTE: We acknowledge the contribution of all those who participated in the conference "Constitutional Origins, Structure and Change in Federal Democracies" in Calgary, 28 February to 1 March 2003. For their
additional comments and advice, we thank Roger Gibbins, Patrick Fafard, F.L.
Morton, Richard Simeon, Ian Stewart, and Ronald Watts. Their suggestions improved this chapter, and if space had allowed, they would have improved it even
further. We are also grateful for the indispensable organizational and research
support provided by Christopher Alcantera, Dennis Baker, Jeremy Clarke,
David deGroot, Royce Koop, and Christopher Northcott.

1 The largest country is Russia, which has a landmass of 17 million square kilometers.
2 Canada, "E-Book: Complete List of Tables, Gross Domestic Product," *Statistics
   Canada*, 7 January 2003, http://www.statcan.ca/english/Pgdb/econo4.htm.
3 Canada's coastline is 208,080 kilometers. See Canada, "Coastlines," *Atlas of
   Canada*, 21 May 2003, http://atlas.gc.ca/site/english/facts/coastline.htm.
4 The following are the 1 October 2003 populations (and percentages of the total Canadian population) of Canada's jurisdictions: Canada, 31,717,637
   (100%); Ontario, 12,280,731 (38.7%); Quebec, 7,503,502 (23.7%); British
   Columbia, 4,158,649 (13.1%); Alberta, 3,164,400 (10.0%); Manitoba,
   1,164,135 (3.7%); Saskatchewan, 995,003 (3.1%); Nova Scotia, 936,878
   (3.0%); New Brunswick, 750,460 (2.4%); Newfoundland and Labrador,
   520,170 (1.6%); Prince Edward Island, 137,941 (0.4%); Northwest Territories,
   42,040 (0.1%); Yukon, 31,371 (0.1%); Nunavut, 29,357 (0.1%). See Canada,
   "The Daily," *Statistics Canada*, 7 January 2003, www.statcan.ca/Daily/English/
   031218/do31218c.htm.
5 Canada, "Canada's Ethnocultural Profile: The Changing Mosaic," *Statistics Canada*, 21 January 2003, http://www12.statcan.ca/english/census01/Products/
   Analytic/companion/etoimm/contents.cfm.
6 Canada, "Religions in Canada," *Statistics Canada*, 13 May 2003, http://www12.
   statcan.ca/english/census01/Products/Analytic/companion/rel/contents.cfm.
7 Neil Nevitte, *The Decline of Deference: Canadian Value Change in Cross-National Perspective* (Peterborough, ON: Broadview Press, 1996), pp. 210–11.
8 Section 93 protects denominational schools but only in five provinces: Ontario,
   Nova Scotia, New Brunswick, British Columbia, and Prince Edward Island.

Active but modified versions of Section 93 can also be found in the statutes constituting Manitoba (Sec. 22, 1870), Saskatchewan (Sec. 17, 1905) and Alberta (Sec. 17, 1905). Quebec and Newfoundland are not subject to the Section 93 protections for denominational schooling by virtue of Constitutional Amendment Proclamation 1997 (Quebec), Can. Stat. Instruments, SI 97-141, and of Constitutional Amendment Proclamation 1997 (Newfoundland Act), Can. Stat. Instruments, SI 98-25. See Peter Hogg, *Constitutional Law of Canada*, loose-leaf edition (Scarborough, ON: Carswell, 1997), p. 53–24.1.

9 Britain retroactively confirmed Ottawa's authority to do so in 1871.

10 Canada Act 1982, UK, 1982 c. 11, s. 2.

11 Section 52 refers to a list found in the Schedule to the Constitution Act 1982.

12 See, for example, Albert J. Smith, in the New Brunswick House of Assembly, 14 March 1866, *Canada's Founding Debates*, ed. Janet Ajzenstat et al. (Toronto: Stoddart, 1999), pp. 129–30. See also Robert Pinsent, in the Newfoundland Legislative Council, 14 February 1865, Azjenstat et al., eds, *Founding Debates*, p. 149.

13 Charles Tupper, in the Nova Scotia House of Assembly, 10 April 1865, Ajzenstat et al., eds, *Founding Debates*, p. 170.

14 Some Americans thought that by ending reciprocity, the BNA colonies would be forced by economic circumstances to seek union with the United States on their own. See R.D. Francis, *Origins: Canadian History to Confederation* (Toronto: Harcourt Brace Canada, 1996).

15 George-Etienne Cartier, in the Legislative Assembly of Canada, 7 February 1865, Ajzenstat et al., eds, *Founding Debates*, p. 183.

16 Christopher Moore, *1867: How the Fathers Made a Deal* (Toronto: McClelland and Stewart, 1997), p. 42.

17 Garth Stevenson, *Unfulfilled Union: Canadian Federalism and National Unity*, rev. ed. (Toronto: Gage, 1982), pp. 199–200.

18 "[L]egislative union would be preferable ... it would be the best, the cheapest, the most vigorous, and the strongest system of government we could adopt." John A. Macdonald, in the Legislative Assembly of Canada, 6 February 1865, Ajzenstat et al., eds, *Founding Debates*, p. 279.

19 R. MacGregor Dawson, *The Government of Canada*, 5th ed., rev. Norman Ward (Toronto: University of Toronto Press, 1970), p. 27.

20 Robert C. Vipond, *Liberty and Community: Confederation and the Failure of the Constitution* (Albany: State University of New York Press, 1991), pp. 22–3.

21 John A. Macdonald, in the Legislative Assembly of Canada, 13 March 1865, Ajzenstat et al., eds, *Founding Debates*, p. 314.

22 Constitution Act 1867, Section 90.

23 Ibid.

24 Ibid., Sections 55 and 57.

25 In *Re Resolution to Amend the Constitution* [1981] 1 S.C.R. 753 at 802, the Supreme Court noted that "reservation and disallowance of provincial legislation,

although in law still open, have, to all intents and purposes, fallen into disuse."
See also Hogg, *Constitutional Law of Canada,* p. 5–19 n. 70.

26 For a historical account of how the powers of disallowance and reservation have
been used, see Guy V. LaForest, *Disallowance and Reservation of Provincial Legislation* (Ottawa: Queen's Printer, 1965). See also, generally, Vipond, *Liberty and
Community;* and Hogg, *Constitutional Law of Canada,* p. 5–19.

27 Constitution Act 1867, Section 92(10)(c). According to Hogg, this declaratory
power has been used 472 times, mostly for the construction of railways but also
for bridges, harbours, mines, and so on. Hogg also notes, however, that the federal government is "sensitive to the anomalous character of the power" and is
"now inclined to use the power only sparingly" (22–18). The failed Charlottetown Accord of 1992 would have required provincial consent for the exercise
of Section 92(10)(c). See Hogg, *Constitutional Law of Canada,* pp. 22–15 to
22–18.

28 Constitution Act 1867, Section 93(4). Section 93(4) has never been used.

29 Constitution Act 1867, Section 96.

30 K.C. Wheare, *Federal Government,* 4th ed. (London: Oxford University Press,
1963), p. 19.

31 Vipond, *Liberty and Community,* chapter 5.

32 See discussion of *Fort Frances Pulp and Power Co. v. Manitoba Free Press* [1923]
A.C. 695 in Peter H. Russell, Rainer Knopff, and F.L. Morton, eds, *Federalism
and the Charter: Leading Constitutional Decisions,* 2nd ed. (Ottawa: Carleton University Press, 1989), pp. 68–72.

33 The broad scope of Section 92(13) is demonstrated by Lord Atkin's comments
in *Attorney General of Canada v. Attorney General of Ontario (Employment and Social
Insurance Act Reference)* [1937] A.C. 355. H. Carl Goldenberg described Section
92(13) as "wide enough to cover nearly all legislation outside of criminal law"
in "Social and Economic Problems in Canadian Federalism," *Canadian Bar Review* 12 (September 1934): 422–30 at 423. See Alan C. Cairns, "The Judicial
Committee and Its Critics," *Canadian Journal of Political Science* 4, no. 3 (September, 1971): 301–45 at 306.

34 Keith Archer et al., *Parameters of Power: Canada's Political Institutions,* 2nd ed.
(Scarborough, ON: ITP Nelson, 1999), p. 158.

35 For instance, the cost-shared (federal transfer based on provincial expenditure)
Established Programs Financing and the Canada Assistance Plan were replaced
by the "block-grants" (federal transfer based on population, regardless of provincial need) of the Canada Health and Social Transfer (CHST), although some
believe that the CHST's effects on federal expenditure have been only modest.
See Tracy R. Snodden, "The Impact of the CHST on Interprovincial Redistribution in Canada," *Canadian Public Policy* 24 (March 1998): 49–70.

36 Ronald L. Watts, *Comparing Federal Systems,* 2nd ed. (Kingston, ON: Institute of
Intergovernmental Relations, Queen's University, 1999).

37 Archer et al., *Parameters of Power,* p. 80.

38 Peter Russell, *Constitutional Odyssey: Can Canadians Become a Sovereign People?*
    2nd ed. (Toronto: University of Toronto Press, 1993), pp. 96–7.

39 Pierre Elliott Trudeau, *Federalism and the French Canadians* (Toronto: Macmillan
    of Canada, 1968).

40 Rainer Knopff and F.L. Morton, *Charter Politics* (Scarborough, ON: Nelson Can-
    ada, 1992).

41 Archer et al., *Parameters of Power*, p. 95.

42 Only Ontario and New Brunswick initially supported it.

43 Archer et al., *Parameters of Power*, pp. 90–1.

44 *Re Constitution of Canada* (1981) 125 D.L.R. (3d). For a discussion of this case,
    see Michael Mandel, *The Charter of Rights and the Legalization of Politics in Canada*
    (Toronto: Wall and Thompson, 1989), pp. 24–34.

45 Russell, *Constitutional Odyssey*, p. 111.

46 For a discussion of the nature of the decision and how it contributed to federal-
    provincial compromise, see Rainer Knopff, "Legal Theory and the 'Patriation'
    Debate," *Queen's Law Journal* 7, no. 1 (1981–82): 41–65 at 41. See also Peter
    Russell, "Bold Statescraft, Questionable Jurisprudence," *And No One Cheered:
    Federalism, Democracy & The Constitution Act*, ed. Keith Banting and Richard
    Simeon (Toronto: Methuen Publications, 1983), pp. 210–38.

47 Constitution Act 1982, Section 33.

48 Alan Cairns, "Citizens (Outsiders) and Governments (Insiders) in Constitution
    Making: The Case of Meech Lake," *Disruptions: Constitutional Struggles from the
    Charter to Meech Lake*, ed. Douglas E. Williams (Toronto: McClelland and Stew-
    art, 1991), pp. 108–38 at 110.

49 See *Re: Objection to a Resolution to Amend the Constitution (Québec Veto Reference),
    1982,* [1982] 2 S.C.R. 793, in which the Supreme Court subsequently rejected
    this claim that Quebec retained a two-nations veto. See Russell, Knopff, and
    Morton, eds, "Québec Veto Reference," *Federalism and the Charter*, pp. 760–70 at
    p. 760. For a critical analysis of this decision, see Marc E. Gould, "The Mask of
    Objectivity: Politics and Rhetoric in the Supreme Court of Canada," *Supreme
    Court Review* 7 (1985): 455–510.

50 Russell, *Constitutional Odyssey*, pp. 111–12.

51 From the "two-nations" perspective, an equal senate would give one-half of the
    political community only one-tenth of the representation.

52 Alan Cairns, *Charter versus Federalism* (Kingston, ON: McGill-Queen's University
    Press, 1992), pp. 114–18.

53 Patrick Monahan, *Meech Lake: The Inside Story* (Toronto: University of Toronto
    Press, 1991); Ronald L. Watts, "Canadian Federalism in the 1990s: Once More
    in Question," *Publius: The Journal of Federalism* 21 (Summer 1991): 169–87.

54 Kenneth McRoberts and Patrick Monahan, eds, *The Charlottetown Accord, The
    Referendum and The Future of Canada* (Toronto: University of Toronto Press,
    1993); Robert C. Vipond, "Seeing Canada Through Referendums: Still a House
    Divided," *Publius: The Journal of Federalism* 23 (Summer 1993): 39–56.

55 See Constitution Act 1930.

56 *Reference re Secession of Quebec* [1998] 2 S.C.R. 217, paragraph 88. See also Peter Leslie, "Canada: The Supreme Court Sets Rules for the Secession of Quebec," *Publius: The Journal of Federalism* 29 (Spring 1999): 135–51.

57 Constitution Act 1982, Section 43.

58 See Nelson Wiseman, "Clarifying Provincial Constitutions," *National Journal of Constitutional Law* 6 (March 1996): 269–94. See also Campbell Sharman, "The Strange Case of a Provincial Constitution: The British Columbia *Constitution Act*," *Canadian Journal of Political Science* 17 (March 1984): 87–108.

59 Jean Chrétien's appointment of Jean-Louis Roux as lieutenant governor of Quebec in September 1996 is a rare example of the appointment being made over the objections of the provincial government. Roux had spoken against the sovereigntist position in the 1995 referendum, thus making him an attractive candidate to the federal Liberals but unacceptable to the Parti Quebecois government. Roux resigned in November 1997 as a result of a minor scandal (Roux had worn a swastika in 1942 to express his contempt for conscription).

60 *Re Initiative and Referendum Act* [1919] A.C. 935.

61 This is the case by virtue of Quebec's and Manitoba's place in the national Constitution. *Attorney General of Manitoba v. Forest* [1979] 2 S.C.R. 1032; *Attorney General of Quebec v. Blaikie* [1979] 2 S.C.R. 1016.

62 These are Quebec, Ontario, Prince Edward Island, Nova Scotia, and New Brunswick.

63 *Ontario (Attorney General) v. Pembina Exploration Canada Ltd* [1989] 1 S.C.R. 206.

64 Andrew Sancton, "Municipalities, Cities and Globalization: Implications for Canadian Federalism," *Canadian Federalism: Performance, Effectiveness, and Legitimacy*, ed. Herman Bakvis and G. Skogstad (Oxford: Oxford University Press, 2002), pp. 261–77. Sancton notes that former Toronto mayor Mel Lastman "speculated that Toronto might be better off comprising its own province" (271).

65 For instance, both Ontario and Quebec have recently incorporated a number of formerly autonomous communities into their largest cities: Toronto in 1998 and Montreal in 2001 respectively.

66 See Peter H. Russell, "The End of Mega Constitutional Politics in Canada?" *PS: Political Science and Politics* 26 (March 1993): 33–37 at 37. Although a comprehensive land claim was negotiated between the Cree in northern Quebec and the Quebec government in 1975, the number of land claims has grown exponentially since 1992.

67 The Nisga'a final agreement came into effect on 11 May 2000.

68 Bill C-19, the proposed First Nations Fiscal and Statistical Management Act, was introduced in the House of Commons and read the first time on 2 December 2002. It was read a second time and referred to the House of Commons Standing Committee on Aboriginal Affairs on 25 February 2003. The bill was referred back to the House on 24 September 2003 but died on the *Order Paper* when the Parliament was prorogued on 12 November 2003.

69 *The Queen v. Hauser* [1979] 1 S.C.R. 984 (approving federal prosecutions under the Narcotics Control Act); *Attorney-General of Canada v. C.N. Transportation* [1983] 2 S.C.R. 206 (approving federal prosecutions under the Combines Investigation Act); and *R. v. Wetmore* [1983] 2 S.C.R. 284 (approving federal prosecutions under the Food and Drugs Act).

70 See, for instance, Section 21 of the Alberta Police Act.

71 *Reference re Anti-Inflation Act* [1976] 2 S.C.R. 373.

72 *Attorney General for Canada v. Attorney General for Ontario et al.* [A.C. 326] 1937. The "watertight compartments" metaphor competed with another strand of jurisprudence that did not emphasize exclusivity: the "double aspect" theory, which allowed both orders of government to legislate on the same matters from different angles.

73 *Citizens Insurance Co. v. Parsons; Queen Insurance Co. v. Parsons* (1881) 7 App. Cas. 96.

74 *Re Board of Commerce Act* [1922] 1 A.C. 191; *Toronto Electric Commissioners v. Snider* [1925] A.C. 396.

75 This change was emphasized by the Supreme Court of Canada in *Severn v. the Queen* [1878] 2 S.C.R. 70.

76 Fields such as securities regulation present a "double aspect," where one aspect of the law falls within federal jursidiction (in the case of securities, the federal power to incorporate companies, and power over criminal law) while another aspect falls within provincial jurisdiction (the provincial power over property and civil rights). In such cases, concurrence is granted (*Multiple Access Ltd. v. McCutcheon* [1982] 2 S.C.R. 161). Where there is an operational conflict between "double aspect" laws, the federal law is paramount (*Law Society of British Columbia v. Mangat* [2001] 3 S.C.R. 113).

77 See, for example, *Switzman v. Elbling and Attorney General of Quebec* [1957] S.C.R. 285.

78 See James B. Kelly, "Reconciling Rights and Federalism during Review of the Charter of Rights and Freedoms: The Supreme Court of Canada and the Centralization Thesis, 1982 to 1999," *Canadian Journal of Political Science* 34 (June 2001): 321–55.

79 In *obiter dicta,* Justice La Forest has included Section 121 as part of the "common market," which forms "one of the central features of the constitutional arrangements incorporated in the Constitution Act, 1867." *Morgaurd Investments Ltd. v. De Savoye* [1990] 3 S.C.R. 1077 at 1099; *Hunt v. T&N plc* [1993] 4 S.C.R. 289 at 322.

80 Kevin Clifford Wasson, "Non-Tariff Barriers to Trade in Canada," MA thesis, University of Toronto, Faculty of Law, 1990, p. 1; Thomas Courchene, *Economic Management and the Division of Powers* (Toronto: University of Toronto Press, 1986), p. 215. These barriers have been reduced somewhat by the 1995 Agreement on Internal Trade.

81 See Ajzenstat et al., eds, *Founding Debates,* chapter 2.

82 Jeffrey Simpson, *The Friendly Dictatorship* (Toronto: McClelland and Stewart, 2001).

83 James Madison, "Federalist No. 47," in Alexander Hamilton, James Madison, and John Jay, *The Federalist Papers* (New York: Mentor Books, 1961), pp. 300–308 at 301.

84 Constitution Act 1867, Section 53.

85 Constitution Act 1982, Section 47(1).

86 Constitution Act 1985.

87 Donald J. Savoie, *Governing from the Centre: The Concentration of Power in Canadian Politics* (Toronto: University of Toronto Press, 1999).

88 Peter McCormick and Ian Greene, *Judges and Judging* (Toronto: Lorimer, 1990), p. 18.

89 Cases that had begun prior to 1949 could be decided after that date.

90 However, there appear to be limits to how far the federal government may move in this direction. See Peter H. Russell, *The Judiciary in Canada* (Toronto: McGraw Hill, 1987), pp. 68–9.

91 See, for example, *Vriend v. Alberta* [1998] 1 S.C.R. 493.

92 *Re Constitution of Canada* (1981) 125 D.L.R. (3d); *Reference re Secession of Quebec* [1998] 2 S.C.R. 217.

93 See, for example, Peter H. Russell and Jacob S. Ziegel, "Mulroney's Judicial Appointments and the New Judicial Advisory Committees," *University of Toronto Law Journal* 41 (Winter 1991): 4–37; and F.L. Morton, "Debate: Should there be Confirmation Hearings for Supreme Court Judges? Affirmative," *Law Politics and the Judicial Process in Canada*, ed. F.L. Morton, 2nd ed. (Calgary: University of Calgary Press), pp. 117–19.

94 See, Richard Simeon, *Federal-Provincial Diplomacy: The Making of Recent Policy in Canada* (Toronto: University of Toronto Press, 1972).

95 Donald Smiley, "An Outsider's Observations of Federal-Provincial Relations among Consenting Adults," *Confrontation and Collaboration: Intergovernmental Relations in Canada Today*, ed. Richard Simeon (Toronto: Institute of Public Administration of Canada, 1979), pp. 105–13.

96 See *Black v. Law Society of Alberta* [1989] 1 S.C.R. 591.

97 Hogg, *Constitutional Law in Canada*, p. 43–11.

98 Constitution Act 1867, Section 91(3).

99 Ibid., Section 92(2 and 9).

100 The classic definition is John Stuart Mill's in book 5, chapter 3, of *Principles of Political Economy*, 7th ed., ed. William J. Ashley (London: Longmans, Green, and Co., 1909). Mill's definition has been accepted by the courts. The leading case is *Bank of Toronto v. Lambe* (1887) 12 App. Cas. 575. See Hogg, *Constitutional Law of Canada*, p. 30–6.

101 *Atlantic Smoke Shops v. Conlon* [1943] A.C. 550.

102 Only the federal government may levy taxes on offshore resources (as territorial waters are a federal responsibility). The federal government owns and

taxes natural resources in the territories. Territories are granted taxation powers under federal statute, and a number of indigenous communities have taxation powers granted them by federal and provincial statutes. Municipalities have access to property taxes and some other miscellaneous taxation via provincial legislation.

103 Constitution Act 1867, Sections 91(4) and 92(3).

104 Some provinces have introduced balanced-budget legislation; in some cases, they apply this to municipalities.

105 *Attorney General of Canada v. Attorney General of Ontario* [1937] A.C. 327.

106 Hogg, *Constitutional Law of Canada*, p. 11–16.

107 Ibid., pp. 34–5, 43–5 n. 17.

108 *Andrews v. Law Society of British Columbia* [1989] 1 S.C.R. 143.

109 *Lavoie v. Canada* [2002] 1 S.C.R. 769.

110 Constitution Act 1982, Section 3.

111 *Reference re Prov. Electoral Boundaries [Sask.]* [1991] 2 S.C.R. 158.

112 Ibid., 173. Even greater deviations are permitted in sparsely populated northern constituencies.

113 *Sauvé v. Canada (Chief Electoral Officer)* [2002] 3 S.C.R. 519.

114 Russell, *The Judiciary in Canada*, pp. 255–56.

115 See, for example, *Reference Re Alberta Statutes*, [1938] 2 S.C.R. 100, p. 133.

116 The statutory bills of rights are still important because they extend to matters not covered by the Charter of Rights. For example, the federal Bill of Rights covers property rights.

117 Some of the Charter's rights contain their own similar qualifiers. Thus the document's "legal rights" preclude only "unreasonable" searches and seizures (Sec. 8) and "cruel and unusual" punishments (Sec. 12) and guarantee that no one will be deprived of "life, liberty, and security of the person … except in accordance with the principles of fundamental justice" (Sec. 7).

118 Tsvi Kahana, "The Notwithstanding Mechanism and Public Discussion: Lessons from the Ignored Practice of Section 33 of the Charter," *Canadian Public Administration* 44 (Fall 2001): 255–91.

119 *Andrews v. Law Society of British Columbia* [1989] 1 S.C.R. 143.

120 *Egan and Nesbitt v. Canada* [1995] 2 S.C.R. 513.

121 Alexander Alvaro, "Why Property Rights Were Excluded from the Canadian Charter of Rights and Freedoms," *Canadian Journal of Political Science* 24, no. 2 (1991): 309–29.

122 For example, Section 23, which gives parents who were educated anywhere in Canada in the minority official language (i.e., French) the right to educate their children in this language, was designed to overcome Quebec's restriction of English-language schooling to children whose parents had been educated in English in Quebec.

123 The constitutional text simply requires that statutes be "printed and published" in both languages, but the Supreme Court has ruled that it requires

"enactment" in both languages as well. *Attorney General of Quebec v. Blaikie* [1979] 2 S.C.R. 1016 at 1022.

124 *Vriend v. Alberta* [1998] 1 S.C.R. 493.

125 *Eldridge v. British Columbia (Attorney General)* [1997] 3 S.C.R. 624.

126 Hogg, *Constitutional Law of* Canada, p. 4–22. Hogg's "regional veto statute" does not have an official short title. Its long title is: An Act Respecting Constitutional Amendments, S.C. 1996, c. 1.

127 Six of the eight constitutional amendments since 1982 have used the Section 43 mechanism. See Hogg, *Constitutional Law of Canada*, p. 1–7 n. 28.

128 Some believe that the "citizens' constitution" has changed the Canadian consciousness in such a way as to render the "top-down" accommodation of elites an illegitimate method of substantive constitutional change. See Russell, *Constitutional Odyssey*; and Alan C. Cairns, *Disruptions: Constitutional Struggles from the Charter to Meech Lake* (Toronto: McLelland and Stewart, 1991).

129 Hogg lists eight amendments since 1982: 6 using Section 43 (1987, Nfld; 1993, NB; 1993, PEI; 1997, Nfld; 1997, QC; 1998, Nfld), 1 using Section 38 (1983) and 1 using Section 44 (1985). Hogg, *Constitutional Law of Canada*, p. 1–7 n. 28.

130 *Reference re Secession of Quebec* [1998] 2 S.C.R. 217.

131 These items include the division of the national debt, borders, the rights of aboriginals, and the protection of minorities.

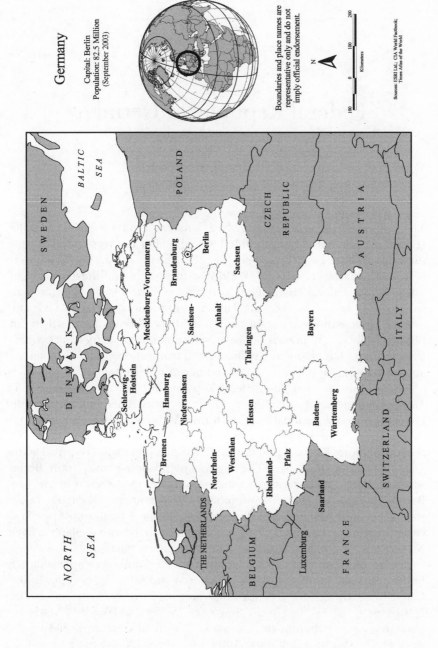

Germany

Capital: Berlin
Population: 82.5 Million
(September 2003)

Boundaries and place names are
representative only and do not
imply official endorsement.

N

Kilometers

100   0   100   200

Sources: ESRI Ltd.; CIA World Factbook;
Times Atlas of the World

NORTH

SEA

SWEDEN

BALTIC

SEA

DENMARK

POLAND

Mecklenburg-Vorpommern

Schleswig-
Holstein

Brandenburg

Berlin

Sachsen

Hamburg

Bremen

Niedersachsen

Sachsen-
Anhalt

Thüringen

CZECH

REPUBLIC

Bayern

AUSTRIA

THE NETHERLANDS

Nordrhein-
Westfalen

Hessen

Baden-
Württemberg

ITALY

BELGIUM

Rheinland-
Pfalz

Saarland

SWITZERLAND

Luxemburg

FRANCE

Federal Republic of Germany

JUTTA KRAMER

The Federal Republic of Germany "is a democratic and social federal state" (Basic Law, Art. 20I). It was founded in 1949, after the Western Allies gave the prime ministers of the *Länder* (i.e., the constituent states), which were reestablished after the Second World War, the task of drafting a new constitution with a federal character in order to prevent a strong central state from arising in Germany again. However, the federal order in Germany does not follow the example of the United States Constitution, which emphasizes a division of powers between governments, but rather the German tradition, which is characterized by mutual connections, interconnections, and overlapping of the centralized and decentralized state units.[1]

When it was founded, the Federal Republic of Germany consisted of 11 *Länder* (without Berlin, which was a city-state under Allied control) that did not conform to the boundaries of the former Weimar Republic. Since reunification in 1990, Germany has consisted of 16 *Länder*, including three city-states: Hamburg, Bremen, and Berlin. Germany's population is spread across 357,000 square kilometres. The highest population density is in Berlin, which has 3,800 inhabitants per square kilometre; the lowest is in the *Land* Brandenburg, which has only 88 inhabitants per square kilometre. *Länder* sizes differ considerably as well. The smallest *Land*, Bremen, consisting of two cities (Bremen and Bremerhaven), has 680,000 inhabitants; the largest *Land*, North Rhine-Westphalia, has more than 17.9 million inhabitants.

The ethnicity of Germany's population of 82.5 million people is largely homogeneous. German is the only national and official language. Ethnic minorities with a distinct culture and language live only in the extreme Northwest (Frisians) and in the Southeast (Sorbs and Wends of Slavic origin). In addition, there is the national minority of German Danes on the northern border with Denmark. At the end of 2002, more than 7.3 million foreigners were living in Germany. Compared with the end of 1989, this figure had risen by roughly 2.3 million. The proportion of foreigners within the total population rose from 6.4 percent in 1989 to 8.9 percent in 2002. Many foreign families have lived in Germany for two or three generations. Roughly 55 million Germans are Christians, 28.2 million of them being Protestant and 27 million being Roman Catholic; in addition, there are approximately 1.7 million Muslims and only 54,000 Jews (representing a mere 10 percent of Germany's 1933 Jewish population before the Holocaust). The gross domestic product per capita (real) was us$32,962 in 2001.[2]

After 45 years of the East-West political division of Germany due to the Cold War conflict, the reunification of Germany took place in 1990, when the German Democratic Republic (GDR) joined the territory covered by the Basic Law *(Grundgesetz)* after the GDR collapsed politically and economically. Simultaneously, five new *Länder* were established within the territory of the former GDR. On this occasion, no use was made of the possibility, provided for in Article 146 of the Basic Law, of creating a new constitution and of allowing the German people to vote on it. This option had not been exercised in 1949 either, when the Basic Law likewise came into force without a popular vote. Sixty-five years after the outbreak of the Second World War, however, Germany regards itself as a community open to the world that promotes the European process of integration as a member of the European Union (EU) and contributes to the creation of a democratic, social, and federal Europe based on the rule of law and a peaceful coexistence (Art. 23I).[3]

CREATION OF THE FEDERAL CONSTITUTION

The constitution of the Federal Republic of Germany, called the Basic Law, was drafted and passed by the Parliamentary Council in 1948–49. This council consisted of 65 members delegated by the *Länder* parliaments. The constitution came into force on 23 May 1949. The basis for the council's discussions and decisions was the so-called Herrenchiemsee Draft, drawn up by a group of senior civil servants and leading politicians from the *Länder.* In addition to the desires expressed and conditions laid down by the Allies, the new constitutions of these *Länder,* dating from 1946–47, had a considerable influence on the content of the Basic Law.

The main goal of the majority of the founding fathers was to establish a Western-style democratic federal state that would guarantee freedom, peace, and security and enable a free-market economy to come into existence. All of these goals were, however, politically controversial in the Parliamentary Council because, at that time, the Cold-War conflict between the Eastern and Western political systems was already dominant. While conservatives preferred a more decentralized type of federalism in agreement with the Allies, left-wing circles were more in favour of a unitary federal state that would, in their view, enable Germany to overcome more easily the difficult problems of postwar reconstruction. As for the form of the democratic system, it was decided, in contrast to the plebiscitary examples in some of the *Länder* constitutions, that the political will should be formed in a purely representative body because, after the experience with the Weimar Republic and National Socialism, there was fear of providing demagogic leaders with a public platform. Finally, the free-market economy was also suspected by some founders of having favoured National Socialism because some business tycoons had supported Adolf Hitler; therefore, the free market was rejected by most people, including many liberals and conservatives. Thus, despite its neutrality regarding economic policy, the Basic Law still contains an article that permits the socialization of the means of production, of banks, and of land (Art. 15). Another heavily debated issue was the structure of the second chamber of the Parliament; the two alternatives have been either the establishment of a senate with directly elected members or the readoption of the former federal council composed of members nominated by the *Land* governments.

Taking a lesson from the inhuman regime of National Socialism, the founders laid special emphasis on guaranteeing human rights and civil rights, which they regarded as fundamental rights, placing them in the first section of the Basic Law ahead of all the other articles, and which they made directly and legally binding for all three branches of government: legislature, executive, and judiciary. In addition, they guaranteed that in the case of any violation of these rights by the state, a person has recourse to independent courts. Apart from the classic civil rights and liberties, guaranteeing the equality of all people before the law also played a special role for the founders. In the future, no one was to be favoured or disfavoured due to his or her language, race, homeland, origin, gender, or political opinions. Basic political rights, such as the freedoms of expression, assembly, and association, were also guaranteed. Thus the authors of the Basic Law not only complied with the wishes of the Allies, but also followed the Western traditions of constitutionalism, basing their ideas in particular on models like those developed in the nineteenth century after the bourgeois revolution in the years 1848–49, which produced the first attempts to draw up a federal constitution in St Paul's Church in Frankfurt.

The Basic Law was thus more a product of political elites than the result of broad participation by the population. After a 12-year break caused by the Hitler regime, the Basic Law replaced the Weimar Constitution of 1919, which, just like its predecessor, the Imperial Constitution of 1871, had established a federal state characterized by the principle of allegiance to the federation in the relationship between the federation and the *Länder* and between the *Länder* themselves. Thus a tradition dating back to the early Middle Ages was resumed in 1949.

The Holy Roman Empire founded by Charlemagne in 800 was later provided with the first federal-like structure through the Constitutional Charter of 1356, called the "Golden Bulle." This federal structure consisted of the imperial organs (i.e., emperor, electoral princes, imperial court counsellors, and imperial supreme court) and imperial administrative districts (with their own administrations and armies). After the Thirty Years' War (1618–48), the individual duchies and principalities were given restricted sovereignty in the Treaty of Westphalia of 1648; thus from this time on, the German Empire can be regarded as having been a federal-like polity (not merely a confederation of states). Whereas the federal state came into existence at that time by way of decentralization (through the creation of autonomous subnational states), the creation of today's federal order in Germany was achieved by precisely the opposite means – namely, through the amalgamation or accession of individual *Länder* in 1949.[4]

CONSTITUTIONAL PRINCIPLES OF THE FEDERATION

In accordance with the founders' intentions, the Basic Law was designed with a strongly noncentralized system of federalism in mind. Thus Article 30 stipulates that the exercise of state powers and the discharge of state functions are matters for the *Länder*. Any divergence from this rule governing the distribution of responsibilities must be laid down expressly in the Basic Law. Nevertheless, even during the early days of the Federal Republic, there were numerous interconnections between the responsibilities of the federation and those of the *Länder* (i.e., no "dual federalism" as in the United States). Thus, for example, legislation concerning taxation has always been a federal responsibility shared between the federal Parliament and the Federal Council *(Bundesrat),* while the *Länder* are entitled to a share of the revenues from the taxes collected. From the very beginning, the framework of responsibility in the field of legislation allowed the federal government to draw up such detailed regulations that the *Länder* had hardly any freedom to make decisions about their own political programs.[5]

Since 1969 the trend toward a unitary federal state has been considerably increased (1) by the fact that, in practice, a comprehensive integrated system has developed in which the federation partly finances tasks that were originally financed solely by the *Länder* (e.g., building and expanding institutions of higher education, strengthening regional economic structures, improving agriculture, enhancing coastal protection, and funding scientific research) and (2) by the enlargement of the mechanism of common taxes — namely, the income and corporate taxes and the turnover tax. Taking a cue from the American model, this integrated system was called "cooperative federalism." However, this system has proved to be not only crippling, but also problematic from the democratic point of view because everybody can be made responsible for everything, and therefore nobody is responsible for anything. For this reason, there has been much discussion about instituting reforms to produce greater transparency with regard to decision making and responsibility and about permitting more competition between the federal government and the *Länder*. However, Germany is still far from having a system of competitive federalism.[6]

From the outset, the Basic Law tried to create a proper balance between unity and diversity. On one hand, it gave the federation the task of creating equivalent living conditions everywhere in Germany; on the other hand, with an extensive catalogue of so-called concurrent legislative responsibilities, it provided the *Länder* with the potential power to shape their own policies. In addition, the Basic Law still mandates that the costs of carrying out state tasks must, in each case, be borne by the order of government that is also responsible for carrying out the tasks in question (the so-called principle of division).

Regarding the assignment of state tasks, the Basic Law merely distinguishes between two orders: the federation and the *Länder*. This means that all the *Länder* must fulfil the same tasks regardless of their size, number of inhabitants, and economic or financial strength. They also have equal rights in dealing with the federation. Thus Germany's federalism can be considered symmetric if one disregards the different weighting of *Land* votes in the Federal Council *(Bundesrat)*. It is surprising that the authors of the constitution decided in favour of symmetry of this kind in 1949, when the *Länder* were burdened to differing degrees by an influx of refugees from the East. It was probably decisive here that traditional reasons spoke in favour of the legal equality of all the *Länder*. The German constitutions of 1871 and 1919 had established a symmetric federal state even though two-thirds of the territory of the Reich at that time consisted of one *Land*, Prussia. The costs of this symmetric federalism are obvious, as the great economic and social differences between the *Länder* must be compensated for by means of an extensive system of equalization payments.

The federal order and also, in particular, the participation of the *Länder* in the legislation of the federation are guaranteed by the so-called "eternity clause" (Art. 79III) of the Basic Law. This clause is not subject to any constitutional change and therefore cannot be removed even with a 100 percent majority in the legislative bodies. In turn, the *Länder* have no right of secession; in fact, the unilateral withdrawal of a *Land* from the Federal Republic would result in a state of emergency and, in the most extreme case, could be prevented by military means. Political parties that pursue the goal of secession can be banned by the Federal Constitutional Court. However, this does not mean that the present system, with its 16 *Länder*, must be maintained forever. Reorganization of the federal territory (Art. 29) could either increase or reduce the number of *Länder*. However, at least two *Länder* would have to be left in place in order to satisfy the demands of the federal system guaranteed by the "eternity clause."

The Länder

Like the federation, each *Land* has the quality of a state. The *Länder* can write their own constitutions, and, like the federation, they have their own constitutional jurisdiction, enforced by independent constitutional courts. The Basic Law is bound merely to create homogeneous constitutional structures. The *Land* constitutions must be in accordance with the principles of the German democratic and social state, which is governed by the rule of law, and must have a republican character (Art. 28). Adherence to these principles can be examined by the Federal Constitutional Court, and in the most extreme case, the principles can be enforced by federal compulsion (Art. 37). Apart from this proviso, the *Länder* are free to choose their own system of government. Bavaria, for example, was for many years the only *Land* to have a bicameral legislative system. The *Länder* can create their own organs of government and complement the parliamentary system (with or without a constructive vote of no confidence) with processes of direct democracy. The direct election of the prime ministers in the *Länder* by the people would also be permissible, but so far, this option has only been discussed in some *Länder*. All the members of the government and senior civil servants in the *Länder* are elected or appointed; the federation has no possibility of influencing the filling of these positions.

Differences between the *Länder* constitutions are largely due to the fact that some of them had already come into force in 1946–47, before the promulgation of the Basic Law. They are so-called full constitutions, which also contain a comprehensive catalogue of basic rights. In the case of the *Länder* constitutions that came into force after 1949, either the basic rights were omitted, or those of the Basic Law were simply adopted, or rights declarations were restricted to those basic rights that fall within *Land* responsibility (i.e., education, schools, religion, and churches). The constitutions of the new *Länder* that came into existence after reunification in 1990 are different. Although they again contain full catalogues of basic rights, which are largely modelled on the basic rights of the federation, they nevertheless complement these rights with social rights (Art. 142).

Most *Land* constitutions were drawn up and passed by the *Land* parliaments. Only in a few cases were there referenda. The parliaments of the *Länder* are also primarily responsible for changes to the constitution, for which a two-thirds majority of their members is required. Only a few *Länder* (e.g., Baden-Württemberg and Bavaria) can hold a referendum on alterations to their respective *Land* constitutions. The Basic Law takes precedence in any contradiction between the Basic Law and a *Land* constitution

(Art. 31). However, the organs of a *Land*, in particular the constitutional court of a *Land*, are responsible for interpreting their own constitution.[7]

Municipalities

In Article 28II the Basic Law expressly guarantees the rights of municipalities to regulate all local affairs. This guarantee also extends to the bases of financial autonomy; these bases include the right of municipalities to a source of tax revenues based on the economic ability of each. However, municipalities are not incorporated as a third order in the governmental system; rather, they are a part of *Land* administration. There is, therefore, no direct legal relationship between the federation and the municipalities. Supervision of the municipalities is exclusively the task of the *Land* authorities. In political reality, however, the municipalities are strongly influenced by federal policies. For example, they must fund all social aid from their own budgets. Nevertheless, the relevant laws always require the consent of the Federal Council *(Bundesrat)*, wherein the represented *Land* governments not infrequently ease their financial burdens at the expense of their municipalities by passing costs on to them. The financing gaps thus arising for the municipalities are not always completely compensated by the redistribution of funds to them within the *Land*. This is why municipal officials continually complain about a structural financial crisis.

In the Basic Law, the names of the *Länder* are listed only in the preamble, without any distinction being made between the city-states and the other states. The city-states of Hamburg and Berlin are at the same time municipalities divided into dependent districts. Here the state characteristic of being a *Land* coincides with the self-governing character of being a municipality. The situation in the city-state of Bremen is different, as it consists of two municipalities: Bremen and Bremerhaven. Here, the Bremen city parliament acts simultaneously as the *Land* parliament and as the body representing the municipality of Bremen.

Although the municipalities' right to self-government includes only a small amount of tax power, self-government otherwise covers all matters concerning the local community (and its own sphere of government). In particular, these include cultural matters (i.e., museums, theatres, sports facilities, and schools) and public services (e.g., provision of water and power, waste disposal, abattoirs, cemeteries, and hospitals) as well as the maintenance of public roads and streets within a municipality. In this field, municipalities are also independent in matters regarding planning and personnel and have their own independent administration, which is not subject to the specialist supervision of the *Land* administration but only to its legal supervision.

In addition, municipalities carry out *Land* tasks (transferred sphere of government) for the federation and the *Länder,* for the fulfilment of which they have a right to adequate funds (called the principle of connection). Examples of these tasks are the administration of traffic (e.g., driver's licenses and vehicle registration) and matters concerning registration of the population, aliens, food inspection, job safety, and health control. Within this framework, in addition to legal supervision, municipalities are subject to supervision by the *Land* authorities, which have a right to examine the effectiveness of each local measure. If the municipalities do not observe the instructions of the supervising bodies of the *Land,* the supervising bodies can take over the task themselves (substitution measure). In the most extreme case, they can also replace the head of the municipal administration with a *Land* commissioner (Art. 28III).

The federation itself has no supervisory rights over municipalities. However, if a *Land* does not fulfil its supervisory duties regarding its municipalities, or does not fulfil them satisfactorily, the federation can take steps to compel the *Land* to comply with its duties (Art. 37). If, in the case of an internal emergency, the *Land* is willing to combat the disturbance of internal order but is not able to do so with its own forces, it can request other *Länder* to provide help or call upon the Federal Border Police (Art. 91II). However, this provision has never been applied in the history of the Federal Republic, and it is hard to imagine that this situation will ever occur in the future.

The Basic Law does not contain special regulations concerning the self-government of national minorities or original inhabitants (e.g., Aboriginals). Some *Land* constitutions (e.g., Schleswig-Holstein, Lower Saxony, and Saxony) merely include regulations that compel the *Land* and its municipalities to protect the language and culture of ethnic minorities (e.g., Frisians, Wends, and Sorbs).

THE ALLOCATION OF POWERS: GENERAL

The Basic Law lists only the individual tasks and responsibilities of the federation. Consequently, all the tasks and responsibilities not mentioned therein must be fulfilled by the *Länder* and the municipalities. In Article 30 this is laid down in such a way that the discharge of state functions and the exercise of state powers is a matter for the *Länder* except as otherwise determined by the Basic Law. Thus the residual powers lie solely with the *Länder.* The federation is responsible only for foreign relations, defence, protection of the civilian population, questions of nationality and passports, immigration and emigration, the monetary system, customs and foreign trade, air traffic, the railways, and highways. The federation and the

Länder are jointly responsible for all other legislative tasks, but here the federation takes precedence. In particular, these tasks include civil law, criminal law, procedural law, commercial law, labour law, social-security law, antitrust law, environmental law, and state liability.

This means that only a small number of legislative powers are exercised exclusively by the federation; the greater part of legislative authority lies within the sphere of the concurrent competence of the federation and the *Länder.* In the area of concurrent responsibilities, federal law takes precedence over any concurrent *Land* law when there is a conflict (see Art. 31). However, a conflict of this kind rarely occurs because when authority for a concurrent competence is claimed by the federation, the concurrent *Land* law becomes void. The federation's assumption of authority regarding a concurrent competence, therefore, has a blocking effect on any conflicting *Land* laws. However, the federation can exercise this authority only when it is absolutely necessary in order to guarantee legal and economic unity or to establish equivalent living conditions everywhere in the federal territory. Recently, the Federal Constitutional Court reviewed these criteria and denied them in a special case.[8]

With the introduction of joint tasks, joint-planning committees consisting of representatives from the federation and the *Länder* were also established under the constitution. These committees decide on the distribution of the funds for carrying out the joint tasks. The Basic Law does not provide for further institutions for intergovernmental relations between the federation and the *Länder* or among the *Länder* themselves. Nevertheless, numerous forums and conferences have come into existence to coordinate policy within the federation and among the *Länder.* These include, above all, the Conference of Prime Ministers and the conferences of the ministers of special portfolios. These forums are of particular importance in matters for which the *Länder* are exclusively responsible, such as education. The Education Ministers' Conference ensures almost uniform courses of instruction and educational qualifications for the whole of the republic in order to make it possible for people to move from one *Land* to another without any difficulty, thus guaranteeing the freedom of movement laid down in the Basic Law.

In addition, at the administrative level, there are more than 950 discussion and working groups in which experts responsible for a particular subject area meet regularly to exchange information and to coordinate their decisions. These networks are one of the essential reasons why the high degree of federal entanglement often paralyzes the nation's political decision-making processes. Because majority decisions are not made in the field of intergovernmental relations, and because the principle of consensus is the determining factor, agreement is achieved in most cases only by means of appeal to the lowest common denominator, which leads to a certain rigidity and inflexibility in the decision-making process.[9]

JURISDICTIONAL CONFLICTS BETWEEN
THE FEDERAL GOVERNMENT AND THE *LÄNDER*

As far as conflicts of competence between the federation and the *Länder* are concerned, a distinction must be made between legislative and administrative disagreements. If the federation and the *Länder* cannot agree on which government is responsible for legislation in a particular case, both can call on the Federal Constitutional Court to make a direct decision under the rules dealing with so-called federation-*Länder* conflict. For example, if in the field of concurrent jurisdiction, the federation passes a law for which a *Land* claims to be either entirely or partly responsible, this *Land* can apply to the Federal Constitutional Court to have this federal law declared invalid due to the lack of federal jurisdiction. The reverse is also true, and such cases have occurred many times.

In the field of administration, German federalism is characterized by an atypical peculiarity. In accordance with the Basic Law, the *Länder* implement not only their own laws but also the laws of the federation. As long as the *Länder* are active on their own behalf, the federation has only the right of legal supervision. A special procedure is provided with regard to the federation's right of supervision. Initially, the federation must send representatives to the highest *Land* authorities, and if these representatives determine that legal errors have been made in implementing the federal laws, the *Land* authorities are reprimanded. If these errors are not addressed by the *Land*, and if the *Land* feels that its rights have been violated, the federation or the *Land* can appeal to the Federal Council *(Bundesrat)*, which determines whether the *Land* has violated federal law. The federation or the *Land* can appeal the decision of the Federal Council to the Federal Constitutional Court, which then makes the final decision (Art. 84IV). This procedure of federal overview is only of minor practical importance because the *Länder* have been obedient to the federal government in the past.

However, if the *Länder* become active in executing federal laws when obligated to do so by the federation (which must be expressly provided for in the Basic Law), then they are also subordinate to the expert supervision of the federation, which covers not only the legality but also the suitability of the implementing action. The *Länder* are then obliged to follow the directives of the federation without contradiction, even if the directives are unconstitutional. Disputes associated with this complicated procedure have been mostly settled by several decisions of the Federal Constitutional Court, such that conflicts of this kind hardly occur any more.[10]

FEDERALISM AND THE STRUCTURE AND OPERATION
OF GOVERNMENT

The federation and the *Länder* all have parliamentary systems based on the British model to the extent that the government's formation and continued existence depend on the confidence of the majority of the Parliament. The decision in favour of parliamentary systems was strongly influenced by negative experiences with the semipresidential system during the Weimar Republic. When the Reichstag could no longer form a majority at the end of the 1920s, the excessive use of emergency decrees by the German president aided the Nazis' assumption of power. Today the only *Land* with a semipresidential form of government is the Free State of Bavaria. Because its constitution neither provides for a constructive vote of no confidence nor grants the premier the right to dissolve the Parliament during its elected term of office, a change of government can take place only if the government resigns voluntarily. The *Land* Parliament cannot bring about a change of government of its own accord.

Although the separation of government powers is a normative feature of the Basic Law, it is only indirectly standardized in the text of the constitution. Article 20II mentions the "specific organs" of the legislature, the executive, and the judiciary (separation of organs), whose members are, in most cases, permitted to belong to only one body (incompatibility). The one exception is the compatibility of a seat in the Parliament and the position of a minister. In addition, all three organs, or branches, of government are mentioned once more in Article 1III (commitment to the basic rights) and in Article 20III (commitment to the constitution, law, and justice), ensuring the separation of government functions. Finally, the independence of judges is derived from Article 97I.

Although a balance formally exists between all three organs, due to the parliamentary system, the legislative power nevertheless takes precedence in practice because a law is necessary for every state measure that affects the rights of citizens (legal reservation). However, as in every parliamentary system, the legislative and the executive powers are not strictly separated but are concentrated in the governing majority. While the government and its parliamentary majority form a political unit for action, their governance is scrutinized in the Parliament by the parliamentary minority, or opposition. As a result of the multiparty system and the proportional electoral system in Germany, there is, as a rule, a coalition government on the one side and a heterogeneous opposition on the other. As a result of this intermingling of powers, one can even speak of the breaking of the principle of the separation of powers in the legal sense or of the political separation of powers between the majority and the opposition.

The Federal Parliament

Four constitutional organs are involved in the legislative process of the federation: the *Bundestag* (Federal Diet) and *Bundesrat* (Federal Council), the federal government (i.e., the executive branch), and the federal president. Legislative initiatives can be introduced by the federal government, by the *Bundesrat*, and from within the *Bundestag* when at least 5 percent of its members support such a measure. If the federal government introduces a legislative initiative, it is first submitted to the *Bundesrat*, which then expresses its opinion. It is then returned to the federal government, which can then make a counterstatement. Only after the completion of this process is the proposed legislation submitted to the *Bundestag*. If the *Bundesrat* introduces a legislative initiative, it is sent to the federal government (i.e., executive) for its comments and is then submitted to the *Bundestag*. This so-called "first stage" provides the *Bundestag* with the opportunity to learn the opinion of the *Länder* in the case of government initiatives and to hear the opinion of the federal government in the case of *Bundesrat* initiatives before it deals with the draft bill. Initiatives from within the Parliament initially remain in the *Bundestag* without the federal executive or the *Bundesrat* having the opportunity to express an opinion on them.

As a rule, each bill is given three readings in the *Bundestag* (i.e., general discussion, special debates, and final vote). If the bill receives support by a parliamentary majority, it then becomes a so-called adopted bill. It is then submitted to the *Bundesrat*, which has an absolute right of veto over legislation requiring its consent. In the case of so-called laws with the right of objection, the *Bundesrat* can force the *Bundestag* to decide once again on the *Bundesrat*'s objection, in which case the *Bundestag* must override this objection in order for the law to be adopted. Whether the *Bundesrat*'s consent is required for a law's adoption or whether the *Bundesrat* can only object to a law depends on its content. If it contains organizational or procedural regulations about its implementation by the *Länder* and municipalities, this will always justify the necessity for consent. If the law has come into existence either because the *Bundesrat* has given its consent or has raised no objection to the law or because the objection by the *Bundesrat* has been rejected by the *Bundestag*, the law is submitted to the federal president, who signs and promulgates it. Finally, the law is published in the *Federal Law Gazette*.

In Germany there is neither a unicameral system nor a genuine bicameral system. The legislature does consist of two bodies, the *Bundestag* and the *Bundesrat*; however, the two bodies do not have equal competences and functions. In the case of laws to which it has the right of objection, the *Bundesrat* has merely a suspensive veto that can be overruled by a majority in the *Bundestag*. Only in the case of laws requiring the *Bundesrat*'s consent does the absolute right of veto enable the *Bundesrat* to block laws – creating a situation similar to that of a bicameral system. However, before the *Bundesrat* can object or refuse to give its consent, a so-called mediation process normally takes place with the goal of achieving a compromise between the majority of the *Bundestag* and the majority of the *Bundesrat*. The adopted bill is submitted to the so-called mediation committee, which consists of 32 members (1 member for each *Land* and 16 members of the *Bundestag*, who are not nominated by the majority but are nominated by the parliamentary caucuses in accordance with their relative strength in the Parliament). The subject of the continuing legislative procedure in the *Bundesrat* is always the version of the bill that has been agreed upon in the process of mediation. The mediation committee can deal with the same bill three times at most: once on application by the *Bundesrat* (normal case), once by the federal government, and once by the *Bundestag*.

For legislation, the *Länder* are represented in the *Bundesrat*, but this representation extends only to the *Land* governments. The *Land* parliaments have no influence either on the composition of the *Bundesrat* or on the voting behaviour of their *Land* governments. Unlike the members of the United States Senate, the members of the *Bundesrat* are not elected directly by the people. Thus the *Bundesrat* represents only the *Länder* executives; consequently, it is also called the "parliament of the public officials." The members of the *Bundesrat* and their alternates are at the same time members of their respective *Land* cabinets, but they can also be represented by alternates, who, as a rule, are senior civil servants.

The number of votes (and members) in the *Bundesrat* is determined by the number of inhabitants in the *Länder*. Each *Land* has at least three votes (i.e., Bremen, Hamburg, Mecklenburg-Pomerania, and Saarland). *Länder* with more than 2 million inhabitants have four votes (i.e., Berlin, Brandenburg, Rhineland-Palatinate, Saxony, Saxony-Anhaltina, Schleswig-Holstein, and Thuringia); *Länder* with more than 6 million inhabitants have five votes (i.e., Hessia); and *Länder* with more than 7 million inhabitants have six votes (i.e., Baden-Württemberg, Bavaria, Lower Saxony, and North Rhine-Westphalia). Each *Land* in the *Bundesrat* must cast its votes as a unit (block votes). This block commitment of votes is often a problem for multiparty coalition governments in the *Länder*, which the *Länder* representatives have tried to solve by abstention or by means of special provisions in a coalition agreement, but an abstention is still effectively a "No" vote. Each decision of the *Bundesrat* requires the absolute majority of its votes, which at present means at least 35 of the 69 votes and members.

From the constitutional point of view, the *Bundesrat*'s most important task is its participation in passing or blocking federal legislation through its rights of consent and of objection. However, because it is composed of delegates from the *Land* cabinets, it does, in fact, exert some executive powers. Thus one can also talk of an element of executive federalism in Germany, whereby policy is negotiated and formulated by Land and federal executives. The *Bundesrat*'s executive power is even increased, first, by its required participation in approving important statutory orders of the federal government (so-called statutory instruments requiring its consent under Article 80II) and, second, by the fact that its European chamber has its own right to make final decisions in matters concerning the European Union (Art. 23). Apart from its authority in these matters, the *Bundesrat* has no exclusive or special competence.

The participation of the *Bundesrat* in federal legislation and administration, as well as in European affairs, has a double-edged effect. On one hand, the *Bundesrat* provides the *Länder* governments with a means to introduce their interests and demands directly in the federation's decision-making process. However, because the *Bundesrat* is constructed as, and remains, the representative body of the *Länder*, it is a federal organ and is thus also partly responsible for federal policy as a whole. On the other hand, this dual nature of the *Bundesrat* leads to considerable conflicts when the political majorities in the *Bundestag* and in the *Bundesrat* are comprised of different political parties, which has almost become the rule in the Federal Republic, especially since 1971. When a political group wins the federal elections and forms the federal government over a period of four or more years, the opposition in the federation has regularly succeeded in winning a number of subsequent *Land*-parliament elections, thus gaining the majority in the *Bundesrat*. This situation can lead to a deadlock of federal policy if the large parties do not come to an agreement along the lines of a hidden grand coalition in the *Bundestag* and in the *Bundesrat*. The mixing of responsibilities associated with this situation regularly leads to public irritation and frustration because the voters do not know to which political actors they can attribute particular decisions. For this reason, reform of the *Bundesrat* is being discussed, as is a change at least to its voting procedure, which would force coalition governments in the *Länder* to make a clear decision for or against a measure introduced by the ruling majority in the federation. There is certainly agreement that the present situation not only represents a danger to the functioning of the parliamentary system, but is also, in the view of many observers, a deficit of democracy.[11]

Whereas the *Länder* governments can introduce their own legislative initiatives in the federal arena via the *Bundesrat*, neither the municipalities nor ethnic or national minorities can participate formally in the federation's legislative procedures. At best, they appear as lobbying groups (e.g., the German Conference of Municipal Authorities). Given that *Bundesrat* initiatives introduced by the majority of the *Länder* governments can be blocked by the *Bundestag*, they are introduced either for demonstration purposes in order to sharpen the political profile of an issue or only when there is a good chance that the majority of the *Bundestag* will endorse them. Initiatives from within the *Bundestag* itself are fairly rare; they mostly serve only to shorten the procedure in order to avoid the *Bundesrat*'s participation during the first stage of consideration. Thus more than 80 percent of all bills originate with the federal government with the expectation that they will be supported by its parliamentary majority in the *Bundestag*. However, the governments of the *Länder* can prevent these bills from becoming law through the majority in the *Bundesrat*, or the *Bundesrat* can alter such bills if they pertain to laws requiring its consent according to the results of a mediation procedure.

The Federal Executive

The executive power of the federation lies with the federal government and the federal administration. The number of ministries and the areas of their jurisdiction are not laid down in the constitution; the federal chancellor formally decides on this matter by recommending to the federal president the appointment of certain ministers. In practice, however, in the case of coalition governments, the decisions about appointing ministers as well as the responsibilities of their ministries and the delimitation of their portfolios are all agreed upon in the preceding negotiations, and the results of these negotiations are included in the coalition agreement. The organization of the federal executive is therefore de facto the concern of the entire federal government. The federal government is made up of the federal chancellor and the federal ministers (i.e., the Cabinet). Each minister is responsible for a ministry, which is headed by a deputy minister, who is an appointed civil servant. The chancellor chairs the Cabinet. The chancellor also determines, and is responsible for overseeing adherence to, the general guidelines on policy. Within these limits, each federal minister conducts the affairs of his or her portfolio independently and according to his or her own responsibility and is therefore responsible to the Parliament. The federal government resolves differences of opinion between federal ministers.

Because the *Länder* execute the majority of federal laws, Germany has only a very small direct federal administration, which is restricted essentially to the exclusive responsibilities of the federation (Art. 87), namely the foreign service, the federal financial administration, the administration of federal waterways and shipping, the Federal Border Police, and the federal armed forces. The federation's further administrative tasks are fulfilled on the basis of a law concerning the highest independent federal authorities. These tasks include, among others, weather forecasts, transport administration, radiation protection, defence of the constitution, and intelligence services. Therefore, the *Länder* do not participate directly in the federal administration. However, the constitution provides that civil servants employed by the highest federal authorities are to be drawn from all the *Länder* in appropriate proportions (Art. 36), but in practice, these civil servants are drawn from all applicants without taking the regional proportions into account. If a particular federal authority is not situated in the capital of Berlin but in one of the *Länder*, its employees, as a rule, are drawn from the *Land* in which they serve.

The Federal Judiciary

The federal courts are exclusively courts of appeal; they examine the decisions of the courts within the *Länder* for legal errors but not with regard to the correctness of the facts. Thus the federal courts' only task is the legal review of decisions rendered by the lower courts of the *Länder*. These federal courts include the Federal Court of Justice (civil and criminal law), the Federal Administrative Court (administrative conflicts), the Federal Finance Court (disputes concerning taxes), the Federal Labour Court (labour law), the Federal Social Court (social jurisdiction), and the Federal Constitutional Court (Arts 93 and 95). The federation has also created other courts (Art. 96) — namely, the Federal Patent Court (legal protection of industrial property) and the Federal Antitrust Court (antitrust law). The Federal Constitutional Court is responsible for all constitutional disputes arising from the application or interpretation of the Basic Law.

Federal judges are jointly appointed by the federal minister with competence and by a committee for the selection of judges consisting of the *Land* ministers with competence and an equal number of members of the *Bundestag* (Art. 95II). Half of the members of the Federal Constitutional Court are elected by an electoral committee of the *Bundestag*, the other half are elected by the *Bundesrat*.

The Basic Law does not provide for a supreme federal court that would have the final right of decision over all the other federal courts. All the federal courts are on a par with each other. It is true that the Federal Constitutional Court can reverse decisions of the other federal courts if they violate the constitution, but this does not make it a supreme court because it becomes active only when requested; moreover, through its decisions, it expresses only the precedence of the constitution over ordinary law. So far, no use has been made of the possibility provided for in the Basic Law of guaranteeing the uniformity of judicial procedure by forming a joint chamber of the above-mentioned supreme federal courts – that is, a supreme court of justice (Art. 95III). All the other courts are those of the *Länder*, which are lower courts subordinate to the federal courts. To this extent, one can speak of a certain hierarchy of judicial power in Germany. Once again, the constitutional courts of the *Länder* are an exception here because they exclusively have the task of overseeing the compatibility of acts undertaken by a *Land* under its own constitution.

The right to declare federal laws invalid is concentrated in the Federal Constitutional Court. There are three ways to have a law declared invalid. For one, if a lower court considers a law, or parts of a law on whose validity the court's decision depends, to be unconstitutional, it must stay the proceedings and obtain a decision from the Constitutional Court (concrete judicial review), as provided for in Article 100. Second, the federal government, any *Land* government, and/or one-third of the members of the *Bundestag* can have any federal law, or parts of it, examined with regard to its compatibility with the Basic Law; these bodies can also have any *Land* law examined with regard to its compatibility with federal law. In the case of incompatibility with the constitution or with a federal law, the Constitutional Court declares the law in question to be invalid (abstract judicial review), as provided for in Article 93I, No. 2. Third, any person can file a constitutional complaint after exhausting all other legal means to reverse an executive decision or law that affects him or her directly (Art. 93I, No. 4a). In such cases, the Constitutional Court examines whether the act of public authority that occasioned the complaint is itself based on a law contrary to the constitution; if so, the Constitutional Court declares both the law and the act of public authority to be invalid. Until 1954 it was possible to obtain an advisory legal opinion from the Constitutional Court on the conformity of prospective laws with the constitution, but this practice was discontinued because experience showed that in this way the Constitutional Court could have a massive influence on the political decision-making process, even before the process had been completed, and that, in addition, the Constitutional Court was in danger of being used by the political powers for their own purposes. The constitutional courts of the *Länder* (including Schleswig-Holstein, which employs the Federal Constitutional Court as its own state constitutional court) make the final decision about the validity of *Land* laws and their compatibility with *Land* constitutions; their decisions are not subject to any further examination by the Federal Constitutional Court.

The *Länder* do not present their candidates directly for the federal courts. However, through their ministers of justice, who are members of the parliamentary committee for the selection of judges, they have considerable influence on filling the posts of the federal courts. In the case of the Federal Constitutional Court, the *Bundesrat,* as the representative of the *Land* governments in the federal arena, even selects half the judges. In this way, the posts at all the federal courts have a personnel composition that is oriented along the lines of the proportional representation of the *Länder,* without any individual *Land* being able to claim a certain quota of posts. Membership on a federal court does not necessarily require that a person have previously been a judge. Any person who has fulfilled the criteria for admission to the profession of attorney and is at least 40 years old can be elected as a federal judge.

The Basic Law provides only for state courts to decide on all legal disputes. Extraordinary courts for ethnic, traditional, or religious minorities are expressly forbidden (Art. 101I). This ban is based on Germany's experiences with extraordinary courts for Jews and for political dissidents under the Nazi dictatorship. It is only at the municipal level that some *Länder* have justices of the peace or arbitration services, participation in which is a precondition for being able to apply to a general court.

Institutions of the Constituent Polities

The institutional regulations in the constitutions of the *Länder* generally reflect the constitutional structures of the federation. The constitutional order in the *Länder* must have a republican character and must conform to the principles of a democratic and social state governed by the rule of law. The *Länder* and municipalities must also have bodies representing the people, which are elected in general, direct, free, equal, and secret elections (Art. 28I). All the *Länder* have unicameral parliaments and governments elected by the people of the *Länder* according to the principles of the parliamentary system. The governments consist of the prime ministers and the ministers. The *Länder* have no head of state, such as a president. One part of a president's functions (e.g., external representation, the right of appointment, and the right of reprieve) is exercised by the prime minister, and another part (e.g., the drafting and proclaiming of laws) is carried out in some *Länder* by the Speaker of the parliament.

In addition, processes of direct democracy have been introduced in all the *Länder*, some of which have two stages (petition for a referendum and the referendum itself) and some of which have three stages (with a preliminary motion for a petition for a referendum). A derogative referendum, with which the people, as in Switzerland, can rescind a law directly through a single decision, does not exist in Germany. However, using the path of normal popular legislation, the rescinding of a law could be demanded.

The *Länder* have no independent (autonomous) courts whose decision would not be reversible by superior federal courts; it is rather the case that they are built into the prescribed channels of jurisdiction as a whole. As far as the institutions of the administration of justice are concerned, despite their formal independence, Germany has more of a hierarchical than a dual system of courts. Only the constitutional courts of the federation and the *Länder* are totally separated from each other. Therefore, on matters in

which a constitutional court of a *Land* is bound by the *Land*'s constitution
rather than by the Basic Law, it can come to decisions that are different
from those of the Federal Constitutional Court.

Relations Between the Constituent Polities

In accordance with the Basic Law, the Federal Republic of Germany forms
one legal area. This means that all the legal actions of one *Land* are recognized in all the other *Länder*. In accordance with Article 33I of the Basic
Law, every German has the same political rights and duties in every *Land*
and – according to his or her aptitude, qualifications, and professional
achievements – has equal access to any public office. Thus the freedom of
movement of all German citizens is guaranteed throughout the federal territory (Art. 11), and any discrimination against them is forbidden. The
rights to transfer capital, goods, services, and labour are guaranteed by the
constitution. Because both the penal code as well as the code of criminal
procedure are standardized by federal laws, borders between the *Länder*
play no role in the prosecution of offences and in the punishment of criminals even though the severity of sentences declines as one moves from the
South to the North. In civil-law procedures, the domicile of the debtor or
the defendant is decisive in determining which court is responsible for trying a case, provided that no other court of jurisdiction has been agreed
upon under private law between the litigants. In cases of disputes over administrative decisions by governments, the seat of the state authority that
made the initial decision is decisive. In criminal cases, the decision always
lies with the court in whose area of responsibility the crime took place or in
which the commission of the crime began.

The Basic Law does not provide for any formal mechanisms or institutions to deal with relationships between the *Länder*. In practice, however,
numerous forums have been developed (see above), in which the *Länder*
forge policy agreements among themselves (so-called self-coordination of
the *Länder* on a "third level"). These include the regular prime ministers'
conferences (with informal "fireside discussions"), the conferences of the
individual ministers, and the numerous working groups and discussion
groups of experts. The *Länder* also have the right to conclude state agreements between each other and with the federation. As long as these agreements are within the framework of their exclusive legislative responsibilities
(i.e., culture, education, mass media, and internal security), the *Länder* do
not require the consent of federal organs.

Only when the *Länder* conclude treaties with foreign states within these
responsibilities must the federal government give its consent (Art. 32III).
In the course of working toward European unification, there is now active
cross-border cooperation, which is based partly on international treaties

but mainly on mere administrative agreements that do not require the consent of the federation. In order to guarantee cooperation of this kind under administrative law and under constitutional law, the Basic Law permits the *Länder*, with the consent of the federal government, even to transfer sovereign jurisdiction for tasks to transfrontier institutions in neighbouring regions – provided that the *Länder* are responsible for fulfilling these tasks in the first place (Art. 24IIa). As a rule, these transfrontier institutions deal with such questions as regional planning and traffic management, environmental protection, and joint public services (e.g., Neue Hansa in the Baltic region and the ARGE-Alp in Bavaria, Austria, Switzerland, and Italy).[12]

FISCAL AND MONETARY POWERS

Germany has an entangled system of (1) revenue and tax legislation vested mainly in the federation, (2) tax allocation and revenue apportionment shared jointly by the federation and the *Länder*, and (3) revenue collection administered by the *Länder*. One of the most eminent and distinctive characteristics of German fiscal federalism is a highly developed mechanism of financial equalization between the federation and the *Länder* as well as among the *Länder* themselves.

The Basic Law establishes a system of burden sharing between the federation and the *Länder* in accordance with two principles and many exceptions. The federation and the *Länder* separately finance the expenditures (principle of separation) resulting from the discharge of their respective tasks (principle of connection) insofar as the Basic Law does not provide otherwise. Where the *Länder* act as agents of the federation, the federation must meet the resulting expenditure. Federal laws to be executed by the *Länder* make provision for payments to be met wholly or partly by the federation. Where any such statute provides that the federation shall meet one half of the expenditure or more, the statute must be implemented by the *Länder* as agents of the federation. Where any such statute provides that the *Länder* shall meet one-quarter of the expenditure or more, the consent of the *Bundesrat* is required. The federation and the *Länder* meet the administrative expenditure incurred by their respective authorities and are responsible to each other for ensuring proper administration.

The federation has exclusive power to legislate on customs and fiscal monopolies and concurrent power to legislate on all other taxes, the revenue from which accrues to it wholly or partly. The *Länder* can legislate on local excise taxes as long, and insofar as, these taxes are not identical to taxes imposed by the federation. Federal laws relating to taxes whose yield accrues in whole or in part to the *Länder* or to municipalities and associations of municipalities require the consent of the *Bundesrat* (Art. 105). The municipalities are entitled to establish minor local taxes (e.g., real-property and trade taxes) within the framework of existing legislation and local excise taxes (Art. 106VI). Although the constitution grants the federation exclusive power over customs legislation and the accrual of related revenue, this is one of the powers that has been shifted to the European Union.

Neither the Basic Law nor a *Land* constitution gives any government ownership of or tax authority over natural resources wherever they are located. In the northern part of Germany, however, there are some oil and gas fields that are exploited by private companies. They have to pay a so-called extracting fee *(Förderzins)*. This fee accrues in total to the *Land* in which the natural resources are located (Lower Saxony and Schleswig-Holstein), and the fee counts as revenue in the horizontal fiscal-equalization scheme.

The Basic Law guarantees the individual right to property and thus creates an inherent limit on the tax authority of both the federation and the *Länder* (Art. 14). The taxes of the federation and the *Länder,* therefore, have to be coordinated in order to establish a fair balance that prevents excessive burdens on the taxpayer, such as confiscation, and to ensure uniformity of living standards in the federal territory (Art. 106III, No. 2). Following the requirement of preventing excessive burdens on the taxpayers, the Constitutional Court recently declared the existing property tax unconstitutional.[13]

The Basic Law also establishes limits on the tax authority of the *Länder* governments insofar as it prohibits the duplication of taxes by two orders of government. The legislative competence of the federation creates a limit on the authority of the *Länder* to legislate on the same tax base. The requirement of equivalent living conditions throughout the federation inhibits competitive taxes between the *Länder* (Arts 28I, No. 1, and 72II). This obstacle is disputed nowadays, as some *Länder* argue that this, together with the highly developed financial-equalization system, is one of the reasons why *Länder* officials do not feel inclined to make an adequate effort to promote their economies and to spend their revenues efficiently.

Customs duties, fiscal monopolies, excise taxes subject to federal legislation, including an import turnover tax, and levies imposed within the framework of the European Union are collected and administered by federal revenue authorities. The organization of these authorities is regulated by federal legislation. The heads of intermediate authorities are appointed in consultation with the respective *Land* government. All other taxes are collected and administered by *Land* revenue authorities. The organization of these authorities and the uniform training of their civil servants is regulated by federal legislation with the consent of the *Bundesrat.*

To the extent that taxes accruing to the federation are also collected by *Land* revenue authorities, the latter act as agents of the federation. In this case, the *Land* authorities have to comply with the directives from the federal Ministry of Finance. Federal legislation provides for (1) cooperation between federal and *Land* revenue authorities on matters of tax collection and administration in the cases of customs duties, fiscal monopolies, and excise taxes, including an import turnover tax and levies within the framework of the European Union, (2) collection and administration of taxes by *Land* revenue authorities, and (3) in the case of other taxes, collection and administration by federal revenue authorities where, and to the extent that, this considerably improves or facilitates the implementation of tax laws.

The collection and administration of taxes, the revenue from which accrues exclusively to the municipalities (or associations of municipalities), are delegated by the *Land* revenue authorities to the municipalities (or associations of municipalities). The procedure to be used by the *Land* revenue authorities is laid down by federal legislation. The procedure to be applied by *Land* revenue authorities for taxes whose revenue accrues exclusively to the municipalities (or associations of municipalities) or by the municipalities (or associations of municipalities) is also laid down by federal legislation requiring the *Bundesrat*'s consent. The federal government issues general administrative rules which, to the extent that administration is entrusted to *Land* revenue authorities or municipalities (or associations of municipalities), require the consent of the *Bundesrat* (Art. 108).

For each fiscal year, borrowing funds and assuming surety obligations, guarantees, or other commitments (deficit spending) require special authorization by a federal law specifying or permitting computation of the amounts involved. Revenue obtained by borrowing must not exceed the total of investment expenditures provided for in the budget estimates; exceptions are permissible only to avert a disturbance of the overall macroeconomic equilibrium (Art. 115). For the *Länder* there are similar limits on borrowing contained in their own constitutions. Furthermore, in accordance with an intergovernmental agreement, all the *Länder*, together with the federation, have to comply with a debt limit that is equal to 3 percent of the total federation budget and that is required by the European Union's stability pact. Following a decision of the Federal Constitutional Court,[14] the federation is obliged to give additional grants to the *Länder* in cases of "fiscal emergency" (i.e., if *Länder* or local governments fail to pay their debts) under the condition that the *Länder* provide for a recovery plan.

The allocation and distribution of tax revenue are governed by detailed rules in the Basic Law. The yield from fiscal monopolies and revenue from the following taxes accrue to the federation: customs duties; taxes on consumption (e.g., the tobacco tax) insofar as they do not accrue to the *Länder*, or jointly to the federation and the *Länder*, or to the municipalities; highway-freight tax; taxes on capital transactions; insurance and bills of exchange; nonrecurring levies on property and equalization-of-burdens levies (nonexistent); income and corporation surtaxes (nonexistent); and levies imposed by the European Community (nonexistent). The yield from the following taxes accrues to the *Länder*: property tax (nonexistent), inheritance tax, motor-vehicle tax, such taxes on transactions as do not accrue to the federation or jointly to the federation and the *Länder*, beer tax, and levies on gambling establishments. All these taxes and levies together do not account for more than 20 percent of the overall revenue of both the federation and the *Länder*.

Revenue from income taxes, corporation taxes, and turnover taxes (i.e., 80 percent of the overall revenue) accrue jointly to the federation, the *Länder*, and the municipalities (joint taxes). The income and corporation taxes are equally shared by the federation and the *Länder* (42.5 percent each), plus 15 percent of the income tax is distributed to the municipalities on a per capita basis. The respective shares of the federation and the *Länder* in the revenue from the turnover tax (a value-added tax, VAT) are determined by a federal law requiring the consent of the *Bundesrat*. Such determination is based on the following principles: (1) The federation and the *Länder* have an equal claim on current revenues required to cover their necessary expenditures; (2) the extent of such expenditures is determined with due regard to multiyear financial planning; and (3) the financial requirements of the federation and of the *Länder* are coordinated in such a way as to establish a fair balance, avoid excessive burdens on taxpayers, and ensure uniformity of living standards throughout the federal territory. For the time being, the federation receives 45 percent of the VAT, and the *Länder* receive 55 percent, distributed per capita. The municipalities receive a share of the revenue from the income tax (15 percent), the turnover tax, taxes on real property and trade, and local taxes on consumption and expenditures. Furthermore, they receive unconditional grants from the *Länder* according to a specific formula, called the "key system" (Art. 106).

In 1949 the system of allocating and distributing revenue was incomplete due to some highly disputed interventions by the Allied Powers that favoured a very decentralized order. However, the necessity of reconstruction in Germany led to a reform of the system, which came into force in 1955. A second major change based on Keynesian ideas took place in 1969 in order to fight an economic crisis in Germany. The third and last series of reforms started after the reunification in order to finance the five new *Länder* of the former German Democratic Republic (GDR) and to bring their economic standing up to the level of the western *Länder* in accordance with the constitutional requirement for equivalent living conditions in the entire country.

The Basic Law also authorizes the federal government to spend revenue for purposes benefiting the *Länder* and the municipalities (Art. 104a) by two means. First, the federation may grant the *Länder* financial assistance for particularly important investments by the *Länder* or by municipalities or associations of municipalities, provided that such investments are necessary to avert a disturbance of the overall macroeconomic equilibrium, or to equalize differences of economic capacities within the federal territory, or to promote economic growth. Details, especially concerning the kinds of investments to be promoted, are regulated by a federal statute requiring the consent of the *Bundesrat* or by administrative arrangements under the federal budget law. Second, the federation's fiscal equalization policy provides for federal grants to be made to financially weak *Länder* in order to supplement the coverage of their general financial requirements (Art. 107II, No. 3). These complementary grants have to cover, for example, special burdens for the entire country (e.g., harbours and waterways) and promote economic growth in the five new *Länder* of the former GDR.

The Basic Law provides for a highly developed scheme of fiscal equalization (Art. 107). Revenue from *Land* taxes and the *Länder's* share of revenue from income and corporation taxes accrue to the individual *Länder* to the extent that such taxes are collected by revenue authorities within their respective territories (principle of local yield). The *Länder's* share of revenue from the turnover tax accrues to each *Land* on a per capita basis (principle of inhabitants).

In accordance with the Basic Law, the equalization procedure follows four steps. First, there is the splitting of the local yield. A federal law (the Financial Equalization Act) requiring the consent of the *Bundesrat* (i.e., the majority of the votes of the *Länder*) regulates the delimitation as well as the manner and scope of allotment of local revenue from corporation and wage taxes. This law may also provide for the delimitation and allotment of local revenue from other taxes. Second, there are supplementary *Land* shares of the turnover tax. A federal law requiring the consent of the *Bundesrat* may provide for the grant of supplementary shares of the *Land* revenue from the turnover tax (not exceeding one-quarter of a *Land's* share) to *Länder* whose per capita revenue from *Land* taxes and from income and corporation taxes is below the average of all *Länder* combined. Third, there is a horizontal equalization. The same federal law has to ensure a reasonable equalization of the disparate financial capacities of the different *Länder*, with due regard to the financial capacities and needs of municipalities. It specifies the conditions governing the claims of *Länder* entitled to equalization payments (receiving *Länder*) and the liabilities of *Länder* required to make such payments (donating *Länder*) as well as the criteria for determining the amounts of such payments. Fourth, there are additional grants from the federation. A federal law provides for additional grants to be made to financially weak *Länder* from the federation's own funds to assist them in meeting their general financial needs (supplementary grants).[15]

This equalization scheme upgrades the 12 receiving *Länder*, even the poorest, to 98.5 percent of the average *Land's* tax revenue per capita, and downgrades the 4 donating *Länder* (i.e., Baden-Württemberg, Bavaria, Hamburg, and Hesse) from 130 percent to 103.5 percent of the average. When three of the donating *Länder* took the other *Länder* to the Federal Constitutional Court, the Court confirmed the constitutionality of the system in principle but stated that the federal legislator has to avoid any diminution of the capacity of the *Länder* to raise taxes.[16]

Fiscal policy with respect to spending is assigned to both the federation and the *Länder*. In their budget management, the federation and the *Länder* are autonomous and independent. Through federal legislation requiring the consent of the *Bundesrat*, principles applicable to both the federation and the *Länder* were established governing budgetary law, budget management reflecting economic situations, and five-year financial planning. With a view to averting disturbances of the macroeconomic equilibrium, federal legislation requiring the consent of the *Bundesrat* has provided for maximum amounts, terms, and timing of loans raised by local authorities or joint authorities and obliged the federation and the *Länder* to keep interest-free deposits at the German Federal Reserve Bank (anticyclical reserves). Only the federal government, with the consent of the *Bundesrat*, is empowered to issue statutory orders in this matter, but these orders can be repealed if the federal Parliament so requires (Art. 109).

The Basic Law provides for the establishment of a Federal Reserve Bank responsible for issuing notes and stabilizing the currency (Art. 88). The *Länder* are represented on the board of directors of this bank by representatives of their own central banks. However, the responsibilities and the powers of both the Federal Reserve Bank and the central banks of the *Länder* have been transferred to the European Central Bank, which was established in 1998 to manage the European Union's currency union and which is also independent and aims primarily to safeguard price stability within the EU.[17]

FOREIGN AFFAIRS AND DEFENCE POWERS

The responsibilities for foreign affairs and defence – apart from a few exceptions – lie exclusively with the federation, or to be more precise, with the federal government and the federal legislative bodies: the *Bundestag* and *Bundesrat* (Art. 73I, No. 1). The federal government is responsible for all foreign policy, the diplomatic service (Art. 87I), and the signing of internationally binding treaties in cases where the federal president does not formally represent the Federal Republic of Germany (Art. 59I). In addition, the federal government, or more precisely, the minister of defence, organizes external security and part of internal security (Arts 80a, 87a, and

115aI). In peacetime, command of the armed forces is vested in the minister of defence (Art. 65a); when Germany is in a state of defence, the power of command over the armed forces passes to the federal chancellor (Art. 115b). The legislative bodies are responsible for the ratification of international treaties (Art. 59II). The committees for foreign policy control the foreign policy of the federal government.

In addition, the deployment of the federal army outside the area of the North Atlantic Treaty Organization (NATO) must be authorized by a special resolution of the *Bundestag* in each case. This reservation of power to the Parliament is not enshrined in the Basic Law but is based on a decision of the Federal Constitutional Court, which expressly characterizes the armed forces as a parliamentary army in accordance with German constitutional law (unlike the German army during the Weimar Republic).[18] Given that, in accordance with the Basic Law, the federal army has the power only of defence against an attack on federal territory or on the territory of another NATO member state, any deployment outside these territories, as in Kosovo, Macedonia, or Afghanistan, requires special parliamentary decisions. In the field of defence, the *Bundestag* makes the decision on measures of mobilization (state of tension), as provided for in Article 80a, and determines whether the federal territory or the territory of a NATO member state is under attack by a hostile armed force (state of defence), as provided for in Article 115a.

The responsibilities of the *Länder* in foreign affairs and defence are strictly limited. The *Länder* have neither their own armed forces nor any other militia. Coastal protection is a task of the Federal Border Police and the customs service and thus also a federal matter. To the extent that the *Länder* are responsible for legislation, they can sign treaties with foreign states; however, such treaties require the agreement of the federal government (Art. 32III). The procedure to be followed is laid down in a special agreement between the federation and the *Länder,* the so-called Lindau Agreement. In addition, through the *Bundesrat,* the *Länder* have an influence on the ratification of international treaties by the federation (Art. 59II). The *Länder* also only have an influence on decision-making processes in the field of defence and external security to the extent that the *Bundesrat* is involved. Any determination that federal territory is under attack, for example, requires the consent of the *Bundesrat* (Art. 115I).

Civilian political control of the armed forces takes place in three ways: (1) through the command of the federal minister of defence and, in the event of a state of defence, through the federal chancellor; (2) through the *Bundestag*'s Committee on Defence, which can also be constituted as an investigative committee (Art. 45a); and (3) through the parliamentary commissioner for the armed forces, who assists the *Bundestag* in exercising parliamentary control of the infringement of soldiers' rights (Art. 45b).

Apart from this, in accordance with Article 4III, no person can be compelled against his or her conscience to render military service. If necessary, one can be guaranteed this basic right by making a complaint about infringement of the constitution to the Constitutional Court. For some time, there has been no special procedure for determining the existence of such conscience-based grounds. As an alternative, community service has been introduced, which lasts three months longer than the term of military service. It is assumed that this disadvantage is sufficient to counteract any abuse of the right to refuse to render military service against one's conscience. Since the end of the East-West conflict, however, the abolition of all general military service and the establishment of a professional army have been under discussion.

European politics play a special role in Germany's governance and are becoming more and more important. Formally, European policy is still a matter of foreign affairs, for which the federation is responsible; in many cases, however, one can talk already about a European internal policy that is no longer foreign policy. Although federal organs also represent the Federal Republic of Germany externally in this field, in recent years, the *Länder* have acquired substantial rights to participate in and shape European policy. These rights are essentially exerted by the *Bundesrat* (Art. 23II-V). For example, if the federation transfers to the European Union a field of sovereign jurisdiction that mainly concerns the legislative rights of the *Länder,* the federation must, to this extent, essentially take the opinion of the *Bundesrat* into account. In the case of the relevant decisions undertaken by the European Union in Brussels, the representation of the Federal Republic of Germany can even be transferred from the federation to a representative of the *Länder* nominated by the *Bundesrat.* The *Bundesrat*'s opinion is even important whenever the federation acts within the framework of its exclusive legislative competence and its action also affects the interests of the *Länder* (Art. 23V). Further details are regulated in two so-called Federal Cooperation Laws. Apart from this, all the *Länder* have their own offices at the headquarters of the European Union in Brussels, and today they occasionally even have a kind of "secondary foreign policy" of their own.[19]

The Basic Law contains no explicit regulations about the membership or participation of the federation, a *Land,* or municipalities in international organizations. Article 24II states merely that the federation may enter into a system of mutual collective security with a view to maintaining peace. This regulation refers primarily to NATO. In fact, the Federal Republic of Germany is a member of almost every international organization (e.g., the United Nations, International Labour Organization, World Trade Organization, and World Health Organization). The only body in which the *Länder* and municipalities are directly represented at the supranational level is the Committee of the Regions of the European Union, which participates in the legislative process of the EU in an advisory capacity.

CITIZENSHIP

In Article 116I the Basic Law contains a definition of German citizenship. A German is a person who possesses German citizenship or who has been admitted to the territory of the German Reich within the boundaries of 31 December 1937 as a refugee or expellee of German ethnic origin. Further details are regulated by the Citizenship Act, for which the federation has the exclusive legislative powers (Art. 73II). The concurrent legislative competence to regulate citizenship within the *Länder*, which was provided for in 1949, was abolished only in 1994. Since then, only the federal legislator can decide about citizenship and the preconditions for naturalization, although the *Länder* play an essential part through the *Bundesrat*. However, dual nationality in the federation and the *Länder*, as would have been possible until 1994, has never actually existed.

For a long time, citizenship in the federation was based exclusively on the pure principle of descent *(ius sanguinis)*. This principle has been relaxed slightly. Children of foreigners living in Germany are provisionally given German citizenship from birth until the age of 23, when they must decide whether they want to remain German or to adopt the citizenship of their parents. Apart from this exception, for which there is a time limit, dual nationality is not permitted in Germany in principle, although examples do exist in practice. The purpose of this exception is to enable the large number of often second or third generation foreigners (mostly Turks) living in Germany to integrate more effectively.

Although all the citizens of the European Union have the right to vote in local government elections in each member state, no citizenship comparable to nationality yet exists in the EU; however, this might be included in the new constitution of the European Union.

VOTING, ELECTIONS, AND POLITICAL PARTIES

Article 38 of the Basic Law regulates the right to vote in elections to the *Bundestag*. However, it lays down only the basic principles involving voting rights (i.e., general, direct, free, equal, and secret ballots), which also apply to *Land*-parliament, county, and municipal elections (Art. 28I). It does not determine the electoral system, the number of constituencies, and the size of the federal Parliament. In addition, it makes the right to vote and eligibility for political office dependent on reaching the age of 18. All the other regulations for elections to the *Bundestag* are found in the Federal Electoral Act and the Federal Election Regulations. Elections to a *Land* parliament are governed by the laws and regulations of the *Land*, just as county and municipal elections are governed by the laws and regulations of the counties and municipalities. With uniform basic principles concerning voting rights, every order of government thus has its own election rules, which vary considerably with regard both to the electoral system and to voting (one or two votes).

Because the Federal Election Act, like all federal laws, is administered by the *Länder*, they are also mainly responsible for registering voters and running the elections. Because elections are a state matter, the *Länder* have transferred this task to the municipalities. The municipalities are responsible for the electoral register, polling cards, and the administration of postal votes. Assistants from the municipality work in the polling stations; they also count votes after the polling stations have closed. The individual election results are then passed on to the federal returning officer via the *Land*'s returning officer in the case of *Bundestag* elections. In the case of *Land*-parliament, county, and municipal elections, they are passed on to the *Land*'s returning officer. The federal or *Land* returning officers then announce a provisional final result and, after examination, the final election result.

In accordance with the principle of the general vote, the conditions for participation in elections for the *Bundestag*, a *Land* parliament, the counties, and municipalities are German nationality (in county and municipal elections, persons who possess citizenship of a member state of the European Union are also eligible to vote) and the age of at least 18 for federal elections and in some *Länder* at least 16 for the election of *Land* legislators. In addition, the voters must be in possession of their civil rights, of which they can, in special cases, be deprived by a penal judgment. There are no other reasons for exclusion from the right to vote in Germany.

For the first time in German history, Article 21 of the Basic Law regulates the constitutional status of political parties. Thus the parties are required to participate in the formation of the political will of the people. They may be established freely, and their political activities may be freely conducted; to this extent, they can also have recourse to basic rights. In reaction to the "Fuehrer" principle of dictatorship in the platform of the National Socialist German Workers' Party (NSDAP), the Basic Law requires that the internal organization of parties conform to democratic principles. Given that the parties are also partly financed by the state (i.e., up to a maximum of half of their total income), the Basic Law demands that they publicly account for the sources and uses of their funds as well as for their assets.

Parties whose aims and behaviour seek to undermine or abolish the free democratic order and to endanger the existence and the security of the federation or *Länder* are considered unconstitutional but can be banned only by the Federal Constitutional Court. In the case of a ban, their assets and seats in the federal and *Land* parliaments are also forfeited. So far, the Constitutional Court has made use of this possibility of a ban only twice: in 1952 against the *Sozialistische Reichspartei* (a successor organization to the NSDAP) and in 1956 against the Communist Party of Germany (KDP). The procedure to ban the radical right-wing National Democratic Party (NDP), which was introduced a few years ago by the *Bundestag, Bundesrat,* and federal government, failed recently because the identities of informers from the intelligence agencies were not revealed to the Constitutional Court.

PROTECTION OF INDIVIDUAL AND COMMUNAL RIGHTS

Since it came into existence, the Basic Law has contained a complete catalogue of human rights and basic freedoms. It also makes reference to international human-rights agreements. Taking a lesson from the time of the Nazi regime, the Basic Law attaches exceptional importance to basic freedoms and human rights, which is also expressed by the inclusion of these rights in the first article of the constitution. In accordance with Article 1II, the German people acknowledge inviolable and inalienable human rights as the basis of every community, of peace, and of justice in the world.

Insofar as human rights are part of the fundamental rules of an international organization, such as the United Nations' Declaration of Human Rights of 1948, then in accordance with Article 25, they form an integral part of the general rules of international law and thus take precedence over the laws of the federation and the *Länder,* although not over the constitution of the federation. Insofar as human rights are contained in multilateral international conventions, such as the European Convention on the Protection of Human Rights (EMRK/HCPHR), they are, like every international treaty, part of federal law in accordance with Article 59II.

All of Germany's courts, governments, and administrative authorities must observe these human rights and guarantee their validity. Even the legislatures are bound by this stipulation. Overall, one can, therefore, state that basic civil rights and human rights in Germany are binding on the legislature, the executive, and the judiciary as directly applicable law (Art. 1III).

The Basic Law guarantees individual rights as both defensive rights against the state (negative rights) and rights of performance and participation (positive rights). The *defensive rights* include the classic civil rights (e.g., the freedoms of opinion, assembly, association, faith, and occupation). The *rights of performance and participation* include the classic rights of equality, such as the right against discrimination on the grounds of origin, race, sex, homeland, or political or religious opinion as well as the right to the establishment of equal opportunities for disadvantaged groups (e.g., women, the disabled, children, the aged, and the sick). Property rights and inheritance are also guaranteed. In addition, there are the rights to life, freedom from bodily harm, and protection of the personal sphere (e.g., data protection, inviolability of the home and family, and the privacy of mail and telecommunications). Finally, in accordance with the decisions of the Constitutional Court, people have a direct claim on the state for the provision of a minimum living income in the form of social aid.

Insofar as these rights are contained in the Basic Law, they are directed only against the state powers of the federation; most of the constitutions of the *Länder* contain their own lists of basic rights that bind the *Länder* authorities. At both levels, the lists of basic rights contain directly applicable law, which, from the perspective of constitutional law, is protected by the fact that a person can claim that an infringement of his or her rights has occurred. This is done by making a complaint about an infringement of the constitution before the Federal Constitutional Court or the constitutional court of a *Land*.

However, all these rights protect a person only against interventions by the state or justify the special obligation of the state to provide the right of protection; they are not directed immediately against infringements by private persons of others' rights, although the labour law is an exception. However, the courts are obliged to observe the basic rights in a conflict concerning civil rights between private persons. If this does not occur, the judgment in question can also be a matter of complaint about an infringement of the constitution that produces a direct infringement of a person's civil rights by another individual.

Whoever abuses the basic rights, particularly the freedom of expression, freedom of the press, freedom of teaching, freedom of assembly, freedom of association, the rights of property, or the right of asylum, in order to destroy the free democratic order can be required to forfeit these basic rights. However, this forfeiture can only follow a decision by the Federal Constitutional Court (Art. 18). This procedure has been initiated only once – against the publisher of a right-wing newspaper – but the procedure was not completed. The suspension of these basic rights is not provided for. Even in an emergency, these basic rights cannot be revoked or suspended; they can only be restricted. Nor can any person renounce his or her basic rights.

In contrast to the constitutions of some *Länder*, the Basic Law contains no social rights (e.g., rights to housing, education and training, work, social security, and health checkups). However, the constitutional courts tend to deduce the right of action on the part of the legislature from the state's obligations to protect certain basic freedoms, such as life and freedom from bodily harm. The legislature must create proper conditions for exercising such civil rights and liberties.

The Basic Law contains no special group rights or rights for ethnic, cultural, religious, or linguistic minorities. However, all individual rights can also be exerted by a number of people jointly. Thus, for example, freedom of assembly and also assembly as such are protected, as are freedom of association and association as such; the freedom of coalition also protects employers' associations and trade unions. In addition, all domestic legal entities can take advantage of these basic rights to the extent permitted by the nature of such rights (Art. 19III). This even applies to public institutions, as in the case of academic freedom for universities, the freedom of broadcasting for public broadcasting corporations, and the freedom of religion for churches and religious communities.

The basic rights in the Basic Law and in the constitutions of the *Länder* are partly formulated as human rights and partly only as civil rights (i.e., rights for Germans). The human-rights protections are also valid for all people in the country who are not German citizens, such as foreign workers and tourists.

Most of the constitutions of the *Länder* also contain lists of basic rights or, in particular, those basic rights that are associated with the special responsibilities of the *Länder* (e.g., culture and internal security). These lists of basic rights do not differ essentially from those of the Basic Law. The *Länder* are also bound by the basic rights in the Basic Law, but in their own *Land* constitutions, they can incorporate other or more extensive rights. Here, however, they must not contradict the Basic Law and must not fall below the minimum standard of the federal basic rights (Art. 142). For example, the constitution of Saxony contains a right to co-determination in the public service, which, although it does not exist in the Basic Law, is valid in Saxony. In contrast, the constitution of Hesse contains a ban on lockouts by employers, whereas lockouts are permitted to a limited extent in the Basic Law; the regulation in Hesse is therefore invalid.

The basic rights in the *Länder* constitutions are legally protected only in those *Länder* in which a complaint about infringement of the constitution can be made to the constitutional court of the *Land* in question (e.g., in Bavaria, Berlin, Brandenburg, Hesse, Rhineland-Palatinate, and Saxony). Given that the possibility of legal protection for the basic rights of the *Länder* exists in only a few *Länder*, the significance of these rights has remained fairly small in practice.

CONSTITUTIONAL CHANGE

The Basic Law can be amended at any time but only by means of a law that expressly alters or complements the wording of the Basic Law. Simple additions without changes to the text of the Basic Law are not permitted.

International treaties that deal with the regulation of peace or serve the defence of the Federal Republic of Germany must not contradict the Basic Law, and any resulting changes or additions to the Basic Law that are needed in order to comply with a treaty must be restricted to the treaty in question. Laws that change the constitution are passed in a normal legislative process, but they require the agreement of two-thirds of the members of the *Bundestag* and two-thirds of the votes of the *Bundesrat*. Procedures of direct democracy with the aim of changing the Basic Law by popular votes are not available.

In addition, the Basic Law provides limits beyond which an amendment to the constitution cannot go. The division of the federation into *Länder*, as well as the rules concerning the participation of the *Länder* in the legislation of the federation, cannot be altered by a change to the constitution, nor can the basic principles of Articles 1 and 20 be altered. These principles include the respect for and the protection of human dignity and the acknowledgement of human rights; the separation of government powers and functions; the commitment of the three branches of government to law and justice and, in particular, to the basic rights; as well as the decisions in favour of the republican form of state, the rule of law, democracy, the welfare state, and the federal order. In accordance with Article 79III, these principles are subject to the so-called eternity clause. The limits to constitutional change also apply if the German people should give themselves a completely new constitution through a total revision (Art. 146).

Constitutional change in Germany is based only partly on changes to the Basic Law. The Federal Constitutional Court plays an essential role by amending the Basic Law through interpretation and especially by adapting it to more recent technical developments or to social and economic challenges. In comparison, the government and the legislature work much less creatively in interpreting the constitution. Since it was passed in 1949, the Basic Law has been amended 50 times, which means once a year on average. Most of the changes concerned shifts of responsibilities to the federation at the expense of the *Länder*.

The number of changes has neither increased nor decreased in the last few years, and one cannot say what form the future development of the constitution will take. The changes to the constitution of the past ten years have been reactions partly to reunification, partly to necessary adaptations to modern social developments, and partly to European integration. Some changes have been brought about by European law (e.g., the admission of women to the federal armed forces). Currently, the governments of the federation and the *Länder* are preparing a comprehensive reform of the German federal system, which will be reflected in the Basic Law within the next few years.

NOTES

1 Ute Wachendorfer-Schmidt, *Politikverflechtung im vereinigten Deutschland* (Wiesbaden: Westdt. Verlag, 2003); Jürgen Faulenbach, *Föderalismus in Deutschland* (Bonn: Bundeszentrale für politische Bildung, 2002); Roland Sturm, *Föderalismus in Deutschland* (Opladen: Leske und Budrich, 2001); Karl Eckart, *Föderalismus in Deutschland* (Berlin: Duncker and Humblot, 2001); and Heinz Laufer and Ursula Münch, *Das föderative System der Budesrepublik Deutschland* (Opladen: Leske und Buderus, UTB für Wissenschaft, 1998).

2 Statistisches Bundesamt, *Datenreport 2002* (Bonn: Bundeszentrale für politische Bildung, 2002). See also www.destatis.de, *Facts about Germany* (Frankfurt am Main: Societätsverlag, 1996); and Federal Council, *Handbuch 2002/03* (Baden-Baden: Nomos Verlag, 2002).

3 Hans-Peter Schneider, "Entwicklungen, Fehlentwicklungen, Reformen des deutschen Föderalismus und der Europäischen Union," *Föderalismus: Leitbild für die Europäische Union*, ed. Michael Piazolo and Jürgen Weber (München: Olzog Verlag, 2004), pp. 46–57; and Charley Jeffery, *Recasting German Federalism: The Legacies of Unification* (London: Pinter, 1999).

4 Maiken Umbach, *Federalism and Enlightenment in Germany, 1740–1806* (London: Hambledon Press, 2000); and Ernst Deuerlein, *Föderalismus: Die historische und philosophische Grundlagen des föderativen Prinzips* (München: List Verlag, 1972).

5 Maiken Umbach, *German Federalism: Past, Present, Future* (Basingstoke: Palgrave, 2002); Hans-Peter Schneider, "Fünfzig Jahre Grundgesetz: Vom westdeutschen Provisorium zur gesamtdeutschen Verfassung," *Neue Juristische Wochenschrift* (1999): 1497–1504; and Hans-Peter Schneider, "Federalism in Continental Thought during the 17th and 18th Centuries," *Federalism and Civil Societies: An International Symposium*, ed. Jutta Kramer and Hans-Peter Schneider (Baden-Baden: Nomos, 1999), pp. 43–52.

6 On the concept of competitive federalism, see, for example, Daphne A. Kenyon and John Kincaid, eds, *Competition among States and Local Governments: Efficiency and Equity in American Federalism* (Washington, DC: Urban Institute Press, 1991).

7 Arthur B. Gunlicks, *The Länder and German Federalism* (Basingstoke: Palgrave, 2003); Hans-Georg Wehling, *Die deutschen Länder: Geschichte, Politik, Wirtschaft*, 2nd ed. (Opladen: Leske und Buderus, 2002); Cesare Onestini, *Federalism and Länder Autonomy: The Higher Education Policy Network in the Federal Republic of Germany* (New York: RoutledgeFalmer, 2002); and Hans-Peter Schneider, "German Unification and the Federal System: The Challenge of Reform," *Recasting German Federalism: The Legacies of Unification*, ed. Charlie Jeffery (London: Pinter, 1999), pp. 58–84.

8 BundesVerfassungsGerichtsEntscheidung (BVerfGE) [Decision of the Constitutional Court Volume] "Altenpflegegesetz" ["Health care for elderly people act"] 106, p. 62 ff.

9 Hans-Peter Schneider, "The Distribution of Powers in the Federal Republic of Germany," *African Journal of Federal Studies* 1 (2000): 19–33; Ute Wachendorfer-Schmidt, *Federalism and Political Performance* (London: Routledge, 2000); and Fritz W. Scharpf, *Politikverflechtung* (Kronsberg/TS: Scriptor Verlag, 1976).

10 BVerfGE 81, pp. 310–31.

11 Sven Leunig, *Föderale Verhandlungen: Bundesrat, Bundestag und Bundesregierung im Gesetzgebungsprozess* (Frankfurt am Main: Lang, 2003); and Hans-Peter Schneider, "Die Aufgabenverteilung zwischen Bund und Ländern nach dem Grundgesetz: Eine Ausprägung des Subsidiaritätsprinzips?" *Die Entwicklung des Staates der Autonomien in Spanien und der bundesstaatlichen Ordnung in der Bundesrepublik Deutschland*, ed. Jutta Kramer (Baden-Baden: Nomos, 1996), pp. 37–47.

12 Hans-Peter Schneider, "Grenzen der Rechtsangleichung in Europa: Warum der Europäische Gerichtshof die Gemeinschaftsorgane in die Schranken wies," *Frankfurter Allgemeine Zeitung*, no. 240 (16 October 2000): 12; Rudolf Hrbek, *Europapolitik und Bundesstaatsprinzip: Die Europafähigkeit Deutschlands und seiner Länder im Vergleich mit anderen Föderalstaaten* (Baden-Baden: Nomos Verlagsgesellschaft, 2000); and Rudolf Hrbek, ed, *Aussenbeziehungen von Regionen in Europa und der Welt* (Baden-Baden: Nomos Verlagsgesellschaft, 2003).

13 BVerfGE 93, p. 121 ff.

14 BVerfGE 86, p. 148 ff.

15 Hans-Peter Schneider, "Comment on Art. 107 Basic Law," *Kommentar zum Grundgesetz für die Bundesrepublik Deutschland (AKGG)*, ed. Erhard Denninger, Wolfgang Hoffmann-Riem, Hans-Peter Schneider, and Ekkehard Stein, vol. 3. (Neuwied: Luchterhand Verlag, 2001), pp. 64–83; and Kai A. Konrad and Helmut Seitz, *Fiscal Federalism and Risk Sharing in Germany: The Role of Size and Difference* (Berlin: WZB, 2001).

16 BVerfGE 72, p. 330 (418 f.); 86, p. 148 (250).

17 Hans-Peter Schneider, "Föderative Gewaltenteilung in Europa: Zur Kompetenzabgrenzung zwischen der Europäischen Union und ihren Mitgliedstaaten," *Tradition und Weltoffenheit des Rechts: Festschrift für Helmut Steinberger*, ed. H.-J. Cremer, T. Giegerich, D. Richter, and A. Zimmermann (Berlin: Springer, 2002), pp. 1401–24; and Richard Deeg and Suzanne Lütz, *Internationalization and Financial Federalism: The United States and Germany at the Crossroads?* (Köln: MPIFG, 1998).

18 BVerfGE 100, p. 266 ff.

19 Hans-Peter Schneider, "Entwicklungen, Fehlentwicklungen, Reformen des deutschen Föderalismus und der Europäischen Union"; and Rüdiger Gerst, *Föderalismus in Deutschland und Europa: Was bleibt den deutschen Ländern?* (Bamberg: Leibniz-Verlag, 2000).

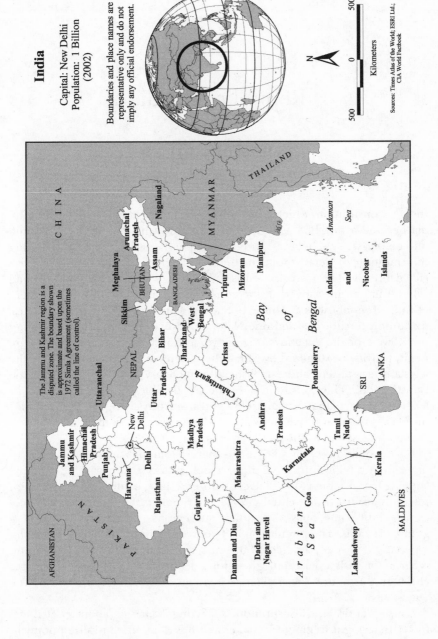

India

Capital: New Delhi
Population: 1 Billion
(2002)

Boundaries and place names are
representative only and do not
imply any official endorsement.

The Jammu and Kashmir region is a
disputed zone. The boundary shown
is approximate and based upon the
1972 Simla Agreement (sometimes
called the line of control).

N

500   0   500
Kilometers

Sources: Times Atlas of the World; ESRI Ltd;
CIA World Factbook

CHINA

AFGHANISTAN

PAKISTAN

Jammu
and Kashmir

Himachal
Pradesh

Punjab

Haryana

Uttaranchal

NEPAL

New
Delhi

Delhi

Rajasthan

Uttar
Pradesh

Bihar

Sikkim

BHUTAN

Meghalaya

Assam

Arunachal
Pradesh

Nagaland

Manipur

Mizoram

Tripura

BANGLADESH

West
Bengal

Jharkhand

MYANMAR

THAILAND

Gujarat

Madhya
Pradesh

Chhattisgarh

Orissa

Maharashtra

Daman and Diu

Dadra and
Nagar Haveli

Goa

Andhra
Pradesh

Karnataka

Pondicherry

Bay

of

Bengal

Andaman

Sea

Andaman,

and

Nicobar

Islands

Tamil
Nadu

Kerala

SRI

LANKA

A r a b i a n
S e a

Lakshadweep

MALDIVES

Republic of India

AKHTAR MAJEED

India's Constitution, which came into force on 26 January 1950, when India became a republic, is the world's longest, with 395 articles (divided into 22 parts), 12 schedules, and three appendices. The framers, following the tradition of detail found in the Government of India Act 1935, rejected brevity. The Constitution is, in fact, a detailed legal code dealing with all important aspects of the constitutional and administrative system of India. It establishes a "Union of States," which now consists of 28 states, six "union territories," and one National Capital Territory. It also defines the powers of the executive, legislative, and judicial branches of government; provides a standard by which the validity of the laws enacted by the legislature is tested; and establishes the judiciary as the guardian of the Constitution.[1] The Constitution is generally flexible but rigid in many of its "federal" matters that pertain to the states, and any change in the "federal" provisions requires a special two-thirds majority in Parliament and ratification by at least half of the legislatures of the states.

Having a land area of 3,287,263 square kilometres and a population of more than a billion, India is an extremely plural society with 18 national languages and some 2,000 dialects, a dozen ethnic communities and seven religious groups (fragmented into a large number of sects, castes, and subcastes), and some 60 socio-cultural subregions spread over seven geographic regions. The population is 83 percent Hindu, 11 percent Muslim, 2 percent Christian, 2 percent Sikh, and 1 percent Buddhist. The country is also poor, with a per capita gross domestic product of US$2,840 in 2001, although this figure does reflect accelerated economic growth during the 1990s.

Consequently, the Constitution, reflecting concerns about centrifugal forces that might fragment India, establishes a rather centralized polity in which the Union government is vested with sufficient powers to ensure not only its dominance, but also its ability to rule in a unitary fashion if necessary and politically feasible. Equally important, the country's diversity and socio-economic conditions, coupled with the ideological influences of socialism, drove the Constitution toward a kind of organically unitary federalism in the name of justice, equality, and rights protection.[2] Only a strong centre, thought many of the founders, could effectively drive economic development and ensure equity across territorial jurisdictions, religions, languages, classes, and castes. Hence the trend generally was toward ever more centralization under the Congress Party from independence to the 1980s. During this decade, however, Union-state relations became more rancorous, the Congress party began to decline, and a coalition government, the National Front, assumed power in New Delhi as a result of the 1989 elections in part because centralized federalism driven by a monopoly party for some 40 years had fallen far short of achieving the objectives set forth in the Constitution. Since 1989, coalition governments at the Centre, proliferating regional and state parties across the country, and liberalization of the economy have served to decentralize the federal political system in many respects.

The Constitution also establishes a Westminster-style parliamentary federation in which, politically, emphasis is placed on the power of the lower house of parliament, the *Lok Sabha*, and the government's primary responsibility is to this house rather than to the upper house of the states *(Rajya Sabha)*. However, unlike Australia and Canada, which also are parliamentary federations, India is a republic that jettisoned the British monarch upon independence. At the same time, while India's Constitution rejects presidentialism, the country does have an elected president, who, moreover, formally appoints the prime minister and the governors of the constituent states. Additionally notable is the survival and comparative success of India's Constitution and federal democratic arrangement compared to the fates of those implemented by other British colonies – such as the East African Federation, Malaysia, Nigeria, Rhodesia and Nyasaland, and the West Indies – that attempted to establish postindependence constitutional federalism and democracy.

HISTORICAL BACKGROUND AND DEVELOPMENT

During British colonial rule, the Government of India Act 1919 had introduced a system of "dyarchy" in the provinces in which subjects were classified as central or provincial. The latter were divided into (1) transferred subjects administered by the governor and his Council of Ministers responsible to the Legislative Council and (2) reserved subjects administered by the governor and his Executive Council.[3] However, the Government of India remained, with the governor general in council, responsible only to the British Parliament (through Great Britain's secretary of state for India).

The central legislature consisted of the Council of Ministers (six members) and the Legislative Assembly (144 members). Each had a large number of unelected and nominated members.[4] It was a unitary system in which the central legislature could legislate on any matter.

The Government of India Act 1935 divided powers between the Centre and the provinces, providing for the concurrent exercise of power over some matters. The British governor general could also assign residual powers to either the Centre or the provinces. This act established a federal system of government in place of the unitary one. The constituent units of the federation included the governors' provinces and the 562 Indian (princely) states. Provinces were established as per administrative requirements and exigencies. The governor general had powers to legislate on a reserved subject or a subject of special responsibility by means of a temporary ordinance or a permanent act. It also was possible for the governor general, in case of a breakdown of the constitutional machinery in a province, to assume all or any of the powers entrusted to the province. The federal legislature consisted of the British monarch (represented by the governor general) and two houses: the Legislative Assembly consisting of 500 members and the Council of States consisting of 260 members. A seven-member federal court exercised exclusive original jurisdiction in any dispute between the federation and the constituent units or between these units.

In 1946 a Constituent Assembly was established to frame the Constitution of India.[5] It completed its work on 24 January 1950, with the Constitution coming into effect on 26 January 1950. The British Parliament passed the India Independence Act 1947 on 18 July 1947, and India became independent on 15 August 1947, being divided in the process into two independent dominions: India and Pakistan. The Indian Independence Act 1947 terminated the paramountcy of the British Crown over India's princely states and granted their independence; however, by 1948 all the princely states had acceded to India. In 1956, on the recommendations of the States Reorganization Commission, all 27 states were reorganized on a linguistic basis into 14 states, each of which had a dominant regional language. Subsequent reorganizations increased the number of states to the present 28, in addition to six territories administered directly by the Union government.

Constitutional Nation Building

The leaders of India's Freedom Movement, the founding fathers of the Constitution, reconciled many diverse forces and ideologies and agreed on a set of principles as the basis of the Indian Constitution: universal adult franchise, democratic liberal-federal republicanism, secularism, universal and fundamental rights, state intervention against inherited inequalities, and social justice. To give effect to these principles, the federal Union was formed to (1) put in place a mechanism of federal governance with a strong parliamentary centre, (2) guarantee cultural autonomy to regions with strong linguistic, religious, tribal, and/or territorial identities, (3) create a mixed economy with sectors demarcated for state and private enterprise, and (4) reduce regional and economic disparities through fiscal federalism and planning.[6]

The Constituent Assembly decided not to use the term "federalism" in the Constitution; in fact, amendments to describe India as a federation were defeated in the Assembly (and the word "federal" is still rarely used in official documents). If one asks what the principal aims of the drafters of the Constitution were with regard to federalism, the answer is that they were not thinking of federalism in the usual sense at all. If one examines the debates in the Constituent Assembly and its working committees, one finds that the overriding aim of the members of the Constituent Assembly was to build a united polity out of a highly fragmented and segmented society.[7] With this in mind, they placed the residual powers in the hands of the Union. They also granted more powers to the Union because the Constitution was being finalized in the aftermath of the partition of India into India and Pakistan. Their second aim was to develop this highly undeveloped country, to eliminate poverty, illiteracy, backwardness, and obscurantism, and to build a modern nation-state.

The impetus for national unity, as represented by the Freedom Movement, was so strong that the subnational identities of citizens were given little consideration. Only later was it realized that federalism could help solve conflicts rooted in territorially based ethnic, religious, linguistic, and other characteristics. In a very limited sense, Indian federalism can be called asymmetrical because there are special provisions for Kashmir, Nagaland, and Meghalaya. Otherwise, states cannot choose their own governmental and political arrangements, and the movement of more and more subjects from the Constitution's State List to the Concurrent List during the twentieth century partly reflected attempts to make things more symmetrical nationwide. However, even though mobilization at the grass roots is working to the advantage of women and backward sections of society, the overall progress of more recent decentralization efforts is slow.

MAIN FEATURES OF THE CONSTITUTION

The purpose of the Constitution is to identify the sources of constitutional authority and the objectives it seeks to establish and promote. The Objectives Resolution of the Constituent Assembly (22 January 1947) had declared that all powers and authority of the Sovereign Independent India, its constituent units, and its organs of government are derived from the people and that adequate safeguards shall be provided for minorities, backward and tribal areas, and depressed and other backward classes. The Preamble lays down the objectives of constituting India as "a Sovereign, Socialist, Secular, Democratic Republic" and of securing to all the citizens justice, liberty, equality, and fraternity.

The Forty-Second Amendment Act 1976 inserted "Socialist" into the Preamble out of political expediency during the Emergency of 1975–77. Demands to insert "Socialist" into the Preamble during the framing of the Constitution were rejected by the Constituent Assembly after B.R. Ambedkar pointed out that the Directive Principles in Part IV were declared to be "fundamental in the governance of the country" and that the state was mandated to implement them by applying the principles in making laws. Referring, in particular, to these provisions of the Constitution, Ambedkar had observed that if these Directive Principles were not socialistic in their direction and in their content, then it was difficult to understand what socialism was.[8] Socialism, as rationalized today, aims at eliminating inequality and exploitation and at providing a decent standard of life for all citizens, which is precisely what these Directive Principles seek to ensure for the governance of the country.

Sovereignty and Citizenship

The institutions of governance derive their authority from the Constitution, and they function within the limits demarcated by it. It is the people of India, according to the Preamble, who have given to themselves this Constitution, and it is the people of India who have resolved to constitute India as a sovereign democratic republic. This implies that sovereignty lies with the whole people of India. The Constitution describes India as "a Union of States" and implies that its unity is indestructible. The Constitution prescribes not only the structure of the Union government but also that of the state governments. It does not envisage dual citizenship; there is only one citizenship for the whole of India.

Flexible and Rigid

The Constitution is partly rigid and partly flexible because the procedures for its amendment are neither very easy nor very difficult. Only for a few of the constitutional provisions (dealing with federal provisions) does the amendment process require ratification by state legislatures, and even in these cases, ratification by only half of them suffices. The rest of the Constitution may be amended by a majority of not less than two-thirds of the members of each house of Parliament present and voting (Art. 368).

Cabinet Government

Both for the Union and the states, a "cabinet-type" system of parliamentary government has been instituted in which the executive is continuously responsible to the legislature. The Union Cabinet is composed of the prime minister and his Council of Ministers. The president (who is the head of state) formally appoints the prime minister and, on the latter's advice, appoints other ministers.[9] The president is aided and advised, in the exercise of his functions, by the Council of Ministers (Art. 74). Similarly, the governor (appointed by the president) is the head of a province or state and similarly appoints the chief minister and the Council of Ministers for his or her state. The prime minister for the Union and the chief minister for a state remain in office as long as they enjoy the confidence of the majority in the legislature (lower house). The president and a governor are the constitutional heads, and the executive power is vested in the prime minister and the chief minister and in their Councils of Ministers.

Independence of the Judiciary

There is a single integrated judicial system for both the Union and the states that administers both the Union's and the states' laws. The Supreme Court has "original jurisdiction" (Art. 131) in any dispute between the Government of India and any state or states as well as between two or more states. For the appointment of judges (by the president), there are rigid qualifications, and the chief justice of India has to be consulted in the appointment of judges of the Supreme Court of India and of the high courts of the states. A judge of the Supreme Court remains in office until he or she attains the age of 65 years, resigns, or is removed by impeachment on grounds of proved misbehaviour or incapacity. The conduct of the judges is beyond the subject of discussion in the legislature unless the process is in motion for a judge's removal from office through a rigid impeachment procedure by the Parliament. The judiciary has been given the power to declare a law to be unconstitutional if it is beyond the jurisdiction of the legislature according to the distribution of powers provided for by the Constitution or if it is in contravention of the fundamental rights or of any other mandatory provisions of the Constitution (Art. 13). The judiciary can thus look into matters respecting the jurisdiction of the legislature but not into the "wisdom" of legislative policy.

Fundamental Rights, Directive Principles of State Policy, and Fundamental Duties

The fundamental rights, in Chapter III (Arts 14–32) of the Constitution, are "justiciable," inviolable, and binding on the legislature and the executive.

A citizen has a right to seek judicial protection if any right is violated, and any act of the legislature or order of the executive at any level of governance can be declared null and void if it violates the fundamental rights of the citizens. The Constitution elaborates these rights as: the right to equality, the right to freedom, the right against exploitation, the right to freedom of religion, cultural and educational rights, and the right to constitutional remedies. Six freedoms are conferred under the right to freedom in Article 19: speech and expression, peaceable assembly, association and unionization, cross-country movement or mobility, residence and settlement anywhere in India, and profession, occupation, trade, or business.

Part IV (Arts 36–51) of the Constitution provides for Directive Principles of State Policy, which are to supplement the fundamental rights in achieving a welfare state. These are in the nature of general directions or instructions to the state, embodying the objectives and ideals that the Union and state governments must bear in mind while formulating policy and making laws. The principles are not justiciable; that is, they are not legally enforceable by any court, and the state cannot be compelled through the courts to implement them. The principles are aimed at the establishment of a social and economic democracy in consonance with the nature of a welfare state, as promised in the Preamble to the Constitution. These principles emphasize that the Indian polity is a welfare state with a duty to ensure for its citizens social and economic justice and the dignity of the individual. They comprise ideals, particularly economic and social, for which the state is expected to strive, which it has mostly done. They are intended as "instruments of instruction" in the governance of the country.

The Forty-Second Amendment Act 1976 incorporated a set of Fundamental Duties in a separate part added to Chapter IV (Art. 51-A). These duties are intended to encourage modern and scientific values and a feeling of common nationality. Just as the Directive Principles are addressed to the state, the Fundamental Duties are addressed to the citizens. Examples of these citizen duties are obligations "to abide by the Constitution and respect its ideals and institutions, the national Flag and the National Anthem" and "to safeguard public property and to abjure violence."

Basic Structure Doctrine

The Preamble to the Constitution specifies certain objectives that reflect the basic structure of India's Constitution and that cannot be amended, as the Supreme Court of India emphasized in *Keshavanada Bharati v State of Kerala* (1973). In this case, the Court opined: "The true position is that every provision of the Constitution can be amended provided in the result the basic foundation and structure of the Constitution remains the same. The basic structure may be said to consist of the following features:

(1) Supremacy of the Constitution; (2) Republican and Democratic form of Government; (3) Secular character of the Constitution; (4) Separation of powers between the legislature, the executive, and the judiciary; (5) Federal character of the Constitution."[10]

Elements of the above ruling were reinforced in *Indira Nehru Gandh v Raj Narain* (1975)[11] and in *Minerva Mills Ltd. v Union of India* (1980).[12] In 2000 the Supreme Court reinforced the principle of separation of powers between the legislature, the executive, and the judiciary and emphasized the principle of an independent judiciary.[13] The Court also has elaborated other items. Most notably, it has upheld as part of the "basic structure" (1) the democratic form of life, as distinct from mere adult franchise, (2) guarantees of fundamental rights, and (3) the secular nature of the state, such that there is no state religion.

THE STATES IN THE UNION

The Constituent Assembly of India set up a federal system by encompassing the provinces in a federal union and placing them all on the same legal footing. Use of the term "union" indicates that Indian federalism did not come into existence due to some mutual agreement or compact among the constituent units and that these units have no freedom to secede from the union. The reason there are no provisions or safeguards for the protection of states' rights is that the states were not sovereign entities when the Union was formed. Given that the Union is not the result of any agreement between the states, there is no concept of equality of states' rights and, consequently, no equality of representation of states in the Council of States (the second chamber of the Union Parliament). The second chamber is thus not a "federal" chamber. The states did not exist prior to the Constitution except as administrative divisions of a unitary state. They have no powers or rights of their own apart from those delegated to them by the central authority. Therefore, the states cannot claim any inviolability as regards their territory, boundaries, area, or even name.

Indeed, in contrast to Article IV, Section 3, of the US Constitution, under Article 3 of India's Constitution, Parliament is empowered by ordinary legislative processes to (1) form a new state by separating territory from any state, or by uniting two or more states or parts of states, or by uniting any territory with a part of any state, (2) increase or diminish the area of any state, or (3) alter the boundaries or name of any state. The states have no say in the matter except if the proposed bill affects the area, boundaries, or name of any state, in which case the bill is referred to the legislature of the affected state so that it can express its opinion within a specified time. The president thus ascertains the views only of the state legislature on the proposal before the Union Parliament. The states are not indestructible units.[14]

The division of powers between the Union and the states reflects the distribution of responsibilities between them. The Union has been assigned the duty of nation building, maintenance of unity, protection of territorial integrity of the country, and maintenance of constitutional-political order throughout the country. The states are to cooperate with the Union in performing these functions and in discharging their own constitutional duties with regard to local issues. But as soon as any subject ceases to be "local," the Union may intervene to legislate on the matter.

Article 257(1) of the Constitution elaborates that "the executive power of the Union shall extend to the giving of such directions to a State as may appear to the Government of India to be necessary for that purpose." Under this provision, the Union can issue a direction only where some action of a state government is likely to prejudice the exercise of the executive power of the Union, as noted by the Supreme Court in *State of Rajasthan v Union of India* (1977).[15] When matters fall within state jurisdiction, such as the maintenance of law and order, Article 257(1) cannot be applied.

The power of the Union government to give directions to the state governments is fortified by Article 365. If a state government flouts directions provided by the Union government, the president can conclude that "a situation has arisen in which the Government of [a] State cannot be carried on in accordance with the provisions of this Constitution." If one carefully analyzes this provision, the operative word appears to be *cannot,* implying an impossibility of governance rather than any difficulty in governance. It is clear that a presidential proclamation under Article 356 is for emergencies; it is not to be made based upon a consideration that is extraneous to the purpose for which the power is conferred – that is, a breakdown of constitutional machinery in a state. Such a provision should not be seen as contrary to the federal principle. For the federal Constitution to function, the Union executive must have the power to give directions to the state executives, as the executive authority of the federation also extends to states.

The status of the states under the Constitution can be summed up as follows:

1 The Constitution does not grant to any state the right of secession.
2 The states have no a priori rights or powers but only rights or powers expressly granted to them by the Constitution. Even the residual powers are vested in the Union government. In the field of concurrent powers, Union law prevails over a state law that conflicts with a Union law.
3 There is a single constitution for both the Union and the states. No state has the right to adopt its own constitution. Part VI of the Constitution provides the framework for the government of the states.
4 There is a single unified judiciary for the whole country and an integrated civil service under the supervision and control of the All-India Services.

5 There is a single citizenship for the people of the country and no separate citizenship for the people of any state.

6 The governors of states are appointees of the Union government (i.e., of
the president), and besides being the constitutional head of state, a governor also is the eyes and ears of the Union in the state.

7 The Constitution guarantees individual rights and rights of certain
groups, such as scheduled castes, scheduled tribes, and minorities, but
not of states as such. It does not concede even the right of equal representation to the states in the upper house of the Union Parliament.

In turn, the Constitution requires the Union to (1) protect every state
against external aggression and internal disturbance and (2) ensure that the
government of each state is carried on in accordance with the Constitution.

The Union government can acquire the features of a unitary system in
an emergency, in which case its legislative power extends to state subjects.
Even in normal circumstances, the Council of States can, by a two-thirds
vote, transfer a subject from the State List to the Union List if such legislation is necessary for the "national interest." There is likewise a kind of paramountcy of the Union in provisions for the suspension of state
governments and the imposition of President's Rule. Union-state cooperation, as worded in Part XI of the Constitution, leaves ample scope for conflict over interpretation of definitional phrases such as "national interest"
and "Union's direction." Article 263, therefore, allows the president to establish an Inter-State Council to work out modalities for continuing cooperation and to forge procedures for coordination between the Union and
the states as well as among the states themselves. The text of Article 263 is
so phrased as to allow the council to discuss, debate, and recommend suitable policy measures on any subject, whether characterized as "national"
or as "public." There is scope for enlarging the ambit of the council, as it
would be lawful for a presidential order "to define the nature of the duties
to be performed by it and its organization and procedure." As an advisory
body, the council may inquire into disputes that "have arisen between
states"; investigate and discuss subjects "in which some or all of the States,
or the Union and one or more of the States, have a common interest"; or
recommend better coordination of policy and action on any subject necessitating interaction between the Union and the states.

However, all of the foregoing does not mean that states are mere append-
ages of the Union. In the sphere allotted to them, the states are supreme and
have an independent constitutional existence. The Constitution is in the nature of a covenant among the people as such, and the states are the creation
of this Constitution. The Constitution therefore guarantees individual rights
and freedoms and singles out minorities for double protection, first under
provisions of general rights and freedoms (Arts 14, 19, 20–23) and again

under provisions specifically pertaining to freedom of religion and cultural and educational rights (Arts 15, 16, 25–30). In addition, government can engage in affirmative action, or positive discrimination, by making special provisions "for the advancement of any socially and educationally backward classes of citizens or for the Scheduled Castes and the Scheduled Tribes."[16]

THE CONSTITUTIONAL AMENDMENT PROCESS

Three procedures for amendment are detailed under Article 368: amendment by simple majority, by special majority, and by ratification by the state legislatures.

Amendment by simple majority. A number of articles in the Constitution are of a transitory nature and can be changed by Parliament through a law enacted by a simple majority. Examples include changes in the names and boundaries of the states, creation or abolition of the legislative councils in the states, and changes in the salaries and allowances of the president, governors, and judges of the Supreme Court and high courts, among others.

Amendment by special majority. Under this procedure, an amendment to the Constitution may be initiated only by the introduction of a bill for this purpose in either house of Parliament. After the bill is passed in each house by a majority of the total membership of each house and by a majority of not less than two-thirds of the members present and voting, and after it has received the president's approval, the Constitution stands amended.

Ratification by the state legislatures. For the amendment of certain other provisions of the Constitution (mainly the "federal" provisions), a bill has to be passed by each house of Parliament by a majority of the total membership of each house and by a majority of not less than two-thirds of the members present and voting. The amendment then must be ratified by the legislatures of not less than one-half of the states before being presented to the president for assent. This requirement of ratification by one half of the state legislatures can be viewed as an additional check on the Parliament's constitutive authority.

The following provisions of the Constitution fall under this latter category: (1) election of the president (Art. 57), (2) extent of the executive power of the Union (Art. 73), (3) extent of the executive power of the states (Art. 162), (4) the Union judiciary (Ch. IV of Prt V), (5) high courts in the states (Ch. V of Prt VI), (6) any of the lists in the Seventh Schedule, (7) the representation of states in Parliament, and (8) provisions dealing with amendment of the Constitution.

India's Constitution is not a covenant, or compact, between the states; rather, the states are the creation of the Constitution and subsequently of Parliament. Consequently, the states do not have an inherent right to share in the amending process, except insofar as the Constitution provides for state legislative participation in the matters listed above – all of which impinge significantly upon the states. In turn, in all cases but one, the states cannot initiate a move for any constitutional amendment, the exception being that the Constitution leaves to the initiative of the state legislatures the creation or abolition of a second chamber in a state legislature.

DUAL POLITY: LOCAL *PANCHAYATS* AND MUNICIPALITIES

The Seventy-Third and Seventy-Fourth Amendments (1992), which introduced Parts IX and IXA of the Constitution, give constitutional status to local bodies, both urban and rural, as almost a third order of government, but the character of India's federal polity remains otherwise unaltered. These local governments have been granted some powers but must depend mostly on financing from the state governments in order to perform the functions assigned to them. Part IX of the Constitution outlines the framework of institutions of rural self-government: a three-tier system of units known, in ascending order, as the village, intermediate, and district *panchayats*.[17]

Part IXA sets forth the framework of urban local government. Three types of institutions of local self-government have been provided for urban areas, namely *nagar panchayats* for transitional areas (i.e., areas that are being transformed from rural to urban), municipal councils for small urban areas, and municipal corporations for large urban areas. Every state is obliged to constitute such units. Local government remains an exclusive state subject. The Seventy-Third and Seventy-Fourth Amendments outline the scheme by which the states can bring their laws on local government into conformity with these amendments.

The Constitution provides for the direct election of local bodies every five years. The noteworthy provisions include: (1) the reservation of local legislative seats for women and for scheduled castes and tribes, (2) a state election commission to conduct elections, (3) a state finance commission to ensure the financial viability of these institutions, and (4) devolution of powers and responsibilities to the local bodies with respect to (a) the preparation of plans and implementation of schemes for economic development and social justice, (b) the subjects listed in the Eleventh Schedule for the *panchayats* and in the Twelfth Schedule for the municipalities, (c) devolution of financial powers to the local bodies, and (d) endowment of these institutions with powers, authority, and responsibility to prepare plans for economic development. Thus these local bodies are empowered to raise revenue with which to undertake various community-welfare programs.

Variations exist from state to state in terms of structure, number of levels, degree of autonomy, length of term, and so on, but today this local-government system is functional in almost all of the states.

DIVISION OF POWERS

The states derive their powers, including their fiscal powers, directly from the Constitution. They are not dependent on the Centre for their legislative or executive authority. The states exercise powers in the administrative, legislative, and financial spheres, and they have their own civil services as well.

The Constitution regulates in elaborate detail the legislative and administrative relations between the Union and the states as well as the distribution of revenues between them. It has been noted that the Constitution tilts in favour of the Union in the distribution of powers and revenue sources. The outcome is that the Union is invested with wider jurisdiction for the operation of its legislative and executive authority than are most other federal systems.

Several considerations support this assessment. First, the Union has exclusive power to legislate on the 97 subjects on the Union List and concurrent power to legislate on the 47 subjects on the Concurrent List. Second, although the Union shares with the states the power to legislate on subjects on the Concurrent List, Union law has priority over any state law in the event of a conflict between the two. Third, the residual powers, as in Canada but unlike in the United States and Switzerland, are vested in the Union. Fourth, the Union Parliament can make laws on subjects on the State List if (1) the *Rajya Sabha* (upper chamber of Parliament), by a resolution passed by not less than two-thirds of the members present and voting, declares that it is expedient or necessary, as a matter of national interest, to do so (Art. 249); (2) a proclamation of national emergency is in operation (Art. 250); (3) the legislatures of one or more states pass resolutions to that effect (Art. 252); or (4) the Union law is to give effect to "any treaty, agreement or convention with any other country or countries or any decision made at any international conference, association or other body" (Art. 253).

In this way, the Union may legislate in the field of the states in specified circumstances. The powers of the Union are such as to enable the Indian central state to fulfil its basic national obligations of (1) safeguarding the nation's unity and integrity, (2) promoting economic development and growth, (3) adopting social-reform measures, (4) promoting higher education, science, and technology, (5) fostering social security and the welfare of labour, and (6) advancing trade, commerce, industries, agriculture, banking, and the like. For this reason, all subjects deemed to be of national importance and subjects said to require uniformity of treatment throughout the country are included on the Union List. These include defence and foreign affairs; citizenship; railways; posts and telegraphs; telephone, wireless, and other like means of communication; currency, coinage, and foreign exchange; interstate trade and commerce; banking; insurance; patents and copyrights; standards of weights and measures; industries; oilfields and mines; census matters; and the higher judiciary.

The Concurrent List contains items that enable the Union to undertake measures of social reform and economic planning and growth. These include criminal law and procedure and civil procedure; marriage and divorce; adoption; succession (inheritance); forests; protection of wild animals and birds; adulteration of foodstuffs and other goods; economic and social planning; trade unions; social security; employment and unemployment; labour welfare; education; weights and measures; price control; factories; electricity; and acquisition and requisitioning of property. The general principle behind these items is that Parliament can initiate policy on matters in which central initiative is considered necessary to secure nationwide uniformity or to guide and encourage state efforts.

The subjects that by their very nature require variation in treatment in order to suit local conditions and circumstances are located on the State List. The state legislature has the exclusive power to make laws for any subject contained on the State List, albeit within limits. The state law must not be repugnant to any provision of a law made by Parliament that is within Parliament's authority. In the event of a conflict between the two, the law made by Parliament prevails, and the state law, to the extent that it conflicts, is void. This means that state legislation can be subordinated in its own field or in the field of concurrent power.

The broad powers given to the Union under the Union and Concurrent Lists and the limited powers given to the states under the State List must not be seen in terms of the "either-or-federalism" of the past, which rested on a dichotomy between the Centre and the states and construed the division of powers as being a zero-sum game, such that any gain for one order of government was thought to come at the expense of the other. The two should no longer be seen as competing centres of power but as co-partners in the task of nation building.

Administrative Relations

The primacy of the Union over the states in the legislative field is carried over into the administrative arena as well, the basic constitutional premise being that the executive power is co-extensive with the legislative power.

The Constitution directs that the executive power of every state be so exercised as to ensure compliance with, and not to impede or prejudice, the exercise of the executive power of the Union, and the Union has the power to give such directions to a state as may appear necessary for the purpose of ensuring compliance with Union laws (Art. 256). However, the Supreme Court has held that this does not empower the Union to interfere in any matter pertaining to the exclusive concern of a state.[18] The president, with the consent of the state government, may entrust to that government, or its officers, functions in relation to any matter falling within the domain of the federal executive. A law made by Parliament that applies in any state may confer powers and impose duties upon the state or its officers and authorities (e.g., the power of subordinate legislation to help carry out the law).

The governor of a state may also, with the consent of the Government of India, entrust to his or her state functions in relation to any matter as may appear to the Union government to be necessary for the matter's administration. When the Union government, in the exercise of its executive power, issues any directions to a state government (under Articles 256–57 of the Constitution), it becomes the duty of the governor to keep the Union government informed of how such directions are being implemented by the state government. The governor becomes an "agent" of the Union when a proclamation of emergency under Article 356 is in operation. Under this article, the president may by proclamation assume to himself the executive powers of the state and declare that the powers of the state legislature shall be exercised by or under the authority of the Union Parliament. When a proclamation of emergency is in operation, the Union executive is empowered to give directions to any state on how the executive power thereof is to be exercised.

There are other institutional arrangements whereby the Union may exercise superintendence, direction, and control over state administrations. The head of the state executive is the governor, who is appointed by the Union president. The governor acts not merely as the constitutional head of state, but also as the agent of the Centre – that is, as its eyes and ears in the state. The Union government may bring a state under President's Rule via Article 356 if it is satisfied on its own that such a measure is necessary or if it receives a report from the governor that the state government "cannot be carried on in accordance with the provisions of this Constitution." In such a situation, the powers and functions of the state government are assumed by the Union government. Article 356 provides the Centre with the possibility of dismissing any state government that it deems politically unacceptable – in addition to providing a way out when no political party or coalition of parties is able to command majority support in the state legislature.[19] However, in a 1994 judgment having far-reaching consequences, the Supreme Court held that the Court can examine whether the president issued a proclamation based on bad faith *(mala fides)* or on irrelevant considerations because the Court is not precluded from calling upon the Union government to disclose to the Court the material upon which the president formed his or her judgment.[20] In this way, the Court sought to contain the Union government's attempts to ride roughshod over the states by threatening them with dismissal.[21]

Another institutional device by which the Union can secure the superintendence, direction, and control of the state administrative apparatus is by superimposition of the All-India Services on the corresponding state services, the provincial civil service, and the provincial police service.

Financial Relations

Fiscal federalism in India can be traced back to the Government of India Act 1919. This act sought to secure for the provinces a greater measure of financial autonomy by abolishing the "divided heads" of revenue and effecting a complete separation between the central and provincial heads. Under the 1919 Act, heads of specific revenue departments were assigned wholly to the provinces, while the Centre retained responsibility for the revenues administered by the remaining department heads. The framework set up in 1919, however, remained unaltered until the Government of India Act 1935. Subsequent reviews of the financial situation kept the structure of Centre-state relations unchanged while altering their respective shares of centrally collected revenue. A principal objective of these endeavours was to equip the provincial governments with greater financial resources. It was not until the enactment of the Constitution in 1950 that a Finance Commission was appointed to overhaul the financial system of the Indian federation and make recommendations about the distribution of revenues between the Union and the states under Articles 273 and 275.

The Constitution clearly demarcates the revenue resources of both the Union and the states, with financial autonomy being secured for the Union government as well as, to a lesser degree, for the states.[22] The Union's sources of revenue are listed in entries 82 to 92A of the Union List; those of the states are indicated in entries 45 to 63 of the State List. An important feature of India's financial framework is revenue sharing between the Union and the states. This takes several forms. There are duties levied by the Union but collected and appropriated by the states, such as stamp duties and excise duties on medicine and toilet preparations. There also are taxes levied and collected by the Union but whose proceeds are assigned wholly to the states – for example, succession (inheritance) duties; estate duties; and as per Article 270, which was added to the Constitution under the Eightieth Amendment (2000), terminal taxes on goods or passengers carried by railway, sea, or air, taxes on the consignment of goods in the course of interstate trade, and taxes on railway fares and freights involving interstate trade. Certain taxes are levied and collected by the Union and distributed between the Union and the states. An important example is taxes on income other than agricultural income. Other taxes and duties are levied and collected by the Union and may be distributed between the Union and the states if Parliament so provides by law. Among these are excise duties other than duties on medicines and toiletries. Finally, Parliament is empowered to make such grants as it deems necessary to providing financial assistance for any state in need. Such grants can be block grants or specific categorical grants.

The Constitution provides that the distribution between the Union and the states of the net proceeds of taxes that are to be divided between them and the allocation between states of the respective shares of such proceeds shall be done on the recommendations of a Finance Commission that is appointed by the president every five years. The commission also recommends the principles that should govern grants-in-aid to the states. The grants are both a means to assist development schemes in states lacking adequate financial resources and an instrument to exercise control and coordination over the states' welfare schemes.

There is a clear vertical imbalance between (1) the powers of taxation assigned to the Union and the states and (2) the social and economic responsibilities assigned to the states. That is, the states' responsibilities exceed their own-source revenues. This arrangement is intended to permit each order of government to do what it is thought to do best; that is, it recognizes that the Centre is perhaps in the best position to collect certain kinds of taxes and to expend and redistribute tax revenues for equitable purposes nationwide, while states and their local governments are in the best position to manage developmental programs and to deliver most services because they are closest to the people. Furthermore, the Finance Commission, the Planning Commission, and the National Development Council provide mechanisms for periodically correcting this imbalance and for allowing the states to better discharge their responsibilities. These forums cater to the grievances of the states, which they redress to the extent possible.

In recognition of the limitations on the financial resources of the states and the growing needs of states and local communities in a welfare state, the Constitution contains specific provisions empowering Parliament to set aside a portion of its revenue for the benefit of the states, the proportion being determined by states' needs. The resources of the Union are not meant exclusively for the benefit of Union activities, although the mandate of each of these bodies (i.e., the Finance Commission, Planning Commission, and the National Development Council) has differing implications for the states' ability to set their own developmental priorities. As conceived, the Union and the states together form one organic whole for the purposes of utilizing the resources of India as a whole. The Union is intended to play the role of equalizer between the greatly disparate states that constitute the Indian Union.

Provisions for Financial Emergency

The Constitution provides that while a proclamation of emergency is in operation, the president may by order modify or suspend the provisions relating to the distribution of revenues between the Centre and the states as may be specified in the order. While a proclamation of financial emergency under Article 360 is in operation, the Union is empowered to give directions to any state to observe such canons of financial propriety as may be specified in the directions. Such direction may include a provision requiring the reduction of salaries and allowances of state officials and a provision requiring all money bills to be reserved for consideration by the president after they are passed by the legislature of the state. While a state is under President's Rule (Art. 356), the powers of the state legislature are exercisable by the Union Parliament, including the power to adopt the state budget and pass the money bills. In this way, during an emergency, the constitutional barriers between the Union and the states are scaled down, and the Indian federation can function more or less like a unitary state.

MECHANISMS OF CONFLICT MANAGEMENT

There are both formal institutional and informal political arrangements for Centre-state coordination. Among the formal mechanisms are the Planning Commission, Finance Commission, National Development Council, Inter-State Council, National Integration Council, zonal councils, tribunals for adjudicating specific disputes, and various commissions and committees to look into specific aspects of Union-state relations. The informal mechanisms include ministerial and departmental meetings, conferences of constitutional functionaries and of political executives, and the governors' and chief ministers' conferences that are convened by the president and the prime minister. These informal arrangements are aimed at laying down procedural norms of conduct, particularly over such issues as the sharing of central taxes and the Union's intervention in states' affairs, and at evolving a common policy on such transgovernmental issues as the environment, communications, and health. Similarly, such informal mechanisms evolve conventions of governance on questions of states' rights, interstate trade and commerce, sharing of river waters, interstate communications, and other matters.

For resolving interstate disputes, the Constitution provides for an Inter-State Council (ISC). Article 263 states:

If at any time it appears to the President that the public interests would be served by the establishment of a Council charged with the duty of (a) inquiring into and advising upon disputes which may have arisen between States; (b) investigating and discussing subjects in which some or all of the States, or the Union and one or more of the States, have a common interest; or (c) making recommendations upon any such subject and, in particular, recommendations for the better co-ordination of policy and action with respect to that subject, it shall be lawful for the President by order to establish such a Council and to define the nature of the duties to be performed by it and its organisation and procedure.

The first Inter-State Council (ISC), composed of six Union Cabinet ministers and all the state chief ministers, was constituted in 1990. This council has been entrusted with the tasks of (1) inquiring into and advising upon disputes between states, (2) investigating and discussing subjects in which the Union and the states have a common interest, and (3) recommending steps for coordinating policy and action with respect to these common-interest subjects. Given that the ISC is an advisory body, it is difficult to assess the efficacy of its policy performance. With the Union government becoming weaker since 1989, with different political parties ruling at the Centre and in several states, and with the Union government enjoying majority support in the Parliament without the major party being in the majority, and with the exigencies of coalition politics, the Union government has to share power with the states. The bargaining power of the states with the Centre has increased markedly, and they no longer need a mechanism like the ISC to bargain with the Centre.

However, subject-specific councils have been established from time to time by the Union government, such as the Central Council of Health, Central Council of Local Self-Government, Transport Development Council, Central Council of Indian Medicine, Central Family Welfare Council, All-India Council of Technical Education, and University Grants Commission. These councils have been set up to investigate and discuss subjects of common interest between the Union and the states or between two or more states and to make recommendations for coordinating policy and action relating to their respective subject areas.

It was the start of central planning in the country that encouraged the establishment of institutions such as the Planning Commission, National Development Council (NDC), Finance Commission, and zonal councils. Whereas the Planning Commission was to make use of national expertise at various levels of government in devising national development plans, the NDC (comprised of the prime minister, chief ministers of states, and members of the Planning Commission) was to review and finalize the development plans made by the Planning Commission. The five zonal councils are advisory bodies on issues pertaining to each region's development planning.

After the States Reorganisation Act 1956, five zonal councils were set up, each composed of the chief ministers of the states in a council's zone, the development ministers and chief secretaries of these states, and a member of the Planning Commission, with each council headed by the Union's home minister. The zonal councils are intended to foster the psychological integration of the country by mitigating regional consciousness; helping the Union and state governments to evolve uniform social and economic policies; assisting with effective implementation of development projects; and evolving a degree of political equilibrium among the regions of the country. It was hoped by the first prime minister of India that, without becoming a fifth wheel of the coach and without disrupting close relations between the Union and the states, the zonal councils would help to solve day-to-day problems and assist in economic planning. The idea is integration through decentralization, but in reality the councils have met with only limited success.

Informal arrangements are in place that, at times, can be more effective. These include intergovernmental conferences, such as those convening state governors, chief ministers, and ministers of various departments. With the emergence since the late 1980s of Union coalition governments, which have the supportive presence of various regional parties, such informal arrangements have generally become more effective than the formal mechanisms of intergovernmental conflict resolution.

THE FEDERATION AT WORK

The division of powers between the Union and the states has not been static but has fluctuated with political and socio-economic circumstances, such that several patterns are discernible in the actual implementation of the Constitution during the past 55 years.

Planning

During the early periods of the republic, one ideological input was added to a political context characterized by the hegemony of one party (i.e., the Congress party) under leaders of mass appeal in their respective states and beyond: namely, economic planning for a socialistic pattern of society and, later on, for building democratic socialism. This was the goal that was said to transcend party lines and cut across state boundaries. Therefore, planning soon came to be looked upon by some observers as a threat to federalism in India since the planning process necessarily meant central

initiative and leadership in plan formulation, along with centralized superintendence, direction, and control of the states in plan execution and performance evaluation.

In 1950 a Planning Commission was set up, with the prime minister as its
ex officio chairman, to prepare five-year plans for social and economic development and to secure the "most effective and balanced utilisation of the
country's resources" that would "initiate a process of development which
will raise living standards and open out to the people new opportunities
for a richer and more varied life." Besides the prime minister, the ministers
of finance, home, and defence are members of the commission. Additionally, there are several full-time members who are experts in finance, agriculture, economics, and the like.

In deference to the federal nature of the polity, the National Development Council was set up in 1952 to involve the states in the formulation of
the plans and "to strengthen and mobilise the efforts and resources of the
nation in support of the plans." More specifically, the NDC reviews the implementation of the national plan from time to time and recommends
measures for achieving the aims and targets set out in the plan. The prime
minister is the ex officio chairman of the NDC, while the members of the
Planning Commission and the chief ministers of all 28 states are its ex officio members.

The NDC is required to supervise the work of national planning, to recommend measures for achieving plan targets, and to consider important
questions of social and economic policy affecting national development.
The state governments submit their five-year plans to the Planning Commission, which prepares the national plan. After its approval by the central
government, the plan is executed by the NDC. The recommendations of
the NDC are taken into consideration by the Planning Commission before
the plan is given final shape. The process represents the principle of cooperative federalism. While its terms of reference originally mandated the
NDC to review the implementation of the national plan from time to time,
in practice the NDC makes recommendations pertaining to the overall size
and structure of the plan. Also, the NDC ensures a coordinated implementation of the plan. Because of the coordinated approach of involving the
Union and the states, the NDC is able to promote a balanced development
in different regions of the country.

The NDC is a policy-making body, and its recommendations are not just
advisory suggestions but policy decisions and policy directives. It is a national forum for planning that gives informal sanction to the underlying
concept of cooperation between the Union and the states. It brings the
states into an organic relationship with the Union because, through national planning, states become an integral part of the Union's body politic.
The NDC occupies an important position in the Indian federal set up

because it consists of the chief executives of the central and state governments and, therefore, its advice can hardly be distinguished from a clear mandate. The NDC was visualized as a bridge between the two orders of government and, by becoming organizationally and operationally strong, it has started to play this role.

The draft of the plan is prepared by the Planning Commission in consultation with Union ministries and state governments, and after approval by the Union Cabinet, it is placed before the NDC for approval. Thus mutual cooperation is institutionalized in the NDC, which is the highest national forum for planning. It has in practice embodied and given informal sanction to the underlying concept of partnership and cooperation between the Union and the states over the whole range of development issues, thereby bringing the state governments into an organic relationship with the organization of planning at the national level.

Resource transfers authorized (under Art. 275) on the recommendations of the Finance Commission are known as statutory grants; those authorized (under Art. 282) on the recommendations of the Planning Commission are known as discretionary grants. When grants to the states are recommended by the Finance Commission – which is a statutory body – the Union government is constitutionally obligated to authorize the grants; hence the Union's authority with respect to grants does not add to its powers. But discretionary grants recommended by the Planning Commission – which is not a statutory body – are at the discretion of the Union government and thus political in nature. As such, they are criticized for causing the states' abject dependence on the Union – a dependence that is said to further enable the Union government to discriminate between states.[23] Plan grants, provided for under Article 282, are 50-50 matching grants, which means that the Union government issues a grant equal to the sum that the state has raised through its own resources. It also means that states have to fall in line with Union policies, priorities, and preferences in issuing matching grants and also dovetail their own funds to Union allocations.

Vertical Federalism

Because the Union grants are routed through central ministries to their counterparts in the states, each Union ministry is in a position to use the strings of financial power to superintend, direct, and control the corresponding state department. In this way, besides the territorial or horizontal federation set up by the Constitution, a sort of vertical federation has come into being. The central ministries and corresponding state departments each constitute a separate single unit for planning, programming, and funding plan projects in a manner similar to what some American scholars have called picket-fence or stovepipe federalism.

Besides the projects approved for the states in the national plan, there are some projects known as "Centrally sponsored schemes" that must necessarily be located in one or another state. These schemes are financed by the Union but executed by the state concerned under the technical guidance and supervision of the related Union ministry. That is, the Union decides the fund allocation, while the states essentially act as spending agencies. In these schemes, programs are cost-shared, such that the Union necessarily influences the functions within the states' spheres of jurisdiction through its matching grants.

The Union government's discretion in choosing locations for public-sector undertakings, which encompass most of the infrastructure industries, such as steel, electricity, heavy engineering, and fertilizers, has been cause for interstate rivalry in view of the many impacts such undertakings have on the local economy and on employment potential. The choice of one site in preference over another is yet one more case in which the Union can exercise discretion in its patronage of the states. Even though most of these schemes relate to state subjects, the Union is able to transform them into subjects of Union jurisdiction because their funding is at the discretion of the Union government. Given past experience, therefore, state officials see these schemes as restrictions on state autonomy.

NEW TRENDS AND THE GROWING ROLE OF STATES IN NATIONAL POLITICS

Unitarian federalism, as Union-state relations came to be described during the long years of one-party Congress rule at the Centre, was the consequence of the dominance of one party in both the Union and the state governments. Since 1989 there have been coalition governments at the Centre, sustained by support from parties in power in various states.[24] Therefore, the system of one-party domination that fostered and sustained unitary federalism for some 40 years has been replaced by more competitive party politics rooted in regionally based and state-based political parties. One-party hegemony subsumed regional politics and regional political forces that were bound to bubble up to the surface with the end of this hegemony.

What is now called competition in India's transactional federalism actually developed as a result of the emergence of coalition politics and power sharing. In this way, the Union and the states under the impact of competitive party politics and increasing regionalism have become more like coordinate centres of power. Howsoever strong the position of the Union in planning, programming, and financing, the execution of plans and projects rests in the hands of the state governments. No other large federal government is as dependent as India's on theoretically subordinate, but actually rather distinct, units responsible to a different order of government for so much of the administration of what are recognized as national programs. In the final analysis, the authority organically exercised in New Delhi is influence rather than power.

Under the Constitution, the relationship between the Union and the states is that between the whole and its parts rather than between a centre and its periphery; otherwise, the image created would be that the centre of authority is in New Delhi, while the states are at the periphery. Nevertheless, the different units of the constituent federal system are to a degree subsidiaries of the Union government. The mechanisms of intergovernmental relations in India are tilted in favour of the Union government. There are intergovernmental institutions meant to ensure some uniformity in administrative relations, but these mechanisms have not been employed in improving the system of governance. The Supreme Court has on occasion put pressure on the state governments to follow certain principles in respect of governance or the welfare of the people, but this does not, in any way, take away the rights of the states to improve their own systems of administration. The hegemony of the Union's governmental institutions over the state governments is meant to bring about some uniformity of standards in administrative procedures.

In some respects, states have also acquired a certain say in matters that used to be the domain of the Union, one reason being that regional parties share political power at the Centre. In terms of foreign affairs, for instance, states that have performed well economically, and that have attracted foreign direct investment, have influenced the foreign economic policy of the Union. States are now more conscious of their role in foreign affairs with neighbouring countries as well as in international organizations, such as the World Trade Organization, World Bank, and Asian Development Bank. Nevertheless, this remains an area in which the states still have little autonomy. It is true that in recent years chief ministers of the states have embarked on foreign junkets, but these initiatives have required concurrence from the Centre. Although bilateral and multilateral international donors finance projects run by state governments, all such projects must be sanctioned by the central government because, ultimately, only it can provide sovereign debt guarantees. Thus intergovernmental relations reflect the tendencies of both conflict and cooperation. Moreover, these relations are always changing, thus requiring the country to continue rethinking its federalism.[25]

The states have been demanding a greater role for the Finance Commission than for the Planning Commission on the grounds that the latter is a political body and is likely to be susceptible to greater central-government control. With the introduction of economic liberalization and the "New Economic Policy," it seems that now the Centre also shares the views of the states on this point. If the "disinvestment" and withdrawal from various fields of activity continues, the Union government is bound to reduce the role of the Planning Commission. In the fiscal sphere, it may force the states toward more competitive performance, producing greater disparities among them.

Issues of fiscal federalism have been thorny even though intergovernmental jurisdiction over taxation is clearly demarcated on the Union and State Lists in the Seventh Schedule of the Constitution. Given that more than 60 percent of the resource transfers from the Union to the states are made through the Planning Commission and the central government's ministries, rather than via the Finance Commission, Union intervention in the states' development programs has increased. Economic planning and development require coordinated efforts, and for these, cooperative federal arrangements are needed, which are best provided by the concerted ventures of the National Development Council and the Inter-State Council. In the past, these institutions have attempted to even out the imbalances in the growth of different states by giving preference to backward areas. Now some of the better-performing states are complaining that rewarding backwardness in effect punishes the stronger states for performing well.

The Indian Constitution would seem, in the end, to create a "cooperative union" of states rather than a dual polity. Planning for the mobilization of national resources and their most effective and balanced utilization for the social and economic development of the country as a whole now appears to be an integral part of this concept. Through substitution and through centralized planning, the Union had extended its role into areas that lie constitutionally within exclusive state fields. What is being observed now is federal restructuring through politically developed rules and conventions, without disturbing the basic scheme of the Constitution. The actual working of cooperative federalism in India has entailed the Union's exercising its influence rather than its constitutional authority. Exigencies of coalition politics have forced the Union and state governments to share power. The Union has more often played the role of a facilitator in interstate disputes than that of an arbitrator. A redistribution of powers – through decentralization and the devolution of authority from the Union to the states and from the states to the *panchayats* and municipalities — is serving to facilitate the attainment of the objectives of the Constitution: unity, social justice, and democracy.

All this suggests steps in the direction of cooperative federalism, although the future course of Indian federalism is, as always, subject to change. Will the states continue to assert themselves in their efforts to become full co-partners with the Union government or even dominant in the system, or will the federal system recentralize, and, if so, will this be the case for an extended period of time? In addition, what impact will the liberalization of India's economy have on the federal system? Will a growing, internationally integrated national economy benefit all states equally, produce greater competition between states, and/or increase economic and fiscal differences between states?

The Constitution envisages a "creative balance" between the need for an effective centre and the need for effectively empowered states. The federal system that has emerged has become a sound framework for the working of the Constitution. Overcoming many problems of maintaining balance, the system has survived even though many of its federal features have been eroded over time. Despite great odds and great complexity, India has survived because it is united as a nation with the voluntary and natural agreement of its constituent units. Largely, this is because the Constitution has provided a mechanism not only for resolving intergovernmental disputes, but also for maintaining a workable, if not always stable, constitutional balance between the key orders of government.

NOTES

1 For the text of the Constitution with some commentary, see P.M. Bakshi, *The Constitution of India,* 5th ed. (Delhi: Universal Law Publishing, 2003). See also M.V. Pylee, *Our Constitution, Government and Politics* (New Delhi: Universal Law, 2002); Granville Austin, *Working a Democratic Constitution: A History of the Indian Experience* (New Delhi: Oxford University Press, 1999); and B. Shiva Rao, *The Framing of India's Constitution: Select Documents* (New Delhi: Indian Institute of Public Administration, 1968).

2 Neera Chandhoke, *The Concept of Civil Society* (New Delhi: Oxford, 2003); Akhtar Majeed, ed., *Nation and Minorities: India's Plural Society and its Constituents* (New Delhi: Kanishka Publishers, 2002); Zoya Hasan, *Politics and the State in India* (New Delhi: Sage, 2000); Partha Chatterjee, *State and Politics in India* (New Delhi: Oxford, 1997); and Balveer Arora and Douglas Verney, *Multiple Identities in a Single State: Indian Federalism in a Comparative Perspective* (New Delhi: Konark, 1995).

3 N. Gangulee, *The Making of Federal India* (London: James Nisbet and Co., 1936).

4 D.D. Basu, *Introduction to the Constitution of India,* 3rd ed. (New Delhi: Wadhwa, 2002), pp. 6–7.

5 The Assembly is indirectly elected by members of the provincial legislative assemblies. The number of representatives from a province and from each religious community within a province is to be proportional to the province's population in the ratio of 1 representative per 2 million people, and the representatives are to be elected by the method of proportional representation with a single transferable vote. D.D. Basu, *Introduction to the Constitution of India,* 2nd ed. (New Delhi: Prentice Hall, 1995), p. 19.

6 Jawaharlal Nehru (India's first prime minister), moving the Resolution on Aims and Objectives of the Constitution, 13 December 1946, Constituent Assembly. Also, Sir Aladi Krishnaswami Ayyar, 25 July 1847, Constituent Assembly. *Constituent Assembly Debates* (CAD), vol. 1 (New Delhi: Lok Sabha Secretariat, 1999), pp. 57–9.

7 Sarvepalli Radhakrishnan (India's second president) and Frank Anthony, 1 December 1946, Constituent Assembly. *Constituent Assembly Debates*, vol. 1, pp. 37–41.

8 *Constituent Assembly Debates*, vol. 5, pp. 494–95.

9 As a practical matter, state governors are actually appointed by the prime minister and the home minister.

10 *Keshavanada Bharati v State of Kerala*, All-India Reporter (AIR) 1973 Supreme Court (SC) 1461. See also H.M. Seervai, *Constitutional Law of India*, vol. 2 (Bombay: N.M. Tripathi, 1993), p. 1355; and Austin, *Working a Democratic Constitution*, p. 258.

11 AIR 1975 SC 2299, quoted in J.N. Pandey, *Constitutional Law of India* (Allahabad: Central Law Agency, 2003), 71.

12 AIR 1980 SC 1789, quoted in Pandey, *Constitutional Law of India*, p. 319.

13 *State of Bihar v Bal Mukund Sah*, AIR 2000 SC 1296, quoted in Pandey, *Constitutional Law of India*, p. 147.

14 By comparison, the US Constitution, "in all its provisions, looks to an indestructible Union, composed of Indestructible States." *Texas v White*, 74 US (7 Wall.) 700 (1869).

15 AIR 1977 SC 1361. See also Alice Jacob and Rajeev Dhavan, "The Dissolution Case Politics at the Bar of the Supreme Court," *Journal of the Indian Law Institute* 19 (1977): 355–97; and Rajeev Dhavan, *President's Rule in the States* (Bombay: N.M. Tripathi, 1979), pp. 126–58.

16 Article 15(4). Scheduled Castes and Tribes are backward communities that constitute some 24 percent of India's population and are identified in Schedules 5 and 6 of the Constitution.

17 George Mathew, ed., *Status of Panchayati Raj in the States and Union Territories of India, 2000* (New Delhi: Institute of Social Sciences, 2000).

18 *S.R. Bommai v Union of India*, 3 SCC (1994), and *State of Rajasthan v Union of India*, AIR 1977 SC 1361, both quoted in A.G. Noorani, *Constitutional Questions in India* (New Delhi: Oxford, 2000), pp. 268 and 253 respectively.

19 Amal Ray and John Kincaid, "Politics, Economic Development, and Second-Generation Strain in India's Federal System," *Publius: The Journal of Federalism* 18 (Spring 1988): 147–67.

20 *S.R. Bommai v Union of India*, 3 SCC (1994).

21 *State of Rajasthan v Union of India*, AIR 1977 SC 1361.

22 See M. Govinda Rao, "Indian Fiscal Federalism from a Comparative Perspective," *Multiple Identities in a Single State*, ed. Arora and Verney, *Multiple Identities in a Single State*, pp. 272–316.

23 *Report of the Commission on Centre-State Relations* [the Sarkaria Commission], vol. 1
   (Nasik: Government of India Press, 1988), p. 387.
24 "Emerging Issues in Indian Federalism," *Publius: The Journal of Federalism* 33
   (Fall 2003): entire issue; M. Govinda Rao, *Development, Poverty and Fiscal Policy:
   Decentralisation of Institutions* (New Delhi: Oxford, 2002); and Akhtar Majeed,
   ed., *Coalition Politics and Power Sharing* (New Delhi: Manak Publishers, 2000).
25 Rasheeduddin Khan, *Rethinking Indian Federalism* (Shimla: Inter-University Centre for Humanities and Social Sciences, Indian Institute of Advanced Studies,
   1997).

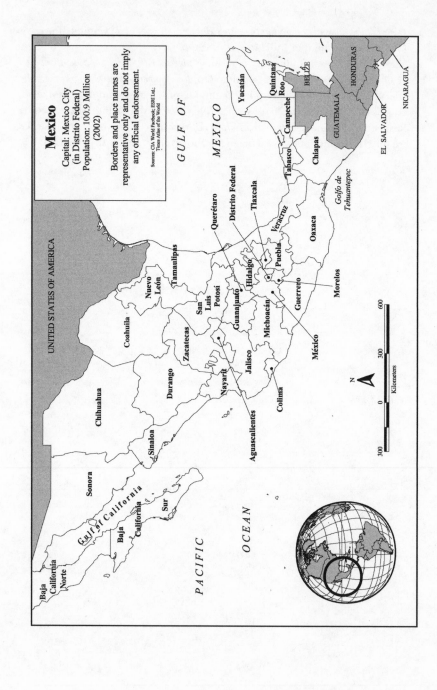

Mexico

Capital: Mexico City
(in Distrito Federal)
Population: 100.9 Million
(2002)

Borders and place names are
representative only and do not imply
any official endorsement.

Source: CIA World Factbook; ESRI Ltd.;
Times Atlas of the World

United Mexican States

JUAN MARCOS GUTIÉRREZ GONZÁLEZ

The Constitution of Mexico – officially, the United Mexican States – does not formally set forth any purposes in a lofty preamble. However, the provisions of the Constitution of 1917 clearly reflect major issues and concerns still prevalent in Mexico.[1] One overriding objective was to limit the power of the president as well as the perpetuation of this power through reelection. Decentralization and establishing a federal system were also at the top of the framers' agenda, as Mexico has a long tradition of centralism extending back through the colonial period and into the eras of the Aztec and Mayan civilizations.

In addition, extensive provisions on religion impose a very strict separation of church and state that seeks to reduce and often prohibit the involvement of religious institutions and clergy in government, education, land and property ownership, and other important facets of society. The Constitution, which vests "ownership of the lands and waters within the boundaries of the national territory ... in the Nation," also contains extensive provisions on land titles, acquisition and disposition of land, protections for certain lands, and national control through the federal government of various on-shore and off-shore lands and natural resources. Efforts to cope with official corruption are reflected in seven articles on the responsibilities of public officials (Arts 108–14), and efforts to address poverty are reflected in very extensive provisions on labour and social security (Art. 123).

Thus the Constitution established a federal system based on the principle that substantial powers should reside in a highly secular social-welfare state largely under the purview of a federal government with authority to intervene in such matters as foreign and domestic trade, agriculture, food supplies, labour, health care, education, and energy. This system facilitated the centralization of government in Mexico, and state ownership of land and natural resources fostered a highly nationalized economy. Therefore, during the twentieth century, the story of Mexican federalism was mostly one of centralization, which has been countered only since about 1982 by demands for policies favouring governmental decentralization, political democratization, and economic liberalization.[2]

HISTORICAL AND CULTURAL CONTEXT OF MEXICO'S CONSTITUTION

Mexico, whose territory comprises 1,967,183 square kilometres, had an estimated population of 103,510,471 in 2004.[3] Spanish is the country's predominant language, but speakers of indigenous languages number about 6,274,418, representing 6.3 percent of the population. Although most Mexicans are of *mestizo* origin (mainly a mix of Spaniards and indigenous peoples), there are 56 ethnic groups, the largest being the Otomí, Mazahua, Mazateco, Nahua, Maya, Huasteco, Tarahumara, and Totonaco.[4] The religious orientation of the Mexican populace is as follows: 82.9 percent are Roman Catholics; 4.9 percent are Protestants and Evangelicals; 2.6 percent are other Evangelicals; 1.5 percent are Pentecostals and Neopentecostals; and 8.1 percent claim other affiliations. The gross domestic product per capita in 2003 was estimated at US$5,701.[5]

Mexico's Constitution, promulgated in 1917, incorporates elements from several federal constitutions that came into effect after the War of Independence (1810–21). The constitutional ideas of the independence movement itself were influenced by the Spanish Constitution of Cadiz (1812)[6] and by the failed Constitution of 1814, known as the Constitution of Apatzingán. The 1917 Constitution, as well as the federal constitutions that preceded it, also reflected the social transformations and political struggles taking place throughout the nineteenth and early twentieth centuries.

Although Mexico's legal system embodies the tradition of Roman law[7] (in contrast to the common-law tradition in the United States), the Mexican Constitution clearly shows influences of the federal principles adopted in the Constitution of the United States of America. Mexico's Constitution may be relatively young, but its federal principles stem directly from the first federal constitution, which came into effect in 1824. Although Mexico had a centralist constitution from 1836 to 1854, the country's experiences under this constitution triggered a resurgence of federalist ideas, culminating in what was called the Plan of Ayutla (launched in 1854) and the federal Constitution of 1857. This Constitution, which failed to stem centralization, remained in effect until the outcome of the Mexican Revolution led to the 1917 Constitution, which remains in effect today. This Constitution, which has 136 articles, was approved in the City of Querétaro, State of Querétaro, on 31 January 1917 and promulgated on 5 February 1917. The Constitutional Congress that assembled to draft the Constitution of 1917 was convened in Querétaro in deference to the ideal of decentralization and at the urging of one of the principal leaders of the

Mexican Revolution, Don Venustiano Carranza, who noted that all previous congresses had been held in Mexico City. Therefore, one can say that federalism has at least circulated in the blood of Mexican society for more than 180 years.

The drafters of Mexico's Constitution had clear federalist and democratic objectives partly because the revolution had begun as a rebellion in several states against the centralized, dictatorial regime of Porfirio Díaz. Originating with the constitutional ideas of the Mexican Revolution (1910–20), one objective was to settle the issue of not allowing the president of the republic to stand for reelection, an issue that had been one of the main causes of the revolution. Thus, as stipulated by the Constitution of 1917, the president can serve only one six-year term. As well, the new federalist regime was organized as "a federal, democratic, representative Republic composed of free and sovereign States in all that concerns their internal government, but united in a Federation established according to the principles of this fundamental law" (Art. 40).[8]

However, under the federal model framed in the Constitution, the legislative and judicial branches of the federal government are essentially subservient to the executive and its overweening powers. Consequently, from 1920 to 1995 the federal system was characterized by a constitutional centralization of powers in the federal government, an arrangement that considerably diminished the decision-making powers of the states and municipalities. This system produced a socio-political phenomenon that characterized Mexico's political life throughout the twentieth century: the powerful presidential system. In addition, a single political party, the *Partido Revolucionario Institucional* (PRI/Institutional Revolutionary Party), maintained nearly monopolistic control over the country's political life. From its founding in 1929 until 1989, the PRI controlled the presidency, the Congress of the Union, the 31 state governments, the Federal District, and most of the nation's 2,448 municipal governments. The PRI lost the presidency for the first time only in 2000, after opposition parties had already gained control of a number of state and municipal governments.

The Constitution of Mexico is divided into two sections. The first, known as the "dogmatic" part, is an extensive list of individual guarantees[9] protecting the right to liberty, equality, property, lawful procedure, and a fair hearing and defence before a court of law as well as other human rights. The second section is known as the "organic" part. Specifically, it addresses the organization of the federation, the separation of powers (i.e., legislative, executive, and judicial), intergovernmental relations, and the existence of autonomous government agencies,[10] such as the *Banco de México* (Central Bank of Mexico), which, due to their structure, characteristics, and activities, tend to transgress in practice the Constitution's rigid stipulations regarding the separation of powers – particularly because they have both independent and multibranch functions.

Customary doctrine holds that individual rights are guaranteed in Articles 1 to 29 of the Constitution and that "organic" matters are treated in Articles 30 to 136. However, this distinction is relative because, throughout the Constitution, there is no distinct separation of the provisions concerning individual rights and those respecting organic matters.

The Federation

Mexico comprises 31 states plus an autonomous Federal District coextensive with Mexico City. The 31 states and the Federal District, which today make up the federation, were not configured in exactly the same way in 1917. During the decades following 1917, the states of Nayarit, Quintana Roo, Baja California, and Baja California Sur were created from areas previously considered federal territories. Admitting new states into the federal union is one of the powers of the Congress of the Union under Article 73, Parts I and II of the Constitution, as is the formation of new states within the boundaries of existing ones, according to the provisions in Part III of Article 73.

The procedures for creating a new state are similar to those for reforming the Constitution. The Constitution requires that (1) a new state have at least 120,000 inhabitants, (2) the opinions of both the executive branch of the federation and the states affected by the creation of the new entity be heard, and (3) the new state have sufficient resources to provide for its political existence. Creating a new state requires the approval of two-thirds of the members present in the federal Chamber of Deputies and in the Senate. A majority of state legislatures must also approve a corresponding decree. However, if the creation of a new state within the boundaries of existing states were proposed by a two-thirds vote of the Congress, the affected states would have to give their consent. If they refused to consent, the new state's creation would require the approval of two-thirds of the legislatures of all the other unaffected states. It is also within the powers of the federal Congress to render a final ruling concerning the boundaries and areas of the states. The only exception to this arrangement arises when a boundary dispute is contentious in nature, in which case the competent (or jurisdictional) authority is the country's Supreme Court of Justice.

CONSTITUTIONAL PRINCIPLES OF THE FEDERATION

General Focus of the Federal Constitution

The Constitution initially tended toward a division of powers and functions between the federal and state governments. However, a new design for cooperative, rather than dual, federalism emerged as a result of constitutional reforms (i.e., amendments) made during the following decades – reforms that established important mechanisms for concurrent federal-state action.[11]

This concurrency is expressed by the shared responsibilities of the national and subnational governments in matters involving education, health, the environment, human rights, and fiscal federalism, among others. Nevertheless, the specific distribution of powers (or competences) among the three orders of government is such that the predominance of the federal government persists, reflecting the existence of a federal but centralized governmental system in Mexico. Although the federal system has succeeded in fostering unity among its diverse constituent polities and communities under a predominant national government, it has done so without adequate recognition of local realities and thus has not fostered balanced and equitable development among the country's regions, states, localities, and classes. In effect, the federal system has weakened the independence of the constituent states and their municipalities while aggravating many regional and socioeconomic inequalities.

The Constitution does not mandate an official language or religion, but statutory legislation recognizes Spanish as the predominant language. With respect to religion, Article 130 of the Constitution guarantees freedom of beliefs, thus making no provision for any official religion. Even though most Mexicans define themselves as Roman Catholic, the Constitution contains no element explicitly influenced by Catholicism. The Constitution of 1917 mandated a strict separation of church and state. However, in 1991 the federal Congress approved a constitutional amendment allowing the recognition of churches by the government, the possession of property by churches (although church buildings remain state property), and the enfranchisement of priests.[12]

Generally, the Mexican federal republic has experienced long periods of highly centralized authority. This has been the case because the victors in the Mexican Revolution were the framers of the 1917 Constitution and because the Constituion was drawn up at a time when participation and support among the citizenry were limited. The Mexican Constitution is an authentic constitution in the sense that it is the result of an internal pact and a constitutional congress; however, it cannot necessarily be regarded as a document that is federal in origin – that is, as a compact among previously free and independent states that united to build a federation – because the framers of the Constitution envisioned a single nation from the moment Mexico became independent from Spain. Moreover, based on a conservative thesis that favoured a centralized republic, the centripetal force – political, economic, and social – was Mexico City.

Status of the Constituent Political Communities

As part of its symmetrical federalism, all of Mexico's constituent entities (i.e., states and municipalities)[13] have the same authority, powers, and structure.[14] This design was probably a response to the initial desire that the distinct regions making up the union be of equal strength and be given equal opportunities for development. The Federal District (i.e., Mexico City) is the only special government; like Washington, DC, it is not considered a constituent unit but a product of the federal agreement.

The Constitution provides for, and guarantees, the rights and powers of the constituent states in Article 124, which is called *the residual clause* because it stipulates that any powers the Constitution does not expressly assign to the federation shall reside with the states. As mentioned above, there are provisions in the Constitution both to create and to admit new states to the federal union, but there is no provision for a state's secession from the federation, which is thus considered unlawful.[15]

Theoretically, the states have the power to create their own institutions and governmental procedures with regard to matters affecting their internal governance. However, contradicting this idea of autonomous internal governance, the Constitution determines the fundamental characteristics and requirements of the powers granted to the states, as well as their basic institutions, including their municipalities. Nevertheless, it is relevant to highlight that some states at least include certain important rights in their own constitutions, such as the state of Oaxaca, which forcefully and in great detail had recognized the rights of indigenous peoples even before the adoption of the federal reform of 2001.[16]

Due to a 1999 reform of Article 115, the Constitution now creates and regulates the existence of municipalities as component parts of the states and, thus, of the federation.[17] This reform was introduced in 1999 on the premise that by including municipalities as an order of government, their existence and powers would no longer depend as much upon the states as upon constitutional standards. In turn, municipalities would be able to oppose any state-initiated reforms intended to change their original structure or powers of government as stipulated in the Constitution. In this sense, the municipalities are not, unlike in the US Constitution, "creatures of the states"; rather, they are "creatures of the Constitution." This is the case, moreover, given that state constitutions usually stipulate the same basic governmental institutions and procedures as those found in the federal Constitution. Any conflict between a state constitution and the federal Constitution is always resolved in favour of the latter, according to the prevailing principle of the supremacy of the federal Constitution.

The legal status given to municipalities distinguishes Mexico's Constitution from many other federal constitutions. This legal status assigns municipalities a legal personality, a list of exclusive powers, and the right to challenge other orders of government.[18] These attributes make municipalities an essential part of the states and, consequently, an essential part of the federation.[19]

Since the 1980s, municipal governments have gained more autonomy.[20] Municipalities have been constitutionally guaranteed federal and state fiscal transfers as well as broad spending autonomy, although they are still limited in their power to levy taxes. While the municipalities have been granted authority over real-property taxation as well as the right to collect user charges for the public services they deliver, the state legislatures authorize the rates and charges as well as the levels of municipal indebtedness. However, budgetary approvals for spending levels and for the objects of spending are an autonomous municipal power, subject to the constitutional principle that municipal budgets must be in accordance with the income previously approved by the state Congress (Art. 115, Sec. IV). Consequently, the municipalities cannot spend more than they receive from their various fiscal sources, including from legally acquired debt. In addition, municipalities have exclusive jurisdiction in matters respecting basic public functions and services, such as potable water, sewerage and drainage, cleaning of public places, waste collection and disposal, wastewater treatment, construction of urban infrastructure, urban land-use control and development, markets and supply centres, public safety (i.e., police), and transit. State constitutions can expand these autonomous functions but not limit them.

For their part, the states have wide powers to run their institutions despite possible regulation or overregulation by the federal government under the terms of the federal Constitution. The constitutional limitations to this exercise of federal regulation are enforced by the Supreme Court of Justice of the Nation, which has jurisdiction to settle this type of dispute under Sections I and II of Article 105 of the Constitution.

State constitutions are approved by a state Constituent Congress. State constitutional reform can be achieved through two fundamental procedures. In some states, it occurs through a Permanent Constituent congress according to a special procedure for reforming a state constitution. This procedure requires that a qualified majority of two-thirds of the members of the state's unicameral Congress vote to reform its constitution. This procedure is used in the state of Yucatan, among others. The second procedure, likewise undertaken by a Permanent Constituent Congress, is in force in the majority of states. In addition to the first procedure's requirements for changing a state constitution, the second procedure also requires the vote of 50 percent plus 1 of the *ayuntamientos* (i.e., municipal councils).[21] This procedure reinforces the principle that municipalities are an integral part of the federation in a way that is closer to the Brazilian than to the American model.

Although state constitutions can create institutions and procedures that are not regulated by the federal Constitution, they usually deal with matters of minor importance, such as simple administrative organization and some alternative legal ways of implementing federal regulations. That is, given the high degree to which state powers and structures are tailored to those contained in the federal Constitution, the state constitutions deal less with fundamentals than they do with issues of minor significance.

Article 2 of the Constitution, which prohibits slavery, was amended in 2001 to impart greater legal status to indigenous peoples, to protect their ways and customs, and to guarantee them access to development. However, the autonomy of indigenous peoples in governmental matters can be expressed only in municipal arenas or through institutions designed by the states in their fields of competence. Particularly, regarding the administration of justice, the application of indigenous customs to legal proceedings requires validation or agreement from the regular agencies or courts of the indigenous group's state government.

The Distribution of Powers

Mexico's Constitution (Art. 124) stipulates that all powers not expressly allocated to the federation are "reserved to the States." In turn, the Constitution guarantees a list of municipal powers in Sections II through V of Article 115 that the states cannot limit. However, frequent amendments to the Constitution over the years have resulted in a long list of powers being shifted to the federation, leaving the states' residual powers much diminished.[22]

The federal government, using formulas of alleged concurrency and cooperation provided for in the Constitution, has intervened in many policy fields that were originally state responsibilities. As a result, the states' autonomy in these fields of concurrency has been weakened and the federation's powers have been expanded. Nevertheless, to ensure equity in the distribution of powers, Article 73 of the Constitution lists both the powers reserved to the states and those concurrent powers shared by the states and the federation with respect to taxation, spending, public debt, social policy, economic development, education, health, the environment, labour relations, trade, human settlements, and public security, among others.

With regard to public security and the prosecution of crime, the statutory catalogue of federal crimes is lengthy. Currently, there is debate about whether it would be preferable for the states to pursue and prosecute criminals concurrently for such offences as drug trafficking. Preventive public security is the concurrent responsibility of the three orders of government, but the fiscal resources for this activity are concentrated in the federal government. Article 97 of the Constitution also grants the federal government the legal authority, known as the *facultad de atracción* (power of attraction), to bring under its own jurisdiction specific matters originally in the states' sphere of competence.

Although the federation wields greater power than do the states with respect to the implementation of constitutional powers, the following constitutional powers are listed in Article 73 as concurrent: taxation, education, health, preventive measures for public security, human settlements, economic and social planning and development, the environment and environmental protection, civil protection against natural disasters, and sports. In most of these matters, mechanisms for intergovernmental coordination, with representation from both the federal and state governments, as well as from municipal governments when appropriate, have been established by federal laws. However, the federation is often dominant, resulting in its subordination of, rather than its coordination with, the constituent states. This is the case, for instance, with the federation's implementation of both the *Sistema Nacional de Coordinación Fiscal* (National System of Fiscal Coordination) and the *Consejo Nacional de Seguridad Pública* (National Council for Public Security).

The constitutional basis for the supremacy of the federal government and for the privileging of the federal Constitution's rules is found in Article 133: The "Constitution, the laws of the Congress of the Union that emanate therefrom, and all treaties" made in accordance with the Constitution "shall be the supreme law of the whole Union." This inclusive article also requires state courts to comply with the Constitution and with federal treaties and laws regardless of any contradictory provisions that might exist in the constitutions or laws of the states. Indeed, the Supreme Court of Justice recently ruled that Mexico's federalist system functions according to a hierarchy of law.[23] The highest level of authority resides in the federal Constitution, followed by international treaties approved by a majority of the Senate, and then by the ordinary laws enacted by the Congress of the Union. This hierarchy gives a treaty greater standing than both the domestic laws of the federation and the laws of the states.

Intergovernmental Conflicts of Competence

The Constitution includes provisions for settling competency conflicts among the three orders of government. Article 105 provides for two methods of governmental litigation: *constitutional controversies* and *actions of unconstitutionality*.[24] In the first instance, litigation can be initiated by any federal, state, or municipal public body to challenge a law, act, or generally observed regulation of another order of government that, in the view of the challenger, violates the Constitution and thus violates a competence constitutionally assigned to the challenging government. Originally, constitutional controversies between orders of government were restricted exclusively to competency conflicts. However, in 1995 an amendment to Article 105 made it possible to initiate litigation respecting a conflict over any matter of constitutionality.

In the second instance (i.e., the case of actions of unconstitutionality), litigation can be initiated to challenge the constitutionality of laws and regulations of general observance, regardless of whether the perceived violation concerns an invasion of a field of competence. However, this right of litigation is intended for use by legislative minorities that disagree with a law approved by the majority of a federal or state legislative body. In this instance, litigation against federal laws or laws of the Federal District passed by the Congress of the Union can go forward with the approval of only 33 percent of the members of either chamber. In the case of challenges to treaties signed by Mexico, litigation can proceed with the approval of only 33 percent of the members of the Senate. Similarly, the approval of 33 percent of the members of either a state legislative body or the Assembly of Representatives of the Federal District is required in order to challenge a state law or a Federal District law. Finally, the *procurador general de la república* (attorney general of the republic) can independently table an action of unconstitutionality against any federal or state law, any law of the Federal District, and any treaty. Political parties can also initiate an action of unconstitutionality regarding an electoral law that they believe violates the Constitution.

These rights of litigation have been increasingly utilized with the advance of Mexico's democratic reforms and as the political-party system has become more pluralistic in both the federal and state governmental arenas. Mexico's transition into a more democratic polity began in the 1980s and continued up through the achievement, finally, of *political alternance* (political change) with the election of Vicente Fox to the federal presidency in 2000. If the institutions of constitutional controversy and actions of unconstitutionality had existed in previous decades, they would have had little effect because the country was governed by a single, hegemonic party able to control state and municipal governments as well as the Supreme Court.

Moreover, it is remarkable that since the restoration in the 1990s of the freedom and autonomy of the federal judicial branch and its highest agency, the Supreme Court of Justice, there has been a significant increase in the number and frequency of these types of controversies. At the same time, the Supreme Court has acted with greater judicial firmness, effectiveness, and rigor, in contrast to the decades when the judicial branch was subordinated to the enormous power of the president of the republic.[25]

FEDERALISM AND THE STRUCTURE AND OPERATION OF GOVERNMENT

The Constitution of Mexico declares that: "It is the will of the Mexican people to organize themselves into a federal, democratic, representative Republic."[26] Mexico has a presidential system, with the single leader of the federal executive branch being elected by popular vote. Given the Constitution's basis in the fundamental principle of the separation of powers, this person exercises only the executive power. Despite the system of checks and balances implicit in this division of powers and allocation of responsibilities, Article 80 of the Constitution refers to "the supreme executive power of the Union" because the president of the republic is both the head of government and the head of state – unlike, for example, the executive provision in the German Basic Law, which stipulates a head of state in the person of the president and a head of government in the person of the chancellor. Mexico's system can perhaps be explained by the history of its evolution from a colony into a nation and, of course, by the influence of the Constitution of the United States of America, which provides effectively for a singular executive.

The Allocation of Powers

The principle of the allocation of powers contained in the Constitution aims to define and limit the role of the president and to distribute, according to areas of expertise, the main governmental responsibilities. In Mexico, aside from the allocation of powers, there is a mechanism for checks and balances that involves what Mexicans call "collaboration between powers," which involves one branch of government participating in, or even integrating with, the activities of another branch of government or of autonomous state agencies. The most common case is the administration of justice in labour disputes, which is overseen by the executive branch instead of the judicial branch.

Federal Legislature

The powers of the federal legislature are divided among the following functions: legislation, control and enforcement, taxation, integration of other public agencies and powers, and matters related to extraordinary functions, such as admitting new states into the union, declaring war, preventing interstate trade restrictions, and granting a leave of absence to the president of the republic as well as designating the president's replacement on an interim, provisional, or substitute basis, to mention only a few.

Obviously, the main duty of the federal legislature is to pass bills. The matters on which it can legislate are included in Article 73 of the Constitution, and are, in general terms: currency, taxation, education, health, sports, weights and measures, natural-disaster response systems, public security, federal crimes, the environment, hydrocarbons, oceans, waters and shorelines, trade, energy, mining, the motion-picture industry, banking, federal justice, public administration, defence, and external relations, to mention only some.

The federal legislative branch is divided into two chambers, the Chamber of Deputies and the Senate, which work together in the process of drawing up legislation by means of *successive debate*[27] on proposals. That is, according to Article 72, a bill must be approved by both the Chamber of Deputies and the Senate. The law-making process can start in either chamber, with the exception of fiscal bills (i.e., taxes and annual budgets of expenditures), which must always start in the lower house (Chamber of Deputies). Each chamber also has some exclusive powers. For example, the Chamber of Deputies approves the federation's budget of expenditures and reviews public accounts (Art. 74); the Senate approves international treaties (Art. 76).[28]

Both chambers clearly represent the Mexican people more than they do the constituent jurisdictions. The Chamber of Deputies consists of 500 members, out of which 300 are elected every three years from districts within the states, the Federal District, and the territories. The other 200 deputies are elected by national partisan lists every three years. Although it has been claimed doctrinally that the members of the Senate represent the constituent states because each state and the Federal District has three senators (who serve six-year terms), there is no constitutional provision expressly stating that senators represent their states per territorial criteria. Also, in the Senate, there is a method for proportional representation of electoral minorities by which 32 of the total of 128 senators are elected through national partisan lists, while the remaining 96 senators are chosen by direct election state by state (3 per state).

State and local legislative bodies cannot veto federal laws and regulations because it is solely in the power of the federal executive to veto bills, with some exceptions. In turn, the federal legislature cannot veto state legislation. However, minorities in both legislatures can contest the constitutionality of federal or state laws before the Supreme Court through an action of unconstitutionality, as mentioned above, based on Section II of Article 105.

The Congress is limited, however, to meeting in ordinary sessions only from 15 February to 31 April and from 1 September to 31 December of each year. As a consequence, the Constitution provides for a Permanent Committee of 37 members composed of 19 deputies and 18 senators appointed by their respective chambers (see Art. 78). This Permanent Committee can give its consent to use of the National Guard; call one or both chambers of the Congress into extraordinary sessions; administer the oath of office for the president, members of the Supreme Court, and magistrates of the Federal District and territories; refer bills to committees for future action; grant a 30-day leave of absence to the president and appoint an interim president; and grant or deny approval of a wide range of appointments proposed by the president.

Federal Executive

The federal executive branch possesses substantial powers vested in a single individual, named the *Presidente de los Estados Unidos Mexicanos* (President of the United Mexican States), who serves a single six-year term. The president is elected directly by a national popular vote, and there is no provision for a direct, permanent substitute or vice president to replace him; so, if necessary, the Congress of the Union has the power under Articles 84 and 85 to appoint an interim, substitute, or provisional president, as the case may require.

The constituent states are not represented in the national executive branch; however, with regard to the president's public administration duties, there are constitutional provisions (Art. 73; Art. 115, Sec. III; and Art. 116, Sec. VII) for intergovernmental coordination and collaboration, for delegating powers, and for agencies of intergovernmental cooperation in which the states and municipalities effectively participate.

Federal Judicial Branch

The federal judiciary is represented by its highest body, the Supreme Court of Justice, which is composed of 11 ministers, each of whom is selected and appointed by the Senate from a short list of candidates proposed by the president. The ministers serve for 15 years and are entitled to a life pension thereafter. Pursuant to Article 100, the lower-court federal-circuit magistrates and district judges are appointed to six-year terms by the Supreme Court through its Judiciary Council. The powers of the judicial branch are bolstered by the autonomy the judiciary possesses to organize itself in accordance with a law passed by the Congress of the Union.

The federal courts decide all controversies arising from (1) laws or acts (federal, state, or local) that violate individual rights, (2) federal laws or acts that restrict or encroach on the sovereignty of the states, and (3) state laws or acts that "invade the sphere of federal authority" (Art. 103). The Supreme Court has exclusive jurisdiction in all controversies between states, between the powers (i.e., branches) of a state government over the constitutionality of each other's acts, and "between the Federation and one or more States" (Art. 105). The Court also settles "questions of jurisdiction that arise between courts of the Federation, between the latter and State courts, or between the courts of one State and those of another" (Art. 106). The federal courts also have jurisdiction over controversies involving federal law,[29] treaties, admiralty law, and members of the diplomatic and consular corps; controversies in which the federation is a party; and controversies between a state and any residents of another state.

The federal courts' basic duties are to dispense ordinary justice in disputes to which the federation is a party, to act as a tribunal for constitutional control through which the Court can invalidate a law of any order of government, and naturally, to resolve issues of legality and constitutionality through a mechanism called the *juicio de amparo* (writ of relief). The *juicio de amparo* is a broad writ that allows the federal courts to protect any kind of constitutional guarantee, not only liberty or life. Through the use of the *juicio de amparo*, any state or municipal matter becomes a federal matter. The purpose of the writ is to nullify constitutional violations and infringements of individual-rights guarantees caused by the creation and application of regulations by any order of government. The Supreme Court also has some extraordinary powers, such as investigating serious infringements of individual-rights guarantees or general violations of the public-election laws.[30]

Pursuant to Article 99, election disputes are resolved by a special tribunal, the *Tribunal Electoral del Poder Judicial de la Federación* (TRIFE/Electoral Tribunal of the Judicial Branch of the Federation). This tribunal reports to the Supreme Court but has great autonomy in carrying out its functions. However, many matters of administrative, fiscal, agrarian, and labour justice are handled by autonomous specialized courts dependent on the executive branch, such as the Agrarian Court, the Fiscal and Administrative Courts, and the labour tribunals. The Supreme Court also has jurisdiction over matters of administrative, fiscal, agrarian, and labour justice at their final stage through the *juicio de amparo* mentioned above. Nevertheless, the legislative and executive branches concur in the formation of these specialized courts insofar as the president appoints the magistrates, but according to Article 76, they must have the confirmation of either the Senate or, during recess, the Permanent Committee.

The Constitution does not recognize any other judicial jurisdiction than that of the federal and state courts. The federal courts are accountable to the Supreme Court and are known as *tribunales unitarios y colegiados de circuito* (full-circuit courts) and as *tribunales de primera instancia* (courts of first instance) in the case of first-district courts.

Each state has its own judicial branch consisting of a Superior Justice Tribunal (called the Supreme Tribunal of Justice in a few states), first-instance state courts, and minor courts staffed by judges named by each state's Superior Tribunal. The members of a state's Superior Tribunal are proposed by the state governor and confirmed by the state Congress. Although these superior state courts are the "last word" on criminal and civil matters under state law, their decisions can be reviewed by federal courts via a *juicio de amparo*. A jurisdiction distinct from the courts mentioned may be recognized only in cases involving either indigenous peoples or conventional systems of arbitration, but these procedures must be validated by their respective state courts according to Article 2.

Institutions of the Constituent Units

The constitutional organization of the constituent units is very similar to the national government's organization (see Title V). This is due to the centralist nature of the Constitution and its excessive regulation of subnational governments. For example, the Constitution limits state governors to a single six-year term. It also declares that "the Congress of the Union and the state legislatures shall immediately enact laws designed to combat alcoholism" (Art. 117, Part IX). Article 115 declares that for "their internal government, the States shall adopt the popular, representative, republican form of government, with the free Municipality as the basis of their territorial division and political and administrative organization." The states' governments are also constitutionally divided into executive, legislative, and judicial branches, and while they have independent courts that embody the state judicial power, the state courts are subject to the criteria of the federal courts through the rulings of the above-mentioned *juicio de amparo.*

It is relevant to mention that this centralist structure did not always exist in Mexico. Although during the twentieth century the states' structures were basically a mirror image of the federal government, with the design of their institutions being subordinated to federal influence, during the nineteenth century the states enjoyed considerably more autonomy, as reflected in their ability to create their own institutions.

The Constitution also prohibits the states from limiting commercial activity and trade with each other; specifically, the right to mobility of labour, capital, goods, and services is guaranteed under the principle of freedom of movement. Thus the constitutional limits on the states include stipulations against (1) making "any alliance, treaty or coalition with another State, or with foreign powers," (2) coining money, (3) issuing paper money or stamps, (4) taxing persons or goods that are passing through their territory, (5) prohibiting or taxing domestic or foreign goods that are entering or leaving their territory, (6) discriminating against out-of-state goods, (7) "levy[ing] duties on the production, storage, or sale of tobacco in a manner distinct from or with quotas greater than those authorized by the Congress of the Union," (8) establishing ship tonnage dues or any other port charges, (9) levying imposts or taxes on imports or exports, (10) possessing permanent troops or ships of war, and (11) making war themselves on any foreign power.

Relations among the Constituent States

Article 120 of the Constitution obligates the governor of each state to publish and enforce federal laws. Article 121 holds that each state must give "complete faith and credence" to the public acts, registries, and judicial proceedings of all the other states.[31] However, the laws of any one state have effect only in its own territory, whereas the rulings pronounced by the courts of one state on property rights and real goods have executive effect in the other states. Additionally, the civil acts – such as marriage, divorce, birth, adoption, and death certificates – of one state have validity in the other states, and professional and university degrees issued by the authorities of one state under its laws must be respected in the other states.[32]

In criminal matters, a state may ask for extradition of a criminal from another state as provided for by interstate agreements or with the intervention of the federal government under the *Sistema Nacional de Coordinación en Seguridad Pública* (System for National Coordination of Public Security), which exercises the power of apprehension. However, the alleged criminal is judged by the court of the state where the crime was committed, regardless of the origin of either the criminal or the victim. In the case of disputes between individuals concerning written transactions, the dispute usually comes under the jurisdiction of the state whose laws govern the contract or agreement of reference. In other cases, the competent court is determined by the location where the action occasioning the conflict occurred. However, in all laws for judicial proceedings, there are regulations to rule on which court is competent to hear a particular case.

The constituent units can make agreements among themselves but only on matters strictly within their competence. States also "have the power to fix their respective boundaries among themselves" (Art. 116), although such boundary agreements must be approved by the Congress. With regard to relations between the federal government and the states, formal agencies for coordination and communication are mandated in federal laws and, in some cases, by intergovernmental compacts. However, this type of agency is more often used in concurrent matters.

FISCAL AND MONETARY POWERS

Taxation

The federal, state, and municipal governments all have independent powers to levy taxes. However, some concurrency between the federal and state spheres is recognized by the Supreme Court,[33] which has held that while not all sources of taxation are concurrent, the main ones (i.e., income, sales, and special taxes on the production of such goods as gasoline, sugar, tobacco, beer, and tequila) are concurrent. Although concurrent taxation exists in general terms, the Constitution also imposes limits on the states' ability to tax foreign trade, hydrocarbons, energy resources, and banking, among others. In some cases, these revenue sources, such as the taxation of electricity and petroleum products, are reserved exclusively for the federal government.

Natural resources are understood to be the property of the whole nation and can be exploited only through federal concessions or authorization. However, a great part of the revenues from natural resources is shared with the state and municipal governments under the National System of Fiscal Coordination.

The tax powers of the three orders of government are limited by the principles of equity and proportionality of taxes and, obviously, the principle of legality – as provided in Article 31, Part IV, of the Constitution. Such authority is further limited by the requirement that levies must be sufficient enough to finance the public spending expressed in the budget, including the financial burden of servicing legally acquired debt. That is, the budgets of the federal, state, and local governments must be balanced by year's end. The major concurrent revenue sources are collected by the federal government, which, by law, must share these revenues with the states and municipalities. However, some areas of tax-revenue collection are coordinated between the three orders of government – for example, an income tax for low-income persons, known as the "regime of small taxpayers." According to Article 3B of the Fiscal Coordination Law, this tax is collected by the states and municipalities, which keep the revenues for themselves, although, in some cases, they pay a percentage to the federal government. Nevertheless, the most important taxes are collected by the federation. Real-property taxes (Art. 115, Sec. IV) are collected only by the municipalities, which may, as a means of support, make agreements with their states to have the latter administer the collection of these taxes in exchange for a share of the revenues collected.

One of the problems with the *Sistema Nacional de Coordinación Fiscal* is precisely that the Constitution does not provide for it. This system has resulted from the concurrency recognized by the Supreme Court of Justice. For this reason, the Congress of the Union passed a special law in 1978, called the *Ley de Coordinación Fiscal* (Fiscal Coordination Act), which has no inherent authority because it requires that the states subscribe to it through agreements authorized by the state legislatures. However, since the system was born, every state, including the Federal District, has subscribed to the agreements and kept them in force. In this way, subnational governments suspend their ability to levy certain taxes in exchange for a share of the funds, more or less equal to the revenues they would obtain if they imposed these various taxes themselves. This Fiscal Coordination Act provides the mechanisms and formulas by which the federal government distributes the respective shares owed to the states and municipalities.

It is also important to highlight how taxes are collected by states and municipalities. For example, people who live in one state but work in another state pay taxes on their income in the state where they work or where their employer is located. But, for example, real-property taxes are paid entirely where one's house or property is located.

Borrowing

The three orders of government are permitted to acquire debt, but this must be done through procedures established in federal or state law, as the case may be, and with the approval of the respective legislature. In the case of municipalities, indebtedness is also approved by the state legislature. State and municipal governments in their turn are limited by the principle that public debt may be incurred only to fund what the Constitution calls productive public investments, namely "the construction of works intended to produce directly an increase in their revenues."[34] However, this principle is not always followed in practice because borrowing is authorized even to fund deficits in current spending.

In Mexico, the state and local governments cannot incur debt to foreigners or in foreign currency, except through the federal government. In recent years, states and municipalities have been issuing bonds for the first time through the national private stock market, something that had not been done for decades because the sole source of financing was the National Development Bank, private banks, or co-investment with the private sector. Although credits from international banks have been channelled to subnational governments under Section VIII of Article 117, these credits are funnelled first through the National Development Bank.

Furthermore, the federal government has been building a public policy for the reduction of borrowing levels. This policy insists on not financing more than 0.5 percent, in terms of the gross domestic product, of the annual spending budget. There is no constitutional guideline that limits the budgetary debts of the state and local governments or establishes a balance point, but some state legislatures have enacted such guidelines. In addition, the public credit market acts as a constraint because investors are reluctant to grant loans to a government that exceeds manageable levels of debt.

As a result of recurring economic crises, such as the financial crisis of 1995 and excessive borrowing during recent decades, state and local governments have not been able to pay all their debts, and the federal government has implemented diverse support programs for debt restructuring.[35] However, the Constitution does not oblige the federation to take such rescue measures; consequently, any bail-out support is regarded as a temporary, ad hoc public policy.

Distribution of Tax Revenues

The *Sistema Nacional de Coordinación Fiscal,* under which federal resources are distributed to the state and local governments, is not a feature of the Constitution. However, even if this conventional system did not exist, Article 73, Part XXIX, of the Constitution does establish that the federal government shall share with the states, and the states shall share with the municipalities, revenues (in proportions not stated in the Constitution) from the *contribuciones especiales* (i.e., special taxes) that the federal government levies on some of its exclusive sources of revenue, such as electrical energy, tobacco products, gasoline and other products derived from petroleum, matches, maguey and its fermented products, forestry exploitation, and the production and consumption of beer.

In addition to the above mechanisms for distributing tax revenues, the Fiscal Coordination Act was approved in 1978 and came into force in 1980. Since then, changes have been made to increase the amounts and broaden the concepts of federal revenue to be shared with the states and municipalities. Changes have also been made to the formulas determining the share of tax revenue to be received by each state and municipality. Today states and municipalities receive about 26 percent of the *Recaudación Federal Participable* (RFP), or federal tax revenue subject to sharing. Not all federal revenue is subject to sharing, as the RFP represents only 60 percent of the federal government's total revenue.

From another perspective, an average of 94 percent of all states' revenues came from the federal government in the form of transfers in 2003, while federal transfers to the municipalities represented from 50 percent to 98 percent of all municipal revenues, depending on the size and performance of each municipality. This shows the huge dependence of subnational governments on federal-government revenue transfers.

Spending

Constitutionally, the federal executive branch's spending power is limited to those areas strictly authorized in the federal spending budget, which must be approved by the Chamber of Deputies.[36] Furthermore, many kinds of spending have been predetermined by legal or conventional obligations; thus only 13 percent of the annual federal spending budget is actually available in the programmable budget (*presupuesto programmable*) for use by the executive branch. The programmable budget permits adjustments to the objects and levels of spending (e.g., for new road construction and new equipment), while the remainder of the budget (non-programmable) is already committed, its uses often being designated by law or contracts (e.g., with respect to salaries for preexisting payrolls and financial service on debt). Similarly, neither the executive branch nor the Chamber of Deputies can approve federal spending that is not related to their essential duties; doing so would be unconstitutional.

The state and municipal governments have full autonomy to spend their own revenues, this authority being limited only by the decrees established by state legislatures or municipal councils and, of course, by the requirement that expenditures be related to their essential duties and powers. They are equally free to spend, as their own, their shares of the federal resources transferred through the *participaciones* (revenue shares).

State and municipal governments also have access to other types of transfers, such as *aportaciones federales* (federal contributions). These are grants-in-aid and represent larger amounts than those received through revenue shares of federal taxation, the *participaciones*. Federal contributions account for 34 percent of the RFP[37] compared to 26 percent of the RFP accounted for by the revenue shares. These federal contributions are not established in the Constitution. They are simply a legal mechanism recently added to the Fiscal Coordination Act, but their nature is different from the "revenue shares." The fundamental difference is that the contributions may or may not exist depending on what is decided by the Congress of the Union. Moreover, the state and municipal governments are subject to conditions and requirements established in the same law for expending these federal contributions, unlike the total autonomy with which they expend the "revenue shares."

Finally, the states and municipalities are subject to transfer mechanisms called spending reallocations or subsidy programs. Through these mechanisms, the federal government distributes predetermined resources among state and municipal governments for specific purposes, which are stipulated in intergovernmental agreements.

FOREIGN AFFAIRS AND DEFENCE POWERS

In principle, the Constitution entrusts external relations and defence to the federal government. The federal Congress has the power to legislate on such matters as nationality, foreigners, emigration and immigration, organization of the diplomatic service, and treaties. In the latter case, the *Ley sobre Tratados Internacionales* (International Treaties Act) alone regulates the procedure for creating treaties; however, treaties are signed only by the federal executive, with their ratification being the prerogative of the Senate. Under Article 89 of the Constitution, however, it is the president of the republic who directs external policy. High-level diplomats are appointed by the federal executive branch with the approval of the Senate.

With respect to defence, the president of the republic is the commander in chief of the armed forces, which include the army, navy, and air force. The president has the power to declare war on behalf of Mexico pursuant to a prior special law approved by the Congress of the Union.

Article 117 of the Constitution prohibits the participation of the states in alliances, treaties, or coalitions with foreign powers. However, Article 119 establishes the obligation of the federal government to protect the states from any invasion or violence emanating from outside the country and, in the case of internal revolt or disturbances, to provide adequate military or police protection when requested by any state legislature or governor.

Despite the above, with regard to foreign relations, the states and the municipalities can make agreements and engage in exchanges with foreign governments or international agencies. This kind of activity is regulated by the *Ley para la Celebración de Tratados* (Treaties Act), which establishes the ability of states, municipalities, and public agencies to make what are called *acuerdos interinstitucionales* (inter-institutional agreements). These agreements must pertain solely to exchanges of technical, educational, cultural, or developmental support, to commercial transactions, to promotion of investments, or to other affairs within the jurisdiction of a state or municipality. These agreements must never have the nature of a law or legal regulation in Mexico. Moreover, under the Treaties Act, prior to the signing of this type of agreement, a *dictamen de no inconveniencia* (ruling of no impropriety) must be obtained from the federal *Secretaría de Relaciones Exteriores* (Secretariat of External Relations). Using this regulatory procedure, state and municipal authorities frequently tour abroad to promote relations with other countries, including establishing representative offices. At all times, however, they are regulated by the principle that none of these relations can compromise the country or its sovereignty.

Under the Constitution, the constituent polities cannot form any type of army. They can establish only police forces that provide public security to their inhabitants or investigate crimes that fall within state jurisdiction. The Constitution does not provide for advisory bodies in which state or local governments are represented in intergovernmental consultation about external relations or defence; however, when dealing with certain international-treaty proposals, the federal government has at times directly consulted with the states and municipalities, depending on the issue.

In Mexico, the North American Free Trade Agreement (NAFTA) has had both favourable and unfavourable impacts on a number of commercial sectors of state and local governments. However, NAFTA has not been a factor in creating or eliminating the powers of the subnational governments because trade matters are under federal jurisdiction (Art. 73, Part X). Mexico's participation in international organizations, as a member or associate, also comes under the powers of the federal executive branch according to the same procedure used for making international treaties.

CITIZENSHIP

Mexico's Constitution clearly distinguishes the concept of nationality (Art. 30) from the concept of citizenship (Art. 34). Mexican nationals are individuals who were born in the territory of the republic or who were born in a foreign country but are the children either of a Mexican father or mother born in Mexico or of a naturalized Mexican father or mother. Mexican civilian or military vessels or aircraft are considered to be Mexican territory as well. Foreign nationals who obtain a naturalization card in accordance with the law also have Mexican nationality. Article 31 of the Constitution obligates Mexicans to (1) see that their children or wards under age 15 attend school, (2) receive civic and military instruction on days and hours specified by their *ayuntamientos* (i.e., municipal councils), (3) enlist and serve in the National Guard, and (4) "contribute to the public expenditures of the Federation, and the State and Municipality in which they reside, in the proportional and equitable manner provided by law."

Apart from Mexican nationality,[38] to be a citizen, an individual must be 18 years of age and have an honest means of earning a living. Citizens have the constitutional rights to vote in elections, to stand for election to any public office or be appointed to any other public employment, to "associate together to discuss the political affairs of the country," to "bear arms in the Army or National Guard," and to "exercise in all cases the right of petition" (Art. 35). Citizens are constitutionally obligated to register on the tax lists of their municipalities and electoral poll-books, to enlist in the National Guard, to vote in popular elections, to serve in federal or state elective offices, to "serve in municipal council positions," and to "fulfill electoral and jury functions."

The Mexican Constitution, unlike the US Constitution, does not explicitly recognize dual (i.e., federal and state) citizenship. However, in the matter of citizenship, the state constitutions may add requirements for being a citizen of a particular state, especially with respect to the exercise of political rights. For example, in some states, a person must have been born in the state to become its governor. This means that a citizen of any state is a Mexican citizen, but to exercise certain rights or enjoy certain public privileges in a state, there may be additional requirements. This does not mean that there are two types of citizenship in Mexico, only that there are certain circumstances governing the exercise of some rights in the state and municipal spheres.

In other words, Mexican nationality can be acquired through the principles of both *jus soli* and *jus sanguinis*, but the right to citizenship is more strongly linked to *jus soli*, especially with regard to citizenship rights in the subnational spheres.

ELECTIONS, VOTING, AND POLITICAL PARTIES

The Constitution establishes important principles regarding political rights. The executive and legislative authorities in the three orders of government must be elected by free, secret, universal votes. Also, Article 41 defines political parties as institutions of public interest. Only Mexican citizens can vote. They must be 18 years old and of sound mind, and they cannot be serving a sentence for any crime, in which case their rights are suspended. By comparison, the right to vote cannot be denied or suspended for any religious, ethnic, gender, or political reason.

The Constitution created an autonomous public body called the *Instituto Federal Electoral* (IFE/Federal Electoral Institute), in which the Congress of the Union, the national political parties, and citizens participate. The IFE's operations are regulated by the principles of assurance, legality, independence, impartiality, and objectivity. The special electoral court, the *Tribunal Electoral del Poder Judicial de la Federación*, also rules on electoral matters and citizens' political rights.

The state governments likewise have autonomous organizations equivalent to the federal IFE that are responsible for organizing elections and for registering state or municipal candidates, who are elected by popular vote. To this end, the states also have courts of first instance for electoral matters. Dealing with voter registration in subnational governments, official identification documents, and elector credentials can be done autonomously by the states or with the support of the IFE, including the organization of elections through agreements with the IFE.

Although states and municipalities are granted autonomy with respect to elections, legal review of these elections may go to the federal tribunal mentioned above. Through a ruling of constitutional review, the tribunal assures that the democratic principles contained mainly in Article 41 are fully respected by state and local officials.

PROTECTION OF INDIVIDUAL AND COLLECTIVE RIGHTS

The Constitution sets out a series of rights known as *garantías individuales* (individual guarantees) while also listing important collective and social rights. Included in the first category are the rights to equality before the law, equality between men and women, and equality to own property as well as the rights to liberty, freedom of movement, freedom of association, freedom of religious worship, lawful trade, legality, defence before the courts, and a speedy and expeditious delivery of justice. The rights to vote and to stand for election are included in the category of political rights, conditional only upon citizenship criteria and the requirement that one's rights have not been suspended (e.g., subsequent to a criminal conviction).

With respect to social rights, the Constitution protects the rights to employment, education, housing, farming, health care, and a safe environment; children's rights; and the communal rights of indigenous peoples and their communities.

Because international treaties are also part of the Constitution and because Mexico is a signatory of the United Nations Universal Declaration of

Human Rights, all the rights established by this declaration must be protected in Mexico. In general, when rights are expressly established in the Constitution as well as in the Universal Declaration of Human Rights, they become mandatory and must be enforced by the state and local governments and, of course, by the federal government.

Indigenous peoples are the only group of ethnically defined individuals granted special status by the Constitution, which guarantees them the right to self-determination in the interest of preserving their culture, religion, and language. Apart from this right, indigenous groups commonly exercise their right to freedom of association through various forms of social organization. Three important examples are labour unions; the *ejido* (common land), which represents a means of organizing agrarian land ownership; and churches or religious associations.

Individual guarantees and human rights apply to any person in Mexico's territory; therefore, enjoyment of these rights does not necessarily require a person to be a citizen or a person of Mexican nationality. However, only Mexican citizens are entitled to certain social and political rights, such as the right to vote, to housing, and to education.

As previously indicated, the states are obliged not only to protect these rights, but also to incorporate them, in some form, into their own constitutions.[39] The fundamental protection of rights is achieved through three mechanisms: jurisdictional protection of persons through the law of *juicio de amparo* (roughly, *habeas corpus* in many such cases); the extended control of the Constitution, which mandates any public authority or power to directly implement the Constitution and the rights that it protects, even when a law contravenes it; and the role of the ombudsman,[40] or human-rights official, who is charged with vigilantly monitoring the conduct of the authorities but who has the power only to make recommendations based on "*auctoritas*," the moral and public authority held by the head of the human-rights protection agency.

In Mexico, the federal duty to protect human rights resides with the National Human Rights Commission, as provided by the Constitution (Art. 102, Part B). The states may create similar autonomous bodies functioning in the same manner as the national body in order to make recommendations about the best way to protect human rights and to investigate and remedy violations of these rights.[41] All 31 states and the Federal District now have such a body.

CHANGES TO THE CONSTITUTION

Over time the Constitution has evolved with respect to many matters, such as human rights and the division of powers, but it has generally retreated from federalism, moving instead toward centralization. For instance, the Constitution was amended 415 times between 1917 and August 2004;[42] Article 73 (federal Congress powers) was amended 47 times, Article 123 (national labour regime) 21 times, and Article 27 (land-property regime) 16 times. Almost half of these reforms were aimed at "strengthening" the federal government and thus, given the nature of Mexico's presidential system, also at increasing the federal executive power. Although the municipalities have experienced an evolution toward decentralization during the past 20 years,[43] the states, in contrast, have suffered a deep reduction of their autonomy.

The weaknesses of the federal system in Mexico are due not so much to an absence of an appropriate constitutional design as to the historical indifference of presidents, governors, and politicians to observing the federal pact. One consequence of this indifference is that states and municipalities are now fiscally dependent upon the federal government, an arrangement that has rendered nonexistent many aspects of their autonomy. To address this problem, Mexico started a process at the beginning of 2004 called the "National Convention for Public Finance," which aims to reach a new fiscal pact that will give more powers, resources, and autonomy to states and municipalities.

It is a principle in Mexico that the people shall have the right, at all times, to alter or modify their form of government and that national sovereignty shall be understood as essentially residing in and originating with the people.[44] To this end, the people are represented in the Permanent Constituent Congress (Art. 135), which carries out the procedure for modifying any article of the Constitution. Article 135 establishes that the Constitution may be amended, or added to, by a vote of approval from two-thirds of the members present in each chamber of the Congress of the Union. For this vote to be valid, at least half plus one of the total members of each chamber must be present. The next step is to obtain a "yes" vote from 50 percent plus one of the state legislatures. This is the means for changing any article of the Constitution, without exception.

The dominant political regime in the twentieth century was extremely active in constitutional reform, making exactly 400 amendments between 1917 and the year 2000.[45] Today, the system of checks and balances characterizing Mexico's democratic transition away from one-party rule means that possibilities for constitutional amendment arise less frequently and that the pace is somewhat slower. Thus only 15 reforms were enacted from late 2000 to August 2004. However, unlike past reforms, which served the purposes of specific public policies or particular styles of government, there are now plans to reform the Constitution with regard to its fundamental institutions. This effort is referred to as the *Reforma del Estado* (state reform) and has the aim of modernizing the Constitution and its fundamental institutions. This objective has been embraced to such an extent that some sectors are now even proposing that a completely new constitution be written.

In either case, one of the central themes of the *Reforma del Estado* is reform of the federal system. Therefore, different political players have advocated the redesign of the federal agreement along the following lines in order to solve a number of perceived problems:

1 Limiting, perhaps substantially, the powers of the president of the republic with respect to the counterbalancing powers of the legislative and judicial branches
2 Strengthening the notion of Mexico as a federal republic by more clearly specifying the three orders of government: federal, state, and municipal
3 Allowing the states and municipalities to recover major and minor taxation powers as sources of revenue
4 Increasing the amounts of federal transfers to the states and municipalities
5 Redefining federal, state, and municipal responsibilities by listing them in the Constitution, with a residual clause outlining that the responsibilities not provided for and not expressly attributed to the federation or the municipalities are under direct control of the states
6 Limiting the system of concurrent actions to what is strictly necessary.

However, at the same time, proponents of these possibilities for redefining Mexico's federal model face opponents who wish only to limit the centralized power of the president of the republic by transferring some executive functions to the federal legislative branch. That is, there are those who think that it is sufficient to remove power from the president but otherwise keep it within the federal purview through the Congress of the Union. Thus over the decades various reforms and initiatives have limited the president's power without necessarily giving more power to the states; instead, the federal government has retained its regulatory, quasi-executive powers in the legislative branch.

The above-mentioned trend is observed in the growing number of proposals to amend Article 73 of the Constitution, each of which has sought to invest more legislative duties in the federal Congress, leaving very few such duties to the state legislatures. This is exemplified in amendments enacted in the early 1990s that made matters of education, health, public security, the environment, sports, and civil protection, in addition to the historically concurrent fiscal powers, shared competences of the federal Congress and the state legislatures.

Mexico is thus debating whether to redefine the list of functions for each order of government with a residual clause in favour of the states, leaving a minor margin for concurrent actions, or to pursue another model that simply limits the federal executive's power but still concentrates great power in the federal legislative branch. This latter option would open the way for more concurrent federal powers and actions, with the almost certain risk that clear differentiations between the functions of federal and state governments would be eroded in the name of concurrency and coordination, which would effectively rebound to the benefit of federal power over the states.

NOTES

1 At the time of this writing, no English translation was available of the complete, fully amended Mexican Constitution. An English translation readily available on the Internet was not complete.

2 See also David Merchant and Paul Rich, "Prospects for Mexican Federalism: Roots of the Policy Issues," *Policy Studies Journal* 31 (Fall 2003): 661–67; Paz Consuelo Márquez-Padilla and Julián Castro Rea, eds, *El Nuevo Federalismo en América del Norte* (Mexico City: Centro de Investigaciones sobre América del Norte, Universidad Nacional Autónoma de México, 2000); Peter M. Ward and Victoria E. Rodríguez, with Enrique Cabrero Mendoza, *New Federalism and State Government in Mexico: Bringing the States Back In* (Austin: Lyndon B. Johnson School of Public Affairs, University of Texas at Austin, 1999); Victoria E. Rodríguez, "Recasting Federalism in Mexico," *Publius: The Journal of Federalism* 28 (Winter 1998): 235–54; Alicia Hernández Chávez, ed., *Hacia un nuevo federalismo?* (Mexico City: Fondo de Cultura Económica, El Colegio de México, 1996); and Carlos Fuentes, *A New Time for México* (New York: Farrar, Straus and Giroux, 1996).

3 Conapo (National Population Council).

4 Secretaría de Educación (Public Education Secretariat), Mexico.

5 Banco de México, or Banxico (Mexico's central bank).

6 Arguably, the Constitution of Cadiz was as much Mexican as it was Spanish because many American deputies contributed to its creation. Among the institutions adopted under this influence was the *Diputaciones Provinciales,* a result of the recommendations of Miguel Ramos Arizpe (Mexican), representative of the *provincias internas de oriente* (western internal provinces). See also Nettie Lee Benson, "Spain's Contribution to Federalism in México," *Essays in Mexican History,* ed. Thomas Cotner and Carlos Castaneda (Austin: Institute of Latin American Studies, University of Texas, 1958), pp. 90–103.

7 Both federal and state secondary legislation reflect their origins in Roman law (i.e., the code of commerce, which is within the federal government's purview, and the states' civil-rights codes).

8 This idea came directly from the federal Constitution of 1857.

9 There was a fundamental change in concepts between the 1857 and 1917 constitutions. The 1857 phrase *derechos del hombre* (rights of man) was changed to *garantías individuales* (individual guarantees) in 1917 precisely to guarantee judicial means of protecting human rights, thanks to the theory of the French

intellectual Pierre Claude Francois Daunou (1761–1840), who was very popular in late-nineteenth-century Mexico.

10 The *órganos autónomos del estado* (autonomous state agencies) are public entities created by the Constitution. Although traditional powers concur in their formation (mainly the executive and legislative branches), the Constitution grants them autonomy to exist and function independently from the executive and legislative branches of the federal government. Thus in Mexico there are such autonomous constitutional agencies as the *Banco de México,* under Article 28 of the Constitution; the *Instituto Federal Electoral* (Federal Electoral Institute); the IFE, under Article 41; and the *Comisión Nacional de Derechos Humanos* (CNDH/ National Commission for Human Rights), under Article 102, Part B.

11 Manuel González Oropeza, *El Federalismo* (Federal District, Mexico: Editorial Porrúa, 1995).

12 Mexico established diplomatic relations with the Vatican in September 1992.

13 According to the Supreme Court's recent interpretation of Article 115, "The municipalities are constituents of the States and therefore of the Federation," as pronounced in Constitutional Controversy 6/95 "*Tijuana v. Presidencia de la Republica y otros,*" 1995.

14 The constitutional provisions of the constituent units are regulated primarily by Articles 40, 41, 115, and 116. See also Wayne A. Cornelius, Todd A. Eisenstadt, and Jane Hindley, eds, *Subnational Politics and Democratization in Mexico* (La Jolla: Center for US-Mexican Studies, University of California, San Diego, 1999).

15 But see, for example, Debora Montesinos, "Northern Bosses Consider Breakaway," *México City Times,* 10 September 1996, p. 1.

16 On 18 July 2001, final approval was given for constitutional reform of Articles 1, 2, 4, and 115, which include the rights of indigenous peoples and communities, as published in the *Diario Oficial de la Federación,* 14 August 2001.

17 Juan Marcos Gutiérrez González and Loza Salvador Santana, *Articulo 115 Constitucional: Historia y reformas de 1999* (Mexico: Ed. INDETEC, 2002), pp. 251–60.

18 See Article 105 and Sections II, III, IV, and V of Article 115 of the Constitution of Mexico.

19 See also Quintana Roldán Carlos, *Derecho Municipal,* 6th ed. (Federal District, Mexico: Editorial Porrúa, 2002).

20 As effected in 1983 through reform of Article 115 of the Constitution and in 1991 through another significant reform, mentioned above.

21 Mexico adopted the Spanish word *ayuntamiento* to designate the corporation that governs a municipality; such corporations are equivalent to municipal councils in other countries. *Ayuntamientos* include a municipal president or mayor and a varying number of aldermen or councillors, depending on the municipality's population size.

22 To this end, during the twentieth century, the dominant political party made a great many reforms to Article 73 of the Constitution, in which the powers of the federal legislative branch are established.

23 *Jurisprudencia* no. 77, 1999, approved 28 October 1999, by Mexico's Supreme Court, published in *"Semanario Judicial de la Federación y su Gaceta, tomo X, Noviembre 1999."*

24 See Article 105 of the Constitution, which gives rise to a special regulatory law that governs proceedings in these types of cases.

25 Jorge Vargas, "The Rebirth of the Supreme Court of Mexico: An Appraisal of President Zedillo's Judicial Reform," *American University Journal of International Law and Policy* 11 (Spring 1995): 295–341; Michael Taylor, "Why Do Rule of Law in México? Explaining the Weaknesses of Mexico's Judicial Branch," *New Mexico Law Review* 27 (Winter 1997): 141–66.

26 See Article 40 of the Constitution.

27 Bicameral discussion for approval of bills or decrees is provided for in Article 72 of the Constitution.

28 Compare the United States Constitution, which requires revenue bills to originate in the House of Representatives and treaties to be ratified by the Senate.

29 However, under Article 104: "Whenever such controversies affect only the interests of private parties, the regular local judges and courts of the States, or the Federal District and Territories may also assume jurisdiction, at the election of the plaintiff."

30 See Article 97 of the Constitution.

31 Compare Article IV, Section 1, of the Constitution of the United States of America.

32 However, in contrast to the United States, where legalization of homosexual marriages in one state might require recognition in other states, Article 4 of the Mexican Constitution stipulates that marriage may occur only between a man and a woman.

33 The federal Constitution does not provide for delimitation of the federal and state powers to establish taxation but follows a complex system, the basic premises of which are (1) concurrent taxation by the federation and the states in the majority of revenue sources (Arts 73, Part VII, and 124); (2) limitations on the levying powers of the states by expressly and concretely reserving designated matters to the federation (Art. 73, Parts X and XXIX); and (3) express restrictions on the states' levying powers (Arts 117, Parts IV–VII, and 118). See 310/953/2°, *Construcciones Alpha Sociedad Anónima y coagraviados,* 27 August 1954, *Jurisprudencia, Quinta Época,* Appendix to vol. 118, p. 1026.

34 See Article 117 of the Constitution. In other countries, these might be called capital investments.

35 The most recent support program was implemented in 1995 due to the financial crisis of that year.

36 The power to approve the spending budget is not bicameral; it is an exclusive power of the Chamber of Deputies under Article 74 of the Constitution.

37 The *Recaudación Federal Participable* (RFP) is defined in Article 2 of the *Ley de Coordinación Fiscal* (Fiscal Coordination Act) as all federal taxes, less refunds owed

to those who paid these taxes, as well as (1) additional taxes and additional or extraordinary rights for petroleum and (2) direct contributions and incentives paid to the subnational governments for their administrative collaboration respecting federal contributions.

38 Article 37 of the Constitution establishes the possibility of Mexicans having dual nationality once certain requirements of the regulatory law have been fulfilled.

39 See also Caroline Beer and Neil J. Mitchell, "Democracy and Human Rights in the Mexican States: Elections or Social Capital?" *International Studies Quarterly* 48 (June 2004): 293–312.

40 The Swedish word *ombudsman* is the generic term used in many countries to refer to the representative, commissioned or mandated by the government, to hear complaints regarding violations of human rights and, with distinct differences in each country, usually to make recommendations to the other authorities on how to proceed.

41 The first state to have such a body was Guerrero.

42 Source: *Subdirección de control e información legislativa, Congreso de la Unión.*

43 Municipal government enhanced its autonomy through the reforms to Article 115 in 1983 and 1999.

44 See Article 39 of the Constitution.

45 Source: *Subdirección de control e información legislativa, Congreso de la Unión.*

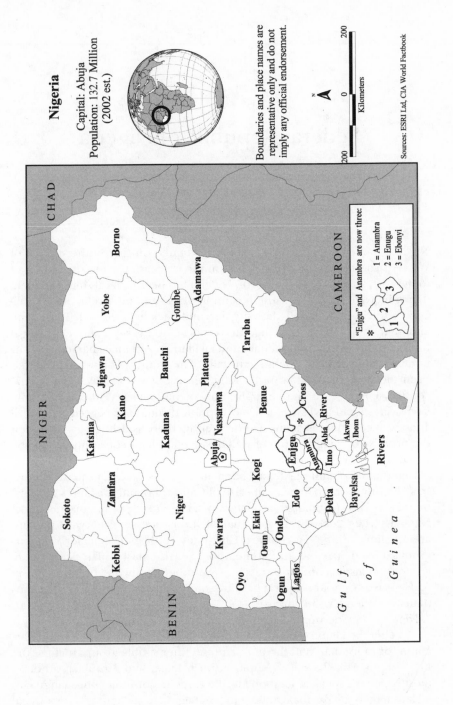

Nigeria

Capital: Abuja
Population: 132.7 Million
(2002 est.)

Boundaries and place names are
representative only and do not
imply any official endorsement.

200   0   200

Kilometers

Sources: ESRI Ltd, CIA World Factbook

"Enjgu" and Anambra are now three:

1 = Anambra
2 = Enugu
3 = Ebonyi

Federal Republic of Nigeria

IGNATIUS AKAAYAR AYUA AND

DAKAS C.J. DAKAS

Nigeria, named after the River Niger, is situated on the southern coast of West Africa. It shares borders with Benin to the west, Cameroon and Chad to the east, and Niger to the north. Nigeria has been federal since independence in 1960 mainly because it is multiethnic and multireligious, yet Nigeria's territorially based diversity also militates against both federalism and democracy by producing, in response to divisive and centrifugal forces, highly centralized military and civilian governance characterized by undemocratic or weakly democratic rule. The country's oil wealth, too, has been more of a curse than a blessing because it has aggravated regional conflict, encouraged the centralization of national revenue, and stimulated widespread and systematic corruption throughout Nigeria's political and socio-economic systems. Consequently, there is a huge gap between the promise of Nigeria's rather well-designed federal constitution and the practice of Nigeria's federal democracy.

Nigeria, the "Giant of Africa," has a land area of 923,733 square kilometres (slightly more than twice the size of California) and the largest population in Africa (estimated at between 120 and 133 million people).[1] Nigeria's 1963 census reported that of the nation's citizenry 48 percent are Muslims and 34 percent are Christians (with many smaller religious groups mixed in), but the contemporary Muslim-Christian ratio is unknown and also a contentious issue. Given that nearly one out of every six Africans is a Nigerian, Nigeria has both more Christians and more Muslims than any other African country.

Nigeria is made up of more than 250 ethnic groups,[2] the three major ones being the Hausa/Fulani, the Igbo, and the Yoruba, which together account for more than half the population. Other sizable groups include the Edo, Ibibio/Efik, Ijaw, Tiv, Nupe, Kanuri, Igala, and Urhobo. Although most Nigerians speak at least one of the three major indigenous languages – Hausa, Igbo, or Yoruba – some 250 languages are spoken, and the official language, a colonial inheritance, is English. The predominantly Muslim Hausa/Fulani mostly inhabit the Northwest. The predominantly Christian Igbo, who are arguably the most mobile ethnic group (owing partly to their commercial dexterity), mostly inhabit the Southeast. The Yoruba are, religiously, a mixed group and live mostly in the Southwest. However, almost a century of living under one rule has dispersed people of all ethnic and religious groups throughout all parts of Nigeria. While this dispersion has reduced the country's traditional divide between the Muslim North and Christian South, it has also produced interreligious and interethnic violence in some parts of Nigeria, such as Kano in the North, resulting in more than 10,000 deaths in recent years.

THE FEDERAL CONSTITUTION IN HISTORICAL-CULTURAL CONTEXT

One can speak of four periods of modern Nigerian history: colonial, early democratic, military, and contemporary democratic.

Constitution Making During the Colonial Era

The creation of Nigeria's federation is rooted in the country's colonial history. Before the Europeans' arrival, there was no political entity known as Nigeria. Precolonial Nigeria consisted of a bewildering variety of communities and entities of varying sizes, levels of political and social development, and degrees of independence and autonomy.[3] Sometimes, and in some places, powerful entities, such as the Benin Kingdom, the Kwararafa, Kanem-Borno, the Hausa states, the Sokoto Caliphate, and the Oyo Empire, brought their neighbours as well as distant groups under their nominal jurisdiction, but at no time before the British arrived was Nigeria even loosely ruled by one government. At all times, many groups of various sizes, such as the Tivs of the Middle Belt, the Ijaws of the Niger Delta, the hundreds of autonomous Igbo communities, and many lesser-known peoples maintained a separate and self-sufficient status.

British colonization began officially in 1861 with the establishment of the Colony of Lagos. British encroachments continued northward from the coast in imperialist competition for territory, particularly with the French. This process concluded with Britain's 1900 declaration of its Protectorate of Northern Nigeria in addition to that of Southern Nigeria. Since then, Nigeria's boundaries have not changed, except that the Northern Region was augmented after the First World War by accessions from the ex-German Cameroons.[4] The Protectorates of Northern and Southern Nigeria and the Colony of Lagos were amalgamated under a single British administration in 1914, and from then until 1954, Nigeria was formally governed as a unitary state.[5]

Thus Nigeria was created not by a voluntary union of previously existing, closely related, and freely contracting political units but by the imposition of union by an imperial power on an artificially demarcated territory containing a heterogeneous population of strangers. Although these strangers had established many economic, social, and political links among themselves long before British rule, they did not recognize themselves as one people or as one political community. In the context of the emergence of the Nigerian federation, the absence of an enabling environment for a credible negotiation of federal-state relations in part accounts for why Nigeria's federal system tilts in favour of the federal government.

The British did introduce a truncated version of English law as the basic law of Nigeria, but they allowed the indigenous peoples to be governed mostly by their own customary laws and interfered little in the day-to-day workings of Nigeria's subunits and communities. The British also embarked on state building, but in doing so, they treated the North and South differently. In 1923, for example, Britain created an Advisory Legislative Council to advise the governor in the South, but such a body was denied to the North. In 1939 Britain divided the Southern Region into the Western and Eastern provinces. This differential treatment was perhaps in recognition of the diversities of language, culture, and religion in Nigeria, the contrasting political communities and economies of the North and South, and the size of the territory, but by adopting this method of administration, the British implicitly conceded to federalism as a mode of governing Nigeria and to asymmetric differences in regional policies.

Although formally governed as a unitary state for 40 years, Nigeria came to be composed of three distinct administrative regions: the Western Region, dominated by the Yorubas; the Eastern Region, dominated by the Igbos; and the vast Northern Region, dominated by the Hausa/Fulani ruling class of the ex-Sokoto Caliphate. During the late colonial period, moreover, the British gave Nigerians more access to legislative and executive authority. The Richards Constitution of 1946 provided for a Legislative Council representing the whole country and also for Northern, Western, and Eastern councils. This creeping federalism was reinforced by the Macpherson Constitution of 1951, which made the three regions more autonomous. When Nigeria was converted into a federation under the so-called Lyttleton Constitution of 1954, these three regions were the federating units, with the ex-Colony of Lagos becoming the Federal Capital Territory. Although the Lyttleton Constitution was not replaced before independence, it was often amended, most notably in 1959 by the insertion of a full bill of Fundamental Human Rights based largely on the European Convention on Human Rights of 1950.[6]

During the last three colonial years, efforts were made to constitute a cabinet to bring the three regions into a nascent national government through a coalition of the three main political parties: the Northern Peoples Congress (NPC), the National Council of Nigeria and the Cameroons (NCNC), and the Action Group (AG), each of which was based in one region. Between 1954 and 1960, when Nigeria achieved its independence, the three regions gradually established all the organs of self-government and began to exercise legislative, executive, and judicial powers. Britain's final constitutional enactment – The Nigeria (Constitution) Order in Council, 1960[7] – promulgated not only the new Constitution of the Federation of Nigeria, but also the constitutions of the three federating regions.

Early Democratic Constitutions: October 1960 to February 1966

Nigeria has had nine constitutions since 1914. The four colonial documents were promulgated by the British and named after the British governors: Clifford (1922), Richards (1946), Macpherson (1951), and Lyttleton (1954). During the postcolonial era, the country has had five constitutions interspersed with long years of extraconstitutional military rule.[8]

The "Independence Constitution" of 1960 was federal. It provided for an exclusive list of legislative powers for the federal government, plus a concurrent list of shared powers, with the residual powers left to the regions. It instituted British-style cabinet government, with the Queen of England as the head of state. Although Sections 64–7 gave the federal government authority to intervene in the conduct of regional governments under certain conditions, the constitutional potential for centralization was not fully realized because the regional governments were politically and economically stronger than the federal government.

The Constitution provided for an upper chamber (the Senate), with equal representation from the three (later four) regions; however, it was designed only as a cooling chamber. It could not delay legislation for more than six months and thus could not compete with the House of Representatives, the more important legislative house. The same was largely true of second chambers (the houses of chiefs) in the regional governments.

Reflecting a further effort to cope with Nigeria's heterogeneity, the 1960 Constitution mandated balanced regional representation on the Supreme Court. The judges included the chief judge of each region, the chief justice of the federation, and "such number of Federal Judges (not being less than three) as may be prescribed by Parliament." Regional representation also prevailed in the Judicial Service Commission.

The Constitution incorporated fundamental rights to protect individuals as well as the political, civil, cultural, religious, and educational attributes of minority ethnic groups. It also included several institutional schemes to protect minorities. For instance, Section 27 provided for fair representation of ethnic minorities in the public-service systems of the regions. Additionally, minority fears of victimization led to deregionalization of Nigeria's police forces and their replacement by a single, federal police force controlled by the Central Police Council.

The 1963 "Republican Constitution" was substantially the same as the 1960 document, except that it severed Nigeria's tie to the British monarchy (although Nigeria remained a member of the Commonwealth). This constitution continued arrangements developed in 1960 to pacify minorities and foster a sense of belonging for all Nigerians. Under this constitution, as under that of 1960, each region had its own constitution.

Several factors explain the failure of these first attempts at federal, constitutional democracy. First, many Nigerians believed that the political system was unsuitable because it had a mixture of federalism and Westminster parliamentarianism as well as "winner takes all, loser gets nothing" elections that created bitter battles among the regional political parties seeking to form the federal government. Nigeria's Westminster system created further problems within the executive. The presence of both a president and a prime minister, combined with a cabinet chosen from members of Parliament, introduced numerous tensions within the executive branch. For instance, the president served as head of state and commander in chief, yet his office was primarily symbolic. The prime minister actually ruled as the chief executive. This created a clash of personalities that generated political upheavals and threatened Nigeria's unity.

Second, the confrontational parliamentary system hindered nation building because the three political parties – the NPC in the North, the NCNC in the East, and the AG in the West and Mid-West – were based in the three regions controlled by the major ethnic groups. The absence both of a truly national party and of a nationally elected chief executive who owed allegiance to the nation and its people rather than to a regionally based ethnic party greatly weakened the nation-state. Third, fragmentation was compounded by the fact that some parties were associated with Islam and others with Christianity. Fourth, the deteriorating political situation was exacerbated by the inefficiency and corrupt tendencies of the political leaders.

Constitutional Change During the First Military Era

The first period of military rule (15 January 1966 to 1 October 1979) created an authoritarian order. The first military leader believed that the solution to Nigeria's problems lay in abolishing federalism. His first constitutional change was the promulgation of Unification Decree No. 34 of 1966, which ushered in unitary government. This decree was a fatal mistake, for it produced a bloody countercoup that reintroduced federalism. The Unification Decree also prompted the Eastern Region to secede from the federation in 1967, declaring itself the independent Republic of

Biafra. The resulting civil war, which lasted from July 1967 to January 1970, restored the territorial integrity of Nigeria.

To foster stability and reduce ethnic tension, General Yakubu Gowon's government reorganized the country by creating 12 states in 1967 in place of the previous four regions. Murtala Mohammed created seven more states in 1976. Thus the strong regional governments were replaced by numerous and smaller states. This was intended to undermine monopolization of power as well as to increase the political influence and safety of minority groups. The restructuring also enhanced the federal government's power vis-à-vis the states.

Under increasing pressure to restore democracy, in 1976 the military established a Constitution Drafting Committee (CDC) comprising a small body of experts charged to prepare a draft constitution for public discussion. This document was then sent to the Constituent Assembly, an elected body, for amendment and ratification.

The Presidential Constitution of 1979

On 1 October 1979 civilians took over the reins of power. The new constitution replaced Nigeria's cabinet-style of government with a US-style presidential system in an effort to enhance the federal government's ability to deal with national problems and thereby hold the country together. There was a separation of powers between the three branches of government, an independent judiciary, and complete freedom for the people to choose all their representatives on the basis of universal suffrage with secret ballots. This constitution also sought to reduce ethnic tensions by affirming the differences among Nigeria's ethnic groups under a robust federal structure and through such concepts as federal character (i.e., affirmative action) and the Fundamental Objectives and Directive Principles of State Policy. Pursuant to local government reforms of 1976, the Constitution established local governments (of which there are now 774) as the third order of government.

The 1979 Constitution provided a good framework for solving the nation's social, economic, and political problems. Yet it lasted only until December 1983 in part because it was frequently abused and violated by politicians. Also, in the early 1980s some state governments, particularly in the Southwest and East, refused to comply with federal-government decisions and used their state-controlled media to attack the federal government. Many states created barriers to appointment to state public services, to admission to state schools, and to intrastate trading for nonresidents in violation of the universality of Nigerian citizenship and the freedoms of movement and residence guaranteed by the Constitution. In many states, those in power excluded opposition parties from policy making, monopolized the bureaucracy, and implemented government programs in a partisan fashion. The situation was aggravated by weak and incompetent national leadership and gross mismanagement of the economy. Corruption assumed alarming proportions, and there was no serious effort to fight poverty. Hence many losers in this corrupt system welcomed military intervention.

Military Rule Redux and the 1989 Partial Constitution

Nigeria, therefore, endured another period of military rule from 31 December 1983 to 29 May 1999. During this period, the military retained parts of the 1979 Constitution, but then a new constitution, formulated with input from a constitutional convention, was partially promulgated by the military in 1989. That is, the 1989 Constitution went into effect for state and local governments only after elections were held for state and local offices in 1991. Thus a transition back to civilian governance had begun by 1992 in the state and local arenas, but implementation of civilian rule for the national government was aborted in June 1993 after a botched presidential election on 12 June. Hence there was no return to civilian democratic rule.[9]

Remarkably, then, during the 45 years following independence in 1960, Nigeria has experienced rule by democratically elected civilian regimes for fewer than 16 years: from 1 October 1960 to 15 January 1966 under Alhaji Sir Abubakar Tafawa Balewa as prime minister and Nnamdi Azikiwe first as governor general and then (after 1963) as president; from 1 October 1979 to 31 December 1983 under President Alhaji Shehu Shagari; and from 29 May 1999 to date under President Olusegun Obasanjo.[10] Nigeria's other rulers – the military juntas[11] – ruled the country for 30 years. Of course, the perpetrators of Nigeria's military coups and countercoups always predicated their action on an altruistic mission to rescue the country from unruly, corrupt, and inept officials. As a result, under pressure from the international community and civil-society organizations, several of the military regimes eventually embarked on a transition to civilian rule and, as part of this process, set in motion the drafting of a new constitution. Thus three of Nigeria's five postcolonial constitutions (1979, 1989, and 1999) emerged under the tutelage of undemocratic military regimes that arrogated to themselves the authority to midwife the birth of democratic constitutions. Given this postindependence history, it is still common to hear references to Nigeria's "nascent democracy," and infidelity to the Constitution and law is still often excused as being part of "the learning process."

The 1999 Constitution

The current constitution went into effect on 29 May 1999 and was the outcome of a transition process led by the military government of General

Abdusalami Abubakar after more than 15 years of failed attempts to re-store civilian rule. Two major constitution-making efforts had failed during these years: the short-lived 1989 Constitution that was never implemented fully and a 1995 draft constitution that was abandoned in 1998 after the sudden death of General Sani Abacha, its chief sponsor.[12]

As part of the transition, General Abubakar appointed a Constitution Debate Coordinating Committee headed by Justice Niki Tobi (then a justice of the Court of Appeal but now a justice of the Supreme Court), charging it to organize nationwide consultations on a new constitution and to make a report and recommendations. One idea debated was to base the new constitution on the 1995 Abacha draft, which never came into force, but "Nigerians raised compelling reservations" about the 1995 draft, the most serious of which were that it was "a product of disputed legitimacy" and suffered from a "crisis of authenticity in the public consciousness."[13] Similar considerations applied to the 1989 Babangida Constitution. The Tobi Committee found, rather, that Nigerians "were near unanimous that the 1979 Constitution had been tried and tested and, therefore, provides a better point of departure in the quest for constitutionalism in Nigeria."[14] Making only minor adjustments to the 1979 document,[15] the Tobi Committee recommended adopting the adjusted document as the new constitution. General Abdulsalami promulgated the Constitution, with a few amendments,[16] in early May 1999 and handed power to the newly elected civilian regime of President Obasanjo on 29 May.

Thus the Constitution retains presidential government and a federal system with three orders of government, and it addresses various political issues that have divided ethnic and cultural groups. The issue of sharing political power among ethnic groups is addressed by the principle of rotation in executive office. The marginalization of disadvantaged minorities has been ameliorated by the establishment of the Federal Character Commission to enforce equity (i.e., affirmative action or positive discrimination) in public-service appointments. The distribution of wealth has been improved by entrenchment of a new revenue-sharing formula. Surpassing all its postcolonial predecessors, the 1999 Constitution has been in force for more than five years and survived its first major test: countrywide general elections conducted in 2003, which resulted in large turnovers in federal and state legislators and regime changes in many state and local governments.

The 1999 Constitution, like its 1979 predecessor, is a very long document. It includes a brief Preamble, eight chapters divided into 320 sections, and seven schedules, and its standard edition comprises 160 closely printed pages. One reason for this length is that the Constitution provides not only for the governance of the federation but also for that of the states – separate constitutions for constituent entities having been abolished in the 1979 Constitution – as well as, more briefly, for local governance.

Another reason is that the document provides at considerable length for matters that in other countries are left to ordinary statutes.

THE QUESTION OF THE CONSTITUTION'S LEGITIMACY

The Preamble to the Constitution proclaims: "We the People of the Federal Republic of Nigeria, HAVING firmly and solemnly resolved [on various things], DO HEREBY MAKE, ENACT AND GIVE TO OURSELVES the following Constitution" (emphases in the original). Despite this proclamation, in large measure "We the People" resolved on nothing and enacted nothing because the Constitution was decreed into existence[17] by the departing military government. How, then, can the Constitution claim "legitimacy?"

Its derivation from the 1979 Constitution is one important legitimating factor. As the Tobi Committee concluded, the 1979 Constitution had been "tried and tested." It was not only in place during the four years of the civilian Shagari administration, but also remained in partial force under the military right up to 1999. The 1979 Constitution, moreover, had been drafted in 1975–76 by a 50-man[18] Constitution Drafting Committee (CDC) appointed by General Murtala Mohammed as part of his program to return the country to civilian rule.[19] The CDC received hundreds of memoranda from individuals and groups from all over Nigeria. Its two-volume report, containing its draft constitution and full discussions of the principles adopted therein, was published in September 1976 and widely distributed.[20] This stimulated "The Great Debate": a year of impassioned public discussion of the draft constitution.[21] In October 1977 a Constituent Assembly, composed of 230 members, of which a large majority (203) were elected by local government councils, convened in Lagos to debate and amend the CDC draft. The Constituent Assembly, whose debates were public,[22] completed its work and adjourned on 5 June 1978. The Constituent Assembly's draft constitution was presented to the head of state, who promulgated it on 21 September 1978, to take effect on 1 October 1979. Thus the 1979 Constitution reflected a broad agreement among most Nigerians.

The 1999 Constitution's derivation from the 1979 Constitution, therefore, lends it a measure of legitimacy. However, there is a widely held view that this lineage is tainted by the fact that the Constitution Drafting Committee of 1975–76 was appointed by the military, as was the entire leadership and 20 members of the 230-member Constituent Assembly. Neither of these bodies was fully representative of the whole population; in particular, there were no women on the CDC, and only five women served in the Constituent Assembly – four of them, incidentally, being among the 20 military appointees.[23] The 1999 Constitution was not put to a plebiscite or ratified by elected bodies in the states but was – once again – simply promulgated by military decree. The worst of it, however, is that the constitution that took effect on 1 October

1979 was not the constitution upon which the Constituent Assembly had agreed. Retracting prior assurances, the military government made 17 amendments to the Constituent Assembly's draft before it was promulgated[24] and then made further amendments just before it took effect.[25]

Consequently, questions about the Constitution's legitimacy keep recurring. This happened, for instance, almost immediately after the 1999 Constitution came into force. Taking advantage of the new democratic dispensation, the House of Assembly of Zamfara State, under the leadership of the state's new governor and with the approval of its predominantly Muslim residents, enacted a series of laws implementing new *sharia* (Islamic law) penal and criminal procedure codes complete with such classical punishments as flogging, limb amputation, and death by stoning. New *sharia* courts were created to administer the codes.[26] The politicians of other northern Muslim states were pressed by popular demand to follow Zamfara's lead. Floggings soon started, and the hand of the first thief was cut off;[27] calls for stonings followed in due course.[28] These widely reported events caused an uproar in the rest of Nigeria and called into question the legitimacy of the 1999 Constitution.

Many non-Muslims saw *sharia* implementation as a violation of the constitutional prohibition of any state religion, a threat to Christians and animists, and "an open, if somewhat disguised, secessionist move by the states concerned."[29] Others contended that the "core North" should be severed from the country and allowed to go its Islamist way alone. Yoruba and Igbo groups, in particular, called for a "Sovereign National Conference" "to decide whether Nigeria will continue to exist as a nation and on what terms."[30]

In the negotiations leading up to the 1960 Constitution, the Northern Region, which "was the only place outside the Arabian peninsula in which the Islamic law, both substantive and procedural, was applied in criminal litigation – sometimes even in regard to capital offences,"[31] was persuaded to give up *sharia* criminal law in return for the continuation of Islamic personal and civil law and the establishment of a *sharia* court of appeal for the region. After the Northern Region was divided into ten states with ten *sharia* courts of appeal, Muslim leaders advocated a Federal *Sharia* Court of Appeal under the 1979 Constitution. This was rejected; instead, appeals were routed to the Federal Court of Appeal, which was constitutionally mandated to include at least three justices learned in Islamic personal law. This arrangement was reproduced in the 1999 Constitution. Hence opponents of the enactments of *sharia* criminal codes between 1999 and 2001 saw these enactments as betrayals of settled constitutional compromises and disruptive of national unity.

Union, however, had been "forced on the country in 1914, and ever since then, the question of whether the amalgamation should continue has never been freely and openly discussed among all nationalities."[32] The

1999 Constitution itself was "an imposition by the military which does not represent the wishes and aspirations of the Nigerian people because it was not made by them."[33] It was said that the Tobi Committee, which had made this constitution, "hardly reflected any awareness of strategies of process-led constitution-making ... It sidetracked serious contentious issues ... and did not attempt to encourage Nigerians to see the document as their own constitution, to be owned, studied, defended, and used to defend democracy ... [T]he structural issues that have bedeviled the country's ability to enthrone a truly accountable, transparent, and democratic political order [were ignored]."[34]

Consequently, while the Constitution "is seen as a legal document," its legitimacy "has been questioned,"[35] prompting both the president and the National Assembly to appoint committees to review the document and recommend changes.

CONSTITUTIONAL PRINCIPLES OF THE FEDERATION

Fundamental Objectives and Directive Principles of State Policy

One innovation made by the CDC was to incorporate the Fundamental Objectives and Directive Principles of State Policy. This was a departure from the 1960 and 1963 Constitutions, which emphasized power and rights but not duties. The objectives, set out in Chapter II of the 1999 Constitution, are long-term goals toward which all governments must work; the directive principles are the paths and policies by which they are to reach these goals. The gist of the provisions is that government power is a trust held on behalf of the people and that sovereignty belongs to the Nigerian people from whom government derives its authority. Powers are given to government for the security and welfare of the people as a whole rather than for the personal aggrandizement of those who wield power. Nigeria is a polity based on principles of democracy and social justice, and government is called upon to ensure the people's participation in their government.

Federalism

A recurring theme in Nigerian federalism is the federal government's dominance vis-à-vis the states and local governments. Illustrations include, for example, the exclusive federal monopoly over the police and armed forces, a sizable list of exclusive federal legislative authority, and federal judicial power to appointment and discipline the judges of both federal and state superior courts of record. A common cliché is that "the federal government's powers are too sprawling."[36] Thus the Presidential Committee on the Review of the 1999 Constitution (set up in 1999 by Obasanjo's administration) observed that "[o]ne of the dominant issues which featured in a large number of submissions and representations is the preferred political structure for Nigeria."[37] Noting that there was an overwhelming agreement that Nigeria should be restructured into a true federation, the committee found that "so strong is the concern and agitation for the desired restructuring that Nigerians cannot seem to wait longer for them to witness the emergence of a True Federation with more powers, responsibilities and resources ... decentralized and devolved in favor of the lower tiers of Government."[38] At the same time, and in light of the Biafran secession attempt, there is apprehension that a weak federal centre would be unable to give the country a sense of security and, in the face of centrifugal forces, prevent national disintegration.

What accounts for the centralizing trend? Apart from the apprehension that a weak federal centre could enable secession, there are two major factors. The first is the manner in which the Nigerian federation was created: By amalgamation under colonial rule, a process bereft of a credible opportunity for a meaningful negotiation of federal-state relations. The second is the dominance of the polity by the military, which, given its hierarchical command structure, is centrist in orientation. That most of Nigeria's postcolonial constitutions, including the 1999 Constitution, were born when the military was the self-imposed midwife reinforces this point.

The dilemma that the Nigerian federation continues to grapple with is how, as Lord Bryce posited in the context of federal systems generally, "to keep the centrifugal and centripetal forces in equilibrium, so that neither the planet states shall fly off into space, nor the sun of the central government draw them into its consuming fires."[39]

Federal Character and the Interface of Unity and Diversity

The Constitution, therefore, sets out to "actively encourage" national integration as well as the "federal character" of the country. To this end, it prohibits discrimination on the basis of place, origin, sex, religion, status, and ethnic or linguistic associations.[40] The Constitution obliges the federation to "foster a feeling of belonging and of involvement among the various peoples of the Federation, to the end that loyalty to the nation shall override sectional loyalties."[41] The Constitution further charges the federal government to reflect, in the conduct of its affairs, the "federal character" of Nigeria and the "need to promote national unity, and also to command national loyalty, thereby ensuring that there shall be no predominance of persons from a few States or from a few ethnic or other sectional groups in [the federal] Government or in any of its agencies." Likewise, the Constitution obliges a state or local government to conduct its affairs "in such manner as to recognise the diversity of the people within its area of authority and the need to promote a sense of belonging and loyalty among all the peoples of the Federation."[42]

The federal-character principle, first introduced in the 1979 Constitution, is part of the nonjusticiable Chapter II. Nonetheless, the Constitution establishes a Federal Character Commission, with membership drawn from all the states and the federal capital territory, and mandates it to (1) work out an equitable formula, subject to the approval of Parliament, for the distribution of all posts in the public service of the federation and of the states, the armed forces of the federation, the police, other government security agencies, government-owned companies, and state parastatals (e.g., government corporations and enterprises); (2) promote, monitor, and enforce compliance with the principle of proportional sharing of all bureaucratic, economic, media, and political posts at all levels of government; and (3) take legal-enforcement measures, including prosecution of the head or staff of any ministry or government body or agency that fails to comply with any federal-character principle or formula prescribed by the commission.[43]

Federal character is a euphemism for ethnic balance – that is, a basis for building unity in diversity by balancing official appointments among groups. Federal character also affects the allocation of public revenue among the federation's constituent units. This principle is criticized by some people as a sacrifice of merit principles and equal opportunity on the altar of mediocrity and political expediency, but federal character has as its justification the idea of promoting social justice through the redistribution of public revenues among the federation's constituent units and social integration of minorities similar to that effected by the systems of affirmative action in India and the United States.

The Constitution also imposes a duty on the federal government to promote national integration by providing adequate facilities for and encouraging the free mobility of people, goods, and services throughout Nigeria; securing full resident rights for every citizen in every part of Nigeria; encouraging intermarriage among persons of different places of origin and religious, ethnic, or linguistic backgrounds; and fostering a feeling of belonging and of involvement so that loyalty to the nation will override sectional and sectarian loyalties. Other provisions aim to ensure social and economic justice.

The viability of these principles, however, depends on three factors: voluntary compliance by the leaders of government, creation of a public opinion that values these principles and insists on their application, and judicial activism to enforce them when possible.

Status of the Constituent Political Communities

The Federal Republic of Nigeria consists of states of disparate sizes and populations. However, the Constitution establishes symmetrical federalism. A contrary stipulation would have evoked memories of the Northern

Table 1
Subdivision of Nigeria's former regions into states

Year (governing official)	Northern Region	Western Region	Eastern Region	Total states
1967 (Gowon)	6	3	3	12
1976 (Murtala and Obasanjo)	10	4	5	19
1987 (Babangida)	11	5	5	21
1991 (Babangida)	16	7	7	30
1996 (Abacha)	19	9	8	36

Region's leverage under Nigeria's previous regional structure and heightened fears of majority domination of minorities. The Constitution does not discriminate between old and new states. Once a new state is created, it has the same powers as the old states.

One prominent theme of Nigeria's federal history has been an urge to subdivide. Agitation for subdividing the original three regions into smaller states began even before independence. One motivation was the sheer size of the Northern Region, which was larger than the other two regions put together, encompassing 75 percent of the country's land area and 60 percent of its population. This imbalance has been described as "[p]erhaps the most astonishing peculiarity of [early] Nigerian federalism"[44] and gave rise to fears in the other two regions of domination by the North. The other cause was that minority ethnic groups in all regions feared the tyranny of local majorities and thus expressed desires to govern themselves in their own territorial states, which resulted in agitation to subdivide not only the North but the other two regions as well.

In the run-up to independence, as part of the constitutional negotiations then taking place, the British appointed a commission to inquire into this matter, and a lengthy report, still read in Nigeria, was produced.[45] In the end, the British refused to subdivide the country, but since independence, subdivision has proceeded apace. The first exercise was carried out according to constitutional procedures in 1964, when a new Mid-Western Region was carved out of the West. Wholesale subdivision of the country into multiple states began in 1967, decreed extraconstitutionally by the federal military government of General Yakubu Gowon. All subsequent state-creation exercises were likewise decreed by military rulers. The table above shows the numbers of states that have resulted from all subdivisions to date.

Today, there are 36 states. A new Federal Capital Territory of Abuja was established in the former Northern Region in 1976, and the capital officially moved there from Lagos in 1991. Agitation for further state creation continues, and there is a very complex provision for it in the 1999 Constitution.[46] However, the Constitution contains no provision on the admission of new territories as states should such a situation arise, nor is there any provision for the reorganization of states in such a way as to *decrease* their number.

What of secession? Unlike the 1995 Ethiopian Constitution,[47] which sets out, among other things, to rectify "historically unjust relationships"[48] and proclaims that "[e]very Nation, Nationality and People in Ethiopia has an unconditional right to self-determination, including the right to secession,"[49] there is no provision for secession either *within* or *from* the Nigerian federation. Instead, the Preamble to the Constitution expresses the firm resolve of Nigerians to live in unity and harmony as "one indivisible and indissoluble Sovereign Nation." Section 2(1) fortifies this resolve: "Nigeria is one indivisible and indissoluble Sovereign State to be known by the name of the Federal Republic of Nigeria."

The significance of these phrases is better appreciated against the background of the civil war, or Biafran War, fought to thwart the secession of the then Eastern Region. Following the country's first military coup (15 January 1966) and countercoup (29 July 1966), a number of factors, including the killing of many Igbos in northern cities and the mass exodus of Igbos from the North to their homelands in the East, led to the proclamation on 30 May 1967 of a new, independent state – territorially identical to the Eastern Region – christened the "Republic of Biafra." The civil war, fought by the North and West against the East, finally ended on 12 January 1970 with the surrender of Biafra and its reintegration into the federation – now subdivided, however, into the East-Central, South-Eastern, and Rivers states. There have been no further attempts to secede from Nigeria, but secessionist agitation has not died out. The recent emergence of a Movement for the Actualization of the Sovereign State of Biafra (MASSOB) underscores the imperative need for a federal system conducive to the symbiotic interface of centrifugal and centripetal forces.

Unlike in the United States and several other federal polities, there is only one constitution in Nigeria. The constituent polities do not have their own constitutions. The federal Constitution sets out in separate parts of the same chapters provisions relating to the federal and state governments, with the exception of miscellaneous and transitional provisions common to both orders of government, which are dealt with in the same sections, as is the case with such issues as citizenship, the Fundamental Objectives and Directive Principles of State Policy, and fundamental rights. By contrast, the 1960 and 1963 Constitutions made provisions for separate regional constitutions. The 1976 Constitution Drafting Committee attributed its preference for a single, national constitution to the convenience of drafting in light of the number of states, 19, in existence at the time. The centrist posture of the Constitution reinforces the views of critics who fault the structure of the Nigerian federation and crave a return to the arrangement that existed under the 1960 and 1963 Constitutions.

Local Government

Section 7(1) of the current Constitution, like the 1979 document, guarantees a system of local government by "democratically elected local government councils." However, the second component of Section 7(1) makes the "establishment, structure, composition, finance and functions" of local governments dependent on state law. Furthermore, the Constitution makes it possible for state governments to cripple local government councils financially by routing the amount of money standing to the credit of local governments in the Federation Account through a State Joint Local Government Account rather than directly to local councils.[50] This arrangement adversely affects the financial viability of most councils. Some state governors make inexplicable deductions or unduly delay the release of funds from the joint accounts to local-government chief executives whom they regard as political adversaries. Ironically, President Obasanjo, whose earlier military administration undertook a major reform of the local-government system in 1976, the basic tenets of which found expression in the 1979 Constitution and then again in the 1999 Constitution, became so disenchanted with the performance of local government that he set up a Presidential Technical Committee to examine the desirability of retaining local government as the third order of government. He believes that inefficiency and high costs bedevil the system.

As of 2004 the Constitution recognized 768 local-government areas in addition to six municipal-area councils (in respect of the Federal Capital Territory of Abuja), thus making the total 774 local government councils. There is a raging controversy (involving several ongoing litigations) as to who, between the federal government and the states, has the final say over the creation of new local-government areas.[51]

The Allocation of Powers

In allocating powers, the Constitution distinguishes between an exclusive legislative list and a concurrent legislative list. The federal government has exclusive authority to exercise the former powers, while both the federal and state governments have concurrent authority to exercise the latter to the extent prescribed in the Constitution. However, states have exclusive legislative authority in residual matters.[52]

The exclusive list consists of as many as 68 items. When compared with the 12 items on the concurrent list, it provides the critics of Nigeria's federal system with another weapon. The matters exclusive to the federal government include, among others, defence; foreign affairs; extradition; police and other government security services; arms, ammunitions, and explosives; prisons; evidence; currency, coinage, and legal tender; taxation of income, profits, and capital gains; stamp duties; mines and minerals (including oil fields, oil mining, geological surveys, and natural gas); copyright; aviation; bankruptcy and insolvency; banks, banking, bills of exchange, and promissory notes; trade and commerce; regulation of political parties; and creation of states.

Both the federal government and the states can enact laws on any matters found on the concurrent list. This list deals with, among other things, the allocation of revenue; antiquities and monuments; archives; tax collection; electoral law; electric power; exhibition of cinematographic films; industrial, commercial, and agricultural development; scientific and technological research; statistics; trigonometric, cadastral, and topographical surveys; and university, technological, and postprimary education. The executive power is similarly distributed between the two orders of government, and is normally coextensive with the concurrent legislative powers.

Pursuant to concurrent powers, if a law made by a state government conflicts with a law "validly made" by the federal government, the latter prevails. In the words of Section 4(5), the former "shall to the extent of the inconsistency be void." Where, however, a law made by a state is not necessarily inconsistent with a validly enacted federal law but relates to a subject matter in respect of which the federal law has, to use a common parlance, covered the field, the state legislation is not necessarily void but is merely "in abeyance," and if, for any reason, the federal law is repealed, the state legislation "is revived and becomes operational."[53]

Apart from normal administrative and political-party mechanisms, there are no explicit constitutional mechanisms designed to promote consensual rather than hierarchical resolution of conflicts between the federal government and the constituent governments. However, such conflict resolution is implicit in the establishment and composition of certain bodies, such as the National Council of States and the Federal Character Commission, whose membership consists of federal and state representatives.

Conflicts of Power and Jurisdiction between the Federal Government and the States

After years of prolonged military rule, Nigeria's current democratic experience has been beset with intergovernmental conflicts on issues ranging from the authority to prescribe the tenure of local government councils[54] to the authority to enact legislation on corruption.[55] However, the Constitution does not expressly employ any mechanisms to forestall the development of power conflicts between the federal government and the states.[56]

The Constitution vests the Supreme Court with the original jurisdiction, to the exclusion of any other court, to determine any legal dispute between the federation and a state or between states. Because the Supreme Court is the court of last resort, this expedites litigation because such cases do not have to wind their way up through the normal, often slow, judicial hierarchy.

FEDERALISM AND THE STRUCTURE AND OPERATION OF GOVERNMENT

System of Government

The current Constitution, like its 1979 precursor, opts for a US-style presidential system. The CDC, which played a significant role in making the 1979 Constitution, preferred the presidential system on the grounds that the separation of the head of state from the head of government under the parliamentary system involved a division between real authority and formal authority that was "meaningless in the light of African political experience and history" and was prone to "a clash of personalities and of interests, a conflict of authority and an unnecessary complexity and uncertainty in governmental relations."[57]

Responding to apprehension that an executive presidency would concentrate too much power in the hands of one person, the CDC asserted that "the ultimate sanction against usurpations of power is a politically conscious society jealous of its constitutional rights to choose those who direct its affairs."[58] The CDC did not say, however, whether a "politically conscious society" existed in Nigeria or was on the verge of emergence. Interestingly, Nigeria's recent experience with presidential government is reigniting debate about the propriety of the presidential, as against parliamentary, government. Charges of civilian dictatorship predicated on a deliberate and systematic weakening of other orders and branches of government are being levelled against President Obasanjo. An attempt to impeach the president for contempt of the legislature and constitutional precepts was averted only after the intervention of the ruling Peoples Democratic Party and elder statesmen, such as former President Shehu Shagari and his military counterpart, Yakubu Gowon. Incidentally, President Obasanjo, a retired army general and Nigeria's military head of state between February 1976 and September 1979, bequeathed the 1979 presidential Constitution to Nigerians. Whether Obasanjo's sometimes vilified style of administration stems from his military background or from the enormous powers the Constitution vests in the presidency, or both, is uncertain, but the domination of politics by retired military and paramilitary officers is one of the challenges facing Nigeria's efforts to enthrone democratic constitutionalism and federalism.[59]

Separation of Powers

A separation of powers is prominent in Nigeria's Constitution. Sections 4, 5, and 6 enumerate the respective powers of the legislative, executive, and judicial branches. However, in light of provisions on checks and balances, the Constitution does not engender a "pure" separation of powers because each branch has some influence over the others. For example, the legislature checks the executive through its oversight functions, the impeachment weapon, and legislative confirmation of certain executive nominees such as ministers, commissioners, and ambassadors. The executive initiates bills and has the prerogative of approving or vetoing a bill passed by the National Assembly. Both the legislature and the executive play important roles in the appointment and discipline of judges, and the judiciary has the power of *Marbury*-style judicial review over both legislative and executive actions.[60]

However, the separation of powers between the executive and legislature does raise potential problems. Unless these two branches agree on policy, a stalemate develops – something that has occurred already. Unless there are mechanisms for consensus building and cooperation, as well as a tolerant rather than competitive attitude, it is difficult for either branch to achieve not only its own goals, but also important national goals.

Federal Legislature

The Constitution establishes a bicameral legislature called the National Assembly, consisting of a lower chamber (House of Representatives) and an upper chamber (Senate). Each Nigerian state is divided into three senatorial districts, with each electing a senator. The federal capital territory has one senator (unlike Washington, DC, which has no senator). The Senate, therefore, consists of 109 senators. Thus, as in the US Senate, each state is equally represented in Nigeria's Senate; however, unlike in the United States, where each senator is elected by his or her entire state electorate, Nigeria's senators are elected from districts within their state. For the House, the Constitution prescribes 360 federal constituencies "of nearly equal population as far as possible," with each constituency electing one House member. Hence, like the differential state representation in the US House of Representatives, the states are not equally represented in Nigeria's lower chamber. The size of a state's representation in the House depends on the size of its population.

The Constitution mandates the National Assembly to make laws for the "peace, order and good government" of the federation or for any part thereof with respect to any matter included in the exclusive legislative list set out in Part 1 of the Constitution's Second Schedule, but subjects the exercise of the Assembly's powers to "the jurisdiction of courts of law and of any judicial tribunals established by law." Accordingly, the Constitution precludes the legislature from enacting any law "that ousts or purports to oust the jurisdiction" of such judicial bodies. The legislature is further prohibited from making, in relation to any crime, a law that has a retroactive (ex post facto) effect. The Assembly, however, can make laws on any matter on the concurrent legislative list and on any other matter with respect to which, under the Constitution, it is empowered to make laws.

In addition, when a state house of assembly is unable to perform its functions by reason of a situation prevailing in that state, such as where the legislature is crisis-ridden, the National Assembly can make laws for that state "until such time as the House of Assembly is able to resume its functions."[61] In recent times, the National Assembly threatened to invoke this power in some states, especially in the East, where power tussles paralyzed the operation of their state houses of assembly. This provision, however, does not authorize the federal legislature to impeach a state governor.

When there is a conflict between a valid federal law and a state law, the state law is rendered void up to the extent of its inconsistency with the federal law. As a general rule, the National Assembly does not have a concurrent approval, veto, or amendment power over legislation enacted by the state governments and vice versa. However, this rule does not extend to legislation respecting the creation of new states and local governments, boundary adjustments, the domestication of certain treaties, and amendment of the Constitution.[62]

Federal Executive

Federal executive power is vested in the president, who has the discretion to exercise such power either directly or through the vice president, ministers of the federal government, or officers in the federation's public service. The president's executive power extends to the execution and maintenance of the Constitution, all federal legislation, and all other matters with respect to which the National Assembly has power to make laws. The president's powers are awesome when considered in light of the broad and expansive nature of the exclusive legislative list – although these powers must be exercised in accordance with the Constitution and laws enacted by the National Assembly.

The president also participates in certain aspects of law making. The president's assent is required for a bill passed by the Assembly to become law,[63] although the Assembly can override a presidential veto by a two-thirds majority. The president's legislative role may take the form of legislative initiative as well. Under Section 81 of the Constitution, the president also can cause estimates to be laid before and acted upon by the legislature. The president has authority under Section 315 to modify by way of addition, alteration, omission, or repeal any existing law in order to bring it into conformity with the Constitution.

Consistent with the federal-character principle, the Constitution obliges the president to appoint to his Cabinet at least one minister from each state of the federation. The constituent polities, as such, do not play any role in electing the president because the outcome of presidential elections is determined by majority votes. However, to win, a presidential candidate must garner not less than one-quarter of the votes cast at the election in at least two-thirds of the states of the federation and the federal capital territory.

Federal Judiciary

The Constitution establishes a three-tier hierarchy of federal courts. The bottom consists of the courts of the federal capital territory and the Federal High Court. The intermediate court, the Court of Appeal, is the second tier, while the Supreme Court, which is the court of last resort, constitutes the top tier.

The Supreme Court is primarily an appellate court. However, it exercises original jurisdiction, to the exclusion of any other court, in respect of matters either between a state and the federal government or between states. Consistent with the power of judicial review, and in light of the principle of the supremacy of the Constitution, the Supreme Court and other superior courts of record can declare a federal law or any other law to be unconstitutional and, therefore, null and void.[64]

The Supreme Court can hear reference cases involving "a substantial question of law" relating to the "interpretation or application" of the Constitution.[65] Through this "leap frog" procedure, the higher court gives its opinion on the question and provides such directives as it deems fit to the court below, but the court does not give advisory opinions to the federal executive and/or to the federal legislature and/or to the governments of the constituent polities.

The Supreme Court justices are appointed by the president on the recommendation of the National Judicial Council, which in turn acts on the advice of the Federal Judicial Service Commission. The constituent polities are represented in the federal judiciary through the federal-character principle, but the Constitution does not mandate, as is the case with ministerial appointments, a specific minimum from each state.

The judiciary occupies a powerful position. Its powers extend, notwithstanding anything contrary to the Constitution, to all inherent powers and sanctions of a court of law. Judicial powers extend also to all legal matters arising between persons or between government (or authority) and any person and to all actions and proceedings for determining any question as to the civil rights and obligations of a person. However, the Fundamental Objectives and Directive Principles of State Policy are not subject to judicial enforcement. Furthermore, judicial power does not extend to any actions or proceedings relating to any existing law made on or before 15 January 1966 (the date of Nigeria's first coup) for determining any issue or question as to the jurisdiction of any authority or person to have made any such law.

With reference to customary or religious courts, the Constitution establishes appellate *sharia* and customary courts for the federal capital territory and permits any state "that requires it" to establish such courts. Individuals are at liberty to choose between regular courts and customary courts so long as both courts possess jurisdiction over the subject matter. *Sharia* courts have jurisdiction only over Muslims, but no constitutional stipulation precludes the parties to a case, even if both are Muslim, from choosing regular courts. In practice, however, opting out of *sharia* courts is rare because many Muslims fear that it could be construed as infidelity to the Islamic faith. Appeals of decisions rendered by *sharia* and customary courts of appeal go to a federal Court of Appeal, whose composition, as a matter of constitutional stipulation, includes at least three justices learned in Islamic personal law and at least three justices learned in customary law. Thereafter, the final appeal lies with the Supreme Court.

Institutions of the Constituent Polities

The states' institutions generally resemble those of the federal government because they are mandated by the federal Constitution. For instance, subject to respective powers, the institutional arrangements for the state executive branch are, with the necessary adjustments, those at the federal level. That is, after vesting powers in the federal president, the Constitution vests powers in the state governors.

The same is true of each state's judiciary to the extent that the state system is hierarchical. However, state courts, other than each state's high court (which is established by the Constitution), are established by state law. These include state *sharia* and customary courts of appeal (if a state chooses to create them), magistrate or district courts, and customary or area courts. State high courts have both original and, to a limited extent, appellate jurisdiction. However, no state has a court of appeal or a supreme court. Cases from state courts eventually wind up, on appeal, in a federal Court of Appeal or in the Supreme Court.

Unlike the National Assembly, the Constitution establishes a unicameral house of assembly for each state. Like the National Assembly, each state legislature is subject to the jurisdiction of the courts and judicial tribunals established by law, and no state law can oust the jurisdiction of a court of law or a judicial tribunal established by law. Also, like the National Assembly's role in approving certain presidential appointments, each state house of assembly collaborates with its governor in the appointment of persons to key executive and judicial posts.

Section 7 of the Constitution guarantees a system of democratically elected local-government councils. Subject to Section 8, each state must ensure their existence under a law that provides for the establishment, structure, composition, finance, and functions of such councils. The Fourth Schedule provides for the main functions of local government councils. A council has the authority to make bylaws and regulations with respect to local functions stated in Schedule 4. Local government arrangements do vary somewhat from state to state because such matters are the subject of state regulation. Otherwise, however, local governments have no judicial branch.

Interstate Relations

The Constitution does not specifically address relations among the constituent polities with respect to such matters as full faith and credit, mutual recognition of each other's legal acts, or the service and/or enforcement of court processes. Such matters are regulated by the laws of the respective states.

In civil suits, jurisdiction is determined by the nature of the subject matter (e.g., a contract, tort, or land matter) and/or by the residence of the litigants. However, in criminal cases, jurisdiction is determined by the place of the commission of the crime. This rule is subject to the proviso that breaches of the provisions of the 1949 Geneva Conventions are, by the provisions of the Geneva Conventions Act,[66] subject to the jurisdiction of the courts in the federal capital territory, irrespective of the nationality of the accused or the place of the alleged crime's commission.

FISCAL AND MONETARY POWERS

Taxation

The federal and state governments have exclusive powers to levy taxes in their respective spheres; there is no concurrent power of taxation. The federal government has broad and elastic taxation powers. For instance, corporate income taxes, customs and excise duties, export duties, stamp duties, and taxes in respect of oil and solid minerals (exclusive ownership of which is vested in the federal government)[67] fall under the exclusive legislative list, thus leaving the states with a residual taxation power that provides only limited room for them to generate their own financial resources.

Nonetheless, it is important to underscore that all revenues collected by the federal government do not belong to the federal government per se but are paid into a distributable pool account, known as the Federation Account (discussed below). In terms of transparency and accountability, the Constitution establishes a Revenue Mobilization Allocation and Fiscal Commission, with membership drawn from each state of the federation and from the federal capital territory. The commission's mandate includes "monitor[ing] the accruals to and disbursement of revenue from the Federation Account."[68] Thus the proceeds of many federal taxes are either given exclusively to the states (i.e., capital-gains tax, personal income tax, including taxation of dividends, and stamp duties on documents or transactions) or shared between the federal, state, and local governments (e.g., value-added tax).

The states do have power to raise revenue from, among others, a land tax, land registration fees, estate duties, and license fees. Also, whereas the federal government can levy a sales tax on interstate trade and commerce, the power to legislate on intrastate trade and commerce is vested in state governments.[69] Local governments have very few fiscal powers. Their revenue sources are limited, among others, to entertainment taxes, motor-park duties, property taxes, and trading and marketing license fees.

The Constitution empowers the National Assembly, in exercise of its powers to impose certain specified taxes or duties, to provide that the collection of such taxes or duties be "carried out by the Government of a State or other authority of a State," with a proviso that such taxes or duties not be levied on the same person by more than one state.[70] The Constitution also obligates each state to pay to the federation, in respect of each financial year, "an amount equal to such part of the expenditure incurred by the Federation during that financial year for the purpose of collection of taxes or duties which are wholly or partly payable to the State ... as is proportionate to the share of the proceeds of those taxes or duties received by the State in respect of that financial year."[71]

The Constitution contains no explicit provisions on tax harmonization, coordination, cooperation, or competition among the states and/or local governments. However, there is a statutory scheme under which provision is made for a Joint Tax Board. This board, with membership drawn from the federal and state boards of internal revenue, meets periodically, affording the members the opportunity to exchange ideas on best practices; makes proposals for the reform of tax laws; and, in appropriate cases, recommends uniform rates for adoption by the relevant authorities.

Borrowing

The federal and state governments can borrow money on capital markets. The Constitution does not limit the federal government's borrowing authority, but states need the approval of the federal government to secure foreign loans. An emerging trend has been for states to issue bonds on capital markets. However, critics charge that the federal government has not exercised sufficient supervision over states unable to pay off their bonds. As of mid-2004, 18 states were practically bankrupt and unable to fulfil Irrevocable Standing Payment Orders (ISPOs) that they had signed with the federal government. ISPOs allow the federal Ministry of Finance to deduct specified percentages from states' statutory allocations of federal revenue as indemnity against defaults on bond payments.

The Constitution neither requires nor encourages the federal government to pay the debts of state and/or local governments when these governments fail or refuse to pay their debts. However, the Constitution envisages the financial viability of the federal government and enjoins it to make grants to a state to supplement the revenue of that state in such a sum and subject to such terms and conditions as may be prescribed by the National Assembly.

Allocation of Revenues

The Constitution establishes a Federation Account into which, with a few specified exceptions, "shall be paid all revenues collected by the Government of the Federation."[72] The Constitution further establishes a fiscal-equity commission, the Revenue Mobilization Allocation and Fiscal Commission, and charges it to, among other things, "review, from time to time, the revenue allocation formulae and principles in operation to ensure conformity with changing realities."[73] Consistent with its mandate, the commission advises the president on proposals for revenue allocation. Upon receipt of such advice, the president tables it before the National Assembly, which in turn prescribes a revenue-allocation formula, taking into consideration allocation principles such as population, equality of states, internal revenue generation, land mass, terrain, and population density.

The federal government has exclusive ownership of oil and solid-mineral resources. However, petroleum – the mainstay of Nigeria's economy – is found mostly in the South. The politics involved in controlling and allocating revenues from natural resources (especially oil) is highly contentious. The Constitution ameliorates the plight of the states from which such resources are extracted by requiring that a minimum of 13 percent of the revenue accruable to the Federation Account from natural resources extracted from any state be returned to that state. This so-called derivation principle "shall be constantly reflected in any approved formula." Whereas the current Constitution otherwise leaves the determination of the exact derivation percentage to the National Assembly, the 1960 and 1963 Constitutions had prescribed 50 percent in favour of regions from which such resources were extracted. A recent attempt by the federal government to deprive Nigeria's coastal states of revenue from offshore natural resources, particularly on the basis of the derivation principle, received judicial backing;[74] however, the government eventually opted for a political solution pursuant to which the National Assembly passed an executive bill abolishing the onshore-offshore distinction.[75]

Revenues accruing to the Federation Account are distributed among the federal, state, and local governments. However, the allocation formula tilts heavily in favour of the federal government. The formula, crafted under General Babangida's rule, prescribes 48.5 percent for the federal government, 24 percent for state governments, 20 percent for local governments, and 7.5 percent for special funds. Following the Supreme Court's invalidation of the percentage prescribed for special funds,[76] President Obasanjo invoked his power of adaptive legislation[77] and added this percentage to the federal government's share, thus making a total of 56 percent in favour of the federal government.[78] However, pursuant to the Constitution, arrangements have also been made for statutory grants-in-aid and loans from the federal government to the states.

The issue of fiscal federalism remains contentious, with some reformers, particularly from the South, clamouring for "resource control" by the states. The Presidential Committee on the Review of the 1999 Constitution reports that "the twin issues of derivation formula and resource control stand out and constitute the greatest test of the political will ... to effect the desired restructuring of the federation so that justice is done to all stakeholders in the Nigerian nation."

Spending of Revenues

Subject to budget limitations that might be imposed by an appropriation act, the Constitution places no limits on the power of the federal government to spend revenues for any or various legal purposes of its own choice. In like manner, the Constitution does not place any limits on the power of the constituent governments to spend own-source and/or grant-in-aid revenues for various legal purposes of their own choice unless, in the case of grants-in-aid, the granting authority prescribes otherwise. Similarly, the Constitution does not limit the authority of the states to spend revenues accruable to them from the Federation Account or otherwise direct how or where such funds are spent. Spending rules for local governments are prescribed by state legislation.

The Constitution assigns monetary policy exclusively to the federal government. A central bank, the Central Bank of Nigeria, was created by statute.

In summary, the division of policy and fiscal powers is heavily weighted toward the national government at the expense of the states. This distribution has prompted calls for devolution and greater state autonomy and also raised the possibility of amending the Constitution to redress the imbalance. However, a number of factors are said to justify a strong national government. The first is the need for national unity. When regions are more powerful than the centre, divisive forces take advantage of the federal government's weakness. Second, the uneven development of regions and peoples is often said to require a strong federal government able to protect the weak and assist less-developed jurisdictions. Third, a strong federal government is said to be necessary to meet external threats. Fourth, a strong federal government is said to be needed to develop the nation's resources and promote economic development.

FOREIGN AFFAIRS AND DEFENCE POWERS

Power in respect of foreign affairs is exclusive to the federal government, and states cannot belong to international or supranational organizations. However, a federal bill that seeks to domesticate an international treaty with respect to matters not included in the exclusive legislative list requires ratification by a majority of all the state houses of assembly.

Defence, too, is an exclusive federal competence. The constituent polities do not possess their own militias or other military forces. However, some states, such as Anambra, have established vigilante groups whose constitutionality is the subject of controversy. The Constitution explicitly provides for civilian control of all armed forces, to the extent that the president is the commander in chief of the Nigerian Armed Forces. The president cannot, without prior legislative approval, deploy any member of the armed forces on combat duty outside Nigeria unless "he is satisfied that national security is under imminent threat or danger."[79] The Constitution explicitly provides for conscientious objection to military service in the specific context of its delineation of the scope of the right to human dignity.[80]

The Constitution does not provide for intergovernmental consultation in foreign affairs or defence. Additionally, the development of supranational institutions (e.g., the African Union, of which Nigeria is a member) has not affected the constitutional allocation of foreign affairs and/or defence powers or otherwise compelled constitutional change to provide for intergovernmental consultation in foreign affairs and/or defence, representation of constituent governments in external negotiations, or external-relations authority (e.g., a limited treaty power) for the federation's states or local governments.

CITIZENSHIP

Chapter III of the Constitution, which is devoted to citizenship, establishes three categories of citizens: by birth (on the basis of ancestral blood ties), by registration (restricted to non-Nigerian female spouses of Nigerian men, which, if literally construed, excludes non-Nigerian male spouses of Nigerian women), and by naturalization (without restrictions but subject to the fulfilment of certain specified conditions relating to domicile and good behaviour). The Constitution recognizes dual citizenship (i.e., Nigerian citizenship and that of a foreign country), but in an effort to emphasize the oneness of Nigerians, it does not recognize or authorize dual citizenship in terms of national and constituent-polity citizenship, such as dual federal and state citizenship in the United States.

Citizenship is determined by the federal government, with a proviso that the grant of an application for citizenship by naturalization requires certification by the governor of the state where the applicant proposes to be resident that the applicant "is acceptable to the community" and "has been assimilated into the way of life of Nigerians in that part of the Federation."[81] An immigrant wishing to obtain citizenship applies to the federal government through the Nigerian Immigration Service. Section 32 of the Constitution authorizes the president to make regulations prescribing all matters for carrying out or giving effect to citizenship and for granting special immigrant status to the non-Nigerian spouse of a Nigerian citizen.

VOTING, ELECTIONS, AND POLITICAL PARTIES

The Constitution established an Independent National Electoral Commission (INEC) that conducts all federal and state elections in Nigeria. Local-government elections are conducted by state independent electoral commissions (SIECs). Registration of eligible voters is the exclusive responsibility of the INEC. The Constitution makes provisions for voter qualifications and elections based on universal adult suffrage, but the details (including a minimum voting age of 18) are set out in Electoral Act 2002.

Nigeria has a multiparty system. As of 2004 there were 30 registered political parties, which are regulated by the INEC. An attempt to constrict the political space, through the imposition of stringent registration requirements, was successfully challenged in court.[82] However, in a deliberate move to discourage past practices whereby most political parties confined themselves to their regional cocoon or were mono-ethnic or mono-religious, the Constitution renders ineligible for registration as a political party any association whose name, symbol, or logo contains "any ethnic or religious connotation or gives the appearance that the activities of the association are confined to a part only of the geographical area of Nigeria."[83] Parties are barred from holding or possessing any funds or other assets outside Nigeria and are not entitled to retain any funds or assets remitted or sent to them from outside Nigeria.[84] There is no provision for independent candidates. The Constitution does not exclude anyone from voting because of gender, race, ethnicity, religion, or conviction for a crime. However, non-Nigerians, whether resident in the country or not, are ineligible to vote.

PROTECTION OF INDIVIDUAL AND COMMUNAL RIGHTS

Constitutional entrenchment of human rights in Nigeria dates back to the recommendation of the Willink Commission of 1958, which was appointed by the colonial government to inquire into the fears of minorities and ways of allaying these fears. The 1999 Constitution incorporates four categories of rights.

Category One includes personal freedoms, such as the right to life, human dignity (e.g., no torture, inhuman or degrading treatment, slavery, and/or forced labour); personal liberty; and guarantees with respect to the privacy of citizens, their homes, correspondence, and telephone and telegraphic communications.

Category Two includes political and moral rights, such as freedom of thought, conscience, expression, and religion (including freedom to change one's beliefs and to worship, teach, and practice one's religion). Section 38 forbids the imposition on a person attending an education institution of a requirement to receive religious instruction or to participate in a religious denomination that is not one's own or of which one's parents or guardians do not approve. These rights are in furtherance of Section 10, which prohibits a state religion. Freedom of the press is protected, along with the right to assemble freely and peacefully and to form or belong to any political party, trade union, or other association, the right to move freely throughout Nigeria and to reside in any part of Nigeria, and freedom from discrimination.

Category Three rights pertain to criminal and judicial proceedings, including a fair hearing by a court within a reasonable time. Category Four refers to property rights, including provisions that eminent domain be exercised only with equitable compensation to property owners.

An omnibus derogation clause validates any law that is "reasonably justifiable in a democratic society – (a) in the interest of defence, public safety, public order, public morality or public health; or (b) for the purpose of protecting the rights and freedoms of other persons."[85] These rights are guaranteed against the federal government, the constituent governments, and/or private abridgment and are enforced primarily by the judiciary, especially by federal and state high courts. These rights apply to Nigerians as well as to non-Nigerians, except where, as is the case with the freedom of movement and the right to nondiscrimination, the rights are, in certain specific contexts, restricted to "every citizen." Constituent governments, individually or collectively, cannot opt out of any or all provisions of the

fundamental-rights provisions. However, nothing stops constituent governments from enacting specific statutes *in furtherance* of the constitutional human-rights regime. For instance, some states have outlawed female genital
mutilation or other harmful religious or traditional practices (e.g., obnox-
ious widowhood rites).

The Constitution does not guarantee economic, social, and cultural
rights. At best, what would have constituted the fulcrum of these second-
generation rights is christened the "Fundamental Objectives and Directive
Principles of State Policy." But these are nonjusticiable.

International human-rights instruments have no force of law unless they
are domesticated through specific legislation. The African Charter on Human and Peoples' Rights, for instance, has been domesticated into Nigerian law[86] and has been the subject of several lawsuits.[87] Human-rights
provisions, whether constitutional, statutory, or domesticated, are enforceable through federal and state high courts. A National Human Rights
Commission complements the enforcement regime.

CONSTITUTIONAL CHANGE

Amendment or review of the Constitution is primarily a legislative responsibility. The Constitution prescribes a two-step amendment process, involving
both the National Assembly and state houses of assembly.[88] There is no referendum requirement in the Constitution amendment or review process.

No provision of the Constitution is immune from amendment. As a general rule, a proposal for an amendment requires the votes of not less than a
two-thirds majority of the members of each house of the National Assembly. However, any proposal to amend sections that (1) prescribe the
amendment procedure, (2) relate to the creation of new states, boundary
adjustment, or the creation of new local-government areas, or (3) contain
fundamental rights requires the votes of not less than a four-fifths majority
of the members of each house of the National Assembly. In either case, the
proposal must be approved by resolution of the houses of assembly of not
less than two-thirds of all the states.

Thus far, no provision of the 1999 Constitution has been amended.
However, shortly after assuming office in 1999, President Obasanjo, in response to criticisms of the Constitution and agitation for its review, constituted an all-party Presidential Committee on the Review of the 1999
Constitution.[89] The committee identified 17 major issues that should engage the amendment process.[90] These include illegitimacy of the Constitution, the framework for defending the Constitution against military
adventurism, the structure of the federation, devolution of powers, the local-
government system, the interface of state and religion, revenue allocation,
and "genderizing" the Constitution's language. A National Assembly Joint

Committee on the Review of the 1999 Constitution made similar findings. A draft bill to amend the Constitution in terms of some of these issues was being debated by the National Assembly in 2004. However, critics, such as the Citizens' Forum for Constitutional Reform (a broad coalition of non-governmental human-rights and democracy organizations), have faulted the process, alleging that it is not sufficiently guided by principles of inclusiveness, diversity, participation, transparency, openness, autonomy, accountability, and legitimacy, which, they contend, are key to any review of the Constitution in terms of producing a people's constitution.[91]

CONCLUSION

Nigeria's Constitution emerged under circumstances that constrain its capacity to respond adequately to the challenges of federalism and constitutionalism that bedevil the polity. Decades of military dictatorship have led to a centrist federal structure and "the curtailment of opportunities for political institutionalization and democratic consolidation."[92] An appraisal of the Constitution since 1999 must reckon with these realities, as well as with its still-young lifespan. Neither the legitimacy of federal constitutionalism nor the practice of federal constitutionalism is yet firmly entrenched in Nigeria.

The country continues to grapple with military predominance, and while a constitutional framework for bolstering the defence of democracy is important, there is a broad public consensus that the best recipe against a military coup is good governance. Civilian officials must act properly in defence of democracy and in demonstration of its superior performance over other forms of government. Nigeria, which is ranked as one of the world's most corrupt countries, must shed its corruption and foster economic development, modernization, and social justice.

Properly utilized, the ongoing constitutional review process could afford "We the People" the opportunity to embark on candid dialogue and negotiation on the thorny issues that hold the key to the success of Nigeria's democratic odyssey and to the very existence of the Nigerian federation. The active involvement of civil-society organizations portends a good omen and gives a sense of the hopefully positive direction of things to come.

NOTES

1 The website of the Nigerian government (http://www.nigeria.gov.ng) estimates the country's population at 120 million; the *World Fact Book* estimated Nigeria's population in July 2003 at 133,881,703 (http://www.odci.gov/cia/publications/factbook/print/ni.html). A national census is scheduled for 2005.

2 See also Rotimi T. Suberu, *Federalism and Ethnic Conflict in Nigeria* (Washington, DC: United States Institute of Peace Press, 2001) and Okwudiba Nnoli, *Ethnicity and Development in Nigeria* (Aldershot, UK: Ashgate, 1995).

3 J. Isawa Elaigwu and Erim O. Erim, eds, *Foundations of Nigerian Federalism: Pre-Colonial Antecedents*, 2nd ed. (Jos: Institute of Governance and Social Research, 2001).

4 However, in a recent land and maritime dispute between Cameroon and Nigeria, the International Court of Justice adjudged part of the Lake Chad area, whose ownership Cameroon claimed, to be part of Nigerian territory. The court adjudged certain other parts of the Lake Chad area and the Bakassi Peninsula, sovereignty over which Nigeria claimed, to be part of Cameroon. See *Case Concerning the Land and Maritime Boundary between Cameroon and Nigeria (Cameroon v Nigeria: Equatorial Guinea Intervening)*, 10 October 2002, General List No. 94. The judgment is obtainable at: http://www.icj-cij.org/icjwww/idocket/icn/icnjudgment/icn_ijudgment_20021010.PDF.

5 See also J. Isawa Elaigwu and G.N. Uzoigwe, eds, *Foundations of Nigerian Federalism: 1900–1960*, 2nd ed. (Jos: Institute of Governance and Social Research, 2001).

6 Nigeria (Constitution) (Amendment No. 3) Order in Council, 1959, effective 24 October 1959.

7 1960 No. 1652, effective 1 October 1960.

8 See also J. Isawa Elaigwu and R.A. Akindele, eds, *Foundations of Nigerian Federalism: 1960–1995*, 2nd ed. (Jos: Institute of Governance and Social Research, 2001).

9 Ladipo Adamolekun, ed., "Federalism in Nigeria: Toward Federal Democracy," *Publius: The Journal of Federalism* 21 (Fall 1991): entire issue.

10 This excludes two years of limited civilian rule between 1991 and 1993, when elected officials ran state and local governments while General Ibrahim Babangida remained the country's military head of state. After his program for transition to civil rule was aborted in June 1993, Babangida resigned in favour of an interim national government headed by Chief Ernest Shonekan, a civilian. Shonekan's brief tenure was terminated on 17 November 1993 by yet another military take-over, this time led by General Sani Abacha.

11 Led by General Aguiyi Ironsi (January to July 1966, when Ironsi was assassinated); General Yakubu Gowon (July 1966 to July 1975, when Gowon was deposed); General Murtala Mohammed (July 1975 to February 1976, when Mohammed was assassinated); General Olusegun Obasanjo (February 1976 to October 1979, when he handed power over to civilians); General Muhammadu Buhari (December 1983 to August 1985, when Buhari was deposed); General Ibrahim Babangida (August 1985 to August 1993, when he handed power to an interim government); General Sani Abacha (November 1993 to June 1998, when he died); and General Abdulsalami Abubakar (June 1998 to May 1999, when he handed power to civilians).

12 See also J. Isawa Elaigwu, P.C. Logams, and H.S. Galadima, eds, *Federalism and Nation Building in Nigeria: The Challenges of the 21st Century* (Abuja: National Council on Intergovernmental Relations, 1994).

13 *Report of the Constitution Debate Coordinating Committee (CDCC), Volume 1, Main Report* (Abuja: Government Printer, December 1999), p. 56.

14 Ibid.

15 For example, insertion of a new provision allowing recall of federal and state legislators (§69 and 110).

16 For example, establishment of a new National Judicial Council (§153 and Third Schedule Part 1 (I)), whose mandate encapsulates both federal and state judges. The Tobi Committee had rejected a proposal to establish such a unified council on the grounds that it would infringe on Nigeria's federal structure.

17 Constitution of the Federal Republic of Nigeria (Promulgation) Decree No. 24 of 5 May 1999.

18 Later 49, following the withdrawal of one of the committee members.

19 After Murtala was assassinated in February 1976 in a failed coup attempt by junior army officers, his successor, General Olusegun Obasanjo, carried through Murtala's program for a return to civilian rule as planned and on schedule.

20 *Report of the Constitution Drafting Committee,* 2 vols (Lagos: Government Printer, 1976).

21 See, for example, W.I. Ofonagoro, A. Ojo, and A. Jinadu, eds, *The Great Debate: Nigerian Viewpoints on the Draft Constitution, 1976/1977* (Lagos: Daily Times Publications, 1977); S. Kumo and A. Aliyu, eds, *Issues in the Nigerian Draft Constitution* (Zaria: Institute of Administration, Ahmadu Bello University, 1977); and *National Seminar on Islam and the Draft Constitution* (Kano: Islamic Foundation, 1977).

22 The debates can be read in *Debates of the Constituent Assembly* of 1977–78, 3 vols (Lagos: Government Printer, 1978).

23 See ibid., vol. 1, pp. 4–9.

24 Constitution of the Federal Republic of Nigeria (Enactment) Decree 1978, 21 September 1978. Most controversial was the elimination from the Constituent Assembly draft of a provision disqualifying from election to office (for a limited time) anyone who, since independence, had been found guilty of corruption, unjust enrichment, or abuse of office.

25 Constitution of the Federal Republic of Nigeria (Amendment) Decree 1979, 28 September 1979.

26 J. Isawa Elaigwu and Habu Galadima, "The Shadow of Sharia Over Nigerian Federalism," *Publius: The Journal of Federalism* 33 (Summer 2003): 123–44.

27 *The (Nigerian) Guardian,* 12 February 2000, p. 1: "Bashiru Sule, a Moslem, was given 80 lashes before an enthusiastic crowd of about 500 people near the Emir's palace in Gusau last Thursday, for drinking beer. Afterwards, Ibrahim Abubakar Ruwon-Dorawa, the judge who handed down the summary sentence, said 'I am happy. It is a good day for Zamfara.' Sule was caught drinking alcohol by members of a vigilante group raised by the state governor Ahmed Sani to

monitor the observance of the strict Islamic code which was introduced to Zamfara on 27 January, officials said." *The Guardian*, 18 February 2000, p. 5: "18-year-old Sani Mamman was yesterday given 100 lashes for having premarital sex. His partner, a 16-year-old, had her punishment deferred due to illness." *The Guardian*, 24 March 2000, p. 1 ff.: The first amputation was on 22 March 2000, when the right hand of Bello Buba Jangebe was cut off for theft of a cow, to which he had confessed. Jangebe was given 30 days to appeal the sentence before the punishment was imposed; he declined to appeal.

28 The two most famous stoning cases, involving Safiya Husseini (Sokoto State) and Amina Lawal (Katsina State), attracted worldwide attention. Both women were eventually discharged by the state *sharia* courts of appeal.

29 "Nigeria At Cross Road," a statement by Ohaneze Ndigbo, the umbrella body of all Igbo organizations, printed in *The Guardian*, 3 July 2000, p. 67.

30 Per the Lagos State House of Assembly, reported in *The Guardian*, 16 November 1999, p. 3.

31 J.N.D. Anderson, *Law Reform in the Muslim World* (London: The Athlone Press, 1976), pp. 27–8. The only limitations were on forms of punishment. From the beginning of their rule, the British had abolished mutilation and torture and had subjected other penalties to a repugnancy test.

32 Editorial in *The Guardian*, 6 December 1999, p. 20.

33 Per the Ondo State House of Assembly, reported in *The Guardian*, 24 November 1999, p. 7.

34 *Report of the Presidential Committee on the Review of the 1999 Constitution, Volume 1, Main Report* (Abuja: Government Printer, February 2001), pp. 3–4.

35 Ibid., p. 4. See also *The Position of the Citizens' Forum for Constitutional Reform (CFCR) on the Review of the Constitution of the Federal Republic of Nigeria, 2001*.

36 J. Isawa Elaigwu, *Nigeria: A Rebirth for the Twenty-First Century* (Jos: Institute of Governance and Social Research, 2000), p. 17.

37 *Report of the Presidential Committee on the Review of the 1999 Constitution, Volume 1, Main Report*, February 2001, p. 3.

38 Ibid., p. 37.

39 Lord James Bryce, quoted in Paul E. Peterson, *The Price of Federalism* (Washington, DC: Brookings Institution, 1995), p. 175.

40 Section 15(2) and Section 42.

41 Section 15(4).

42 Section 14(3)(4).

43 Section 153 and Paragraph c, Part 1 of the Third Schedule to the Constitution. The military government of General Sani Abacha had earlier established a similar commission.

44 B.O. Nwabueze, *A Constitutional History of Nigeria* (New York: Longman, 1982), p. 153.

45 See *Report of the Commission appointed to enquire into the fears of Minorities and the means of allaying them* (London: Her Majesty's Stationary Office, 1958).

46 1999 Constitution § 8.

47 Constitution of the Federal Democratic Republic of Ethiopia, Proclamation
    No. 1/1995, reprinted in *Constitutions of the Countries of the World*, Release 97–1,
    (Gisbert H. Flanz, ed., 1997).

48 Ibid., Preamble.

49 Ibid., Art. 39.

50 Section 162.

51 See, for instance, "New LGs: Lagos Warns of Imminent Crisis," *This Day*,
    22 April 2004, available at http://www.thisdayonline.com. The procedure,
    which is the subject of varying interpretations, is set out in Section 8(3).

52 Section 4(7)(a); *Attorney General of Abia State & Ors v Attorney General of the Feder-
    ation* (2002) 6 N.W.L.R. (Part 763) 1.

53 Per Eso, JSC, in *Attorney General of Ogun State & Ors v Attorney General of the Feder-
    ation & Ors* (1982) 1-2 SC 13, at p. 35. See also Ogundare, JSC, in *Abia State &
    Ors v Attorney General of the Federation (Supra)*, at p. 435. To hold otherwise would
    attribute to a concurrent power an exclusive effect.

54 *Attorney General of Abia State & Ors v Attorney General of the Federation (Supra)*.

55 *Attorney General of Ondo State v Attorney General of the Federation & Ors* (2002)
    6 S.C. (Part I), 1.

56 By Decree No. 89 of 1992, a National Council on Intergovernmental Relations
    (NCIR) was established by General Babangida and mandated to, among other
    things, study and advise on potential conflict areas in intergovernmental rela-
    tions, promote cooperation among the orders of government, and provide reg-
    ular forums for the interaction of the officials of the different orders of
    government in the search for solutions to common problems. However, the
    NCIR, whose expertise would have been better appreciated in a democratic set-
    ting, no longer exists.

57 *Report of the Constitution Drafting Committee Containing the Draft Constitution*, vol. 1
    (Lagos: Federal Ministry of Information, 1976), p. xxix.

58 Ibid., p. xxx.

59 In the 19 April 2003 presidential elections, the leading contenders for the of-
    fice of president were mostly retired military officers: Olusegun Obasanjo of the
    Peoples Democratic Party (PDP), Muhammadu Buhari of the All Nigeria Peo-
    ples Party (ANPP), Odumegwu Ojukwu of the All Progressive Grand Alliance
    (APGA), and Ike Nwachukwu of the National Democratic Party (NDP). In the
    run up to the 2007 presidential elections, apart from the incumbent vice presi-
    dent, Atiku Abubakar (who is a retired officer of the Nigerian Customs Service),
    Generals Ibrahim Babangida, Muhammadu Buhari, and Buba Marwa are being
    touted as leading contenders.

60 This reference is to the US case *Marbury v Madison*, 5 US 137 (1803), in which
    the US Supreme Court asserted its authority to declare acts of Congress to be
    unconstitutional.

61 Section 11(4).

62 Sections 8, 9, and 12(3).

63 Section 58(3).
64 Section 4(8). See, for example, *Attorney General of Bendel State v Attorney General of the Federation & Ors* (1982) 3 NCLR 1; and *Attorney General of Ondo State v Attorney General of the Federation & Ors (Supra)*.
65 Section 295.
66 Cap. 162, Laws of the Federation of Nigeria, 1990.
67 Section 44(3).
68 Section 153 and Paragraph 32(a), Third Schedule.
69 *Attorney General of Ogun State v Aberuagba* (1985) 1 N.W.L.R. (Part 3), 395.
70 Paragraph D, Part II, Second Schedule.
71 Section 165.
72 Section 162(1).
73 Section 153(1)(n) and section 32(b), Part 1, Third Schedule.
74 *Attorney General of the Federation v Attorney General of Abia State & Ors* (2002) 4 S.C. (Part I), 1.
75 Prior to that, the federal government established, pursuant to an executive bill enacted by the National Assembly, a Niger Delta Development Commission to cater to the interests of oil-producing communities.
76 *Attorney General of the Federation v Attorney General of Abia State & Ors (Supra)*.
77 Section 315.
78 A bill for a new revenue-allocation formula that, in large measure, still favours the federal government is pending before the National Assembly.
79 Section 5(4)(5).
80 Section 34(2)(c).
81 Section 27(2)(d).
82 *Musa v INEC* (2002) 11 N.W.L.R. (Part 778) 223.
83 Section 222(e).
84 Section 225(3)
85 Section 45(1).
86 African Charter on Human and Peoples' Rights (Application and Enforcement) Act, Cap. 10, Laws of the Federation of Nigeria, 1990.
87 For example, *Abacha v Fawehinmi* (2000) 6 N.W.L.R (Part 660) 228.
88 Section 9.
89 The committee called for memoranda, held nationwide tours (at which both written and oral submissions were obtained), organized local town meetings, and held state public hearings and zonal conferences at designated universities around the country.
90 *Report of the Presidential Committee on the Review of the 1999 Constitution, Volume 1, Main Report*, February 2001, pp. 4–5.
91 Otive Igbuzor, *A Critique of the 1999 Constitution Making and Review Process in Nigeria*, Citizens' Forum for Constitutional Reform (CFCR) Monograph Series, No. 1, 2002.
92 *Report of the Presidential Committee on the Review of the 1999 Constitution, Volume 1, Main Report*, February 2001, p. 2.

**Russia
(Overview)**

Capital: Moscow
Population: 144 Million
(2002 est.)

Boundaries and place names are
representative only and do not
imply any official endorsement.

N

| 1000 | 0 | 1000 | 2000 | 3000 |

kilometers

Sources: ESRI Ltd.; CIA World Factbook;
Times Atlas of the World

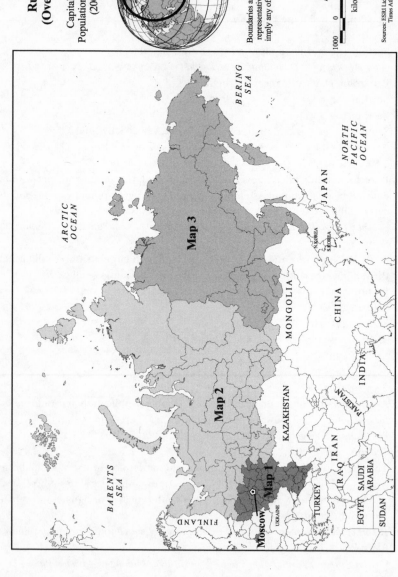

ARCTIC
OCEAN

BARENTS
SEA

BERING
SEA

Map 3

Map 2

Map 1

Moscow

FINLAND

UKRAINE

KAZAKHSTAN

MONGOLIA

CHINA

KOREA
KOREA

JAPAN

NORTH
PACIFIC
OCEAN

INDIA

PAKISTAN

IRAN

TURKEY

IRAQ

SAUDI
ARABIA

EGYPT

SUDAN

Russian Federation (Map 1)

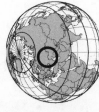

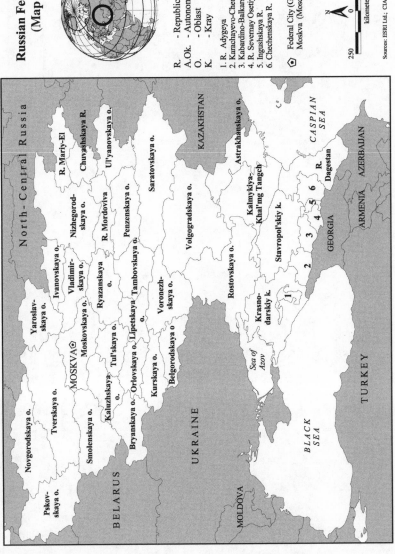

R.   - Republic
A.Ok. - Autonomous Okrug
O.   - Oblast
K.   - Kray

1. R. Adygeya
2. Karachayevo-Cherkesskaya Resp.
3. Kabardino-Balkarskaya Resp.
4. R. Severnay Osetiya
5. Ingushskaya R.
6. Chechenskaya R.

⊕ Federal City (Gorod) of
   Moskva (Moscow)

250   0   250
kilometers

Sources: ESRI Ltd.; CIA World Factbook

Map labels

North-Central Russia

Pskovskaya o.
Novgorodskaya o.
Tverskaya o.
Yaroslavskaya o.
Ivanovskaya o.
Vladimirskaya o.
Nizhegorodskaya o.
R. Mariy-El
Chuvashskaya R.
Ul'yanovskaya o.
Smolenskaya o.
MOSKVA⊕
Moskovskaya o.
Ryazanskaya o.
R. Mordoviva
Penzenskaya o.
Saratovskaya o.
Kaluzhskaya o.
Tul'skaya o.
Orlovskaya o.
Lipetskaya o.
Tambovskaya o.
Bryanskaya o.
Kurskaya o.
Belgorodskaya o.
Voronezhskaya o.
Volgogradskaya o.
Astrakhanskaya o.
KAZAKHSTAN
Rostovskaya o.
Krasnodarskiy k.
Stavropol'skiy k.
Kalmykiya-Khal'mg Tangch
CASPIAN SEA
R. Dagestan
Sea of Azov
BLACK SEA
TURKEY
GEORGIA
ARMENIA
AZERBAIJAN
MOLDOVA
UKRAINE
BELARUS

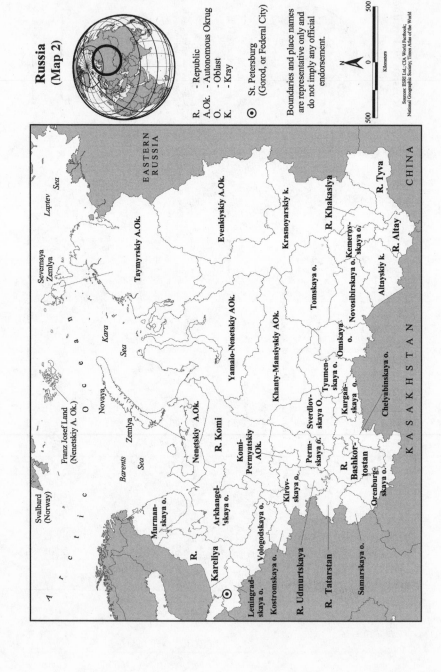

Russia
(Map 2)

R. - Republic
A.Ok. - Autonomous Okrug
O. - Oblast
K. - Kray

⊙ St. Petersburg
(Gorod, or Federal City)

Boundaries and place names
are representative only and
do not imply any official
endorsement.

Kilometers

500   0   500

Sources: ESRI Ltd., CIA World Factbook;
National Geographic Society; Times Atlas of the World

EASTERN
RUSSIA

*Laptev
Sea*

Severnaya
Zemlya

Taymyrskiy A.Ok.

Evenkiyskiy A.Ok.

Krasnoyarskiy k.

R. Tyva

R. Khakasiya

*Kara
Sea*

Yamalo-Nenetskiy AOk.

Tomskaya o.

Kemerov-
skaya o.

R. Altay

Altayskiy k.

Novosibirskaya o.

Omskaya
o.

Khanty-Mansiyskiy AOk.

Tyumen-
skaya o.

Kurgan-
skaya
o.

Chelyabinskaya o.

K A S A K H S T A N

CHINA

Novaya

Zemlya

*Barents
Sea*

Franz Josef Land
(Nenetskiy A. Ok.)

Nenetskiy
A.Ok.

R. Komi

Komi-
Permyatskiy
AOk.

Perm-
skaya o.

Sverdlov-
skaya O.

R.
Bashkor-
tostan

Orenburg-
skaya o.

A r c t i c   O c e a n

Svalbard
(Norway)

Murman-
skaya o.

Arkhangel-
'skaya o.

R.
Kareliya

Vologodskaya o.

Kirov-
skaya o.

R. Udmurtskaya

R. Tatarstan

Samarskaya o.

Leningrad-
skaya o.

Kostromskaya o.

⊙

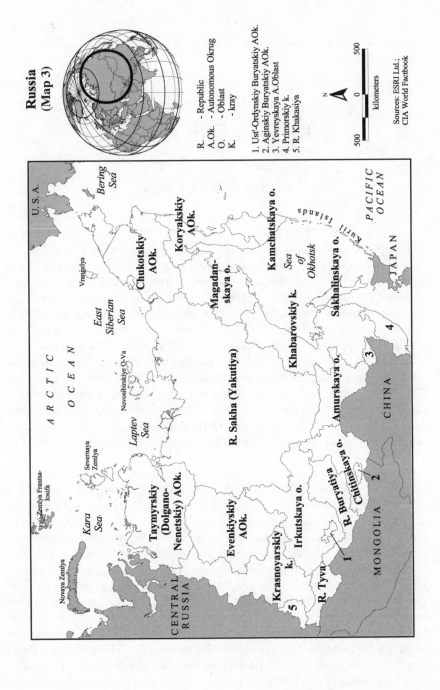

**Russia
(Map 3)**

R. - Republic
A.Ok. - Autonomous Okrug
O. - Oblast
K. - kray

1. Ust'-Ordynskiy Buryatskiy AOk.
2. Aginskiy Buryatskiy AOk.
3. Yevreyskaya A.Oblast
4. Primorskiy k.
5. R. Khakasiya

N

kilometers

500   0   500

Sources: ESRI Ltd.;
CIA World Factbook

U.S.A.

*Bering
Sea*

Vrangelya

Koryakskiy
AOk.

Chukotskiy
AOk.

*East
Siberian
Sea*

Magadan-
skaya o.

Kamchatskaya o.

ARCTIC

OCEAN

Novosibirskiye O-va

*Laptev
Sea*

*Sea
of
Okhotsk*

Kuril Islands

R. Sakha (Yakutiya)

Khabarovskiy k.

Sakhalinskaya o.

*PACIFIC
OCEAN*

*Severnaya
Zemlya*

*Zemlya Frantsa-
Iosifa*

*Kara
Sea*

Taymyrskiy
(Dolgano-
Nenetskiy) AOk.

JAPAN

Novaya Zemlya

Evenkiyskiy
AOk.

Amurskaya o.

3

CHINA

4

**CENTRAL
RUSSIA**

Krasnoyarskiy
k.

Irkutskaya o.

R. Buryatiya

Chitinskaya o.

2

5

R. Tyva

1

MONGOLIA

Russian Federation

MARAT SALIKOV

Geographically, Russia is the world's largest country, with a land area of 17,075,200 square kilometres. It dominates northern Eurasia, stretching northward to the Arctic Ocean, eastward to the Pacific Ocean, and westward to Central Europe, and it is bordered by (among other countries) Azerbaijan, Belarus, China, Poland, and the Ukraine. Russia's population numbers about 145 million. Russians comprise the most numerous ethnic group (81.5 percent of the population), and Russian is the predominant language. However, Russia includes a variety of other ethnic groups, including Tatars (3.8 percent of the population), Ukrainians (3.0 percent), Chuvash (1.2 percent), and Bashkirs (0.9 percent). These groups tend to be geographically concentrated, and some groups retain their own language. The main religion is Russian Orthodox, although there is a substantial Muslim population and some representation of other religions. As of 2000 the per capita income was US$4,200.

Russia has not only the world's largest national land area, but also one of its most complex federal systems. The Russian Federation combines both ethno-federalism and territorial federalism. Its 89 constituent units, typically referred to as "subjects of the federation," are divided into six different types – republics, autonomous areas, one autonomous region, territories, regions, and federal cities – although the asymmetrical features of this division have been muted since the adoption of the 1993 federation Constitution. This Constitution also gives federal constitutional status to local governments. In addition, it authorizes the president of the federation to enter into treaties with the executives of constituent units, further particularizing the allocation of power between the national government and the various subjects of the federation. Finally, in 2000 President Vladimir Putin superimposed seven federal districts on the federal structure, each with its own presidential representative, potentially introducing even greater complexity as well as hierarchy into Russia's federal system.

Putin's reform highlights another key aspect of Russian constitutionalism, namely its evolving character. The current Constitution of the Russian Federation dates from 1993, and the federal arrangements under it remain dynamic.[1] To understand the structure and operation of contemporary Russian constitutionalism and in particular its federal dimensions, one must examine the historical development of federalism in Russia.

THE FEDERATION CONSTITUTION IN HISTORICAL CONTEXT

Creation of the Federation

Federalism was formally introduced by the federal Constitution of Russia in 1918. Before this date, however, there were precursors of federalism in Imperial Russia. These precursors involved tendencies toward federalization, or toward decentralization of a unitary state in favour of some autonomy for subunits. For example, although before 1918 Russia was a unitary state, several territories within the boundaries of the state – such as Finland, Poland, and the Ukraine – enjoyed special autonomy.[2]

The demise of Imperial Russia provided the occasion for the creation of a federation. Even before the Russian revolutions in February and October 1917, different plans for the structure of the Russian state had been proposed, including federative and quasi-federative models. For example, in 1905 the Party of Constitutional Democrats proposed the establishment of a bicameral parliament, with one house including representatives from local governments. At the same time, the Radical Party suggested the creation of a United States of Russia (i.e., a classic federation). Anarchists such as Mikhail Bakunin and Peter Kropotkin offered their own plans for an encompassing global federal structure.[3] However, the Bolshevik (Communist) Party, headed by Vladimir Lenin, initially rejected the idea of federalism for Russia, insisting that it was necessary to retain a centralized, indivisible state.

The Communists' position shifted after they came to power in the October Revolution of 1917 and faced the outbreak of civil war. Lenin accepted a federal arrangement in order to combat disorder, win the support of non-Russian minorities, and prevent the disintegration of the country. The federation in Russia was instituted by the Declaration of the Rights of the Toiling and Exploited People, which was accepted on 10 July 1918 by the Fifth Soviet Congress. The legal establishment of the federal form of state structure occurred with the first written Russian Constitution in July 1918, which proclaimed that the Soviet regions could be united in autonomous regions and could "enter the Russian Socialist Federated Soviet Republic on a federal basis." Thus the stage of prefederal relations in Russia might also be regarded as its preconstitutional stage because the Russian Federation was created by Russia's first written constitution.

Federal Development During the Soviet Era

The most significant federalist development during the Soviet era was the incorporation of the Russian Socialist Federated Soviet Republic (RSFSR) into the Union of Soviet Socialist Republics (USSR), which was officially proclaimed in 1924. Despite its professed commitment to "socialist federalism," the USSR was very much a unitary state, and policies of the RSFSR had to conform to those determined by the leadership of the USSR. The USSR was based on a one-party political system rooted in Marxist-Leninist ideology, with an emphasis on "democratic centralism,"[4] a centrally planned economy, and a powerfully repressive state machinery. The Constitution's apparent grants of power to constituent units were undermined by broad grants to the central government to set "general principles" for public policy as well as to legislate on all "questions of all-union significance." The Soviet system was administered through regional Communist Party officials, with each republic within the Soviet Union being headed by a first secretary of the Communist Party drawn from the indigenous population of the republic. These party secretaries functioned as envoys from the central government rather than as representatives of the regions in which they governed, and they remained dependent on Moscow rather than on local supporters for their political position. Thus a huge gap separated constitutional prescription and political practice, giving rise to a sort of fictive or sham federalism in which, among many other things, the constitutional right of secession was a dead letter.

What was true of the USSR was likewise true of the RSFSR; federalism was more a pretence than a reality. Nevertheless, two aspects of this fictive federalism should be highlighted. First, the adoption of the 1918 Constitution did not complete the USSR's federal development because federal relations changed as a result of constitutional amendments and the adoption of three new constitutions during the Soviet era (1924, 1936, and 1977). Second, federalism during the Soviet era set the stage for federalism under the Russian Federation by providing the underpinnings for its distinctive combination of ethno-federalism and territorial federalism. The RSFSR acknowledged the multiethnic character of its population by according special status – as autonomous republics, *oblasts* (regions), or *okrugs* (areas) – to areas in which non-Russian populations were concentrated, while creating purely territorial *oblasts* and *kraya* (territories) in areas in which the population was predominantly Russian. These territorial units did not have the status of subjects of the federation. Rather, they were governed directly by the central government and, therefore, their relations to the centre were unitary rather than federal in character.

The RSFSR's federal arrangements did not survive the dissolution of the Soviet Union and the move toward democratization. These developments transformed federal-regional relations, leading to greater assertions of autonomy by subjects of the federation. In the early 1990s, for example, when Boris Yeltsin declared that republics could take as much sovereignty as they could swallow, most autonomous republics adopted Declarations of State Sovereignty that proclaimed their sovereign status. The Constitution was amended to eliminate the term "autonomous" from the title of the republics, the title RSFSR was replaced by "Russian Federation," and the territories, regions, and federal cities were all recognized as members of the new federation. However, under the three-part Federation Treaty of 1992,[5] signed by federal authorities and by all of the constituent units of the Russian Federation except Chechnya and Tatarstan, these new members did not enjoy rights equal to those of the republics. Only with the adoption of the 1993 Constitution, Russia's current constitution, were the equal rights of all subjects of the federation recognized. In this and other respects, this Constitution has played a crucial role in promoting democratic reform and encouraging the development of federalism.

CONSTITUTIONAL PRINCIPLES
OF THE RUSSIAN FEDERATION

The Status of Subjects of the Federation

Whereas the federation as a whole is sovereign, its constituent units are not. This was confirmed by the Constitutional Court in a 2000 case involving the Republic of Altai's assertion that it was a sovereign republic. The Court concluded that the federation Constitution does not recognize any source of power other than the multinational people of Russia; therefore, it does not presume any sovereignty other than the sovereignty of the Russian Federation. The sovereignty of the federation precludes the existence of two orders of sovereign power, each enjoying independence in a single system of state power; consequently, it does not allow for even "limited" sovereignty on the part of republics or of any other unit of the Russian Federation.[6]

Yet, although the constituent units lack sovereign authority, they still enjoy considerable autonomy, and their position in the federation is guaranteed in a number of ways, including the following. First, all constituent units of the federation are recognized as self-governing entities, a shift from the Soviet era when only ethnically based units were recognized as subjects of the federation. All units are now free to adopt their own constitution or charter (quasi-constitution) without seeking approval from federal bodies (as had been required during the Soviet era). They may, therefore, design their own government institutions, allocate power among these institutions, and set the terms of office and modes of selection for officials. However, under the federation Constitution's supremacy clause, federal law is given precedence over these subnational constitutions, and therefore the provisions of these constitutions must conform to federal constitutional requirements. Thus the constitutional arrangements must be based on the fundamental principles of the Constitution (e.g., the separation of powers and a republican form of government) and on the general principles for the formation of legislative and executive bodies that are fixed in federal law.

Second, the territorial integrity of the subjects of the federation is guaranteed. Their borders cannot be changed without their consent as well as the consent of the Federation Council. The constituent units do have the right to merge – that is, to join with another subject of the federation to form a new constituent unit – but only under procedures established by federal law. In recent years, there have been proposals to encourage such mergers, given the small size and economic difficulties of some subjects of the federation – for example, to merge the Perm region with the Komi-Permyak autonomous area and to merge the Irkutsk region with the Ust-Ordyn Byurat autonomous area.

Third, each constituent unit has its own name and is free to change it. As all component units are listed in the federation Constitution, the question arose as to how the new name of a constituent unit would become included in the Constitution. In its decision of 28 November 1995, interpreting Article 137, Section 2, of the Constitution, the federal Constitutional Court ruled that changes in the name of a constituent unit are incorporated in the text of the Constitution by a decree of the president of the Russian Federation, once a constituent entity has adopted a new name according to a procedure of its own choosing. However, a change of name that affects the foundations of the constitutional system, human and civil rights and freedoms, the interests of the other constituent units of the federation, the interests of the federation as a whole, or the interests of other states and that presupposes a change in the composition of the federation or in the constitutional legal status of the constituent units, cannot be accomplished under this procedure.[7] Moreover, the legal status of a constituent unit may be changed only with mutual consent of the federation and the constituent unit in accordance with the federal constitutional law.

Fourth, subjects of the federation can protect their interests against federal intrusion. They are represented in the Federation Council, which is one chamber of the bicameral parliament (i.e., the Federal Assembly). Each constituent unit has two representatives, one from its legislature and the other from its executive. If the federal government challenges their authority, constituent units can seek protection from the Constitutional Court. However, the federation can protect its interests against centrifugal tendencies. It can establish its own agencies in the component units; for example, federal bodies with executive power (e.g., ministries, services, agencies, and state committees) maintain branches in the constituencies.

Finally, the constituent units exercise both exclusive powers and concurrent powers. These powers extend even into foreign affairs. Constituent units may enter into international economic agreements (but not treaties) with the constituent parts of other countries and, with the consent of the federation, even with foreign nations. However, their powers do not extend to a right of secession. According to Article 4, Section 3, of the Constitution, "The Russian Federation shall ensure the integrity and inviolability of its territory."

Thus far, this chapter has emphasized features common to all subjects of the federation. The 1993 Constitution confirms the equal legal status of these units. Each has equal representation in the federal government, can devise its own institutions, can exercise legislative authority, and so on. Further, Article 72, Section 2, which lists the concurrent powers of the federation and its component units, states that "the provisions of this Article shall equally apply to the republics, territories, regions, federal cities, the autonomous region and autonomous areas." Nevertheless, this asserted equality of rights is in tension with the diversity among the constituent units and even with other legal authority, namely the Federation Treaty of 1992 – although this treaty was demoted to subordinate status in Section 2, Point 1, of the 1993 Constitution. It is useful to consider the six types of constituent units that make up the Russian Federation.

THE DIVERSITY OF CONSTITUENT UNITS

The subjects of the federation include 32 ethnically based units (21 republics, ten autonomous areas, and one autonomous region) and 57 territorial units (six territories, 49 regions, and two federal cities). Of the 32 ethnically based constituent units, only nine have a native ethnic population that constitutes more than 50 percent of the population: the Aginsky Buryat autonomous area, the Komi-Permyak autonomous area, the Kabardin-Balkar Republic, the Republic of Dagestan, the Republic of Northern Ossetia-Alania, the Republic of Tatarstan, the Republic of Tyva, the Chechen Republic, and the Chuvash Republic.

The federation's constituent units vary dramatically in population, size, and economic development. Seven constituent units boast populations of more than 3 million, while eleven have fewer than 300,000 inhabitants. Six units encompass more than 500,000 square kilometres, while six include less than 20,000 square kilometres. Several are economically prosperous, such as the Tyumen region, Sakha (Yakutia), Sverdlovsk, and Krasnoyarsk, while others are economically backward, such as the Penza region, the Republic of Mordovia, the Republik of Tuva, and the Republic of Dagestan.

Nine out of ten autonomous areas and Russia's two federal cities – Moscow and St Petersburg – are located wholly within the borders of other constituent units. This circumstance requires these compound units to forge agreements regulating areas of mutual concern. Among the compound constituent units are the Nenets autonomous area (inside the Arkhangelsk region), the Komi-Permyak autonomous area (inside the Perm region), the

Ust-Ordyn Buryat autonomous area (inside the Irkutsk region), the Aginsky Buryat autonomous area (inside the Chita region), the Koryak autonomous area (inside the Kamchatka region), the Khanty-Mansi and Yamal-Nenets autonomous areas (inside the Tyumen region), and the Taimyr (Dolgan-Nenets) and Evenk autonomous areas (inside the Krasnoyarsk region).

Republics

Republics resemble nation-states in several respects. They have their own constitutions, while other constituent units have charters; they have state languages that are used in legislation, administration, and schools along with Russian (the official language of the federation); they have the right to establish constitutional courts (which has been done by about half of the republics), while other constituent units have charter courts; the heads of the republics are usually denominated as presidents, while those in other constituent units are called governors; and the republics have capitals, while other subjects of the federation have so-called administrative centres. Most of these distinctive features of the republics have historical roots, reflecting the fact that the republics were members of the Russian Federation from the outset. But under the 1993 Constitution, these differences are matters more of terminology than of substance and do not detract from the equality of rights among constituent units proclaimed in the Constitution.

The Autonomous Region and the Autonomous Areas

The autonomous region and autonomous areas, which are commonly called "autonomies," were designed to reflect the distinctive ethnic composition of the populations they contain. Historically, these jurisdictions were – and many still are – less developed economically; thus previous Russian constitutions contained economic and social welfare guarantees for these units, some of which have been carried over in the current Constitution. For example, whereas the status of other constituent units is determined by the federation Constitution and by regional constitutions or charters, in the case of autonomies, their status can be determined not only by federal and regional constitutional legislation, but also by a special federal law that can be adopted on the initiative of one or more of the autonomies. (To date none has proposed such an initiative.) Nevertheless, in view of the Constitution's equal-rights clause, there is little basis for distinguishing the autonomies from other subjects of the federation.

The Territories and the Regions

Historically, territories *(kraya)* had autonomous regions within their borders, whereas regions *(oblasts)* did not. Because this distinction no longer exists, the difference between these constituent units is a matter of terminology rather than substance. Both territories and regions are based on territory rather than ethnicity and are populated mostly by Russian speakers. These constituent units were recognized as members of the federation in 1992 when the Federation Treaty was signed.

The Federal Cities

Like the regions, the two federal cities – Moscow and St Petersburg – are based on territory, not on ethnicity. They contain mostly Russian populations and were recognized as members of the federation in 1992. What distinguishes the federal cities is that they are both cities and constituent units of the federation (thus resembling the three *Land* cities in Germany). These enclaves are situated within the territory of other units. Moscow is surrounded by the territory of the Moscow region, and St Petersburg is surrounded by the territory of the Leningrad region. Moscow has a particularly complicated status, with four distinct legal identities. It is simultaneously a city, a constituent unit of the federation, the administrative centre of another constituent unit (the Moscow region), and the capital of the Russian Federation.

Local Government

Article 12 of the Constitution recognizes a right of local self-government that citizens exercise directly through referenda and elections and indirectly through the institutions of local government. The Constitution grants these local governments constitutional status and guarantees to them a range of independent powers. This represents a major innovation. In the past, local governments in Russia had no independent authority but were controlled by higher levels of government. The new status of local governments has not yet been fully assimilated, as uncertainty about the division of powers between the subjects of the federation and local governments has led to numerous conflicts.

The federation Constitution assigns the structuring of local government to both the federation and the constituent units of the federation as a joint power. Under this arrangement, the federation has promulgated framework legislation for the organization of local government – the federal Law on General Guidelines for the Organization of Local Self-Government in the Russian Federation. Most subjects of the federation have adopted their own laws that regulate the field of local government in detail. However, the Constitution imposes limits on what subjects of the federation may prescribe, as shown by the Constitutional Court's invalidation in 1997 of the Udmurtian Republic's Law on the System Governing the Organs of State Authority in the Urdmurtian Republic.[8]

The Udmurtian Constitution had dealt with the structuring of local government within the republic. It listed the *raions* (territorial units that may include more than one municipality) and main cities as territorial administrative entities of the Republic of Udmurtia. However, it did not give this status to territorial entities at a different level, namely to *raion* capitals, towns, and villages within the *raion* and other urban areas (such as parts of towns, subdistricts, and residential complexes). For this reason, the Court held that the legislature of the republic could not create structures of government for these latter entities. Because these entities are not part of the state authority system, only the local citizenry exercising its power of self-government has the authority to determine their governmental structure. For the Republic of Udmurtia to intervene and set up governing structures thus violated the federal constitutional right of citizens to exercise local self-government.

As this example indicates, under Article 133 of the Constitution, the judiciary plays an important role in guaranteeing local self-government. Chapter 8 of the Constitution, which is devoted to local government, ensures that the local population retains authority over local issues, such as the ownership, use, and disposal of municipal property, the approval and execution of the local budget, the establishment of local taxes, and the maintenance of law and order. Either the federation or a subject of the federation may grant to local governments additional state powers, which are exercised under the supervision of the granting government. However, the Constitution requires that the granting government provide the material and financial resources necessary to carry out these transferred responsibilities.

Indigenous Peoples

The Constitution recognizes rights of indigenous peoples in two ways. First, some peoples enjoy the status of a member of the federation. For instance, ten autonomous areas have been created for the aboriginal peoples of Siberia, the North, and the Far East. Second, the Constitution imposes a responsibility on both the federal and regional governments for guaranteeing the rights of indigenous peoples. Thus Article 71 empowers the federal government to regulate and protect the rights of national minorities, and Article 72 empowers both the federal government and the constituent units to protect the rights of ethnic minorities as well as the original natural environment and traditional way of life of small ethnic communities. Acting under this authority, the Federal Assembly enacted a federal Law on Guarantees of the Rights of the Aboriginal Small Peoples of the Russian Federation that grants the right to create different types of communities in order to preserve and develop the original environment, traditional way of life, and culture of aboriginal peoples having small populations. Some constituent units have established a fixed number of seats in their legislatures for the representatives of aboriginal peoples in order to ensure that their interests are taken into account in adopting new laws.

ALLOCATION OF POWERS

Under the Soviet constitutions, power was centralized, and the constituent units had few powers. With the fall of the Soviet Union in the early 1990s, latent conflicts emerged in Russia over the allocation of powers. The republics sought to maintain their exclusive status, while some strong regions demanded an equality of rights with the republics. The Sverdlovsk region even proclaimed itself the Urals Republic, but the central government refused to recognize this change in status. The Federation Treaty between the federal government and the governments of almost all the constituent units, signed in 1992, proposed one solution to this conflict, namely distinguishing between federal powers and concurrent powers, with republics being awarded more concurrent powers than were other constituent units. Bilateral treaties between the federal government and regional governments further complicated the allocation of powers.[9] The 1993 federation Constitution rejected the Federation Treaty's approach and asserted an equality of rights for all constituent units, assigning the same concurrent powers to all constituent units, such that republics and nonrepublics alike now have equal powers.

Federal Powers

Article 71 of the Constitution assigns to the federal government those powers that concern the country as a whole. These include the adoption and amendment of the Constitution and federal laws; supervision of the implementation of federal law; the establishment and organization of the federal legislative, executive, and judicial branches; the regulation and protection of rights and liberties; the establishment of criteria for citizenship; and the delineation of federal state property and of how it is to be managed. Article 71 also lists the branches of law on which the federal government may legislate, including criminal law, civil law in its procedural aspects, and intellectual property. Article 76, Section 1, states that on issues within the jurisdiction of the Russian Federation, federal constitutional provisions and laws shall have direct effect throughout the entire territory of the federation.

Concurrent Powers

The sphere of concurrent powers is the most complicated and innovative aspect of the Russian Federation's system of allocation of powers, and both the federal and regional governments are still experimenting with how best to allocate and implement these powers. Among the concurrent powers listed in Article 72 are the establishment of general guidelines for organizing the institutions of state power and local self-government; regulation of the possession, use, and management of land, mineral resources, water, and other natural resources; delimitation of state property; protection of historical and cultural monuments; general questions of upbringing, education, science, culture, physical culture, and sports; establishment of general guidelines for taxation and levies in the Russian Federation; and protection of the original environment and the traditional way of life of small ethnic communities. Both the federal and regional governments have the authority to adopt acts in the fields of administrative, administrative-procedural, labour, family, housing, land, water, and forestry legislation as well as in matters of legislation regarding the subsurface (e.g., minerals) and environmental protection. Article 76, Section 2, of the Constitution confirms that in matters within the concurrent jurisdiction of the Russian Federation and its constituent units, federal law is supreme and that subjects of the federation may adopt only laws and regulations that are consistent with federal law.

Powers of the Subjects of the Federation

Although the Constitution does not list regional powers, Article 73 indicates that those powers that do not fall within the jurisdiction of the Russian Federation or within the joint jurisdiction of the Russian Federation and its component units shall be exercised by the subjects of the federation. If a list of regional powers were drawn from the constitutions and charters of the constituent units, it would likely include the adoption and amendment of regional constitutions or charters and laws plus measures designed to ensure compliance with them; the structure and territory of the component units; the establishment of regional bodies both of legislative, executive, and judicial power and of local self-government; the management of regional state property; and fiscal powers, including preparation of the regional budget, imposition of regional taxes and levies, and expenditures of regional funds.

Recent Initiatives

Although the federation Constitution confirms the precedence of federal law over conflicting laws of the subjects of the federation, the enactment of regional legislation incompatible with federal law emerged as a serious problem during the initial years of the Russian Federation. This sparked a concerted effort to eliminate this contradictory legislation during President Vladimir Putin's early years in office. Relying on the prosecutor's office, the federal courts, and presidential representatives in federal districts, Putin was able to get rid of most of the contradictory regional legislation quite quickly, although there was considerable nonviolent resistance by some subjects of the federation.

Another presidential initiative with important implications for federalism involves the formation by presidential decree of seven so-called federal districts – the Central district, Northwest district, South district, Urals district, Siberian district, Privolzhsky district, and Far East district – each made up of six to seventeen constituent units.[10] The Constitution does not provide for the creation of such districts; thus the districts are not constituent members of the federation and do not have the powers of subjects of the federation. The federal districts are administered by representatives appointed by the president, whose responsibilities are to coordinate the activity of all federal bodies situated in the district; to promote cooperation among federal, regional, and local bodies as well as among political parties and public and religious associations; and to oversee the implementation of laws, decrees, and regulations of the president and the federal government. Some commentators suggest that the federal districts serve to ensure the integrity of the federation and to control centrifugal tendencies, while other commentators view them as a centralizing mechanism inconsistent with federalism. Whichever interpretation is correct, it may be that these districts will serve as a basis for merging existing constituent units and creating newly consolidated subjects of the federation.

STRUCTURE AND OPERATION OF THE FEDERAL GOVERNMENT

The 1993 Constitution establishes a system of separation of powers, with the executive power vested in the president and the government; the legislative power located in a bicameral Federal Assembly consisting of the Federation Council and the State Duma; and the judicial power residing in the Constitutional Court, the Supreme Court, the Supreme Arbitration Court, and the lower federal courts.

The Constitution assigns broad powers to the president, which enable him to play a leadership role, even a dominant role, in the federal government and in the federation as a whole. This feature of the constitutional design reflects the circumstances in the country at the time the Constitution was drafted. It was widely believed that Russia needed very strong leadership in order to confront the myriad challenges associated with the transition to a democratic polity and market economy in the 1990s as well as to combat centrifugal tendencies within the Russian Federation in order to prevent it from dissolving, as had the Soviet Union. Significant opposition to this model did develop, particularly among left-wing parties. There was even an alternative draft constitution circulated that provided for a parliamentary republic with a weak president.

Ultimately, however, the position espoused by President Yeltsin, a presidential republic with a very strong presidency, prevailed. President Putin's approach to his broad powers has been more cautious and secretive than that of his predecessor. For instance, unlike Yeltsin, he has never used his power to dissolve Parliament. Indeed, Yeltsin's disbanding of Parliament in September 1993 via Decree 1400 was an extraconstitutional act that had no legal basis in the then governing RSFSR Constitution. Under the 1993 Constitution, the president does have the power to dissolve Parliament under certain circumstances. Yeltsin threatened to use this power several times, but never did so. By contrast, in an address to the Federal Assembly in 2003, Putin announced his willingness to form the government based on the results of the parliamentary elections, although the Constitution does not require this of him.

The Federal Legislature

Legislative powers are vested in the bicameral Federal Assembly. The upper house, the Federation Council, has 178 seats, which are filled by executive and legislative representatives from each of the 89 constituent units, with members serving terms equal to the terms of the regional executive and legislature but not exceeding five years. The Federation Council is an unusually strong upper house. It has the power to approve changes of borders between constituents of the Russian Federation; approve presidential decrees on the introduction of martial law and a state of emergency; call elections for the presidency; impeach the president; appoint the judges of the Constitutional Court, the Supreme Court, and the Supreme Arbitration Court; and review all bills passed by the State Duma.

The lower house of the Federal Assembly, the State Duma, includes 450 members, with half elected by proportional representation from the party lists of parties winning at least 5 percent of the vote and the other half elected from single-member constituencies. Members are elected by direct popular vote for four-year terms. The State Duma has broad power, in conjunction with the Federation Council, to enact legislation on subjects on the federal- or concurrent-powers lists. In addition, the State Duma can grant consent to the president for the appointment of the chairman of the government, conduct votes of confidence on the government, appoint and dismiss the chairman of the Central Bank, bring charges against the president for his impeachment, pass federal laws, and undertake other responsibilities.

The Federal Executive

The president of the Russian Federation is the head of state and defines the basic domestic and foreign-policy guidelines for the country. The president is directly elected for a term of four years by the citizens of the Russian Federation by secret ballot, and no one may hold the office of president for more than two successive terms.

The president serves as supreme commander in chief of the armed forces and appoints and dismisses the supreme commander of the armed forces. In addition, he can appoint the chairman of the government, with the consent of the State Duma; decide on the resignation of the government; dissolve the State Duma in circumstances stipulated in the Constitution;[11] form and lead Russia's Security Council; introduce draft laws in the State Duma; sign and publish federal laws; conduct negotiations with foreign nations and sign international treaties in the name of the Russian Federation; issue decrees and executive orders; resolve issues of citizenship in the Russian Federation; and grant political asylum. In undertaking these responsibilities, he is assisted by the Presidential Administration, which provides staff and policy support to the president, drafts presidential decrees, and coordinates policy among government agencies.

The Federal Judiciary

The Constitution provides for a federal judicial system consisting of the Constitutional Court, a subsystem of general courts headed by the Supreme Court, and a subsystem of arbitration courts headed by the Supreme Arbitration Court.

The Constitutional Court was initially established in 1991, consisting of 15 judges (only 13 were actually appointed). The Constitution in operation at this time and the Law on the Constitutional Court (adopted on 12 July 1991)[12] granted the Constitutional Court full powers and proclaimed it to be the supreme judicial body charged with protecting the constitutional system. The Court is empowered to try cases on the constitutionality of international treaties and statutory acts (e.g., laws, presidential decrees, and government regulations), to regulate the activities of political parties and other public associations, to oversee law-enforcement practices, to settle jurisdictional disputes among various government entities, and to resolve other cases as prescribed by law. Under the law, the Court has authority to take up cases on its own initiative. The creation of the Constitutional Court marked a major shift in the government of Russia. With the short-lived exception of the USSR's Committee on Constitutional Supervision,[13] never before had there been a specialized body to ensure conformity with the Constitution, and never before had the judiciary served as a counterbalance to legislative and executive powers.

The operation of the Constitutional Court must be divided into two periods: up to late 1993 and since mid-1994. During the earlier period, the Court issued several important rulings protecting the rights of citizens. For example, it invalidated dismissal from office on the basis of age as a violation of the right against discrimination, and it struck down an eviction from an unlawfully occupied housing unit, which had been approved by a prosecutor but which had afforded the evicted no right to lodge a complaint against the prosecutor's action. The Court held that this restricted the right to judicial protection. The Court confirmed the principle of equality in contractual relations between the state and a citizen. It also responded to citizen complaints by acknowledging the responsibility of the state to meet its obligations concerning special-purpose cheques[14] for the purchase of cars and indexation[15] of citizens' money incomes and savings. However, unfamiliar with the political limits on supreme courts in other democratic systems, the Constitutional Court let itself become embroiled in the political conflict between President Yeltsin and Parliament in 1993, thereby sacrificing its reputation for independence and impartiality. This involvement led several judges who did not agree with the Court's stance to refuse to participate in its work; thus, unable to proceed with only part of its membership, the Court ceased to operate in October 1993. President Yeltsin, moreover, issued a decree suspending the Court in October 1993. The Constitutional Court was reconstituted only after the federation Constitution was adopted and a new federal Law on the Constitutional Court of the Russian Federation was enacted in July 1994.[16]

Under this new law, the Court's membership was increased to 19. The president nominates candidates for appointment to the Constitutional Court, and the Federation Council may either accept or reject these nominees. Members of the Court must meet several qualifications. They must be no younger than 40 years of age and citizens of the Russian Federation, with a legal education, a widely recognized high level of qualification in the field of law, an irreproachable reputation, and at least 15 years of legal experience. Judges on the Court serve a single 15-year term or until they reach the retirement age of 70.

The main responsibilities of the Constitutional Court continue to be to interpret the federation Constitution and, through the exercise of judicial review, to ensure that the legislation and other acts of the Russian Federation and its constituent units comply with constitutional mandates. The power of the Court was enhanced in 2001 by an amendment to the Law on the Court, under which, when regional authorities disobey Court decisions and/or refuse to take required action, the regional legislature may be dissolved and the regional governor removed from office.

Cases come to the Constitutional Court directly from citizens alleging violations of their constitutional rights and on request from lower courts that the Court review the constitutionality of a law applied or due to be applied in a specific case. Other cases reach the Court on request by the president, the State Duma, one-fifth of either the members of the Federation Council or the deputies of the State Duma, the government, the Supreme Court, the Supreme Arbitration Court, and the legislative and executive branches of subjects of the Russian Federation.

Since 1994 the Constitutional Court's federalism rulings have not consistently favoured either the federal government or the regional governments, although they have confirmed that the Court stands for an indivisible Russian state. What is striking is that the number of cases coming to the Court that deal with human rights and liberties has increased considerably. Emblematic is a 1996 ruling[17] in which the Court struck down the acts of a number of subjects of the federation that regulated the registration of citizens, holding that they violated the civil right to freedom of movement and choice of residence. This case reveals that the Court is quite willing to address possible violations of, or restrictions on, fundamental rights and freedoms, even in cases that arise from requests by state bodies rather than from citizen complaints.[18] However, the Court does face challenges, as indicated by the fact that this ruling was not implemented by the city of Moscow, the main offender, because the city's mayor pleaded special circumstances.

The Supreme Court of the Russian Federation is the highest judicial body dealing with civil, criminal, administrative, and other matters justiciable by general-jurisdiction courts. Its judges are nominated by the president and appointed by the Federation Council. The Supreme Court hears appeals from the lower federal courts, including general courts operating within the constituent units of the federation (one court in each unit), general courts operating within municipalities (e.g., district courts and city courts), and military courts operating in military units. It will also oversee the rulings of the specialized courts (e.g., administrative courts, labour courts, and juvenile courts) once they are established.

The Supreme Arbitration Court, whose judges are nominated by the president and appointed by the Federation Council, is the highest judicial body for resolving economic disputes concerning sales contracts, property, taxes, evaluation of acts of taxation bodies, insolvency (bankruptcy), loan contracts, insurance, the proclamation of acts of state bodies and other official bodies null and void, and other like matters. The Supreme Arbitration Court supervises the activity of lower arbitration courts, which include 82 arbitration courts operating within the constituent units of the federation and ten district arbitration courts to which the rulings of these lower courts can be appealed.

INSTITUTIONS OF THE CONSTITUENT UNITS

Article 77 of the Constitution grants the subjects of the federation the authority to establish their own government institutions, provided that they

are in accordance with the basic principles of the constitutional system of
the Russian Federation and the general principles governing the organization of legislative and executive bodies found in federal law. The pertinent
law was adopted in 1999: the Law on General Principles of the Organization of Legislative (Representative) and Executive Bodies of Power of the
Constituent Units of the Russian Federation.[19]

Legislatures of the Constituent Units

The legislatures of the constituent units of the federation vary in their
names, size, length of legislative terms of office, and other matters. Many
legislatures are called the Legislative Assembly, State Council, or Legislative Duma. The names for legislatures in some ethnically based units reflect ethnic traditions – for example, the Legislative Suglan of the Evenk
autonomous area, the State Assembly-Kurultayi of the Republic of Bashkortostan, and the Peoples Khural of the Republic of Buryatia.

The membership of regional legislatures ranges from 11 in the Taylmyr
(Dolgan-Nenets) autonomous area to 190 in the Republic of Bashkortostan. Most regional legislatures are unicameral, but some republics have
established bicameral legislatures – for example, the Republic of Bashkortostan's State Assembly-Kurultayi consists of a House of Representatives
and a Legislative House. Among territorial constituent units, only the Sverdlovsk region's Legislative Assembly consists of two chambers: the House
of Representatives and the Regional (Oblastnaya) Duma. Under federal
law, the term of office for regional legislators cannot exceed five years.

In the years immediately following the adoption of the federation Constitution, the Constitutional Court closely supervised the organization of
regional powers to ensure that they did not violate constitutional mandates. A key case involved the Altai territory, where the Legislative Assembly had assigned itself broad powers over the executive branch, including
the right to elect the head of the administration, to review the structure of
the administrative council, and to remove members of the administration
through a vote of no confidence. In addition, the chairman of the Legislative Assembly was assigned the right to sign laws into being. In January
1996, the Constitutional Court invalidated this attempt to subordinate the
executive.[20] Although it recognized that Article 77 of the Constitution authorizes constituent units to establish their own systems of government, the
Court emphasized that regional institutions must conform to the Russian
Constitution and its principle of separation of powers. Altai's charter violated this requirement by not creating a proper system of checks and balances, thereby allowing a single branch of government to both approve
and promulgate laws. In addition, Altai transgressed Article 3, Section 2, of
the Constitution by providing for indirect election of the head of the executive branch rather than for a direct expression of the people's will.[21]

More recently, enactment of the federal Law on General Principles of the Organization of Legislative (Representative) and Executive Bodies of Power of the Constituent Units of the Russian Federation has provided the regions with clearer guidelines as to how regional governments can be organized without violating the principle of separation of powers.

Constituent-Unit Executives

Just as regional legislatures have different names, so also do the executive officials in the constituent units of the federation. In most republics, the title for the highest official is president, although some republics use other titles, such as the head of the republic (the Republic of Komi), chairman of the government (the Republic of Karelia and the Republic of Khakassia), or chairman of the state council (the Republic of Dagestan). The other constituent units use the title of governor for their top official.

The president (or governor) of a constituent unit is elected by its residents for a term of no longer than five years on the basis of a general, equal, and direct vote by secret ballot. No person may hold this office for more than two consecutive terms. The federal Law on General Principles of the Organization of Legislative (Representative) and Executive Bodies of Power of the Constituent Units of the Russian Federation requires that the highest official of the constituent unit be at the same time the head of the regional government. The president (or governor) exercises many of the same powers exercised by the president of the federation. He or she appoints the regional government, decides on a resignation of the government, introduces draft legislation, signs and publishes regional laws, vetoes regional laws, conducts negotiations and signs international agreements, issues decrees and executive orders, and dissolves the legislature in circumstances stipulated in his or her region's constitution (or charter).

Constituent-Unit Judiciaries

The federal Law on the Judicial System of the Russian Federation authorizes two types of regional courts: justices of the peace and constitutional (charter) courts. Justices of the peace, like the federal courts of general jurisdiction, consider a wide range of civil and criminal cases. However, they occupy a position at the lowest level of the judicial hierarchy, just below municipal courts. A district or a city is divided into several sectors, and a justice of the peace sits within each.

Although justices of the peace are considered to be regional courts, they are, in actuality, federal because they act under federal law, implement federal law, and are even financed in part (i.e., justices' salaries) from the federal budget. The federal Law on Justices of the Peace in the Russian Federation specifies their jurisdiction and the legal effects of their decisions. Constituent units of the federation may regulate how justices of the peace are appointed, but federal law prescribes that they must either be appointed by the regional legislature or be elected by the population of the judicial district. The federal Civil Procedural Code and the Criminal Procedural Code detail the procedural rules governing justices of the peace and confirm that the decisions of justices of the peace may be appealed to the federal courts.

Constitutional courts may be established by the republics, and charter courts may be established by other constituent units, although federal law does not oblige constituent units to create such courts. Only twelve constitutional courts (in the Republics of Tatarstan, Bashkortostan, Buryatia, Mari El, Sakha (Yakutia), Adygea, Dagestan, Kabardino-Balkaria, Komi, Karelia, Tyva, and Northern Ossetia-Alania) and three charter courts (in the Sverdlovsk region, in the federal City of St Petesburg, and in the Kaliningrad region) had been established as of 2003.

A regional constitutional (charter) court is responsible for interpreting the constitution or charter of its constituent unit. These courts also exercise judicial review by resolving disputes over whether the laws and other actions of the regional and local governments are consistent with the regional constitution or charter. The jurisdiction of the regional constitutional and charter courts was established by Article 27, Section I, of the Law on the Judicial System of the Russian Federation. However, two republics (Tatarstan and Bashkortostan) challenged the law, arguing that it unconstitutionally narrowed the jurisdiction of the regional constitutional courts. In 2003 the federal Constitutional Court agreed, ruling that the jurisdiction awarded in this law could not be considered exhaustive lest it conflict with Article 27, Section 1, of the federation Constitution. The Court therefore held that constituent units may grant additional powers to their constitutional courts, provided that these powers are consistent with the aims of these courts and do not intrude upon the jurisdiction of the federal courts.[22]

The decisions of regional constitutional (charter) courts are final and cannot be appealed to any federal court of general jurisdiction or to the federal Constitutional Court. The only exception (which is quite rare) is when a case can be considered by both the federal Constitutional Court and a regional constitutional (charter) court – for example, when a treaty between the federal and regional governments is at issue. Then a party dissatisfied with the decision of a regional constitutional (charter) court may apply directly to the federal Constitutional Court. If the federal Constitutional Court reaches a different decision, its ruling will be authoritative.

INTERJURISDICTIONAL RELATIONS

Article 8 of the Constitution guarantees unity of economic space; the free movement of goods, services, and financial resources; support for economic competition; and freedom to undertake any economic activity throughout the Russian Federation. Article 74 prohibits customs frontiers, duties, levies, or any other barriers to the free movement of goods, services, or financial resources within the federation, but it permits federal law to impose restrictions on the movement of goods and services if necessary to protect the people's safety, lives, or health, the natural environment, or cultural values. The subjects of the federation have no power to establish such restrictions; they may only be imposed by federal law and then only for constitutionally envisaged aims.

The Russian Constitution does not contain any provision that expressly requires subjects of the federation to give mutual recognition to each other's legal acts. However, all acts of constituent units that were adopted through lawful procedures are binding on the whole territory of the federation. For example, according to the federal Family Code, the middle name of a child is determined by the name of a child's father. However, not all peoples living in the Russian Federation have a tradition of giving a child a middle name. The subjects of the federation, therefore, determine whether to fix a middle name or not. If a particular subject makes no requirement for a child's middle name, this act will be binding on the territories of all other subjects of the federation. Generally, the Constitution places family law within concurrent jurisdiction, which means that subjects of the federation can legislate if there is no overriding federal law. If there is a federal act, it overrides regional laws. For example, Article 1 of the federal Family Code defines marriage as a union of a man and a woman; consequently, subjects of the federation cannot legalize homosexual marriages.

Given that Article 71 proclaims the regulation of the rights and liberties of the human being and citizen to be a federal power, the federal authorities are responsible for providing equal status for all citizens, no matter from what subject of the federation they come. The Constitutional Court has in several decisions confirmed that subjects of the federation have no power to enact any law that discriminates against residents from other constituent units within the federation. In 1996, for example, the Court struck down a law that imposed a tax on nonresidents of Moscow who came to live in the city and purchased an apartment there.[23]

Because criminal law is a federal power, crimes are tried in federal court, unless the punishment for a crime is two years of imprisonment or less, in which case it is tried by a justice of the peace. However, both federal courts and justices of the peace apply the federal Criminal Code of the Russian Federation in trying cases. Extradition of criminals who flee from one constituent polity to another is thus not an issue in Russia because any court will apply federal criminal law. The issue of regional courts' jurisdiction could arise in civil cases if a resident of one constituent unit sued a resident of another constituent unit in a justice-of-the-peace court. In such a situation, the federal procedural code prescribes that the residence of the defendant determines the court in which the case is heard.

FISCAL FEDERALISM

The Constitution lists the establishment of the general principles of taxation and the imposition of taxes among the joint powers exercised by the Russian Federation and its constituent units. Operating under this authority, the federal government has devised a tax code to replace the contradictory and confusing mass of tax laws that had prevented the efficient operation of the government. In 1998 the first part of the Tax Code of the Russian Federation was enacted, establishing the system of taxes and duties collected for the federal budget. It outlines the common principles of taxation and taxes in the Russian Federation, including the types of taxes and duties; the procedure for collecting taxes and duties; the rights and duties of taxpayers, tax institutions, and other participants in the tax system; the mechanisms by which tax laws and obligations are to be enforced; and the penalties for nonpayment of taxes. The second part the Tax Code discusses various types of taxes and duties in detail. Enacting federal tax legislation was a major step in restoring the integrity of fiscal federalism because the legislation put an end to the tax concessions granted earlier by the national government to some subjects of the federation through bilateral treaties.

At present, all three orders of government – federal, regional, and local – impose taxes and duties. The chief federal taxes and duties include the value-added tax, the income tax, fees for the use of natural resources, taxes on corporate profits, federal license taxes, excises, and the ecological tax. The level of taxes that constituent units pay to the federal budget varies considerably. For example, in 2002 the total amount of profit tax contributed to the federal budget was 180 billion rubles. Of this total, Moscow paid 85 billion rubles, the Khanty-Mansi autonomous area paid 18 billion rubles, and St Petersburg delivered 11 billion rubles, while the Koryak autonomous area paid only 64 million rubles, the Komi-Permyak autonomous area paid 54 million rubles, the Republic of Tyva remitted 28 million rubles, and the Ust-Ordyn autonomous area delivered 14 million rubles.

Constituent units can impose regional taxes, but the federal Tax Code limits their authority. Regional legislatures can establish tax rates (for taxes within their authority), determine the order and terms of payment of taxes, and prescribe the system of tax reporting. But they cannot introduce new taxes that are not specified in the Tax Code. The regional taxes and duties include property taxes for organizations, real-estate taxes, highway taxes, transport taxes, taxes on gambling, regional license taxes, sales taxes, and others. Revenues gleaned from the property tax for organizations are divided equally between regional budgets and local budgets.

As of 1 January 2003, 74 constituent units had introduced sales taxes, most at the 5 percent level. Revenues from the sales tax are funnelled into the budgets of the subjects of the Russian Federation (40 percent) and into local budgets (60 percent). The sales tax is not the main source of revenue for constituent units. Some constituent units have not established it, and in those that have, some enterprises do not pay the sales tax because they use a so-called simplified system of taxation. Nevertheless, in those subjects of the federation that have introduced the sales tax, it has replaced various regional taxes, such as the tax for the needs of educational establishments, the tax on dog owners, and the liquor-license tax. Finally, in addition to revenues from regional taxes, constituent units share in the revenues from such federal taxes as the income tax, the tax on corporate profits, excise taxes, and others.

Both the Tax Code and acts adopted by local governments impose local taxes. The Tax Code limits the authority of local governments to impose taxes. Local governments can establish tax rates (on taxes they are authorized to impose), prescribe the order and terms of payment of the taxes, and provide for a system of tax reporting. Local governments also may introduce tax privileges for certain groups of taxpayers. Among the important local taxes are the land tax, the property tax on individuals, the advertising tax, the tax on inheritance and on the acquisition of property, and local license taxes.

All taxes – whether federal, state, or local – are collected by the federal Tax Ministry, which has offices in each constituent unit of the federation. Neither constituent units nor local governments have their own tax bodies. The revenues are then allocated as directed by the Tax Code and other laws. This system of tax collection and distribution was inherited from the highly centralized Soviet model.

The Russian Federation faces numerous problems relating to intergovernmental fiscal relations. Although the Budget Code of the Russian Federation is supposed to determine the authority of the federal, regional, and local governments in the budget system, the code is badly in need of modernization because the distribution of authority among the orders of government is not well defined. Regional and local governments lack taxing and budgeting autonomy, which undermines the incentives for effective financial management. Also, unfunded mandates from the federal government skew regional budgets; that is, the federal government assigns duties to the subjects of the federation without allocating any funds to fulfil these duties. In addition, most of the federal financial assistance to the constituent units is provided without clearly defined rules and procedures that would ensure accountability.

To address these and other problems, the Federal Assembly in 2001 enacted a reform of the budget system, which will be implemented by 2005.

The main aim of this reform is to define clearly the federal, regional, and local budget responsibilities within Russian law and to demarcate revenues and expenditures between the levels of the budget system.

FOREIGN AFFAIRS AND DEFENCE

The conduct of foreign policy and international relations, including the adoption of international treaties and foreign-trade agreements, are federal powers. The federal government has exclusive authority to determine the country's relations with other countries. The president conducts negotiations and signs international treaties of the Russian Federation, while both chambers of the Federal Assembly ratify them.

At the same time, the Constitution grants to the constituent units a limited role in dealing with foreign countries. Article 72 lists among the concurrent powers the coordination of the international and external economic relations of the constituent units of the Russian Federation and compliance with international treaties of the Russian Federation. This means that constituent units may have international and external economic relations and conclude corresponding agreements with the constituent units of other federations or structural parts of unitary countries. The federal Law on Coordination of the International and External Economic Relations of the Constituent Units of the Russian Federation of 1999 states that the possibility of concluding such an agreement with a country as a whole may be granted to a constituent unit by the federal government. The function of coordination is vested in the federal Ministry of Foreign Affairs. Many constituent units have concluded such agreements both with subunits of the foreign countries and with the countries themselves, dealing mostly with matters of economic and cultural cooperation.

Defence powers – including questions of war and peace; defence and security; defence production; procedures for the sale and purchase of arms, ammunition, military hardware, and other equipment; and the production of fissionable materials, toxic substances, and narcotics, and the procedure for their use – are also exclusively in the hands of the federal government. Constituent units have no armed forces. As the supreme commander in chief of the armed forces, the president appoints and dismisses the supreme commander of the armed forces, introduces martial law under certain circumstances, and declares a state of emergency under certain conditions.

Indeed, the powers exercised by the president extend beyond those elaborated in the federation Constitution. In the famous "Chechen case" of 1995, the Constitutional Court noted that the outbreak of a major, domestic, armed conflict on Russian territory had given rise to widespread violations of the constitutional rights and freedoms of citizens and also that it posed a threat to the security of the country and to its territorial integrity. In such circumstances, the Court held, in the absence of legislation prescribing the course to be followed in resolving the crisis, the president, as the guarantor of the Constitution, can and should, within the limits of his constitutional powers, determine all the measures necessary – including the use of the armed forces – to settle the conflict.[24]

VOTING, ELECTIONS, AND POLITICAL PARTIES

The Constitution devotes relatively few provisions to voting and elections. Article 3, Section 3, states that referenda and free elections shall be the supreme direct manifestation of the power of the people. According to Article 32, Section 2, citizens of the Russian Federation have the right to participate in referenda and the right to elect and to be elected to bodies of state governance and organs of local self-government. Article 81 describes the basic procedures for presidential elections. Section 1 states that the president shall be elected for a term of four years by the citizens of the Russian Federation on the basis of a general, equal, and direct vote by secret ballot. Section 2 lists the qualifications for a presidential candidate: a citizen of the Russian Federation, 35 years of age or older, and a resident of the Russian Federation for not less than ten years. Section 3 mandates that no one shall hold the office of president for more than two successive terms. Section 4 delegates to the Federal Assembly the responsibility to enact laws detailing the process for electing the president of the Russian Federation.

Article 96 addresses the election of the State Duma. Under Section 1, the State Duma is elected for a term of four years. Section 2 delegates to federal law the right to establish the procedure for electing deputies to the State Duma. Finally, Article 97, Section 1, states that any citizen of the Russian Federation who is at least 21 years of age and has the right to participate in elections may be elected to the State Duma.

Because only the main principles of voting and elections are included in the Constitution, the Federal Assembly has enacted a series of laws – such as the Laws on Basic Guarantees of Electoral Rights and the Right of the Citizens of the Russian Federation to Referendum, on Providing Constitutional Rights of the Citizens of the Russian Federation to Elect and to be Elected to the Organs of Self-Government, and on Elections of the President of the Russian Federation – to establish an integrated electoral code for federal elections. The constituent units have adopted their own electoral laws; for instance, the Sverdlovsk region has adopted a code that details the procedures for electing the governor and the deputies of both chambers of the regional legislature. Of course, federal laws guaranteeing electoral rights prevail over any conflicting regional laws.

The Constitution does not address the subject of political parties, except by protecting the general right of association (Art. 30, Sec. 1). The procedures for creating political parties, establishing their rights and responsibilities, determining the order of their participation in elections, and so forth are established in the 2001 federal Law on Political Parties.[25]

CITIZENSHIP AND THE PROTECTION OF RIGHTS

The adoption of the federal Law on Citizenship of the Russian Federation in 2002 clarified the issue of citizenship by establishing a single federal citizenship. Prior to the law's adoption, it was widely assumed that the republics could award their own citizenship. This new law envisages only federal citizenship although, in fact, some republics continue to assert a dual citizenship in their constitution.

The president has responsibility for resolving issues of citizenship in the Russian Federation. He may resolve individual cases through the exercise of presidential discretion, aided by his Commission on Issues of Citizenship, which performs the necessary investigative work. He may also address broader issues – for example, the plight of citizens of the former Soviet Union who were not granted citizenship by their former union republic – through executive ministries.

Even before the 1993 Constitution came into effect, the Russian Federation had already adopted the 1991 Declaration of the Rights and Liberties of Man and Citizen, and its provisions were subsequently included in Chapter 2 of the Constitution. Among the civil rights guaranteed are the right to life, the right to freedom and personal inviolability, the right to privacy and to personal and family secrets, freedom of movement, freedom of conscience and religious worship, and freedom of thought and of speech. Political rights guaranteed by the Constitution include the right to seek, get, transfer, produce, and disseminate information by any lawful means; the right of association; the right to gather peacefully, without weapons, to hold meetings, rallies, and demonstrations, and to engage in marches and picketing; the right to elect and to be elected to bodies of state governance and organs of local self-government; the right to participate in referenda; and the right of equal access to state services. Various economic and cultural rights and liberties are also fixed in the Constitution, such as the right to private property; the right to make free use of one's abilities for work and to choose one's own occupation; the right to collective bargaining in labour disputes under federal law; the right to strike; the right to social security in old age and in cases of disease, handicap, or the loss of the family breadwinner; the right to raise one's own children; the right to health care and medical assistance; the right to education; and the right to participate in cultural life, to use the institutions of culture, and to have access to cultural values.

It should be noted that the Constitution does not guarantee all social and economic rights to the fullest extent possible. For instance, it guarantees basic general education, permitting state or municipal education institutions to condition access to higher education on payment of tuition or success on a competitive examination. Similarly, the Constitution states that medical assistance shall be made available by state and municipal health-care institutions to citizens free of charge, with the money coming from the relevant budget, insurance payments, and other revenues. However, this means that medical assistance delivered by health-care institutions other than the state and municipal ones is not free of charge, even if there is not enough funding provided for state and municipal health-care institutions.

Article 71 indicates that the regulation and protection of the rights and liberties of the human being and citizen are within the scope of the federal powers, while Article 72 includes the protection of the rights and freedoms of man and citizen among the concurrent powers. Taken together, these provisions suggest that the federal government has primary but not exclusive responsibility in this area. The subjects of the federation can supplement federal efforts with their own guarantees, but they cannot of course impede the operation of the federal guarantees.

The Constitution contains some important principles governing the protection of rights and liberties by the state. Among them are that the basic rights and liberties of the human being shall be inalienable and shall belong to everyone from birth; that the rights and liberties of the human being and the citizen shall have direct effect; that these rights and liberties shall determine the meaning, content, and application of the laws and activities of the legislative and executive branches and of local self-government and shall be secured by the judiciary; that all people shall be equal before the law and in a court of law; that the state shall guarantee the equality of rights and liberties regardless of sex, race, nationality, language, origin, property status, employment status, residence, attitude to religion, convictions, membership in public associations, or any other circumstance; that any restrictions of the rights of citizens on social, racial, national, linguistic, or religious grounds is forbidden; and that women and men have equal rights and liberties and equal opportunities for the pursuit of rights and liberties.

According to the Constitution, rights and liberties may be restricted by federal law only to the extent required for the protection of the fundamentals of the constitutional system, namely to preserve morality, health, rights, and the lawful interests of other persons and to ensure the defence of the country and the security of the state. From this provision, several major conclusions can be drawn. First, rights and liberties may be restricted only by federal law; that is, neither a federal regulation (such as a presidential decree) nor a regional law can provide a basis for restricting human rights and freedoms. Second, rights and liberties may be restricted only for the aims listed in the Constitution – that is, for protecting the fundamentals of the constitutional system (morality, health, rights, and lawful interests of other persons) and for ensuring the defence of the country and the security of the state. Third, constitutional rights and liberties may be restricted only to the extent required to achieve these aims; that is, the absolute necessity of restricting a certain right or liberty by means of a federal law must be proved.

CONSTITUTIONAL CHANGE

The 1993 Russian Constitution establishes stringent procedures for constitutional change, which may explain why few constitutional amendments have been adopted. There are three separate procedures for amending the constitutional text, depending on the provisions to be changed.

When a proposal is made to amend any provisions of the Constitution's Chapters 3–8, it takes the form of a special legal text, the Russian Federation Law Amending the Constitution, that has a special status and differs from both regular federal law and regular federal constitutional law. Both chambers of the Federal Assembly must approve the amendment by a majority of at least three-quarters of the total number of members of the Federation Council and at least two-thirds of the total number of deputies of the State Duma. Unlike with regular legislation, the president has no veto authority. The amendment comes into effect when it is approved by no less than two-thirds of the constituent units of the Russian Federation. Then the amendment is signed by the president of the Russian Federation within 14 days and published. No amendments had been adopted utilizing this procedure as of 2004.

Changes to Article 65 of the Constitution, which determines the composition of the Russian Federation, are made on the basis of the federal constitutional law dealing either with admission of constituent units to the Russian Federation, with the formation within the Russian Federation of a new constituent unit, or with a change in the constitutional and legal status of a constituent unit of the Russian Federation. In these three cases, then, federal constitutional laws are adopted, and when the Constitution is to be republished, they are incorporated into the Constitution. No amendments had been made under this procedure as of 2004.

Changes to Article 65 of the Constitution are made on the basis of the president's decree in the event of a change in the name of the particular constituent unit. There are only five cases of amendments to the Constitution being made under this procedure, four republics and one autonomous area having changed their names: the Republic of Ingushetia (formerly the Ingush Republic), the Republic of Kalmykia (formerly the Republic of Kalmykia-Khalm Tangch), the Republic of Northern Ossetia-Alania (formerly the Republic of

Northern Ossetia), the Republic of Chuvashia (formerly the Chuvash Republic), and the Khanty-Mansi autonomous area-Yugra (formerly the Khanty-Mansi autonomous area).

The provisions of Chapters 1, 2, and 9 of the Constitution may not be revised by the Federal Assembly. If a proposal to revise any provisions in these chapters is supported by three-fifths of the total number of members of the Federation Council and the deputies of the State Duma, a constitutional assembly is to be convened in accordance with the federal constitutional law. The constitutional assembly may either confirm the inviolability of the Constitution or develop a new draft of the Constitution that shall be adopted by two-thirds of the total number of members of the constitutional assembly or submitted to a popular vote. Ratification of the proposed constitution requires majority approval by the electorate, with at least half of the electorate taking part in the vote. However, the mandated federal constitutional law on the constitutional assembly had not been enacted as of 2004. Without such a law, the adoption of a new constitution in order to change Chapters 1, 2, and 9 of the previous one remains impossible.

Constitutional change may also occur through judicial interpretation of the Constitution. Federal legislation on the Constitutional Court, adopted in 1994, expressly recognized the power of judicial review. From 1994 to 2004, the Constitutional Court interpreted the Constitution's provisions 13 times, with its decisions addressing such matters as the legislative process, the order of nomination by the president of the candidates for chairman of the federal government, and the meaning of the constitutional terms relating to the executive power.

EMERGING TRENDS AND DEVELOPMENTS

Russia's federal system developed out of a unitary state, and there are still vestiges of the unitary tradition not only in the law, but also in popular consciousness. The historical tendency of Russia's development has been from the supercentralized state of the Russian Empire and the Soviet Union/RSFSR to a decentralized federation, although President Putin's policy on federalism shows signs of a new centralization. In the decade since the adoption of the federation Constitution, Russia has made notable advances in instituting federal democracy, but important challenges remain.

One continuing issue involves the structure of the Russian Federation because the delineation of the current subjects of the federation occurred only recently, with the adoption of the 1993 Constitution. Controversy continues over whether Russian federalism will be symmetrical or asymmetrical, whether subjects of the federation will have equal rights and powers, or whether the ethnically based republics should enjoy different status. There are also pressures in some political circles to enlarge the constituent units and reduce their number given that many undeveloped subjects of the federation are heavily reliant on federal subsidies.

The constitutional division of powers between the federal government and the subjects of the federation also raises concerns, particularly given the implementation of concurrent powers. In theory, the exercise of these powers should involve framework legislation by the federal government coupled with more detailed regulation by subjects of the federation in accordance with local conditions. In practice, however, the general guidelines in federal laws have often become detailed legislation that leave almost no role for regional legislators.

The central government's attempts to harmonize federal-regional relations (strengthening vertical relations) could lead to a highly centralized federalism, although resistance to centralization remains entrenched in certain parts of the federation, such as Bashkortostan, Sakha, Sverdlovsk, and Tatarstan.

The most difficult challenge facing the Russian federal system is the Chechen crisis – a major armed conflict on Russian territory sparked by the Chechen Republic proclaiming itself independent, although the federation Constitution does not provide for secession. This declaration has led to two wars (federal interventions), one from 1994 to 1996 and the other from 1999 to 2000. Even now, when there are no massive battles, separatist-minded units continue to fight with federal forces and to mount terrorist attacks. Despite these hostilities, in the spring of 2003 voters in a referendum in Chechnya adopted a republican constitution and laws governing the election of the Parliament and the president of Chechnya. In fall 2003 the president of the Chechen Republic (Akhmad Kadyrov) was elected; however, he was killed by a terrorist bombing on 9 May 2004. New presidential and parliamentary elections are scheduled for fall 2004, and President Putin has expressed his desire to sign a treaty with the newly elected officials of the Chechen Republic in order to fix the division of powers between the federal government and the Chechen Republic.

Despite these problems, the federation Constitution is far superior to its predecessors, and a combination of constitutional amendments and interpretations of the Constitutional Court should serve to correct whatever deficiencies remain. Russia is on a path toward a more rational, more democratic, more federal, and more perfect union.[26]

NOTES

1 On emerging federalism in Russia and its development, see, for example, Jorge Martinez-Vazquez and Jameson Boex, *Russia's Transition to a New Federalism* (Washington, DC: World Bank, 2001); G. Alan Tarr, "Creating Federalism in

Russia," *South Texas Law Review* 40 (Winter 1999): 689–713; Steven L. Stolnick, *Stealing the State: Control and Collapse in Soviet Institutions* (Cambridge: Davis Center for Russian Studies Series, no. 89, Harvard University Press, 1999); Marat Salikov, "Russian and American Federations: A Comparative and Legal Analysis of Their Origins and Developments," *Tulsa Journal of Comparative and International Law* 3 (Spring 1996): 161–82.

2 See also, for example, Gregory Gleason, *Federalism and Nationalism: The Struggle for Republican Rights in the USSR* (Boulder: Westview Press, 1990).

3 E.B. Alaev, R.B. Arkhipov, I.P. Barabanov, L.F. Boltenkova, et al., "Federalism," *Entsiklopedichesky Slovar,* ed. Sergei Valentei (Moskva: Infra-M, 1997), pp. 25–6, 117–19.

4 Democratic centralism can be defined as a system in which all state organs are elected and thus presumably held accountable to the people, but lower state organs must comply with the decisions of higher state organs.

5 Although written as a singular, "the treaty" actually consisted of three treaties corresponding to the different categories of constituent units discussed below.

6 Vestnik Konstitutsionnogo Suda Rossiiskoi Federatsii [Russian Federation Constitutional Court review], 2000, no. 5.

7 Ibid., 1995, no. 6.

8 Ibid., 1997, no. 1.

9 Vladimir Lysenko, "How Strong Are the Treaty Foundations of Federative Relations?" *Anthropology and Archeology of Eurasia* 36 (Summer 1997): 33–55.

10 Sobranie Zakonodatelstva Rossiiskoi Federatsii [Russian Federation Legislation Collection], 2000, no. 20, Art. 2112.

11 The president may dissolve the State Duma if the latter rejects three successive candidates proposed by the president for chairman of the government, if the State Duma adopts two no-confidence votes in the government within three months, or if the State Duma denies a vote of confidence requested by the chairman.

12 Vedomosti Siezda Narodnykh Deputatov RSFSR i Verkhovnogo Soveta RSFSR [Congress of People's Deputies of the RSFSR and the Supreme Soviet of the RSFSR Register], 1991, no. 19, Art. 621; no. 30, Arts 1016, 1017.

13 The first specialized body of constitutional supervision was the USSR Committee on Constitutional Supervision, which was founded in April 1990 according to the USSR's Law on Constitutional Supervision in the USSR. See Vedomosti Siezda Narodnykh Deputatov RSFSR i Verkhovnogo Soveta RSFSR [Congress of People's Deputies of the USSR and the Supreme Soviet of the USSR Register], 1988, no. 49, Art. 727.

14 Special-purchase cheques for the purchase of cars were designed for construction workers in a number of regions of Russia, including the North and the Far East. According to a federal government regulation, the salaries of such workers are saved in the federal Savings Bank, and after 3 to 5 years the workers may get a special-purchase cheque to buy a car at an earlier determined price. The

Court ruled unconstitutional the federal government regulation that unilaterally changed the terms of the government's obligations.

15 "Indexation" means the automatic adjustment of citizens' wages and bank savings to compensate for inflation. Such obligations were fixed in a number of laws and regulations.

16 Sobranie Zakonodatelstva Rossiiskoi Federatsii [Russian Federation Legislation Collection], 1994, no. 13, Art. 1447.

17 Ibid., 1996, no. 2.

18 On the analysis of cases on civil rights and freedoms examined by the Constitutional Court, see Marat Salikov, "Russia's Transition to Democracy: Constitutional Justice and the Protection of Civil Liberties," *The Future of Freedom in Russia*, ed. William J. Vanden Heuvel (Philadelphia and London: Templeton Foundation Press, 2000), pp. 17–47.

19 See also Kathryn Stoner-Weiss, *Local Heroes: The Political Economy of Russian Regional Governance* (Princeton: Princeton University Press, 1997); and Peter Kirkow, *Russia's Provinces: Authoritarian Transformation versus Local Autonomy?* (Houndmills, UK: Macmillan, 1998).

20 Vestnik Konstitutsionnogo Suda Rossiiskoi Federatsii [Russian Federation Constitutional Court Review], 1996, no. 1.

21 William Pomeranz, "The Russian Constitutional Court's Interpretation of Federalism: Balancing Center-Regional Relations," *Parker School Journal of East European Law* 4 (Fall 1997): 401–44.

22 Vestnik Konstitutsionnogo Suda Rossiiskoi Federatsii [Russian Federation Constitutional Court Review], 2003, no. 4.

23 Ibid., 1996, no. 2.

24 Ibid., 1995, nos 4–5.

25 On parties, see, for example, Kathryn Stoner-Weiss, "Central Governing Incapacity and the Weakness of Political Parties: Russian Democracy in Disarray," *Publius: The Journal of Federalism* 32 (Spring 2002): 125–46.

26 For various perspectives, see Blair A. Ruble, Jodi Koehn, and Nancy E. Popson, eds, *Fragmented Space in the Russian Federation* (Washington, DC: Woodrow Wilson Center Press, 2001); and Rafael Khakimov, ed., *Federalism in Russia* (Kazan: Kazan Institute of Federalism, Institute of History of Tatarstan Academy of Sciences, 2001).

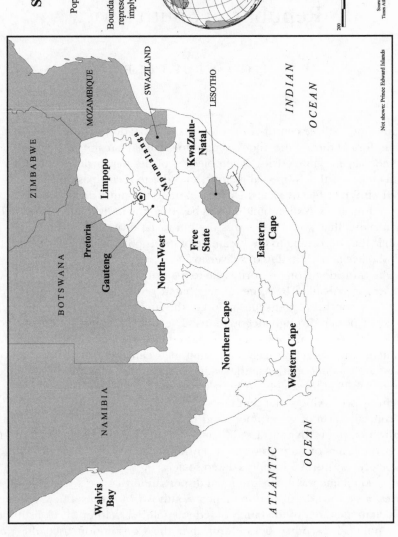

South Africa

Capital: Pretoria
Population: 43.5 Million
(2002 est.)

Boundaries and place names are
representative only and do not
imply official endorsement.

N

200   0   200   400
Kilometres

Sources: CIA World Factbook; ESRI Ltd;
Times Atlas of the World; UN Cartographic Dept.

ZIMBABWE

MOZAMBIQUE

SWAZILAND

BOTSWANA

Limpopo

Pretoria

Gauteng

Mpumalanga

KwaZulu-
Natal

LESOTHO

North-West

Free
State

Eastern
Cape

NAMIBIA

Northern Cape

Western Cape

Walvis
Bay

ATLANTIC

OCEAN

INDIAN

OCEAN

Not shown: Prince Edward Islands

Republic of South Africa

NICO STEYTLER

At the end of three centuries of colonial and racial domination, two constitutions, forged during the 1990s, sought to establish a majoritarian, nonracial democracy in South Africa. The objective of the new order was to liberate and empower the oppressed majority in order to rectify past injustices. Coupled with this objective was the desire to unite a country divided along racial and ethnic lines. Nation building was based on the individualist thrust of human rights that would cut across the old racial divisions, establishing a republic that, according to the Preamble of the 1996 Constitution, "belongs to all who live in it, united in our diversity."

The transition from minority rule to majority rule was, however, a negotiated process, called by some a "negotiated revolution." The majority did not take control of the state by force; the incumbent white regime relinquished power through negotiations. The Interim Constitution of 1993, which ushered in majority rule, was passed by the apartheid tricameral Parliament, thus effecting legal continuity between the old and the new orders. In the negotiations, the white regime and sections of the black "homeland" elites sought to limit the power of the new majority government by preserving some remnants of their powers and privileges through decentralization of government and by protecting certain communal and individual rights. In contrast, the majoritarian objective was to gain control over the levers of state power in a centralist government that could fundamentally transform a racially skewed society.

The outcome was a constitutional dispensation that has some federal features but ensures central dominance. South Africa is thus a new, although reluctant, member of the family of federal polities. Neither the Constitution nor political discourse before and after the Constitution used the word "federalism." Given that South Africa does not self-identify as a federal country, debate continues on the nature of the state.[1] Despite its unofficial status as a federal country, South Africa's Constitution is of interest to other federations for the way power has been dispersed between three spheres of government (national, provincial, and local) and for its explicit articulation of principles of cooperative government.

THE CONSTITUTION IN
HISTORICAL-CULTURAL CONTEXT

Creation of the South African State

Situated on the southern tip of Africa, the Republic of South Africa, with a land area of 1,219,090 square kilometers, has a multilingual, multicultural, and multiracial population of 44 million residing in nine provinces and 285 municipalities. In seven of the provinces, there are linguistic majorities.[2] The population is predominantly Christian (84 percent), with 13 percent adhering to traditional indigenous belief systems. There are small proportions of Muslims (1.5 percent) and Hindus (1.5 percent). Within the Christian community, 10 percent are Protestant and 9.5 percent are Roman Catholic, while the vast majority belong to African independent churches. It is a racially divided country. In terms of the apartheid system of classification – still used for Census purposes – 77.8 percent are regarded as African, 10.1 percent white, 8.7 percent coloured, and 2.4 percent Indian.[3] With a gross national product per capita of US$3,160, South Africa is classified by the World Bank as an upper-middle-income economy.[4]

The Constitution of 1996 is both a product of and an answer to the previous eight decades of apartheid constitution making.[5] The Union of South Africa was formed in 1910 from the merger of four British colonies. Despite the models of uniting British colonies in federations, such as Canada (1868) and Australia (1901), federalism was not favoured by the national convention of 1909 because of the need for nation building and the fear of provincial dominance. A strong union was seen as necessary to promote nation building between the two older British colonies (Cape and Natal) and the two recent acquisitions (Transvaal and Orange River Colony), which had been engaged in war with the British Empire less than a decade before. As a sop to federal sentiments, an upper house, called the Senate, was instituted to represent provincial interests, with each provincial legislature electing an equal number of senators. Provincial legislatures and executives were created, but their powers were restricted with an automatic national legislative override. The provinces thus had no protected or residual powers.

The "homeland" policy of apartheid introduced some devolution. The objective was to create independent black nation-states, thereby robbing all Africans of their South African citizenship. Four "independent" homelands were created (Transkei in 1976, Bophutatswana in 1978, Venda in

1979, and Ciskei in 1981). In addition, there were self-governing territories that received extensive powers (i.e., KwaZulu, Kangwane, Qwa-Qwa, Gazankulu, and KwaNdebele). The territories were demarcated along ethnic lines as much as possible. The aim, in contrast to the sentiments underlying the 1909 convention, was to separate Africans from each other, as well as from whites, as far as possible in a grand strategy of divide and rule.

When it came to the coloured community, the "homeland" solution was first attempted; the coloureds were deemed to be a "nation in the making." A Colored Representative Council was set up with limited legislative powers. This attempt to create a coloured homeland soon failed. With regard to Indians originating from the Indian subcontinent, the apartheid state, after abandoning fairly late in the 1960s the objective of repatriation to India, sought to accommodate them in a separate forum, the South African Indian Council, a body that had no effective legislative or executive powers.

A tricameral parliament was created in 1983 to bring coloureds and Indians into an alliance with the whites. Racial segregation was maintained, as each group had its own parliamentary chamber, which had legislative competence over its "own affairs," while all three had to deliberate jointly over "general affairs." The upshot of the tricameral parliament was the disappearance of the Senate and the provincial legislatures, while limited executive authority was retained by the provinces.

With apartheid's demise and the unbanning of the liberation movements in 1990, a process of political negotiations commenced that saw the adoption of an Interim Constitution in 1993 and the holding of democratic elections in April 1994. This was a protracted process "often marred by widespread public disturbance, acrimonious debate and unspeakable violence."[6] At the outset, the African National Congress (ANC) insisted that adoption of a constitution be done by an elected body, arguing that a new nonracial state could only be built on a firm democratic basis.[7] The South African government and its allies opposed the idea, fearing defeat at the polls and loss of all power and privilege. They proposed a multiparty negotiating forum in which all political parties, without regard to their possible electoral support, would agree by sufficient consensus on a new constitution.[8] In this way, the incumbent governments could make constitutional deals disproportionate to their possible electoral support. The negotiated compromise eventually reached was that the Multi-Party Negotiating Process at Kempton Park would draft a constitution under whose terms the first nonracial election was to be held. Because the Constitution was not based on the will of the people but negotiated by elites, it was an interim measure to be replaced within two years by a final constitution, the 1996 Constitution. The new democratically elected Parliament would then double up as the Constitutional Assembly. However, the Constitutional Assembly would not have a free hand. Apart from the two-thirds majority required for the Constitution's adoption, the Assembly would be bound by a set of Constitutional Principles that would form the backbone of the final Constitution. Moreover, the Constitutional Principles would be enforced by the Constitutional Court, which had to certify that the Constitution accorded with the Constitutional Principles.

The democratic elections of April 1994 unified the country formally. The "independent" homelands ceased to exist, each becoming part of one of the country's new nine provinces. The Transvaal, incorporating Venda and Bophuthatswana, was split into four provinces: Gauteng, North West, Northern Province (now Limpopo), and Mpumalanga. The Cape Province – now including Transkei and Ciskei – devolved into three provinces: Western Cape, Northern Cape, and Eastern Cape. Only the old provinces of Natal and the Orange Free State retained their borders and parts of their names, being renamed KwaZulu-Natal and Free State respectively.

In the Interim Constitution, provision was made to divide the Eastern Cape into two provinces, hiving off the homeland areas of Transkei and Ciskei, if there was sufficient support. Continuation of the Northern Cape as a province could also be reconsidered. In the end, there was no electoral support for border changes. Because the carving up of two provinces into seven new ones was done in a hurry, many borders were contested by local communities along the borders. Provision was also made for border adjustments between provinces. No border changes had, however, been effected by February 1997, when the 1996 Constitution came into effect, thus confirming the 1994 border determinations.

The 1996 Constitution makes no provision for border adjustments or the creation of new provinces. Any changes would have to be effected by a constitutional amendment. When demarcating the country's municipalities in 2000, the artificiality of some provincial borders became apparent; functional communities were split by borders. To solve this problem, the Constitution was amended in 1998 to provide for cross-border municipalities. This compromise has not worked in practice, and the adjustment of provincial borders to eliminate the need for cross-border municipalities is on the national political agenda.

The Interim Constitution was lengthy, comprising over 251 sections and a further six schedules. Six amendments were enacted between 1994 and 1996. Two crucial amendments, which came into effect in April 1994, were aimed at bringing in political groups that had withdrawn from the political negotiations.[9] The first democratic Parliament amended the Constitution no less than eight times in the following two years, mostly with respect to technical issues. As the aim of the Interim Constitution was to be an insurance policy for the outgoing white political elite, the style was legalistic. The 1996 Constitution, however, has slightly fewer sections (243) and six schedules. In addition, a lengthy schedule and two appendices deal with transition arrangements. Unlike the Interim Constitution, which was drafted with an eye for detail to cover every eventuality, the 1996 Constitution was written in a general, open-text style.[10] The objective was also to write it in plain language, making it accessible to ordinary people.

The 1996 Constitution has been amended nine times, the most significant amendments being the establishment of cross-border municipalities; changes to the judiciary; permitting members of the national, provincial, and local legislatures to change party allegiance without losing their seats; and tightening national control over local fiscal matters.

Drafting the 1993 and 1996 Constitutions

A key issue in the negotiations between the liberation movements and the then government and its allies in the homelands was the devolution of power to subnational entities. The Inkatha Freedom Party (IFP), with a strong ethnic power base in KwaZulu-Natal, ardently advocated a federal system. The homeland leaders of Bophuthatswana and Ciskei also expressed interest in devolution. The National Party (NP), which during the apartheid era institutionalized a strong centralist state, made common cause with the homeland leaders in advocating strong regional government. Their interest was to block a strong central government under ANC control. This was coupled with the hope that the NP, in alliance with the homeland leaders, could capture some of the regional spaces. To the right of the government were the conservative Afrikaners who sought an extreme form of federalism: self-determination in their own *volkstaat*. Aligned with this grouping were key elements in the then military and police establishments.

The ANC saw the claims for federalism simply as excuses to thwart majority rule. Moreover, creating strong federal units would legitimate the homelands and create a separate white *volkstaat*. The fear was that federalism would preserve white minority privileges. A strong central state, the ANC argued, was necessary to effect the transformation of a society based on racism into one that would foster nonracialism and correct past injustices.

The end product was a pragmatic, negotiated settlement with elements of both centralism and federalism. When the NP and the ANC concluded the deal, two important players – the IFP and conservative Afrikaners – did not participate, but two months prior to the April 1994 elections, the Interim Constitution was amended to accommodate the IFP and conservative Afrikaners. The principle of self-determination was entrenched in the Interim Constitution and as a Constitutional Principle. A *Volkstaatraad* was established as well, namely a council in which Afrikaners could articulate and advocate their desire for self-determination. These provisions brought the majority of right-wing Afrikaners into the fold. Increasing the powers of provinces and making special accommodation for KwaZulu-Natal similarly appeased the IFP.

The 1993 Interim Constitution was the product of a negotiated settlement driven by two concerns. First, national unity was of prime importance. To break with the apartheid past, the racial and ethnic division of
South Africa was to be avoided at all cost. A nonracial democracy that
united the people of the country was the objective. Second, because of the
threat that both conservative Afrikaners and the conflict in KwaZulu-Natal
posed to the peace and stability of the country, the federal features of the
Interim Constitution were aimed at peace making. The 1993 document is
described as a peace treaty while the 1996 Constitution is a true constitution, being an exercise in constitution making by elected representatives.

The popular legitimacy of the 1996 Constitution lies in both the legitimacy of the 1994 election and the process of drafting the Constitution.
The Interim Constitution envisaged a referendum on the Constitution
only as a deadlock-breaking mechanism if the Constitutional Assembly
could not produce a two-thirds majority. Reflecting this approach to legitimacy, the opening words of the Preamble to the 1996 Constitution, "We
the people," are coupled with the words, "through our freely elected representatives, adopt this Constitution as the supreme law of the Republic." As
a two-thirds majority was reached on the final text, the issue of a referendum did not arise. The popularity of the Constitution is, no doubt, attributed to the public relations efforts of the Assembly, which canvassed more
than two million public submissions. Although these submissions did not
directly shape the Constitution, the participatory process may have facilitated popular ownership.[11]

When the Constitutional Assembly convened in 1994, it was bound by
the Constitutional Principles, four of which were critical for decentralization. First, the legislative and executive powers of the provinces had to be
"appropriate" and "adequate," and such powers were to promote "legitimate provincial autonomy." Second, the new Constitution had to include
exclusive and concurrent powers and functions for national and provincial
spheres of government. Third, the powers and functions of the provinces
could not be substantially less than those provided for by the Interim Constitution. Fourth, "[a] framework for local government powers, functions
and structures" had to be set out in the Constitution.

The Constitutional Assembly passed the new Constitution in May 1996. It
provided for provincial legislatures and executives, which had concurrent
and exclusive powers with respect to items listed in Schedules 4 and 5. When
the document was submitted to the Constitutional Court, it refused to certify
that the text conformed to the Constitutional Principles.[12] In the main, the
Court found that there was a substantial diminution of provincial powers as
compared with the Interim Constitution. When the Court reviewed the
amended text three months later, it found that there was still a diminution of
provincial powers, but this was no longer deemed substantial. Accordingly, it
certified the text,[13] which then came into effect on 4 February 1997.

In the context of decentralization, both the interim and the 1996 constitutions articulated two important points of departure. First, the basis of the constitutional dispensation was a classical liberal democracy based on individualism rather than on the protection and entrenchment of groups, be they ethnic, racial, or linguistic. Second, although subnational entities were established, there was not to be a competitive relationship between the subnational entities and the centre; nation building was the overriding concern.

The individual-rights basis of the constitutions was inevitable. Within the ANC, there has been a long rights-based tradition stemming from the Freedom Charter, an ANC policy document dating from 1955, which coupled social and economic demands with individual rights.[14] No such claim could be made by the NP, which developed an interest in human rights in the 1980s but sought to couple it with group rights. However, during the transition of the early 1990s, the outgoing white elite saw individual rights as a refuge against state intrusions into the private sphere. Both sides, it has been argued, were constrained in the negotiations by the emerging international consensus that an acceptable democratic transition required democratic constitutionalism.[15]

In answer to the demands by conservative Afrikaners for cultural and linguistic protection of minority groups through the recognition of group or communal rights, the ANC argued that such concerns would be accommodated by the individual rights set forth in the Bill of Rights. They would include freedom of association and expression as well as language rights. Only with regard to the right to education was a limited communal element recognized in the Interim Constitution. A person had the right (1) "to instruction in the language of his or her choice where this is reasonable and practicable" and (2) "to establish where practicable, educational institutions based on a common culture, language or religion, provided that there shall be no discrimination on the ground of race" (Sec. 32). In the 1996 Constitution, the communal element was more pronounced with regard to language and culture: "Persons belonging to a cultural, religious or linguistic community may not be denied the right, with other members of that community (a) to enjoy their culture, practice their religion and use their language; and (b) to form, join and maintain cultural, religious and linguistic associations and other organs of civil society" (Sec. 32). However, a group's exercise of these rights must not be inconsistent with the Bill of Rights. Here, the nondiscrimination clause would be the most important limiting factor.

While the Constitution is premised on individual rights, language and cultural diversity are guaranteed. The Constitution recognizes 11 official languages: Sepedi, SeSotho, Setswana, siSwati, Tshivenda, Xitonga, Afrikaans, English, isiNdebele, isiXhosa, and isiZulu. The national and provincial governments may use any official language for the purpose of government, depending on usage, practicality, and expense, but there should be at least two official languages. There is no explicit requirement for municipalities to have more than one language in government; they need take into account only the language usage and preferences of their residents. In practice, English is the country's lingua franca and forms, in effect, the language of government. In court an accused has the right to be tried in any language he or she understands or to have the proceedings interpreted in that language.

As a sop to communal interests, the Constitution mandates the creation of a Commission for the Promotion and Protection of the Rights of Cultural, Religious and Linguistic Communities. However, although the commission must promote respect for cultural, religious, and linguistic rights, it must also pursue "friendship," "tolerance," and "national unity" among groups (Sec. 185). It has proved to be extremely difficult to establish such a body with a diverse mandate cutting across language, religion, and culture;[16] in the South African context, there is little or no commonality between culture and language, on the one hand, and religion, on the other. The enabling legislation was passed only six years after the commencement of the Constitution, and the commission was established in 2003.

Given that the decentralization of the South African polity was a negotiated compromise and that majoritarian nation building was a key objective, the form of decentralization should not be incompatible with nation building. Put differently, the decentralized units should not launch platforms promoting divisive political competition. One of the reasons why the ANC accepted decentralization was the attractiveness of the German model of cooperative government. Although there was no reference to federal comity in the Interim Constitution, the Constitutional Court found that it was inherent in the system. In the 1996 Constitution, however, cooperative government was explicitly made the bedrock of decentralization.

CONSTITUTIONAL PRINCIPLES OF THE SOUTH AFRICAN POLITY

The Constitution states that "government is constituted as national, provincial and local spheres of government which are distinctive, interdependent and interrelated" (Sec. 40(1)). In contrast to the Interim Constitution's reference to "levels" of government, the term "spheres of government," used in the 1996 Constitution, intends to avoid any sense of hierarchy – a promise that the national and provincial governments' powers of supervision over provinces and municipalities respectively contradict.[17] The "distinctive" element refers to the *autonomy* enjoyed by both the provinces and local governments. The spheres are "interdependent" in the sense that each must exercise its autonomy for the common good of the country by cooperating with the other spheres. Each sphere is "interrelated" in the sense that the exercise of autonomy by a sphere is supervised by the other spheres of government. Because of the strong emphasis on supervision by the national government of both provinces and local governments, the polity is centre-dominated. It has thus been described as a hybrid-federal system.

In the Interim Constitution, the dispersal of powers had some asymmetrical elements. Accommodating the conservative Afrikaners and the Zulu nationalists meant that specific provisions were made for a *Volkstaatraad* and for recognition of the right to self-determination as well as for recognition of the Zulu monarch. As the political process moved from peace making to constitution making, the principle of symmetry prevailed; the *volkstaat* idea disappeared, and provinces and municipalities all have the same constitutional powers.[18]

Although the principle of symmetry of powers is the starting point, as in Australia and Germany, the development of provinces and municipalities with asymmetrical powers is possible. First, on the legislative field, the National Assembly may assign any of its legislative powers, except the power to amend the Constitution, to a provincial legislature or a municipality (Sec. 44). A provincial legislature may do the same with respect to a municipal council (Sec. 104). Second, in a provision drawn from the German Basic Law, a province is entitled to implement all national legislation dealing with concurrent and exclusive powers if it has the administrative capacity to do so (Sec. 125(3)). Moreover, the national and provincial governments must assign to a municipality the administration of provincial matters that necessarily relate to local government if these matters would most effectively be administered locally and if the municipality has the capacity to administer them (Sec. 156(4)). The provisions establish the principle of subsidiarity, according to whose terms the asymmetrical assignment of powers to provinces and municipalities may take place. Even so, no province or municipality, however capable, has yet been assigned additional powers.

The functional and territorial integrity of the different spheres is guaranteed in Chapter 3 on Co-operative Government. While affirming the national unity and indivisibility of the republic, and the loyalty owed to the Constitution, the republic, and its people, Section 41(1) also guarantees the existence and functioning of provinces and municipalities. It binds all spheres of government to:

(e) respect the constitutional status, institutions, powers and functions of government in the other spheres;

(f) not assume any power or function except those conferred upon them in terms of the Constitution;

(g) exercise their powers and perform their functions in a manner that does not encroach on the geographical, functional or institutional integrity of government in another sphere.

There are additional constitutional guarantees for local government. A municipality "has the right to govern, on its own initiative, the local government affairs of its community, subject to national and provincial legislation, as provided for in the Constitution" (Sec. 151(3)). The national and provincial governments, in turn, "may not compromise or impede a municipality's ability or right to exercise its powers or perform its functions" (Sec. 151(4)).

The Constitution makes no provision for secession. Indeed, Section 1 of the Constitution proclaims: "The Republic of South Africa is one, sovereign democratic state." The right to self-determination, which was included in the Interim Constitution and through Constitutional Principle XXXIV replicated in the final Constitution, is not regarded as providing any authority for secession. Section 235 reads:

The right of the South African people as a whole to self-determination, as manifested in this Constitution, does not preclude, within the framework of this right, recognition of the notion of the right of self-determination of any community sharing common cultural and language heritage, within a territorial entity in the Republic or in any other way, determined by national legislation.

The right to self-determination, in the legal sense, has been reduced largely to a political claim; any federating process along the route of self-determination will not be in the hands of any self-selected community relying on the Constitution directly but will be governed by Parliament.

Limited freedom is given to provinces and municipalities to create their own governments, political institutions, and processes of government. First, in Chapter 6 the Constitution prescribes the political, legislative, and executive institutions of provinces. However, a province may, in adopting a constitution, establish its own legislative and executive structures and procedures. Second, Chapter 13 on finance requires national legislation to regulate the financial management of provinces. The Public Finance Management Act 1 of 1999 governs both national departments and provinces. Third, the Constitution requires national legislation that structures the public service of provinces. There is a single public service "which must function, and be structured, in terms of national legislation" (Sec. 197(1)). This includes the terms and conditions of employment in the public service. The provinces are confined to the hiring and firing of public servants, but this must occur even within a national framework (Sec. 197(4)). In this area, the Public Service Act of 1994 regulates both the national and provincial administrations in detail. Fourth, Chapter 7 broadly sets out the political structures and procedures of municipalities and requires national legislation on a host of matters. The Municipal Structures Act of 1998, the Municipal Systems Act of 2000, and the Municipal Finance Management Bill of 2003 give effect to these constitutional provisions.

Apart from adopting national legislation on matters that fall within the exclusive domain of provinces (Sec. 44(2), see below), the national executive may intervene in a province when the province fails to comply with any constitutional or statutory executive obligation (Sec. 100). Directives may be issued, and the national executive may even assume responsibility for the execution of the neglected executive obligation if a number of conditions are present, including the need to maintain essential national standards, economic unity, and national security. Provinces have more extensive intervention powers with regard to municipalities. A constitutional amendment in 2003 empowers, and in some situations compels, provinces to intervene in case of a financial crisis by taking steps that include the dismissal of a municipal council.

Although the regulation of provinces and municipalities is extensive, the principles of cooperative government provide some guarantee that such regulation will not be excessive. The Constitutional Court accepted that national-framework legislation may be assessed in terms of the cooperative-government principle that all spheres of government "must exercise their powers and perform their functions in a manner that does not encroach on the geographical, functional or institutional integrity of the government of another sphere" (Sec. 41(1)(g)). This provision, the Court held, is concerned "with the way power is exercised, not with whether the power exists."[19] Thus, the Court continued, "the power given to the national legislature is one which needs to be exercised carefully in the context of the demands of section 41(1)(g) to ensure that in exercising its power, the national legislature does not encroach on the ability of the provinces to carry out the functions entrusted to them by the Constitution."[20]

In as much as the geographical and institutional integrity of a province or a municipality is protected, subnational units are also bound through the principles of cooperative government to act in the national interest as set out in Section 41 of the Constitution. In particular, they must "preserve the peace, national unity and indivisibility of the Republic, secure the well-being of the people of the Republic; provide effective, transparent, accountable and coherent government for the Republic as a whole; [and] ... co-operate with one another in mutual trust and good faith."

The contours of the provinces' power to draft their own constitutions were the product of the negotiations aimed at ensuring the participation of the IFP in the 1994 elections. The scope of the power in terms of both the Interim Constitution and the 1996 Constitution has turned out to be limited. A provincial legislature may pass a constitution with the support of at least two-thirds of its members. Because a provincial constitution must be drafted within the narrow confines set by the Constitution, it must be certified by the Constitutional Court.[21]

The constitutional space accorded to a province is limited: A provincial constitution must be consistent with the national Constitution except for

(1) legislative and executive structures and procedures that may differ from those provided for in the Constitution and (2) the inclusion of the institution, role, authority, and status of a traditional monarch (Sec. 143). Different structures and procedures must further comply with the founding values of the Constitution set out in Section 1 and with the principles of cooperative government and intergovernmental relations set out in Chapter 3. In reviewing the Western Cape Constitution in 1997, the Constitutional Court adopted a restrictive stance by holding that a separate provincial electoral system did not fall within the exception of a legislative structure or procedure that differs from the national norm.[22]

A provincial constitution is subservient to the national Constitution to the extent that it may not be inconsistent with it except on the two matters referred to above. The conformity between the two is secured through the certification process. The issue of conflict then arises only between a provincial constitution and national legislation. In the case of conflict with a national law that the Constitution specifically requires or envisages, the national legislation prevails. In all other cases, the national-override clauses pertaining to conflict with regard to exclusive and concurrent provincial legislation apply with equal force to provincial constitutions (Sec. 147(1)). As the judiciary is a national function, the national courts, with the Constitutional Court at its apex, are the interpreters of provincial constitutions.

Local Government

The Interim Constitution included a chapter on local government, but local government was placed on the list of shared provincial powers, thus placing it under the direct control of provinces. The 1996 Constitution fundamentally changed this concept of local government being the lowest tier by elevating it to a "sphere" of government alongside the national and provincial governments. This followed the trend in some modern federal constitutions of recognizing local government as constitutional state institutions, as evidenced in the constitutions of Germany (1949), Spain (1978), and Brazil (1988) and in the 1992 amendments to India's Constitution.

A number of domestic factors contributed to the shift in status.[23] Politically, within the liberation movements, local communities played a significant role in the protracted struggle against apartheid, giving rise to a strong civic movement. The drafters sought to direct this social movement toward people-centered development. The vision of local government as a driver of development also reflected modern theories of development, where local buy-in and initiative are seen as indispensable to social and economic development. Finally, given the ANC's ambivalence about provinces, there was little hesitation to strengthen local government at the expense of provinces.

The autonomy of municipalities is evident in the following areas. First, their powers and functions are listed in the Constitution. Second, they derive their main taxation powers – rates on property and surcharges on fees charged for services rendered – directly from the Constitution. Third, because local government officials fall outside the national and provincial public service, their conditions of employment are set by municipalities, and the hiring and firing of personnel are their prerogative.

Although local government, as a sphere, is guaranteed a measure of autonomy, there is still considerable supervision by both the national and provincial governments. First, the national government, in terms of the Constitution, must pass legislation providing a broad framework for local-government structures and operating procedures. Second, provinces are given specific powers to regulate defined aspects of local government. Third, both the national and provincial governments have the legislative and executive authority to regulate how municipalities exercise their executive authority in order to ensure that they perform their listed functions effectively (Sec. 155(7)). Fourth, the national and provincial governments have broad powers to monitor local government.

The Constitution creates three categories of municipalities: The first is metropolitan areas; the second is local municipalities; and the third is district municipalities, with which a district's local municipalities share their legislative and executive authority. The object of the latter category is to coordinate local municipalities and equalize services within districts. The demarcation of six large metropolitan areas creating municipalities with budgets rivaling those of provinces has de facto created city-states.

Indigenous Peoples

Given that South Africa's democratic revolution resulted in majority rule, the concept of indigenous people does not feature in the Constitution. Although there is a provision that the languages of the Khoi, Nama, and San – arguably the first peoples on the subcontinent – should be promoted and conditions created for their development (Sec. 6(5)), these groups are not accorded a different status than that of any other group.

Traditional forms of government were given only limited constitutional recognition. In Chapter 12, "the institution, status and role of traditional leadership, according to customary law, are recognized, subject to the Constitution" (Sec. 211(1)). To deal with issues affecting traditional leaders and customary law, provinces and the national government may establish houses of traditional leaders. For traditional leaders or institutions to participate directly in governance, national legislation may provide a role for them as "an institution at local level on matters affecting local communities" (Sec. 212(1)). Finally, traditional leadership is a matter included on the list of concurrent national and provincial powers. With democratically elected municipalities covering the entire surface of the country, the governance role of traditional leaders in matters of local government has theoretically been eclipsed. However, despite the constitutional status of municipalities, traditional leaders continue to play a significant, albeit a contested, governance role in the old "homeland" areas.

Allocation of Powers

The highly centralized nature of South Africa's decentralized system is evident from the way power is dispersed to subnational units. Although provinces and local governments are allocated powers in discrete functional areas, the national government retains a strong supervisory role. Much influenced by the German notion of cooperative government and the constitutional architecture giving effect thereto, concurrency of powers is a central feature in the Constitution.

Like their counterparts in Germany, India, and Nigeria, provinces have both "concurrent" powers (listed in Schedule 4) and "exclusive" powers (listed in Schedule 5). Schedule 4 includes agriculture, casinos and gambling, consumer protection, cultural matters, education at all levels (excluding tertiary education), environment, health services, housing, industrial promotion, population development, public transport, regional planning and development, tourism, trade, and welfare services. Provincial powers also cover matters that are reasonably necessary for, or incidental to, the effective exercise of a power concerning any matter listed in Schedule 4. The "exclusive" powers are more restricted, and the list consists of abattoirs, ambulance services, archives other than national archives, libraries other than national libraries, liquor licenses, museums other than national museums, provincial planning, provincial cultural matters, provincial recreation and amenities, provincial sports, provincial roads and traffic, and veterinary services, excluding regulation of the professions.

Local government's powers are listed in Part B of Schedules 4 and 5. Schedule 4B includes electricity distribution, firefighting, municipal health, public transport, and water and sanitation. Schedule 5B includes street cleaning, cemeteries, control of undertakings selling liquor to the public, markets, roads, refuse removal, and traffic.

Outside the two schedules, the Constitution confers a few additional powers on provinces and municipalities. For example, while provinces may not have their own police forces, they have a limited role in monitoring and overseeing the uniform branch of the national police service. In contrast, municipalities may establish municipal police forces within the framework of national legislation.

Residual powers reside, as in Canada and India, with the national government, which may also legislate with respect to most of the provincial powers. In the case of "concurrent" powers, both the provinces and the national

Parliament may validly legislate on the same matter at the same time. With respect to the "exclusive" provincial powers, national legislation is possible only when national legislation is deemed necessary "(a) to maintain national security; (b) to maintain economic unity; (c) to maintain essential national standards; (d) to establish minimum standards required for the rendering of services; or (e) to prevent unreasonable action taken by a province which is prejudicial to the interest of another province or the country as a whole" (Sec. 44(2)).

The only incidences of truly provincial exclusive powers are naming a province (Sec. 104(2)), writing a provincial constitution (Sec. 142), and adopting a language policy (Sec. 6).

Local government's powers are also circumscribed by the other spheres' powers in the same functional areas.[24] Under Schedule 4B, the national and provincial governments may regulate – by setting standards and minimum requirements – only how municipalities exercise their executive authority. With regard to Schedule 5B matters, the national government must comply with the requirements of Section 44(2), quoted above, and provinces may regulate only by setting the legal framework within which municipalities exercise their powers.

When a conflict arises between national and provincial legislation in a concurrent functional area, a broad and generous override clause applies. National legislation that applies uniformly to the country as a whole prevails if:

(a) the matter cannot be regulated effectively by provinces individually;
(b) the matter, to be dealt with effectively, requires uniformity across the nation, and such uniformity is established by norms and standards, frameworks, or national policies;
(c) such legislation is necessary for
    (i)   the maintenance of national security;
    (ii) the maintenance of economic unity;
    (iii) the protection of the common market in respect of the mobility of goods, services, capital and labour;
    (iv) the promotion of economic activities across provincial boundaries;
    (v)   the promotion of equal opportunity of equal access to government services; or
    (vi) the protection of the environment. (Sec. 146(2))

National legislation also prevails if it is aimed at preventing unreasonable action by a province that (1) is prejudicial to the economic health or security interests of either another province or the country as a whole or (2) impedes the implementation of national economic policy (Sec. 146(3)). If a court finds that the usual rules of paramountcy cannot resolve a conflict, the national legislation prevails over the provincial legislation or constitution

(Sec. 148). Conversely, provincial legislation prevails if the requirements for a national override are not met (Sec. 148(5)). Depending on the Constitutional Court's interpretation, an expansive reading of the override clauses will place few fetters on the national government's supremacy over concurrent matters, while a narrow reading will leave some space for provinces.

In the case of a province's "exclusive" powers, the criteria for valid national legislation, set out in Section 44(2), serve also to determine the question of conflict. If national legislation meets the required criteria, it is valid and thus overrides any provincial legislation (Sec. 147(2)). If the national legislation prevails, the provincial law is not invalidated; it simply becomes inoperative but only as long as the conflict remains (Sec. 149). However, the override is confined to the area of the conflict; the entire provincial law is not necessarily rendered inoperative.

With regard to municipal bylaws, the basic rule of paramountcy is that a bylaw in conflict with national or provincial legislation is invalid. However, in a novel provision, a bylaw may trump even a national law. A national or provincial law will not prevail if it "compromise[s] or impede[s] a municipality's ability or right to exercise its powers or perform its functions" (Sec. 151(4)). This may be interpreted to mean that the national and provincial governments may not use their legislative powers in an unduly intrusive or excessively prescriptive manner.[25]

Despite the extensive overlapping of legislative powers, the level of conflict has been very low.[26] The main reason is extensive national legislation in the area of concurrent jurisdiction. There are only a limited number of provincial laws in the same areas. In turn, the national government has only once entered the provinces' "exclusive" functional area, namely with the passing of the Liquor Bill in 1999. This bill dealing with regulation of the liquor industry was challenged with partial success on the ground that the Parliament exceeded its legislative authority. With the dominance of national legislation, provinces have not come into their own legislatively. In the main, they have become administrative bodies, implementing national laws with regard to education, welfare, and health care. A few factors contribute to the dearth of provincial legislation. First, with hardly any revenue-raising powers, provinces are reluctant to adopt laws whose implementation may add to their financial burden. Second, the dominance of the ANC in eight of the nine provinces inhibits the passing of competing legislation. Third, some provinces lack the capacity to develop their own legislation in order to exploit the available legal space.

The allocation of powers should be placed in the context of the overarching framework of cooperative government. Conflicts about the exercise of powers should be managed through participation by the spheres in various structures facilitating intergovernmental relations. Moreover, a principle of cooperative government is the avoidance of litigation to resolve intergovernmental disputes, including those that arise from con-currency.[27] All organs of state must, in complying with their duty to cooper-ate in mutual trust and good faith, avoid legal proceedings against one another (Sec. 41(1)). The Constitutional Court put this duty positively: Or-gans of state must "try and resolve their dispute amicably."[28] The rationale is, in the words of the Court, that the Constitution does not embody "com-petitive federalism," but, to the contrary, "co-operative government."[29] The latter entails, the Court said, that "disputes should where possible be re-solved at a political level rather than through adversarial litigation."[30] The duty to avoid litigation is demanding because Section 41(3) requires that every organ of state "must make every reasonable effort to settle the dispute ... and must exhaust all other remedies before it approaches a court to resolve the dispute." The courts may enforce this duty by referring a dispute back to the parties if the requirements of Section 41(3) have not been met. The Constitutional Court has taken compliance with this duty se-riously. It has said that a court, including itself, will "rarely decide an inter-governmental dispute unless the organs of state involved in the dispute have made every reasonable effort to resolve it at a political level."[31]

STRUCTURE AND OPERATION OF GOVERNMENT

Separation of Powers

Locked into the Westminster mode of thinking for historical reasons, the negotiators of the Interim Constitution showed little enthusiasm for Amer-ican-style presidentialism; consequently, they opted, as did most former British colonies (except for Nigeria in its Constitutions of 1978 and 1999), for a parliamentary system in the national sphere. The separation of pow-ers was, however, elevated to Constitutional Principle VI: "There shall be a separation of powers between the legislature, the executive and judiciary, with appropriate checks and balances to ensure accountability, responsive-ness and openness." The Constitutional Court held that this principle does not require the formal separation of personnel between the legislature and executive.[32] A parliamentary system in both the national and provincial governments, therefore, does not violate this principle. However, although there is an overlap of personnel, the functions of the legislature and the executive have to be kept separate. In an early decision, the Constitutional Court struck down as unconstitutional an act that gave the president the power, in effect, to amend the act.[33] The Court held that the granting of regulatory powers to the president exceeded the bounds of the legislative powers that could be delegated to the executive because they entailed the power to amend the act itself.

National Parliament

National legislative authority is vested in Parliament, consisting of the National Assembly and the National Council of Provinces (NCOP). The Assembly may consist of between 350 and 400 members directly elected in terms of an electoral system that results, in general, in proportional representation for a period of five years. As of 1994, the number of members was 400, elected from closed party lists. To ensure that the Assembly is as inclusive as possible, a party need only receive 0.25 percent of the overall vote to get one member elected. In the 2004 election, in addition to the three large parties (the ANC, Democratic Alliance, and IFP), a further eight small parties gained representation.

The NCOP was created to draw the provinces into the national legislative process. In line with American and Australian models of equal representation of states, each province, irrespective of size, has ten representatives in the NCOP. In loosely following the German *Bundesrat* model, four members of each provincial delegation are members of the provincial legislature with one seat reserved for the provincial premier. The other six members are appointed on a permanent basis by the provincial legislature, with the power of recall. Organized local government, represented by the South African Local Government Association, may also participate but not vote in proceedings dealing with local matters.

The NCOP's legislative authority is limited to provincial issues. With regard to legislation falling outside the provinces' concurrent and exclusive powers, the NCOP has merely a delaying power. In these cases, each NCOP member has an individual vote. Should the NCOP reject a bill, the National Assembly may adopt it with an ordinary majority. When a matter falls within the provinces' concurrent or exclusive powers, the law-making processes of the German *Bundesrat* have been followed in the main. The voting is by province, each provincial delegation having one vote. As representatives of the provinces, each delegation must obtain a mandate from its provincial legislature on how to cast its vote. Where there is a conflict between the Assembly and the NCOP, provision is made for a mediating committee. If the conflict still persists, the will of the NCOP may be overridden by a two-thirds majority in the National Assembly.

The NCOP does not yet have high political status, and considerable practical difficulties exist in getting mandates from the provinces.[34] The dominance of the ANC in eight of the nine provinces ensures concordance between the National Assembly and the NCOP, and legislation approved by Cabinet is rarely challenged by these provinces. The lack of resources, skills, and expertise of the NCOP and the provincial legislatures, coupled with a short period within which to obtain mandates on national legislation, has meant that no substantial provincial value has been added to the Parliament by the NCOP. On a structural level, in much the same way as intergovernmental relations in Canada are dominated by an extensive system of "executive federalism" because parliamentary government concentrates powers in the executive, the executive institutions of intergovernmental relations – the meetings of the president and the nine premiers (called the president's Coordinating Council) and the meetings between national ministers and their provincial counterparts (called MinMECs) – have eclipsed the NCOP's deliberative function.[35] After national legislation has been negotiated at the executive level, provincial executives are unlikely to add or raise anything of substance during the NCOP proceedings that conclude the legislative process.

Although Parliament has no veto over laws made by provincial legislatures or municipal councils, it may pass countervailing legislation, the supremacy of which will then be determined by the override rules. The provinces have, through the NCOP, a number of veto powers over national executive action. First, the NCOP may terminate an intervention by the national government in a province because all interventions must be confirmed by the NCOP (Sec. 100). Second, it may terminate the national Treasury's decision to stop the transfer of funds to a province because of the latter's alleged persistent or serious breach of financial management rules (Sec. 216). Third, along with the National Assembly, the NCOP must ratify all international treaties concluded by the national executive. Finally, as a component part of Parliament, the NCOP must approve declarations of "a state of national defense" (Sec. 203(3)).

National Executive

The president, who is the head of state and head of the national executive, is elected from among the elected MPs. To the extent that half of the 400 members of the National Assembly are elected on a provincial list via proportional representation, provinces participate in an attenuated way in the eventual election of the president. Except for a possible two members, the president must select the Cabinet from the National Assembly. On election, he or she vacates his or her seat in Parliament, but this does not terminate the president's or the Cabinet's accountability to the Assembly. Apart from the power to impeach the president by a two-thirds majority, in accordance with the true Westminster system, the National Assembly may, by a majority vote, remove the president and the Cabinet by passing a motion of no confidence.

Judiciary

In the 1996 Constitution, one of the founding values of the new democratic state is the "supremacy of the constitution and the rule of law" (Sec. 1(c)).

Within this dispensation, the judiciary plays a key role in safeguarding and enforcing the Constitution. During the multiparty negotiations, the future of the judiciary appointed during the apartheid area was contentious. The liberation movements argued that the existing judiciary, mainly white, male, and comprised of enforcers of the apartheid legal order, could not be trusted as the guardians of the new democratic constitutional order. The National Party, however, sought their continuation in office. Although their tenure of office was eventually accepted, a compromise was struck on the guardians of the Constitution. On all constitutional matters, a new court, called the Constitutional Court, has the final say, while on all other matters, the then existing Appellate Division is the highest court of appeal. Given the years of executive dominance of the appointment of the judiciary, the objective was to depoliticize the appointment process by establishing the Judicial Service Commission (JSC). Both institutions, the Constitutional Court and the JSC, were retained in the 1996 Constitution.

As in India, there is one national judiciary. At the apex on matters constitutional, in the same mold as the German Constitutional Court, is the Constitutional Court, the ultimate interpreter and enforcer of the Constitution. On other matters, the Supreme Court of Appeal is the highest court. Below these two courts is the High Court, divided into a number of divisions, which eventually will coincide with the new provincial boundaries. The current divisions are based on pre-1994 jurisdictional boundaries, including the "independent" homelands.

At the base of the appointment of members of the judiciary is the JSC, which has a broad membership that includes representatives of the judiciary and the legal profession, six members of the National Assembly, and four permanent delegates to the NCOP. The premier of a province becomes a member of the JSC when considering a judicial appointment to a provincial division falling within the province. The president, after consulting the JSC, among others, appoints the judges heading the Constitutional Court and the Supreme Court of Appeal. The appointment of judges to the Constitutional Court is done by the president from a list prepared by the JSC. All other judges are appointed by the JSC.

Only the Constitutional Court may decide disputes between organs of state in the national and provincial spheres concerning the constitutional status, powers, and functions of any of these organs. The Court also makes the final decision on whether national or provincial legislation is constitutional. It decides the constitutionality of any amendment to the Constitution and whether Parliament or the president failed to fulfil a constitutional obligation. The certification of a provincial constitution is a further duty. Finally, before a national or provincial act is put into operation, the Court has the power to review its constitutionality on application by the president, the National Assembly, or a provincial legislature.[36]

Provincial Governments

The provincial institutions largely mirror the national ones. Provincial legislatures are, however, unicameral. Their size varies between 30 and 80 members, with the exact number determined by a formula prescribed in national legislation. Members are elected for five years through a system of proportional representation based on closed party lists. The premier is elected from among members of the provincial legislature and appoints all members of the executive council from the legislature. As pointed out above, a province may in its constitution provide for executive and legislative structures that differ from those in the national Constitution. The Western Cape did so in the Western Cape Constitution of 1997 with regard to the size of the provincial legislature.

Municipalities

Democratic governance is mandated for local government across the country. The fully elected municipal councils combine both the legislative and executive in one. The interim measure that entitled a traditional leader *ex officio* to be a member of a council without voting rights lapsed with the implementation of the final phase of the local-government dispensation in December 2000. The Constitution further set out the basic internal procedures of the council to ensure democratic governance.

National-Provincial-Local Relations

Within the context of those principles of cooperative government that focus on the unity of the people and a strong ethos of equality, the consequences of residency in a province are, in terms of the Constitution, not significant. To the contrary, if a province discriminates on the basis of residency, the national government may intervene. National legislation prevails over provincial legislation if the former is necessary for the "promotion of equal opportunity or equal access to government services" (Sec. 146(2)). Further, national legislation is supreme if it is necessary for the "protection of the common market in respect of the mobility of goods, services, capital and labour" (Sec. 146(2)).

Although the Constitution does not establish mechanisms to facilitate intergovernmental relations, it requires the enactment of national legislation to do so (Sec. 41(2)). No such legislation is yet in place, but statutory mechanisms have been established in discrete areas, such as intergovernmental fiscal relations. As intergovernmental relations are left largely unregulated in the Constitution, there is no prohibition against interprovincial or inter-municipal agreements.

FISCAL AND MONETARY POWERS

When South Africa reentered the international financial world after apartheid's years of isolation, it encountered a consensus that emphasized fiscal discipline and a strict monetary policy. The impact of this consensus on the constitution-making process is not clear, but it may have had an influence on what some commentators refer to as the two constitutions: a "political constitution" featuring most elements of a federal system and a "fiscal constitution" that has the hallmarks of a very centralized system. With the fiscal side of the 1996 Constitution largely determining how the political side functions, the end result is national dominance.

Taxation

There appear to be no limits to the national government's taxation power, a power that is not explicitly mentioned in the Constitution. The taxation powers of provinces and municipalities are listed explicitly. Severe limitations are placed on the provinces' powers, whereas the powers of local government are more substantial.

Under the Constitution, a province may impose taxes, levies, and duties other than an income tax, a value-added tax, a general sales tax, rates on property, or custom duties. In addition, a province may impose a surcharge on any nationally imposed tax, levy, or duty other than on a corporate income tax, value-added tax, rate on property, or customs duty (Sec. 228(1)). However, these powers must be regulated in terms of an act of Parliament. If there is no such act, as currently is the case, then there are no taxation powers. Arguably, there is a limit on the extent to which the national government could deny provinces taxation powers by failing to pass the necessary legislation; the Constitutional Court could well entertain a constitutional claim that the national government is obliged to pass the requisite legislation.

In contrast, municipalities' taxation powers of imposing rates on property and surcharges on fees for services (Sec. 229) are not dependent on national legislation, but they may be regulated by national legislation. In addition, if authorized by national legislation, municipalities may impose other taxes, levies, and duties except an income tax, value-added tax, general sales tax, or customs duty.

Apart from the limitation that provincial taxation powers are to be exercised in terms of national regulatory legislation, the Constitution provides that provincial taxation powers "may not be exercised in a way that materially and unreasonably prejudices national economic policies, economic activities across provincial boundaries, or the national mobility of goods, services, capital and labour" (Sec. 228(2)). Similar principles apply to the exercise of local government's taxation powers (Sec. 229(2)). With only municipalities currently exercising significant taxation powers, the issue of tax harmonization is relevant only to this sphere. National legislation may regulate any aspect of local government's taxation powers, and the harmonization of rates on property was being sought through the national Property Rates Act of 2004.

The "fiscal constitution" has resulted in an extreme case of vertical fiscal imbalance in which provinces are almost entirely dependent on national-government transfers while responsible for the execution of most social services. At present, provinces raise less than 5 percent of their total revenue. The main sources of their own revenue are gambling taxes and some user fees. This contrasts sharply with the 92 percent of total revenue that municipalities raise themselves. The remainder of municipal revenue comes from national transfers, with hardly any coming from the provinces. The main sources of municipal revenue are rates on property (21 percent), surcharges on service fees (32 percent), and licenses, fees, and fines (32 percent). With the budgets of some of the six metropolitan municipalities rivaling the budgets of the provinces in which they are located, the significance of local government in South Africa is apparent.

Borrowing Powers

The Constitution regulates the borrowing powers of provinces and municipalities but is silent with regard to the national government. The borrowing powers of provinces and municipalities are subject to more or less the same conditions in the Constitution (Secs 230 and 230A). These powers are to be exercised in terms of national legislation adopted after considering the recommendations of the Financial and Fiscal Commission. Borrowing may be for capital or current expenditure, but in the latter case, borrowing may be done only when necessary for bridging purposes during a fiscal year. Provincial borrowing is governed by the Borrowing Powers of Provincial Government Act 48 of 1996 and the Public Finance Management Act 1 of 1999. Because these acts impose a tight framework, provinces engage in little borrowing.

Guarantees

In contrast to the Constitution's silence on loans incurred by the national government, loan guarantees provided by any of the three spheres of government (standing surety for the financial obligations of another body) must be subject to conditions set out in national legislation (Sec. 218). No explicit provision makes the national government the guarantor for provincial and local debt. The only reference in the Constitution that may suggest that the national government must come to the rescue of provinces is the constitutional obligation that the national government must, by legislative or other means, help provinces develop the administrative capacity required for the effective exercise of their powers and functions (Sec. 125(3)). With respect to local government, both the national and the provincial governments must "support and strengthen the capacity of municipalities to manage their own affairs" and to exercise their powers and functions (Sec. 154(1)). However, when the Supreme Court of Appeal interpreted the constitutional obligation of provinces to "support" municipalities, it held that support did not include standing in for a municipality's bad debt.[37]

Allocation of Revenues

The provinces' main source of income is national government transfers, which consume 58 percent of the national budget. Transfers are of two kinds. First, each province is entitled to an "equitable share" of revenue raised nationally, which forms the bulk of transfers. Second, conditional grants are issued at the national government's discretion. Municipalities are also entitled to their equitable share of the revenue raised nationally and may receive conditional grants. Every year, an act of Parliament must provide for the "equitable division" of revenue raised nationally between the three spheres of government as well as within the provincial sphere. The division is made in terms of guiding principles set out in the Constitution (Sec. 214(1)) that seek to secure equalization among the provinces and municipalities. The division of local government's equitable share among the 284 municipalities is done administratively by the national Treasury.

The "equitable share" of each sphere is determined through a three-stage process. First, the Financial and Fiscal Commission, composed of representatives of the three spheres, recommends how the cake must be sliced in accordance with the broad criteria set forth in Section 214. The commission has been guided mainly by provincial population size and measurable poverty. The second step is to consult with the provinces and local governments in the Budget Council and Budget Forum respectively. These bodies for intergovernmental fiscal relations are composed of representatives of the three spheres of government. The final determination is made by the national minister of finance subject to parliamentary approval of the annual Division of Revenue Bill.

Spending of Revenues

There are no constitutional limits on how the national government spends its share of the revenue raised nationally. The Constitution requires, however, that the procurement of goods and services by all three spheres of government must be in accordance with a "fair, equitable, transparent, competitive and cost-effective" system prescribed in national legislation (Sec. 217(1)) and that such policy must include provisions to protect or advance persons or categories of persons disadvantaged by past discrimination (Sec. 217(2)).

Although there are no constitutional restrictions on how provinces use their equitable share, in practice spending is largely prescribed by the national government. The bulk of provincial expenditure goes to education, health, and social security. Most of the spending objects are determined by national standards. For example, in social welfare, pensions are determined nationally; the provinces are concerned only with the distribution of these grants. The end result is that 85 percent of all the funds a province receives have already been preallocated by the national government.

Monetary Policy

The Constitutional Assembly sought to insulate monetary policy from the vagaries of politics. The Constitution thus establishes a central bank, the South African Reserve Bank. Its primary objective is to protect "the value of the currency in the interest of balanced and sustainable economic growth" (Sec. 224(1)). In pursuing this objective, the bank must perform its functions "independently and without fear, favor or prejudice." However, there must be regular consultation between the bank and the minister of finance (Sec. 224(2)).

FOREIGN AFFAIRS AND DEFENCE POWERS

International relations fall to the national government: "The negotiating and signing of all international agreements is the responsibility of the national executive" (Sec. 231(1)). Furthermore, the president is responsible for diplomacy. Although provinces and municipalities do not have foreign-affairs powers under the Constitution, they have engaged in international relations, concluding a variety of memoranda of understanding and other agreements based on a general plenary power to conclude agreements in general.[38]

Provinces are brought indirectly into international relations through their participation in the NCOP. In contrast to the NCOP's limited veto powers over national legislation that directly affects provinces, it has a veto power over the ratification of international agreements. Except for self-executing executive agreements, "[a]n international agreement binds the Republic only after it has been approved by resolution in both the National Assembly and the National Council of Provinces" (Sec. 231). No evidence has yet emerged that the NCOP has asserted its role in this field, which is symptomatic of its overall marginal role in Parliament.

The security services are a national concern. The Constitution provides for "a single defense force," which is "the only lawful military force" in the country (Sec. 199(1),(2)). The president, as the head of the national executive, has the authority to deploy the defence force (Sec. 201). As security is also subject to the authority of Parliament (Sec. 198(d)), the provinces may play an important role through the NCOP. A declaration of war ("a state of national defense") by the president lapses unless it is approved by Parliament within seven days of the declaration (Sec. 203(3)). Although the NCOP's consent is not expressly required, as a component part of Parliament, it codetermines the question.

VOTING, ELECTIONS, AND POLITICAL PARTIES

In a clear break from South Africa's apartheid past of race-based voters' rolls, the Constitution proclaims in Section 1 that the founding values of the republic include "[u]niversal adult suffrage, [and] a national common voters roll." The common voters' roll applies to all elections to the National Assembly, provincial legislatures, and municipal councils. The Bill of Rights further entrenches the right of every adult citizen, with a minimum voting age of 18 years, to vote in elections and to stand for office in these legislative bodies (Sec. 19(3)). Precluded from standing as candidates are public servants, persons declared insolvent, those declared to be of unsound mind, and those convicted to serve a prison sentence of more than a year. In addition, every citizen has the right "to free, fair and regular elections" with respect to all political institutions (Sec. 19(2)).

The entire responsibility for registering voters, conducting elections, and declaring results has been entrusted to the Independent Electoral Commission. It is one of the State Institutions Supporting Constitutional Democracy listed and described in Chapter 9, which are, in terms of the Constitution, "independent, and subject only to the Constitution and the law and ... must be impartial and must exercise their powers and perform their functions without fear, favor or prejudice" (Sec. 181(1)). The Constitutional Court held that because of its independence and the absence of control by the national government, it does not form a part of the national sphere of government for the purposes of adhering to the principles of cooperative government, including the duty to avoid litigation.[39]

The Bill of Rights guarantees every citizen the right to form a political party (Sec. 19(1)). There are no restrictions on the nature of a party, but other provisions of the Bill of Rights, such as freedom of expression, may impose limits. Freedom of expression does not extend to "propaganda for war" or "advocacy of hatred that is based on race, ethnicity, gender or religion, and that constitutes incitement to cause harm" (Sec. 16(2)). There is no explicit regulation of political parties, but the Constitution requires that "[t]o enhance multi-party democracy, national legislation must provide for the funding of political parties participating in national and provincial legislatures on an equitable and proportional basis" (Sec. 236).

PROTECTION OF RIGHTS

In the same way as Germany responded to its Nazi past in 1949 by guaranteeing individual rights, including the right to equality, the protection of individual rights was high on the agenda of the constitution makers in the wake of apartheid's race discrimination and repression. The Interim Constitution of 1993 contained a chapter on "fundamental rights," while the final Constitution's Chapter 2 refers to a "Bill of Rights." In the latter, both the content of the rights and their application are innovative.

Because the struggle against apartheid was waged also in terms of international law, international human-rights law features prominently in the Constitution. The Constitution maintains the dualist system; that is, international conventions become part of South African law only on incorporation by domestic law unless they are regarded as part of customary international law. International human-rights law applies indirectly: In interpreting the Bill of Rights, any court or tribunal must "consider international law" (Sec. 39(1)). Furthermore, in interpreting any legislation, a reasonable interpretation that conforms with international law must be preferred (Sec. 232).

The Bill of Rights contains an extensive array of rights, from the classical civil liberties and political rights to modern socio-economic rights. Taking pride of place is the right to equality, followed by the rights to human dignity, life, freedom, security of person, and privacy. The freedoms of religion, belief, opinion, expression, association, movement, and residence are also guaranteed. Extensive rights are accorded to detained and accused persons.

Limited only to citizens are political rights, rights relating to citizenship, and the right to choose a trade, occupation, or profession. Section 3 of the Constitution provides that there "is a common South African citizenship." This entails that all citizens are "equally entitled to the rights, privileges and benefits of citizenship" as well as being "equally subject to the duties and responsibilities of citizenship." This section provides further that national legislation determines the acquisition, loss, and restoration of citizenship.

Controversial in the constitutional negotiations were rights relating to education, labour relations, and property.[40] Individual rights are recognized with regard to language, culture, and education. Having considered the Indian approach to second-generation rights through nonenforceable Directive Principles of State Policy, the Constitutional Assembly included enforceable socio-economic rights relating to housing, health care, food, water, social security, and education. Specific rights are bestowed on children, too. There are also rights of access to information, just administrative action, and access to courts. As mentioned above, the right of persons to belong to a cultural, religious, or linguistic community is the only right with a communal element.

The Bill of Rights binds all spheres of government. In addition, rights may apply horizontally to natural and juristic persons, depending on the suitability of the right and the nature of the duty imposed by the right. Influenced by Canada's Charter of Rights and Freedoms, the Bill of Rights also contains a limitation clause. In states of emergency, certain rights may be suspended temporarily. However, a number of rights are nonderogable, including equality with respect to unfair discrimination solely on the grounds of race, colour, ethnic or social origin, sex, religion, language, human dignity, and life. This emergency-suspension provision has not yet been used.

The principal method of enforcing rights is through the courts. Any law or conduct inconsistent with the Bill of Rights is invalid and must be declared as such by a court. The Constitutional Court has invalidated numerous laws dating from the apartheid era (e.g., the death penalty). Less frequent has been the invalidation of laws passed by the new democratic Parliament. The Court has also been willing to enforce the socio-economic rights. With regard to the right of access to housing, the Court found the national government wanting for not having a policy on emergency shelter for persons in destitute situations.[41] In enforcing the right of access to health, it set aside a national policy on HIV/AIDS for being unreasonable.[42] In the latter case, the Court explicitly rejected the argument that its review of government policy violated the separation of judicial and executive powers. The Court asserted in this case and others that, as guardian of the Constitution, it has the power to review all aspects of executive actions.

With human rights high on the constitution makers' agenda, a number of independent commissions and institutions are provided for, namely the Public Protector, the South African Human Rights Commission, the Commission for Gender Equality, and the Commission for the Promotion and Protection of the Rights of Cultural, Religious and Linguistic Communities. The Human Rights Commission is tasked, in general, with promoting respect for human rights and, in particular, with monitoring the measures taken by government to realize the socio-economic rights.

Although the Constitution is silent about bills of rights in provincial constitutions, the Constitutional Court held in its judgment on certification of the KwaZulu-Natal Constitution that it is permissible for a province to adopt a bill of rights but only within the parameters of the province's constitution-making powers.[43] The KwaZulu-Natal Constitution was thus rejected by the Court on the ground, *inter alia*, that through its provincial Bill of Rights, the province had arrogated for itself additional powers. The scope of a provincial bill of rights is limited: It may deal only with matters falling within the province's powers and may not subtract from the national Bill of Rights. When the Western Cape drafted its provincial constitution, it opted instead for a set of unenforceable Directive Principles of Provincial Policy.

CONSTITUTIONAL CHANGE

Constitutional entrenchment was a highly contested issue. For the National Party, the Constitution was to serve as an insurance policy against oppressive majoritarianism. Thus, at the outset of the negotiations, the NP sought constitutional entrenchment with majorities as high as 75 percent for the Bill of Rights and regional governments.[44] This was opposed by the ANC. In the end, the standard two-thirds majority prevailed in the Interim Constitution. The norm for the 1996 Constitution is also a two-thirds majority, but there are special majorities and procedures for some aspects of the Constitution. The role of the NCOP in the amending procedure depends on the provision at issue. Amending Section 1, the founding values of the 1996 Constitution, requires the supporting vote of 75 percent in the National Assembly and six of the nine provinces in the NCOP. The Bill of Rights may be amended only with the support of a two-thirds majority in the National Assembly and six provinces in the NCOP. With regard to all other matters, a two-thirds majority is required in the National Assembly. On these amendments, the support of six provinces in the NCOP is required only when the amendment relates to a matter affecting the NCOP, alters provincial boundaries, or deals with a provincial matter. When an amendment bill concerns a specific province (or provinces), the NCOP may not pass the bill unless it has been approved by the legislature(s) of the affected province(s). This gives provinces veto power over amendments directed at them.

As indicated above, the Interim Constitution was amended ten times during its less than three-year life. The first two amendments – enlarging the powers of provinces and recognizing the principle of self-determination and the *Volkstaatraad* – gave shape to the eventual form that decentralization took in the 1996 Constitution. Some of the ten amendments to the 1996 Constitution have facilitated a slow rolling back of the reach of decentralization. In 1998 the significance of provincial borders was tempered by making provision for the establishment of cross-border municipalities.[45] In the same year, the dissolution of a municipal council by a province was authorized indirectly.[46] In 2001 an amendment extended local government's borrowing powers by enabling municipal councils to bind themselves and future councils in order to secure loans or investments. By a second amendment in the same year, the hand of the national Treasury was strengthened vis-à-vis the other spheres.[47] The Treasury must now "enforce compliance" with measures ensuring transparency and expenditure control in all three spheres. The national law relating to procurement, applicable to all spheres, *must* prescribe a framework for affirmative action. National legislation may now determine a framework for the operation of the provincial revenue funds. The amendment also removed the limitation that national legislation may impose only "reasonable conditions" on the raising of loans by provinces. The representation that each province had in the Financial and Fiscal Commission has been replaced by three provincial representatives appointed by the president. A 2003 amendment eased the provisions for intervention by the national government in provinces as well as in municipalities.[48] Instead of having to secure the approval of the NCOP for an intervention within 30 days, the period was extended to 180 days. In the case of a financial emergency in a municipality, the provincial government is obliged to intervene, and if it does not do so adequately, the national government may do so in its place. The overall objective is greater national control over the financial affairs of provinces and local governments.

THE FUTURE

The 1996 Constitution is the product of negotiations and compromise. Structured by the Constitutional Principles of the Interim Constitution, the 1996 Constitution secured a strong majoritarian national government functioning within the limits of an individual-rights regime. In the first decade of democratic rule, constitutionalism has been the norm. The role of the courts in enforcing the Constitution has not been questioned by the new political elite, and the courts have not shied away from their responsibility.

The establishment of provincial governments was an important part of the "negotiated revolution." It was an uneasy compromise that left open the question of whether the country would move toward more or less decentralization. Amendments over the past four years suggest that the trend is toward greater centralization. Even if decentralization survives as the basic form of the state, the present dispersal of power between provincial and local governments may not remain intact. With the establishment of local government as a strong sphere of government, led by six megametropolitan cities, the place and role of the provinces will come under increasing pressure. The result might thus be an hourglass configuration, with the provinces squeezed thin between the national and local spheres of government.

Whether South Africa will proceed down the road of decentralization mapped out by the Constitution depends on a number of factors. First, the Constitution establishes a normative framework consisting of a complex set of institutional and procedural rules. Governing within the constitutional framework and the laws that give it effect requires skill and resources, raising the question of whether the country has the institutional capacity to make decentralization work. Insufficient human and other resources may undermine the capacity of provinces and local authorities to fulfil their constitutional mandates, thereby creating the need for a more centralized government.

Second, the dominance of one party, the ANC, which governs nationally with 70 percent of the vote and is in control of all nine provinces (being the major party in coalition governments in KwaZulu-Natal and the Western Cape),[49] raises the question of whether the party, with its strong centralist organization and philosophy, will centralize the constitutional structure. Given that central-party control is a guiding tenet of the ANC and that all provincial premiers are thus appointed centrally rather than through provincial party structures, the ANC's dominance in South Africa's political life may not result in the development of strong provincial or local governments. However, the converse is also possible: Current practice in some provinces suggests that the federal dimension of the constitutional structure might make the party more federal in the long run.

How the question resolves itself may depend on whether a federal society or federal political culture comes to underpin the Constitution. Unlike in some other federations, decentralization in South Africa was not driven principally by historical nationalities or by ethnic or language groups. Although conservative Afrikaners and Zulu nationalists influenced the shape of the decentralized state, they were not the main drivers of the process. The desire to secure a strong central government was the main impulse. Consequently, the essential federal society or federal political culture that props up federal political structures is weak, leaving these structures vulnerable to any push toward centralization. However, political culture is not static, and if South Africa proceeds along the decentralization road, a federal culture might grow apace in the provinces and municipalities.

Third, given that "party dominance is not a permanent state" and that the fortunes of parties fluctuate,[50] will the system of decentralization, in the absence of a dominant ANC, be able to deliver effective government to the people? Will a multiparty system be able to produce decisive ruling majorities in Parliament, and will the system of cooperative government deliver government across party lines? More broadly, is there a liberal democratic political culture capable of sustaining a multiparty system? The evidence emerging from KwaZulu-Natal on cross-party government is not always encouraging. The governing ANC and IFP coalition in this province between 1994 and 2004 has been fractious and unstable. Cooperative structures and relations between the province and the municipalities across ANC and IFP party lines are also tenuous.

Although multiparty politics pose a challenge to South Africa's constitutional democracy, decentralization provides an opportunity for its entrenchment. Multiparty democracy entails more than competition at the polls to determine who will be the governing party. It includes the notion that, first, different political parties may govern in different spheres of government and, second, that different parties so governing may work together to the benefit of the people of a province and the country as a whole. The establishment of a vibrant local democracy, then, is of immense value to deepening democracy nationally. The experience internationally is that pluralist politics must be learned, and subnational governments make a good school. A key challenge, then, is making multiparty democracy work in the subnational spheres within the cooperative government framework.

The Constitution was forged in the heat of political negotiations and compromise of the 1990s. It was intended to inspire nation building based on liberal democracy. Transforming society and political culture in this image of the Constitution is under way. In this endeavour, South Africa's Constitution will both influence and be influenced by the political culture in which it operates.

NOTES

1 See Ronald L. Watts, "Is the New Constitution Federal or Unitary," *Birth of a Constitution*, ed. Bertus de Villiers (Cape Town: Juta, 1994), pp. 75–88 at p. 86; Richard Simeon, "Considerations in the Design of Federations: The South African Constitution in Comparative Context," *SA Public Law* 13, no. 1 (1998): 42–71.

2 Eastern Cape (iziXhosa 82.8%); KwaZulu-Natal (isiZulu 79.8%); Northern Cape (Afrikaans 69.3%); Western Cape (Afrikaans 59.2%); North West (Setswana 67.2%); Free State (Sesotho 62.1%); and Limpopo (Sepedi 52.7%). Statistics South Africa, *Stats in Brief 2002* (Pretoria: Statistics South Africa, 2002), Table 2.11.

3 Ibid., p. 11. Less than 1 percent of the population was classified as "unspecified or other."

4 Countries with a gross national product per capita of between US$2,996 and US$9,265 are classified by the World Bank as upper-middle-income countries.

5 See Nico Steytler, "South Africa," *Federalism and Civil Societies*, ed. Jutta Kramer and Hans-Peter Schneider (Baden-Baden: Nomos, 1999), pp. 295–317 at pp. 295–97; Nico Steytler, "Constitution-making: In Search of a Democratic South Africa," *Negotiating Justice: A New Constitution for South Africa*, ed. Mervyn Bennun and Malyn D.D. Newitt (Exeter: University of Exeter, 1995), pp. 63–80 at pp. 62–71.

6 Penelope Andrews and Stephen Ellman, "Introduction: Towards Understanding South African Constitutionalism," *The Post-Apartheid Constitutions: Perspectives on South Africa's Basic Law*, ed. Penelope Andrews and Stephen Ellman (Johannesburg and Athens: Witwatersrand University Press and Ohio University Press, 2001), pp. 1–19 at p. 1.

7 See Cyril Ramaphosa, "Negotiating a New Nation: Reflections on the Development of South Africa's Constitution," *The Post-Apartheid Constitutions: Perspectives on South Africa's Basic Law,* ed. Penelope Andrews and Stephen Ellman (Johannesburg and Athens: Witwatersrand University Press and Ohio University Press, 2001), pp. 71–84.

8 See Roelf Meyer, "From Parliamentary Sovereignty to Constitutionality: The Democratisation of South Africa, 1990 to 1994," *The Post-Apartheid Constitutions: Perspectives on South Africa's Basic Law,* ed. Penelope Andrews and Stephen Ellman (Johannesburg and Athens: Witwatersrand University Press and Ohio University Press, 2001), pp. 48–70.

9 See Nico Steytler and Johann Mettler, "Federal Arrangements as a Peacemaking Device during South Africa's Transition to Democracy," *Publius: The Journal of Federalism* 31 (Fall 2001): 93–106.

10 Christina Murray, "Negotiating beyond Deadlock: From the Constitutional Assembly to the Court," *The Post-Apartheid Constitutions: Perspectives on South Africa's Basic Law,* ed. Penelope Andrews and Stephen Ellman (Johannesburg and Athens: Witwatersrand University Press and Ohio University Press, 2001), pp. 103–27 at p. 106.

11 Carmel Rickard, "The Certification of the Constitution of South Africa," *The Post-Apartheid Constitutions: Perspectives on South Africa's Basic Law,* ed. Penelope Andrews and Stephen Ellman (Johannesburg and Athens: Witwatersrand University Press and Ohio University Press, 2001), pp. 224–304.

12 *In re: Certification of the Constitution of the Republic of South Africa, 1996,* 1996 (10) BCLR 518 (CC).

13 *In re: Certification of the Amended Text of the Constitution of Republic of South Africa, 1996,* 1997 (1) BCLR 1 (CC).

14 Heinz Klug, "Participating in the Design: Constitution-making in South Africa," *The Post-Apartheid Constitutions: Perspectives on South Africa's Basic Law,* ed. Penelope Andrews and Stephen Ellman (Johannesburg and Athens: Witwatersrand University Press and Ohio University Press, 2001), pp. 128–63 at p. 133. See also Nico Steytler, ed., *The Freedom Charter and Beyond: Founding Principles for a Democratic South African Legal Order* (Cape Town: Wyvern, 1991).

15 Klug, "Participating in the Design," p. 133.

16 Steytler and Mettler, "Federal Arrangements."

17 Christina Murray, "The Constitutional Context of Intergovernmental Relations in South Africa," *Intergovernmental Relations in South Africa: The Challenges of Cooperative Government,* ed. Norman Levy and Chris Tapscott (Cape Town: School of Government, University of the Western Cape and Political Information and Monitoring Service, IDASA, 2001), pp. 66–83 at p. 77.

18 Steytler and Mettler, "Federal Arrangements."

19 *Premier of the Province of the Western Cape v. President of the Republic of South Africa,* 1999 (4) BCLR 382 (CC), para. 57.

20 Ibid., para. 60.

21 See Rassie Malherbe and Dirk Brand, "Sub-national Constitutional Law: South Africa," *International Encyclopedia of Laws*, ed. P. Blanpain (Deventer: Kluwer, 2001).

22 *In re: Certification of the Constitution of the Western Cape, 1997*, 1997 9 BCLR 1167 (CC).

23 Rudolf Mastenbroek and Nico Steytler, "Local Government and Development: The New Constitutional Enterprise," *Law, Democracy and Development* 1, no. 2 (1997): 233–50.

24 See Jaap de Visser, "Powers of Local Government," *SA Public Law* 17, no. 2 (2002): 223–43.

25 Ibid., 234.

26 See Nico Steytler, "Concurrency and Co-operative Government: The Law and Practice in South Africa," *SA Public Law* 16, no. 2 (2001): 241–54.

27 See Nico Steytler, "The Settlement of Intergovernmental Disputes," *Intergovernmental Relations in South Africa: The Challenges of Co-operative Government*, ed. Norman Levy and Chris Tapscott (Cape Town: School of Government, University of the Western Cape and Political Information and Monitoring Service, IDASA, 2001), pp. 175–206.

28 *National Gambling Board v. Premier of KwaZulu-Natal*, 2002 (2) BCLR 156 (CC), para. 4.

29 *In re: Certification of the Constitution of the Republic of South Africa, 1996*, 1996 4 SA 744 (CC), para. 287.

30 Ibid., para. 291.

31 *Uthukela District Municipality and others v. President of the Republic of South Africa*, 2002 (2) BLCR 1220 (CC), para. 14.

32 *In re: Certification of the Constitution of the Republic of South Africa, 1996*, 1996 4 SA 744 (CC).

33 *Executive Council, Western Cape Legislature v. President of the Republic of South Africa*, 1995 (4) SA 877 (CC).

34 Richard Simeon and Christina Murray, "Multi-Sphere Governance in South Africa: An Interim Assessment," *Publius: The Journal of Federalism* 31 (Fall 2001): 65–92 at 78–9. See also Nicholas Haysom, "The Origins of Co-operative Governance: The 'Federal' Debates in the Constitution-making Process," *Intergovernmental Relations in South Africa: The Challenges of Co-operative Government*, ed. Norman Levy and Chris Tapscott (Cape Town: School of Government, University of the Western Cape and Political Information and Monitoring Service, IDASA, 2001), pp. 43–65 at p. 58.

35 Steytler, "Concurrency and Co-operative Government," p. 246.

36 See, generally, Rassie Malherbe, "The Role of the Constitutional Court in the Development of Provincial Autonomy," *SA Public Law* 16, no. 2 (2001): 255–85.

37 *MEC for Local Governemnt, Mpumalanga v. IMATU*, 2002 (1) SA 76 (SCA).

38 See Dirk Brand, "The Role of Provinces in International Relations," *Tradition und Weltoffenheit des Rechts: Festschrift für Helmut Steinberger*, ed. H-J. Cremer,

T. Giegerich, D. Richter, and A. Zimmermann (Berlin: Springer, 2001), pp. 677–92 at p. 677; Nico Steytler, "Cross-Border External Relations of South Africa's Provinces," *External Relations of Regions in Europe and the World,* ed. Rudolf Hrbek (Baden-Baden: Nomos Verlagsgesellschaft, 2003), pp. 247–56.

39 *Independent Electoral Commission v. Langeberg Municipality,* 2001 (9) BCLR 883 (CC).

40 See Katherine Savage, "Negotiating South Africa's New Constitution: An Overview of the Key Players and the Negotiating Process," *The Post-Apartheid Constitutions: Perspectives on South Africa's Basic Law,* ed. Penelope Andrews and Stephen Ellman (Johannesburg and Athens: Witwatersrand University Press and Ohio University Press, 2001), pp. 164–93.

41 *Government of Republic of South Africa v. Grootboom,* 2000 (11) BCLR 1169 (CC).

42 *Minister of Health and Others v. Treatment Action Campaign and Others (1),* 2002 (10) BCLR 1033 (CC); see also, Nico Steytler, "Federal Homogeneity from the Bottom Up: Provincial Shaping of National HIV/AIDs Policy in South Africa," *Publius: The Journal of Federalism* 33 (Winter 2003): 59–74.

43 *In re: Certification of the Constitution of the Province of KwaZulu-Natal, 1996,* 1996 (11) BCLR 1419 (CC).

44 Meyer, "From Parliamentary Sovereignty to Constitutionality," p. 54.

45 Constitution Amendment Act 87 of 1998.

46 Constitution Amendment Act 65 of 1998.

47 Constitution Second Amendment Act 61 of 2001.

48 Constitution Second Amendment Act 3 of 2003.

49 Based on the results of South Africa's 2004 general election.

50 Steven Friedman, "No Easy Stroll to Dominance: Party Dominance, Opposition and Civil Society in South Africa," *The Awkward Embrace: One Party-domination and Democracy,* ed. Hermann Giliomee and Charles Simkins (Cape Town: Tafelberg, 1999), pp. 97–126 at p. 104.

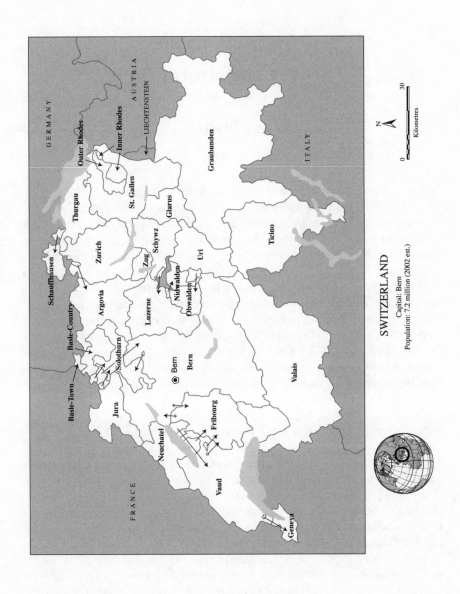

SWITZERLAND

Capital: Bern
Population: 7.2 million (2002 est.)

Swiss Confederation

NICOLAS SCHMITT[1]

Denis de Rougemont characterized Swiss federalism as a "love of complexity." The distinguishing feature of Switzerland is its diversity: There are 26 cantons, four national languages, and a kaleidoscope of cultures and religions as well as a varied geography (towns, countrysides, and mountain regions). Switzerland is not a nation in the traditional sense of the term but a *willensnation* forged by the desire of its citizens to renew constantly the links that unite them: "Together, we defend the right to remain different."[2] It is this very unity in diversity that makes Switzerland a paradigm of political integration. The Preamble to the Swiss Constitution expresses the determination of the cantons "to live together with our diversities, with respect for one another and in equity." Indeed, it is the Constitution's creation of governmental institutions and its definition of the nation's democratic procedures that permanently contribute to national integration and to preserving the federal polity according to the wishes of its citizens.

THE SWISS CONSTITUTION IN CONTEXT

Switzerland, covering an area 41,285 square kilometres (225 times smaller than the United States) and located in the heart of Europe, is home to 7,261,000 people, of whom 20.1 percent are foreigners. The country consists of 26 cantons and 2,900 municipalities. Forged over centuries, this political mosaic reflects Switzerland's geographical, linguistic, and religious diversity and expresses a multitude of social and cultural contrasts.

Geographically, the country is divided into five zones. The Alps, which span from east to west, constitute a wide dividing line. The Alps may be vast, but they are sparsely populated due to their inhospitable living conditions. The Pre-Alps in the North are a zone of mountains of average altitude. They provide a transition to the third zone, Mittelland, a relatively narrow tract (50 to 100 kilometres) that stretches from Lake Geneva to

Lake Constance. This zone is the most densely populated region and boasts the most fertile soils in Switzerland. It borders the fourth zone, comprising the Jura Mountains in the West and Northwest. On the south side of the Alps, the Canton of Ticino and parts of the Engadine Valley enjoy certain characteristics of Mediterranean culture. The importance of Switzerland's mountainous landscape is underlined in Article 50 of the Constitution (Para. 3), which states that the Confederation shall take into account the possible consequences of its activities for the mountain regions in order to protect the ecological integrity of these regions.

Switzerland has four national languages – German (spoken by 63.7 percent of Swiss), French (20.4 percent), Italian (6.5 percent), and Romansch (0.5 percent)[3] – each of which, in accordance with Article 4, is of equal importance. The remaining 8.9 percent of people in Switzerland speak other languages. In terms of their actual use, Article 70 (Para. 1) recognizes German, French, and Italian as the official languages of Switzerland. If the three official-language versions of a federal law differ, it falls to a judge to choose the one that best conveys the will of the legislator because no language has precedence over the others. Romansch speakers may use Romansch in their official dealings with the federal administration; thus in federal-government matters, Romansch is a semiofficial language.[4] The Confederation wishes to preserve and promote linguistic diversity. According to Article 70 (Para. 3), the Confederation is obliged to provide financial support to the four plurilingual cantons in order to help cover the costs of working in multiple languages (e.g., bilingual schools, translation services, and publication of laws in several languages). There is also great diversity within two of the national languages. Swiss Germans usually speak Schwyzertütsch, a German dialect of which there are more variations than there are German-speaking cantons. In Ticino various Italian dialects are spoken, particularly in the valleys. Only in French-speaking Switzerland (Suisse Romande) has "French from France" crowded out the regional patois. This language situation brings with it communication problems. Some Swiss believe that the solution lies with adopting English as the country's lingua franca and with favouring the teaching of English in schools over the other national languages.

In terms of religion, Switzerland is equally diverse. There are Roman Catholics (41.8 percent of the Swiss population), Protestants (35.3 percent), Orthodox Christians (1.8 percent), Christian Catholics (0.2 percent),[5] Muslims (4.3 percent), and Jews (0.2 percent); other religious communities and citizens who state that they have no religion comprise 15.4 percent. Article 72 of the Constitution provides that the regulation of the relationship between church and state falls to the cantons. Articles 8 (equality) and 15 (freedom of religion) prohibit discrimination. Cantons are, therefore, constitutionally obligated to respect the principle of the confessional neutrality of the state, which is inherent in religious freedom, but public authorities are not required to be entirely neutral toward, or totally uninvolved with, religious affairs. After all, the Preamble to the Constitution declares: "In the name of almighty God!"

This flexibility has enabled the cantons to develop their relations with religious institutions in different ways, ranging from declaring their main religion or religions status in public law and maintaining close links between church and state to favouring a system of (relative) separation based on the French secular model.

Religion is no longer a reason for conflict in Switzerland. In 1848 the Protestants imposed their vision of the federal state; yet over time, Catholics became the majority, and Catholic federal councillors soon joined the government. The anticlerical clauses in the Swiss Constitution, such as a ban on Jesuits, gradually disappeared. The last anticlerical clause to disappear was a requirement that the Federal Council approve the creation of new bishoprics, which was repealed on 10 June 2001.

Creation of the Federal Polity

In 1291 the first three cantons – Schwyz, Unterwalden, and Uri – founded a confederal alliance, although their pact of 1291 makes reference to an earlier *antiqua confoederatio* of 1273.[6] These three were later joined by Lucerne in 1332, Zurich in 1351, Glarus and Zug in 1352 (when the allied communities first became known as Switzerland), Berne in 1353, Fribourg and Solothurn in 1481, Basle and Schaffhausen in 1501, and Appenzell in 1513. The last three cantons – Geneva, Neuchatel, and Valais – joined as part of the Pact of 1815 following the defeat of Napoleon.[7] Thus it took more than 500 years to complete Switzerland's integration process.[8] After the short-lived war of the *Sonderbund* (i.e., Protestants versus the Catholic separatist league) in 1847, Switzerland, as we know it today, began to take shape. Its foundation rests on the first federal Constitution of 1848, which reflected the outcome of the Sonderbund War as well as the popular revolutions that had swept through Europe at the time. In 1874 a total revision of the Constitution, which was undertaken to correct problems with the 1848 version but which did not significantly alter the Swiss system, was approved by a double majority (the population and the cantons). Although subject to 155 partial revisions, it remained in force for 125 years. A new constitution, an "update" of the previous text undertaken to modernize the document and clarify the jumble of 155 revisions, was adopted by popular vote on 18 April 1999 and entered into force on 1 January 2000. In most basic respects, then, the Swiss political system has remained largely unchanged since 1848.

Although not as famous as their American counterparts, the founding fathers of the Swiss Confederation pursued a worthy and noble goal: to bring peace, security, freedom, and reconciliation of diversity to their country by means of a modern federal constitution. They had to find a subtle compromise between creating national unity and preserving the specific diversities of the cantons, a preservation demanded by conservatives.

To this end, they drew on the federalism and bicameralism developed in the United States.[9] They also drew on ideas from the 1798 Swiss Constitution, the 1830 French Revolution (and the regeneration that it brought to the Swiss cantons), the works of Jean-Jacques Rousseau, and the practical, imperial legacy of Napoleon Bonaparte. Indeed, a part of the 1848 achievement has its origins in the 1789 French Revolution and its introduction into Switzerland during Napoleon's invasion of 1798. The French imposed a constitution on Switzerland in 1798 that established a centralized state that was "one and indivisible," converted the cantons into administrative subdivisions of the new national government, created a single Swiss citizenship and universal democratic suffrage for men, introduced fundamental rights and liberties, and abolished traditional, hierarchical rights and privileges among citizens.

Beyond these outside intellectual influences, the authors of the 1848 Constitution were not subject to external pressures. This was fortunate because a heterogeneous country like Switzerland would have risked imploding if its larger neighbours had become involved in its affairs. Many Swiss resented the French invasion and, thereafter, the interferences of the allies who defeated Napoleon. This helps to explain the ambivalent attitude of the Swiss to the outside world. Sometimes, the country appears to close in on itself, as reflected in its delicate relations with the European Union and its long-standing neutrality. Yet not everyone in Switzerland wants isolation. Switzerland also operates a universalist policy based on neutrality in which Switzerland is seen as a member of the world and a global actor. Thus the Swiss welcomed, first, the League of Nations and, later, the European headquarters of the United Nations, plus a host of other international organizations, to locate in Switzerland. Switzerland's accession to the United Nations in 2002 following a popular vote extended this universalist approach.[10]

Before 1848 Switzerland was a confederation of sovereign cantons bound together by numerous alliance treaties. The 1848 Constitution created a real federation, characterized by certain undisputed structural principles: the rule of law, democracy, federalism, and the welfare state. The old alliance between the states was replaced by a compact among individuals as well as among peoples (i.e., the peoples of the cantons). Although the 1848 Constitution was rejected by eight cantons, due in part to the citizens' fear of its modernity, it soon acquired full legitimacy. Cantons were able to preserve their individual identities, even a certain patriotism, to the point that they could be considered microstates. In their constitutions, some cantons refer to themselves as a "Free State," "Sovereign Canton," "Republic and Canton," and the like. In the interests of national cohesion, it was decided to retain *Eidgenossenschaft* (Confederation) rather than *Bundesstaat* (federal state) as the official title of the country. Hence the formal title of the Constitution is the Federal Constitution of the Swiss Confederation.

Cantonal cohesion is a permanent concern for a country that fears the re-emergence of conflicting alliances, such as those that led to the *Sonderbund* upheaval in 1847. Because the Confederation has only a few, restricted means to impose its views, the principle of confederal loyalty is of great importance. Article 44 (Para. 1) of the Constitution provides that the Confederation and the cantons shall support each other in the fulfillment of their tasks and also cooperate in general.[11] This clause remains above all a political maxim[12] because cantons enjoy a high level of freedom with regard to organizing and managing their institutions. Other clauses of the Constitution require cantons not to act in breach of federal law or against the interests of the Confederation and the other cantons (particularly Art. 48, Para. 3, and Art. 56, Para. 2).

Since 1848 no national conflict has threatened the internal order of the Confederation, although on ten occasions the federal government has been forced to deploy the armed forces in varying numbers in order to safeguard public order in certain cantons; the last time was in 1932 in Geneva. The question of secession has never arisen since 1848, even in the context of the one important territorial change that has occurred since 1848: The 1979 creation of the Canton of Jura, the breakaway French-speaking Catholic part of the mostly German-speaking and Protestant Canton of Berne. Creating this one canton required tough negotiations between the relevant parties, followed by a series of three popular referenda, which were finally ratified by the entire electorate of Switzerland. Fortunately, Switzerland was able to resolve this contentious issue peacefully, even if the process was often painful, particularly for Laufen, one of the seven districts in Jura.[13] The procedure followed to create the Canton of Jura proved very complicated, so much so that the 1999 Constitution contains an article (53) providing for a simplified procedure for territorial changes within one canton. Changes to the territories of several cantons or to their status remain subject to the Constitution's revised Article 1.

Updating the Constitution in 1999

The protection of diversity as a unifying element of the Swiss people is by now a well-established idea (see the Constitution's Preamble or Art. 70, Para. 2). As democracy, federalism, and the search for consensus gradually became anchored in Swiss society and its Constitution, reforming the system became increasingly difficult.

The 1999 Constitution is, therefore, the result of a long process of attempting to update and rationalize the text. The Federal Assembly had first given the Federal Council the mandate to prepare a new constitution back in 1966. A proposal for a very modern text was submitted in 1977, but strong reservations were expressed during the consultation process largely because the proposed changes seemed to sacrifice the general clause, which privileged cantonal responsibilities, in favour of a detailed catalogue of federal and cantonal powers. The process was only relaunched on 3 June 1987 with a request from the Federal Assembly to "update" the 1874 text. This implied that the Constitution did not require fundamental changes but rather that the written and unwritten constitutional law, having lost its coherence after 155 partial revisions, should be presented in an understandable form by systematically restructuring the earlier Constitution and by harmonizing the style of its language. It was thus decided that the new constitution should be adopted for the year 2000.

The proposals of the Federal Council were subject to a consultation procedure in 1995 and 1996. Different versions of contentious proposals were presented for consultation in order to weed out the most contentious issues and thereby avoid the risk of the proposed new constitution being rejected by the population. The definitive text was not developed by a constituent assembly but by Parliament during the course of 1998. The new constitution was accepted by a popular vote of 59.2 percent and by majorities of voters in 13 cantons on 18 April 1999.[14] The new constitution entered into force on 1 January 2000.

The scope of the resulting text exceeded what had originally been planned. Updating the Constitution was not limited to a simple "facelift." New clauses were introduced, many reflecting existing practices that had never been set out in the Constitution. A number of these new clauses relate to federalism. In fact, during the 1990s, the cantons began to assert their rights more strongly, notably by founding the Conference of Cantonal Governments (CdC) in a convention of 8 December 1993. The CdC strove for better recognition of the cantons in the 1999 Constitution because many cantonal leaders felt that the cantons had transferred too many of their powers to the Confederation over the decades. They wanted to remind the Confederation that the cantons have, and should have, powers and identities of their own. The CdC's efforts were rewarded by the adoption of Articles 42–48 as well as of Articles 55 and 56 of Title 3, "Confederation, cantons and municipalities." These clauses clarify, secure, and in some ways, enhance cantonal autonomy and participation in the Confederation's decision-making processes.

Nevertheless, several fundamental reforms did not find their way into the 1999 Constitution; instead, they were left for discussion at later dates. For example, a concept for reform of the justice system has been accepted but has yet to enter into force via implementing legislation. With regard to democracy, an ambitious project affecting democratic rights was toned down by Parliament before being accepted by popular vote on 9 January 2003. Its key innovation was to establish a "general initiative."[15] Reforms of federalism and governance are still in preparation. So far Swiss involvement in the European integration process has been confined mainly to the conclusion of bilateral agreements with the European Union (EU), some of which, in effect, partially integrate Switzerland with the EU.

CONSTITUTIONAL PRINCIPLES OF THE CONFEDERATION

Status of the Cantons

Elmer de Vattel was the first to call for the equality of states regardless of their size. Conforming to this principle, the Swiss cantons are member states with their own powers and the largest possible degree of autonomy – in terms of their organization, funding, and definition of their tasks – allowable within the limits of the constitutional and legal federal constraints imposed upon them (Art. 43). Despite the use of the term "sovereign" in Article 3, the cantons are not states in the sense of international law because they do not have "jurisdiction concerning jurisdiction" *(Kompetenz-Kompetenz)*.

The 26 cantons listed in Article 1 are all constitutionally equal, including the six cantons with one representative rather than two representatives in the Council of States (Art. 150, Para. 2) and whose votes count as a half-vote for decisions on constitutional change (Art. 142). But this equality de jure hides significant de facto differences, leading to a certain imbalance in how public policies are implemented by the cantons. For example, the population of the Canton of Zurich is almost 100 times that of the Canton of Appenzell-InnerRhoden, which has led some experts to recommend a weighting of the cantons in terms of both popular votes and representation in the Council of States, as is the case in the German *Bundesrat*.

The Constitution contains two guarantees for the integrity of the cantons. The first is Article 1, which lists the cantons; the second is Article 53, according to which the Confederation is obliged to protect their existence, status, and territories. Some cantonal constitutions mention that the canton's territory is guaranteed by the Confederation.[16]

According to Article 51, each canton shall have a democratic constitution, which must be approved by the population and can be revised on the request of the majority of the electorate. The democratic principle implies, as a minimum, a constitutional initiative, a mandatory constitutional referendum, and a parliamentary democracy for each canton. However, the doctrine is also largely held to imply the separation of powers. The cantonal constitutions and their partial revisions must be guaranteed by the

Confederation, which is the case when they do not contravene federal law. There are few institutions that cantons are not allowed to set up. Cantonal constitutions appear very similar on the surface, but each canton includes its own specifics, often hidden in the details. Several cantons have recently adopted new constitutions in order to improve their governance structures and to strengthen their cantonal parliaments. These cantonal constitutions, however, are not equal to the Federal Constitution due to the primacy of federal law (Art. 49).

Judicial interpretation of cantonal constitutions as the final word on their meaning is not really an issue in Switzerland because the Swiss do not have such a judicial-review tradition in either the federal or the cantonal arenas. It would be unthinkable, as well, to introduce a clause granting such a right to the cantonal parliaments, for example. Insofar as the Swiss Constitution reflects and incorporates the will of the sovereign people, only they can interpret it. Some cantons (e.g., Jura, Nidwalden, and Graubünden) have nevertheless set up constitutional courts. Yet the Federal Constitution obliges all authorities in charge of applying a law to make a so-called pre-judicial determination of the law's compatibility with any superior laws and the Constitution. In addition, authorities are barred from applying cantonal laws that contravene the allocation of powers between the Confederation and the cantons. This obligation follows from the primacy of federal constitutional law, and it is known as the pre-judicial control of norms or standards.

Allocation of Powers

Article 3 of the Swiss Constitution has remained unchanged since 1848. This article provides that the cantons are sovereign insofar as their sovereignty is not constrained by the Constitution. This means that the cantons exercise the Confederation's residual powers – that is, all powers that have not been transferred to the Confederation through the original Constitution or through a constitutional change accepted by a majority of the population and of the cantons (Art. 42, Para. 1). Furthermore, the Confederation exercises only those powers that are said to require uniform enforcement, as stipulated by Article 42 (Para. 2); however, although not stated explicitly, this clause is supposed to incorporate the principle of subsidiarity.[17]

Hence an important function of the Constitution is to catalogue federal powers. Conversely, it has been deemed appropriate to state explicitly that some powers fall to the cantons, which also means that they have the obligation to exercise them (e.g., Art. 78, Para. l, on the protection of nature and natural resources within cantons; Art. 69, Para. 1, on culture; Art. 62, Para. 1, on education; and Art. 70, Para. 2, on the national languages).

The clarity of Article 3 may seem to imply, typologically speaking, that the allocation of powers is clear-cut. Yet the Constitution does not contain any official typology. That is, while the Constitution does have a list of powers, it does not clearly say which government shall exercise which powers. There are no clearly exclusive or shared powers. Clarification has been established instead through jurisprudence and doctrine, which characterize powers according to their *scope* and to their *effects*.

In terms of their *scope*, some federal powers are *global* (such as the protection of the environment, Art. 74); some are *restricted to principle* (e.g., land-use planning, Art. 75, and fiscal harmonization, Art. 129); others are *fragmentary*, such that only part of a power (e.g., health protection, Art. 118) has been delegated to the Confederation; and still others are merely *incentivizing*, such that the Confederation can provide incentives (e.g., financial) for cantonal action on certain matters (e.g., promoting understanding between linguistic communities, Art. 70, Para. 3, and protecting cultural heritages of national importance, Art. 78, Para. 3).

In terms of *effects*, some powers are (1) *exclusive* to the Confederation (e.g., customs, Art. 133, and money and currency, Art. 99); (2) *concurrent*, whereby the cantons have jurisdiction as long as the Confederation has not exercised its authority (e.g., maternity insurance, Art. 116, Para. 3); (3) *limited*, such that the federal legislator must limit itself to setting out principles (e.g., land-use planning, Art. 75); and (4) *parallel*, such that the exercise of a federal power does not affect the cantonal equivalent (e.g., languages, Art. 70, and income tax, Arts 128 and 129).

Over time, a number of jurisdictions (e.g., agriculture, energy, and transportation) have been transferred to the Confederation. Also, that cantons in principle enforce legislation adopted by the federal government *(fédéralisme d'exécution* or *Vollzugsfoederalismus)* has often led the Confederation to legislate so thoroughly that the cantons are rendered mere executive bodies. This is seen, for example, in relation to general environmental protection, such as combating air pollution – an area in which the federal legislator leaves very little room for independent cantonal action. This trend could increase if Switzerland becomes a member of the European Union.

It is therefore not surprising that the most important political project under way in Switzerland is a new allocation of tasks and a reorganization of financial equalization (RPT), which has been studied for many years and is still unfinished. Along the way, Parliament has rescinded several parts of the reform for fear of provoking a backlash and possible rejection by a popular vote. One matter on which Parliament has exercised caution is possible transfers of financial burdens from the Confederation to the cantons and their taxpayers.

The aim of the RPT is twofold. First, it is designed to unbundle the financial burdens and tasks of the Confederation and the cantons. Under the current draft, the Confederation would have exclusive responsibility for six areas (e.g., national defence, national roads, agriculture, and old-age insurance), while the cantons would have exclusive responsibility for thirteen areas (e.g., special schools, student grants, school sports, noise control, traffic, and nursing homes). Collaboration between the Confederation and the cantons would be improved in twelve areas called joint tasks (e.g., hunting and fishing, flood protection, protection of nature, airports, and supplementary old-age pensions), and intercantonal cooperation would be strengthened in relation to nine joint cantonal tasks (e.g., jail sentences, universities, cultural institutions, waste treatment, urban public transportation, and services for the handicapped). Some proposals, however, remain controversial, in particular the "cantonalization" of residential homes and workshops for the disabled and the elderly, which would make the cantons responsible for these matters.

Second, the RPT aims to harmonize cantonal financial capacity. Whereas currently half of fiscal equalization occurs through subsidies, the reform provides that the financial capacities of the cantons would be equalized using three separate and independent financial-assistance instruments. The first would be an equalization of resources based on the fact that the cantons are ranked according to their income per-capita and categorized as cantons with either strong or weak resource potential – in other words, as "rich" or "poor" cantons. The poor cantons would receive assistance from the rich cantons and the Confederation, the ideal effect being a growth in their capacity to provide public services close to the national norm as well as lower tax rates if appropriate. The second instrument would be a sharing of burdens with the aim of compensating cantons for expenditures linked to factors either geo-topographical (e.g., mountain regions) or socio-democratic (e.g., major cities) over which the cantons have no control. Third, temporary adjustment assistance would serve to smooth the transition to the new system. But this is for the future.

Currently, one area that is difficult to ignore is security. The allocation of powers here is complex. The application of federal law and the enforcement of law and order are primarily organized and implemented by the cantons. Because this often carries a heavy financial burden, particularly for the smallest cantons, all cantons have signed mutual cooperation conventions, known as "concordats." The federal police force, which has long played an essentially administrative role, now has certain penal jurisdiction. In the event of an upheaval or a serious threat to public order, the army may be deployed (Art. 52, Para. 2).

From a judicial perspective, there have been no legal differences between Swiss citizens in terms of their origin (Art. 24) since 1798 despite the jurisdictional differences between the cantons and the fact that there are intercantonal disparities in terms of the laws applied to Swiss nationals and foreigners. The 1848 Constitution had provided for the mutual recognition of judgments, a procedure that became obsolete in 1912 with the new standardized Swiss Civil Code of Obligations. It is also due to the Swiss Penal Code, rather than to the Constitution, that offenders are no longer "extradited" from one canton to another. Jurisdictional issues are also dealt with through statutory law.

Conflicts of Jurisdiction

The Constitution explicitly recognizes in Article 189 (Para. 1d) the possibility of jurisdictional conflicts between the federal and cantonal authorities. The Federal Tribunal (supreme court) is responsible for resolving
such cases. Its rule of conflict resolution was developed from doctrine and
jurisprudence, which traditionally referred to the principle of the superior
authority of federal law, now enshrined in Article 49 (Para. 1). Federal law
takes precedence over cantonal law, where the latter contravenes the
former. This principle implies that the cantons do not have the right to enact a law that is contrary to federal law. If a cantonal law already in force
contravenes federal law, the cantonal authorities must refuse to enforce it;
such a law is null and void for want of cantonal jurisdiction.

Although there are elements of competition, confederal life in Switzerland is underpinned by the idea that the cantons and the Confederation
should not view each other as rivals but as partners working toward common goals. Conflicts are to be resolved through negotiation and searches
for compromise, as stated in Article 44 (Para. 3). This clause is not a procedural norm but an exhortation; once opposing sides have formed, it may
be too late to mediate.[18]

In concrete terms, mechanisms exist to prevent conflict. Thus the adoption of every federal law is preceded by a consultation procedure required
by the Constitution and thus by intense political dialogue (Art. 147). Also,
due to the small size of the country, persons in important positions often
know each other, allowing them to iron out problems through informal
talks. The intercantonal conferences, which bring together members of
cantonal governments with responsibility for particular areas (e.g., education, health, or justice and the police), provide a platform for dialogue between all the parties concerned. These conferences can include the
relevant federal councillors in their meetings, and there is always room on
their agendas for discussing contentious issues.

THE STRUCTURE AND FUNCTIONING
OF THE INSTITUTIONS

The System in General

The Swiss federal government consists of an assembly flanked by a collegial
government.[19] The legislature (Federal Assembly) is bicameral, with a National Council made up of 200 popularly elected representatives and a
Council of States comprising 46 likewise elected cantonal representatives.
The executive is the seven-member Federal Council, which, unlike in a parliamentary system, cannot be dissolved by the Federal Assembly. In turn,

Table 1
Allocation of powers within the Swiss government

Jurisdiction	Powers allocated to the Federal Assembly	Powers allocated to the Federal Council
Legislation	Arts 164 and 165	Arts 181 and 182
Foreign affairs	Art. 166	Art. 184
Finances	Art. 167	Art. 183
Federal-cantonal relations	Art. 172	Art. 186
Other	Art. 173	Art. 187

the Federal Council does not have the power to dissolve the Assembly. Each member of the Federal Council is elected individually by the Federal Assembly (Art. 175).

The election of the Federal Council by the people – a possibility being discussed – would necessitate several procedural guarantees to ensure the representation of minorities. Legally, it could prove incompatible with the ultimate supervision that Parliament imposes on the executive (Art. 169) because direct election of the Federal Council could potentially weaken Parliament. The existence of collegial governments in Switzerland, in both the federal and cantonal arenas, reflects a cultural disposition toward and the political necessity of reaching a broad consensus between all constituent parts of the country via the distribution of power.

The separation of powers is a fundamental principle because it is at the heart of republicanism. However, it is more implicit in the federal government than in the cantons, so much so that reality does not always correspond to the strict doctrine. Title 5 (Ch. 2, Sec. 3) of the Constitution provides for an allocation of powers within the Confederation government. This should not be confused with the allocation of powers between the Confederation and the cantons. The relevant clauses show that the powers of the Federal Assembly and the Federal Council often overlap, as indicated in Table 1.

In these cases, the two institutions must exercise their powers jointly, regardless of certain functional differences. For example, although Parliament adopts laws, legislation is drafted mostly by the government. Increasingly, the Assembly has shown a tendency to ask for the executive's draft implementation regulations before adopting new laws. That is, the Assembly wants examples of regulations the executive would issue to implement a proposed law. In foreign affairs, as well, the Constitution allocates powers between Parliament and the government not according to binding rules but in terms of practicality and, particularly, of democratic legitimacy. As this model encourages cooperation, conflicts between the two powers are rare. The concept of "high supervision" of the executive by the Federal Assembly has an important role to play but requires time and energy.

The Federal Assembly

Parliament, being the supreme authority of the Confederation (Art. 148), rules in the case of conflict between the Federal Council and the Federal Tribunal (Art. 173, Para. 1).

In the bicameral Parliament, the 200 deputies in the National Council are elected according to a standardized procedure, with each canton representing an electoral district. The largest cantons have many deputies (e.g., Zurich with 34 and Bern with 26), whereas the smallest cantons (i.e., Apenzell, Glarus, Obwalden, Nidwalden, and Uri) have only one deputy. Because the majority of the cantons have few deputies, changing the cantonal delegation in Bern would require a major political upheaval; thus the National Council's composition can be said to account for the stability of the Swiss Parliament. Over time, there have been changes to how the 46 deputies to the Council of States are elected, as this responsibility has gradually been taken from the cantonal legislatures and given to the people. Nowadays, they are elected by universal suffrage in each canton according to the procedure it has chosen (Art. 159, Para. 3). However, the deputies vote without instructions (Art. 161, Para. 1). The popular election of members of the Council of States implies that they are not cantonal representatives; rather, the Council is merely another forum representating the people and thus functions primarily as a means of ensuring checks and balances. The resulting need for greater cantonal representation was one of the reasons for the creation of the CdC in 1993.

The five most populous cantons theoretically have a blocking majority in the National Council. But the two chambers have exactly the same powers, unlike the chambers of the US Senate or the German *Bundesrat* (Art. 156, Para. 2). The supposed existence of a special relationship between the cantons and the Council of States has aided the cantons fight to maintain a degree of "committed" federalism in which the cantons have a voice and power. However, this effect is decreasing, and even though the links between federal members of Parliament and the cantonal governments remain close, almost all cantons prohibit members of their governments to sit in the Federal Assembly.

The Federal Council

The Constitution sets out the legal basis for the federal administration (Arts 178 and 179) and the Federal Council (i.e., cabinet or government), which comprise the supreme executive authority of the Confederation (Art. 174). The Federal Council's powers are listed in Articles 180 to 187. The cantons are not directly represented in the Federal Council despite the clause providing that the Council represent the geographical and linguistic diversity of the country (Art. 175, Para. 4). The Federal Council is a coalition government of four main national political parties. This is not stipulated by the Constitution but is the product of an unwritten agreement between the largest political parties, itself a result of the specific relations between the Federal Assembly, the Federal Council, and the people in a direct democracy. After 1848 the Free Democratic Party of Switzerland (PRD; liberal right) monopolized the government for 43 years. In 1891 the Federal Assembly elected a Catholic conservative to the Council for the first time, making way for what is now the Christian-Democratic Party (PDC). This was the first step toward the current system of coalition government. The PDC obtained its second seat in 1919. In 1929 the Federal Council saw the election of a member of the Agrarian Party, now the Swiss People's Party (UDC). The first appearance of the Socialist Party (PS) in government dates back to the Second World War, a period that was very favourable to the unions. This development culminated in the partial election of Thursday 17 December 1959 to appoint four new federal councillors. The Federal Assembly opted for a political composition that has become known as the "magic formula": two PRD members, two PDC, two PS, and one UDC. The relative stability of this political equilibrium meant that the "magic formula" remained intact until 2003, when it was called into question as a result of the polarization of Swiss politics: a rise in support for the UDC and the PS, and a loss of public support for the centre parties (PRD, PDC, and Liberal).

The federal elections of October 2003 confirmed a shift to the right. This was clearly in evidence during the reelection of the Federal Council on 10 December, when one of the two PDC representatives was replaced by a UDC candidate to reflect this party's share of the electoral vote. Opinion remains divided as to whether this is the death knoll for the "magic formula" or simply a temporary change to an otherwise stable system.

The stability of the government is due, in part, to the constitutional mechanisms by which it is guaranteed, particularly to the fact that its members are elected for four years (Art. 175, Para. 3), that they cannot be voted out of office during this time, and that they remain in office for an average of ten years. Its collegial nature allows minorities to be represented in the highest bodies of the Swiss polity. Yet this balancing of members of the Federal Council is less a constitutional obligation than a tradition (except for Art. 175, Para. 4), and candidates applying for a vacancy must satisfy several criteria relative to the seat to be filled (e.g., political party, canton, language, and gender).

The Federal Council functions according to the collegiality principle. Once a decision has been adopted, it is backed by the entire Cabinet even if some of its members do not agree on political or personal grounds. Cases of a "break-up of the collegiate" are very rare.

The collegial authority, the Federal Council, is polymorphous, combining the government of the country with the implementation of its policies; it is the head of state, prime minister, and government rolled into one. Each federal councillor is the head of a department, or ministry. This means a heavy workload for the seven members. Certain reform proposals envision a "two-tier" government, with the Federal Council supported by "deputy ministers." Other proposed reforms provide for an increase in the number of federal councillors.

The Federal Supreme Court and the Judicial System

The highest court is the Federal Tribunal, or supreme court, governed by Articles 188 to 191. Its members are elected by the Federal Assembly, the procedures for which are set down in legislation. Article 188 (Para. 4) states that the official languages must be represented in the Tribunal. Because the Tribunal is made up of 39 judges from 26 cantons, it is clear that a fair representation of the different linguistic regions can be easily guaranteed. The supreme court's seat is in Lausanne, partly to symbolize its independence from Parliament and the government. The Federal Insurance Court has its seat in Lucerne. This court hears public-law cases involving social insurance (e.g., accident, disability, and old-age).

Article 189 of the Constitution catalogues the powers of the Federal Tribunal. Its decisions are final in Switzerland, although they may be subject to individual appeals to the European Court of Human Rights in Strasbourg for violations of rights upheld by the European Convention of Human Rights.

The most significant characteristic of the organization of the Swiss judicial system is that, with the exception of the Tibunal and a few federal appeals commissions, almost all judicial authority is a product of cantonal law. This very marked judicial federalism explains why there are 29 codes of criminal procedure in Switzerland.

In this context, the Federal Tribunal has a double role. First, it is the guardian of federal law. It enforces federal law and sees to its uniform application. The paths of appeal enable it to fulfil this function according to the areas of law: appeal, petition for annulment, or appeal of administrative law. Second, the Federal Tribunal is the guardian of the federal and cantonal constitutions. Legally, it exercises this role through public-law appeals filed against cantonal acts, be they cantonal laws or administrative decisions.

One feature of the system is that constitutional jurisdiction is not comprehensive because neither the Tribunal nor any other authority can review the constitutionality of federal laws and international treaties ratified by Switzerland (Art. 191). With regard to federal laws, this specificity has its origins in the fact that the authors of the 1874 Constitution gave precedence to the separation of powers and direct democracy over jurisdictional control. That is, neither the Tribunal nor any other authority can review the constitutionality of federal law. With regard to international law, this principle serves to ensure the international credibility of Switzerland. However, this principle is somewhat softened by the fact that federal law can be partially superseded by a restrictive interpretation of Article 191 either by the federal supreme court[20] or by the electorate.[21] In concrete terms, the length of the legislative process and the consultative procedure makes it unlikely that laws with an element of nonconstitutionality will go undetected.

Less than three months after it entered into force, the new Constitution was subject to a reform of the justice system, accepted by popular vote on 12 March 2000. The aim is to alleviate the burden on the Federal Tribunal and, at the same time, to improve the legal protection of private individuals. It should relieve the Federal Council of its jurisdictional powers and enable the unification of civil and criminal procedures. This reform has not entered completely into force, as a number of relevant laws have yet to be adopted. A proposal for the total revision of the federal judiciary, however, provides for further decentralization. An administrative court of first instance, located in St Gallen, is to replace some 30 appeals commissions. In addition, a federal criminal court of first instance will be established in Bellinzona (Ticino).

Cantonal Institutions

The cantons do not have a federal structure, and their parliaments are unicameral. The ancestral *Landsgemeinden* (people's assemblies that bring the citizens of a canton together in a public square once a year) have almost disappeared. For some observers, the *Landsgemeinden* "rather than a bill of rights or a declaration of freedoms" has been the "symbol of Swiss freedom."[22] The pressures of modern life and economics, as well as a reluctance of citizens defending minority positions to express themselves, have combined to erode this institution. A few years ago, Switzerland had five *Landsgemeinden*; now only two remain: in Glarus and Appenzell-Inner-Rhoden. They are, in some sense, only a visible expression of universal suffrage because even each of these cantons has a parliament.

The cantonal institutions are very similar to their federal counterparts, the principal difference being that all cantonal governments (i.e., executive officials) are elected by the people. Although the sizes of their governments and parliaments vary widely, all cantons have a high degree of proportional representation, just like federal institutions. No political party holds absolute power in any canton, and the collegial cantonal governments provide adequate representation for minorities. Cantonal executive bodies are collegial, like the Federal Council. In Valais, for instance, the cantonal Constitution provides that members of the cantonal government be elected in a manner ensuring that the three regions of the canton are taken into account. The Canton of Berne guarantees one seat in the cantonal government to the French-speaking minority in the three districts of Bernese Jura.

Intercantonal Relations

The mechanisms to prevent conflicts of jurisdiction reflect the complexity of intercantonal diplomacy. From a political point of view, two contradictory elements characterize relations between the cantons: On the one hand, federal and European requirements demand greater cooperation; on the other hand, the cantons wish to preserve their "sovereignty."

All attempts at procedural centralization remain contentious, as they are considered a threat to federalism, particularly because the last century saw numerous cantonal powers pass to the Confederation. Given that changes are inevitable, notably due to economic globalization and people's increased mobility, there is a growing need for intercantonal harmonization. This falls primarily to the cantons themselves but also, to some extent, to the Confederation. For example, legal conflicts between the cantons are resolved by the Federal Tribunal, although such conflicts are rare.

The cantons increasingly conclude concordats on matters necessitating interdependence and institutionalize their cooperation, often with the help of the Confederation. The Constitution is accommodating in this area, particularly through Article 48, which authorizes largely intercantonal treaties, to such an extent that the project to reorganize financial equalization (RPT) envisages the possibility of granting these treaties general binding force in certain circumstances. An interesting example, due to its importance and complexity, concerns university policy. A "triangular" structure has been adopted. The aim was to give the Confederation, the university cantons, and the universities a joint body vested with real decision-making powers in this area of shared responsibility. The new federal law on assisting universities has therefore delegated powers to the Swiss Universities' Conference. The university cantons had to conclude a concordat containing a parallel delegation rule, and an administrative convention organizes the joint body and governs the details of its activities.

The Confederation is also concerned with harmonization, notably through the creation of a unified Swiss economic area (Art. 95, Para. 2). This aspiration dates back to 1848, but until now its achievement has been limited de facto, in certain sectors, by the immobility of the workforce. In the current era of globalization, the European Union has helped to speed up this process by introducing greater freedom of movement of persons, goods, and services. This poses a challenge for Swiss federalism because it entails, among other things, the mutual recognition of titles and certificates.

The Municipalities

Switzerland is a three-tier federation: confederation, cantons, and municipalities. The latter are the "basic units" of society, and their importance is evident notably in the fact that anyone who has municipal citizenship necessarily has Swiss citizenship (Art. 37, Para. 1) because to obtain citizenship in Switzerland, one must first obtain citizenship in a Swiss municipality. (There is no dual cantonal and Swiss citizenship.) In this regard, a recent controversy has been the naturalization process. Some municipalities employ procedures involving a secret ballot; this has often led to people from some Eastern European countries being refused Swiss citizenship. Subject to an appeal against a municipality in the Canton of Lucerne, the Federal Tribunal ruled on 9 July 2003 that such a procedure is no longer acceptable.[23] This judgment was criticized by some politicians and experts who are opposed to preventing the population from exercising its democratic right.

The Constitution has never contained many clauses pertaining to municipalities. They are mentioned four times in the 1874 Constitution and five times in that of 1999. This is because most authors of the Constitution judged that, as the status of the municipalities falls under cantonal law, cantons should remain the main interlocutors. Until 1999 municipal autonomy was not guaranteed by the Constitution but through the jurisprudence of the Federal Tibunal. A section of the Constitution now deals with municipalities, although it consists of only one article (Art. 50), of which the first paragraph states that municipal autonomy is guaranteed within the limits fixed by cantonal law. This implies that the status of the municipalities varies from canton to canton. Furthermore, the Confederation must take into account the consequences of its activities on the municipalities as well as on towns, agglomerations, and mountain regions (Art. 50, Para. 3).

POPULAR SOVEREIGNTY AND DIRECT DEMOCRACY

Like its predecessors, the 1999 Constitution attaches great importance to the political rights of the population, notably when it declares that their protection is one of the aims of the Confederation (Art. 2). In Title 4 the Constitution defines the composition of the federal electorate and lists its prerogatives, namely the rights to participate in the elections for the National Council and in votes on federal questions (e.g., national referenda), to launch and to sign popular initiatives, and to call for a referendum. These rights are then specified in detail. The Constitution thus respects popular sovereignty. However, this does not mean that the population can decide on everything. In fact, what best characterizes popular sovereignty in its truest sense is the autonomy granted to the people because, according to the framework in which sovereignty is proposed by the Constitution, the people can express their opinion independently of any other state body.

Brief Historical Background

During the 1830s many cantons adopted liberal constitutions that expressed the principle of pure representation. That is, the people could only influence affairs of state during periodic legislative elections and through rights of petition, which still had a certain importance. In cantons where the Liberals held the majority in Parliament, there was intense legislative activity aimed at reforming the state according to the rationalist principles of natural law. However, these reforms were often imposed somewhat dogmatically, with little consideration for the opposing views of Catholics, Protestant conservatives, small tradesmen, and farmers. These conservative circles felt that the Liberals were moving too quickly and soon realized that periodic elections were not sufficient to afford them a lasting influence on government policy in the spirit of Rousseau's "general will."

Certain theorists contended that the representative system favoured by the Liberals contradicted the principle of popular sovereignty anchored in the Constitution. They also argued that this system enabled a new aristocracy to appear, albeit a slightly improved version of its predecessor. Hence a section of the population, having come to see the representative system as a substitute for ancient oligarchies, rejected it. Furthermore, the majority of the Liberal constitutions contained clauses that forbade revisions for a long period of time, to the extent that the path to constitutional change was too long for the coordination of the will of the people with government policy. There were riots, some motivated by revolutionary aims.

Some cantons tried to find a more civilized approach – for example, through the introduction of a veto that allowed citizens to block laws they opposed. Until the 1860s, the representative principle largely dominated. Only when the Democrats finally succeeded in denouncing the parliamentary sovereignty of the Liberals could the position of the population in the legislative process be strengthened through the introduction of the legislative initiative and referendum.

Concepts of Direct Democracy

Direct democracy denotes a political regime in which the authorities are not only elected by the citizens, but also bound by their decisions. Therefore, in addition to elections (a classic feature of the representative system), there are popular votes in Switzerland that enable the people to express their opinion on specific issues.

Swiss direct democracy, combining elections and popular votes, establishes a dialogue between elected representatives and the people. The electorate must be consulted and can decide conclusively, hence the title "sovereign people." However, parliaments and governments, federal and cantonal, are involved at the beginning and the end of voting procedures, enacting texts that will be subject to referenda and possibly proposing countermeasures with respect to the tabled initiatives. In all cases, the elected officials implement the decisions of the ballot. This dialogue even exists in the two cantons that have kept the *Landsgemeinde*.

Two institutions allow the population to exercise its direct democratic rights: the popular initiative and the popular referendum. The former is exerted *at the beginning* of a legislative procedure, the latter *at the end.* To a certain degree, this is guaranteed by the Federal Constitution (Arts 138–42). However, it should be noted that cantonal law offers a broader guarantee with respect to cantonal initiatives and referenda.

The Popular Initiative

The popular initiative is the right, attributed to a certain number of citizens, to submit a constitutional proposal (nonconstitutional legislative proposals having been excluded at the federal level until 2003) to the electorate; by extension, the term also denotes the subject of the proposition – that is, the text to be approved by the voters. The option of calling for a total revision of the Constitution through a popular initiative is a legal right set out in the Federal Constitution (Art. 139 for the Confederation and Art. 51, Para. 1, for the cantons). For federal matters, there was no other type of initiative before the introduction in 2003 of the "general initiative." This did not stop the cantons from introducing the "legislative initiative," the "cantonal constitutional initiative," and others.

The procedural details are complex and varied. An initiative must have a certain number of signatures, gathered by an initiative committee, which is also authorized to withdraw the initiative. This number varies according to cantons not only in absolute terms (1 to 15,000 signatures in various cantons; 100,000 signatures for the Confederation), but also as a percentage of the number of eligible voters (0.007 percent to 4.6 percent). The partial initiative deals with a subject that is defined more or less broadly by the Constitution. It can be "set out in general terms" or "formulated in full" (Art. 139, Para.) – a procedure not possible for a total revision – giving rise to two distinct procedures. In all cases, however, its validity is subject to certain formal and material criteria – notably unity of form and of substance. It is put to a ballot, the practical details of which differ according to whether a countermeasure has been proposed. To be enacted, an initiative on the Constitution needs a majority vote of the people of Switzerland plus a majority of the people's votes in a majority of the cantons.

The Popular Referendum

The popular referendum is the right of citizens to express their opinion on a law already adopted by an elected body, generally Parliament; a new law cannot be enforced until it has been subject to popular scrutiny. To be successful, a federal referendum must garner a majority of the vote of the people of Switzerland and a majority of the people's votes in a majority of the cantons. The referendum procedure can be triggered automatically (compulsory referendum) or at the request of a certain number of citizens (optional referendum). The compulsory referendum exists in all cantons because it is prescribed in Article 51 (Para. 1) of the Constitution. The adoption of a federal constitution or a cantonal constitution, as well as any changes to them, must be approved by the people via a compulsory referendum, regardless of the procedure that has led to constitutional change. Nevertheless, the cantons can widen or narrow the scope of a constitutional referendum by making the content of their constitutions more or less precise. There is no compulsory referendum relating to federal legislation, but it does exist in eight cantons where the citizens, together with the legislative authority they have elected, are thus the ordinary legislator. Increasingly, the compulsory legislative referendum is being replaced by the optional referendum due mainly to the fall in voter turnout. Otherwise, a few cantons provide for a compulsory referendum on matters of public finance (e.g., taxing, spending, or borrowing).

The optional referendum exists for federal legislation but is not required for the cantons. Nonetheless, all cantons have instituted it, thus exceeding federal requirements. Similar to the popular initiative, an optional referendum can be triggered by a fraction of the electorate (50,000 signatures for the Confederation). Having been adopted by Parliament, a law that is subject to an optional referendum is published in the *Official Gazette*, including the expiration date for the submission of a referendum request as well as the length of time that can be taken to collect the signatures (from 30 days to three months). In general, such a law cannot be enforced until it is known whether a request for a referendum has been submitted and, when applicable, until the electorate has spoken. Article 165, however, allows for emergency legislation that changes the nature of a referendum from suspensive to rescinding. Otherwise, unlike the many US states that during the early twentieth century adopted the recall of elected officials, along with Swiss-style initiative and referendum procedures, only a few cantons have adopted the popular recall of elected officials during their tenure in office, and no canton has yet removed an elected official from office via a popular recall vote.

Utility and Necessity

One merit of direct democracy is to confer a share of public responsibility on the population at large. Furthermore, it underpins one of Switzerland's special characteristics: collegial governments. Direct democracy encourages politicians to find solutions that are as acceptable as possible in order to avoid the risks involved in a popular vote, hence the constant search for consensus. Before the introduction of the popular referendum in 1874, the Federal Council was made up of representatives from a single party.

Subsequently, it had to integrate representatives from other parties to broaden its basic legitimacy.

Direct democracy is also the driving force of political life. Although initiatives are rarely accepted by voters, their launch, and the discussions to which they give rise, moves debate forward. A telling example was the initiative to abolish the Swiss army in 1989. It was rejected, but its impact caused the government to undertake a sweeping reform of the army in 1995.

Finally, in a country as diverse as Switzerland, the increase in the number of subjects that do not cut along traditional divides often enables classical ethnic and religious divisions to be blurred rather than exacerbated. Votes are so frequent (almost every three months) and concern so many different subjects (e.g., highway speed limits, new military aircraft, status of imported wine, swamp protection, tax increases or reductions, nuclear-power plants, and life sentences for murdering sex offenders) that the proponents and opponents of various measures often divide along class, gender, age, and other such demographic lines rather than along Catholic versus Protestant lines or French-speaking versus German-speaking lines. Today, classical religious and ethnic divides show up on only a few issues, such as European integration, which is generally supported by the Swiss French and opposed by the Swiss Germans.[24]

Direct democracy, however, also has some disadvantages. The desire to consider all opinions in order to avoid a referendum slows down the legislative process. Furthermore, voter participation rates tend to be low (averaging about 40 percent) due to the frequency of referenda and to the fact that often the subject is not disputed, is of little interest, or is complex. In fact, then, questions are often decided by a minority of the Swiss population, with some very technical proposals testing the limits of direct democracy. Finally, it must be admitted that, practically, only lobbyists, political parties, and large pressure groups have the necessary political instruments to launch (and especially to win) an initiative or referendum; this removes direct democracy slightly from regular citizens.

PROTECTION OF BASIC RIGHTS

Basic rights, such as those enshrined in substantive law, are found in the Federal Constitution, in the cantonal constitutions, in the European Convention on Human Rights, and in United Nations' protocols as well as in a series of specific international conventions and in constitutional jurisprudence defining their scope and limits.

The protection of individual rights is based on the US model. However, before 1999 the situation had been less clear-cut because several rights were enshrined and developed only by the Federal Tibunal, often on the basis of Article 4a of the 1874 Constitution, which provided for the equality of citizens before the law. Nowadays, the new Constitution contains a detailed Bill of Rights (Arts 7–34). But it does not contain any typology of these rights, just as there is no typology for the allocation of powers; this was left up to development through legislative and judicial doctrines.

The list begins with the principle of human dignity, which is the cornerstone of the whole system. It then distinguishes freedoms, the rule of law, social rights, and political rights.

The list of *freedoms* includes freedom of religion and conscience, opinion and information, the press and media, languages, science, art, assembly, association, and residence as well as economic freedom and freedom to unionize. In principle, the protection of these rights is not absolute, although government limitations of these rights are subject to the strict conditions provided for in Article 36.[25]

Among the *guarantees of the rule of law*, there are the rights, among others, to equality before the law, to protection against arbitrariness, and to procedural guarantees as well as the right to petition government officials.

Social rights, such as those stipulated in Article 12 (right to aid in distress) and Article 19 (right to a basic education), must be clearly distinguished from the social objectives set out in Article 41, which has its own specific chapter. This chapter provides, for example, that all persons be covered by social security and guaranteed basic health care. Yet the fourth paragraph limits the scope by specifying that these social objectives cannot be interpreted as conferring any special rights to state services.

Article 34 does not directly grant *political rights*, such as the right to vote, because they are governed by cantonal constitutional law and by Article 136 of the Federal Constitution. Nevertheless, Article 34 provides for the free and regular exercise of political rights, where they exist.

In accordance with Article 35, basic rights must be implemented throughout the entire legal system. Doctrine accepts, however, that they do not have a horizontal effect; that is, they cannot be invoked directly by private persons, with the exception of Article 8 (Para. 3, Phrase 3) relative to the right to equal pay for men and women. The basic rights do not per se protect individuals against rights infringements by other individuals.

The application of these rights is carried out by the appropriate procedural instruments established by both the cantonal and the federal governments (Art. 35).

The Constitution ensures only a few substantive rights (e.g., Art. 19, on the right to a basic education, and Art. 28, Para. 3, on the right to strike) that can be invoked in court. There is no tradition of collective rights in Switzerland. This was reflected in the difficulty of including the right to strike in the 1999 Constitution.

The constitutions of the cantons also contain bills of rights, but the cantonal guarantees of basic rights do not have their own legal significance relative to the corresponding federal guarantees. Cantonal rights have a basically educational function; in the past, they often inspired extensions of federal basic rights. Traditionally, any new features of federal constitutional law had first been introduced and "tested" in one or more cantons. This was true not only for basic rights, but also for political rights, direct democracy, organization of the government and Parliament, and administrative jurisdiction. As such, the cantons have been what US Supreme Court Justice Louis Brandeis called "laboratories of democracy."[26]

That cantonal guarantees can surpass the protection of rights set down in the Federal Constitution is uncontroversial. Some cantons, for instance, have added the right to information, a requirement that government publish all administrative acts, or protection against laws applied retroactively. In Bern constitutional rights are declared to be inviolable, something that is specific to this canton. In addition, the rights recognized by the European Convention on Human Rights, ratified by Switzerland on 28 November 1974, are regarded in Swiss law as constitutional rights in the sense of Article 189 (Para. 1a). This was quickly accepted by the Federal Tribunal for procedural reasons. Finally, the International Protocol on Civil and Political Rights of 16 December 1966 entered into force in Switzerland on 18 September 1992.

TAXES AND FINANCES

Taxation

Fiscal authority is divided between the Confederation, the cantons, and the municipalities. Each order of government has direct access to several sources of revenue (vertical coordination). The allocation of fiscal powers and tax revenues between cantonal and municipal jurisdictions, when the tax base covers several cantons or several municipalities (horizontal coordination), is carried out on request by the Federal Tribunal.[27] The only clause in the Constitution that deals with horizontal coordination is that which prohibits intercantonal double taxation (Art. 127, Para. 3).

In principle, direct taxes are the reserve of the cantons, while indirect taxes belong to the Confederation. The latter, however, can levy direct taxes on the incomes of individuals, on net profits, and on the capital and reserves of corporations for a limited, but regularly extended, period of time. The current direct federal tax (IFD) will be in effect until the end of 2006, as per Article 196, Ch. 13. The maximum rates are fixed by the Constitution (Art. 128). Taxation and tax collection are carried out by the cantons, which can retain three-tenths of the gross IFD revenue. The Confederation can define the principles of cantonal direct-tax harmonization. It has no say, however, on tax scales, tax rates, and exemptions (Art. 129). Tax harmonization is therefore only a concept in the Federal Constitution, which has subsequently been implemented by federal and cantonal law.

Indirect taxes (Arts 130–33) are exclusively the responsibility of the Confederation. It can levy a value-added tax (VAT), special consumption taxes, stamp duties, and a withholding tax on income from financial assets, on lottery winnings, and on insurance payments. Customs duties are also an exclusive federal responsibility.

The fiscal sovereignty of the cantons is limited only by the jurisprudence of the Federal Tribunal and the few constitutional norms mentioned above. Nevertheless, considerable efforts are being made by all governments to promote harmonization. The undertaking is very delicate. A series of such fiscal measures, adopted by the Federal Assembly in June 2003, produced the first-ever national referendum launched by 11 cantons (although only 8 are needed to launch such a referendum), in which the federal fiscal package was rejected by 60 percent of the voters and all 26 cantons in May 2004.

Borrowing

The Constitution does not contain any clause on government borrowing. However, both the federal government and the cantonal governments are permitted to borrow, although not from the Central Bank, which is prohibited from extending credit to federal or cantonal governments in accordance with the federal law on the Swiss National Bank. Currently, the Constitution does not force the federal government to present a balanced budget every year. However, Article 126 provides that the Confederation must balance its expenditure and receipts in the medium term.[28] The Federal Constitution does not impose a limit (borrowing limit or budgetary balance) on the cantonal authorities. Nevertheless, some cantons (particularly Bern, Fribourg, and Vaud) have constitutional requirements demanding that the operating budget be balanced, while capital-investment expenditures may be financed through borrowing.

Distribution of Revenue and Expenditure

In 2001 (latest statistics available), the income and wealth taxes levied by the cantons and municipalities generated US$40.4 billion. The direct federal tax produced US$9.8 billion, of which US$2.9 billion was redistributed to the cantons. Revenue from the IFD, special consumption taxes, and the withholding tax is partially shared among the cantons to guarantee them a source of additional income. For most taxes, sharing is done as a function of the financial strength of the cantons because the Confederation supports financial equalization (Art. 135, Para. 1).

The cantons can also count on two-thirds of Swiss National Bank profits (Art. 99, Para. 4), divided up according to the population and financial strength of each canton. The recent sale of part of the National Bank's gold reserves has generated substantial returns, the distribution of which is a source of fierce debate.

With the exception of the curb on debts provided for in Article 126 and in Article 130 (Para. 2), which stipulates that 5 percent of the VAT revenue be used in favour of lower-income groups, the Constitution sets only a few limits on the freedom of federal, cantonal, and local authorities to spend their revenues.

FOREIGN AFFAIRS AND DEFENCE

Foreign Affairs

In regard to foreign affairs, the 1999 Constitution is more explicit than its predecessor. Article 54 (Para. 1) clearly states that foreign affairs is the responsibility of the Confederation. Even though this was effectively the case in the nineteenth century, too, the 1874 Constitution did not contain such an unambiguous declaration.

Articles 184 and 185 of the Constitution set out the powers of the Federal Council with respect to both foreign affairs and internal and external security. However, the Constitution does not address the issue of neutrality, a complex concept of international public law and policy, which refers to the nonparticipation of a state in the wars of other states. Neutrality is inextricably linked to the history of the Swiss Confederation and has marked its destiny for centuries. Since the Swiss defeat by the French at Marignano in 1515, the guiding principle of Swiss foreign and security policies has been noninterference in the affairs of others. Neutrality was also a requirement of domestic policy in a confederation of states with different religious beliefs and interests.

Over the centuries, neutrality became an integral part of the legal and political order in Switzerland, and it was recognized in 1815 by the great powers as being "in the true political interests of all of Europe." Later, thanks in particular to permanent neutrality, Switzerland was able to resist most of the upheavals of the nineteenth century and even the ravages of the two world wars. This is undoubtedly why neutrality is engraved so deeply in the minds of Swiss citizens. Yet it has never been declared a constitutional aim. Since 1977, however, there has been a requirement for a compulsory referendum on international treaties that would provide for Swiss membership in collective security organizations or supranational communities (Art. 140, Para. 1b). In this way, the Constitution indirectly includes the subject of neutrality.[29]

The Constitution contains several references to the openness of Switzerland to the world (e.g., Preamble; Art. 2, Para. 4; and Art. 54, Para. 2). Switzerland is a member of the United Nations and its specialist bodies, the Council of Europe, the European Free Trade Association (EFTA), the Organization Internationale de la Francophonie (OIF), and the World Trade Organization (WTO). It is even a partner of the European Union through bilateral agreements, which had been preceded since 1972 by a free-exchange treaty with the then European Economic Community (EEC). The Constitution makes no mention of relations between Switzerland and Europe. These relations are not made any easier by the compulsory referendum on new collective-security and supranational treaties; accession to the European Union would have to be approved by popular vote with a double majority (the population and the cantons), making this a sensitive political issue.

For many years, the cantons have developed a dense network of cross-border relations, and their openness to external relations is recognized by the Constitution. Article 55 deals with their participation in deciding foreign policy, which includes European issues. Article 56 concerns the cantons' relations with foreign states. From the perspective of federalism, the development of supranational institutions has strengthened the cantons through what one might call a reaction in anticipation, which can be attributed to the CdC. That is, the CdC has sought to bolster cantonal powers against challenges to these powers likely to arise from future treaties and supranational obligations. Given that foreign affairs are by nature the "domain of princes," they are an ideal ground on which to acquire cantonal powers and, thereby, to reaffirm cantonal sovereignty as expressed in Article 3.

Defence

The 1848 Constitution allowed for the creation of a federal army made up of cantonal troops. The 1874 Constitution unified the army without centralizing it completely. Nowadays, national defence is exclusively under federal jurisdiction, with only a trace of cantonal military sovereignty. The Constitution states that (1) military legislation, (2) organizing, training, and equipping the armed forces, and (3) mobilizing the armed forces are federal responsibilities. Yet Article 60 (Para. 2) alludes to the possible existence of "cantonal troops," which will soon disappear as a result of the complete reorganization of the Swiss army according to the so-called Army XXI model.

The Swiss army is a useful tool of social integration because it is essentially an army of conscripts; every Swiss man is a citizen-soldier (Art. 58, Para. 1, and Art. 59, Para. 1). The Constitution allows for four categories of professional soldiers, categories that can be extended to include operators of complex and expensive equipment. The Constitution also allows for alternative civilian service for conscientious objectors,[30] although it was only in 1992, after the failure of various parliamentary and popular initiatives, that a generally well-received solution could be found for the age-old issue of conscientious objectors. Another recent development in the army's activities, in addition to its traditional task of defending the country, is foreign peacekeeping activities, depending on the political willingness of the federal legislator. In June 1999 the Federal Council decided to assist the UN peacekeeping force in Kosovo by providing an army corps of 220 volunteers, known as SWISSCOY. In June 2001 the Swiss population accepted a change to the Constitution that authorizes the arming of Swiss soldiers during peacekeeping missions abroad.

CONSTITUTIONAL AMENDMENTS

Constitutional amendments (formally governed by Articles 192–95) represent a classical form of political decision making in Switzerland. In terms both of their political impact and of their underlying procedures, they represent the essence of Swiss federalism.

A partial revision (i.e., a change to only one part of the Constitution) can be proposed by the Federal Assembly (often at the request of the Federal Council, which submits a message to the Assembly) or by the people (Art. 194, Para. 1) through a popular initiative. The text of the Constitution provides for a basic rule that guarantees subsidiarity; that is, any constitutional amendment must obtain a double majority (the population and the cantons; Art. 140, Para. 1a, and Art. 142, Para. 2). Votes that attract only a single majority have been rare (eleven in total), but they are on the increase.

The Constitution does not expressly provide that certain clauses are inviolable. Only the peremptory norms of general international law could be inviolable despite the difficulty in determining the content of the *ius cogens* (see Art. 193, Para. 4, and Art. 194, Para. 2). One might, of course, argue in support of certain fundamental structural principles being peremptory.

There have been numerous partial amendments, and they continue to accumulate. The 1848 Constitution was amended only once, in 1865; that of 1874 was amended 155 times; and since entering into force in 2000, the 1999 Constitution has already been amended six times, and 25 provisions have been altered. Since the first federal referendum in 1866, some 510 questions have been submitted to the electorate, the first half between 1866 and 1970, and the second half from 1970 to today. This means that the average frequency of popular votes has quadrupled in 30 years. However, the rate of acceptance and rejection has not changed over time. More than seven times out of ten, the people have voted in line with the authorities' recommendations.

Some of the authorities' notable referendum successes have concerned important subjects, such as new taxes, creation of the Canton of Jura, and membership in the UN. Yet, as Federal Councillor Arnold Koller declared, "The Swiss do not seem to have an irresistible desire for change,"[31] so much so that the Constitution progresses slowly along the path of modernity, its pace dictated by pragmatism and a deep suspicion of ideologies. Since 1848 the number of cantons that have not accepted the Swiss Constitution has continued to grow; the 1848 Constitution was rejected by eight cantons,[32] the 1874 Constitution by ten cantons,[33] and the 1999 Constitution by twelve cantons.[34] This means that 6 cantons out of 26 (Appenzell-Inner Rhoden, Obwalden, Nidwalden, Schwyz, Valais, and Uri) have never accepted any of modern Switzerland's three constitutions.

CONCLUSION

With its adoption in 1848, the Swiss Constitution transformed a centuries' old confederation into a federal state – for only the second time in modern history (the first time was in the United States). This was, in some sense, revolutionary because it happened within a European context characterized by numerous outspoken liberal movements, none of which enjoyed comparable success in the nineteenth century.

In time, the revolution settled down, with the Swiss turning toward traditionalism and conservatism. This was confirmed by the difficulty in radically modifying the original 1874 text; the 1999 Constitution is a mere "update" of the 1874 original. Thus the Federal Constitution has successfully integrated the specificities and needs of Swiss citizens thanks to its creation of adept institutions and the flexibility of the revision methods it prescribes. In the absence of a "Swiss nation" in the customary sense, the Constitution created a *willensnation* while insisting on the importance of diversity. In doing so, it made federalism the foundation on which modern Switzerland could develop and prosper. In 1935, against the background of a troubled political situation, 72.7 percent of the electorate rejected the only popular initiative ever submitted on the total revision of the Constitution; this had been launched by ultra-conservative forces taking their lead from the rise in nationalism elsewhere in Europe. Its clear rejection showed to what point the Swiss were committed to the democratic and liberal order established by the 1874 Constitution. However, the 155 partial amendments to the Constitution since 1848 and the changes they implied are a reminder that Swiss federalism is a system in perpetual movement. At the dawn of the twenty-first century, it must rise to new challenges.

This brings us to relations with the European Union. Will the EU continue to agree to negotiate increasingly complex bilateral agreements with such a small country as Switzerland, located in the heart of Europe and rich in federalist experience? This remains a very sensitive issue for the Swiss. Because the country suffered less than others from the ravages of the two world wars, some Swiss citizens do not fully appreciate the significance of building a united Europe, and they believe that a degree of Swiss insularity in the heart of the EU could be an advantage, notably in economic terms. However, it is undeniable that substantial reforms of political institutions would be necessary prior to Swiss membership in the EU. The cantons would see an increase in constraints on their sovereignty, an increase in purely executive tasks, a weakening of parliamentary democracy and thus of direct democracy, and greater restrictions on municipal autonomy. Consequently, enhanced participation in the European integration process would likely strengthen cooperation within the Confederation by obliging the cantons and the Confederation to cooperate more quickly on various matters. The cantons may fear that their sphere of autonomy would shrink to a simple executive federalism. It would be a difficult undertaking to find a counterbalance to these developments.

Finding consensus has become more difficult due to the growing polarization of Swiss politics, which is reflected in the composition of the Federal Assembly. The centre is losing ground to the left and right of the political spectrum. The change in the composition of the Federal Council in December 2003 after 44 years of continuity illustrated this vividly. Swiss politics, once rather subdued, are becoming increasingly like those of its neighbouring European countries.

Hopefully, Switzerland will find solutions in this new century that are as workable as those adopted in the nineteenth century and as instrumental in its success. "The habit of concerning themselves with government has inspired in the Swiss a feeling of public duty and patriotic pride unknown among other people ... This little country holds a great place in the history of political institutions worldwide."[35]

NOTES

1 The author wishes to thank Augustin Macheret, professor of public law, former member of the Government of the Canton of Fribourg, and former president of the Conference of Governments of Western Switzerland (Conférence des Gouvernements de Suisse occidentale), who proved invaluable help in rendering a very complex subject both succinct and more understandable. The author's thanks also go to Professor Bernhard Waldmann, head of the National Centre of the Institute of Federalism, and to Me Adriano Previtali.

2 Denis de Rougemont, *La Suisse ou l'histoire d'un peuple heureux* (Lausanne: L'Age d'Homme, 1990), p. 18.

3 Romansch is spoken only in the Canton of Graubünden, the only trilingual canton in Switzerland, where it is the official language alongside German and

Italian. Romansch is not so much a single language as it is a collection of five dialects. Migration and economic development have increased the number of German speakers in the canton, to the extent that Romansch is gradually disappearing, exacerbated by the fact that it does not benefit from sharing the linguistic culture of a large neighbouring country.

4 The recognition of Romansch in 1938 further reflected Switzerland's commitment to diversity in unity. The federal message that proposed this constitutional change inverted Hitler's Aryan rhetoric of "ein Volk, ein Reich, ein Führer," as it aimed to strengthen Swiss national unity not through racial homogeneity and ideological uniformity but through the recognition of diversity. This amendment was approved by a large majority of Swiss voters.

5 Christian Catholics represent a small minority of Catholics who did not recognize two major doctrines concerning the supremacy of the pope, adopted in 1870 at the Vatican I Ecumenical Council.

6 William E. Rappard, *Collective Security in Swiss Experience, 1291–1948* (London: George Allen and Unwin, 1948), p. 4.

7 Aargau, Graubünden, St Gallen, Thurgau, Ticino, and Vaud had become part of Switzerland in 1803.

8 William Martin, *Switzerland: From Roman Times to the Present* (New York: Praeger, 1971).

9 James H. Hutson, *The Sister Republics: Switzerland and the United States from 1776 to the Present* (Washington, DC: Library of Congress, 1991).

10 See also, for example, the essays on "The Idea of Switzerland" published in *Granta* 35 (Spring 1991).

11 See also Wolf Linder, *Swiss Democracy: Possible Solutions to Conflict in Multicultural Societies* (New York: St Martin's Press, 1994).

12 This maxim rests on the principle of good faith in Article 5, Para. 3 of the Federal Constitution.

13 Jura, part of the Canton of Bern, is made up of seven districts. The three southern districts have remained with Bern; the three in the north make up the new canton; and the seventh, Laufen, which is German-speaking and further away, chose to leave the Canton of Bern and to join the nearest canton, Baselland.

14 The refusal of cantons to accept a constitution has never had significant political consequences because the dissenting cantons nevertheless accept the decision of the majority of voters and cantons.

15 The general initiative expresses an intention and is not concerned with integration of the proposed initiative in the legislation. It is for Parliament to decide whether the initiative should be implemented at the constitutional or the legislative level. Of importance is that the intention be realized. If the promoters of the initiative feel that Parliament has not been faithful to the content of the initiative, they can take their case to the Federal Tribunal (supreme court), which will not impose its solution but will invite Parliament to legislate in accordance with the initiative.

16 Consequently, Article 138 of the 1977 Constitution of Jura, providing that the new canton could welcome any new part from the Canton of Bern, which is legally separated from the latter, did not receive a guarantee from the Federal Assembly (Art. 51, Para. 2, of the Federal Constitution).

17 The principle of subsidiarity demands that any government function that can be performed adequately and sufficiently by the smallest unit of government closest to the people (e.g., municipal government) should be performed by that government rather than by a larger unit of government such as that of a canton or of the Confederation.

18 A well-documented example was the fiscal dispute between Vaud and Geneva, which could not be resolved through mediation. Therefore, it was the subject of an appeal under public law in the Federal Tribunal (Art. 83 OJF, ATF 125 I 458).

19 For further background, see also Nicolas Schmitt, *Federalism: The Swiss Experience* (Pretoria: HSAC Publishers, 1996); Oswald Sigg, *Switzerland's Political Institutions* (Zürich: Pro Helvetia, Arts Council of Switzerland, 1991); Hans Huber, *How Switzerland is Governed* (Zürich: Schweizer Spiegel Verlag, 1968); George Arthur Codding, *The Federal Government of Switzerland* (Boston: Houghton Mifflin, 1961); and George Sauser-Hall, *The Political Institutions of Switzerland* (Zürich and New York: Swiss National Tourist Office, 1946).

20 For example, the Federal Tribunal can examine pre-judicially federal laws for compliance with the European Convention on Human Rights; likewise, the interpretation of the convention must also comply with the Constitution.

21 This will be the case if the RPT is approved.

22 Benjamin R. Barber, *The Death of Communal Liberty: A History of Freedom in a Swiss Mountain Canton* (Princeton: Princeton University Press, 1974), p. 11.

23 Rule of the Federal Tribunal: ATF/BGE, 129, I, 217.

24 See also, Yannis Papadopoulos, "Connecting Minorities to the Swiss Federal System: A Frozen Conception of Representation and the Problem of 'Requisite Variety,'" *Publius: The Journal of Federalism* 32 (Summer 2002): 47–65.

25 All limitations of a basic right must have a legal basis, justified in the interest of the public and proportionate to the stated aim. However, the essential character of basic rights remains inviolable.

26 *New State Ice Co. v Liebman*, 285 US 262, 311 (1932).

27 See note 17.

28 This concerns a "curb on debt," which was accepted by popular vote on 2 December 2001 but which has yet to be written into the law.

29 See Article 173, Para. 1a, and Article 185, Para. 1, which also refer to the obligations of the Federal Assembly and the Federal Council to preserve Switzerland's neutrality.

30 The federal law on alternative civilian service is currently being amended.

31 Presentation of the project on the revision of the Constitution in *Le Nouveau Quotidien*, 27 June 1995.

32 Appenzell-InnerRhoden, Nidwalden, Obwalden, Schwyz, Ticino, Uri, Valais, and Zug.

33 Appenzell-InnerRhoden, Fribourg, Lucerne, Nidwalden, Obwalden, Schwyz, Ticino, Uri, Valaiws, and Zug.

34 Aargau, Appenzell-InnerRhoden, Appenzell-AusserRhoden, Glarus, Nidwalden, Obwalden, St Gallen, Schaffhausen, Schwyz, Thurgau, Uri, and Valais.

35 Charles Seignobos, *Histoire politique de l'Europe contemporaine, 1814–1914,* 7th ed., vol. 1 (Paris: Armand Colin, 1924), p. 323.

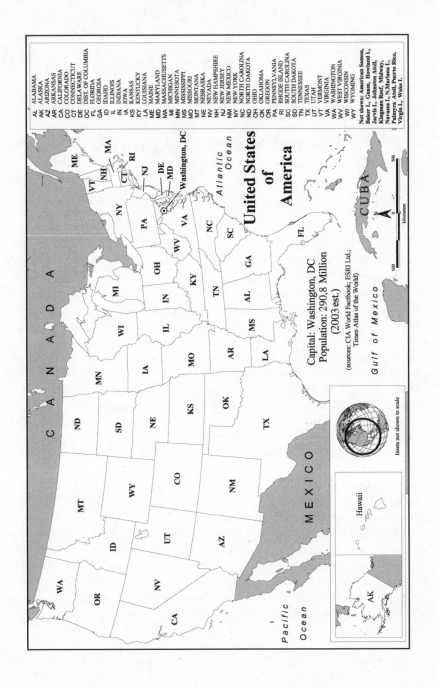

United States of America

Capital: Washington, DC
Population: 290,8 Million
(2003 est.)

(sources: CIA World Factbook; ESRI Ltd;
Times Atlas of the World)

Insets not shown to scale

AL ALABAMA
AK ALASKA
AZ ARIZONA
AR ARKANSAS
CA CALIFORNIA
CO COLORADO
CT CONNECTICUT
DE DELAWARE
DC DIST. OF COLUMBIA
FL FLORIDA
GA GEORGIA
ID IDAHO
IL ILLINOIS
IN INDIANA
IA IOWA
KS KANSAS
KY KENTUCKY
LA LOUISIANA
ME MAINE
MD MARYLAND
MA MASSACHUSETTS
MI MICHIGAN
MN MINNESOTA
MS MISSISSIPPI
MO MISSOURI
MT MONTANA
NE NEBRASKA
NV NEVADA
NH NEW HAMPSHIRE
NJ NEW JERSEY
NM NEW MEXICO
NY NEW YORK
NC NORTH CAROLINA
ND NORTH DAKOTA
OH OHIO
OK OKLAHOMA
OR OREGON
PA PENNSYLVANIA
RI RHODE ISLAND
SC SOUTH CAROLINA
SD SOUTH DAKOTA
TN TENNESSEE
TX TEXAS
UT UTAH
VT VERMONT
VA VIRGINIA
WA WASHINGTON
WV WEST VIRGINIA
WI WISCONSIN
WY WYOMING

Not shown: American Samoa,
Baker I., Guam, Howland I.,
Jarvis I., Johnston Atoll,
Kingman Reef, Midway,
Navassa I., N.Mariana I.,
Palmyra Atoll, Puerto Rico,
Virgin I., Wake I.

United States of America

G. ALAN TARR

The United States of America is the world's oldest, continuing, modern federal democracy. Indeed, the framers of the United States Constitution are widely regarded as the inventors of modern federalism, as distinct from ancient forms of federalism, especially confederalism. The US Constitution has been influential as a model of federal democracy, and key principles of the Constitution – such as federalism, the separation of powers, an independent judiciary, and individual rights – have gained acceptance worldwide. Americans believe that the nation's success owes much to the brilliance of the Constitution's drafters. Yet neither the Constitution, nor the federal polity it created, has remained static. Amendments adopted after the Civil War (1861–65) altered the federal-state balance, and the authorization of a federal income tax in the Sixteenth Amendment (1913) greatly augmented the fiscal power of the federal government. The Constitution has also both influenced and been influenced by political and social developments, including the transformation of the United States from a few states hugging the Atlantic Coast to a continental nation and also from a country recently liberated from colonial rule to an economic and military superpower.

The United States now encompasses 50 states, a federal district (Washington, DC) that serves as the capital, 11 island territories (e.g., Guam and Puerto Rico), and some 600 federally recognized Native American tribes that have the status of "domestic dependent nations."[1] The country spans the middle of the North American continent from east to west, with Alaska and Hawaii, the most recent additions to the union in 1959, separated from the contiguous 48 states. With a 2003 population of 291 million, a land mass of 9,629,091 square kilometers, and a per capita gross domestic product of $36,200, the United States today is far different from the 13 states with a population of 2.5 million that declared independence from Great Britain in 1776. The transformation extends to the population's ethnic character. In 1776 about two-thirds of Americans were English, Welsh, and

Scottish, with Germans comprising about 9 percent and slaves of African ancestry about 17 percent of the population. The country's population today reflects massive immigration from throughout Europe during the nineteenth and twentieth centuries and from Latin America and Asia, particularly during the late twentieth century. As of 2002, the US population was 13.4 percent Hispanic, 12.2 percent African American, and 3.9 percent Asian American. English is the de facto national language, although the US Constitution mandates no official language.

The population remains overwhelmingly Christian and predominantly Protestant although immigration has increased religious diversity. Americans accept a separation of church and state, but they are also highly religious. This religiosity is reflected in vigorous conflicts over moral issues such as abortion. The country's predominant religious belief systems have, however, been generally supportive of constitutionalism, democracy, and rights. Key rights movements, such as the abolition of slavery and the civil-rights revolution of the 1960s led by the Reverend Dr. Martin Luther King, Jr, have been driven by religious leaders. Liberal individualism has been a powerful force in American life as well, but so has communitarianism: the desire of people to build and maintain communities, especially local communities, that reflect their beliefs and preferences and also to use government, especially state and local governments, to tame the excesses of liberal individualism.

CREATION OF THE FEDERAL CONSTITUTION

The United States Constitution is the nation's second, drafted in 1787 to replace the weak Articles of Confederation of 1781. Under the Articles, each state had an equal vote in Congress, with state delegations subject to recall by state legislatures; consequently, representatives were tied mostly to the interests of their states. The Articles limited the confederal government to a few specified responsibilities (e.g., war and foreign affairs) and gave it no control over the internal affairs of the states. Most important, the confederal government exercised no direct authority over the states or over the citizens of those states; it could not tax or conscript citizens, nor could it subject them to its laws (e.g., economic regulations). As a result, the states could, and did, disregard mandates and requests for funding by the confederal government. The absence of adequate national authority reduced the United States to, in the words of Alexander Hamilton, "the last stage of national humiliation."[2]

Problems in the states also provided an impetus for a new constitution. Most early state constitutions concentrated governing power in the legislature and subjected legislators to annual election. The absence of checks and balances, plus the lack of restraints on popular enthusiasms, led to abuses (e.g., laws freeing debtors from their debts or allowing them to pay debts with worthless paper money). These are examples of what James Madison regarded as the tyranny of the majority in democratic polities.[3] In addition, commercial competition among the states led to a proliferation of trade barriers designed to shield local producers against out-of-state competitors, contributing to a stagnant economy and to interstate conflicts.

The convention that met in Philadelphia in 1787 was charged by the confederal Congress with proposing amendments to the Articles of Confederation, but most of the 55 delegates concluded that only a new constitution, erected on different principles, could remedy the country's problems. The delegates proposed a system that blended elements of confederal and unitary government, or what Madison called "federal" and "national" principles.[4] The delegates sought to augment federal power, while protecting against tyranny, in order to protect individual liberty (including property rights), promote commercial prosperity (e.g., through free trade), secure domestic peace, and enhance national defence. The constitutional limits imposed on federal and state powers also served to advance the framers' objectives, as did the few requirements imposed on the states. Individual liberty was protected by key rights embedded in the Constitution, such as the right to a jury trial, but even more by the constitutionally limited powers of the federal government, by its accountability to the people, and by the reservation of the police power to the states.[5]

With the exception of the "peculiar institution" of southern slavery, the framers were not concerned with accommodating territorially based linguistic, ethnic, or religious diversity, although they were greatly concerned about protecting the individual rights of persons with diverse linguistic, ethnic, and religious identities. President George Washington's 1790 letter to a Jewish congregation in New York City assuring protection and a safe haven for Jews in the United States exemplified this policy of toleration.[6]

Furthermore, the constitutional requirements that members of the US House of Representatives be at least 25 years old and "seven Years a citizen of the United States" and that members of the US Senate be at least 30 years old and "nine Years a citizen" ensure that the federal union's legislative body is open to immigrants who obtain US citizenship.[7] In turn, except for the federal Constitution's ban on religious tests for federal officeholders, the Constitution is silent about language, culture, ethnicity, and religion.[8] Authority in these matters was reserved to the states or, implicitly, to the private sphere of life. Thus the president's oath of office found in Article II, Section 1, obliges the president to "protect and defend the Constitution," not the American people, nation, or nation-state.

Among the most important new federal powers were the powers to tax, regulate interstate and foreign commerce, raise an army and navy, and subject the people to federal laws. In sharp contrast to the Articles, the Constitution also granted Congress implied powers, namely the authority to enact laws "necessary and proper" to implementing its expressly delegated powers. As a consequence of these new general powers and in conformity with the Revolutionary War slogan, "No taxation without representation," the Constitution made all federal officials either directly or indirectly accountable to the people. In addition, it instituted checks and balances and a separation of powers, and it continued to divide power between the nation and the states. It bears emphasis that the US Constitution affords the federal government only limited, delegated powers. Because all powers originally belonged to the sovereign peoples of the constituent states, the people and their states retained all powers that they did not delegate to the new federal government. Thus, although the Constitution prohibits some state powers, it does not delegate powers to the states, nor does it contain a list of powers that the states share with the federal government.

The Constitution sought to address the problems posed by interstate rivalry and majority tyranny in the states by delegating certain powers to the federal government, including the powers to establish uniform rules of bankruptcy, make currency, regulate commerce among the states, and borrow money. It also prohibited states from making currency, passing laws impairing the obligation of contracts, or laying duties on imports or exports, "except what may be absolutely necessary for executing [their] inspection laws" (Art. I, Sec. 9). The delegates believed that the federal government could be entrusted with enhanced powers because, with its checks and balances, it was better constructed than the state governments and thus less likely to tyrannize. In addition, as Madison argues, majority faction (tyranny) tends to flourish in small, homogeneous political societies, in which a single group might dominate. In contrast, the federal government, encompassing an extended commercial republic with a multiplicity of groups, would be less susceptible to the formation of majority factions.[9]

Furthermore, the Constitution provides for the admission of new states to the Union, contemplating an expanding country, with new states admitted on an equal footing with the original states, a revolutionary novelty in the 1780s. Most nonoriginal states were formed from territory governed by the United States, with Congress (under Art. IV, Sec. 3, of the Constitution) controlling the admission of states and the delineation of their boundaries. Texas was an independent republic before its admission in 1845, and five states (Vermont, Kentucky, Tennessee, Maine, and West Virginia) were carved out of the territory of older states. In the first four cases, the legislature of the older state gave its consent. West Virginia was part of Virginia, but it remained loyal to the federal Union when Virginia seceded in 1861 during the Civil War, and it was admitted through questionable constitutional procedures while that war was being fought.

The vigorously fought ratification of the Constitution in 1788, together with the inauguration of the new government in 1789 and the adoption of the Bill of Rights in 1791 (insisted upon by the anti-Federalist opponents of the Constitution), completed the nation's founding. Successful as the Constitution was, it left the issue of slavery unresolved. Many founders opposed slavery but believed that it was not viable economically and would soon die out. However, the slave economy of the South flourished, particularly after the invention of the cotton gin in 1793, and regional conflict – fueled partly by southern fears of northern antislavery sentiment – led eventually to civil war.

The conclusion of the Civil War prompted the adoption of three constitutional amendments: The Thirteenth Amendment (1865) outlawed slavery; the Fourteenth Amendment (1868) extended federal protection to citizens against state violations of rights; and the Fifteenth Amendment (1870) forbade states from prohibiting men from voting because of "race, color, or previous condition of servitude." All three amendments gave Congress the power to enforce their mandates by "appropriate legislation," and all established legal standards upon which the laws and actions of state officials may be challenged in the federal courts. Some commentators believe that these amendments completed the work of the nation's founding, eliminating the Constitution's compromise on slavery and realizing the commitment in the Declaration of Independence (1776) to the proposition that "all men are created equal."[10] Other commentators view the amendments as dramatically shifting the balance of power from the states to the federal government, thus inaugurating a fundamental change in the Constitution's design.[11]

Either way, one key to understanding federal constitutional development since the Civil War is to recognize that President Abraham Lincoln and other slavery opponents elevated the Declaration to the status of a morally, although not legally, binding guidepost for interpreting the federal Constitution, especially with respect to individual rights. Every civil-rights movement – by women, black Americans, Hispanics, Indians, persons with disabilities, gays and lesbians, and others – has appealed to the Declaration as a moral basis for its claims to constitutional rights. This, in turn, has served to increase federal power. Because the Declaration declares Americans to be one people, groups facing discrimination and exclusion have declared their right to inclusion and, thus, to full and equal protection by all the rights and privileges afforded the American people by the federal Constitution.

THE STATES IN THE FEDERAL UNION

The US Constitution confirms the key role of the states in the constitutional system. The states are mentioned more than 50 times in the Constitution, and crucial aspects of the federal government (e.g., selecting presidential electors and conducting congressional elections) depend on the exercise of state power. Thus the Constitution is an "incomplete constitution," which depends for its operation on state constitutions that "complete" and consequently form a part of the overall constitutional system.[12]

The American federal system is symmetrical. All states enjoy equal constitutional status. Their existence and their powers are constitutionally guaranteed rather than under the control of the US government. The Constitution safeguards the position of the states in several ways. First, it grants only limited powers to the federal government and reserves residual powers to the states, or to the people. The Tenth Amendment (1791) states that "[t]he powers not delegated to the United States by the Constitution, nor prohibited by it to the States, are reserved to the States respectively, or to the people." Although this may initially have been the most important protection for the states, the expansion of national power since the 1930s, together with the US Supreme Court's acquiescence in its expansion, has raised questions about whether this amendment remains an effective safeguard of state autonomy. Since the early 1990s, the Supreme Court has shown greater interest in safeguarding state power and curtailing federal power, but its rulings have blocked the further expansion of federal power rather than reversing the effects of earlier rulings that encouraged expansion.[13]

Second, the Constitution grants extraordinary protection to the territorial integrity of the states, forbidding tampering with state boundaries not only by congressional legislation but also by the normal processes for constitutional amendment.[14] Third, the Constitution secures to the states a role in the selection of federal officials and in the processes of the federal government. Initially, state legislatures selected US senators, who directly represented the interests of their various states. The Seventeenth Amendment (1913) instituted popular election of senators, but states still enjoy equal representation in the Senate (two senators each), and this is the one provision of the Constitution that may not be amended by future generations. In addition, as long as they do not discriminate on the basis of race, gender, or other factors, the states also set eligibility requirements for voting in both federal and state elections. Finally, under Article V, constitutional amendments require ratification by three-quarters of the states. Taken together, these protections for state autonomy and state interests justify Madison's claim that the system created by the Constitution was partly national and partly (con)federal.

One independent authority vested in the states is the power to create their own governmental institutions. The federal Constitution imposes few limitations on this power. It directs the federal government to "guarantee to every State in this Union a Republican [i.e., representative democracy] Form of Government," and it upholds the supremacy of federal law within its constitutional sphere over "any Thing in the Constitution or Laws of any State."[15]

The Fifteenth, Nineteenth, Twenty-Fourth, and Twenty-Sixth Amendments limit the states' ability to restrict the franchise. Nevertheless, the states retain broad discretion in creating their own institutions and processes of government. Every state adopts its own constitution, and the state supreme court is the ultimate interpreter of this constitution and of state law more generally. Every state elects or appoints its own officials without the intervention or approval of the federal government. Finally, every state adopts its own laws, and these operate unless they conflict with federal law.

In contrast, the country's 87,900 local governments receive no recognition under the federal Constitution. For most federal constitutional-law purposes, local governments are mere creatures, or creations, of state governments. In most states, the legislature may create, abolish, and change the boundaries of local governments. In a few states with major cities, such as New York, the state's Constitution grants the city some constitutional status or recognition. A recent important development has been the insertion of provisions in state constitutions prohibiting state legislatures from imposing "mandates" on local governments without also providing adequate funding for local governments to carry out the mandated functions, duties, or responsibilities. About half of the states have limits on "unfunded mandates," although some of these limits are found in statutes rather than in the states' constitutions.

Federally recognized Indian tribes have a distinct status. They devise their own constitutions, elect their own leaders, and exercise significant governing authority. Nevertheless, the prevailing US Supreme Court case law recognizes no constitutional limits to Congress's power to act as trustee for Indian nations; thus the tribes' right of self-determination is ultimately a matter of congressional grace rather than a matter of rights.[16]

THE ALLOCATION OF POWERS

Constitutional Principles

Article I, Section 8, of the Constitution enumerates the legislative powers of Congress, and the Tenth Amendment confirms that powers not granted to the federal government are reserved to the states, or to the people of the states. Complications arise, however, in determining how the enumeration of powers in the Constitution affects the powers of the states. Hamilton observes that "the State governments would clearly retain all the rights of sovereignty which they before had, and which were not, by the ratification of the Constitution *exclusively* delegated to the United States."[17] This statement suggests that the powers delegated to the federal government may be divided into (1) exclusive powers, which cannot be exercised by the states; (2) concurrent powers, whose delegation to the federal government does not restrict state power; and (3) powers that are neither entirely exclusive nor entirely concurrent, whose delegation to the federal government limits but does not completely preclude their exercise by the states.

The Constitution grants exclusive authority to the federal government in various ways. Some exclusive powers, such as jurisdiction over the seat of government (Art. I, Sec. 8), are granted expressly. Other powers are both granted to the federal government and denied the states. For example, the Constitution both authorizes the president to make treaties, with the advice and consent of the Senate (Art. II, Sec. 2), and forbids the states to make them (Art. I, Sec. 10). Finally, some powers granted to the federal government, such as the power to declare war (Art. I, Sec. 8), are by their very nature exclusive and thus cannot be exercised by the states.

In granting yet other powers to the federal government, the Constitution neither expressly nor implicitly precludes state legislation. A prime example is the concurrent power to tax. Under the supremacy clause (Art. VI), state enactments may still be unconstitutional if they conflict with federal legislation. In this way, the exercise of federal power can diminish state power, but in the absence of conflicting federal legislation, the states remain free to exercise their concurrent powers.

Finally, some constitutional grants of power are neither wholly exclusive nor wholly concurrent. If the states exercised these powers to the fullest possible extent, the federal government would be prevented from achieving the ends for which the powers were intended. However, elimination of all state authority would imperil legitimate state autonomy. By far, the most important power in this category is the commerce power. Excessive state regulation of interstate commerce could threaten the national common market that the Constitution sought to create. At the same time, states have a valid interest in protecting the health, safety, welfare, and morals of their citizens and should thus not be precluded from legislating for those purposes. The us Supreme Court plays a central role in balancing the competing interests of the nation and the states, ensuring that the states can protect their citizens while not unduly restricting the flow of commerce.

Constitutional Development

The paramount feature of American constitutional history has been the expansion of the power of the federal government. This process has been aided by the Supreme Court's broad interpretation of the powers granted to Congress and by constitutional amendments – especially the Fourteenth and Sixteenth Amendments – that have conferred important additional powers on Congress. The states themselves have often agitated for increased federal power to meet their own needs and interests and have also fostered it by their eagerness for federal grants-in-aid. Interest groups, too, have played an important role in expanding federal power, in part be-cause, as business leaders often say, they would rather be regulated by one 500-pound gorilla than by 50 monkeys.

As a result of these factors, although the Tenth Amendment provides for the states to retain those powers not delegated to the federal government, the areas of exclusive state control have progressively narrowed. Since the early 1930s, the federal government has entered a variety of policy areas – for example, pollution control, race relations, and consumer protection – that previously had been predominantly state concerns. This expansion of federal power has not invariably produced conflict because federal and state policies often have been complementary. Nevertheless, as the federal government has come to regulate areas traditionally dominated by the states, collisions between state and federal claims of authority have in-creased. When federal and state policies have clashed, the supremacy clause (Art. VI) mandates that federal policies prevail over (preempt) in-consistent state policies.

In its early years, the Supreme Court, particularly under Chief Justice John Marshall (1801–35), asserted the supremacy of the federal govern-ment. From the 1840s until the New Deal of the 1930s, however, the Court sought to strike more of a balance by limiting the ability of Congress to ex-pand its powers at the expense of the states. At first, the Court struck down key New Deal legislation in the mid-1930s as violating principles of federal-ism, but under intense political pressure from President Franklin D. Roosevelt, a new majority emerged on the Court that began to uphold ex-panded federal power. The Court thereafter became a strong supporter of the growth of federal power, especially in the areas of commerce, social policy, and civil rights. In recent years, however, the Court has shifted course. A slim 5-4 states' rights majority on the Court under the leadership of Chief Justice William Rehnquist has worked to strike down some federal legislation as undercutting the constitutional autonomy of the states. The Court has resurrected the idea that the federal government cannot legis-late away the "sovereign immunity" of states, thereby reducing the extent to which citizens may sue states for failure to uphold federal laws.[18] It has also ruled that the federal government cannot "commandeer" state legisla-tures or executive officials, requiring them to carry out federal programs.[19]

The understanding of federal-state relations has changed over time as well. A contrast has historically been drawn between dual and cooperative federalism. Dual federalism emphasized the separateness of the two orders of government and the need to confine each to its own sphere of responsi-bility and to prevent either from encroaching on the sovereignty of the other. Others noted that the framers' vague wording in the Constitution intended a more nuanced system of overlapping powers necessitating a more cooperative federalism based on sharing powers and supporting each other as the federal government helped states to fulfil basic functions and as states helped the federal government to fulfil national objectives. Cooperative federalism especially characterized federal-state-local relations from 1932 to the late 1960s, during which time the federal government poured ever more money into state and local governments and all public policy became intergovernmental. Since the late 1960s, however, many observers have characterized the system as one of regulatory or coercive federalism, in which the federal government is predominant and cooperation is viewed as the willingness of states to cooperate with federal directives. This period has been marked by unprecedented increases in federal rules attached to grants-in-aid, mandates on the states, federal preemption of state laws, federal intrusions into state tax bases, federal court orders, and a federalization of state criminal law.[20]

In reaction to this centralization, several presidents – especially Republicans Richard M. Nixon (1969–74) and Ronald Reagan (1981–89) – proposed a "new federalism" to return powers to the states; however, there has been little movement in this direction beyond grants of more administrative flexibility for states to implement federal policies. President Reagan, for example, while rhetorically advocating states' rights, signed more federal laws preempting state powers than had any previous president.

THE STRUCTURE AND OPERATION OF GOVERNMENT

The Federal Government

In designing the Constitution, the delegates to the Constitutional Convention sought to create a government to which one could safely entrust the extensive powers it needed in order to serve the ends for which it was created. Making the government dependent on the people was part of the answer, as was extending the commercial republic. Another means by which they sought to realize this objective was establishing a system based on checks and balances and on a separation of powers. The delegates were aware that "the accumulation of all powers legislative, executive, and judiciary in the same hands, whether of one, a few, or many, and whether hereditary, self-appointed, or elective might justly be pronounced the very definition of tyranny"; therefore, "the preservation of liberty requires that the three great departments of power should be separate and distinct."[21] Thus they sought to construct a government consisting of three coordinate and equal branches, with each performing a blend of functions, thereby balancing governmental powers. Their goal was to structure the government so that the mutual relations between the three branches would keep each in its proper place.

The Constitution creates a presidential system, in which the president is elected and serves both as chief executive and as chief of state, in which a bicameral Congress exercises the legislative power and in which independent federal courts exercise the federal judicial power. The "national" house of Congress, the House of Representatives, includes 435 members, elected from districts within each state for two-year terms, with representation apportioned among the 50 states on the basis of population (although each state is guaranteed at least one representative). Districts are reapportioned by state legislatures every ten years based on data from the federal Census, and the Supreme Court ruled in *Wesberry v. Sanders* (1964) that congressional districts within a state must be of equal population.[22] The "(con)federal" house, the Senate, has 100 members, two from each state, elected statewide to staggered six-year terms (one-third of the senators are elected every two years). In addition to its legislative powers, the Senate has the power to advise and give consent on treaties (by a two-thirds vote) and on presidential appointments to executive offices and to the federal judiciary (by majority vote).

The founders expected that the division of Congress into two houses of different sizes, with different systems of apportionment, different modes of selection, and different terms of office, would produce distinctive perspectives in the two chambers, thereby encouraging more thorough consideration of proposed statutes. They also expected that the representation of the states in the Senate would ensure that the federal government took state interests and concerns into account in its policy making. Here the evidence is less clear. The ratification of the Seventeenth Amendment, replacing the selection of senators by state legislatures with their direct election by the people, removed one of the principal structural devices the founders employed to protect the interests of the states as states. In *Garcia v. San Antonio Metropolitan Transit Authority* (1985), a five-member majority on the US Supreme Court concluded nevertheless that "[t]he Framers chose to rely on a federal system in which special restraints on federal power over the States inhered principally in the workings of the National Government itself" and that the states' interests are principally "protected by procedural safeguards inherent in the structure of the federal system." Four justices disagreed, asserting that "the States' role ... is a matter of constitutional law, not legislative grace."[23]

Article II of the Constitution vests the executive power in the president and awards him or her various powers and responsibilities, such as the power to veto legislation, to appoint executive officials and federal judges, to serve as commander in chief of the nation's armed forces, and to ensure that federal laws are faithfully executed. These powers make the president a formidable participant in the system of checks and balances. Historical developments have also enhanced presidential power. For example, the nation's expanding international presence has augmented presidential power because the Constitution assigns the president a major role in the conduct of foreign policy. In the domestic sphere, the expansion in the size of the federal government and in the scope of its activities has enhanced the significance of the president's powers to make appointments, supervise administration, and implement public policies.

The president is selected by a system known as the electoral college, which was devised to ensure that the chief executive was not dependent on the legislature and would therefore be willing to check it. This system also enhances the electoral weight of small states and of minority groups and requires candidates to build support across various regions. Each state casts electoral-college votes based on its representation in Congress: two senators plus the number of representatives it has in the House of Representatives. Forty-eight states award all their electoral-college votes to the presidential candidate who receives a plurality of the popular vote in the state. Typically, the candidate who receives the most popular votes nationwide also receives the most electoral votes. However, in close elections, this need not be the case. In 2000 the Democratic candidate, Albert Gore, won the nationwide popular vote by 500,000 votes (0.5 percent of the total vote) but lost in the electoral college to the Republican candidate, George W. Bush, by a 271-266 margin.

Article III of the Constitution establishes both the US Supreme Court and "such inferior Courts as the Congress shall from time to time ordain and establish." Congress responded to this invitation by creating a three-tiered system of federal courts. The federal judges are appointed by the president, confirmed by the Senate, and enjoy tenure during "good behavior." The district courts serve as the federal trial courts, with at least one district court in each state. The thirteen courts of appeals hear appeals from the district courts. Eleven of the courts of appeals are organized regionally, with each court's "circuit" made up of three or more states. The Court of Appeals for the District of Columbia serves as a sort of state supreme court for the District of Columbia, and the United States Court of Appeals for the Federal Circuit reviews large numbers of appeals from federal administrative agencies.

At the apex of the federal court system is the US Supreme Court. This nine-member body selectively reviews cases appealed to it from the federal courts of appeals and from state supreme courts. Of the more than 7,000 cases appealed to it in any given year, it typically accepts no more than 100 cases for decision. It also has a very limited original jurisdiction conferred on it by the Constitution, extending to cases involving foreign diplomatic personnel and to cases in which a state is a party. Finally, as Chief Justice John Jay made clear in 1793 in response to a request from

President Washington, the Court does not issue advisory opinions (although several state supreme courts are authorized to issue such opinions).

Article III confers judicial power on the federal courts for four basic purposes. First, in order to vindicate the authority of the federal government, federal courts are empowered to hear cases arising under the US Constitution, cases arising under US laws, and cases in which the federal government is a party. Although the power of judicial review is not mentioned in the Constitution, the Supreme Court ruled in *Marbury v. Madison* (1803) that the power to "say what the [federal] law is" carries with it the power to rule on the constitutionality of federal or state laws, and all federal courts exercise the power of judicial review.[24] Second, in order to maintain exclusive federal control over foreign affairs, the federal courts are empowered to hear admiralty cases, cases arising under treaties, cases affecting ambassadors or other diplomatic personnel of foreign countries, and cases pitting states or their citizens against foreign states or their citizens. Third, in order to maintain interstate comity, the federal courts are empowered to hear disputes between two or more states and disputes between a state and the citizens of another state. Finally, in order to protect out-of-state litigants against the possible bias of state tribunals, federal courts are empowered to hear civil cases between citizens of different states.

State Governments

American state governments have similar political structures. All 50 state constitutions have instituted a "presidential" system in which the chief executive, the governor, is elected by the populace rather than by the legislature. All have established a tripartite division of governmental power (legislative, executive, and judicial), provided for regular periodic elections, and guaranteed an array of fundamental rights. All but Nebraska have created a bicameral legislature, and all but Nebraska elect their legislators in partisan elections. Differences among state governments typically involve the size of the state legislature, the number and powers of separately elected statewide executive offices, the number of separate executive departments, and the structure of the state judicial system. Of these differences, the most important is the number of statewide elective executive offices. The election of various executive officials was introduced during the nineteenth century in order to promote greater democratic control of government, and it has largely survived to the present day despite the claim of twentieth-century reformers that it undermines governmental efficiency and effective leadership by the governor. Executive officials (e.g., the attorney general, secretary of state, and treasurer) who owe their position to the populace, rather than to the governor, exercise considerable political independence, and in many states may be political rivals of the governor.

Interstate and Federal-State Relations

Constitutional provisions addressing interstate and federal-state relations sound several themes. First is a commitment to state autonomy. For example, the federal government cannot intervene to protect states against internal violence without a request from the state legislature or the governor. Although the federal government is to "guarantee to every State in the Union a Republican Form of Government," this enigmatic clause has had little effect on how the states have structured their political institutions. Second is an expectation of conflict over the scope of federal and state authority, aggravated, as Madison observes, by the difficulty of "marking the proper line of partition between the authority of the general and that of the State governments."[25] The Constitution's supremacy clause confirms that the federal government is supreme within its sphere, "any Thing in the Constitution or Laws of any State to the Contrary notwithstanding," and state officials are bound by oath to support the US Constitution, but the enumeration of powers in Article I and the later ratification of the Tenth Amendment indicate that the sphere of federal authority is limited. Third is a concern about state parochialism. The tendency toward parochialism is combated by transferring some powers to the federal government (e.g., the power to regulate commerce among the states), by allowing civil cases between citizens of different states to be tried in federal courts (which are presumed to be more impartial than their state counterparts), and by protecting citizens of one state against discrimination while in another state through the privileges-and-immunities clause of Article IV. Fourth is a desire for interstate comity. The Constitution encourages comity by specifying the obligations owed by one state to another. States are obliged to give full faith and credit to the public acts and judgments of other states (e.g., recognize driver's and marriage licenses issued in other states). They are also required to extradite fugitives from justice in other states and, prior to the Civil War, were required to return fugitive slaves. Fifth is a desire to facilitate interstate cooperation in solving common problems while safeguarding federal interests. Thus the Constitution recognizes the authority of states to compact with one another, although they may do so only with the consent of Congress.[26]

FISCAL POWERS

The framers gave Congress limited power to tax so that the federal government could raise the revenue necessary to finance its operations without having to rely on the states. The Constitution imposes three express limits on this power: Congress may not tax exports, it must apportion direct taxes among the states in relation to their populations, and it must impose taxes uniformly throughout the nation. Only the vague limitation on "direct taxes" has provoked controversy. In *Pollock v. Farmer's Loan & Trust Company* (1895), the Supreme Court held that because taxes on real estate are direct taxes, the same is true of taxes on income from real estate.[27] This decision, which in effect prevented the imposition of any type of federal income tax, was reversed by ratification of the Sixteenth Amendment in 1913.

Granting taxation authority to the federal government does not preclude taxation by the states. The power to tax is a concurrent power because states retain authority to tax anything they wish as long as a tax does not discriminate against persons or businesses from other states, violate anyone's civil rights, or violate the constitutional ban on state taxes on imports or exports. The Constitution contains no provisions for revenue sharing or fiscal equalization; it does not require the federal government or the states to cooperate or coordinate with each other on tax matters, nor does it require the states to harmonize their tax systems. *McCulloch v. Maryland* (1819) established the doctrine of intergovernmental tax immunities, under which states and localities cannot tax instrumentalities of the federal government (e.g., a federal courthouse) and the federal government cannot tax instrumentalities of state and local governments.[28]

The federal Constitution does not require the federal or state governments to balance their budgets, nor does it regulate federal, state, or local borrowing. However, state constitutions do place fiscal constraints on state and local governments; they often include detailed provisions concerning the power of those governments to levy taxes, grant tax exemptions, borrow money through issuing bonds, and spend the money raised by taxing and borrowing. Many state constitutions impose tax uniformity requirements analogous to the requirement found in the federal Constitution – for example, the Pennsylvania Constitution mandates that "all taxes shall be uniform, upon the same class of subjects, within the territorial limits of the authority levying the tax."[29] In addition, several states have adopted amendments by constitutional initiative that restrict the taxation authority of state and local governments. For example, in 1978 California adopted "Proposition 13," which reduced local property taxes and capped future property-tax increases, and in 1992 Colorado adopted the "Taxpayer Bill of Rights," which requires popular approval of all new taxes via referendum.[30] Most state constitutions also require state governments to have balanced operating budgets. Many also restrict state and local borrowing, typically requiring that proposals to incur debt be submitted to popular referendum. Thus, whereas the federal Constitution places few constraints on the fiscal powers of the federal government and the states, state constitutions impose a variety of limitations.

The fiscal arrangements of the federal system have changed dramatically since the early 1930s. Article I, Section 8(1), gives Congress the power to raise certain taxes and impose duties. The federal government levied an income tax during the Civil War but did not implement a permanent, graduated income tax until after the Sixteenth Amendment (1913) removed doubts about its constitutionality. With this power to tax income, the federal government became, by the Second World War, the predominant tax power. The federal government increasingly relied on this power, as well as on deficit spending, to gain leverage over the states, enticing them to enlist in federal programs by offering them conditional grants-in-aid. Acting through its spending power, Congress may extend its reach to many matters normally reserved to the states. It may accomplish its aims indirectly by attaching conditions to federal spending programs or grants. In *South Dakota v. Dole* (1987), the US Supreme Court upheld this use of federal power, noting that "objectives not thought to be within Article I's 'enumerated legislative fields' ... may nevertheless be attained through the use of the spending power and the conditional grant of federal funds."[31] In this case, the Court upheld a condition of federal highway aid that required all states to raise to 21 the age to purchase alcoholic beverages. States failing to raise the drinking age would have lost some of their highway aid.

FOREIGN AFFAIRS AND DEFENCE

The conduct of foreign affairs is preeminently a federal, rather than a state, concern. As Madison writes, "If we are to be one nation in any respect, it clearly ought to be in respect to other nations."[32] The Constitution recognizes this not only by granting pertinent powers to the president and to Congress but also by expressly denying them to the states or ensuring that their exercise by the states does not conflict with federal policy. Thus Article I, Section 10, of the Constitution prohibits states from entering into any treaty, alliances, or confederation with foreign nations, but it allows them to enter agreements and compacts with foreign states with congressional consent, and many states have done so. The Constitution forbids the states from engaging in war unless actually invaded or in imminent danger of invasion, but it safeguards their ability to defend themselves through state militias. In *Crosby v. National Foreign Trade Council* (2000)[33] the Court struck down a Massachusetts law forbidding the state to purchase goods or services from companies that did business with Myanmar because the law conflicted with a federal statute governing trade with that country. However, the Court left unanswered the more fundamental question of whether the Constitution precludes all state actions affecting foreign affairs or even all state economic sanctions against foreign countries.[34] Finally, in *American Insurance Association v. Garamendi* (2003), the Court struck down a California statute designed to help Holocaust survivors receive payment on life-insurance plans purchased during the Second World

War, holding that the law interfered with the president's ability to conduct and control foreign policy and was thus preempted.

Each state has its own armed force, the militia, and the Constitution guarantees the states the authority to appoint militia officers and to train their militias "according to the discipline prescribed by Congress" (Art. I, Sec. 8, Para. 16). Initially, the militia served two purposes. First, the founders feared a large standing army as dangerous to republican liberty, and the militia provided an alternative to such an army, an armed force of all able-bodied free males that could help repel foreign foes or quell domestic disturbances. Thus the Constitution authorizes Congress to call state militias into the service of the United States "to execute the laws of the Union, suppress insurrections, and repel invasions" (Art. I, Sec. 8, Para. 15). (By statute, Congress has delegated this authority to the president, who serves as commander in chief of the militia when it is called into service.) Second, the militia provided a means by which the states could resist federal tyranny. As Madison observes, potential federal usurpers would face "a militia amounting to near a half a million of citizens with arms in their hands, officered by men chosen from among themselves, fighting for their common liberties and united and conducted by government possessing their affections and confidence."[35]

Since the Second World War, the United States has maintained a large standing army, so the militia is less important. Over time, the character of the militia has changed from a force comprised of all citizens into a select and better-trained force, the National Guard. In *Perpich v. Department of Defense* (1990), the Supreme Court upheld over a governor's objections a congressional authorization for training National Guard troops outside the United States, ruling that the exercise of federal powers in foreign affairs supersedes state prerogatives.[36]

The states' role in war and foreign affairs comes primarily from their representation in the us Senate. Although the Constitution designates the president as "commander in chief of the Army and Navy" (Art. II, Sec. 2, Para. 1), Congress has the authority to raise and support military forces, to declare war, to regulate commerce with foreign countries, and to suspend the writ of *habeas corpus* in time of war. The Constitution grants the House of Representatives a role equal to that of the Senate in exercising these military powers because *individuals* might have to be conscripted for war and because *individuals* have to be taxed to pay for war. The Constitution grants the Senate the power to confirm ambassadors and other envoys and to ratify treaties by a two-thirds vote, a concession to the southern states, which feared that a simple-majority rule would allow the northern states to ratify treaties detrimental to their interests. It thus grants the house of Congress representing state interests crucial authority over foreign policy matters that might encroach upon state powers. As the United States became a world power, the president emerged as the dominant figure in setting foreign policy and initiating military action. Nevertheless, the president seeks the support of Congress in order to present a united front to other countries. Thus President George W. Bush sought the concurrence of Congress for taking action against al-Qa'ida in the wake of the attacks on New York City's World Trade Center in 2001 and for war against Iraq in 2003.

CITIZENSHIP

The Preamble to the Constitution indicates that those making the Constitution are "We the People of the United States." Implicit in this language is a fundamental ambiguity about the character of the system that was being created. Nationalist interpreters have read the language to mean "We the People of the whole United States," emphasizing the founders' desire to augment federal power and the recognition of Americans as one people in the Declaration of Independence. Interpreters of states' rights have read the language as "We the People of the several States" that are uniting to form a more perfect union, thus viewing the Constitution as uniting states rather than persons. They note that the Constitution was ratified by conventions in the various states rather than by a popular national referendum and that nowhere does the Constitution permit the whole people to act directly on anything. This seemingly arcane debate has had real consequences – for example, southern proponents of secession argued that if a state could consent to join the Union, it could also withdraw that consent. Moreover, conflict over the nature of the federal Union continues to the present day.

This ambiguity is intensified by the treatment of dual federal and state citizenship in the Constitution. The Constitution mentions both state and national citizens at several points but does not define either type of citizenship or indicate the relationship between them. In the infamous case of *Dred Scott v. Sandford* (1857), the Supreme Court accepted the priority of state over national citizenship, ruling that persons born in the United States derived their citizenship from their status as descendants of those "who were at the time of the adoption of the Constitution recognized as citizens in the several States." The Court also held that black Americans could not attain United States citizenship either from a state or by virtue of birth within the United States.[37] The Fourteenth Amendment (1868) expressly overruled *Dred Scott* and confirmed that "[a]ll persons born or naturalized in the United States and subject to the jurisdiction thereof, are citizens of the United States and of the state wherein they reside" (Sec. 1). The amendment thus recognized the citizenship of African Americans, established the priority of national over state citizenship, and reduced state citizenship to little more than residence within a state.

The Constitution grants Congress the power "to establish a uniform Rule of Naturalization," and in *Chirac v. Chirac* (1817), the Supreme Court confirmed that this is an exclusive, not a concurrent, power.[38] Congress also has the power to exclude aliens from the United States – admission is a privilege granted only on such terms as Congress may prescribe – and to deport or expel aliens who have been admitted. The Supreme Court has imposed some procedural requirements on deportation hearings, but these are considerably fewer than are available to defendants in criminal trials.[39]

VOTING, ELECTIONS, AND POLITICAL PARTIES

The states have primary responsibility for structuring their own processes of self-government, subject to few federal constitutional limitations. They also bear considerable responsibility for structuring national political processes, exercising in the first instance the power to regulate the time, place, and manner of congressional elections, and determining how presidential electors (i.e., the electoral college) are selected.

During the decade between independence and drafting of the federal Constitution, each state established its own eligibility requirements for voting in state elections. Rather than impose a uniform standard for federal elections, which would diverge from the qualifications in some states and thus create distinct state and federal electorates, the Constitution adopted the diverse state qualifications as its own. It mandated that the qualifications to vote for members of the us House of Representatives shall be the same qualifications requisite for electors (i.e., voters) of the most numerous branch of the state legislature.[40] During the nineteenth century, states liberalized voting requirements, thus substantially enlarging the federal and state electorates. Today states continue to determine voter eligibility (e.g., by limiting voting on the basis of residency, mental incapacity, and conviction of a felony crime) and to retain responsibility for voter registration. However, federal constitutional amendments and congressional statutes now limit state discretion in setting eligibility requirements. The Fifteenth Amendment (1870) forbids states from denying the right to vote based on race, colour, or previous condition of servitude. The Nineteenth Amendment (1920) guarantees women the right to vote. The Twenty-fourth Amendment (1964) provides that the right to vote in federal elections shall not be denied for failure to pay a poll tax or any other tax. The Twenty-sixth Amendment (1971) lowered the voting age to 18 nationwide. All of these amendments authorize congressional enforcement through "appropriate legislation." In 1965 Congress enacted the Voting Rights Act, which bars racial discrimination in all voting practices and procedures. The act also requires that before enacting changes to voting practices and procedures, officials in nine states and in portions of seven others in which racial discrimination was once widespread must obtain advance approval from the federal attorney general or from a federal court. Other federal laws with which states must comply proscribe electoral violence and intimidation, require states to maintain voter registration procedures for federal elections that are convenient and easy to satisfy (e.g., the "motor voter" law), and provide standards governing absentee voting by members of the armed forces.[41]

The right to form political parties and other political groups is implicit in the First Amendment's (1791) protections of freedom of speech and the rights to assemble and to petition governments for redress of grievances. In 1976 the US Supreme Court held that the right of individuals and groups to contribute funds to political candidates and political parties is protected under the First Amendment.[42] However, the federal Constitution does not expressly deal with political parties, nor do most state constitutions.

THE PROTECTION OF RIGHTS

The original Constitution included several important rights protections. It forbade bills of attainder (legislative acts declaring persons guilty of crimes and passing sentence without benefit of trial) and *ex post facto* laws. It expressly defined and limited treason so that treason charges could not be used to persecute political opponents. It restricted suspension of the writ of *habeas corpus*, except "when in Cases of Rebellion or Invasion the public Safety may require it." It also forbade religious tests for holding any federal office.[43]

The original Constitution did not include a bill of rights because few delegates to the Constitutional Convention believed one was necessary. When George Mason of Virginia proposed a bill of rights during the final week of the convention, not a single state supported his proposal. However, during the debate over ratification of the Constitution, anti-Federalist opponents of ratification pointed to the absence of a bill of rights as a fatal defect that would allow the growth of a dangerously powerful federal government. In response, Hamilton insisted that a bill of rights would expand federal power because it would imply that the federal government could do anything not prohibited by a bill of rights.[44] However, Hamilton's argument proved unpersuasive, and the Federalists, who supported ratification, agreed to introduce amendments as the price of ratification.

The Bill of Rights of 1791, the first ten amendments to the Constitution, reflects in part the anti-Federalists' concerns. Because the anti-Federalists viewed the federal government as the primary threat to liberty, the amendments imposed limits only on the federal government. Most state constitutions already contained declarations of rights to safeguard against state violations; in fact, these state constitutions were the source of most of the rights in the federal Bill of Rights. Moreover, some amendments also safeguard state prerogatives.

For example, the First Amendment forbids Congress from enacting laws respecting an establishment of religion, thereby leaving the states free to structure church-state relations as they saw fit; the Second Amendment safeguards the right to bear arms, enabling citizens to band together against federal oppression under state leadership if necessary. Finally, the Tenth Amendment confirms that the Constitution grants only limited authority to the federal government and that all powers not delegated to the federal government are reserved to the states or to the people.

The Bill of Rights, moreover, reflects a concern for individual rights. The First Amendment protects basic freedoms of religion, speech, press, public assembly, and petitioning government. The Fourth, Fifth, and Sixth Amendments guarantee a panoply of rights to defendants accused of crime – for example, a right against unreasonable search and seizure, the right to counsel, and the right against self-incrimination. The Sixth and Seventh Amendments secure the right to a jury trial in federal criminal and civil cases. The Eighth Amendment prohibits excessive bail or fines and outlaws "cruel and unusual punishments." The Ninth Amendment confirms that the list of rights in the preceding eight amendments is not comprehensive, that "the enumeration in the Constitution, of certain rights, shall not be construed to deny or disparage others retained by the people."

What is striking, at least from today's perspective, is what the Bill of Rights omits. For one, it does not provide for the suspension of rights during national emergencies. The Constitution permits only suspension of the writ of *habeas corpus* in case of rebellion or invasion. Thus it is largely left to Congress and the judiciary to determine whether curtailment of rights during a war or other emergency is justified by circumstances. Second, the Bill of Rights recognizes no group or communal rights, and even later amendments that protect members of groups do so by protecting their individual rights. Thus the Fourteenth Amendment protects "any person" (Sec. 1) against denial of equal protection by the laws, the Fifteenth Amendment ensures that no citizen will be denied the right to vote on the basis of race or colour, and the Nineteenth Amendment does the same on the basis of gender. Third, the Bill of Rights guarantees negative rights in the form of freedoms from government oppression; it does not protect positive rights, such as rights to government services. For instance, when litigants in *San Antonio Independent School District v. Rodriguez* (1973) insisted that the Constitution guarantees a right to education, the US Supreme Court rejected their argument.[45] (Some state constitutions do protect positive rights, such as the right to education, to a clean and healthful environment, and to housing.) Finally, the Bill of Rights offers no protection against private violations of rights, securing rights only against violation by governments.

Three developments have dramatically altered the protection of rights under American constitutionalism. The first development began with the adoption of the Fourteenth Amendment in 1868. The amendment's immediate aim was to secure the rights of newly freed slaves against state violations. However, the amendment does not mention race, and its language is very broad. It forbids states from "mak[ing] or enforc[ing] any law which shall abridge the privileges and immunities of citizens of the United States," "deny[ing] to any person within their jurisdiction the equal protection of the laws," and "depriv[ing] any person of their life, liberty, or property without due process of law" (Sec. 1). Commentators and judges have disagreed vehemently about the intended scope of the Fourteenth Amendment. Some scholars insist that the amendment applies the Bill of Rights to the states, guarantees other rights against state infringement as well, and gives the federal government broad authority to protect these rights.[46] Others emphasize the attachment to federalism of the amendment's authors, depict the amendment's aims as specific rather than open-ended, and deny that these aims encompassed the application of the Bill of Rights to the states.[47] Initially, the Supreme Court in *The Slaughterhouse Cases* (1873) read the amendment narrowly.[48] However, during the twentieth century – and particularly during the chief justiceship of Earl Warren (1953–69) – the Court read the amendment broadly, and it incrementally ruled that nearly all provisions of the Bill of Rights protect against state, as well as federal, infringements on rights.

Implicit in what has been said is a second major development, the more aggressive stance taken by the US Supreme Court in enforcing rights. Not until the early twentieth century did the Court strike down a state law for violating the Bill of Rights. However, with the extension of the Bill of Rights to the states, the number of cases involving rights claims increased dramatically, leading to landmark Court rulings. For example, the Court's rulings protecting flag burning under the First Amendment, outlawing state-sanctioned religious practices in schools, granting government-provided legal counsel to indigent defendants, requiring police to inform suspects of their rights before interrogating them, and prohibiting the death penalty in rape cases all involved state rather than federal violations of rights.[49] In addition, the Supreme Court has relied on the equal-protection clause of the Fourteenth Amendment to address racial discrimination (e.g., *Brown v. Board of Education*, 1954), legislative apportionment (e.g., *Reynolds v. Sims*, 1964), and more recently, gender discrimination (e.g., *United States v. Virginia*, 1996) and affirmative action (e.g., *Grutter v. Bollinger*, 2003).[50] Finally, the Court has identified rights not expressly found in the Constitution, such as a right to privacy, and thereby struck down state laws held to violate these rights, such as prohibitions of abortion (e.g., *Roe v. Wade*, 1973).[51]

Beginning in the 1970s, another important development took place, namely the rediscovery of state bills (or declarations) of rights. State constitutions have always included rights guarantees. However, for most of the twentieth century, litigants only infrequently looked to these protections, preferring instead to rely on the federal Bill of Rights and on federal courts to secure their rights. Under Chief Justice Earl Warren, the US Supreme Court was very responsive to rights claims. After Warren retired in 1969, however, the Court moved in a more conservative direction, particularly in cases involving the rights of defendants. This led many civil-liberties advocates to take cases into state courts, fashioning legal arguments based on state constitutional declarations of rights. This "new judicial federalism" has enjoyed considerable success, with state courts playing a significant role in cases involving (among other things) the rights of defendants, the rights of gays and lesbians, and the reform of public school finance. Thus rights litigants often engage in forum shopping between state and federal courts.

CONSTITUTIONAL CHANGE

Constitutional change can occur either by altering the text of the document through amendment or revision (replacement) or by altering the interpretation of the text. In the 50 states, constitutional change has proceeded primarily through amendment and revision. But change through interpretation has predominated for the US Constitution. The most important developments in American constitutional history – the extension in the scope of all orders of government, the expansion of federal power, and the growth of presidential and judicial power – have largely occurred without constitutional amendment.

The Constitution has been amended only 27 times in more than 215 years. If one excludes the Bill of Rights (Amendments 1-10) of 1791, the Constitution has been amended less than once every 13 years. The infrequency of formal change reflects in part the difficulty of amendment. Amendments must be proposed by a two-thirds vote in each house of Congress or by a convention called by Congress upon petition by two-thirds of the state legislatures. (The latter approach, inserted to ensure that Congress could not block popular demands for constitutional change, has never been utilized.) Although thousands of amendments have been introduced in Congress, only 33 have been sent to the states for ratification. Ratification requires approval by the legislatures of three-quarters of the states or, if Congress so designates, by specially elected conventions in three-quarters of the states. The ratification procedure thus reflects the federal character of the American polity, requiring that amendments be approved by both partners (federal and state) in the federal system and be supported not merely by a numerical supermajority but also by a geographically dispersed majority.[52]

EMERGING TRENDS AND DEVELOPMENTS

It is highly unlikely that major amendments to the US Constitution will be adopted in the near future. Therefore, the most important influences on the development of American constitutionalism and federalism in the early decades of the twenty-first century will be changes in interpretations of the Constitution and/or political developments within the leeways provided by the Constitution. Three trends bear watching.

First is the US Supreme Court's role in safeguarding state prerogatives and enforcing limits on federal power. Beginning in the 1990s, the Supreme Court reaffirmed and expanded the concept of state sovereign immunity. It also ruled that the institutions of state government (other than courts) cannot be commandeered by Congress to assist in the enforcement of federal law. It placed limits on congressional use of the commerce clause to regulate noneconomic activities. Finally, it imposed new, rather stringent standards for review of congressional legislation adopted under Section 5 of the Fourteenth Amendment, which authorizes Congress to enact "appropriate legislation" to enforce the amendment's mandates. Many of these cases were decided by a narrow 5-4 margin, and the durability of these judicial initiatives in enforcing constitutional federalism are likely to depend on future appointments to the bench, which, in turn, will depend on the outcomes of future presidential and senatorial elections.

Second is the unwillingness of the federal government to limit its activities in areas of concurrent power in order to allow the states to exercise their traditional governing responsibilities. Since the 1970s, a succession of presidents has given rhetorical support to reining in the federal government, thereby permitting state governments to pursue innovative approaches to policy issues and to tailor policy to the needs and circumstances of their citizens.[53] Scholars have also rediscovered the virtues of federalism.[54] Nevertheless, political practice has not always coincided with rhetoric. Presidents have tended to encourage centralized solutions for perceived problems – for example, President George W. Bush's initiatives with regard to elementary and secondary education and tort reform – and Congress has responded to interest-group pressure by federalizing a variety of ordinary state-law crimes, such as drug possession and violence against women. Whether this federal reach can be restrained will be important in determining the future course of American federalism.

Third are the terrorist attacks on the United States of 11 September 2001 and the response to these attacks by the federal government. These attacks and the resulting war on terrorism have concentrated the attention of the federal government on foreign affairs and homeland security and have led to the adoption of legislation (e.g., the USA Patriot Act) designed to forestall future acts of terrorism. This statute has been controversial, as have some of the other actions taken by the federal government, but the controversy has focused on alleged threats to civil liberties from these initiatives rather than on threats to the federal balance. In fact, the effort to combat terrorism has not significantly altered US federalism. The creation of the US Department of Homeland Security within the federal government entailed a major reorganization within this government but did not significantly affect intergovernmental relations. The emphasis has been on improving intergovernmental cooperation and coordination rather than on accelerating centralization. In this sense, the response to 11 September has been adapted to the current federal system.

NOTES

1 This description of the tribes' status is drawn from the opinion of Chief Justice John Marshall in *Worcester v. Georgia*, 31 US (6 Pet.) 515 (1832).

2 Alexander Hamilton, John Jay, and James Madison, *The Federalist Papers*, ed. Clinton Rossiter (New York: New American Library, 1961), p. 74. All subsequent references to *The Federalist Papers* are to this edition.

3 See James Madison's famous discussion in *The Federalist Papers*, no. 10, p. 45.

4 James Madison, *The Federalist Papers*, no. 39, 214.

5 The "police power" is understood in American constitutional law as the power to protect the health, safety, welfare, and morals of the citizenry.

6 George Washington, "To the Hebrew Congregations of Philadelphia, New York, Charleston, and Richmond, December 1790," *The Writings of George Washington*, vol. 31, ed. John C. Fitzpatrick (Washington, DC: US Government Printing Office, 1939), pp. 185–86.

7 US Constitution, Article I, Section 2, Paragraph 2, and Section 3, Paragraph 3.

8 The ban on religious tests is found in US Constitution, Article IV, Paragraph 3.

9 James Madison, *The Federalist Papers*, no. 10. For a penetrating analysis of Madison's argument, see David F. Epstein, *The Political Theory of the Federalist* (Chicago: University of Chicago Press, 1984).

10 See, for example, Michael F. Zuckert, "Completing the Constitution: The Fourteenth Amendment," *Publius: The Journal of Federalism* 22 (Spring 1992): 69–92.

11 See, for example, Robert J. Kaczorowski, "To Begin the Nation Anew: Congress, Citizenship, and Civil Rights After the Civil War," *American Historical Review* 92 (February 1987): 45–68.

12 Donald S. Lutz, "The United States Constitution as an Incomplete Text," *Annals of the American Academy of Political and Social Sciences* 496 (March 1988): 23–32.

13 See, for example, *United States v. Lopez*, 511 US 1029 (1995); *Printz v. United States*, 521 US 898 (1997); and *United States v. Morrison*, 529 US 598 (2000).

14 US Constitution, Article IV, Section 3, Paragraph 1.

15 US Constitution, Article IV, Section 4, and Article IV, Section 2.

16 See David E. Wilkins, *American Indian Sovereignty and the US Supreme Court: The Masking of Justice* (Austin: University of Texas Press, 1997).

17 Alexander Hamilton, *The Federalist Papers*, no. 32, p. 166, emphasis added.

18 See, for example, *Seminole Tribe of Florida v. Florida*, 517 US 44 (1996); and *Federal Maritime Commission v. South Carolina State Ports Authority*, 535 US 743 (2002).

19 See, for example, *New York v. United States*, 505 US 144 (1992); and *Printz v. United States*, 521 US 898 (1997).

20 John Kincaid, "From Dual to Coercive Federalism in American Intergovernmental Relations," *Globalization and Decentralization*, ed. John S. Jun and Deil S. Wright (Washington, DC: Georgetown University Press, 1996), pp. 29–47; John Kincaid, "From Cooperation to Coercion in American Federalism: Housing, Fragmentation, and Preemption, 1780–1992," *Journal of Law and Politics* 9 (Winter 1993): 333–433; US Advisory Commission on Intergovernmental Relations, *Federal Statutory Preemption of State and Local Authority: History, Inventory, and Issues* (Washington, DC: US ACIR, 1992); US Advisory Commission on Intergovernmental Relations, *Regulatory Federalism: Policy, Process, Impact, and Reform* (Washington, DC: US Government Printing Office, 1984); and Thomas J. Maroney, "Fifty Years of Federalization of Criminal Law: Sounding the Alarm or 'Crying Wolf,'" *Syracuse Law Review* 50 (2000): 1317–78.

21 James Madison, *The Federalist Papers*, no. 47, p. 269.

22 *Wesberry v. Sanders*, 376 US 1 (1964).

23 *Garcia v. San Antonio Metropolitan Transit Authority*, 469 US 528 (1995).

24 *Marbury v. Madison*, 5 US (1 Cranch) 137 (1803).

25 James Madison, *The Federalist Papers*, no. 37, p. 195.

26 US Constitution, Article I, Section 10, Paragraph 3.

27 *Pollock v. Farmers' Loan & Trust Co.*, 157 US 429 (1895).

28 *McCulloch v. Maryland*, 17 US (4 Wheat.) 316 (1819).

29 Pennsylvania Constitution, Article XI, Section 1.

30 California Constitution, Article XIIIA, and Colorado Constitution, Article 10, Section 20.

31 *South Dakota v. Dole*, 483 US 203 (1987).

32 James Madison, *The Federalist Papers*, no. 42, p. 232.

33 *American Insurance Association v. Garamendi*, No. 02-722 (2003).

34 *Crosby v. National Foreign Trade Council*, 530 US 363 (2000).

35 James Madison, *The Federalist Papers*, no. 46, 267.

36 *Perpich v. Department of Defense*, 496 US 334 (1990).

37 *Dred Scott v. Sandford*, 60 US (19 How.) 393 (1857).

38 *Chirac v. Chirac*, 15 US (2 Wheat.) 259 (1817).

39 See American Civil Liberties Union, *The Rights of Aliens and Refugees: The Basic ACLU Guide to Alien and Refugee Rights*, 2nd ed. (Carbondale, IL: Southern Illinois University Press, 1990); and Gerald L. Neuman, *Strangers to the Constitution: Immigrants, Borders, and Fundamental Law* (Princeton, NJ: Princeton University Press, 1996).

40 US Constitution, Article I, Section 2, Paragraph 1.

41 The National Voter Registration Act of 1993, also known as the "motor voter" law, requires states to make provision for residents to register to vote at the same time that they obtain or renew their drivers' licenses.

42 *Buckley v. Valeo*, 424 US 1 (1976).

43 US Constitution, Article I, Section 9, Paragraphs 2 and 3; Article III, Section 3, Paragraph 1; and Article IV, Section 3.

44 Alexander Hamilton, *The Federalist Papers*, no. 84.

45 *San Antonio Independent School District v. Rodriguez*, 411 US 1 (1973).

46 See, for example, Michael Kent Curtis, *No State Shall Abridge: The Fourteenth Amendment and the Bill of Rights* (Durham, NC: Duke University Press, 1986).

47 See, for example, Raoul Berger, *Government by Judiciary: The Transformation of the Fourteenth Amendment* (Cambridge, MA: Harvard University Press, 1977).

48 *The Slaughterhouse Cases*, 83 US (16 Wallace) 36 (1873).

49 *Texas v. Johnson*, 491 US 397 (1989); *School District of Abington Township v. Schempp*, 374 US 203 (1963); *Gideon v. Wainwright*, 372 US 335 (1963); *Miranda v. Arizona*, 384 US 436 (1966); *Coker v. Georgia*, 433 US 584 (1977).

50 *Brown v. Board of Education of Topeka*, 347 US 483 (1954); *Reynolds v. Sims*, 377 US 533 (1964); *United States v. Virginia*, 518 US 515 (1996); *Grutter v. Bollinger*, 02-241 (2003).

51 *Roe v. Wade*, 410 US 113 (1973).

52 US Constitution, Article V.

53 Timothy M. Conlan, *From New Federalism to Devolution: Twenty-five Years of Intergovernmental Reform* (Washington, DC: The Brookings Institution, 1998); and David B. Walker, *Slouching Toward Washington: The Rebirth of Federalism* (Chatham, NJ: Chatham House, 1995).

54 See, for example, Alice M. Rivlin, *Reviving the American Dream: The Economy, the States, and the Federal Government* (Washington, DC: The Brookings Institution, 1992).

Comparative Observations

JOHN KINCAID

The 12 constitutions examined here are drawn from a universe of 25 federal countries.[1] The constitutions range from the oldest, that of the United States of America (1788), to the youngest, that of the Republic of South Africa (1996). The countries range from Australia, with only six constituent states, to Russia, with 89 "subjects of the federation," plus Belgium, with its double federation of three territorial regions and three nonterritorial language communities, making for five constituent units because Flanders is both a community and a region. The sample includes common-law and civil-law federations, parliamentary and nonparliamentary federations, and highly homogeneous (e.g., Germany) and highly heterogeneous (e.g., India) federal countries from around the world.

The sample illustrates the diversity of federal constitutionalism and the flexibility of the federal idea as it has been adapted to the circumstances of 12 countries. As such, each constitution reflects its country's history, culture, and political experiences as well as its population characteristics. There exists, therefore, no single model, or ideal, federal constitution but rather a range of designs from which constitution makers can draw ideas. The suitability of any design depends on the objectives of constitution makers and the circumstances they face when organizing a federal system of self-rule and shared rule.

FEDERALISM AND CONSTITUTIONALISM

The word "federal" comes from the Latin *foedus*, meaning "covenant." A covenant signifies a partnership, or marriage, in which individuals or groups voluntarily consent to unite for common purposes without giving up their fundamental rights or identities. A covenant represents a theological concept and political idea[2] that stands in contrast to (1) organic governments based on a common ancestor and (2) governments based on conquest – or what Alexander Hamilton in 1787 termed governments based on accident or on force rather than on "reflection and choice."[3]

Federalism and its related terms (e.g., federal and federation) refer to a type of government and governance that is established voluntarily to achieve unity while preserving diversity by constitutionally uniting separate political communities into a single limited, but encompassing, political community, such as a nation-state. Union may result from the aggregation of separate, even independent, political communities into a federation (e.g., the United States) or from the disaggregation or transformation of a unitary state into a *de jure* or *de facto* federal arrangement (e.g., Belgium and South Africa). Either way, power is divided and shared between (1) a general (federal or national) government that has certain area-wide (or nationwide) responsibilities, such as national defence and monetary policy, and (2) constituent territorial governments (e.g., states, provinces, *Länder*, republics, or cantons) that ordinarily have broad local responsibilities – such as education, land-use planning, highways, health care, and public safety – and that are also represented, often equally, in the federal legislature. Most federations have two orders of government: national and regional. A few (e.g., India, Nigeria, and South Africa) recognize municipal government as a third order.[4] Each order of government, moreover, is authorized to act directly on individuals (e.g., tax, fine, and regulate) within its sphere of authority.

Although, in principle, a federal union is voluntary, in practice, Hobbesian factors and coercive forces, along with positive incentives, also sustain a federation even in the face of disgruntlement on the part of some or all of the federation's constituent political communities. Indeed, in some circumstances, the political choices available are stark: either anarchy or tyranny if not federalism. Consequently, federal polities tend to be dynamic over time as various forces contest for more or less centralization within more or less unity.

One key dynamic in federalism is a contest between majority rule, which is needed for unity, and minority rights, which are needed for diversity. One major rationale for modern federalism first articulated by James Madison in *The Federalist* papers of 1787–88 is the need to restrain simple-majority rule in a large and heterogeneous nation-state so as to prevent the rise of a tyranny of the majority that crushes the rights of minorities or extinguishes their identities. A federal constitution, therefore, ordinarily constrains the rule of any simple national majority (i.e., 50 percent plus one), providing instead for (1) mechanisms of concurrent consent and super-majority rule intended to encourage consensus building, coupled with (2) separations of powers within governments and a division of powers among different autonomous or semiautonomous governments so as to block the concentration of power in any one official or government, along with (3) a high court authorized to resolve legal conflicts and safeguard the constitution.

At the same time, a federation needs to be concerned about majority or minority tyranny emerging in its constituent political communities, such as the existence of slavery in US southern states for the first 75 years of US history, followed by nearly a century of apartheid-like race segregation and oppression. Similarly, the application of strict Muslim *sharia* (law) – such as stoning women for adultery – in several northern states of Nigeria violates commonly accepted human-rights conventions.[5]

The desire of Canada's Francophone minority to protect its rights and preserve its cultural-linguistic identity in the face of the Anglophone majority is an example of a feature common to contemporary federations encompassing racial, cultural, ethnic, religious, and/or linguistic communities that have territorial bases. By contrast, South Africa's constitution makers sought to empower the country's black racial majority after decades of white-minority rule while still protecting everyone from any oppressive majority rule. In more homogeneous federations such as Germany, Mexico, and the United States, the intention, even if not always fulfilled, is to frustrate tyrannical national rule by any single political party or interest group, whether it represent a majority or a minority of the population.

A federal system ordinarily requires a written constitution[6] because a federation is based on a voluntary agreement, which, like any important agreement, is best placed in writing. A constitution also is essential because a federation consists of political communities with different cultures, customs, preferences, and political institutions. Quite often, moreover, a federation encompasses a large territory and/or population. An unwritten constitution, such as that classically attributed to Great Britain, is unsuitable for a federal system because in order to be effective, an unwritten constitution requires shared customs rooted in a common history. Moreover, a written constitution is needed because, in principle, a federation has no inherent powers of its own; it is the creation of the federating units. In practice, of course, there may be a pre-existing regime, but discarding or transforming this regime is likely to require a constitution-writing process. In addition, a written constitution serves to set forth the division and sharing of powers among the federation's orders of government.

A constitution is usually intended to be a fundamental or organic law that embodies a country's basic choices about the purposes, powers, limits, institutions, organization, and operation of its government or governments. A constitution designates public offices, stipulates how they are filled, and allocates powers and responsibilities among these offices. A constitution also serves as a basic norm intended to be binding[7] and is thus a legal mechanism for integration as well. Most important, a constitution establishes the key relationships between the people and their governments, including representation. As originally conceived in the eighteenth century, a constitution was deemed necessary to protect individual rights and personal autonomy against rapacious officials. Thus constitutions place limits on the exercise of power, in part by listing unalienable rights. However, by the twentieth century, a constitution came to be seen also as a mechanism to empower rather than merely to restrain government, especially in order to ensure governmental capacity to provide for social justice and social welfare.

CONSTITUTIONAL GOALS AND PURPOSES

Federal constitutions are framed for a variety of reasons and purposes. Constitution making in Brazil, India, Mexico, Nigeria, and the United States followed the end of colonialism as efforts to maintain unity and establish federal democracy. Some federal constitutions seek to create a democratic order in the aftermath of a history of dictatorship, as in Russia in 1993 and South Africa in 1996. Other federal constitutions are framed to restore a democratic constitutional order, as in Germany in 1949, Brazil in 1988, and Nigeria in 1999. Still other constitutions, such as those of Australia and Canada, reflect rather pragmatic reasons for federation, while others, such as those of Belgium and Switzerland, reflect evolutionary processes of holding together quite different cultural communities.

A common objective of all the federal constitutions is to build a modern nation-state. Indeed, if one takes the founding of the United States as marking the birth of modern federalism as distinguished from premodern confederalism, then modern federalism is aimed at nation-state construction and maintenance. Virtually all federal constitutions aspire to perpetual union. Federalism, of course, is not the only way to build a nation-state, and it is not even the prevalent way, but it may be the appropriate nation-building choice wherever a heterogeneous population and/or large territory and population militate against unitary democratic governance. It is this nation-state orientation that helps to account for trends toward centralization in many federations as well as for the tensions that occur within multinational federations, where construction of a nation-state can remain contested and controversial.

A key purpose of a federal constitution is to establish a stable framework of fundamental law that enables federalism and democracy to work peacefully and effectively over the long term even in the face of pressures for constitutional degradation. For this purpose, institutional design is important, as is the process by which a federal constitution is framed and adopted. Generally, there is a need for good-faith bargaining and negotiation among all relevant actors in an environment of trust, moderation, and pragmatic problem-solving.

Indeed, the objectives to be achieved and problems to be solved in framing a federal constitution are crucial in determining constitutional choices and in designing institutions. Constitutional choices are quite different if the predominant objective is to achieve a common defence, economic development, national unity, the coexistence of cultural communities, a restoration of democracy, or something else. In some cases, the objectives are stated clearly in the constitution, as in the Preamble to the US Constitution and the Preamble to the Indian Constitution. The latter preamble is quite precise in its stated intention to establish "a Sovereign, Socialist, Secular, Democratic Republic." Other constitutions, such as those of Australia, Belgium, and Mexico, do not have clear, formally stated objectives; instead, objectives are embedded in the constitution's design.

In most cases, the participants in the framing of a federal constitution have different objectives. Some might give priority to national unity; others might emphasize the coexistence of cultural communities; still others might emphasize economic development. It may be necessary, therefore, for the framers of a constitution to agree to disagree on certain matters so as to move forward on matters of agreement that will achieve unity and establish institutions to facilitate long-term conflict resolution on other matters. This is another reason why there is no ideal, or model, federal constitution; most federal constitutions have an eclectic character that reflects compromised constitutional choices and value tradeoffs made among actors who have different objectives and who look at different federal constitutions for guidance.[8]

Indeed, a common characteristic of federal constitution-making is that the framers examine existing constitutions for ideas. Today, as well, a number of developed federations, such as Canada, Germany, and Switzerland, promote federal constitutionalism. However, striking characteristics of modern federal constitutions are the legacy of (1) the British colonial tradition, which fostered federal orientations in Australia, Canada, India, Nigeria, South Africa, the United States, and elsewhere, along with (2) the influences of the positive and negative effects of the US Constitution on federal constitution-making in Australia, Brazil, Canada, Germany, Mexico, Nigeria, Switzerland, and elsewhere.

One classical view of the reasons for federation is that the "politicians who offer the [federal] bargain desire to expand their territorial control, usually ... to meet an external military or diplomatic threat," while those "who accept the bargain, giving up some independence for the sake of union, ... do so because of some external military-diplomatic threat or opportunity."[9] These reasons follow from the nation-state premise of modern federalism, but they can also be regarded as a truism because peace and security are necessarily among the objectives of every federal constitution and thus one of the reasons why all or most important foreign-affairs and defence powers are assigned to the national government in a federation. However, these defence reasons fail to explain why a federal constitution is much more than a peace pact and why federal constitutions are dominated by matters that have nothing to do with foreign affairs and defence. Most federal constitutions framed in recent decades have not been motivated by foreign-affairs and defence concerns. Even the US Constitution – the oldest – seeks, in addition to "domestic Tranquility" and a "common defence," to "establish Justice, ... promote the general Welfare, and secure the Blessings of Liberty to ourselves and our Posterity."[10]

Whereas liberty was a prominent objective of the American founders, the establishment or restoration of freedom, democracy, and a republican form of government stands out as a frequent objective of post-Second World War federal constitutions, beginning with Germany in 1949, where federalism was seen, in part, as a structural barrier to a revival of totalitarianism. Not every federal constitution achieves this objective, but the objective is not mere rhetoric.

Another common objective is to foster economic development through the creation of a common market. Consequently, federal constitutions ordinarily vest common-market powers in the national government and seek to lower and eliminate trade and mobility barriers between the federation's constituent political communities. The social-welfare orientation of most federal constitution-makers also produces mechanisms for wealth redistribution (e.g., fiscal equalization) among the federation's constituent political communities in efforts to alleviate poverty and promote even economic development across the federation.

At least half of the federal constitutions – Belgium, Canada, India, Nigeria, Russia, and Switzerland – examined in this volume reflect, as a predominant objective, efforts to accommodate territorially based racial, ethnic, religious, cultural, and/or linguistic diversity and thus to preserve cultural identities along with national unity. The Preamble to the Swiss Constitution, for instance, states the intention of the cantons "to live together with our diversities, with respect for one another and in equity." By giving a country's diverse cultural communities some guaranteed share of national political power coupled with (1) some measure of local self-governing autonomy and (2) procedures for continual negotiation, consultation, and dispute-resolution, a federal constitutional arrangement can, potentially over time, short-circuit secession, dull the sharp edges of militant communalism, foster political and socio-economic integration of cultural communities, and reinforce the constitutional rule of law.

The desire for accommodation can come from cultural minorities that insist on federalism as the price of national unity or from a national majority seeking to construct or maintain national unity against centrifugal forces. Either way, success is likely to require that the positive incentives pulling communities together outweigh both the negative incentives pushing communities together and the counter-incentives pulling communities apart.

However, federations formed mainly around territorially based cultural diversity usually experience recurring rounds, and sometimes crises, of centrifugal versus centripetal pressures. Such federations can also break apart at the first opening of a window of political opportunity (e.g., the former Czechoslovakia, Yugoslavia, and Union of Soviet Socialist Republics). In situations of fractious cultural diversity, those in control of the national government, whether they represent a national majority or minority, may fear that a federal constitution will institutionalize a pathway to fragmentation and secession by draining power and electoral support from the centre and perhaps, as well, opening a Pandora's Box of communal-autonomy claims.

Opponents of federalism, therefore, seize on the examples of failed multicultural federations, especially the bloody break-up of Yugoslavia, in order to discredit federalism. Yet these failed federations were, from the outset, shotgun federations constructed by conquest and held together by an authoritarian political party not democratically accountable to the people. By contrast, the stable and democratic multicultural federations are rooted much more in voluntarism and sustained by virtually continual bargaining and negotiation. Of course, in some situations, militant communalism may reject any offer of a federal bargain and demand, instead, complete national independence. Nevertheless, where federalism is a potential remedy for fractious multiculturalism, there are successful examples from which constitution makers can draw valuable ideas.

A few federal constitutions contain directive principles setting forth instructions for government to pursue certain objectives and ideals, such as the principles of economic and social democracy inscribed in India's Constitution. Nigeria's Constitution contains objectives and principles emphasizing the sovereignty of the people and the idea that government exists to serve the wellbeing of the people pursuant to principles of democracy and social justice. The Constitution also obligates the federal government to promote national integration by providing adequate facilities for and encouraging the free interstate mobility of people, goods, and services; securing full resident rights for every citizen everywhere in Nigeria; encouraging intermarriage among different religious, ethnic, linguistic, and territorial groups; and fostering a sense of belonging and loyalty to the nation that overrides sectional and sectarian loyalties.

Such principles are ordinarily hortatory and not justiciable. Consequently, even though they reflect admirable, agreed-upon aspirations, they are likely to be difficult to realize in practice. Indeed, their very presence in the constitution suggests an attempt to institutionalize on parchment principles and objectives deemed essential for good federal governance but recognized as being only weakly institutionalized in a country's political culture.

A few constitutions also set forth fundamental duties for citizens, such as the obligations of Indian citizens "to abide by the Constitution and respect its ideals and institutions, the National Flag and the National Anthem" and "to safeguard public property and to abjure violence." The Mexican Constitution, which distinguishes between nationals and citizens, stipulates certain duties for each. For example, citizens must, among other things, register on their municipality's tax list, be willing to serve in elected offices, and "fulfill electoral and jury functions."

CHARACTERISTICS OF FEDERAL CONSTITUTIONS

Most federal constitutions are not the product of a big-bang creation but rather of a long gestation, often involving previous successful and unsuccessful constitutional experiences. The US Constitution, for instance, was preceded by the Articles of Confederation of 1781, earlier nonconstitutional agreements of union (e.g., the Continental Congress), 18 state constitutions, and hundreds of regional and local constitution-like documents forged in the colonies for some 170 years. Canada's Constitution Act 1982 followed five earlier constitutional arrangements dating back to the Royal Proclamation of 1763, while Switzerland's Constitution of 1848 reflected 575 years of confederal development involving numerous alliance treaties among various cantons dating back to the *antiqua confoederatio* of 1273. In these and other countries (e.g., Belgium and Germany), previous developments contributed to comparatively successful, contemporary, constitutional, federal democracies.

More problematic are, for example, Brazil's current seventh constitution and Nigeria's current fifth constitution, both of which followed failed constitutions, disruptions of democracy, and military *coups d'état*. Some newer federal constitutions, such as those of Russia (1993) and South Africa (1996), had, by necessity, shorter gestations, although the framers of these constitutions had the benefit of the experiences of many successful and unsuccessful federal arrangements around the world. These newer constitutions, moreover, have yet to withstand the tests of time.

By comparison, two stable, peaceful, and democratic federations – Canada and Switzerland – have important constituent political communities that have not ratified the federal constitution, namely Quebec in Canada and six[11] of Switzerland's 26 cantons, which have never accepted any of modern Switzerland's three constitutions. The 1848 Constitution was rejected by eight cantons; the 1874 Constitution was rejected by ten cantons; and the 1999 Constitution was rejected by twelve cantons. Yet the Swiss and Canadian federations are widely regarded as models of success!

Some federal constitutions are short (e.g., the US Constitution); others are long and complex, such as that of India (the longest), where the challenge of establishing a constitution for a highly diverse nation-state of continental size posed issues never previously addressed by Western constitutionalists. For postcolonial nations, moreover, a constitution is an important symbol of national independence. In turn, some constitutions demonstrate remarkable endurance, such as the 217-year-old US Constitution, which is the world's oldest written national constitution still in operation (and with only 27 amendments). Other constitutions have brief, undistinguished lives. Although Thomas Jefferson argued that a country should adopt a new constitution every 19 years so as to ensure that each living generation is not governed by the dead hand of the past, virtually all constitutional framers have concluded that such frequent change would foster factionalism, incite conflict, perpetuate instability, and undermine democratic government. Instead, framers seek to establish multigenerational stability, but without rigidity, in a federal constitution.

The extent to which a constitution is revered also varies among federal countries. In the United States, the federal Constitution is so highly revered that it is often regarded as the nation's third sacred text, following the Bible and the Declaration of Independence (1776). By contrast, in Australia, the federal Constitution is accorded no particular reverence or even attention by most citizens. Similarly, the extent to which the federal constitution is viewed as a superior law or higher law varies across federations. Generally, the constitution is more likely to be regarded as a higher law where it performs a crucial legitimating function for the federal polity, where statutes can be struck down as violations of the constitution, and where the constitution is not subject to excessive amendment.

Multilayered Hierarchy of Values

An often overlooked characteristic of federal constitutions is their multilayered nature, beginning with a hierarchy of values within the constitution and extending outward to laws, documents, and judicial rulings of a quasi- or para-constitutional nature. Many federal constitutions contain a hierarchy of values that is protected by rules of amendment. That is, in the first place, some provisions (e.g., the German Basic Law's "eternity clause")[12] cannot be amended at all. Some other provisions, while not specifically exempted from amendment, are structured in a manner that makes their amendment virtually unimaginable politically, such as equal representation of each constituent unit in one chamber of the national legislature.

Usually, the provisions immune to amendment are those that concern rights and the federal order. The "eternity clause" in Germany's Basic Law protects the division of the country into *Länder*, the participation of the *Länder* in federation legislation, and basic principles stipulated in Articles 1 and 20 regarding such matters as the separation of powers, protection of human dignity and rights, the rule of law, democracy, and the welfare state. In India, the supremacy of the Constitution, the republican and democratic form of the government, the secular character of the Constitution and secular nature of the state, the separation of powers, and the federal character of the Constitution are regarded as not subject to amendment. In Brazil, amendments cannot be considered to abolish the federal system, the separation of powers, the direct secret ballot, and individual rights. In short, federal constitutions treat federalism not as transitory or transitional but as permanent.

Nevertheless, a number of federal constitutions provide for two or more methods of amending various constitutional provisions, each of decreasing difficulty. Changing some provisions requires a super-majority vote in the legislature, while changing others requires only a simple-majority vote. Likewise, some amendments require the consent of some portion of the constituent political communities, whereas others do not.

The hierarchy of values is often protected as well by rules for super-majority votes (e.g., two-thirds or three-fourths) on certain matters and by requirements for concurrent (or dual or double) majority votes on certain matters. Such rules reflect the general orientation of federal constitutions away from simple majority rule and toward rules of governance that favour super-majoritarian or consensus-based decision-making as a means of protecting minorities and promoting unity.

Another facet of this layering is the extent to which international human-rights law features prominently in some post-1945 federal constitutions (e.g., Germany and South Africa). In South Africa, any court must "consider international law"[13] when interpreting the bill of rights, and priority must be given to interpreting domestic law in conformity with international law whenever possible. These international conventions did not exist when the US Constitution was drafted in 1787, but the Declaration of Independence came to be regarded, especially subsequent to the presidency of Abraham Lincoln (1861–65), as the higher legal mandate for the Constitution. Other important rules may likewise lie outside the constitution, such as the Australia Act 1986, which renounced British sovereignty. In Belgium, special para-constitutional laws specify the details of powers devolved to the regions and communities in light of basic principles expressed in the Constitution. Brazil's Constitution provides for Congress to enact "supplementary laws" in order to carry out certain provisions, such as the conditions for executing concurrent powers.

In some federations, such as the United States, state or provincial constitutions may complete the national constitution in the sense that the national constitution cannot operate without the aid of the institutions and functions established by the state constitutions.[14] Lastly, most federations have a body of constitutional law, contained in judicial decisions, that interprets the national constitution as well as, in a few countries, the state or provincial constitutions. In summary, then, the complete operational constitution of a federation is rarely a single, seamless, uniform document.

Federal-Specific Provisions

In addition to matters addressed by all constitutions, a federal constitution must (1) determine what the constituent units (e.g., states, provinces, or cantons) are and whether there is to be two or three orders of government, (2) set forth the extent of the constituent units' territorial integrity and self-governing autonomy or sovereignty, (3) provide for the admission of new political communities to the union, (4) determine the role of the constituent units in the composition and operation of the national government, (5) provide mechanisms and institutions for accountability to the people by all orders of government, (6) provide for the representation of both individual citizens and the constituent political communities in national-government institutions, (7) distribute powers (or competences) among the orders of government, (8) determine which powers are to be exclusive to each order and which are to be explicitly or implicitly concurrent, (9) conclude where residual powers lie, (10) establish institutions and/or mechanisms to resolve conflicts between the orders of government, especially over the distribution of powers, (11) provide rules for intergovernmental (e.g., federal, provincial, local) and interjurisdictional (e.g., interprovincial and interlocal) relations and mutual obligations, (12) stipulate the supremacy of federal law within the national government's sphere of constitutional authority, (13) provide for a minimum standard of human-rights protections to be guaranteed by the federal government and by all the constituent governments, (14) provide for a high court to umpire or police the division and sharing of powers among the orders of government, and (15) set forth amendment procedures that protect the hierarchy of values chosen by the framers and that strike a balance between constitutional stability and constitutional adaptability to historical change.

At the same time, most of the federal constitutions also contain provisions that are dead, ineffective, or in abeyance. In Canada, for instance, the federal government has the authority to reject provincial legislation through powers of reservation and disallowance. The federal government used these powers in the past, but their use was discontinued by custom. Most federal constitutions also have sleeper provisions that appear innocuous or inconsequential at first but rise to prominence later in the federation's history. Using a Canadian example again, the federal government's spending power eventually became a vehicle for what many provincial officials regard as federal-government intrusions into traditional areas of provincial jurisdiction.

Sources of Legitimate Authority

The sovereign source or sources of power to enact a constitution vary across federal countries. The "We the People" formulation in the US Constitution locates sovereignty in the people, but there is contested ambiguity as to whether "We the People" means the entire people of the whole United States or the different peoples of the 50 separate states. The US Constitution was not ratified by a national referendum but by a popularly elected convention in each state. The constitutions of Brazil, India, and Mexico are regarded as emanating from the people of the nation-state as a whole. The Russian Constitution does not recognize any source of power other than the multinational people of Russia; therefore, the only sovereignty presumed is that of the federation. The federation's sovereignty precludes the existence of two orders of sovereign power, each enjoying independence in a single system of state power; consequently, it does not allow for even "limited" sovereignty on the part of republics or of any other unit of the federation. Similarly, in India, the union is not seen as having come into existence as the result of a covenant or compact among the states because the states possessed no sovereignty prior to the union.

Meanwhile, Belgium's Constitution is seen as emanating from the nation, not directly from the people. The Swiss Constitution is, in effect, a compact among the individuals who constitute the whole people of Switzerland as well as a compact among the separate peoples of the cantons. In Canada, there are contested views as to whether the constitution is, or should be, a compact between two peoples (i.e., the English and the French), a compact among multiple peoples (i.e., the Aboriginals, the English, and the French), a compact among ten provinces and three territories, or a compact among the whole people of Canada.

Only a few federal constitutions, such as those of Australia and Switzerland, were submitted to the people as a whole and/or to the peoples of the constituent political communities for final approval by referendum. In recent decades, there has been a trend to convene a special constituent or constitutional assembly, usually elected, to draft a constitution and engage in widespread public consultations rather than having a constitution drafted by a regular legislative body or handed down by a monarch. Final adoption might involve a regular, national, legislative body and/or the legislative bodies in some or all of the constituent political communities.

NATIONAL CONTENTS OF FEDERAL CONSTITUTIONS

All federal constitutions contain provisions that apply nationwide, apply throughout the intergovernmental order, distribute powers, establish national-government institutions, provide for the operation of national institutions, and so on.

Rights

Except for Australia,[15] all of the constitutions examined here list protected civil rights (e.g., freedoms of speech and religion), procedural rights (especially with respect to criminal justice), and political rights (e.g., the rights to vote and hold public office). The rights protected in these three categories are fairly similar across the constitutions, although there are some variations. Property rights, for example, are protected in some constitutions (e.g., Germany) but not in others (e.g., Canada). There also are some variations in emphasis, such as very stringent provisions on separation of church and state in Mexico's Constitution. In addition, several constitutions (e.g., Germany and Mexico) incorporate international human-rights conventions, such as the United Nations Declaration of Human Rights and the European Convention on the Protection of Human Rights.

Several constitutions – namely those of Brazil, Nigeria, Russia, South Africa, and Switzerland – incorporate a fourth set of rights, commonly called social rights. These include, among others, rights to education, health care, housing, work, leisure, and the like. For example, various economic and cultural rights are fixed in the Russian Constitution, such as the right to collective bargaining and the right to strike; the right to social security in old age and in cases of disease, handicap, or loss of family wage earner; the right to bring up one's own children; the right to free health care and medical assistance; the right to education; and the right to participate in cultural life, to use the institutions of culture, and to retain cultural values. These social rights, however, are often difficult to implement and to adjudicate. The Swiss Constitution sets forth a few social rights (e.g., a right to basic education) but then sets forth several social objectives (e.g., social-security and health-care guarantees) that do not confer any special rights to government services. Thus social-rights declarations are often more hortatory than mandatory, although a few high courts, such as that of South Africa, have attempted to enforce such rights.

Many of the federal constitutions provide for the national suspension of certain rights in times of emergency. The US Constitution, for instance, permits suspension of the writ of *habeas corpus* in times of rebellion or invasion, but no other rights are subject to suspension, at least constitutionally. A variation on this theme is the notwithstanding clause in Canada's 1982 Charter of Rights and Freedoms. This clause permits provinces to opt out of certain rights provisions by allowing a provincial law to operate for five-year renewable periods "notwithstanding" certain Charter rights. Not subject to this clause, however, are democratic rights, mobility rights, and language rights.

Interestingly, in light of federalism's commitment to diversity, there are few direct or explicit protections of group or communal rights in the 12 federal constitutions treated in this volume. Instead, there is an emphasis on individual rights, including individual rights to speak a language and retain a culture. Although South Africa's Constitution, for example, recognizes the "right of self-determination of any community sharing a common cultural and language heritage," there is not only a strong emphasis on individual rights befitting the leading framers' commitment to majoritarian democracy but also a tinge of hostility toward group or communal rights due to the country's apartheid history. Instead, therefore, group rights are usually protected indirectly via the freedoms of association, speech, religion, and the like. Otherwise, group rights are protected structurally through representation, regional and local self-government, power-sharing, service-provision rules, and the like.

Distribution of Powers, or Competences

Every federal constitution must determine a distribution of powers, especially the powers to be exercised by the national government. Certain powers can be delegated exclusively to one or more orders of government, while certain other powers can be regarded as concurrent – that is, capable of being exercised by both the national government and the constituent governments. A federal constitution also ordinarily stipulates the jurisdictional location of the residual powers, namely legitimate powers that might be exercised by a government but are not listed in the constitution.

Powers commonly assigned, mostly exclusively, to national governments in federations include intranational and international trade and commerce, national currency and monetary policy, the central bank, customs and excise duties, value-added taxes (VAT) and income taxes, foreign affairs, national defence, postal services, patents and copyrights, weights and measures, social welfare, citizenship determination, immigration, major public utilities, certain natural resources, criminal law, and aviation. Of course, a much wider variety of powers is differentially assigned to national governments across federations, making an accurate generalization impossible.

Some federal constitutions (e.g., Russia, India, and Nigeria) contain an explicit list of concurrent powers. Among the concurrent (or joint) powers listed in Russia's Constitution, for example, are establishing general guidelines for organizing the institutions of government power and local self-government; regulating possession, use, and management of land, mineral resources, water, and other natural resources; delimiting state property; protecting historical and cultural monuments; addressing general questions of youth socialization, education, science, culture, physical culture, and sports; establishing general guidelines for taxation and levies in the federation; and protecting the original environment and the traditional way of life of small ethnic communities. Both the federal and subject governments can legislate in the fields of administration, administrative procedure, labour, family, housing, land, water, and forestry as well as legislate on sub-surface matters (e.g., minerals) and environmental protection. In Canada there is concurrency with respect to agriculture, forest products, electricity, exportation of nonrenewable energy resources, immigration, and senior-citizen pensions and benefits. In other federal constitutions, such as the US Constitution, there is no list of concurrent powers, but there is, nevertheless, a huge field of politically and judicially accepted concurrency (e.g., the federal government and 42 states levy income taxes entirely independently of each, other). In other cases, such as that of Belgium, there are no truly concurrent powers; instead, the federal system is highly dualistic.

Too much dualism, however, can stifle intergovernmental cooperation and coordination as in Brazil and, potentially, as in Belgium, where there is a high need for coordination and where the system tends to compel cooperation as the only way in which the various orders of government can accomplish their tasks. At the same time, too much cooperation and concurrency can, as in Germany, impede efficient decision-making and even produce gridlock.

In matters within the concurrent or joint jurisdiction of a federation and its constituent units, federal law is almost invariably supreme, and the constituent governments may adopt only laws and regulations that are consistent with federal law. In Canada, however, there is one area of concurrency, old-age pensions and supplementary benefits, where provincial law has paramountcy (so that Quebec can maintain its own pension system). In South Africa, the Constitution attempts to put some constraints on the national government by stipulating that national law usually, but not always, overrides a conflicting provincial law, depending on circumstances.

As a result, the widespread experience in the federations analyzed here is that concurrent powers have served as vehicles for expanding federal power. Although usually, in principle, the national government is intended to enact only framework legislation within concurrent fields, national governments tend to enact increasingly detailed legislation that progressively circumscribes the discretion of the constituent governments, as has been evident, for example, in Germany, India, Mexico, Russia, and South Africa. Indeed, in Mexico, the federal government long sought to expand the concurrent list so that it could, like the proverbial camel's nose in the tent, intrude upon constituent-state powers. (In India, the Union Parliament can even enact laws under certain circumstances in areas of power delegated to the states.) This expansion of federal power through concurrency appears to be enhanced in federations where the national government captures most of the federation's tax revenue and then redistributes revenue to the constituent governments.

A related trend appears to be the growth of federal criminal law in most of the federations examined here, even where criminal law has been exclusively or substantially a constituent-government responsibility. In 1798 Thomas Jefferson pointed out in opposition to the recently enacted federal Alien and Sedition Acts that the US Constitution "delegated to Congress a power to punish treason, counterfeiting the securities and current coin of the United States, piracies and felonies committed on the high seas, and offenses against the laws of nations, and no other crimes whatever."[16] Today there are more than 3,000 federal criminal statutes, including some 50 death-penalty statutes. In the United States, this growth in federal criminal-law is partly the result of members of Congress seeking to present themselves to the voters as being "tough on crime"; however, more generally, modern technological, corporate, and international developments appear to be driving this trend, a trend that could be accelerated by terrorism. In Mexico, however, there has been some agitation to give the states more criminal-law functions in order to increase criminal-justice efficiency and effectiveness.

A further refinement on the distribution of powers is that in contrast to Australia, Canada, and the United States, for example, where each government has executive or administrative powers adequate to give effect to its own legislative powers so that neither order is dependent on the other to carry out its will, in some other federations, such as Germany, India, and Switzerland, there is a constitutional separation between the federal government's legislative powers and the authority to implement federal legislation. That is, while the federal government is empowered to enact legislation in various, usually domestic and concurrent, policy fields, the legislation must be executed or administered by the constituent governments. Thus legislative power is substantially centralized, while administrative power is decentralized.

Another contemporary aspect of the distribution of powers is that it can be either symmetrical or asymmetrical. In a symmetrical distribution, which characterizes all but one (i.e., Russia) of the 12 federations – although India is a partial exception, too – the full-fledged constituent political communities are on an equal footing in terms of having the same constitutionally assigned and/or residual powers and the same status before the national government. In an asymmetrical distribution, the constituent political communities are not on an equal footing, and some have more constitutional and/or residual powers than others. However, it is not uncommon for certain *de facto* asymmetries to emerge over time in a federation characterized by constitutional symmetry.

The residual powers lie with the constituent political communities in Australia, Brazil, Germany, Mexico, Nigeria, Russia, Switzerland, and the United States. The residual powers lie with the national government in Canada, India, and South Africa – all three of which were motivated by centralizing objectives at their founding. In Belgium, the residual powers actually lie with the national government even though the Constitution says that they lie with the regions and communities. Although the residual powers lie with the states in Brazil, the federal Constitution is so detailed that little room is left for state discretion.

The location of the residual powers was once believed to be crucial because the holder of the residual powers was presumed perpetually to be in a situation enabling it to sustain and expand its powers vis-à-vis the other order or orders of government. Experience suggests, however, that this is rarely so. In Mexico the states' possession of residual powers could not counteract the country's long history of highly centralized, one-party, presidential rule. In Canada, the residual powers were lodged in the federal government as part of an effort to create a centralized federation. Today Canada is widely agreed to be one of the most noncentralized federations. In contrast, the US states insisted on holding the residual powers; yet, the US federal system has become highly centralized in most respects. In both Canada and the United States, residual powers proved to be elusive because courts interpreted specified enumerated powers broadly and unspecified residual powers narrowly.

Fiscal and Monetary Powers

Given that he or she who pays the piper calls the tune, the distribution of tax, spending, and borrowing powers is of crucial, often decisive, importance. Among the 12 federations treated herein, there is tremendous variation with respect to the details of their fiscal systems, but generally, either by constitutional design, historical development, and/or constituent-government preference, the national government in most federations captures the largest portion, sometimes the lion's share, of total tax revenues. In Australia, for instance, the Commonwealth government garners nearly 82 percent of the federation's tax revenue. Although tax powers in all federations are allocated to the national, constituent, and local governments so that each order of government can raise at least some portion of its own revenue, local governments usually have the least own-source revenue-raising authority, followed by the constituent governments.

The major taxes are corporation taxes, personal income taxes, consumption taxes (e.g., a VAT and a sales tax), excise and customs duties, and property or real-estate taxes. Customs duties and excise taxes are ordinarily assigned exclusively to the federal government. All the other major taxes are assigned exclusively or concurrently to the federal, state, and local governments, with property taxation being a common local tax power. However, even where there is concurrent tax authority, the federal government frequently gets the tax's largest share of revenue; in some cases (e.g., Brazil), the federal government also determines the rates and rules for state and local tax levies.

Consequently, every federation engages in fiscal transfers, with the national government ordinarily being the source of the largest transfers to its constituent and/or local governments. In turn, state, provincial, and

cantonal governments ordinarily transfer revenues to their local governments. Many federal constitutions mandate that the national government
must share certain revenues with the constituent and/or local governments. In Germany, for instance, revenues from certain taxes, such as income and corporation taxes, accrue jointly to the federation, the *Länder*,
and the municipalities. Other fiscal transfers in a federation are undertaken at the discretion of the national government. Essentially, such transfers can be unconditional or conditional (matters that are sometimes
stipulated in the constitution). Unconditional transfers allow the recipient
government to spend the funds as it sees fit. Conditional transfers require
the recipient to spend the funds in a manner and on matters stipulated by
the national government. Leaders of the constituent political communities
usually prefer unconditional transfers. In turn, some fiscal transfers may
not require the recipient government to put up any funds of its own; other
transfers may require the recipient government to put up matching funds
of some proportion from its own revenues. Some fiscal transfers may be
distributed on a simple per-government or per-capita basis; other transfers
may be distributed according to highly complex and often contested formulas. Occasionally, some fiscal transfers are competitive; that is, receipt of
the funds depends on submitting a successful grant proposal.

Except for the United States, all of the federations examined here engage
in some type of fiscal equalization – that is, a redistribution of revenues
(usually from the federal government but also from wealthy *Länder* in Germany) to poor constituent governments in order to ensure that all constituent governments can provide comparable or equal levels of public services
at comparable levels of tax costs to citizens. Just how equalizing the equalization program is varies across federations. Some programs are based on
an agreed formula (e.g., in Belgium, Canada, Germany, and Switzerland),
while others (e.g., in Australia, India, and Nigeria) are based on periodic
recommendations of permanent or temporary, and usually independent,
commissions. Nigeria's Constitution established a fiscal-equity commission,
the Revenue Mobilization Allocation and Fiscal Commission, that must "review, from time to time, the revenue allocation formulae and principles in
operation [for the states] to ensure conformity with changing realities."

Fiscal equalization is undertaken overtly for equity reasons; however,
such programs are often referred to as "solidarity" or "cohesion" policies
because they function as the fiscal glue of national unity. As such, fiscal
equalization can also be viewed as covert bribery whereby wealthy constituent units entice poorer units to remain in the federation or, alternately, as
covert extortion whereby independence-minded constituent political communities extract redistributive payments as a price for peace or union.
Thus safeguards are crucial to ensuring that constituent governments do
not substitute transfer funds for own-source revenues, thereby delivering

services at an artificially low tax price; that funds given to the governments of poor places actually help poor people; and that fiscal equalization does not reward indolence and therefore retard necessary economic development or migration out of poor jurisdictions.

Generally, intergovernmental fiscal transfers pose issues of accountability and responsibility because the spending decision is separated from the taxing decision. That is, the more that the politicians who enjoy the electoral pleasure of spending tax money must first experience the electoral pain of extracting it from the taxpayers, the more their fiscal behaviour is likely to be responsible and subject to voter accountability. Indeed, this appears to be one factor in the revenue predominance of national governments in most federations. The elected officials of the constituent governments are often content, even eager, to allow the federal government to make the major tax decisions so long as the federal government is generous about sharing its revenues. In some federations (e.g., Australia with respect to the income tax), the constituent governments even refuse to exercise certain revenue authority, preferring instead to leave tax collection to the federal government in return for a share (preferably an unconditional share) of the revenues.

Other tax issues include whether there are rules of intergovernmental tax immunity preventing the national government and the constituent governments from taxing each other's instrumentalities, rules of nondiscrimination ensuring that federal taxes do not discriminate between constituent political communities or parts of those communities, rules of nondiscriminatory taxation between constituent units, and rules governing extraterritorial taxation by the constituent governments.

Rules covering government borrowing also vary among federations. In some, such as the United States, the federal government and the states borrow independently, with each establishing its own rules for its own borrowing. In turn, each order of government is responsible for its own debt and for any problems created by excessive or irresponsible borrowing. Likewise, in Australia, both the federal government and the states can borrow independently, but borrowing must be disclosed fully and subject to oversight by a national Loan Council. In many federations, the national government is authorized to regulate and limit constituent-government borrowing, and in some, constituent governments are prohibited from borrowing directly from foreign sources. A key issue, however, is whether the national government is legally obligated or politically obliged to assume the debt service of defaulting subnational governments because, in the absence of adequate controls, subnational governments are likely to borrow excessively whenever the national government has default duties.

Another source of revenue consists of state enterprises, public corporations, parastatals, and the like. Where such entities exist in a federation, they are likely to be established by the constituent governments and local governments in addition to the national government. However, globalization and economic liberalization have been driving many such entities out of existence or into the private sector.

Rarely subject to sharing is monetary policy. The constituent political communities may have some role in influencing monetary policy through their representatives in the national government and through political pressure, but monetary policy is normally a national-government power, much of which is usually assigned to an independent central bank.

Centralization

The federal constitutions represented in this volume vary significantly in terms of centralization, decentralization, and noncentralization. Constitutionally, Australia, Belgium, Canada, Germany, Switzerland, and the United States can be said to be noncentralized in the sense that "the powers of government within them are diffused among many centers, whose existence and authority are guaranteed by the general constitution, rather than being concentrated in a single center"[17] having unilateral authority to centralize or decentralize the federal system. Brazil, India, Mexico, Nigeria, Russia, and South Africa operate along a centralization-decentralization continuum whereby the constitution and/or the operation of the federal system was designed to be centralized or pushed toward centralization. Countries undertaking major social and economic transformations (e.g., Brazil, India, Nigeria, and South Africa, plus Russia under Vladimir Putin) often choose centralized federalism out of beliefs that a strong centre is necessary to guiding the transformation, driving political integration, promoting economic development, redistributing wealth, and maintaining peace and good order. Several countries (e.g., India and Mexico) have been moving toward decentralization in recent years, while Putin appears to have engineered an exponential increase in centralization in Russia.

In the essentially noncentralized federations, there are, nevertheless, trends toward decentralization or centralization, too. Australia, Germany, Switzerland, and the United States moved, to varying degrees and at variable speeds, in a centralizing direction during much of the twentieth century, while Belgium and Canada moved in a decentralizing direction after the 1950s. Factors that foster centralization include federal dominance of tax revenues, national-government use of its spending powers, expansive interpretations of federal powers by courts and politicians, national-government use of its foreign-affairs powers (e.g., the treaty power), and constituent-government agitation, as well as citizen agitation, for increasing uniformity of policies (e.g., business regulation) nationwide and for national-government

action to solve social problems. Generally, decentralization is more characteristic of multicultural federations where one or more constituent cultural
communities constantly insist on enhancing their own self-rule.

Perhaps even more important is the role of political-party systems in fostering centralization and decentralization.[18] For example, one-party rule
in Mexico for most of the twentieth century produced highly centralized
federal governance. In India, where Congress was the dominant party until
1988, the federal system was decidedly centralized, but the federal system
moved in a decentralizing direction when the Congress party lost national-
majority power, regional and state-based parties entered the political
arena, and coalition governments emerged in the Union government.
Generally speaking, the more nationalized and centralized the party system is, the more centralized is the federal system.

Institutions of the Federal or National Government

The federations examined here have parliamentary systems (e.g., Australia, Belgium, Canada, and Germany), presidential systems (e.g., Brazil,
Mexico, Nigeria, Russia, and the United States), and hybrid systems, such
as India, South Africa, and Switzerland. Ordinarily, the national legislature
is bicameral in some fashion, with one chamber (e.g., a senate) intended
to represent the federation's constituent political communities. At the
same time, whether parliamentary or presidential, most federal constitutions mandate a separation of powers of some type between the branches
of the national government.

No one system is obviously superior to the others, and each has assets
and liabilities. One liability of a parliamentary system is that it can give rise
to executive federalism in which policy making is dominated by national
and regional executives who hammer out agreements, often behind closed
doors, with little or no public participation and even with little participation by many of the elected members of the respective parliaments.

In a parliamentary system, there also may be some tension, as in Australia, between the idea of the constitution as a limit on power and the classical notion that parliament is supreme and should have plenary discretion
and flexibility. There may also be a tension between the constitutional flexibility available within each order of government and the constitutional
limits on flexibility available in relations between the orders of government
and the protection of their respective powers.

One liability of a presidential system is that it can give rise to an imperial
presidency, as in Mexico historically, Russia presently, and Nigeria potentially. A presidential system can accommodate effective and efficient decision-making, perhaps more so than executive federalism, but it can drive a

federal system toward centralization if there are inadequate cultural restraints and institutional checks on presidential power. Yet less-developed
federations where the rule of law has been weak tend to chose a pure or hybrid presidential arrangement, which can go awry. In 2004 President Putin
virtually decreed that regional governors and presidents in Russia will
henceforth be nominated by the federal president and then elected by regional legislatures rather than elected by their constituents. He also declared that district elections for the Duma will be replaced by proportional
electoral representation based on national-party lists. Putin's actions were
supported by many regional leaders.[19] "Russia has always been a single
state," said Dmitriy Rogozin, leader of the Motherland party, who added
that Putin is fashioning a more organic federalism that will, among other
things, "avoid blackmail of the federal centre by overweening regional bar-
ons and oligarchs."[20] Other regional leaders who supported or refused to
oppose Putin were apparently intimated by Kremlin threats.

One striking finding from the 12 case studies presented here is the widespread inability or unwillingness of second chambers representing the constituent political communities to maintain the powers of the federation's
constituent governments against expansions of federal power. Even where
this chamber is strong, as in Australia and the United States, the members
of the senate more often vote along political-party and interest-group lines
than along constituent-government lines. In Brazil the Senate is strong, but
the federal system is Union-dominated. The state governors exercise some
control over federal legislators but rarely for purposes of asserting state
powers over federal powers. In Canada the Senate is simply weak. In South
Africa, parliamentary executive federalism has eclipsed the functions of
the National Council of Provinces, which was modelled after Germany's
Bundesrat. In Germany the *Bundesrat* has arguably been fairly effective in
sustaining *Land* powers vis-à-vis federal power; however, the *Bundesrat* is not
quite a senate because it has an absolute veto only over certain types of federal legislation. Furthermore, the combination of executive federalism and
the tendency of voters to elect parties to the *Bundesrat* that oppose the majority party or coalition in the *Bundestag* and government tends to produce
political deadlocks and policy-making gridlocks.

In addition to the regional representation formally and informally present
in the legislature, regional representation is usually present in the national
executive branch, too, even if not mandated by the constitution. The cabinet
and its ministries are likely to be staffed by people from all the federation's
constituent political communities or, where this is impossible, from all the
country's key regions and constituent communities. In Nigeria the president
must, in the first place, win regionally dispersed support, not just a simple national majority. Switzerland's executive is constitutionally structured as a
seven-member Federal Council. However, even though the Swiss Constitution

mandates the Federal Council to represent the country's geographic and linguistic diversity, it is a coalition council of the four major national political parties. In this respect, there are competing representational forces in every federation. In the United States, for example, demands for adequate representation of racial and ethnic minorities and of women compete with the historical emphasis on regional representation in the president's Cabinet.

Court systems differ across federations as well; however, one virtual constant is the establishment of a supreme court or constitutional court having authority to resolve constitutional and legal conflicts among the federation's governments. Moreover, these courts are the venues of last resort on matters involving the federal constitution, federal law, and treaties. Many of these high courts (e.g., in Australia, Brazil, Canada, Germany, India, Russia, South Africa, and the United States) also have the authority to declare a law enacted by the federal government, a constituent government, and/or a local government to be unconstitutional. Usually, the courts of the federation government have jurisdiction, among other things, over federal constitutional, statutory, and treaty law, cases in which the national government is a party, cases involving foreign governments and persons, cases involving different constituent governments, and cases involving individuals from different constituent political communities.

Some federations, such as Brazil and the United States, have dual (federal and state) court systems that are independent except insofar as cases involving matters of federal constitutional or statutory law can be appealed to federal courts. Australia also has federal and state courts, but the Commonwealth government relied heavily for many decades on state courts to fulfil its judicial needs. Germany also has *Land* courts, and the decisions of *Land* courts can be reviewed by federal courts. Canada has provincial courts, joint federal-provincial courts, and federal courts, all of which exist within a hierarchical judicial system.

The Russian Constitution established federal courts that reach into the constituent units, but a constitutional court can be established by a republic, and a charter court can be created by a constituent unit that is not a republic. Regional constitutional (or charter) courts interpret their own constitution (or charter) and also resolve disputes over whether the laws and other actions of their regional and local governments conform to the regional constitution or charter. A constituent political community can also grant additional powers to its constitutional (or charter) court, provided that the powers are consistent with the aims of the court and do not invade the federal courts' jurisdiction. Virtually all decisions of regional constitutional (or charter) courts are final and cannot be appealed to any federal court of general jurisdiction or to the federal constitutional court.

By contrast, India and South Africa each have a single, integrated, hierarchical judicial system.

In Switzerland the official languages must be represented on the Federal Tribunal (i.e., supreme court), and the court is made up of 39 judges from all 26 cantons. In Canada three of the nine judges on the Supreme Court must be from Quebec, and the other regions must be fairly represented as well. Nevertheless, there is generally less emphasis on regional representation on federal high courts than in federal legislative and executive bodies. Instead, criteria associated with education, legal expertise, judicial experience, partisanship, and philosophical orientation are equally or more important than one's region of origin in the selection of high-court judges.

Intergovernmental Relations

In addition to the division of powers and guarantees of autonomy for the various orders of government, there is a need for rules and mechanisms to facilitate the co-operation and coordination of governments in the overall co-governance and co-management of a federation. The Swiss Constitution even mandates that the cantons and the confederation government cooperate with each other and help each other carry out their respective responsibilities.[21] Other provisions admonish the cantons to comply with federal law and not to act against the interests of the confederation or other cantons. The Constitution of South Africa also places a major emphasis on cooperation and the avoidance of litigation.

However, most federal constitutions say little about institutions or processes of intergovernmental relations beyond the role of the judiciary in resolving intergovernmental legal disputes. There are institutions and processes intended to foster intergovernmental cooperation and coordination in most federations; some are constitutional, but most are not. In Belgium, there is a Concertation Committee consisting of federal and regional officials, but most problems are solved by political-party leaders. In Australia, the Australian Loan Council once performed coordinating functions with respect to borrowing. Also, the Commonwealth government can enact laws on additional matters referred by state parliaments and can make use of state courts and prisons for federal purposes. Germany's Basic Law provides for joint federal-*Land* planning committees for joint tasks, but there are many other intergovernmental mechanisms, such as the Conference of Prime Ministers and conferences of other ministers. India has quite a number of formal institutions, including the Planning Commission, Finance Commission, National Development Council, Inter-State Council, and National Integration Council. Mexico has various statutory institutions such as the System for National Coordination of Public Security and the System for National Fiscal Coordination. Nigeria has a National Council of States and a Federal Character Commission. In response to expansions of federal power, the Swiss cantons formed the Conference of Cantonal Governments in 1993 to assert cantonal interests more effectively. By contrast, Brazil's Constitution does not provide for any intergovernmental mechanisms or institutions. Intergovernmental relations in Brazil tend to be Union-dominated and competitive, such that there are few examples of Union-state and interstate cooperation even though there is considerable intermunicipal cooperation.

No federal constitution explicitly endorses intergovernmental or interjurisdictional competition in an effort to improve service efficiency and taxpayer accountability.[22] Instead, to the extent that intergovernmental relations are mentioned, the emphasis is on cooperation and coordination. Federal constitutions must also provide for relations among the constituent political communities themselves, such as full faith and credit, or mutual recognition, among the constituent units where necessary, as well as provide for guarantees of mobility rights and individual-rights protections for citizens throughout the federation.

In the final analysis, intergovernmental relations are shaped more powerfully by the political-party system, by political leaders and administrators themselves, and by the attitudes they bring to the intergovernmental arena. If national officials favour command-and-control policies and have the ability to implement them, then intergovernmental relations are likely to be more coercive and conflictual than cooperative. If officials from the constituent governments favour excessive self-determination and desire merely to extract concessions and resources from the national government, then intergovernmental relations are likely to be conflictual and competitive.

Citizenship, Elections, and Political Parties

Unlike the United States, which provides for dual (i.e., federal and state) citizenship, most federations do not provide for dual citizenship. Even in Switzerland, where to obtain Swiss citizenship, one must first obtain citizenship in a municipality, there is no dual (i.e., federal and cantonal) citizenship. The Russian Constitution does not recognize dual citizenship either, although some republics assert a dual Russian and republican citizenship.

Usually, only the main principles of voting and elections are enshrined in the federal constitution, such as the principle of nondiscrimination in voting on the basis of race, ethnicity, religion, and gender. Some federal constitutions make provisions for voter qualifications and elections based on universal adult suffrage, but the details (sometimes including a minimum voting age, such as 18) are established by statutes.

Most of the constitutions examined here do not address political parties, although some address election procedures. Mexico's Constitution established the Federal Electoral Institute to oversee elections, and each constituent state has an equivalent body. Similarly, South Africa's Constitution entrusts voter registration and the conduct of elections to the Independent Electoral Commission, which is one of the Constitution's "state institutions supporting constitutional democracy" listed in Chapter 9. Nigeria's Constitution established an Independent National Electoral Commission (INEC) that conducts all federal and state elections and regulates political parties. Local-government elections are conducted by state independent electoral commissions (SIECs). Registration of eligible voters is the exclusive responsibility of the INEC, but an attempt to impose stringent registration requirements was blocked by the courts.

As of 2004, 30 registered political parties were regulated by the INEC. In an effort to discourage political parties from confining themselves to one region or remaining mono-ethnic or mono-religious, the Constitution disqualifies a political party for registration if its name, symbol, or logo contains "any ethnic or religious connotation or gives the appearance that the activities of the association are confined to a part only of the geographical area of Nigeria."[23] Parties cannot hold or possess any funds or other assets outside of Nigeria and are not entitled to retain any funds or assets sent to them from outside Nigeria. There is no provision for independent candidates.

In South Africa, the Bill of Rights guarantees the right to form political parties, although freedom of speech does not include "propaganda for war" or "advocacy of hatred that is based on race, ethnicity, gender or religion, and that constitutes incitement to cause harm."[24] The Constitution does not explicitly regulate parties, but it requires national-government "funding of political parties participating in national and provincial legislatures on an equitable and proportional basis" in order to "enhance multiparty democracy."[25]

Foreign Affairs and Defence

Consistent with modern federalism's nation-building premise and with the world of nation-states, all the important powers and powers relevant to international law that pertain to defence, foreign affairs, and diplomacy are ordinarily allocated exclusively to the national government in a federation. Only the federation can declare war, for example, although constituent political communities may have self-defence rights in the face of an invasion. The federation dispatches and receives ambassadors, negotiates and signs treaties, and the like.

Yet, since the founding of the first modern federation (i.e., the United States), most federal constitutions also have explicitly and implicitly reserved limited roles for constituent political communities in foreign affairs and defence. In the United States, the states even maintain their own army and air-force units, commanded by the governors. The Constitution authorizes states, with the consent of Congress, to enter agreements or compacts with foreign nations. At the same time, the Constitution does not prohibit the states from engaging in various kinds of international activities such as sending agents abroad and opening offices abroad to attract immigrants, tourists, and investment and to promote foreign exports of state products.

Since the 1960s, there has been a marked increase in the level and variety of international activities undertaken by the constituent political communities and municipalities of most federations (e.g., sister-city or twinning relationships)[26] and especially by the developed-country federations, such as Australia, Belgium, Canada, Germany, Switzerland, and the United States. These activities have a substantial economic component involving trade, investment, and tourism as cities and regions seek to be competitive in the global arena. Also common are technical, educational, and cultural exchanges. Frequently, these international activities also have substantial border-management and housekeeping components addressing local matters that cross frontiers, from cows and criminals that slip across borders to such matters as transportation, environmental protection, shared waters, and public health. Indeed, the federations within the European Union have given their constituent political communities substantial authority to conclude agreements and even treaties on cross-broader matters relevant to their jurisdiction. In multicultural federations, international activities also have a strong cultural-identity component as ethnic or linguistic constituent political communities, such as Quebec and Tatarstan, seek to project a quasi-sovereign "national" identity in the international arena. During the 1990s, several Russian republics sought to assert an international status virtually co-sovereign with the federation.

Such activities are less prevalent and more constrained in less-developed-country federations and in federations with more centralist orientations, such as Brazil, India, Mexico, Nigeria, and South Africa.[27] Here, there are usually fears, too, that centrifugal forces might be accelerated or unleashed by too much subnational engagement in international affairs.

One area of controversy in many federations is the impact of treaties and trade agreements on the powers of the constituent political communities. In Australia and the United States, for example, treaties and agreements concluded by the federal government are binding on the states. Consequently, treaties and agreements can, and have, become vehicles for expanding federal powers, sometimes at the expense of state powers. In response to the potential centralizing effects of treaties and agreements, the constituent political communities in most federations have sought certain protections and participation rights. In Canada, for example, where treaties and other agreements do not automatically override the watertight compartments of provincial jurisdiction, the federal government has been compelled to engage in extensive consultations with provincial leaders during international negotiations on matters that affect the provinces;

however, the federal government has declined to share with the provinces its formal powers to negotiate and sign treaties. In Nigeria, a federal bill that seeks to domesticate an international treaty with respect to matters not included on the federal government's exclusive legislative list requires ratification by a majority of the country's state houses of assembly.

Given the deep domestic impacts of the European Union (EU), all of the Western European federations have significantly enhanced the voice and participatory roles of their constituent political communities with respect to EU negotiations, even allowing in some cases (e.g., Belgium) representatives of these communities to sit with full negotiating authority at EU bargaining tables on matters relevant to their jurisdiction. Belgium has perhaps gone the farthest in that the regions and communities have far-reaching foreign-affairs powers, including the authority to conclude treaties and agreements on all matters pertinent to their competences, including international trade.

THE CONSTITUENT POLITICAL COMMUNITIES

The term "constituent political communities" has been used in this chapter to signify that although the constituent parts of a federation are ordinarily more than only parts, units, or levels, they are also frequently less than co-sovereign or semi-sovereign polities. In addition, some federations constitutionally recognize their local governments as a third order of government, even though none of them have been construed as co-sovereign or semi-sovereign polities. Again, then, there is considerable variation among the federations examined here regarding the status of their constituent political communities.

Territorial Integrity

Historically, as in the US Constitution, federal constitutions have guaranteed the territorial integrity of the constituent units of the federation against unilateral alteration by the federal government and/or other constituent units acting collectively. As the US Supreme Court ruled in 1869, four years after the Civil War, "The Constitution, in all its provisions, looks to an indestructible Union, composed of indestructible States."[28] The usual rule has been that a constituent political community's boundaries cannot be changed without its consent. This guarantee can be regarded as a crucial element of the guarantee of political autonomy for the constituent political communities and as a formal recognition of the continuing sovereignty of political communities that were regarded as sovereign prior to union. However, in a few post-Second World War federations, such as India, either the constitutional guarantee of territorial integrity is weak or, as in Nigeria, unconstitutional or extraconstitutional practices vitiated any such guarantees.

In Nigeria, military governments created new states mainly to disperse territorially based ethnic and religious groups. Having begun with three regional states at independence in 1960, Nigeria had 36 states by 1996. In India, where the states are in effect creatures of the national government, the federal Parliament can change boundaries and create new states by ordinary legislative processes. Indeed, India's 27 states were reorganized in 1956 into 14 states along linguistic lines; subsequently, the number of states increased to 28.[29] In Mexico the creation of a new state requires the approval of two-thirds of the members present in the federal Chamber of Deputies and the Senate. A majority of state legislatures must approve a corresponding decree. However, if a new state is proposed by a two-thirds vote of the Congress to be created within the boundaries of existing states, the effected states must give their consent. If they refuse to consent, creation of the new state requires the approval of two-thirds of the legislatures of all the other unaffected states.

Constituent Constitutions

Federations also vary in the levels either of constitutional sovereignty or of self-governing autonomy available to the constituent political communities. In Australia, Brazil, arguably Canada, Germany, Mexico, Russia, South Africa, Switzerland, and the United States, the constituent political communities have, or can have, their own constitutions. In most of these federations, the constituent political communities have substantial constitutional autonomy and broad legal discretion to establish their own governments, political institutions, government processes, and public policies subject only to certain limits and prohibitions set forth in the federal constitution. However, these limits and prohibitions are ordinarily intended only or mainly to protect the sovereignty or autonomy of the federal government, rather than to dictate forms or functions to the constituent political communities. For example, among the few limits explicitly imposed on the states by the US Constitution are that:

No state shall enter into any Treaty, Alliance, or Confederation; grant Letters of Marque and Reprisal; coin Money; emit bills of Credit; make any Thing but gold and silver Coin a Tender in Payment of Debts; pass any Bill of Attainder, ex post facto Law, or Law impairing the Obligation of Contracts, or grant any Title of Nobility.[30]

Consequently, where the constituent political communities have such broad constitutional autonomy, there is usually no requirement to have a constitution approved or certified by the national government.

In Brazil, however, while the states have constitutions, their constitutional autonomy is quite constrained because state constitutions must conform to mandates and rules set forth in the federal Constitution, which determines such detail as the number of state deputies and their pay ceilings. Likewise, in Mexico, state constitutions are not especially important because most of the important details of state government are mandated by the federal document. In South Africa, provinces can adopt a constitution, but they are sharply circumscribed by the national Constitution, and a provincial constitution must be certified by the national Constitutional Court; thus only the Western Cape adopted a provincial constitution.

Local Government

In contrast to such federations as Australia, Canada, Switzerland,[31] and the United States, where local governments are creatures of the constituent political communities, 7 of the 12 federal constitutions represented in this volume accord constitutional status of some sort to local government, usually municipal government, although not all of the seven treat local government as the third order of government. In Germany, for example, municipalities are part of *Land* administration (although three *Länder* are themselves city-states: Berlin, Bremen, and Hamburg), but the Basic Law guarantees municipalities the right to regulate local affairs and gives them some financial autonomy. Brazil's Constitution stipulates three orders of government – federal, state, and municipal – although much of municipal government is prescribed by the Constitution. In 1999, Mexico's Constitution was amended to establish municipal governments as a third order of government so as to afford them more autonomy and constitutional protection against adverse state-government action.

Aside from Moscow and St Petersburg, which are constituent units of the Russian federation, Russia's Constitution recognizes a right of local self-government that citizens exercise through referenda and elections and through local-government institutions. These local governments enjoy constitutional status and various independent powers. The structuring of local government is a joint power of both the federation and the constituent governments. Under this arrangement, the federation has promulgated framework legislation for the organization of local government. Most subjects of the federation have enacted laws that regulate local government in detail. However, the Constitution imposes limits on what subjects of the federation can prescribe; for instance, the judiciary struck down one republic's attempt to set up local governing structures because this action violated the federal constitutional right of citizens to exercise local self-government. Thus the judiciary plays a role in guaranteeing local self-government, while the Constitution ensures that local populations retain authority over local issues, such as the ownership, use, and disposal of municipal property, approval and execution of the local budget, establishment of local taxes, and maintenance of law and order. Either the federation or a subject of the federation can grant to local governments additional state powers, which are exercised under the supervision of the granting government. However, the Constitution requires the granting government to provide the material and financial resources needed to carry out those transferred responsibilities.

India's Constitution was amended in 1992 to grant constitutional status to rural and urban local governments, although these governments are not wholly a third order of government. For rural areas, the Constitution recognizes, in ascending order, village, intermediate, and district *panchayats*. There are *nagar panchayats* for urbanizing areas, municipal councils for small urban areas, and municipal corporations for large urban areas. Every state is obliged to establish such local governments. Although these local governments are granted some powers and autonomy by the Constitution, they depend greatly on financing from their state government, and they remain an exclusive subject of state government. Nigeria's 1979 and 1999 constitutions recognize local government (774 local-government councils as of 2004) as a third order of government; however, the "establishment, structure, composition, finance and functions" of local government depend on state law.

South Africa's Constitution holds that "government is constituted as national, provincial and local spheres of government which are distinctive, interdependent, and interrelated."[32] The word "spheres" is used intentionally to avoid the hierarchical notion of government embedded in the word "levels." Furthermore, the Constitution maintains that the national and provincial governments "may not compromise or impede a municipality's ability or right to exercise its powers or perform its functions."[33]

Globalization and Regional Integration

There have been frequent assertions in recent decades that local rather than national governments, especially municipalities and metropolitan areas, are the key actors in globalization (and thus should have more autonomy). It has been noted, too, that power is generally gravitating "upward" to supranational institutions and "downward" to local institutions worldwide. Nevertheless, the developed-country federations most deeply and successfully integrated into globalization accord little, if any, constitutional recognition to local government. At the same time, however, the constituent political communities may themselves grant substantial self-governing autonomy or home rule to their local governments – self-rule powers that might actually make them more autonomous than local governments accorded national constitutional recognition in other federations.

Instead, constitutional recognition of local government is more characteristic of less-developed-country federations; yet even in these federations, the constitutional recognition of local government is not a response to globalization. On the contrary, such recognition is usually linked to democratization, attempts to empower local citizens (including women), and efforts to protect local-government powers and revenues from corrupt and rapacious officials in the constituent governments and national government.

Likewise, it is often argued that globalization has had substantial impacts on the structure and operations of federal systems. Yet, as the case studies in this volume suggest indirectly, and as other studies indicate more directly,[34] globalization has, for the most part, not yet significantly altered the structure and operations of federal systems and has not generated major constitutional changes.

What has had a major impact on both local governments and the constituent political communities of federations, however, has been regional integration, namely the rise of the European Union. Given that the transfer of powers, or competences, to the EU often reduces the powers and competences of constituent political communities, all of the federations within the EU as well as Switzerland have altered their constitutions to give the constituent governments a greater voice or even a veto in such transfers of power to the EU so that the national governments of these federations cannot simply give away the powers of their constituent governments. However, these federations have not, for the most part, extended comparable constitutional protections to their local governments in part because local governments are presumed to be protected by their regional government.

Indigenous Peoples

Indigenous (or aboriginal) peoples are a significant communal presence in at least 8 of the 12 federations: Australia, Brazil, Canada, India, Mexico, Russia, South Africa, and the United States. Most commonly, indigenous peoples, having been objects of conquest, were not included as constitutional partners in federations, such as Australia, that were established prior to the widespread movement that began in the 1960s to recognize the rights and revive the cultures of indigenous peoples. In Australia aboriginals were regarded as a state responsibility; now they are a concurrent federal and state responsibility. In Canada and the United States, they are regarded as a federal-government responsibility. The US Constitution vests authority for relations with the Indian tribes in the federal government because they were treated as sovereign nations with which the United States concluded treaties during the first century of its history. However, in all of these federations, indigenous peoples were nearly extinguished by the early twentieth century due to warfare, disease, and assimilation.

The revival of indigenous peoples' individual, communal, and treaty rights since the early 1960s has resulted in constitutional, statutory, and/or judicial changes in all of these federations that provide greater protections and, in some cases, such as Canada and the United States, greater self-government and self-determination for territorially rooted indigenous communities (e.g., creation of a third territory, Nunavut, for the Inuit in Canada). These changes have usually been accompanied by efforts to protect indigenous lands and to recover some indigenous lands taken by conquest, theft, and treaty violations. Thus Brazil's Constitution of 1988 and Canada's Constitution Act 1982 provide certain protections for indigenous peoples. Mexico amended its Constitution in 2001 to give more protections and benefits to indigenous peoples. Australia amended its Constitution in 1967 to remove provisions stating that aboriginals were explicitly excluded from Commonwealth power under the Constitution and from any population count taken for constitutional purposes.

Russia's 1993 Constitution recognizes rights of indigenous peoples in two ways. Some peoples are members of the federation. For example, ten autonomous areas were created for the aboriginal peoples of Siberia, the North, and the Far East. Additionally, the Constitution requires both the federal and the regional governments to guarantee the rights of indigenous peoples to create different types of communities and to preserve and develop their original environment, traditional way of life, and culture. Some constituent units have established a fixed number of seats in their legislature for representatives of aboriginal peoples. South Africa's Constitution provides no special status for indigenous peoples, although "the institution, status and role of traditional leadership, according to customary law, are recognized, subject to the Constitution."[35]

Indigenous peoples in some of these federations have agitated for full-scale federation membership as a third or fourth order of government, but they have not been accorded this status. In the United States, Presidents Bill Clinton and George Bush embraced Indian tribes as the fourth partner in intergovernmental administrative relations (i.e., federal-state-local-tribal relations) and thus acknowledged that US relations with the tribes are government-to-government relations, but the US Supreme Court has been issuing decisions generally adverse to tribal autonomy and self-government.[36]

Secession

Secession, which is or has been a concern in three of the federations examined in this volume – i.e., Canada, Nigeria, and Russia – is rarely authorized by a federal constitution. Instead, the Preamble to Nigeria's Constitution, which expresses the firm resolve of Nigerians to live in unity and harmony as "one indivisible and indissoluble Sovereigzn Nation," is typical of anti-secession sentiment. The current exception is Ethiopia's Constitution. In addition, Canada's Supreme Court sketched a secession procedure in 1998, which was then followed by a clarifying federal statute.

Although a leading exponent of the public-choice school of political economy argues that the leverage against tyranny and oppression offered by secession is an essential tool of last resort in an ideal federal system,[37] most theorists and practitioners have been hostile to secession[38] partly because modern federalism has always been associated with nation building. Some theorists argue that a federal polity is intended to be permanent and perpetual.[39] Indeed, the early templates for modern federalism spoke of perpetuity. The US Articles of Confederation (1781) stipulated a "perpetual Union." "The German Federal Act of 1815 stated that the members agreed to a 'permanent federal union'; the Viennese Act of 1820 was said to 'indissolubly join the bond which unites the whole of Germany in harmony and peace' and Article V of this act stated: 'The federation is established as an indissoluble union and therefore no member is free to withdraw.'"[40] The Preamble to Australia's 1901 Constitution Act refers to an "indissoluble federal Commonwealth."

CONSTITUTIONAL CHANGE

All of the federal constitutions examined here provide for lawful constitutional change via amendment procedures. These procedures seek to protect the constitution against arbitrary change, such as that noted by a Jordanian: "We have a constitution, but the King can change it by making two phone calls."[41] They also seek to strike a balance between rigidity and instability. Generally, the procedures also reflect the centralist or noncentralist orientation of the constitution and the extent of sovereignty or autonomy enjoyed by the constituent political communities and, thus, the extent to which their consent is required for constitutional change.

In Australia only the federal Parliament can initiate amendments; however, like the Swiss approval procedure, these amendments must be ratified by a double or concurrent majority of (1) a majority of the people voting nationwide and (2) a majority of the voters in a majority of the states (cantons in Switzerland). However, given Australia's common-law versus Switzerland's civil-law system, there have been few amendments to Australia's Constitution. Furthermore, voters have rejected most proposed amendments, in part because the Constitution is changed through judicial interpretation as well as through issues being referred to the federal Parliament by state parliaments. By contrast, the Swiss Constitution, which is not subject to such judicial interpretation, is amended so frequently that citizens sometimes experience voter fatigue in a climate of amendomania similar to that of California in the United States.

Canada, which has displayed an aversion to constitutional change since the failure of the Meech Lake and Charlottetown Accords, has four amending formulas, each applying to different aspects of the Constitution, plus a fifth formula enabling provinces to amend their own constitutions. Belgium has a complex process in which specific articles must first be identified as needing change. When Parliament approves these specifics, the Parliament is then dissolved. The subsequent new Parliament can change the specified articles by a two-thirds vote in each house. The regions, communities, and people have no direct role. Belgium's special para-constitutional laws are approved by a two-thirds majority in each house, plus a majority of each language group, in the federal Parliament.

In Brazil, where some parts of the Constitution cannot be altered, amendments need the support of three-fifths of the members of Congress on two rounds of roll-call voting in each house. In Germany, where some parts of the Basic Law also are immune to amendment, constitutional amendments pass through the normal legislative process but require the support of two-thirds of the members of the *Bundestag* and two-thirds of the votes of the *Bundesrat*.

In Nigeria no provision of the Constitution is immune from amendment. Most commonly, an amendment proposal requires the vote of not less than a two-thirds majority of each house of the National Assembly. However, any proposal to amend sections that (1) prescribe the amendment procedure, (2) relate to the creation of new states, boundary adjustments, or creation of new local-government areas, or (3) contain fundamental rights requires the vote of not less than a four-fifths majority of the members of each house of the National Assembly. In either case, the proposal must be approved by the houses of assembly of not less than two-thirds of all the states.

In India certain provisions (e.g., those regarding names and boundaries of states) can be changed by a simple-majority vote of the national Parliament. Other provisions can be amended by a majority of the total membership of each house and by a majority of not less than two-thirds of the members present and voting, coupled with the president's approval. Still other provisions require these same parliamentary majorities, but coupled with ratification by one-half or more of the state legislatures, followed by presidential assent. Provisions subject to change only with such state consent include election of the president, extent of the Union's executive power, extent of executive power of the states, the Union judiciary, state high courts, and constitutional amendment procedures.

Russia likewise has three procedures of various stringency and scope of participation for changing the Constitution, depending on the provisions to be changed. South Africa also has several procedures for amending various parts of the Constitution. Most stringent is a requirement that any amendments to Section 1, which sets forth the Constitution's founding values, must garner the support of 75 percent of the members of the National Assembly and six of the nine provinces in the National Council of Provinces.

In Mexico amendments require a two-thirds vote of the members present in each chamber of the Congress of the Union, followed by the approval of 50 percent plus one of the state legislatures. In the United States amendments can be proposed by a two-thirds vote of each house of Congress or by a constitutional convention that must be called by Congress upon the petition of two-thirds of the state legislatures. The latter procedure has never been used, mostly because of fear that it could produce a volatile, runaway convention. Amendments must be ratified by three-fourths of the state legislatures or by popularly elected conventions in three-fourths of the states (used only once). Since 1919, Congress has normally placed a seven-year limit on ratification; however, because the Constitution imposes no time limit, an amendment proposed in 1789 but not ratified by three-fourths of the original 13 states was revived by a university student during the 1980s and ratified in 1992.[42]

POTENTIAL ELEMENTS OF CONSTITUTIONAL SUCCESS

Behind the formal constitution, there is always what was once called "the living constitution"[43] – that is, how the constitution actually works in practice. The constitution comes alive, so to speak, through the attitudes and behaviours of the political actors empowered by it because no constitution is self-executing and because no constitution can describe and prescribe the sum total of political reality. Where the written constitution is reinforced and enriched by the attitudes and behaviours of political actors, federal democracy is likely to be robust. Where the written constitution is ignored and subverted by political actors, it is likely to be little more than a façade hiding a dark reality. Constitutional governance, therefore, requires a culture of democracy and rule of law supporting adherence to principled rules that are predictable and embodied in a legitimate authority above or outside of government officials.

The process of making a constitution, therefore, appears to be as important as the content of the constitution in fostering success. This is the case partly because the content is not likely to be viewed as legitimate if the process is viewed as illegitimate. Today, legitimacy usually requires transparency and public participation, as in South Africa, where the Constitutional Assembly solicited voter input with the slogan, "You've made your mark, now have your say." The assembly received some two million public comments. Likewise, in the drafting of Brazil's Constitution (1988), 12 million voters signed petitions proposing 122 provisions, and individuals sent 72,719 suggestions to the Constituent National Assembly, which wrote the Constitution. Both the breadth and depth of public participation are often important at all stages of constitution making, from initial proposals and drafts through deliberations over the final text and adoption of the constitution. Thus the document is not merely majoritarian but reflects a broad, inclusive consensus, or what was termed a "sufficient consensus" in South Africa, among a country's diverse groups.

The development of a sufficient consensus appears to be a key factor because constitutional development can, under certain circumstances, succeed without broad, direct public participation. The process in Belgium, for instance, has been driven by elites in a consociational fashion in which consensus building among leaders is ordinarily sufficient to ensure tacit public consent. However, these leaders are embedded in a democratic rule-of-law culture.

The use of experts, including foreign experts, seen as being above normal partisan politics has gained considerable acceptance in constitution making, as has the appointment or election of representative constitutional-reform commissions seen as being more trustworthy than normal parliamentary and partisan processes. Similarly, the covering security and assistance of international organizations, such as the United Nations and the European Union, can enhance the success of making and maintaining a federal constitution.

Where the political communities that are to constitute a federation value their autonomy and integrity, it is important that they believe that the constitution will protect them against usurpations of their autonomy and integrity by the federal government and/or the other constituent units. In turn, where the sense of nationhood is weak, it is likely to be important that proponents of union believe that the constitution will sustain the union against secession or usurpations of power by constituent units.

Further elements of success in framing a constitution are likely to include commonly recognized problems that can be resolved or at least mitigated by federal power-sharing, a window of opportunity and neutral ground on which to bring all the relevant political actors together for good-faith deliberations and negotiations, a process of trust and confidence building, a sustained commitment on the part of the key actors to strike a bargain, a commitment by those actors to the wellbeing of the people of the country, bargaining flexibility and accountability, and a pragmatic problem-solving attitude.

It is not necessary to have a common agreement on why federalism is necessary; it can be sufficient to agree only that federalism is necessary for various reasons. More important are efforts by constitution makers to solve problems in ways that optimize benefits for all the parties and the people in a non-zero-sum, or win-win, fashion. Thus success may also require agreements to take certain issues off the table and leave them for future resolution or agreements to leave them in the hands of the constituent political communities or civil society. Indeed, one advantage of a federal system is that certain volatile political issues can be diffused among the constituent political communities for variable resolutions rather than thrust into the white heat of national politics for a single, uniform resolution.

Maintenance of a federal democratic constitution is likely to require continual bargaining and negotiation within the context of the constitution because process is no less important than structure in the success of federal democracy. In turn, the federation must obtain and maintain the support of the people by, among other things, ensuring their safety and security, protecting fundamental rights and freedoms, providing recognizable justice, curing problems of corruption and nepotism, preventing usurpations of power anywhere in the federal system, providing effective and efficient government administration, facilitating economic development throughout the federation, and ensuring that all governments in the federation have the capacity and resources to provide public services responsive to people's needs and preferences.

NOTES

1 Argentina, Australia, Austria, Belgium, Bosnia and Herzegovina, Brazil, Canada, Comoros, Ethiopia, Germany, India, Malaysia, Mexico, Micronesia, Nigeria, Pakistan, Russia, St. Kitts and Nevis, Serbia and Montenegro, South Africa, Spain, Switzerland, United Arab Emirates, United States of America, and Venezuela. See also, Ann L. Griffiths, ed., *Handbook of Federal Countries, 2002* (Montreal and Kingston: McGill-Queen's University Press, 2002) and Ronald L. Watts, *Comparing Federal Systems*, 2nd ed. (Montreal and Kingston: McGill-Queen's University Press, 1999).

2 Daniel J. Elazar and John Kincaid, eds, *The Covenant Connection: From Federal Theology to Modern Federalism* (Lanham, MD: Lexington Books, 2000).

3 Alexander Hamilton, James Madison, and John Jay, *The Federalist*, ed. Jacob E. Cooke (Middletown, CT: Wesleyan University Press, 1961), Federalist No. 1, p. 3.

4 The term "orders of government" is used here instead of "levels of government" because "levels" implies a hierarchy of governments. Hierarchy is a characteristic of some but not all federal systems.

5 J. Isawa Elaigwu and Habu Galadima, "The Shadow of *Sharia* Over Nigerian Federalism," *Publius: The Journal of Federalism* 33 (Summer 2003): 123–44.

6 See also, Cheryl Saunders, "Constitutional Arrangements of Federal Systems," *Publius: The Journal of Federalism* 25 (Winter 1995): 61–79.

7 Hans Kelsen, *General Theory of Law and State*, 20th Century Legal Philosophy Series (1945; reprint, New York: Russell and Russell, 1961), Vol. 1.

8 John Kincaid, "Values and Value Tradeoffs in Federalism," *Publius: The Journal of Federalism* 25 (Spring 1995): 29–44.

9 William H. Riker, *Federalism: Origin, Operation, Significance* (Boston: Little, Brown, 1964), p. 12.

10 Constitution of the United States of America (1788), Preamble.

11 Appenzell-Inner Rhoden, Obwalden, Nidwalden, Schwyz, Valais, and Uri.

12 Article 79III.

13 Constitution of the Republic of South Africa (1996), Section 39(1).

14 Donald S. Lutz, "The United States Constitution as an Incomplete Text," *Annals of the Academy of Political and Social Science* 496 (March 1988): 23–32.

15 Australia's constitution does incorporate a few procedural rights, such as a right to a trial by jury.

16 "Kentucky Resolutions, 1798," *A Source Book of American Political Theory*, ed. Benjamin Fletcher Wright (New York: Macmillan, 1929), p. 322.

17 Daniel J. Elazar, *Exploring Federalism* (Tuscaloosa: University of Alabama Press, 1987), p. 34.

18 See also, David B. Truman, "Federalism and the Party System," *Federalism: Mature and Emergent*, ed. Arthur MacMahon (New York: Doubleday, 1955), pp. 115–36; Riker, *Federalism*; and Morton Grodzins, *The American System: A New View of Government in the United States*, ed. Daniel J. Elazar (Chicago: Rand McNally, 1966), pp. 254–89 and elsewhere.

19 Steven Lee Myers, "From Those Putin Would Weaken, Praise," *New York Times*, 15 September 2004, pp. A1 and A9, and Matthew Kaminski, "KGB Democracy," *Wall Street Journal*, 17 September 2004, p. A15.

20 Quoted in ITAR-TASS, "Mixed Reaction from Russian Party Leaders to Putin's Political Proposals," 13 September 2004, at http://www.eng.yabloko.ru/Publ/2004/AGENCIES/040913_itar_tass.html. Accessed 27 September 2004.

21 Constitution of Switzerland (1999), Article 44, Paragraph 1.

22 See, for example, Daphne A. Kenyon and John Kincaid, eds, *Competition among States and Local Governments: Efficiency and Equity in American Federalism* (Washington, DC: Urban Institute Press, 1991).

23 Constitution of the Republic of Nigeria (1999), Section 222(e).

24 Constitution of the Republic of South Africa (1996), Section 16(2).

25 Ibid., Section 236.

26 See, for example, Francisco Aldecoa and Michael Keating, eds, *Paradiplomacy in Action: The Foreign Relations of Subnational Governments* (London: Frank Cass, 1999); Hans J. Michelmann and Panayotis Soldatos, eds, *Federalism and International Relations: The Role of Subnational Units* (Clarendon: Oxford University Press, 1990); and Ivo D. Duchacek, ed, "Federated States and International Relations," *Publius: The Journal of Federalism* 14 (Fall 1984): entire issue.

27 See, for example, Rob Jenkins, "India's States and the Making of Foreign Economic Policy: The Limits of the Constituent Diplomacy Paradigm," *Publius: The Journal of Federalism* 33 (Fall 2003): 63–81, and Rudolf Hrbek, ed., *Außenbeziehungen von Regionen in Europa und der Welt* (Baden-Baden: Nomos Verlagsgesellschaft, 2003).

28 *Texas v. White*, 7 Wallace 700, 710 (1869).

29 See also Akhtar Majeed, "The Changing Politics of States' Reorganization," *Publius: The Journal of Federalism* 33 (Fall 2003): 83–98.

30 Constitution of the United States (1788), Article I, Section 10.

31 However, Article 50 of the Swiss Constitution holds that municipal autonomy is guaranteed within the limits set by cantonal law.

32 Constitution of the Republic of South Africa (1996), Section 40(1).

33 Ibid., Section 151(4).

34 See, for example, Harvey Lazar, Hamish Telford, and Ronald L. Watts, eds, *The Impact of Global and Regional Integration on Federal Systems* (Montreal and Kingston: McGill-Queen's University Press, 2003).

35 Ibid., Section 211(1).

36 See, for example, David E. Wilkins and Keith Richotte, "The Rehnquist Court and Indigenous Rights: The Expedited Diminution of Native Powers of Governance," *Publius: The Journal of Federalism* 33 (Summer 2003): 83–110.

37 James M. Buchanan, "Federalism as an Ideal Political Order and an Objective for Constitutional Reform," *Publius: The Journal of Federalism* 25 (Winter 1995): 19–27.

38 See recently, for example, Cass R. Sunstein, *Designing Democracy: What Constitutions Do* (Oxford: Oxford University Press, 2001).

39 Carl Schmitt, "The Constitutional Theory of Federation (1928)," *Telos* 91 (Spring 1992): 30.

40 Ibid.

41 Quoted in Amos Elon, "An Unsentimental Education," *New York Review of Books* 50 (29 May 2003): 6.

42 Constitution of the United States (1788), Amendment XXVII.

43 Howard Lee McBain, *The Living Constitution: A Consideration of the Realities and Legends of Our Fundamental Law* (New York: Workers' Education Bureau, 1927).

Contributors

IGNATIUS AKAAYAR AYUA attended Ahmadu Bello University, Zaria, obtaining LL.B (Hons) and LL.M degrees in 1973 and 1976 respectively, and the University of Birmingham, where he completed a PhD specializing in company taxation in 1979. He has held many academic and administrative positions. His major textbooks are *Nigerian Company Law* and *Nigerian Tax Law*. He served as director general of the Nigerian Institute of Advanced Legal Studies for eight years and is currently solicitor general of the Federal Republic of Nigeria. He is a member of several professional bodies, a senior advocate of Nigeria (SAN), and a recipient of the national honour Officer of the Order of the Federal Republic.

RAOUL BLINDENBACHER is vice president and director of global programs at the Forum of Federations. He was the executive director of the International Conference on Federalism 2002 and recently coedited the conference book "Federalism in a Changing World." He has special interests in the methods and theory of institutional and intergovernmental learning and is a member of the Council of the Institute of Federalism at the University of Fribourg. He holds a doctorate in education, with an emphasis on organizational sociology and political science, from the University of Zurich.

DAKAS C.J. DAKAS is a senior lecturer in the Department of International Law and Jurisprudence, University of Jos, Nigeria. The recipient of several meritorious scholarships and distinguished awards, he is the author or coeditor of numerous books and articles dealing with international law and constitutional law, including *International Law on Trial: Bakassi and the Eurocentricity of International Law* (2003) and *The Right to Be Different: Minority Rights, the Cultural Middle-Belt and Constitutionalism in Nigeria* (2001). His current research focuses on recent constitutional issues in the specific context of the opportunities and challenges of federalism in Nigeria's burgeoning democracy.

KRIS DESCHOUWER is a professor of politics at the Vrije Universiteit Brussel. He has been involved in research on political parties, elections, consociational democracy, federalism, and regionalism and has published widely on these topics. He is the editor of the *European Journal of Political Research.*

JUAN MARCOS GUTIÉRREZ GONZÁLEZ is consul general of Mexico in Denver, Colorado. Consul Gutierrez holds a degree in law from the Autonomous University of Baja California, where he is a professor of constitutional law. He has postgraduate certificates in public-finance law, trade-dispute resolutions under the North Americn Free Trade Agreement (NAFTA), and fiscal law. In the past, Gutierrez has served as a general secretary and chief legal officer in the Government of Tijuana, Baja California; as a federal congressman for the National Action Party in Mexico's Chamber of Deputies; as chief of advisors in the Mexican Federal Senate; and as general director of the Institute for the Technical Development of Public Finance.

JOHN KINCAID is the Robert B. and Helen S. Meyner Professor of Government and Public Service and director of the Meyner Center for the Study of State and Local Government at Lafayette College, Easton, Pennsylvania. He is the editor of *Publius: The Journal of Federalism,* editor of a series of books on the governments and politics of the American states, and an elected fellow of the National Academy of Public Administration. He is the former executive director of the US Advisory Commission on Intergovernmental Relations, Washington, DC, and author of various works on federalism and intergovernmental relations.

RAINER KNOPFF is a professor of political science and is associate vice president (Research and International) at the University of Calgary. He has written widely in the areas of public law, human rights, and Canadian political thought. His books include *The Charter Revolution and the Court Party* and *Charter Politics* (both with F.L. Morton), *Human Rights and Social Technology: The New War on Discrimination* (with T.E. Flanagan), and *Parameters of Power: Canada's Political Institutions* (with Keith Archer, Roger Gibbins, Heather MacIvor, and Leslie A. Pal).

JUTTA KRAMER is a lawyer and senior research assistant at the Institute for Federal Studies, University of Hanover. She has served as an expert for various international organizations on federalism and constitutionalism and has been involved in the constitution-making process in South Africa. Her thesis was published as *Apartheid and Constitution: The Constitutional Law as a Tool of Implementation and Abolishment of Racial Discrimination in South Africa* (2001). Currently she is heading the research project "The German Basic Law: Documentations on Its Creation/Making" at the University of Hannover.

AKHTAR MAJEED is a professor of political science and is director of the Centre for Federal Studies at Hamdard University in New Delhi, India. He has taught at the Universities of Allahabad and Aligarh, in India, has been a visiting professor at the University of Illinois at Urbana-Champaign, USA, and is on the faculty that oversees the online program on federalism at Transcend Peace University. His recent publications include: *Federalism within the Union* (2004), *Nation and Minorities* (2002), *Constitutional Nation-Building: Half a Century of India's Success* (2001), and *Coalition Politics and Power-Sharing* (2000). He is editor of the biannual *Indian Journal of Federal Studies*.

MARAT SALIKOV is the director to the dean of the Institute of Justice of Urals State Law Academy, a doctor of juridical science (SJD), and a professor at Urals State Law Academy, Yekaterinburg, Russia. He teaches classes in constitutional law, comparative federalism, and constitutional and judicial procedure and has written or contributed to over 100 publications. He is the author of *Comparative Federalism of the USA and Russia* (1998) and co-author and chief editor of *Constitutional Judicial Procedure* (2003). He has been a visiting professor in the Fulbright Program at Saint Louis University School of Law, where he taught comparative federalism; a visiting scholar at Cologne and Humboldt Universities, Germany; and a guest lecturer at Wayne State University School of Law, Detroit.

CHERYL SAUNDERS holds a personal chair in law at the University of Melbourne and is a Fellow of the Academy of the Social Sciences in Australia. She has specialist interests in constitutional law and comparative constitutional law, including federalism and intergovernmental relations, constitutional design and change, and constitutional theory. She is president of the International Association of Constitutional Law and vice president of both the International Association of Centres for Federal Studies and the Australian Association of Constitutional Law. She is an editor of the *Public Law Review* and a member of the editorial boards of a range of Australian and international journals, including *I.CON* and *Publius*.

ANTHONY SAYERS is an associate professor of political science at the University of Calgary. He has written on both Canadian and Australian politics – and, in particular, on federalism, political parties, election campaigns, and electoral systems. He is the author of *Parties, Candidates and Constituency Campaigns in Canadian Elections* (1999).

NICOLAS SCHMITT is a research fellow at the Institute on Federalism in Fribourg, Switzerland. His areas of interest include the role of regions in the new Europe as well as the relevance of the Swiss federal experience at the international level. Among his recent publications are: "Le processus de centralisation a-t-il atteint ses limites en Suisse?" (*Revue d'Allemagne* 3, 2003); and "Petit aperçu comparatif du fédéralisme en Suisse, en Allemagne et aux Etats-Unis" (in *L'Europe en formation*, 2nd ed., 2004). He has a doctorate in law from the University of Fribourg.

CELINA SOUZA is a professor and researcher of political science and public administration at the Federal University of Bahia, Brazil. Her primary research interests are federalism, subnational governments, and public policies in Brazil. Dr Souza is the author of *Constitutional Engineering in Brazil: The Politics of Federalism and Decentralization* (1997). She has also written a number of journal articles and contributed to anthologies both in English and Portuguese. Her most recent publication in English is "Brazil: The Prospects of a Center-Constraining Federation in a Fragmented Polity," which was published in *Publius: The Journal of Federalism*, Spring 2002.

NICO STEYTLER is the director of the Community Law Centre of the University of the Western Cape, a research and advocacy institute that works for the realization of the democratic values and human rights enshrined in South Africa's Constitution. He has been involved in the development of the new constitutional order for the past decade. He was a technical advisor to the Constitutional Assembly drafting the 1996 Constitution (1995–96) as well as a technical advisor to the Western Cape Provincial Legislature on the drafting of a provincial constitution (1996–97). His main field of research is intergovernmental relations and local government.

G. ALAN TARR is director of the Center for State Constitutional Studies and chair of the Department of Political Science at Rutgers University-Camden. He is the author or editor of numerous books dealing with constitutionalism, including *American Constitutional Law* (5th ed., 2003), *Understanding State Constitutions* (1998), and *Federalism and Rights* (1996). His articles on federalism and constitutionalism have appeared in *Publius: The Journal of Federalism, Rutgers Law Journal, Wisconsin Law Review,* and other legal publications. His research is currently focused on the reform of American state constitutions.

Participants of the Global Dialogue on Federalism

We gratefully acknowledge the assistance of the following individuals who participated in the theme of Constitutional Origins, Structure, and Change. While participants contributed their knowledge and experience, they are in no way responsible for the contents of this book.

José Roberto Afonso, Brazil
Basília Aguirre, Brazil
Peter Akper, Nigeria
Chris Alcantara, Canada ·
E. Alemika, Nigeria
Zinaida Alexandrova, Russia
Miguel Ángel Romo, Mexico
Marta Arretche, Brazil
Jean-François Aubert, Switzerland
Céline Auclair, Canada
I.A. Ayua, Nigeria
E.C.J. Azinge, Nigeria
Janet Azjenstat, Canada
Lynn Baker, United States
Gérald Beaudoin, Canada
Wouter Beke, Belgium
Svetlana Bendyurina, Russia
Gilberto Bercovici, Brazil
C.P. Bhambri, India
Vladimir Boublik, Russia
Dirk Brand, South Africa
Claudine Brohi, Switzerland
A.J. Brown, Australia
César Camacho Quiroz, Mexico
Jaime Cárdenas Gracia, Mexico

Siska Castelein, Belgium
Octavio Chavez, Mexico
Jan Clement, Belgium
Jamison Colburn, United States
Barry Cooper, Canada
Fernando Cosenza, Brazil
Juan José Crispín Borbolla, Mexico
David De Groot, Canada
Kris Deschouwer, Belgium
Hugues Dumont, Belgium
Alex Ekwueme, Nigeria
Vanessa Elias de Oliveira, Brazil
Rebeca Elizalde Hernández, Mexico
Fred Erdman, Belgium
Simon Evans, Australia
Patrick Fafard, Canada
James Faulkner, Australia
Carlos Figueiredo, Brazil
Thomas Fleiner, Switzerland
Rubén Jaime Flores Medina, Mexico
Stephen Frank, United States
Carlos Gadsden Carrazco, Mexico
Brian Galligan, Australia
Roger Gibbins, Canada
Tatiana Gladkova, Russia

Leslie Goldstein, United States
Manuel González Oropeza, Mexico
Karthy Govender, South Africa
Michael Grant, Mexico
Tonatiuh Guillén López, Mexico
Desiree Guobadia, Nigeria
Juan Marcos Gutiérrez González, Mexico
Geoffrey Hale, Canada
Ian Harris, Australia
N. Hembe, Nigeria
Simone Hermans, South Africa
Jan Martin Hoffmann, Germany
Meenakshi Hooja, India
Javier Hurtado González, Mexico
Gennady Ignatenko, Russia
R.B. Jain, India
César Jáuregui Robles, Mexico
Harold Jensen, Canada
Nirmal Jindal, India
B.B. Kanyip, Nigeria
Subhash C. Kashyap, India
Ellis Katz, United States
Cristiane Kersches, Brazil
Arshi Khan, India
Farah Khan, India
John Kincaid, United States
Paul King, Canada
Rainer Knopff, Canada
Alexander Kokotov, Russia
Royce Koop, Canada
Jutta Kramer, Germany
Christopher Kukucha, Canada
T. Ladan, Nigeria
Nicolas Lagasse, Belgium
Natalia Larionova, Russia
Harvey Lazar, Canada
Katy Le Roy, Australia
Dörte Liebetruth, Germany
Geoffrey Lindell, Australia
Marina Lomovtseva, Russia
Augustin Macheret, Switzerland
Akhtar Majeed, India
Christopher Manfredi, Canada

Preston Manning, Canada
Bernardo H. Martínez Aguirre, Mexico
George Mathew, India
David McCann, Australia
Peter McCormick, Canada
Nadezhda Mershina, Russia
Geraldine Mettler, South Africa
Hans Michelmann, Canada
Adrián Miranda, Mexico
Eamon Morann, Australia
F.L. Morton, Canada
Radinaledi Mosiane, South Africa
Christina Murray, South Africa
Marie Nagy, Belgium
A.S. Narang, India
Svetlana Nesmeyanova, Russia
Valeri Nevinski, Russia
A.G. Noorani, India
Charles-Ferdinand Nothomb, Belgium
Ofem Obno-Obla, Nigeria
Alessandro Octaviani, Brazil
Lawal Olayinka, Nigeria
Donald David Onje, Nigeria
Brian Opeskin, Australia
Waldeck Ornelas, Brazil
Sam Oyovbaire, Nigeria
Francisco José Paoli Bolio, Mexico
Victor Perevalov, Russia
Javier Pérez Torres, Mexico
Derek Powell, South Africa
Adriano Previtali, Switzerland
Balraj Puri, India
Paul Rabbat, Australia
H. Ramchandran, India
Fernando Rezende da Silva, Brazil
Horst Risse, Germany
Heather Roberts, Australia
Eduardo C. Robreno, United States
Rocío Arleth Rodríguez Torres, Mexico
Vladimir Rusinov, Russia
Marat Salikov, Russia
Alexander Salomatkin, Russia
Cheryl Saunders, Australia

Peter Savitski, Russia
Rekha Saxena, India
Anthony Sayers, Canada
Nicolas Schmitt, Switzerland
Hans-Peter Schneider, Germany
Rainer-Olaf Schultze, Germany
Pierre Scyboz, Switzerland
Campbell Sharman, Canada
Ronli Sifiris, Australia
Ajay K. Singh, India
Chhatar Singh, India
M.P. Singh, India
Khalipile Sizani, South Africa
Celina Souza, Brazil
Yuri Skuratov, Russia
Donald Speagle, Australia
David Stewart, Canada
Nico Steytler, South Africa
Kumar Suresh, India
Faiz Tajuddin, India
Fauzaya Talhaoui, Belgium
G. Alan Tarr, United States
Maria Hermínia Tavares de Almeida,
 Brazil

Paul Thomas, Canada
Krisztina Toth, Switzerland
Anne Twomey, Australia
A.A. Ujo, Nigeria
Bala Usman, Nigeria
Marnix Van Damme, Belgium
Oscar Vega Marín, Mexico
Francois Venter, South Africa
Ludo Veny, Belgium
Magali Verdonck, Belgium
Andrey Vikharev, Russia
Oscar Vilhena, Brazil
Bernhard Waldmann, Switzerland
Kristen Walker, Australia
Adam Wand, Australia
Ronald L. Watts, Canada
Bernard Wicht, Switzerland
Robert F. Williams, United States
George Winterton, Australia
Lisa Young, Canada
Elman Yusubov, Russia
Vladimir Zadiora, Russia
Mikhail Zatsepin, Russia
Emilio Zebadûa González, Mexico

Index